THE

LIFE OF MAHOMET

FROM ORIGINAL SOURCES

BY

SIR WILLIAM MUIR

LL.D.

NEW EDITION

[ABRIDGED FROM THE FIRST EDITION IN FOUR VOLUMES]

WITH AN INDEX

LONDON

SMITH, ELDER, & CO., 15 WATERLOO PLACE

1878

THE

LIFE OF MAHOMET

PREFACE.

THE present volume is an abridgment of the 'LIFE OF MAHOMET' published in four volumes in 1861. The introductory chapters on the pre-Islamite history of Arabia, and most of the notes, with all the references to original authorities, have been omitted. The text, though here and there slightly enlarged, and throughout amended, is in both editions substantially the same.

The chapter on the Corân and Tradition has been retained as an Appendix, with the view of showing to those interested what reliance may be placed on the materials for this history.

If the reader should wish to verify the authority for any particular statement, I must ask him to consult the references which have been freely given in the larger edition.

W. M.

SIMLA: 1876.

CONTENTS.

———◆◆◆———

INTRODUCTION.

CHAPTER I.

CHAPTER II.

CHAPTER III.

CHAPTER IV.

CHAPTER V.

CHAPTER VI.

CHAPTER VII.

CHAPTER VIII.

CHAPTER IX.

CHAPTER X.

CHAPTER XI.

CHAPTER XII.

CHAPTER XIII.

CHAPTER XIV.

CHAPTER XV.

CHAPTER XVI.

CHAPTER XVII.

CHAPTER XVIII.

CHAPTER XIX.

CHAPTER XX.

CHAPTER XXI.

CHAPTER XXII.

CHAPTER XXIII.

CHAPTER XXIV.

CHAPTER XXXVII.

APPENDIX.

ARABIAN CALENDAR.

Arabian Months	Corresponding Months	
Moharram	April	The Arabian months are lunar, and the year was originally corrected by the intercalation of a month every third year. The reckoning was thus luni-solar until, at the Farewell pilgrimage, Mahomet, by abolishing intercalation, made the Mussulman or *Hegira* year a purely lunar one.
Safar	May	
Rabî I	June	
Rabî II	July	
Jumâd I	August	
Jumâd II	September	This table gives the months as they stood at the time of Mahomet's flight to Medina, and they were so maintained by intercalation with little variation till the Farewell pilgrimage.
Rajab	October	
Shabân	November	
Ramadhân	December	
Shawwâl	January	The calculation is according to M. C. de Perceval.
Dzul Câda	February	
Dzul Hijj	March	

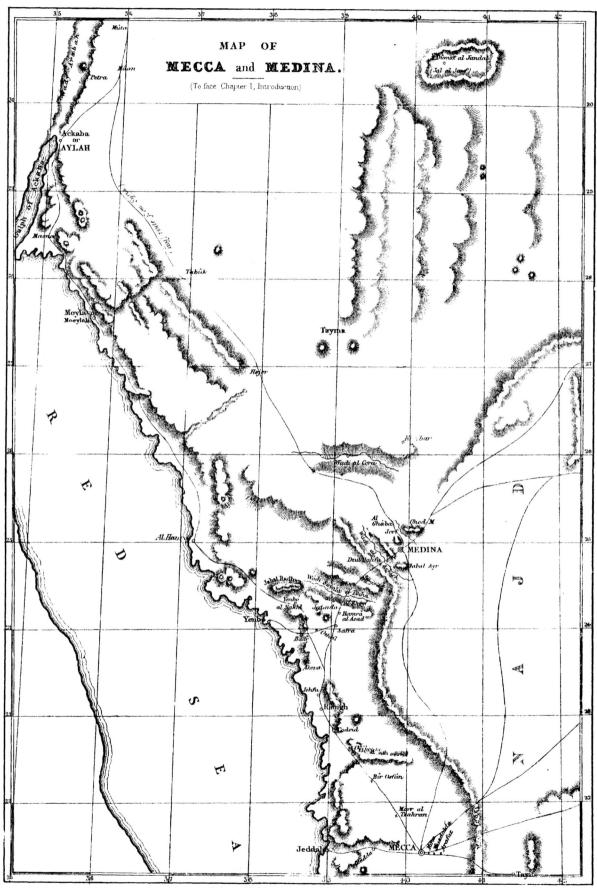

MAP OF
MECCA and **MEDINA.**

(To face Chapter I, Introduction)

Published by Smith, Elder & Co., 15 Waterloo Place, London

INTRODUCTION.

CHAPTER I.

ARABIA BEFORE THE TIME OF MAHOMET.

THE biography of the Prophet of Arabia may be prefaced with advantage by a brief description of his country and native city, and of their condition at his advent.

Arabia is usually described as a triangle, having a right angle at the Strait of Bâb al Mandeb. It may be more correct to regard it as of an oblong shape. The sides bounded by the Red Sea on the one hand, and by the Persian Gulf and the Euphrates on the other, are the longest; while the southern side protracted towards the Strait of Ormuz, and washed by the Indian Ocean, is broader than the northern of which the Syrian confine is narrowed by the westerly bend of the Euphrates.

Along the western side of the peninsula a chain of lofty mountains follows closely the line of the coast, from whence the mariner sees its dismal and repulsive rocks of reddish sandstone and porphyry, at times pressing near enough to be laved by the waves of the sea; at times receding so as to form a broad margin of low land, which is called the Tehâma. Between the sea and the crest of this range is the mountainous region of the Hejâz, in which lie the two cities of Mecca and Medîna. The hills, as you recede from the coast, rise one above another, with vales or *wâdies* between them, till the granite peaks of the chief range overtop the whole. The traveller who has toiled up the weary ascent finds to his surprise that, instead of a similar declivity on the eastern side, he has reached the level of a grand plateau, the Nejd or elevated central steppe of Arabia, stretching away towards the Persian Gulf.

In this great peninsula, 1,400 miles in length, and half as much in breadth, there is not a single river deserving the name. The south-west quarter, indeed, abounds in perennial streams which, watering its fields and groves, have given to it the name of Yemen, or 'the blest.' But elsewhere the leading feature is a

[margin note: Geographical outline of Arabia.]

[margin note: Arid and inhospitable character of the soil.]

weary waste of sand and rock. The floods lose themselves in the thirsty land, and seldom or never reach the sea. But underneath the dried-up channels a stratum of water is often found which supports a rich vegetation, and breaks out here and there in springs. Such are the wâdies or oases of the desert, which, contrasting with the wild bleak wilderness around, charm the traveller by an indescribable freshness and verdure.

Early historical notices of Arabia.

Until the seventh century, when Mussulman conquest drew aside the veil, Central Arabia was an unknown land. Only on the extreme northern and southern confines did it even touch the outer world. In ancient times the notices of Arabia are few and meagre. In the days of Jacob we find the Arab traders carrying the spiceries of Gilead on their camels down to Egypt. During the reign of Solomon a naval station was formed at Elath, the modern Ackaba; the 'kings of Arabia' and its merchantmen supplied Judæa with the rarities of the East; and so widely throughout the peninsula was the fame of the Jewish monarch noised abroad, that the queen of Sheba came from the far south to visit him. In the reign of Augustus, Ælius Gallus, starting with a Roman army from the northern shores of the Red Sea, penetrated to the south probably as far as Mâreb and Saba; but after some months he was forced, by treachery and scarcity of water, to retrace his steps. Comparatively modern as is this expedition in the annals of Arabia, not a vestige of it is traceable in the national traditions and poetry of Arabia; and (which is stranger still) with a very few exceptions it has been found impossible to connect with certainty the many names recorded by Pliny and Strabo in their account of the invasion with any of the known localities or tribes of the country.

Caravan trade.

But though thus hidden for long ages from external view, we know that a great stream of trade was all this time passing through the peninsula, which made the Arabs in fact the carriers of the world between the east and west. In those days the sea was dreaded, and commerce confined almost exclusively to the land. A continent, now the greatest obstacle to traffic, was then its chief facility. The steppes of Central Asia and Arabia were the ocean of the ancients, and companies of camels their fleets. But the way was long and perilous; and hence the necessity for caravans travelling at fixed periods and by determined routes. 'The course of the caravan,' says Heeren, 'was not a matter of free choice, but of established custom. In the vast steppes of sandy deserts, which they had to traverse, nature had sparingly allotted to the traveller a few scattered places of rest, where, under the shade of palm trees, and beside the cool fountains at their feet, the merchant and his beast of burden might enjoy the refreshment rendered necessary by so much suffering. Such places of repose became *entrepôts* of commerce, and not unfrequently the sites of temples and sanctuaries, under the protection of which the merchant prosecuted his trade, and to which the pilgrim resorted.'[1]

Through Arabia there were two great routes. One struck north from Hadhramaut to Gerra on the Persian Gulf, and thence by Palmyra to Palestine and Tyre. The western (with which we are more immediately concerned) started from the same quarter, and ran parallel with the Red Sea, avoiding on the one hand the parched deserts of Nejd, and the impracticable cliffs of the coast upon the other. Mecca, the ancient Macoraba, was probably the half-way station between Arabia Felix and Petræa. The traffic afforded a wide field of employment to the Arab tribes. Some settled in the various emporia, and became traders on their own account. Others, without abandoning their nomad habits, were the carriers of the trade.

Two great routes through Arabia.

The commerce assumed great dimensions, and enriched the nation. About B.C. 600 Ezekiel's denunciation of the haughty Tyre marks the busy intercourse which then replenished the Phenician markets with the products of Arabia and the East.[2] Several centuries later, we learn from Roman writers that the Arabs of the Hejâz still carried on the same traffic; and the stages from Hadhramaut to Ayla are reckoned by them as seventy, which corresponds exactly with the number on the same route at the present day. From the stately ruins which in the Syrian desert still denote the sites of the ancient emporia, some conception may be formed of the prosperity and wealth of the merchant tribes inhabiting them. And no doubt at the southern terminus also, there were in Yemen and Hadhramaut cities which might

Mercantile prosperity of Arabia.

---

[1] *Heeren's Researches : Africa*, vol. i. p. 23. The concluding sentence bears upon the origin and rise of Mecca. But it will still be a question which had the priority, the temple or the mercantile station?

[2] *Ezek.* xxvii. 19–24, which Heeren translates: ' *Wadan and Javan brought thee, from Sanaa, sword blades, cassia and cinnamon, in exchange for thy wares. The merchants of Saba and of Raama traded with thee ; the best spices, precious stones, and gold brought they to thee for thy wares. Haran, Canna, Aden, Saba, traded with thee.*' He adds: ' Some of these places, as Aden, Canna, and Haran, all celebrated sea-ports on the Indian Sea, as well as Sanaa and Saba (or Mariaba), still the capital of Yemen, have retained their name unchanged to the present day ; the site of others, as Wadan, on the Straits of Babel Mandab, rest only on probable conjecture. These accurate statements of the Prophet at all events prove what a special knowledge the inhabitants of Palestine had of Happy Arabia, and how great and active the intercourse with that country must have been.'—*Heeren's As. Res.*, vol. ii. p. 98.

have vied in their ruder and simpler way with the queenly Palmyra.

Failure of the trade and disastrous results.

It was an evil hour for Arabia when Roman enterprise early in the Christian era projected a maritime traffic by the Red Sea direct to Yemen and the East, and thus inflicted a fatal blow on the caravan trade of the peninsula. The land commerce melted away, and the mercantile stations were deserted. Such, after the lapse of sixteen centuries, is the tale which the ruins of Petra Jerash and Philadelphia still attest. The drying up of the tide of merchandise which from time immemorial had fertilised Arabia, and the abandonment of many populous cities dependent on it, cannot fail to have caused widespread disorganisation and distress. The Bedouin carriers might betake themselves to their desert wastes again; but the settled population, with no such resource, were forced to emigrate in quest of some land less overstocked. To this cause may most probably be traced those great emigrations from the south of Codhâite and Azdite tribes, which tradition tells us took place in the second century. These all tended northwards, some to Mecca and Syria, some to Central Arabia, and others to the Persian Gulf and Hîra.

Kingdoms of the Ghassânides and of Hira.

We shall now notice the few points at which in ancient times Arabia touched the outer world. The northern province, stretching from Syria to the Euphrates, was occupied (according to native tradition) in the second century, by some of those tribes which about that time had emigrated from the south; and of them we frequently hear in the later annals of the Roman empire. To the west, in the Syrian desert, with their capital at Palmyra, was the dynasty of the Ghassânides; and to the east, on the banks of the Euphrates, the kingdom of Hîra; the former, as a rule, adhered to the Roman, the latter to the Persian, empire. At some points we can even identify the heroes of Arab story with those of western history. Thus, Odzeina and Zebba of Tadmor are without doubt the Odenathus and Zenobia of Palmyra. In the marvellous tales of Zebba, her beauty, wealth, and knowledge of many languages, and her capture at the tunnel which she had constructed under the Euphrates, we can dimly read the story of Zenobia, her splendid reign, her rebellion and defence of Palmyra, and her seizure by the Romans as she endeavoured to escape across the same river. The princes of Hîra, again, are often mentioned by the Greek and Roman historians, in the wars of the fifth and sixth centuries, as adherents of the Persian cause. Suddenly as a thunder-cloud their troops would darken some fated spot, and sweep in their train devastation, captivity, and death; as suddenly would they disappear, scorning pursuit, and leave no trace behind but in their ravages.

The dynasty of Palmyra and the western tribes embraced Christianity in the time of Constantine; to the east of the desert the religion was later of gaining ground, and indeed was not adopted by the court of Hîra till near the end of the sixth century. Early in the seventh, Hîra fell from its dignity as an independent power, and became a satrapy of Persia. The Ghassânide kingdom also broke up into various petty governments, and eventually merged into the Roman empire. The Persian inroads in the reign of Phocas and early years of Heraclius, gave the Syrian tribes a shock from which they never recovered. And thus the decadence of the kingdoms on both sides of the desert was destined to smooth the victorious path of the Arabian conqueror.

Their decadence in the seventh century.

Turning now to the south of the peninsula, we find Hadhramaut and Yemen ruled by the Himyarites, a dynasty of which tradition carries the origin far back into the obscurity of ages. In the fourth century an embassy from Constantius visited this court, headed by a Christian bishop. In A.D. 523 the throne was seized by a bigoted and dissolute usurper. A proselyte to Judaism, he perpetrated frightful cruelties on the Christians of the neighbouring province of Najrân who refused to embrace his faith. Trenches filled with combustible materials were lighted, and the martyrs cast into the flames. Tradition gives the number thus miserably burned, or slain by the sword, at twenty thousand. However exaggerated, there can be no doubt of the bloody character of the tyrant's reign. One of the intended victims escaped to the court of Justinian, and, holding up a half-burned Gospel, invoked retribution. At the Emperor's desire the Negus, prince of Abyssinia, crossed from Adulis and defeated the usurper; and thus the Himyarites were supplanted by a Christian government under an Abyssinian viceroy. But Abyssinian rule was distasteful to the people; an appeal was made to Persia, and before the end of the sixth century the Abyssinians were vanquished and expelled, and Yemen sank into a simple dependency of Persia.

Kingdom of Hadhramaut and Yemen.

Thus, whether we look to the north or the south, it was but the farther outskirts of the peninsula which came into even casual contact with the civilised world. The rest of Arabia was absolutely unknown to it; and excepting through the medium of their countrymen engaged in merchandise or settled on the confines of Syria, the Arabs themselves had but little knowledge of anything beyond their own deserts. For any community of interest with the nations beyond, they might have been the very antipodes of the Roman empire. It is not till the fifth century that native tradition, as preserved by Mahometan writers, begins

Arabia before Mahomet, unknown to the outer world.

to shed a fitful and imperfect light on the political relations of the leading tribes; and as we approach still nearer the era of Islâm, the history becomes clearer and more distinct.

Political and religious state of Arabia.

Before turning to Mecca, we shall conclude this chapter with a rapid survey of the political and religious state of Arabia, and the relations in which it stood to Mahomet both as a Prophet and a warrior.

The habits of the nomad tribes are singularly unsusceptible of change; and Arabia as we find it in the sixth century probably differed little from the Arabia of Abraham and Job. The distinctive feature has ever been the independence of the tribe, the family, the individual. The counsels of each several tribe or cluster of tribes are guided by a Sheikh, but only as representing the embodied wishes and opinions of the individual members. No bond of permanent union holds them together, and dissentients may secede at pleasure. With a code of honour bordering on jealousy, personal hostilities and tribal wars incessantly occur; and thus tribes often rise or fall, coalesce or become disintegrated, remain in their ancestral haunts or migrate to distant lands. On the other hand, there is a strong cohesive power within each tribe in the *esprit de corps* which binds together the several members and identifies them with its safety and honour. So strong indeed is the bond that, after the lapse of twelve centuries, we find some tribes, as the Bani Adwân and Hawâzin, the same in name and descent, and inhabiting even the same localities, as in the days of Mahomet.

Subdivision and independence of Arab tribes a formidable obstacle to union.

The first peculiarity, then, which attracts attention is the subdivision of the Arabs into innumerable bodies, governed by the same code of honour and morals, exhibiting the same manners, speaking for the most part the same language, but each independent of the others; restless and often at war amongst themselves; and even where united by blood or by interest, ever ready on some insignificant cause to separate and abandon themselves to an implacable hostility. Thus at the era of Islâm the retrospect of Arabian history exhibits an ever-varying state of combination and repulsion such as had hitherto rendered abortive any attempt at a general union. The freedom of Arabia from foreign conquest was owing not so much to the difficulties of its parched and pathless wilds, as to the endless array of isolated clans, and the absence of any head or chief power which might be made the object of subjugation. The problem had yet to be solved, by what force these tribes could be subdued, or drawn to one common centre; and it was solved by Mahomet, who struck out a political system of his own, universally acceptable because derived from elements common to all Arabia; vigorous, because based upon the energy of a new religious life; rapidly and irrepressibly expansive, because borne forward by inducements, irresistible to an Arab, of war and plunder.

The prospects of Arabia before the rise of Mahomet were as unfavourable to religious reform as to political union or national regeneration. The foundation of Arab faith was a deep-rooted idolatry, which for centuries had stood proof, with no palpable symptom of decay, against every attempt at evangelisation from Egypt and Syria. Several causes increased the insensibility of Arabia to the Gospel. A broad margin of hostile Judaism neutralised on the northern frontier the effects of Christian teaching, and afforded shelter to the paganism beyond. The connections of the Jews extended far into the interior, and were supported towards the south by the powerful Jewish settlement in Yemen, which at times even sought to proselytise the neighbouring tribes.

Small prospect of religious reform.

Christianity neutralised by Judaism.

But more than this, the idolatry of Mecca had formed a compromise with Judaism, and had admitted enough of its legends, and perhaps of its tenets also, to steel the national mind against the appeal of Christianity. Idolatry, simple and naked, is comparatively powerless against the attacks of reason and the Gospel; but, aided by some measure of truth, it can maintain its ground against the most urgent persuasion. To advance the authority of Abraham for the worship of the Káaba, and vaunt his legacy of divinely inculcated rites, would be a triumphant reply to the invitations either of Judaism or of Christianity. Moreover, the Christianity of the seventh century was itself decrepit and corrupt. It was disabled by contending schisms, and had substituted the puerilities of superstition for the pure and expansive faith of the early ages.

Combination with Judaical legends strengthened the idolatry of Arabia.

Northern Arabia, long the battle-field of Persia and the Empire, was peculiarly unfavourable to Christian effort. Alternately swept by the armies of the Chosroes and of Constantinople, of Hîra and of the Ghassânides, the Syrian frontier presented little opportunity for the advance of peaceful Christianity.

Unsettled frontier to the North unfavourable to Christianity.

The vagrant habits of the nomads themselves eluded the importunity of missionary endeavour; while their haughty temper and vindictive code equally resented the humble and forgiving precepts of the Gospel. A nominal adhesion to Christianity, as to any other religion, may indeed be obtained without participation in its spirit or subjection to its moral requirements; but such a formal submission could have resulted alone from the political supremacy of a Christian power, not from the persuasion of a religious agency. Let us enquire, then, what political inducements bore upon Arabia from without.

Habits of the Arabs opposed to Christianity.

Political influence of Christianity from without.
1. From the *North*.

To the *North*, we find that Egypt and Syria, representing the Roman empire, exercised at the best but a remote and foreign influence upon Arabian affairs ; and even that limited influence was neutralised by the victories of Persia. The weight of Constantinople, if ever brought to bear directly upon the affairs of Arabia, was but lightly and transiently felt. The kingdom of Ghassân, upon the borders of Syria, was indeed at once Arab and Christian, but it yielded to Hîra the palm of supremacy, and never exercised any important bearing on the affairs and policy of central Arabia.

2. From the *North-east*.

If we turn to the *North-east*, we observe that the prospects of Christianity had improved by the conversion of the court at Hîra and many of its subordinate tribes. But Hîra itself was but a vassal, for its native dynasty, lately fallen, had been replaced by the direct government of Persia, a strong opponent of Christianity. The relations of pagan Persia with the northern and eastern Arabs more than counterbalanced the influence of Christianity in the west.

3. From the *South*.

To the *South*, Christianity had suffered an important loss. The prestige of a monarchy, though but an Abyssinian, was gone ; and in its room had arisen a persian satrapy, under the shadow of which the ancient Himyarite idolatry, and once royal Judaism, flourished apace.[1] On the *East* there was the Christian

4. From the *East*.

kingdom of Abyssinia, but it was divided from Arabia by the Red Sea ; and the negro race, even if brought into closer contact, could never have exercised much influence upon the Arab mind.

The peninsula presented no prospect of hopeful change.

Thus the star of Christianity was not in the ascendant : in some respects it was declining. There was no hope of a change from external aid ; and, apart from such aid, the strong influence of Judaism, and the almost universal submission to national idolatry, rendered the conversion of Arabia a doubtful and a distant prospect. During the youth of Mahomet, the aspect of the peninsula was strongly conservative ; perhaps reform never was at any period more hopeless.

Causes are sometimes conjured up to account for results produced by an agent apparently inadequate to effect them. Mahomet arose, and forthwith the Arabs were aroused to a new and a spiritual faith. Hence the conclusion has been drawn that Arabia was fermenting for the change, and prepared to adopt

---

[1] Gibbon thus marks the importance of the fall of the Christian government in Yemen : 'This narrative of obscure and remote events is not foreign to the decline and fall of the Roman empire. If a Christian power had been maintained in Arabia Mahomet must have been crushed in his cradle, and Abyssinia would have prevented a revolution, which has changed the civil and religious state of the world.'—*Decline and Fall*, chap. xlii.

it.   To us, calmly reviewing the past, pre-Islamite history belies the assumption.   After five centuries of Christian evangelisation, we can point to but a sprinkling here and there of Christian converts;—the Bani Hârith of Najrân; the Bani Hanîfa of Yemâma; some of the Bani Tay at Tayma; and hardly any more.   Judaism, vastly more powerful, had exhibited a spasmodic effort of proselytism; but, as an active and converting agent, the Jewish faith was no longer operative.   In fine, viewed thus in a religious aspect, the surface of Arabia had been now and then gently rippled by the feeble efforts of Christianity; the sterner influences of Judaism had been occasionally visible in a deeper and more troubled current; but the tide of indigenous idolatry and of Ishmaelite superstition, setting strongly from every quarter towards the Káaba, gave ample evidence that the faith and worship of Mecca held the Arab mind in a thraldom rigorous and undisputed.

The writer questions the position that Arabia was prepared for a change.

It was obstinately fixed in the profession of idolatry.

Yet, even amongst a people thus enthralled, there existed elements which a master mind, seeking the regeneration of Arabia, might work upon.   Christianity was well known; living examples existed amongst the native tribes; the New Testament was respected, if not revered, as a book that claimed to be divine; in most quarters it was easily accessible, and some of its facts and doctrines were admitted without dispute.   The tenets of Judaism were even more familiar, and its legends, if not its sacred writings, were known throughout the peninsula.   The worship of Mecca was founded upon patriarchal traditions common both to Christianity and Judaism.   Here, then, was ground on which the spiritual fulcrum might be planted; a wide field already open to the enquirer in close connection with the truth, inviting scrutiny and improvement.   And, no doubt, many an Arab heart, before Mahomet, had responded to the voice, casually heard it may be, of Christianity and of Judaism: many an honest Bedouin spirit had confessed of the law that it was just and good: many an aspiring intellect, as the eye travelled over the spangled expanse of heaven, had concluded that the universe was supported by ONE great being; and in time of need, many an earnest soul had accepted with joy the Christian Sacrifice.   Coss, bishop of Najrân, was not the first, nor perhaps the most eloquent and earnest, of Arab preachers who sought to turn their fellows from the error of their ways, and reasoned with them of righteousness, temperance, and judgment to come.

Still large material had been prepared by Judaism and Christianity.

The material for a great change was here.   But it required to be wrought; and Mahomet was the workman.   The fabric of Islâm no more necessarily grew out of the state of Arabia, than a gorgeous texture grows from the slender meshes of silken

It was Mahomet who worked the material into shape.

filament; or the stately ship from unhewn timber of the forest; or the splendid palace from rude masses of rock. Had Mahomet, stern to his early convictions, followed the leading of Jewish and Christian truth, and inculcated upon his fellows their simple doctrine, there might have been a 'SAINT MAHOMET'—more likely a 'MAHOMET THE MARTYR'—laying the foundation stone of the Arabian Church. But then (so far as human probabilities and analogy indicate) Arabia would not have been convulsed by his preaching to its centre, or even any considerable portions of it converted. He abandoned his early convictions; for the uncompromising severity of principle, he substituted the designs of expediency and compromise; and then, with consummate skill, he devised a machinery, by the adaptive energy of which he gradually shaped the broken and disconnected masses of the Arab race into an harmonious whole, a body politic endowed with life and vigour. To the Christian, he was as a Christian; to the Jew he became as a Jew; to the idolater of Mecca, as a reformed worshipper of the Káaba. And thus, by unparalleled art and a rare supremacy of mind, he persuaded the whole of Arabia, Pagan, Jew, and Christian, to follow his steps with docile submission.

Such a process is that of *the workman shaping his material.* It is not that of the material shaping its own form, much less (as some would hold) moulding the workman himself. It was Mahomet that formed Islâm; it was not Islâm, or any pre-existing Moslem spirit, that moulded Mahomet.

CHAPTER II.

PRE-HISTORICAL NOTICES OF MECCA.

WE shall in this chapter consider such mythical and traditional notices of Mecca as may throw light on the origin of the Káaba and its worship, and on the ancestry of Mahomet.

Mahometan legend ascribes the building of the Káaba to Abraham. Hagar (so the story runs), wandering in the desert with her boy, reaches at length the valley of Mecca. In the agony of thirst she paces hurriedly to and fro between the little hills of Safa and Marwa, seeking for water. Ishmael, whom she had left crying on the ground, kicks around him in childish passion, when behold the spot bubbles forth beneath his feet in a clear stream of sweet water. It is the well Zemzem. Amalekites and Arab tribes from Yemen, attracted by the fountain, settle there; Ishmael grows up amongst them, and marries the daughter of their chief. In fulfilment of the divine command received in a vision, Abraham is about to offer up his son upon an eminence in the neighbourhood, when his arm is stayed and a vicarious sacrifice accepted. On a subsequent visit, the patriarch, assisted by his son, erected the temple where it now stands, and reconstituted the primeval rites of pilgrimage.

Legend of the founding of Mecca by Ishmael.

Descending from this myth, tradition gives us little more than bare genealogical tables (borrowed palpably from the Jews) in which it is pretended to trace up generation by generation the Coreishite stock to Abraham. It is not till we reach the Christian era that tradition commences, and then it soon begins to teem with tales and legends in which, mingled with the mass of fiction, there may be grains of fact. The guardianship of the Káaba (assumed to belong to the Coreishite ancestry in virtue of descent from Ishmael) was usurped by the Jorhomite tribe, which remained long in possession of the temple and the supremacy of Mecca. In the second century some of the numerous tribes migrating from Yemen northwards, settled in the vicinity. Most of them passed on eventually to Medîna, Syria, and Hîra; but a remnant, called the Khozâa, remained behind; and these in their turn seized upon the government of Mecca. The Jorhom dynasty was thus ousted in the third century, and their last king, on retiring from Mecca, buried in

Traditional history to fourth century.

the well Zemzem his treasures; among them were two gazelles of gold, and swords and suits of armour, of which we shall hear more hereafter.

Cossai assumes the government; middle of fifth century. For 200 years the Khozâites remained masters of Mecca, certain inferior offices connected with the worship of the Káaba being alone retained by families of the original stock. It was reserved for Cossai, a bold adventurer of Coreishite descent, to seize upon (or to resume for its rightful owners) the supreme control of Mecca. He gathered all his kindred and settled them in the sacred valley, enlarged the city, and assigned to each family a separate quarter. Near the Káaba he built a council-house in which, under his presidency, was transacted all important business. From thence caravans set forth; there on returning the absent traveller first alighted; and when war was resolved on, the banner was mounted there on its staff, and consigned to the standard-bearer by Cossai himself or one of his sons. Cossai also assumed the chief offices connected with the local worship. The keys of the Káaba were in his hands; the giving of drink to the pilgrims, and providing them with food, were his sole prerogative, which, administered with princely liberality, invested his name in the eyes of the hospitable Arabs with a peculiar lustre. The assumption of these functions consolidated the power of Cossai as the sheikh of Mecca and chief of the surrounding territory; and tradition adds that 'his ordinances were obeyed and venerated, as people obey and venerate the observances of religion, both before and after his death.' This same Cossai was ancestor, at the fifth remove, of the Arabian Prophet.

Rites of the Káaba; the Lesser pilgrimage. The ceremonies of pilgrimage thus handed down by Cossai were substantially the same as we find them in the time of Mahomet; and, with some modifications introduced by Mahomet himself, the same as are practised at the present day. The grand centre is the Káaba, to visit which, to kiss the Black stone imbedded in the eastern angle, and to make seven circuits round the sacred edifice, is at all times and seasons, regarded meritorious. The 'Lesser pilgrimage' (otherwise called *Omrâ*), in addition to these acts, includes the passing to and fro with hasty steps seven times between the eminences of Safa and Marwa. It may be performed with merit at any season of the year, but especially in the sacred month of Rajab. Before entering the holy territory surrounding Mecca, the votary assumes the pilgrim garb, and at the conclusion of the ceremonies shaves his head and pares his nails.

The Greater pilgrimage. The 'Greater pilgrimage' can be performed only in the holy month Dzul Hijj. In addition to the ceremonies of the Lesser, it embraces the tour of Arafât, a small granite hill in a valley within the mountain tract, ten or twelve miles east of Mecca. The pilgrims, starting from Mecca on the 8th of the month, spend the following day at Arafât, and the same evening return three or four miles to Muzdalifa. Next morning, they proceed half way back to Mecca, and spend at Minâ the two or three succeeding days. Small stones are cast by all the pilgrims at certain objects in the Minâ valley, and the pilgrimage is concluded by the sacrifice of victims.

The country for several miles round Mecca was hallowed and inviolable, and had from time immemorial been so regarded. Four months of the year were universally held sacred; three were consecutive, and one separate.[1] During this period war was by unanimous consent suspended, hostile feeling suppressed, and amnesty reigned throughout Arabia. Pilgrims from every quarter were then free to repair to Mecca; and fairs were thronged by those whom merchandise, or the contests of poetry or of rivalry, brought together.

Sacred environs of Mecca and four holy months.

Coupled with this, and bearing the same name, was a privilege by which the last of the three continuous months might be commuted for the one succeeding it. The innovation is attributed to Cossai, who may have wished, by abridging the long three months' recess of peace, to humour the warlike Arabs, as well as to obtain for himself the power of holding a month either sacred or secular as might best suit his purpose.[2]

Commutation of a sacred for a secular month.

There is reason to suppose that the year was originally lunar, and so continued till the beginning of the fifth century, when in imitation of the Jews it was turned, by the interjection of a month at the close of every third year, into a luni-solar period. If by this change it was intended to make the season of pilgrimage correspond invariably with the autumn, when a supply of food for the vast multitude would be easily procurable, that object was defeated by the remaining imperfection of the cycle; for the year being still shorter by one day and a fraction than the real year, each recurring season accelerated the time of pilgrimage; so that when, after two centuries, intercalation was altogether prohibited by Mahomet, the days of pilgrimage had moved from October gradually backward to March.

The luni-solar year of Mecca.

In reviewing the history of Mecca, the origin of the temple and the local worship demands further scrutiny. The Mahometan attributes both to Abraham, and connects part of the ceremonial

Enquiry into the origin of the Kâaba

---

[1] The last two months of the year, *Dzul Câada* and *Dzul Hijj*, with the first month of the new year, *Moharram*; and the seventh, *Rajab*.

[2] For Moharram would thus become secular and Safar (the month succeeding it) become sacred. The office of intercalation and commutation was called *Nasâ*; and the person holding it, *Nâsi*.

and its worship.

with biblical legend; but the narrative is plainly a fable. The following considerations will strengthen the conviction that Mecca and its rites cannot possibly claim any such origin.

No Abrahamic element in main ceremonies of the Káaba.

First. There is no trace of anything Abrahamic in the essential elements of the superstition. To kiss the Black stone, to make the circuit of the Káaba, and perform the other observances at Mecca Arafât and the vale of Minâ, to keep the sacred months and to hallow the sacred territory, have no conceivable connection with Abraham, or with the ideas and principles which his descendants would be likely to inherit from him. Such rites originated in causes foreign to the country chiefly occupied by the children of Abraham. They were either strictly local, or, corresponding with the idolatry that prevailed in the south of the peninsula, were imported by immigrants from Yemen.

Remote antiquity of the Káaba.

Second. A very high antiquity must be assigned to the main features of the religion of Mecca. Although Herodotus does not refer to the Káaba, yet he names as one of the chief Arab divinities, ALILAT; and this is strong evidence of the worship, at that early period, of *Allât* the great idol of Mecca. He likewise alludes to the veneration of the Arabs for stones. Diodorus Siculus, writing about half a century before our era, says of that part of Arabia washed by the Red Sea—' there is, in this country, a temple greatly revered by all the Arabs.' These words must refer to the holy house of Mecca, for we know of no other which ever commanded the universal homage of Arabia. Early *historical* tradition gives no trace of its first construction. Some authorities assert that the Amalekites rebuilt the edifice which they found in ruins, and retained it for a time under their charge. All agree that it was in existence under the Jorhomites (about the time of the Christian era), and, being injured by a flood of rain, was then repaired. It was again repaired by Cossai.

Wide extent of the worship of the Káaba.

Tradition represents the Káaba as from time immemorial the scene of pilgrimage from *all* quarters of Arabia :—from Yemen Hadhramaut and the shores of the Persian Gulf, from the deserts of Syria, and from the distant environs of Hîra and Mesopotamia, men yearly flocked to Mecca. So extensive an homage must have had its beginnings in an extremely remote age; and a similar antiquity must be ascribed to the essential concomitants of the local worship,—the Káaba with its Black stone, the sacred territory, and the holy months. The origin of a superstition so ancient and universal should be looked for within the peninsula itself, and not in any foreign country.

Connection with systems native to Arabia.

Third. The native systems of Arabia were Sabeanism, Idolatry, and Stone-worship, all closely connected with the religion of Mecca.

There is reason for believing that Sabeanism, or the worship of the heavenly bodies, was the earliest departure from pure religion in Arabia. The book of Job contains historical notices of the system, and certain early names in the Himyar dynasty imply its prevalence. As late as the fourth century, we find sacrifices offered in Yemen to the sun, moon, and stars. The seven circuits of the Káaba were probably emblematical of the revolutions of the planetary bodies; and we are told that a similar rite was observed at other idol fanes in Arabia.

1. Sabean-ism.

The practice of idolatry thickly overspread the whole peninsula. We have authentic records of ancient shrines scattered in various parts of Arabia from Yemen to Dûma and even as far as Hîra, some of them subordinate to the Káaba and having rites resembling those of Mecca. A system thus widely diffused and thoroughly organised, may well be regarded as of indigenous growth.

2. Idolatry.

The most singular feature in the fetichism of Arabia was the adoration paid to unshapen stones. Mahometans hold that this practice arose out of the Káaba worship. 'The adoration of stones among the Ishmaelites,' says Ibn Ishâc, ' originated in the custom of men carrying a stone from the sacred enclosure of Mecca when they went upon a journey, out of reverence to the Káaba; and whithersoever they went they set it up and made circuits round about it as about the Káaba, till at the last they worshipped every goodly stone they saw, and forgot their religion, and changed the faith of Abraham and Ishmael, and worshipped images.' This tendency to stone-worship was undoubtedly prevalent throughout Arabia; but it is more probable that, it *occasioned* the superstition of the Káaba and its black stone, than took its rise therefrom.

3. Stone-worship.

Thus the religion of Mecca is, in all essential points, connected strictly with forms of superstition native to Arabia, and we may naturally conclude that it grew out of them. The process may be thus imagined. Mecca owed its origin and importance to its position midway between Yemen and Petra. We have seen that, from ancient times, the merchandise of the East passed through Arabia; and the vale of Mecca lay upon the great western route. A plentiful supply of water attracted the caravans; it became a halting place, and then an *entrepôt* of commerce; a mercantile population grew up in the vicinity, and change of carriage took place there. The carrier's hire, the frontier customs, the dues of protection, and the profits of direct traffic, added capital to the city which may have rivalled, though in a primitive and simple style, the emporia of Petra, Jerash, or Philadelphia. The earliest inhabitants were natives of Yemen, and the ever flowing traffic maintained a permanent intercourse between them and their

Supposed history of the rise of Mecca and its religion.

mother country. From Yemen no doubt they brought with them, or subsequently received, Sabeanism, Stone-worship, and Idolatry. These were connected with the well of Zemzem, the source of their prosperity ; and near to it they erected their fane, with its symbolical Sabeanism and mysterious Black stone. Local rites were superadded; but it was Yemen, the cradle of the Arabs, which furnished the essential elements of the system. The mercantile eminence of Mecca, while it attracted the Bedouins from all parts of Arabia by the profits of the carrying trade, by degrees imparted a national character to the local superstition, till at last it became the religion of Arabia. When the southern trade deserted this channel, the mercantile prestige of Mecca vanished and its opulence decayed, but the Káaba continued the national temple of the peninsula. The floating population betook themselves to the desert; and the native tribes (the ancestry of the Coreish) were overpowered by such southern immigrants as the Jorhom and Khozâa dynasties; till at last Cossai arose to vindicate the honour, and re-establish the influence, of the house of Mecca.

How is this theory reconciled with the legend of the Abrahamic origin of the Káaba?

But, according to this theory, how shall we account for the tradition current among the Arabs, that the temple owed its origin to Abraham ? This was no Moslem fiction, but the popular opinion long before the time of Mahomet. Otherwise, it could not have been referred to in the Corân as an acknowledged fact ; nor would certain spots around the Káaba have been connected, as we know them to have been, with the names of Abraham and Ishmael.

Supposed origin of Abrahamic legend in connection with the Káaba.

It seems probable from tradition that Abrahamic tribes were early and extensively commingled with the Arabs from Yemen, and that a branch descended from Abraham, probably through Ishmael, settled at Mecca and there became allied with the Yemenite race. Abrahamic legends still surviving from this source would be resuscitated and strengthened by later intercourse with the Jews. The mingled stock from Syria and from Yemen required such a modification of the local religion as would correspond with their double descent. Hence Jewish legends were naturally grafted upon the indigenous worship, and rites of sacrifice were now for the first time introduced, or at any rate now first associated with the memory of Abraham.

Combination of the Abrahamic legend with the local superstition.

The Jews themselves were also largely settled in northern Arabia, where they acquired a considerable influence. There were extensive colonies about Medîna and Kheibar, in Wâdi al Cora, and on the shores of the Ælanitic gulf. These maintained a constant and friendly intercourse with Mecca and the Arab tribes, who looked with respect and veneration upon their religion and their holy books. When once the loose conception of Abraham and Ishmael as the great forefathers of the race on one side, was superimposed upon the superstition of Mecca, and had received the stamp of native currency, it will easily be conceived that Jewish tradition and legend would be eagerly welcomed and readily assimilated with native legend and tradition. By a summary adjustment, the story of Palestine became the story of the Hejâz. The precincts of the Káaba were hallowed as the scene of Hagar's distress, and the sacred well Zemzem as the source of her relief. The pilgrims hasted to and fro between Safa and Marwa in memory of her hurried steps in search of water. It was Abraham and Ishmael who built the temple, imbedded in it the Black stone, and established for all mankind the pilgrimage to Arafât. In imitation of him it was that stones were flung by the pilgrims as if at Satan, and sacrifices offered at Minâ in remembrance of the vicarious sacrifice by Abraham in the stead of his son. And thus, although the indigenous rites may have been little if at all altered by the adoption of the Abrahamic legends, they came to be viewed in a totally different light, and to be connected in an Arab's imagination with something of the sanctity of Abraham the Friend of God.[1] The gulf between the gross idolatry of Arabia and the pure theism of the Jews was bridged over. Upon this common   Vantage ground thus gained

[1] It is to this source that we may trace the native doctrine of a Supreme Being, to whom gods and idols were subordinate. The title of *Allah Taâla*, THE MOST HIGH GOD, was commonly used long before Mahomet to designate this conception. But in some tribes, the idea had become so materialised that a portion of the votive offerings was assigned to the great God, just as a portion was allotted to their idols. The notion of a supreme Divinity to be represented by no sensible symbol, is clearly not cognate with any of the indigenous forms of Arab superstition. It was borrowed directly from the Jews, or from some other Abrahamic race among whom contact with the Jews had preserved or revived the knowledge of the 'God of Abraham.'

Familiarity with the Abrahamic races also introduced the doctrine of the immortality of the soul, and the resurrection from the dead; but these were held with many fantastic ideas of Arabian growth. Revenge pictured the murdered soul as a bird chirping for retribution against the murderer; and a camel was sometimes left to starve at the grave of his master, that he might be ready at the resurrection again to carry him.

A vast variety of biblical language and terminology was also in common use, or at least sufficiently in use to be commonly understood. Faith, Repentance, Heaven and Hell, the Devil and his angels, the heavenly angels, Gabriel the messenger of God, are a specimen of ideas and expressions which, acquired from a Jewish source, were either current or ready for adoption. Similarly familiar were the stories of the Fall of man, the Flood, the destruction of the cities of the plain, &c.—so that there was an extensive substratum of crude ideas and unwrought knowledge or conception bordering upon the spiritual, ready to the hand of Mahomet.

ground Mahomet took his stand, and proclaimed to his people a new and a spiritual system, in accents to which all Arabia could respond. The rites of the Káaba were retained, but stripped by him of every idolatrous tendency; and they still hang, a strange unmeaning shroud, around the living theism of Islâm.

CHAPTER III.

THE FOREFATHERS OF MAHOMET.

THE social institutions of Mecca did not essentially differ from those of the wandering Bedouins. They were to some extent modified by their settled habitation and by the pilgrimage and worship of the Káaba. But the ultimate sanctions of society, and the springs of political movement, were in reality the same at Mecca then (so wonderfully have they survived the corroding effects of time) as exist in Arabia at the present day.

Civil polity based on the habits of the Bedouins.

It must be borne in mind that at Mecca there was not, before the establishment of Islâm, any *government* in the common sense of the term. No supreme authority existed whose mandate was law. Every separate tribe was a republic governed by public opinion; and the opinion of the aggregate tribes, who chanced for the time to act together, was the sovereign law. There was no recognised exponent of the popular will; each tribe was free to hold back from that which was clearly decreed by the rest; and no individual was more bound than his collective tribe to a compulsory conformity with even the unanimous resolve of his fellow-citizens. Honour and revenge supplied the place of a more elaborate system. The former prompted the individual, by the desire of upholding the name and influence of his clan, to a compliance with the general wish; the latter provided for the respect of private right, by the unrelenting pursuit of the injurer. In effect, the will of the majority did form the general rule of action, although there was a continual risk that the minority might separate and assume an independent, if not antagonistic, course. The law of revenge, too, though in such a society perhaps unavoidable, was then, even as now, the curse of Arabia. The stain of blood once shed was not easily effaced: its price might be rejected by the heir, and life demanded for life. Retaliation followed retribution: the nearest of kin, the family, the clan, the confederate tribes, one by one in a widening circle, identified themselves with the sufferer, and adopted his claim as their own; and thus a petty affront or unpremeditated blow not unfrequently involved whole tribes and tracts of country in protracted and bloody strife. Still, in a system

General principles of Bedouin government.

which provided no legal power to interfere in personal disputes, it cannot be doubted that the law of retaliation afforded an important check upon the passions of the stronger; and that acts of violence and injustice were repressed by fear of retribution from the relatives or adherents of the injured party. The benefit of the custom was further increased by the practice of *patronage* or guardianship. The weak resorted to the strong for protection; and when the word of a chief or powerful man was once pledged to grant it, the pledge was fulfilled with chivalrous scrupulosity.

Offices of the Káaba conferred authority on Chiefs of Mecca.

At first sight it might appear that, under this system, a chief possessed no shadow of authority to execute either his own wish or that of the people. But in reality his powers, though vague and undefined, were large and effective. The position of chief always secured an important share in forming and giving expression to public opinion; so that, excepting rare and unusual cases, he swayed the councils and the movements of his tribe. It was mainly by the influence derived from the offices attaching to the Káaba and the pilgrimage, that the chiefs of Mecca differed from the sheikhs of the nomad tribes, and exercised a more regular and permanent rule.

Cossai, A.D. 440, and his descendants.

We have seen that about the middle of the fifth century Cossai had concentrated the chief of these offices in his own person. When he became old and infirm, he resigned them into the hands of his eldest son, Abd al Dâr. From him they descended to his sons and grandsons; but the latter, who succeeded to the inheritance in the beginning of the sixth century, were too young effectually to maintain their rights. Abd Menâf, another son of Cossai, had been the powerful rival of his brother; and the sons of Abd Menâf inherited their father's influence. The chief

Discord among Cos-

were, Mottalib, Hâshim, Abd Shams, and Naufal.[1] These con-

[1] This was the branch from which Mahomet was descended. The following table should be studied and referred to as occasion requires. It illustrates the family influences which affected not only the position of the Prophet, but the destinies of the Caliphate in ages long after:—

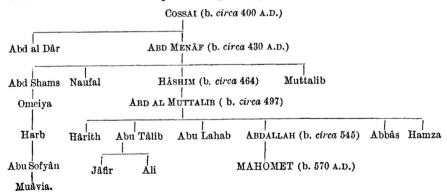

spired to wrest from the descendants of Abd al Dâr the hereditary offices bequeathed by Cossai. Hâshim took the lead, and
grounded his claim on the superior dignity of the family of
Abd Menâf. But the descendants of Abd al Dâr refused to cede
their rights, and an open rupture ensued. The Coreish were
equally divided between the two factions, one portion siding with
the claimants, and the other with the actual possessors of the
offices. The opponents, who had bound themselves by the most
stringent oaths, were already marshalled within sight of each
other when unexpectedly a truce was called. The conditions
were to give Hâshim and his party the offices of providing food
and water for the pilgrims; the descendants of Abd al Dâr retained the custody of the Káaba and the Council-hall, and the
right of raising the banner. Peace was restored upon these
terms.

HÂSHIM, thus installed in the office of entertaining the pilgrims, fulfilled it with princely magnificence. He was himself
rich, and many others of the Coreish had also by trading acquired much wealth. He appealed to them as his grandfather
Cossai had done: '*Ye are the neighbours of God, and the keepers*
of His House. The pilgrims who visit the temple are His guests;
and it is meet that ye should entertain them above all other guests.
Ye are especially chosen unto this high dignity; wherefore honour
His guests and refresh them. For, from distant cities, on their lean
and jaded camels, they come unto you fatigued and harassed, with
hair dishevelled and bodies covered with the dust and squalor of
the way. Then invite them hospitably, and furnish them with water
in abundance.' Hâshim set the example by a munificent provision, and the Coreish were forward to contribute every man
according to his ability. Water sufficient for the great assemblage
was collected in cisterns close by the Káaba, and at the stations
on the route to Arafât. The distribution of food commenced
upon the day on which the pilgrims set out for Minâ and Arafât,
and continued until they dispersed. During this period, that is
for five or six days, they were entertained with pottage of meat
and bread, or of butter and barley, variously prepared, and with
the favourite national repast of dates.

Thus Hâshim supported the credit of Mecca. But his name
is even more renowned for the splendid charity by which in a
time of famine he relieved the necessities of his fellow-citizens.
He proceeded to Syria, purchased an immense stock of bread,
and conveyed it upon camels to Mecca. There the provisions
were cooked, the camels slaughtered and roasted, and the whole
divided among the people. Destitution and mourning were
suddenly turned into mirth and plenty; and it was (the historian

adds) 'as it were the beginning of new life after the year of scarcity.'

Commercial treaties concluded by Hâshim and his brothers.

The foreign relations of the Coreish were conducted by the sons of Abd Menâf. With the Roman authorities, and the Ghassânide prince, Hâshim himself concluded a treaty; and he is said to have received from the Emperor a rescript authorising the Coreish to travel to Syria in security. Abd Shams made a treaty with the Negus of Abyssinia, in pursuance of which the Coreish traded with his people; Naufal and Muttalib concluded alliances, the former with the king of Persia who allowed the merchants of Mecca to traffic in Irâc and Fars, the latter with the kings of Himyar who encouraged their commercial operations in Yemen. Thus the affairs of the Coreish prospered in every direction. To Hâshim is also ascribed the credit of establishing upon a uniform footing the mercantile expeditions of his people, so that every winter a caravan set out regularly for Yemen and Abyssinia, while in the summer a second visited Ghazza, Ancyra, and other Syrian marts.

Hâshim is challenged. by Omeiya, who is vanquished and exiled.

The success and glory of Hâshim exposed him to the envy of Omeiya, the son of his brother Abd Shams. Omeiya was opulent, and he expended his riches in a vain attempt to rival the splendour of his kinsman's munificence. The Coreish perceived the endeavour, and turned it into ridicule. Omeiya was enraged. *Who*, said he, *is Hâshim?* and he defied him to a trial of superiority.[1] Hâshim would willingly have avoided a contest with one so much his inferior both in years and dignity; but the Coreish, who loved such exhibitions, would not excuse him; he consented, therefore, but with the stipulation that the vanquished party should lose fifty black-eyed camels, and be ten years exiled from Mecca. A Khozâite soothsayer was appointed umpire; and, having heard the pretensions of both, pronounced Hâshim to be the victor. Hâshim then took the fifty camels, slaughtered them in the vale of Mecca, and fed with them all the people who were present. Omeiya set out for Syria, and remained there the full period of his exile. The circumstance is carefully and superstitiously noted by Mahometan writers as the first trace of that rivalry between the *Hâshimite* and *Omeyad* factions, which in after ages shook the Caliphate.

Hâshim marries

Hâshim was now advanced in years when, on a mercan-

---

[1] It is difficult to express, in any language but the Arabic, the idea implied by such a contest. It was a vainglorious practice of the Arabs, which consisted in one person challenging another, and claiming to be more noble and renowned, brave or generous, than he. Each disputant adduced facts and witnesses to prove his ambitious pretensions, and the arbiter judged at his discretion.

tile journey to the north, he visited Medîna with a party of the
Coreish. As he traded there, he was attracted by the graceful figure
of a female, who from an elevated position was directing her
people how to buy and sell for her. She was discreet and comely,
and made a tender impression upon the heart of Hâshim. He
enquired of the citizens whether she was married or single, and
they answered that she had been married, but was now divorced.
The dignity of the lady, they added, was so great amongst her
people that she would not marry, unless it were stipulated that
she should remain mistress of her own concerns, and have at
pleasure the power of divorce. This was SALMA, daughter of Amr,
of the Bani Najjâr. Hâshim thereupon demanded her in marriage; and she consented, for she was well aware of his renown
and noble birth. The fruit of this union was a son, who remained with his mother at Medîna.

Salma at Medina, who bears him a son A.D 497.

Hâshim, dying a few years after on a mercantile expedition
to Gaza, left his dignities to Muttalib, his elder brother, who,
when Hâshim's son had grown into boyhood, set out for Medîna
to fetch him thence. On his return, as the inhabitants of Mecca
saw him pass with a lad by his side, they concluded that he had
purchased a slave, and exclaimed *Abd al Muttalib!*—'lo, the
servant of Muttalib!' 'Out upon you!' said he; 'it is my
nephew, the son of Hâshim.' And as each scrutinised the
features of the boy, they swore—'By my life, it is the very
same.' In this incident is said to have originated the name of
ABD AL MUTTALIB, by which the son of Hâshim was called.

Muttalib fetches his nephew Abd al Muttalib from Medina.

In due time Abd al Muttalib was installed by his uncle in the
possession of his father's property; but Naufal, another uncle,
interposed, and violently deprived him of the paternal estate.
Abd al Muttalib (now reached the years of discretion) appealed to his tribe to aid him in resisting the usurpation of his
rights; but they declined to interfere. He then wrote to his
maternal relatives at Medîna, who no sooner received the intelligence than eighty mounted men of his mother's clan started for
Mecca. Abd al Muttalib went forth to meet them, and invited
them to his house; but their chief refused to alight until he had
called Naufal to account. He proceeded straightway to the yard
of the holy House, and found him seated there among the chiefs
of the Coreish. Naufal arose to offer welcome; but the stranger
refused his welcome, and drawing his sword declared that he
would plunge it into him unless he forthwith reinstated the orphan
in his rights. The oppressor was daunted, and agreed to the
concession, which was ratified by oath before the assembled
Coreish.

Abd al Muttalib maintains possession of his paternal estate.

Some years after, on the death of Muttalib, Abd al Mut-

Abd al Muttalib

succeeds to the office of entertaining pilgrims.

He discovers the ancient well Zemzem.

Claim of Coreish negatived by oracle.

Zemzem gives forth an abundant spring.

His son, *Abdallah,* ransomed

talib succeeded to the office of entertaining the pilgrims. But for a long time he was destitute of power and influence; and, having but one son to assist him in the assertion of his claims, he found it difficult to cope with the opposing faction of the Coreish. It was during this period that he discovered the ancient well of Zemzem. Finding it laborious to procure water from the scattered wells of Mecca and store it in cisterns by the Káaba, and perhaps aware by tradition of the existence of a well in the vicinity, he made diligent search, and at last chanced upon the venerable masonry. It was a remnant of the palmy days of Mecca, when a rich and incessant stream of commerce flowed through it. Centuries had elapsed since the trade had ceased, and with it had followed the partial desertion of Mecca, and neglect of the well. It was choked up either accidentally or by design, and the remembrance of it was so indistinct that even the site was now unknown.

As Abd al Muttalib, aided by his son Hârith, dug deeper and deeper, he came upon the two golden gazelles, with the swords and suits of armour buried there (as we have seen) by the Jorhomite king more than three centuries before. The Coreish envied him these treasures, and demanded a share. They asserted their right to the well itself, as the possession of their common ancestor Ishmael. Abd al Muttalib was not powerful enough to resist the oppressive claim; but he agreed to refer it to the decision of the arrows of HOBAL, the god whose image was within the Káaba. Lots were cast for the Káaba and for the respective claimants. The gazelles fell to the share of the Káaba, and the swords and suits of armour to Abd al Muttalib, while the arrows of the Coreish were blank. The Coreish acquiesced in the divine decree, and relinquished their pretensions to the well. Abd al Muttalib beat out the gazelles into plates of gold, and fixed them by way of ornament to the door of the Káaba. He hung up the swords before the door as a protection to the treasures within; but at the same time added a more effectual guard in the shape of a golden lock and key.

The plentiful flow of fresh water, soon apparent in the well Zemzem, was a great triumph to Abd al Muttalib. All other wells in Mecca were deserted, and this alone resorted to. From it Abd al Muttalib supplied the pilgrims; and the water itself soon shared the sacredness of the Káaba and its rites. The fame and influence of Abd al Muttalib now waxed greater and greater; a large family of powerful sons added to his dignity; he became, and continued to his death, the virtual chief of Mecca.

A strange calamity threatened to embitter his prosperity. During his early troubles, while supported by an only son, he had felt so strongly his weakness and inferiority in contending with the large and influential families of his opponents, as to vow that, if Providence should ever grant him ten sons, he would devote one of them to the Deity. Years rolled on, and the rash father at last found himself surrounded by the longed-for number, the sight of whom daily reminded him of his vow. He bade his sons accompany him to the Káaba; each was made to write his name upon a lot, and the lots were made over to the intendant of the temple, who cast them in the usual mode. The fatal arrow fell upon ABDALLAH, the youngest and the best beloved. The vow devoting him to the Deity must needs be fulfilled, but how else than by the sacrificial knife? His daughters wept and clung around Abd al Muttalib, who was willingly persuaded to cast lots between Abdallah and ten camels, the current fine for the blood of a man. If the Deity should accept the ransom, the father need not scruple to spare his son. But the lot a second time fell upon Abdallah. Again, and with equal fortune, it was cast between him and twenty camels. At each successive trial Abd al Muttalib added ten camels to the stake, but the Deity appeared inexorably to refuse the vicarious offering, and to require the blood of his son. It was now the tenth throw, and the ransom had reached a hundred camels, when the lot at last fell upon them. The father joyfully released Abdallah from his impending fate; and taking a hundred camels slaughtered them between Safa and Marwa. The inhabitants of Mecca feasted upon them, and the residue was left to the beasts and to the birds; for Abd al Muttalib's family refused to taste of them. This Abdallah was the father of Mahomet.

The prosperity and fame of Abd al Muttalib excited the envy of the house of Omeiya, whose son Harb, following the example of his father, challenged his rival to a trial of their respective merits. The Abyssinian king declined to be the umpire, and the judgment was committed to a Coreishite, who declared that Abd al Muttalib was in every respect the superior. Harb was deeply mortified, and abandoned the society of his opponent whose companion he had previously been. Thus the ill feeling between the branches of Hâshim and Omeiya was perpetuated and increased.

Abd al Muttalib gained an important accession of stability to his party by concluding a defensive league with the Khozâite inhabitants of Mecca. They came to him and represented that, as their quarters adjoined, such a treaty would be advantageous for both parties. Abd al Muttalib was not slow in perceiving this. With ten of his adherents he met the Khozâites at the Káaba, and there they mutually pledged their faith. The league was reduced to writing, and hung up in the Holy house. No one from the family of Omeiya was present, or indeed knew of the transaction until thus published. The combination was permanent, and in after times proved of essential service to Mahomet.

The viceroy of Yemen invades Mecca A.D. 570,

In the year A.D. 570, or about eight years before the death of Abd al Muttalib, occurred the memorable invasion of Mecca by Abraha the Abyssinian viceroy of Yemen. This potentate had built at Sanâ a magnificent cathedral to which he sought to attract the worship of Arabia, and, thwarted in the attempt, he vented his displeasure in an attack on Mecca and its temple. Upon this enterprise he set out with a considerable army. In its train was an elephant;—a circumstance for Arabia so singular that the commander, his host, the invasion, and the year, are still called by the name of 'the Elephant.' Notwithstanding opposition from various Arab tribes, Abraha victoriously reached Tâif, a city three days' march east of Mecca. The men of Tâif protested that they had no concern with the Káaba, and furnished the Abyssinians with a guide, who died on the way to Mecca. Centuries afterwards, men were wont to mark their abhorrence of the traitor by casting stones at his tomb as they passed.

And threatens the Káaba;

Abraha then sent forward a body of troops to scour the Tehâma, and carry off what cattle they could find. They were successful in the raid, and among the plunder secured two hundred camels belonging to Abd al Muttalib. An embassy was despatched to the inhabitants of Mecca: 'Abraha,' the message ran, 'had no desire to do them injury. His only object was to demolish the Káaba; that performed, he would retire without shedding the blood of any.' The citizens of Mecca had already resolved that it would be vain to oppose the invader by force of arms; but the destruction of the Káaba they refused upon any terms to allow. At last the embassy prevailed on Abd al Muttalib and the other chiefs of Mecca to repair to the viceroy's camp, and there plead their cause. Abd al Muttalib was treated with distinguished honour. To gain him over, Abraha restored his plundered camels; but he could obtain from him no satisfactory answer regarding the Káaba. The chiefs offered a third of the wealth of the Tehâma if he would desist from his designs against their temple, but he refused. The negotiation was broken off, and the deputation returned to Mecca. The people, by the advice of Abd al Muttalib, made preparations for retiring in a body to the hills and defiles about the city on the day before the expected attack. As Abd al Muttalib leaned upon the ring of the door of the Káaba, he is said to have prayed to the Deity thus aloud: 'Defend, O Lord, thine own House, and suffer not the Cross to triumph over the Káaba!' This done, he relaxed his hold, and, betaking himself with the rest to the neighbouring heights, watched what the end might be.

Meanwhile a pestilential distemper had shown itself in the camp of the viceroy. It broke out with deadly pustules and blains, and was probably an aggravated form of small-pox. In confusion and dismay the army commenced its retreat. Abandoned by their guides, they perished among the valleys, and a flood (such is the pious legend) sent by the wrath of Heaven swept multitudes into the sea. The pestilence alone is, however, adequate to the effects described. Scarcely any recovered who had once been smitten by it; and Abraha himself, a mass of malignant and putrid sores, died miserably on his return to Sanâ.[1]

Is discomfited by the pestilence.

The unexpected and seemingly miraculous disappointment of the magnificent preparations of Abraha increased the reverence with which throughout Arabia the Coreish were regarded. They became vainglorious, and sought to mark their superiority by the assumption of special immunities. 'Let us,' they said, 'release ourselves from some of the observances imposed upon the multitude; and forbid ourselves some of the things which to them are lawful.' Thus (says tradition) they gave up the yearly pilgrimage to Arafât, and the ceremonial return therefrom, although they still acknowledged those acts to be an essential part of the 'religion of Abraham,' binding upon others; they also denied themselves the use of cheese and butter while in the pilgrim garb; and, abandoning tents of camels' hair, restricted themselves to tents of leather. Upon pilgrims who came from beyond the sacred limits, they imposed new rules for their own aggrandisement. Such visitors, whether for the Greater or the Lesser pilgrimage, were forbidden to eat food brought from without the sacred boundary; and were compelled to make the circuit of the Káaba either naked, or clothed in vestments provided only by the citizens who formed the league. This association, called the HOMS, included the Coreish, the Bani Kinâna a collateral branch, and the Khozâites. To them the privileges of the league were re-

The Coreish establish the Homs *or ceremonial exceptions in their own favour.*

---

[1] The accounts leave no room to question the nature of the disease as having been a pestilential form of small-pox. Wâckidi, after describing the calamity in the fanciful style of the Corân, adds: '*And that was the first beginning of the small-pox.*' The word signifies likewise 'small stones,' and the name as applied to the small-pox is probably derived from the gravelly appearance and feeling of the hard pustules. The name, coupled with its derivation, probably gave rise to the poetical description of the event in the Corân: '*Hast thou not seen how thy Lord dealt with the army of the Elephant? Did he not cause their stratagem to miscarry? And he sent against them flocks of little birds which cast upon them small clay stones, and made them like unto the stubble of which the cattle have eaten.*'

stricted. All others were subjected to the humiliation of soliciting food and raiment.

There is some doubt as to whether these innovations were only now introduced or existed from an earlier period. Under any circumstances they give proof that the worship of the Káaba was active and vigorous, and that its directors exercised a wonderful influence over the whole of Arabia. The practices then enforced were superseded only by Islâm; and (adopting the latest date assigned for their introduction) they were maintained for more than half a century. The reverence for the Káaba, which permitted the imposition of customs so unreasonable and oppressive, must necessarily have been grossly superstitious as well as widely prevalent.

Let us now review for a moment the state of parties in Mecca towards the latter days of Abd al Muttalib.

There arose, as we have seen, upon the death of Cossai, two leading factions, the descendants respectively of his sons, Abd al Dâr and Abd Menâf. The house of Abd al Dâr originally possessed all the public offices; but since the struggle with Hâshim, when they were stripped of several important dignities, their influence had departed, and they had now sunk into a subordinate and insignificant position. The offices retained by them were still undoubtedly valuable, but they were divided among separate members of the family; the benefit of combination was lost; and there was no steady and united effort to improve their advantages towards the acquisition of social influence and political power.

The virtual chiefship of Mecca was thus in the hands of the descendants of Abd Menâf. Among these, again, two parties had arisen; the families, namely, of his sons Hâshim and Abd Shams. The grand offices of giving food and water to the pilgrims secured to the Hâshimites a commanding and permanent influence under the able management of Hâshim, of Muttalib, and now of Abd al Muttalib who, like his father Hâshim, was regarded as the chief of the sheikhs of Mecca. But the

branch of Omeiya son of Abd Shams, with its numerous and powerful connections, were jealous of the power of the Hâshimites, and repeatedly endeavoured to humble them, or to bring discredit on their high position. One office, the Leadership in war, was secured by the Omeyad family, and contributed much to its splendour. The Omeyads were, moreover, rich and successful in commerce, and by some are thought to have exceeded in influence and power even the stock of Hâshim.

But the 'Year of the Elephant' had already given birth to a personage destined, within half a century, to eclipse the distinctions both of Hâshimite and Omeyad race. To the narration of this momentous event the succeeding chapter will be devoted.

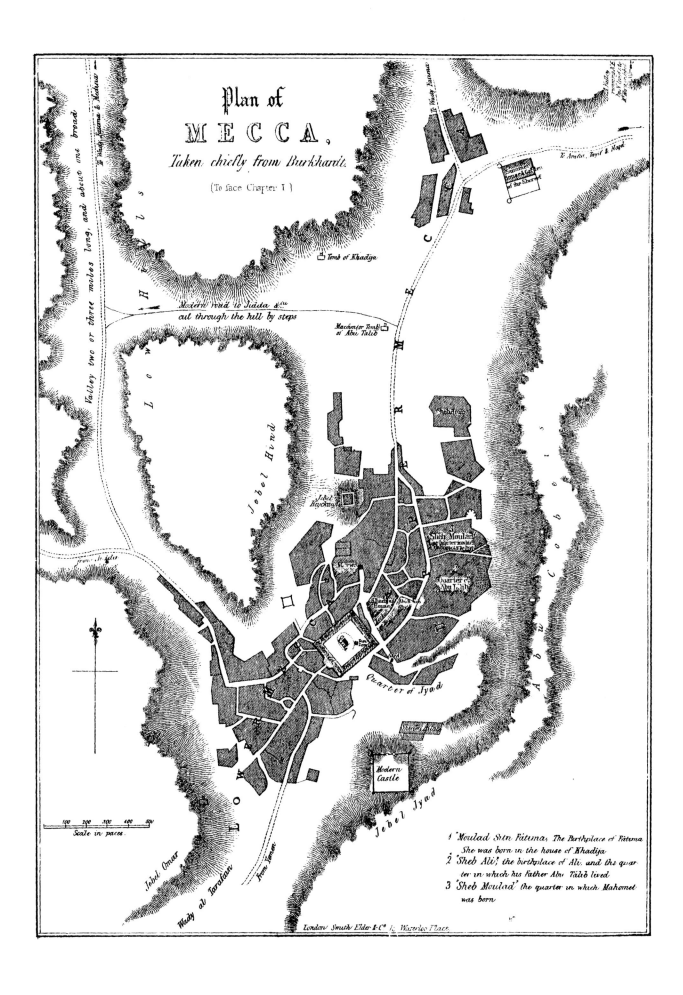

Plan of
MECCA.

Taken chiefly from Burkhardt.

(To face Chapter I)

Valley two or three miles long, and about one broad

To Wady Fatima & Madina

To Wady Fatima & Madina

Hejaz Hills

Lower

Jebel Hind

To Wady Fatima

To Arafat, Tayif & Nejd

Summer residence & Garden of the Shereef

Tomb of Khadija

M E R R O R

Modern road to Jidda &c.
cut through the hill by steps

Macâm (or Tomb)
of Abu Talib

Jebel Kaykaan

Chebilun

Sheb Moulad
the quarter in which
Mahomet is born

Quarter of
Abu Jebb

M. Syad

Khadija Abu Bekr
House

Quarter of Jyad

Abu Cobeys Hills

Sheb Moulad

From Jidda

From Yemen

Jebel Omar

Wady al Taralain

Modern
Castle

Jebel Jyad

100 200 300 400 500
Scale in paces.

1 "Moulad Sitn Fatima, The Birthplace of Fatima
   She was born in the house of Khadija
2 "Sheb Ali", the birthplace of Ali and the quarter in which his father Abu Talib lived
3 "Sheb Moulad" the quarter in which Mahomet
   was born

London Smith Elder & Co. 15 Waterloo Place.

THE LIFE OF MAHOMET.

CHAPTER I.

THE BIRTH AND CHILDHOOD OF MAHOMET.

In the Introduction, the history of Mecca and the ancestors of Mahomet has been traced from the earliest times to the *year of the Elephant*, when the sacred city was marvellously delivered from the army of the Abyssinian viceroy of Yemen. Before proceeding farther, I propose briefly to describe Mecca and the country immediately surrounding it.

Within the great mountain range which skirts the Red Sea, and about equidistant by the caravan track from Yemen and the Gulf of Akaba, lies the holy valley. The traveller from the seashore, after a journey of about fifty miles, reaches it by an almost imperceptible ascent, chiefly through sandy plains and defiles hemmed in by low hills of gneiss and quartz, which rise in some places four or five hundred feet. Passing Mecca, and pursuing an eastward course, he proceeds with the same gentle rise between hills partly composed of granite through the valley of Minâ, and in five or six hours arrives at the sacred eminence of Arafât. Onwards the mountains ascend to a great height, till about eighty miles from the sea the granite peaks of Jebel Kora crown the range, and Tâif comes in sight thirty miles farther east. Between Jebel Kora and Tâif the country is fertile and lovely. Rivulets every here and there descend from the hills ; the plains are clothed with verdure, and adorned by

B

Fertility of Tâif.

large shady trees. Tâif is famous for its fruits. The grapes are of a large size and delicious flavour. And there is no want of variety to tempt the appetite; for peaches and pomegranates, apples and almonds, figs, apricots and quinces, grow in abundance and perfection. Far different is it with the frowning hills and barren valleys for many a mile round Mecca. Stunted brushwood and thorny acacias occasionally relieve the eye, and furnish a scanty repast to the camel; but the general features are rugged rocks unrelieved by a trace of foliage, with sandy stony glens from which the peasant in vain looks for the grateful returns of tillage. Even at the present day, after the riches of Asia have for twelve centuries poured into the city, and a regular supply of water may be secured by a conduit from the springs of Arafât, Mecca can hardly boast a garden or cultivated field, and only here and there a tree.

Sterility of Mecca.

Valley of Mecca.

In the immediate vicinity of Mecca the hills are formed of quartz and gneiss; but a little to the east, grey strata of granite appear, and within one or two miles of the city, lofty and rugged peaks begin to shoot upwards in grand masses. The valley of Mecca is about two miles in length. The general direction and slope are from north to south; but the upper or northern extremity on the way to Arafât bends eastward; and at the southern or lower end, where the roads from Yemen Jedda and Syria meet, there is a still more decided bend to the west. At the latter curve the valley opens out to the breadth of half a mile; and in the spacious amphitheatre thus shut in by rocks and mountains were founded the Káaba, and the main portions of the city both ancient and modern. The surrounding rocks rise precipitously two or three hundred feet, and on the eastern side reach a height of five hundred. It is here that the craggy defiles of Abu Cobeis the most lofty of the hills encircling the valley, overhang the quarter of the town in which Abd al Muttalib and his family lived. About three furlongs to the north-east of the Káaba, the spot of Mahomet's birth is still pointed out to the pious pilgrim, and hard by is the quarter in which Ali resided; both built upon the declivity of the rock.

Climate.

Though within the tropics, Mecca has not the advantage of tropical showers. The rainy season begins about December, but the clouds do not at any time discharge their precious freight continuously or with regularity. Sometimes the rain descends with excessive violence and inundates the little valley with floods from Arafât. Even in the summer, rain is not unfrequent. The seasons are thus uncertain, and the calamities of continued drought are occasionally experienced. The heat, especially in the months of autumn, is oppressive. The surrounding ridges make the valley close and sultry; and the sun, beating with violence on the bare gravelly soil, reflects an intense and distressing glare. The native of Mecca, acclimated to the narrow vale, may regard with complacency its inhospitable atmosphere; but the traveller even in winter complains of stifling warmth and stifling closeness.[1]

Such is the spot, barren and unpromising, on which the Arabs look with fond and superstitious reverence as the cradle of their destiny, and the arena of the remote events which gave birth to their faith. Here Hagar alighted with Ishmael, and in search of water hurried to and fro between the little hill of Safa, a spur of Abu Cobeis, and the eminence of Marwa, an offshoot from the range on the opposite side of the valley. Here the Bani Jorhom established themselves upon the failing fortunes of the ancestors of the Coreish; and from hence they were expelled by the Bani Khozâa, the new invaders from the south. It was in this pent-up vale that Cossai nourished his ambitious plans, and, in the neighbouring defiles of Minâ, asserted them by a bloody encounter with his rivals; and here he established the Coreish in their supremacy. It was hard by the Káaba that his descendants, the children of Abd al Dâr and of Abd Menâf, were drawn up in battle array to fight for the sovereign prerogative. It was here that Hâshim exhibited his princely liberality; and on this spot that Abd al Muttalib toiled with his solitary son till he discovered the ancient well of Zemzem. Thousands of such associations crowd upon the mind of the weary pilgrim, as the minarets of the Káaba rise before his longing eyes; and in the long vista of ages reaching even to Adam, his imagination pictures multitudes of pious devotees in every age and from all quarters of the globe, flocking to the little valley, making their seven circuits of the holy

Fond veneration with which it is regarded by the Arabs.

---

[1] Sprenger thinks the population may have been at this time 12,000. The number seems large; but materials for even the loosest estimate are wanting.

house, kissing the mysterious stone, and drinking of the sacred water. Well then may the Arab regard the fane, and its surrounding rocks, with awe and admiration.

Abdallah (born A D. 545) marries Amina.

At the period of Abraha's retreat from Mecca, Abd al Muttalib, now above seventy years of age, enjoyed the rank and consideration of the foremost chief of Mecca. Some months previous to that event, he had taken his youngest son ABDALLAH,[1] then about four-and-twenty years of age, to the house of Wuheib, a distant kinsman descended from Zohra brother of the famous Cossai; and there affianced him to AMINA [2] the niece of Wuheib, under whose guardianship she lived. At the same time Abd al Muttalib, notwithstanding his advanced age, bethought him of a matrimonial alliance on his own account, and married Hâlah the cousin of Amina and daughter of Wuheib; of this late marriage, the famous Hamza was the firstfruits.

Death of Abdallah.

As was customary in a marriage at the home of the bride, Abdallah remained with her there for three days. Not long after, he left his wife with child, and set out on a mercantile expedition to Ghazza (Gaza) in the south of Syria. On his way back he sickened at Medîna, and was left behind by the caravan with his father's maternal relatives. Abd al Muttalib, learning of Abdallah's sickness from his comrades, despatched his son Hârîth to take care of him. On reaching Medîna, Hârîth found that his brother had died about a month after the departure of the caravan. He returned with these tidings, and his father and brethren mourned for Abdallah. He was but five-and-twenty years of age at his death, and Amina had not yet been delivered. He left behind him five camels fed on wild shrubs,[3] a flock of goats, and *Omm Ayman*, a slave-girl (called also *Baraka*), who tended the infant borne by his widow. This little property, and the house in which he dwelt, were all the inheritance Mahomet received from his father; but, little as it was, the simple habits of the Arab required no more, and, instead of being evidence of poverty, the possession of a female slave is rather an indication of prosperity and comfort.

[1] Abdallah, or *servant of God* (corresponding with the Hebrew *Abdiel*), was a name common among the ante-Mahometan Arabs.

[2] The first syllable of Amina is long, the second short.

[3] That is to say, not reared at home, and therefore of an inferior kind.

Passing over, as fabulous and unworthy of credit, the marvellous incidents related of the gestation of the infant Mahomet, it suffices to state that the widowed Amina gave birth to a son in the autumn of the year A.D. 570. The materials are too vague and discrepant for any close calculation. But we are told that the event occurred about fifty-five days after the attack of Abraha; and we may accept, as an approximation, the date carefully computed by Caussin de Perceval, namely, the 20th of August, A.D. 570.

Amina delivered of a son, August, A.D. 570.

No sooner was the infant born, than Amina sent to tell Abd al Muttalib. The messenger carrying the good tidings, reached the chief as he sat in the sacred enclosure of the Káaba, in the midst of his sons and the principal men of his tribe; and he was glad (so the simple tradition runs), and arose and those that were with him, and visited Amina, who told him all that had taken place. Then he took the young child in his arms, and went to the Káaba; and as he stood beside the holy house, he gave thanks to God. The child was called MOHAMMAD.

Joy of Abd al Muttalib.

The child is called Mohammad.

This name was rare among the Arabs, but not unknown. It is derived from the root *Hamd* and signifies 'The Praised.' Another form is AHMAD, which having been erroneously employed as a translation of '*The Paraclete*' in some Arabic version of the New Testament, became a favourite term with Mahometans, especially in addressing Jews and Christians; for it was (they said) the title under which the Prophet had been in their books predicted. Following the established usage of Christendom, I will style Mohammad MAHOMET.

Derivation of the name.

It was not the custom for the better class of women at Mecca to nurse their children. They procured nurses for them, or gave them out to nurse among the neighbouring Bedouin tribes, where was gained the double advantage of a robust frame, and the pure speech and free manners of the desert.[1]

The infant was not nursed by his mother,

The infant Mahomet, shortly after his birth, was made

---

[1] The practice is still common among the Shereefs of Mecca. At eight days old the infant is sent away and, excepting a visit at the sixth month, does not return to his parents till eight or ten years of age. Burkhardt names several tribes to which the infants are thus sent; and among them the *Bani Sád*, the very tribe to which the infant Mahomet was made over.

but for a few days by Thueiba.

over to Thueiba, a slave woman of Abu Lahab who had lately nursed Hamza. Though suckled by her for a very few days, he retained in after life a lively sense of the connection thus formed. Both Mahomet and Khadîja were wont to express in grateful terms their respect for her. Mahomet used to send her periodically clothes and other presents until the seventh year of the Hégira, when tidings were brought of her death. Then he enquired after her son, his foster-brother; but he too was dead, and she had left no relatives.

Entrusted to Halima, a woman of the Bani Sád.

After Thueiba had suckled the child for several days, a party of the Bani Sád (a tribe of the Bani Hawâzin) arrived at Mecca with ten women who offered themselves as nurses. They were soon provided with children, excepting Halîma who was at last with difficulty persuaded to take the infant Mahomet; for it was to the father that the nurses chiefly looked for reward, and the charge of the orphan child had been already declined. The legends of after days have encircled Halîma's journey home with a halo of miraculous prosperity, but this it does not lie within my province to relate.

Remains among the Bani Sáad till five years old.

The infancy and part of the childhood of Mahomet were spent with Halîma among the Bani Sád. At two years of age she weaned him and took him to his home. Amina was so delighted with the healthy and robust appearance of her infant, who looked like a child of double the age, that she said: 'Take him with thee back again to the desert; for I fear the unhealthy air of Mecca.' So Halîma returned with him to her tribe. When another two years were ended, some strange event occurred to the boy which greatly alarmed his nurse. It was probably a fit of epilepsy; but Mahometan legends have invested it with so many marvellous features, that it is difficult to discover the real facts. It is certain that the apprehensions of Halîma and her husband were aroused; for Arab superstition was wont to regard the subject of such ailments as under the influence of an evil spirit. They resolved to rid themselves of the charge, and Halîma carried the child back to its mother. With some difficulty, Amina obtained from her an account of what had happened, calmed her fears, and entreated her to resume the care of her boy. Halîma loved her foster-child, and was not unwil-

Is seized with a fit.

lingly persuaded to take him once more to her encampment. There she kept him for about a year longer, and watched him so closely that she would not suffer him to move out of her sight. But uneasiness was again excited by fresh symptoms of a suspicious nature ; and she set out finally to restore the boy to his mother, when he was about five years of age. As she reached the outskirts of Mecca, the child strayed and she could not find him. In her perplexity she repaired to Abd al Muttalib, and he sent one of his sons to aid her in the search; the little boy was discovered wandering in Upper Mecca, and restored to his mother.

If we are right in regarding the attacks which alarmed Halîma as fits of a nervous or epileptic nature, they exhibit in the constitution of Mahomet the normal marks of those excited states and ecstatic swoons which perhaps suggested to his own mind the idea of inspiration, as by his followers they were undoubtedly taken to be evidence of it. It is probable that, in other respects, the constitution of Mahomet was rendered robust, and character free and independent, by his five years' residence among the Bani Sád. At any rate his speech was thus formed upon one of the purest models of the beautiful language of the Peninsula; and it was his pride in after days to say : ' Verily, I am the most perfect Arab amongst you ; my descent is from the Coreish, and my tongue is the tongue of the Bani Sád.' When eloquence began to form an important element towards his success, a pure language and standard dialect were advantages of essential moment.

Advantages to Mahomet from residence among the Bedouins.

Mahomet ever retained a grateful impression of the kindness he had experienced as a child among the Bani Sáad. Halîma visited him at Mecca after his marriage with Khadîja. ' It was ' (the tradition runs) ' a year of drought, in which much cattle perished ; and Mahomet spoke to Khadîja and she gave to Halîma a camel used to carry a litter, and forty sheep ; so she returned to her people.' Upon another occasion he spread out his mantle for her to sit upon,—a token of especial respect,—and placed his hand upon her bosom in a familiar and affectionate manner. Many years after when, on the expedition against Tâif, he attacked the Bani Hawâzin and took a multitude of them captive, they found ready access to his heart by reminding him of the days

Grateful remembrance of Halîma's nursing.

when he was nursed among them. About the same time a woman called Shîma was brought in with some other prisoners to the camp. When they threatened her with their swords, she declared that she was the Prophet's foster-sister. Mahomet enquired how he should know the truth of this, and she replied: ' Thou gavest me this bite upon my back, once upon a time when I carried thee on my hip.' The Prophet recognised the mark, spread his mantle over her, and made her to sit down by him. He gave her the option of remaining in honour and comfort with him, but she preferred to return with a present to her people.

The sixth year of his life Mahomet spent at Mecca under the care of his mother. She then planned a visit to Medîna, where she longed to show her boy to the maternal relatives of his father. So she departed with her slave-girl Omm Ayman who tended the child; and they rode upon two camels. Arrived in Medîna, she alighted at the house where her husband had died and was buried. The visit was of sufficient duration to imprint the scene and the society, notwith-

standing his tender age, upon the memory of Mahomet. He used in later days to call to recollection things that happened on this occasion. Seven-and-forty years afterwards, when he entered Medîna as a refugee, he recognised the place, and said: ' In this house I sported with Aynasa, a little girl of Medîna; and with my cousins, I used to put to flight the birds that alighted upon the roof.' As he gazed upon the mansion, he added: ' Here it was my mother lodged with me; in this place is the tomb of my father; and it was there, in that very well (or pond), that I learnt to swim.'

After sojourning at Medîna about a month, Amina be- thought her of returning to Mecca, and set out in the same manner as she had come. But when she had reached about half way a spot called Abwâ, she fell sick and died; and she was buried there. The little orphan was carried back to Mecca by Omm Ayman, who although then quite a girl was a faithful nurse to the child, and continued to be his constant attendant.

The early loss of his mother no doubt imparted to the youthful Mahomet something of that pensive and meditative character by which he was afterwards distinguished. In his seventh year he could appreciate the bereavement and feel the desolation of his orphan state. In the Corân he has alluded touchingly to the subject. While reassuring his heart of the divine favour, he recounts the mercies of the Almighty; and amongst them the first is this: '*Did He not find thee an orphan, and furnished thee with a refuge?*' On his pilgrimage from Medîna to Hodeibia he visited his mother's tomb, and he lifted up his voice and wept, and his followers likewise wept around him. And they asked him concerning it, and he said: 'This is the grave of my mother: the Lord hath permitted me to visit it. And I sought leave to pray for her salvation, but it was not granted. So I called my mother to remembrance, and the tender memory of her overcame me, and I wept.'

Grief on visiting her tomb in after life.

The charge of the orphan was now undertaken by his grandfather Abd al Muttalib, who had by this time reached the patriarchal age of fourscore years. The child was treated by him with singular fondness. A rug used to be spread under the Káaba, and on it the aged chief reclined in shelter from the heat of the sun. Around the carpet, but at a respectful distance, sat his sons. The little Mahomet was wont to run up close to the patriarch, and unceremoniously take possession of his rug; his sons would seek to drive him off; but Abd al Muttalib would interpose, saying: 'Let my little son alone,' stroke him on the back, and delight to listen to his childish prattle. The boy was still under the care of his nurse; but he would ever and anon quit her, and run into the apartment of his grandfather even when he was alone or asleep.

Abd al Muttalib undertakes charge of the orphan A.D. 576.

The guardianship of Abd al Muttalib lasted but two years, for he died eight years after the attack of Abraha. The orphan child felt bitterly the loss of his indulgent grandfather; as he followed the bier he was seen to weep, and when he grew up, he retained a distinct remembrance of his death. The heart of Mahomet in his tender years was thus again rudely wounded, and the fresh bereavement was rendered more poignant by the dependent position in which it left him. The nobility of his grandfather's descent, the deference paid to him throughout the vale of Mecca, and his splendid liberality in providing the pilgrims with food and drink, were witnessed with satisfaction by the thoughtful child. These things no doubt left behind them a proud

Abd al Muttalib dies A.D. 578.

remembrance, and formed the seed perhaps of many an ambitious thought and day-dream of power and domination.

Effect of death of Abd al Muttalib.

The death of Abd al Muttalib left the children of Hâshim without any powerful head; while it enabled the other branch, descended from Omeiya, to gain an ascendency. Of the latter family the chief at this time was Harb, who held the *Leadership* in war, and was followed by a numerous and powerful body of relations.

The sons of Abd al Muttalib.

Of Abd al Muttalib's sons, Hârîth the eldest was now dead; the chief of those who survived were Zobeir and Abu Tâlib (both by the same mother as Abdallah the father of Mahomet), Abu Lahab, Abbâs and Hamza. The last two were still very young. Zobeir was the oldest, and to him Abd al Muttalib bequeathed his dignity and offices. Zobeir, again,

Abu Tâlib and Abbâs.

left them to Abu Tâlib, who, finding himself too poor to discharge the expensive and onerous task of providing for the pilgrims, waived the honour in favour of his younger brother Abbâs. But the family of Hâshim had fallen from its high estate; for Abbâs was able to retain only the giving of drink, while the furnishing of food passed into the hands of another branch. Abbâs was rich, and his influential post, involving the constant charge of the well Zemzem, was retained by him till the introduction of Islâm, and then confirmed to his family by the Prophet; but he was not a man of strong character, and never attained to a commanding position at Mecca. Abu Tâlib, on the other hand, possessed many noble qualities, and won greater respect; but, probably from poverty, he too remained in the back ground. It was thus that in the oscillations of phylarchical government, the prestige of the house of Hâshim had begun to wane, and nearly disappear; while a rival branch was rising to importance. This phase of the political state of Mecca began with the death of Abd al Muttalib, and continued until the conquest of the city by Mahomet himself.

Abu Tâlib becomes guardian of his orphan nephew.

To Abu Tâlib, the dying Abd al Muttalib consigned the guardianship of his orphan grandchild; and faithfully and kindly did Abu Tâlib discharge the trust. His fondness for the lad equalled that of Abd al Muttalib. He made him sleep by his bed, eat by his side, and go with him whenever he walked abroad. And this tender treatment was continued until his nephew had emerged from the helplessness of child-hood.

It was during this period that Abu Tâlib, accompanied by Mahomet, undertook a mercantile journey to Syria. He intended to leave the child behind; for now twelve years of age he was able to take care of himself. But when the caravan was ready to depart, and Abu Tâlib about to mount, his nephew, overcome by the prospect of so long a separation, clung to his protector. Abu Tâlib was moved, and carried the boy along with him. The expedition extended to Bostra, perhaps farther. It lasted for several months, and afforded to the youthful Mahomet opportunities of observation, which were not lost upon him. He passed near to Petra, Jerash, Ammon, and other remains of former mercantile grandeur; and the sight must have deeply imprinted upon his reflective mind the instability of earthly greatness. The wild story of the valley of Hejer, with its lonely deserted habitations hewn out of the rock, and the tale of divine vengeance descending on the cities of the plain over which now rolled the waves of the Dead Sea, would excite apprehension and awe; while these strange histories, rendered more startling and tragical by Jewish tradition and local legend, would win and charm the childish heart ever yearning after the marvellous. On this journey too, he passed through several Jewish settlements, and came in contact with the national profession of Christianity in Syria. Hitherto he had witnessed only the occasional and isolated exhibition of the faith: now he saw its rites in full and regular performance by a whole community. The national and social customs founded upon Christianity; the churches with their crosses, images, or pictures, and other symbols of the faith; the ringing of bells; the frequent assemblages for worship, were all forced on his attention. The reports, and possibly an actual glimpse, of the continually recurring ceremonial, effected (we may suppose) a deep impression upon him; and this impression would be rendered more practical and lasting by the sight of whole tribes, Arab like himself, converted to the same faith and practising the same observances. However fallen and materialised the Christianity of that day in Syria, it must have struck the thoughtful observer in favourable and wonderful contrast with the gross idolatry of Mecca. Once

Mahomet at twelve years of age accompanies Abu Tâlib to Syria A.D. 582.

Impressions probably excited by this journey.

again, in mature life, Mahomet visited Syria, and whatever reflections of this nature were then awakened would receive augmented force and deeper colouring, from the vivid pictures and bright imagery which, upon the same ground, had been impressed on the imagination of his childhood.

No further incident of a special nature is related of Mahomet, until he had advanced from childhood to youth.

CHAPTER II.

FROM THE YOUTH OF MAHOMET TO HIS FORTIETH YEAR.

THE next passage in the life of Mahomet is connected with events of a wider and more stirring interest.

Between the years A.D. 580 and 590, the vale of Mecca and the surrounding country were disturbed by one of those bloody feuds so frequently excited by the fiery pride, and prolonged by the revengeful temper, of the nation. 'Sacrilegious war between A.D. 580 and 590.

In Dzul Cáada, the sacred month preceding the days of pilgrimage, an annual fair was held at Ocâtz, where, within three days' journey east of Mecca, the shady palm and cool fountain offered a grateful resting-place to the merchant and the traveller after their toilsome journey. A fair held annually at Ocâtz.

Goods were bartered, vainglorious contests (those characteristic exhibitions of Bedouin chivalry) were held, and verses recited by the bards of the various tribes. The successful poems produced at this national gathering were treated with distinguished honour. They were transcribed in illuminated characters, and thus styled *Golden*; or they were attached to the Káaba and honoured with the title *Suspended*. The 'Seven suspended poems' still survive from a period anterior even to Mahomet, a wondrous specimen of artless eloquence. The beauty of the language and wild richness of the imagery are acknowledged by the European reader; but the subject of the poet was limited, and the beaten track seldom deviated from. The charms of his mistress, the envied spot marked by the still fresh traces of her encampment, the solitude of her deserted haunts, his own generosity and prowess, the unrivalled glory of his tribe, the noble qualities of his camel;—these were the themes which, with little variation of treatment, and with no contrivance whatever of plot or story, occupied the Chivalrous and poetical contests.

Arab muse;—and some of them only added fuel to the besetting vices of the people, vainglory, envy, vindictiveness, and pride.

Origin of the 'Sacrilegious war.'

At the fair of Ocâtz, a rivalrous spirit had been about this period engendered between the Coreish and the Bani Hawâzin, a numerous tribe of kindred descent, which dwelt (and still dwells) in the country between Mecca and Tâif. An arrogant poet, vaunting the superiority of his tribe, had been struck by an indignant Hawâzinite; a maid of Hawâzin descent rudely treated by some Coreishite youths; an importunate creditor insolently repulsed.[1] On each occasion the sword was unsheathed, blood flowed, and the conflict would have become general unless the leaders had interfered to calm the excited people. Such was the origin of the 'Sacrilegious war,' so called because it occurred within the sacred term, and was eventually carried within the sacred territory.

Precautions for peace.

These incidents suggested the expediency of requiring all who frequented the fair to surrender, while it lasted, their arms, and to deposit them with Abdallah ibn Jodáân, a chief of Mecca. By this precaution peace was preserved for several years, when a wanton murder supplied more serious cause of offence.

Hostilities precipitated by a murder.

The prince of Hîra had despatched to the fair a caravan richly laden with perfumes and musk. It proceeded under the escort of a chieftain of the Bani Hawâzin. Another chief, a friend of the Coreish, jealous at being supplanted in the convoy, watched his opportunity, and falling upon the caravan, slew its leader, and fled with the booty. On his flight he met a Coreishite whom he charged to proceed with expedition to the fair then being held at Ocâtz, and communicate the intelligence to Harb[2] his friend and con-

---

[1] The incident affords a curious illustration of Arab manners. The Hawâzin creditor seated himself in a conspicuous place with a monkey by his side, and said: ' *Who will give me another such ape, and I will give him in exchange my claim on such a one?* '—naming his creditor with his full pedigree from Kinâna, an ancestor of the Coreish. This he kept vociferating to the intense annoyance of the Kinâna tribe, one of whom drew his sword and cut off the monkey's head. In an instant the Hawâzin and Kinâna tribes were embroiled in bitter strife.

[2] Harb was the son of Omeiya and father of Mahomet's opponent Abu Sofiân.

federate, and the other Coreishite chiefs. The message was
conveyed, and Abdallah ibn Jodáân, thus privately informed
of the murder, immediately gave back to all their arms, and
feigning urgent business at Mecca at once departed with his
whole tribe. But the news of the murder began rapidly to
spread at Ocâtz, and as the sun went down it reached the
ears of the chief of the Hawâzin; who, forthwith perceiving
the cause of the precipitate departure of the Coreish, rallied
his people and proceeded in hot pursuit. The Coreish had
already entered the sacred limits, and the Bani Hawâzin
contented themselves with challenging their enemy to a
rencounter at the same period of the following year. The
challenge was accepted, and both parties prepared for the
struggle. Several battles were fought with various success,
and hostilities, more or less formal, were prolonged for four
years, when a truce was proposed. The dead were numbered
up, and as twenty had been killed of the Hawâzin more than
of the Coreish, the latter consented to pay the price of their
blood, and for this purpose delivered hostages. One of these
was Abu Sofiân, the famous antagonist in after days of
Mahomet.

A truce after four years' fighting.

In some of these conflicts, the whole of the Coreish
and their allies were engaged. Each tribe was commanded
by a chief of its own; and Abdallah ibn Jodáân guided the
general movements. The descendants of Abd Shams and
Noufal were headed by Harb son of Omeiya, and took a
distinguished part in the warfare. The children of Hâshim
were present also, under the command of Zobeir the eldest
surviving son of Abd al Muttalib; but they occupied no
prominent position.

Whole of Coreish engaged in the struggle.

In one of the battles Mahomet attended upon his uncles;
but, though now near twenty years of age, he had not acquired
the love of arms. According to some authorities, his efforts
were confined to gathering up the arrows discharged by the
enemy and handing them to his uncles. Others assign to
him a somewhat more active share; but the sentence in which
mention of this is preserved does not imply much enthusiasm in the warfare: 'I remember,' said the Prophet,
' being present with my uncles in the "Sacrilegious war;" I
discharged arrows at the enemy, and I do not regret it.'
Physical courage, indeed, and martial daring, are virtues

Part taken by Mahomet in the fighting.

which did not distinguish the Prophet at any period of his
career.[1]

Probable
influence
upon Maho-
met of at-
tending the
fair at
Ocâtz,

The struggles for pre-eminence and the contests of eloquence, at the annual fair, must have possessed for the
youthful Mahomet a more engrossing interest than the combat of arms. At these spectacles, while his patriotism was
aroused and desire after personal distinction stimulated by
the whole atmosphere of rivalry, he had rare opportunities
of cultivating his own genius, and learning from the greatest

in acquir-
ing the
faculty of
poetry and
rhetoric ;

masters and most perfect models, the art of poetry and the
power of rhetoric. But another and a nobler lesson might
be learned in the concourse at Ocâtz. The Christianity, as
well as the chivalry, of Arabia had representatives there ;
and, if we may believe tradition, Mahomet while a boy heard

and an ac-
quaintance
with Chris-
tians and
Jews.

Coss, the bishop of Najrân, preach a purer creed than that
of Mecca, in accents which agitated and aroused his soul.
And many at that fair, besides the venerable Coss, though
influenced it may be by a less catholic spirit, yet professed
to believe in the same revelation from above, and preach
the same good tidings. There too were Jews, serious and
earnest men, surpassing the Christians in number, and
equally with them appealing to an inspired Book. The scene
thus annually witnessed by Mahomet as he advanced into
mature years, had (we cannot doubt) a deep influence upon

Possible
germ here
of his great
catholic
system.

him. May there not have been here too the germ of his
great catholic design ; of that Faith around which the tribes
of all Arabia were to rally? At the fair, religion clashed
against religion in hopeless opposition ; and yet amid the
discord he might discern some common elements, a book, a
name, to which all would reverently bow. With the Jews
he was more familiar than the Christians, for as a child he
had seen them at Medîna, had heard of their synagogue and
worship, and had learned to respect them as men that feared
God. These glanced bitterly at the Christians, and, even
when Coss addressed them in language which approved itself
to the heart of Mahomet as truth, they scorned his words,

[1] Among the chieftains in command of tribes, it is interesting to notice
Khuweilid the father of Khadîja ; Khattâb the father of Omar ; Othmân and
Zeid, two of the four 'Enquirers' who will be noticed below ; besides other
well-known names.

and railed at the meek and lowly Jesus of whom he spoke.
Not less disdainfully did the Christians regard the Jews.
And both Jews and Christians spurned the Arab tribes as
heathens devoted to the wrath of an offended Deity. Yet
if the enquirer sought, by questioning the parties around
him, to fathom the causes of this opposition, he would find
that, notwithstanding the mutual enmity of Jews and Christians, there was a Revelation equally acknowledged by both
to be divine; that both denounced idolatry as a damnable
sin, and professed to worship the One only God ; and (what
would startle Mahomet and stir his inmost soul) that both
repeated with profound veneration a common name,—the
name of Abraham, the builder of the Káaba and author of
the faith and rites observed there by every Arab tribe.
What, if there were truth in all these systems ;—divine
TRUTH, dimly glimmering through human prejudice, malevo-
lence, and superstition ? Would not that be a glorious
mission to act the part of the Christian bishop, but on a still
wider and more catholic stage, and, by removing the miserable
partitions which hide and sever each sect and nation from
its neighbour, to make way for the illumination of truth and
love emanating from the great Father of all ! Visions and
speculations such as these were no doubt raised in the mind
of Mahomet by association with the Jews and Christians
frequenting this great fair. Certain it is that, late in life,
he referred with satisfaction to the memory of Coss the son
of Sâida, and spoke of him as having preached there the
‘ true catholic faith.’

A confederacy formed at Mecca shortly after the restor- A league
ation of peace, for the suppression of violence and injustice, amongst
the Coreish
aroused an enthusiasm in the mind of Mahomet which the for protecting the
martial exploits of the ‘ Sacrilegious war ’ failed to kindle. oppressed.
The offices of State, and with them the powers of government,
had (as we have seen) become divided among the various
Coreishite families. There was no one now to exercise an
authority such as had been enjoyed by Cossai and Hâshim,
or even by Abd al Muttalib. When any of the separate
tribes neglected to punish its members for oppression and
wrong-doing, no chief at Mecca was strong enough to stand
up as the champion of the injured. Right was not enforced :

wrong remained unpunished. Certain glaring acts of tyranny suggested to the principal Coreishite families the expediency of binding themselves by an oath to secure justice to the helpless. The honour of originating the movement is ascribed to Zobeir, the oldest surviving son of Abd al Muttalib. The descendants of Hâshim, and the families sprung from Zohra and Taym,[1] assembled in the house of Abdallah ibn Jodáân, who prepared for them a feast; and they swore 'by the avenging Deity, that they would take the part of the oppressed, and see his claim fulfilled, so long as a drop of water remained in the ocean, or that they would satisfy it from their own resources.' The league was useful, both as a restraint against injustice, and on some occasions as a means of enforcing restitution. 'I would not,' Mahomet used in after years to say, 'exchange for the choicest camel in all Arabia the remembrance of being present at the oath which we took in the house of Abdallah, when the Bani Hâshim, Zohra, and Taym, swore that they would stand by the oppressed.'[2]

Mahomet's occupation as a shepherd.

The youth of Mahomet passed away without any other incidents of interest. At one period he was employed, like other lads, in tending the sheep and goats of Mecca upon the neighbouring hills and valleys. He used when at Medîna to refer to this employment and to say that it comported with his prophetic office, even as it did with that of Moses and David. On one occasion, as some people passed by with the fruit of the wild shrub *Arak*, the Prophet said to his companions: 'Pick me out the blackest of these berries, for they are sweet;—even such was I wont to gather when I fed the flocks of Mecca at Ajyâd. Verily there hath been no prophet raised up, who performed not the work of a Shepherd.' The hire received for this duty would contribute

---

[1] Zohra the brother, and Taym the uncle, of Cossai.

[2] It is remarkable that only these three tribes joined the league. To the Bani Zohra belonged Mahomet's mother; and his friend Abu Bakr to the Bani Taym. That the league was only a partial one is probable from its name, the Oath of *Fudhúl*, i.e., 'what is unnecessary or supererogatory.' It seems to have been so called by the rest of the Coreish who did not join it. An instance is given in which after the death of Mahomet the league was appealed to by Hosein son of Ali, against Moávia or his nephew.

towards the support of his needy uncle Abu Tâlib, and the
occupation itself was congenial with his thoughtful and
meditative character. While he watched the flocks, his
attention would be riveted by the evidences of natural
religion spread around : the twinkling stars and bright con-
stellations gliding through the dark blue sky silently along,
would be charged to him with a special message ; the loneliness of the desert would arm with a deeper conviction that
speech which day everywhere utters unto day ; while the still
small voice, never unheard by the attentive listener, would
swell into grander and more imperious tones when the tempest swept with its forked lightning and far rolling thunder
along the vast solitudes of the mountains about Mecca. Thus,
we may presume, was cherished a deep and earnest faith
in the Deity as an ever-present, all-directing Agent ;—a
faith which in after days the Prophet was wont to enforce
from the stores of his well-furnished observation, by
eloquent and heart-stirring appeals to the sublime operations of Nature and the beneficent adaptations of Providence.

Probable effect of shepherd life.

Our authorities all agree in ascribing to the youth of
Mahomet a correctness of deportment and purity of manners
rare among the people of Mecca. His modesty is said to have
been miraculously preserved. ' I was engaged one night '
(so the Prophet relates) ' feeding the flocks in company with
a lad of the Coreish. And I said to him, If thou wilt look
after my flock, I will go into Mecca and divert myself there,
even as youths are wont by night to divert themselves.' But
no sooner had he reached the precincts of the city, than a
marriage feast engaged his attention, and he fell asleep.
On another night, entering the town with the same intentions, he was arrested by heavenly strains of music, and
sitting down slept till morning. Thus he escaped temptation.
' And after this,' said Mahomet, ' I no more sought after
vice ; even until I had attained unto the prophetic office.'
Making every allowance for the fond reverence which favoured
the currency of such stories, it is quite in keeping with the
character of Mahomet that he should have shrunk from the
coarse and licentious practices of his youthful friends. Endowed with a refined mind and delicate taste, reserved and

Reserved and tempe- rate youth of Maho- met.

meditative, he lived much within himself, and the ponderings of his heart supplied occupation for leisure hours spent by men of a lower stamp in rude sports and profligacy. The fair character and honourable bearing of the unobtrusive youth won the approbation of his fellow-citizens; and he received the title, by common consent, of AL AMÎN, 'the Faithful.'

Abu Tâlib suggests mercantile expedition. Ætat 25.

Thus respected and honoured, Mahomet lived a quiet and retired life in the family of Abu Tâlib, who (as we have seen) was prevented by limited means from occupying any prominent position in the society of Mecca. At last, finding his family increase faster than the ability to provide for them, Abu Tâlib bethought him of setting his nephew, now of mature age, to earn a livelihood for himself. Mahomet was never covetous of wealth, or at any period of his career energetic in the pursuit of riches for their own sake. If left to himself, he would probably have preferred the quiet and repose of his present life, to the bustle and cares of a mercantile journey. He would not spontaneously have contemplated such an expedition. But when the proposal was made, his generous soul at once felt the necessity of doing all that was possible to relieve his uncle, and he cheerfully responded to the call. The story is as follows:—

Mahomet accompanies a Syrian caravan in charge of Khadîja's venture.

When his nephew was now five-and-twenty years of age, Abu Tâlib addressed him in these words: 'I am, as thou knowest, a man of small substance; and truly the times deal hardly with me. Now here is a caravan of thine own tribe about to start for Syria, and Khadîja daughter of Khuweilid needeth men of our tribe to send forth with her merchandise. If thou wert to offer thyself, she would readily accept thy services.' Mahomet replied: 'Be it so as thou hast said.' Then Abu Tâlib went to Khadîja, and enquired whether she wished to hire his nephew, but he added: 'We hear that thou hast engaged such an one for two camels, and we should not be content that my nephew's hire were less than four.' The matron answered: 'Hadst thou askedst this thing for one of a distant or alien tribe, I would have granted it; how much rather now that thou askest it for a near relative and friend!' So the matter was settled, and Mahomet prepared for the journey. When the caravan was about to set out, his uncle commended him to the men of the company. Meisara, a servant of Khadîja, likewise travelled along with Mahomet in charge of her property.

The caravan took the usual route to Syria, the same which Mahomet had traversed with his uncle thirteen years before. In due time they reached Bostra, a city on the road to Damascus and about sixty miles to the east of the Jordan. The transactions of that busy mart, where the practised merchants of Syria sought to overreach the simple Arabs, were ill-suited to the tastes and the habits of Mahomet ; yet his natural sagacity and shrewdness carried him prosperously through the undertaking. He returned from the barter with the balance more than usually in his favour.

Reaches Bostra, and barters to advantage.

The reflective mind of Mahomet, now arrived at the mature but still inquisitive period of early manhood, must have received deep and abiding impressions from all that he saw and heard upon the journey, and during his stay at Bostra. Though the story of his interview with Nestorius (a monk who they say embraced him as 'the coming prophet') is to be rejected as puerile, yet we may be certain that Mahomet lost no opportunity of enquiring into the practices and tenets of the Syrian Christians or of conversing with the monks and clergy who fell in his way.[1]

Impressions regarding Christianity.

He probably experienced kindness, and perhaps hospitality, from them ; for in his book he ever speaks of them with respect, and sometimes with praise.[2] But for their doctrines he had no sympathy. The picture of Christianity in the Corân must have been, in some considerable degree, painted from the conceptions now formed. Had he witnessed a purer exhibition of its rites and doctrines, and seen more of its reforming and regenerating influences, we cannot doubt but that, in the sincerity of his early search after the truth, he might readily have embraced and faithfully adhered to the faith of Jesus. Lamentable, indeed, is the reflection that so small a portion of the fair form of Christi-

Distorted view presented by Syrian worship and teaching.

---

[1] Arabic was spoken by the subjects of the Ghassânide dynasty, and Mahomet would find little difficulty in effecting an interchange of ideas with those about him. Poets, merchants, and travellers from Medîna used to be guests at the Ghassânide court.

[2] Thus *Sura,* v. 91.—*Thou shalt surely find those amongst them who profess Christianity to be the most inclined to the believers. This cometh to pass because there are priests and monks among them, and because they are not elated with pride.*

anity was disclosed by the ecclesiastics and monks of Syria to the earnest enquirer; and that little, how altered and distorted! Instead of the simple majesty of the gospel,— as a revelation of God reconciling mankind to himself through his Son,—the sacred dogma of the Trinity was forced upon the traveller with the misguided and offensive zeal of Eutychian and Jacobite partisanship, and the worship of Mary exhibited in so gross a form as to leave the impression upon the mind of Mahomet that she was held to be a goddess, if not the third Person and the consort of the Deity.[1] It must surely have been by such blasphemous extravagances that Mahomet was repelled from the true doctrine of Jesus as 'the SON OF GOD,' and led to regard him only as 'Jesus son of Mary,' the sole title by which he is spoken of in the Corân. We may well mourn that the misnamed Catholicism of the Empire thus grievously misled the master mind of the age, and through him eventually so great a part of Asia and Africa.

Mahomet reports in person to Khadija the successful result.

But to return. When Mahomet had disposed of the merchandise and, according to her command, purchased for his mistress such things as she had need of, he retraced his steps in company with the caravan to his native valley.[2]

---

[1] *Sura, v. 125.—And when* GOD *shall say: O Jesus son of Mary! Didst thou speak unto mankind, saying, ' Take me and my mother for two gods besides the Lord? He shall answer, Praise be to thee! It is not for me to say that which I ought not,'* &c.

Mahomet's knowledge of Christianity was apparently derived from the Orthodox party, who styled Mary 'Mother of God.' He may have heard of the Nestorians, and they are possibly referred to among the 'Sects' into which Jews and Christians are said in the Corân to be divided. But, had he ever obtained a closer acquaintance with the Nestorian doctrine, at least in the earlier part of his career, it would (according to the analogy of his practice with respect to other subjects) have been more definitely mentioned in his revelation. The truth, however (as will be shown hereafter), is that Mahomet's acquaintance with Christianity was at the best singularly dim and meagre.

[2] Though the *direct* route from Mecca to Bostra would run a great way east of the Mediterranean, it seems possible that, either now or on the former journey, Mahomet may have seen the Mediterranean Sea. Perhaps, the caravan visited Gaza (*Ghazza*) the favourite *entrepôt* of the Meccan merchants. His references in the Corân to ships gliding majestically on the waters, *like mountains*, point to a larger class of vessels than he was likely to see on the Red Sea. The vivid pictures of sea-storms are among the finest sketches in the Corân, and evidently drawn from nature: the waves and tempests may have been witnessed from the Arabian shore, but the 'mountain ships' more likely refer to the Mediterranean.

The mildness of his manners and kind attention had won the heart of Meisara, and, as they drew near to Mecca, the grateful servant persuaded Mahomet to go in advance of the rest, and himself bear to his mistress the tidings of successful traffic. Khadîja, surrounded by her maidens, was sitting upon the upper story of her house,[1] on the watch for the first glimpse of the caravan, when a camel was seen rapidly to advance from the expected quarter, and as it approached she perceived that Mahomet was the rider. He entered, recounted the prosperous issue of the adventure, and enumerated the various goods which agreeably to her commission he had purchased for her. She was delighted at all she heard; but there was a charm in the dark and pensive eye, in the noble features, and the graceful form of her assiduous agent as he stood before her, which pleased her even more than her good fortune. The comely widow was now forty years of age, she had been twice married, and had borne two sons and a daughter. Yet she cast a fond eye upon the thoughtful youth of five-and-twenty; nor, when he departed, could she dismiss him from her thoughts.

She is charmed

Khadîja was a Coreishite lady, distinguished by fortune as well as by birth. Her father Khuweilid was the grandson of Asád, and Asád was the grandson of Cossei. Khuweilid commanded in the 'Sacrilegious war' a considerable section of the Coreish, and so did his nephew Othmân son of Huweirith. Her substance, whether inherited or acquired through her former marriages, was very considerable; and by means of hired agents she had increased it largely in mercantile speculation. To the blessing of affluence, she added the more important endowments of discretion, virtue, and an affectionate heart; and, though now mellowed by a more than middle age, she retained a fair and attractive countenance. The chief men of the Coreish were not insensible to these charms, and many sought her in marriage; choosing rather to live on in dignified and independent widowhood, she had rejected all their offers. But the tender emotions excited by the visit of Mahomet overpowered her resolution. The servant Meisara continued to sound in her not unwilling

Description of Khadîja.

[1] Her house is still shown, a little to the north-east of the Káaba. It is called the birthplace of Fátima.

ears the praises of his fellow-traveller. At last her love became irresistible, and she resolved in a discreet and cautious way to make known her passion to its object. A sister (according to other accounts, a servant) was the agent deputed to sound his views. 'What is it, O Mahomet,' said this female, adroitly referring to the unusual circumstance of his being unmarried at so mature an age,—'what is it that hindereth thee from marriage?' 'I have nothing,' replied he, 'in my hands wherewithal I might marry.' 'But if haply that difficulty were removed, and thou wert invited to espouse a beautiful and wealthy lady of noble birth, who would place thee in affluence, wouldest thou not desire to have her?' 'And who,' said Mahomet, startled at the novel thought, 'might that be?' 'It is Khadîja.' 'But how can I attain unto her?' 'Let that be my care,' returned the female. The mind of Mahomet was at once made up, and he answered, 'I am ready.' The female departed and told Khadîja.

She sends to negotiate marriage between herself and Mahomet.

Mahomet is married to Khadîja.

No sooner was she apprised of his willingness to marry her, than Khadîja despatched a messenger to Mahomet or his uncle, appointing a time when they should meet. Meanwhile, as she dreaded the refusal of her father, she provided for him a feast; and when he had well drunk and was merry, she slaughtered a cow, and casting over her father perfume of saffron or ambergris, dressed him in marriage raiment. While thus under the effects of wine, the old man united his daughter to Mahomet in the presence of his uncle Hamza. But when he recovered his senses, he began to look around with wonder, and to enquire what these symptoms of a nuptial feast, the slaughtered cow, the perfumes and the marriage garment, should mean. So soon as he was made aware of what had happened—for they told him 'The nuptial dress was put upon thee by Mahomet thy son-in-law'—he fell into a violent passion, and declared that he would never consent to give away to that poor youth, a daughter courted by the great men of the Coreish. The friends of Mahomet replied indignantly that the alliance had not originated in their wish, but was the act of no other than his own daughter. Weapons were drawn on both sides, and blood might have been shed, when the old man became pacified, and at last was reconciled.

Notwithstanding a stormy and inauspicious commence- *The union fortunate and happy.* ment, the connubial state proved, both to Mahomet and Khadîja, one of unusual tranquillity and happiness. Upon him it conferred a faithful and affectionate companion, and, in spite of her age, a not unfruitful wife. Khadîja, on her part, fully appreciated the noble genius and commanding mind of Mahomet, which a reserved and contemplative habit while it veiled from others, could not conceal from her. She conducted as before the duties of her establishment, and left him to enjoy his leisure hours undisturbed, and free from care. Her house was thenceforward his home, and her bosom the safe receptacle of those doubts and longings after spiritual light which now began to agitate his mind.

Within the next ten or twelve years, Khadîja bore to *The children of Mahomet by Khadija.* Mahomet two sons and four daughters. The firstborn was named Câsim; and after him, according to Arabian custom, Mahomet received the appellation of AB UL CÂSIM, or 'the father of Câsim.' This son died at the age of two years. Meanwhile, his eldest daughter Zeinab was born; and after her, at intervals of one or two years, three other daughters, Rockeya, Fâtima, and Omm Kolthûm. Last of all was born his second son, who died in infancy. Salma, the maid of Safia, Mahomet's aunt, officiated as midwife on these occasions. Khadîja sacrificed at the birth of each boy two kids, and one at the birth of every girl. All her children she nursed herself.

Many years after, Mahomet used to look back to this *Mutual love of Mahomet and Khadija.* period of his life with fond remembrance. Indeed so much did he dwell upon the mutual love of Khadîja and himself, that the envious Ayesha declared herself more jealous of this rival whom she had never seen, than of all his other wives who contested with her the affection of the Prophet.

No description of Mahomet at this period has been at- *The person of Mahomet described.* tempted by traditionists. But from the copious accounts of his person in later life, an approximate outline may be traced of his appearance in the prime of manhood. Slightly above the middle size, his figure though spare was handsome and commanding, the chest broad and open, the bones and framework large, the joints well knit together. His neck was long and finely moulded. His head, unusually large, gave space for a broad and noble brow. The hair, thick, jet black, and slightly curling, fell down over his ears. The eyebrows were arched and joined. The countenance thin, but ruddy. His large eyes, intensely black and piercing, received additional lustre from eyelashes long and dark. The nose was high and slightly aquiline, but fine, and at the end attenuated. The teeth were far apart. A long black bushy beard, reaching to the breast, added manliness and presence. His expression was pensive and contemplative. The face beamed with intelligence, though something of the sensuous also might be discerned. The skin of his body was clear and soft; the only hair that met the eye was a fine thin line which ran down from the neck towards the navel. His broad back leaned slightly forward as he walked; and his step was hasty, yet sharp and decided, like that of one rapidly descending a declivity.[1]

His manner and conversation.

There was something unsettled in his bloodshot eye, which refused to rest upon its object. When he turned towards you, it was never partially but with the whole body. Taciturn and reserved,[2] he was yet in company distinguished by a graceful urbanity. His words were pregnant and laconic; but when it pleased him to unbend, his speech was often humorous and sometimes pungent. At such seasons he entered with zest into the diversion of the moment, and now and then would laugh immoderately.[3] But in general he listened to the conversation rather than joined in it.

His emotions under control.

He was the subject of strong passions, but they were so controlled by reason or discretion, that they rarely appeared upon the surface. When much excited, the vein between his eyebrows would mantle, and violently swell across his ample forehead; yet he was cautious if not crafty, and in action fearful of personal danger.

---

[1] This at Medina degenerated into a stoop. Some say he walked like a man *ascending* a hill; others as if he was wrenching his foot from a stone. These descriptions imply *decision* of step. The hollows of his hands and feet were more than usually filled and level: a feature regarded by Orientals with interest.

[2] 'Mahomet was sorrowful in temperament; continually meditating; he had no rest; he never spoke except from necessity; he used to be long silent; he expressed himself in pregnant sentences, using neither too few nor too many words.'

[3] When laughing immoderately, he showed his teeth and gums, and was at times so convulsed that he held his sides.

Mahomet was generous and considerate to his friends, and by his well-timed favour and attention knew how to gain over even the disaffected and rivet them to his service. He regarded his enemies, so long as they continued their opposition, with a vindictive and unrelenting hatred: yet he rarely pursued a foe after he had tendered timely submission. His commanding mien inspired the stranger with an undefined and indescribable awe; but on closer intimacy, apprehension and fear gave place to confidence and love.

Treatment of friends and enemies.

Behind the quiet retiring exterior of Mahomet, lay hid a high resolve, a singleness of purpose, a strength and fixedness of will, a sublime determination, destined to achieve the marvellous work of bowing towards himself the heart of all Arabia as the heart of one man. Khadîja was the first to perceive these noble and commanding qualities, and with a childlike confidence she surrendered to him her will and faith.

Latent force of will.

The first incident which interrupted the even tenor of the married life of Mahomet was the rebuilding of the Káaba, when he was about five-and-thirty years of age. One of those violent floods which sometimes sweep down the valley had shattered the holy house; it was filled with ominous rents, and they feared lest it should fall. The treasury was also insecure, owing to the absence of a roof; and thieves had lately clambered over and stolen some of the precious relics. These were recovered, but it was resolved that similar danger should for the future be avoided by raising the walls and covering them over. While the Coreish deliberated how this should be done, a Grecian ship was driven by stress of weather upon the near shore of the Red Sea. The news reaching Mecca, Walîd son of Moghîra, accompanied by a body of the Coreish, proceeded to the wreck, purchased the timber of the broken ship, and engaged her captain, a Greek by name Bacûm, skilled in architecture, to assist in the reconstruction of the Káaba. The several tribes of the Coreish were divided into four bodies, and to each was assigned the charge of one side. With such mysterious reverence was the Káaba regarded, that apprehensions were entertained lest the apparent sacrilege of dismantling the holy walls should expose even the pious restorers to divine wrath. At last Walîd seized a

Rebuilding of the Káaba, A.D. 605. Ætat 35.

.pickaxe, and invoking the Deity in a deprecatory prayer, detached and threw down a portion of the wall. They then retired and waited till the morning, when, finding that no mischief had befallen the adventurous chief, all joined in the demolition. They continued to dig till they reached a hard foundation of green stones which resisted the stroke of the pickaxe. From thence they began to build the wall. Stones of grey granite from the neighbouring hills were carried by the citizens upon their heads to the sacred enclosure. The whole body of the Coreish assisted in the work, and all proceeded harmoniously until the structure rose four or five feet above the surface. At that stage it became

The Black stone.

necessary to build the Black stone into the eastern corner, with its surface so exposed as to be readily kissed by the pilgrims upon foot. This stone, we learn from modern travellers, is semicircular, and measures about six inches in height, and eight in breadth; it is of a reddish-black colour, and notwithstanding the polish imparted by myriads of kisses, still bears marks in its undulating surface of volcanic origin.

Contention as to which tribe should deposit the stone in its place.

As the virtue of the edifice depended upon this mysterious stone, each family of the Coreish advanced pretensions to the exclusive right of placing it in its future receptacle. The contention became hot, and it was feared that bloodshed would ensue. For four or five days the building was suspended. At last the Coreish again assembled on the spot amicably to decide the difficulty. Then the oldest citizen arose and said: 'O Coreish, hearken unto me! My advice is that the man who chanceth first to enter the court of the Káaba by this gate of the Bani Sheyba, he shall be chosen to decide the difference amongst you, or himself to place the stone.' The proposal was confirmed by acclamation, and they awaited the issue. Mahomet, who happened to be absent on the occasion, was observed approaching, and he was the first to enter the gate. They exclaimed: 'Here comes the faithful Arbiter (al Amín); we are content to abide by

Mahomet is chosen arbiter. His decision.

his decision.' Calm and self-possessed, Mahomet received the commission, and at once resolved upon an expedient which should conciliate them all. Taking off his mantle and spreading it upon the ground, he placed the stone thereon, and said : 'Now let one from each of your four divisions come forward, and raise a corner of this mantle.' Four chiefs approached, and seizing the corner simultaneously lifted the stone. When it had reached the proper height, Mahomet, with his own hand, guided it to its place. The decision raised the character of Mahomet for wisdom and judgment; while the singular and apparently providential call would not pass unnoticed by Mahomet himself. Religious awe not unfrequently with him degenerated into superstition; and there was here a mysterious singling out of himself to be judge among his fellows in a sacred question, which might well have wrought upon a less imaginative and enthusiastic spirit than that of Mahomet, and prompted the idea of his being chosen of God to be the prophet of his people.

After the stone had been thus deposited in its proper place, the Coreish built on without interruption; and when the wall had risen to a considerable height they roofed it in with fifteen rafters resting upon six central pillars. A covering of cloth, thrown over the edifice, according to ancient custom, hung down like a curtain on every side.[1] The Káaba thus rebuilt was surrounded by a small enclosure probably of not more than fifty yards in diameter. To the west stood the Hall of council, with its door towards the Káaba. On the east was the gateway of the Bani Sheyba, close by the sacred well Zemzem. At a respectful distance around were

The Káaba finished.

[1] The custom of veiling the Káaba is of extremely remote date. Originally the cloth covered the whole building, including the top. Before a roof was built by the Coreish it must have constituted the only protection from the weather. The curtain is now attached to the walls.

In the time of Mahomet the curtain was of Yemen cloth. Omar renewed it yearly of Egyptian linen. Various materials, as striped Yemen stuff, red brocade, or black silk, have been at different times used; and the covering has been changed as often as six times a year. To supply it came to be regarded as a sign of sovereignty.

The covering is now worked at Cairo, and renewed yearly at the season of pilgrimage. It 'is a coarse tissue of silk and cotton mixed.' A band of two feet, embroidered with texts, is inserted about a third from the top. Burton describes the new covering thus : 'It was of a brilliant black, and the Hizâm —the zone or golden band running round the upper portion of the building— as well as the Boorka (face veil) were of dazzling brightness.' The Boorka is 'the gold embroidered curtain covering the Káaba door.'

built the houses of the Coreish. The great idol Hobal was placed in the centre of the holy house ; and outside were ranged various other images. The door for entering the Káaba was then, as now, near the Black stone in the eastern side, and several feet above the ground,—a fact attributed by Mahomet to the pride of the Coreish, and the desire to retain in their own hands the power of admission. The building, though now substantial and secure, occupied somewhat less space than its dilapidated and roofless predecessor. The excluded area lay to the north-west, and is still without the sacred walls.[1]

Absence of any paramount authority.

The circumstances which gave occasion for the decision of Mahomet strikingly illustrate the absence of any paramount authority in Mecca, and the number of persons among whom the power of government was at this time divided. Each main branch of the Coreishite stock was independent of the other ; and the Offices of state and religion created by Cossai with the view of securing an undisputed command had, from their distribution among several independent families, lost their potency. It was a period in which the genius of a Cossai might have again dispensed with the

---

[1] The sill of the door is now about seven feet above the level of the ground, and a moveable wooden staircase is used for ascending. It is six feet from the corner of the Black stone. After the conquest of Mecca, Mahomet is related to have said: ' *Verily they have drawn back the foundations of the Káaba from their original limit ; and if it were not that the inhabitants are fresh from idolatry, I would have restored to the building that which was excluded from the area thereof. But in case the people may again after my time need to renew the structure, come, and I will show thee what was left out.*' So he showed a space in the *Hijr* (or excluded area) of about seven yards.

This space at present lies to the north-west of the Káaba, about the distance pointed out by Mahomet as the limit of the old building. It is now marked by a semicircular parapet of white marble, five feet high, facing the Káaba, and is still regarded as equally holy with the temple itself.

Othmân and Ibn Zobeir enlarged the square by purchasing and removing the adjoining houses of the Coreish, and they enclosed it by a wall. Various similar changes and improvements were made by successive Caliphs till, in the third century of the Hegira, the quadrangle with its imposing colonnade assumed the present dimensions.

The Káaba, as it now stands, is an irregular cube, the sides of which vary from forty to fifty feet in length. The quadrangle, or court, corresponds loosely with the direction of its walls. ' Káaba ' is probably the ancient idolatrous name ; while ' Beit-ullah,' *The house of God* (used indifferently with the other in the time of Mahomet), is the more modern title harmonising with Jewish phraseology.

prestige of place and birth, and asserted dominion by strength of will and inflexibility of purpose. But no such leader appeared, and the divided aristocracy moved onward with feeble and distracted step.

A curious story is related of an attempt made about this period to gain the rule at Mecca. The aspirant was Othmân, first cousin of Khadîja's father. He was dissatisfied, as the legend goes, with the idolatrous system of Mecca, and travelled to the court of the Roman emperor, where he was honourably entertained, and admitted to Christian baptism. He returned to Mecca, and on the strength of an imperial grant, real or pretended, laid claim to the government of the city. But his claim was rejected, and he fled to Syria, where he found a refuge with the Ghassânide prince. Othmân revenged his expulsion by using his influence for the imprisonment of the Coreishite merchants who chanced to be at the Syrian court. But emissaries from Mecca, by the aid of gifts, counteracted his authority with the prince, and at last procured his death.

Othmân ibn Huweirith attempts, by aid of the Roman Emperor, to seize the government.

Notwithstanding the absence of a strong government, Mecca continued to flourish under the generally harmonious combination of the several independent phylarchies. Commerce was prosecuted towards Syria and Irâc with greater vigour than ever. About the year A.D. 606 we read of a mercantile expedition under Abu Sofiân, which for the first time penetrated to the capital of Persia, and reached even the presence of the Chosroes.

Commerce flourishes at Mecca.

I proceed to notice some particulars of the domestic life of Mahomet.

Domestic life of Mahomet.

The sister of Khadîja was married to Rabî, a descendant of Abd Shams, and had borne him a son called Abul âs. The son had by this time grown up, and was respected in Mecca for his uprightness and mercantile success. Khadîja loved her nephew, and looked upon him as her own son. She prevailed upon Mahomet to join him in marriage with their eldest daughter Zeinab, who had but just reached the age of womanhood. The union proved to be one of real affection, though during the troubled rise of Islâm it was chequered by a temporary severance, and by several romantic incidents. Somewhat later the two younger daughters, Rockeya and Omm Kolthûm, were given in marriage to Otba and Oteiba,

Marriage of three eldest daughters.

both sons of Abu Lahab, the uncle of Mahomet. Fâtima, the youngest, was yet a child.

Adopts his cousin Ali. Shortly after the rebuilding of the Káaba, Mahomet comforted himself for the loss of his infant son Câsim by adopting Ali, the child of his friend and former guardian Abu Tâlib. The circumstance is thus described: It chanced that a season of severe scarcity fell upon the Coreish; and Abu Tâlib, still poor, was put to shifts for the support of his numerous family. His difficulties were not unperceived by Mahomet, who, prompted by his usual kindness and consideration, repaired to his rich uncle Abbâs, and said: 'O Abbâs! thy brother Abu Tâlib hath a burdensome family, and thou seest what straits all men are brought to. Let us go to him, and relieve him somewhat of the care of his children. I will take one son, if thou wilt take another. And we shall support them.' Abbâs consenting, they proposed the thing to Abu Tâlib; and he replied: 'Leave me Ackîl and Tâlib; and do ye with the others as it pleaseth you.' So Mahomet took Ali, and Abbâs took Jáfar. Ali, at this time not above five or six years of age, remained ever after with Mahomet, and they exhibited towards each other the mutual attachment of parent and child.

Zeid son of Hâritha, a Christian slave, The heart of Mahomet was inclined to ardent and lasting friendships. About the period of Ali's adoption he admitted to his closest intimacy another person unconnected with him by family ties, but of more equal age. This was Zeid son of Hâritha. As he will be frequently alluded to, and his society must have influenced to some extent the course of Mahomet, it is important to trace his previous life. The father of Zeid was of the Bani Odzra, a tribe which occupied the region south of Syria; his mother belonged to a branch of the Bani Tai. Zeid was yet a child when, journeying with his mother, the company was waylaid by a band of Arab marauders, who carried him away captive, and sold him into slavery. When a youth he fell into the hands of Hakîm, grandson of Khuweilid, who presented him to his aunt Khadîja shortly after her marriage with Mahomet. He was then about twenty years of age; and is described as small of stature, and dark in complexion, with a short and depressed nose. He was an active and useful servant; and Mahomet soon conceived a strong affection for him.

Khadîja to gratify her husband made him a present of the slave.

His father searched long in vain for Zeid; and his grief found vent in touching verses, some of which have been preserved to us by tradition. At last a party of his tribe when on a pilgrimage to Mecca recognised the youth, and communicated tidings of him to his disconsolate father, who immediately set out to fetch him home. Arrived at Mecca, Hâritha offered a large payment for his ransom. Mahomet summoned Zeid, and left it in his option to go or stay. He chose to stay. ' I will not leave thee,' he said; ' thou art in the place to me of father and of mother.' Delighted by his faithfulness, Mahomet took him straight-way to the black stone of the Káaba and said: ' Bear testi-mony, all ye that are present. Zeid is my son; I will be his heir, and he shall be mine.' His father contented with the declaration returned home glad at heart; and the freed-man was thenceforward called ' Zeid ibn Mohammad,' *Zeid the son of Mahomet.* At Mahomet's desire he married his old attendant, Omm Ayman. Though nearly double his age, she bore him a son called Usâma, who was the leader in the expedition to Syria at the time of Mahomet's fatal illness.[1]

Is also adopted by Mahomet.

Christianity prevailed in the tribes from which, both on the father's and mother's side, Zeid sprang; and though severed from his home at too early an age to have acquired any extensive or thorough knowledge of its doctrines, yet he probably carried with him some impression of the teaching, and some fragments of the facts or legends, of the faith. These would form subjects of conversation between the youth and his adoptive father, whose mind was now feeling in all directions after religious truth. Among the relatives of Khadîja, too, there were persons who possessed a knowledge of Christianity, and observed perhaps something of its practice. Her cousin Othmân has been already noticed as having embraced Christianity at Constantinople, and made an

Christian influence of Zeid;

Othmân ibn Hu-weirith;

[1] He was probably about six years younger than Mahomet. The difference of age between him and his bride was so great, that tradition tells us Mahomet promised him *paradise* for marrying her.

and Wa-
raca.

unsuccessful attempt to gain the rule at Mecca. Waraca, another cousin, is said also to have become a convert to Christianity, to have been acquainted with the religious tenets and sacred Scriptures both of Jews and Christians, and even to have copied or translated some portion of the gospels into Hebrew or Arabic. In the following chapter it will be seen that this person had an acknowledged share in satisfying the mind of Mahomet that his mission was divine.

The Four
Enquirers.

It is a fancy of the traditionists that, shortly before the appearance of Mahomet, several enquirers were not only seeking after the true faith (or as they style it *the Religion of Abraham*), but, warned by prophecy and by the unguarded admissions of Jews and Christians, were in immediate expectation of the coming prophet. Of such enquirers among the Coreish, Mahometan biographies specify *four*. Two of these, *Othmân* and *Waraca*, have been already mentioned.

Obeidallah
bin Jahsh.

The third, *Obeidallah* (by his mother a grandson of Abd al Muttalib) embraced Islâm, emigrated with his brethren in the faith to Abyssinia, and there went over to Christianity.[1]

Zeid ibn
Amr.

The fourth was *Zeid*, the grandson of Nofail, and cousin of Omar. Of him tradition says that he condemned the idolatrous sacrifices of the Kâaba, reprobated the burying alive of infant daughters, and 'followed the religion of Abraham.' But not content with such assertions, the traditionists add that Zeid possessed distinct knowledge of the coming prophet and left his salutation to be delivered to him when he should appear. Nay, he described his person, stated that he would be of the family of Abd al Muttalib, and foretold that he would emigrate to Medîna! He died while the Kâaba was rebuilding, and was buried at the foot of mount Hîra.

Though such anticipations of the Prophet are to be rejected as altogether puerile, and though the manifest tendency to invent legends of this description makes it difficult to sever the real from the fictitious in the matter of these four Enquirers, yet it may be admitted as highly prob-

---

[1] He died in Abyssinia, and Mahomet married his widow, Omm Habîba, daughter of Abu Sofiân.

able that a spirit of religious enquiry, the disposition to A spirit of enquiry probably abroad. reject idolatry, and a perception of the superiority of Judaism and Christianity, did in some quarters about this time exist. With such enquirers Mahomet would no doubt deeply sympathise, and hold converse on the gross idolatry of the Arabs, and the need of a more spiritual faith for their regeneration.

Mahomet was now approaching his fortieth year. Always Mahomet seeks solitude. pensive, he had of late become even more thoughtful and retiring. Contemplation and reflection engaged his mind. The debasement of his people pressed heavily on him; the dim and imperfect shadows of Judaism and Christianity excited doubts without satisfying them; and his soul was perplexed with uncertainty as to what was the true religion. Thus burdened, he frequently retired to seek relief in meditation amongst the solitary valleys and rocks near Mecca. His favourite spot was a cave in the declivities at the foot of mount Hîra,[1] a lofty conical hill two or three miles north of Mecca. Thither he would retire for days at a time; and his faithful wife sometimes accompanied him. The continued solitude, instead of stilling his anxiety, magnified into sterner and more impressive shapes the solemn realities which agitated his soul. Close by was the grave of the aged Zeid who, after spending a lifetime in the same enquiries, had now passed into the state of certainty;—might he himself not reach the same assurance without crossing the gate of death?

All around was bleak and rugged. To the east and south, Spiritual anxiety and groping after light. the vision from the cave of Hîra is bounded by lofty mountain ranges, but to the north and west there is an extensive prospect, thus described by Burkhardt: 'The country before

---

[1] Since called Jebel Nûr, or Mountain of light, because Mahomet is said to have received his first revelation there. The hill is so lofty as to be seen a long distance off. Burkhardt says: 'Passing the Sherif's garden house on the road to Arafât, a little further on, we enter a valley, which extends in a direction N.E. by N., and is terminated by the mountain, which is conical. . . . In the rocky floor of a small building ruined by the Wahabys, a cleft is shown about the size of a man in length and breadth. . . . A little below this place is a small cavern in the red granite rock, which forms the upper stratum of this mountain.' This valley was often trod by Mahomet on his way to and from the cleft and the cavern.

us had a dreary aspect, not a single green spot being visible; barren, black, and grey hills, and white sandy valleys, were the only objects in sight.' There was harmony here between external nature, and the troubled chaotic elements of the spiritual world within. By degrees his impulsive and susceptible mind was wrought up to the highest pitch of excitement; and he would give vent to his agitation in wild and rhapsodical language, the counterpart of his inward struggles after truth. The following fragments in the Corân may perhaps belong to this period.

Poetical fragments of this period.

Sura ciii.

> By the declining day I swear !
>   Verily, man is in the way of ruin ;
>   Excepting such as possess Faith,
>   And do the things which are right,
>   And stir up one another to truth and steadfastness.

And again—

Sura c.

> I swear by the rushing horses that pant !
> By those that strike fire with their flashing hoof !
> By those that scour the enemy's land,
> And darken it with dust,
> And penetrate thereby the host !
> Verily, man is to his Lord ungrateful ;
> And he is himself a witness thereof ;
> Verily he is keen in the love of this world's good.
> Ah ! wotteth he not, when that which is in the graves shall be
>   scattered abroad,
> And that which is in men's hearts shall be brought forth ;
> Verily, their Lord shall in that day be informed as to them.

Prayer for guidance.

Nor was he wanting in prayer for guidance to the great Being who, he felt, alone could give it. The following petitions (though probably adapted subsequently to public worship) contain perhaps the germ of his daily prayer at this early period.

Sura i.

> Praise be to God, the Lord of creation,
>   The All-merciful, the All-compassionate !
>   Ruler of the day of Reckoning !
>   Thee we worship, and Thee we invoke for help.
>   Lead us in the straight path ;—

The path of those upon whom Thou hast been gracious,
Not of those that are the objects of wrath, or that are in error.[1]

How such aspirations developed themselves into the belief that the subject of them was inspired from heaven, is an obscure and painful theme, which I purpose to consider in the following chapter.

[1] This is the Fâteha, so often recited in public and private worship.

CHAPTER III.

THE BELIEF OF MAHOMET IN HIS OWN INSPIRATION.

Ætat. 40–43.

Mahomet
gives vent
to his agi-
tation in
fragments
of poetry.

OUR sketch of the life of Mahomet has now reached a period when, as we have seen, anxious yearnings after religious truth were springing up within him; and his mind, brooding over the gross superstition and abject worldliness of the inhabitants of Mecca, and bewildered by its own speculations amidst the uncertain flickerings of spiritual light ever and anon flashing around, began to unburthen itself in fragments of wild and impassioned poetry. These often assume the character of soliloquies, full of melancholy reflection upon the state and prospects of mankind; sometimes fraught with burning words and imagery of terror, they seem intended as a warning or admonition to fellow-citizens; at other times, they exhibit a mind intent upon itself, oppressed by perplexity and distress, and seeking for comfort and assurance by fleeing to its Maker.

Such frag-
ments only
partially
preserved
in the
Corân.

Though there is ground for supposing that fragments of such poetry were at this period delivered frequently, yet few are extant, and these only as we find them in the Corân. The reason why more have not been preserved is that they differ in form from the subsequent compositions which claim to be inspired. They did not fit in with the theory which holds every word of the Corân to be a message emanating directly from God. And it is probable that the more remarkable of these pieces, imprinted indelibly on the hearts of those who shared in the early aspirations of Mahomet, have alone found a place in his Revelation. It is thus that in the whole Corân there are only eighteen Suras which can with any likelihood be assigned to this period of his life. To aid in tracing the development of spiritual conception and religious belief in the mind of Mahomet some extracts from these will now be laid before the reader.[1]

Specimens of these fragments.

Of the soliloquies, the subjoined Sura is a specimen :—

Sura ci.

That which striketh ! What is it which striketh ?
  And what shall certify thee what meaneth THE STRIKING ?
On that day mankind shall be like unto moths scattered abroad,
And the mountains shall be like unto wool of divers colours
    carded.
Then truly whose-soever balances are heavy, he shall enter into a
    life of happiness ;
And whose-soever balances are light, to him verily appertaineth
    the Pit.
  And what shall certify thee what the PIT meaneth ?
          A raging FIRE !

Of the following fragment, a part is represented as pronounced directly by the Deity, but probably as yet only by poetical fiction.

Sura xcv.

  I swear by the Fig and Olive,
  By mount Sinai, and by this inviolate Territory !
That WE verily created Man of a most excellent structure,
  Then WE rendered him the lowest of the low ;—
Excepting such as believe and do the things that are right ;
  For unto them shall be given a reward that fadeth not away.
Then, what shall cause thee after this to deny the reckoning ?
  What ! is not God the most righteous of all Judges ?

The voice of expostulation and alarm was raised in accents such as these :—

Warning and expostulation.

Sura civ.

  Woe unto the Backbiter and Defamer ;—
Unto him that heapeth up riches, and numbereth them for the
    future !
He thinketh surely that his wealth shall be with him for ever.

---

[1] The earlier Suras or chapters of the Corân are generally composed each of a single short piece delivered all at once, and the period of their appearance is, therefore, more easily assigned than that of the later Suras, which are made up of fragments delivered on various occasions. The later Suras grow gradually longer ; but in the Corân the Suras have been arranged in an order precisely the reverse of this, the longest being generally placed first and the shortest last. The chronological sequence, in short, has been reversed. Hence it is that the casual reader of the Corân, by perusing it in this inverted order, forms no correct conception of the origin and development of Mahomet's system.

Nay ! for verily he shall be cast into the crushing fire ;
And what shall cause thee to know what the CRUSHING FIRE is ?
　　　The fire of God kindled,
Which shall mount above the hearts ;
It shall verily rise above them as a covering,
　　　Stretched upon lofty columns.

The 92nd Sura, after a variety of wild and incoherent oaths, proceeds thus :—

Sura xcii.

Verily it is OUR part to give Direction,
　　And unto Us belongeth the Future and the Past.
Wherefore I warn you of the fire which breaketh into flame ;
　　There shall not be cast therein but the most wretched,—
　　He that rejected the truth, and turned his back.
But whoso feareth the Lord shall escape therefrom,—
　　He that giveth of his wealth to purify his soul withal ;
And who offereth not his favours unto any with the hope of
　　recompense,
Except the recompense of seeking the face of his Lord Most
　　High ;
　　　And surely he shall be satisfied.

Rhyming style.

The rhyming style which is frequent in the Corân, may be illustrated by the following Sura. Each verse ends with the syllable *hâ* (the feminine pronoun of the third person), and the corresponding word is indicated by italics.

Sura xci.

By the Sun and *his* early splendour !
　　By the Moon when she followeth *him !*
　　By the Day when it showeth forth *its* glory !
　　By the Night when it covereth the *same !*
　　By the Heavens and Him that made *them !*
　　By the Earth and Him that spread *it* forth !
　　By the Soul and Him that framed *it,*
　　And inspired it with its wickedness and *its* virtue !
Verily he is blessed that purifieth *the same ;*
And he is wretched that corrupteth *the same.*
The Thamudites rejected the message of the Lord in *their*
　　impiety ;
When the most abandoned among *them* arose.
(Now the prophet[1] of God had said unto them, 'It is the she-
　　camel of the Lord ; Give ye drink unto *her ;* ')
But they rejected him, and cut *her* in pieces ;

[1] Sâlih, the prophet of the Thamudites.

Wherefore the Lord overthrew them in their iniquities, and
rendered unto them a recompense equal with *their Sin;*
And he feareth not the issue *thereof.*

Allusion is sometimes made, though in a form as yet very
brief and vague, both to Arab and Jewish legend. Thus in
the 89th Sura :— Arab and Jewish legend.

What! hast thou not seen how thy Lord dealt with the
children of AD,— Sura lxxxix.
The Iremites possessed of pillars,
The like whereof have not been builded in any city ?—
And with the THAMUDITES which hewed out the rock in the
Valley ;—
And with PHARAOH that used the stakes ? [1]
These all behaved insolently in the earth,
And multiplied wickedness therein ;
Wherefore thy Lord poured upon them the mingled cup of His
wrath,
Verily thy Lord is upon His watch-tower, &c.

And there was not wanting special appeal to national
considerations. The 105th Sura, which recounts God's
mercies to the inhabitants of Mecca in the overthrow of
Abraha and preservation of their city, belongs probably to
this period. And also the following :— Suras cv. and cvi.

For the stirring up (or uniting) of the COREISH;— Sura cvi.
The stirring of them up unto the Winter and Summer expedi-
tions (of merchandise).
And let them worship the Lord of this House,
He that hath provided them with food against Hunger,
And hath granted them immunity from Fear.[2]

In elucidation of Mahomet's honest striving after Truth
another Sura may be quoted in which the two paths of Virtue
and Vice, and the difficulties of the straight way, are set
forth :— 'The two Paths.'

Verily I swear by this Territory, Sura xc.
(And thou art a resident of this Territory ;)
By the Begetter, and by that which is begotten !
Surely WE have created man in trouble.
Ah! doth he think indeed that no one hath power over him ?
He saith,—'I have wasted much wealth.'

[1] Alluding to the tyrant's mode of punishment.
[2] Inviolability of the sacred territory from foreign attack.

Ah! doth he think that no one seeth him?
What! Have WE not made him two eyes and two lips;
And guided him unto the TWO ROADS.
Yet he applieth himself not unto the ascent;—
And what shall cause thee to know what the ASCENT is?—
Freeing the captive,
And giving food in the day of want
To the orphan that is near of kin,
Or to the poor that lieth in the dust;—
Further, the Righteous must be of those that believe, and stir up
one another unto steadfastness and compassion.
These are the heirs of blessedness.
But they who deny OUR signs, shall be the heirs of wretchedness;
Around them the Fire shall close.

Mahomet's early religious poetry. It is highly probable that Mahomet occupied himself with such thoughts, and gave vent to his feelings in language similar to these quotations, for several years before he assumed the office of a divine teacher. The early Suras, and we may suppose many other reflective and didactic pieces not preserved because not purporting to proceed as inspired from God, would be recorded by the aged Waraca, by Ali who was still a boy, and possibly by Khadîja herself or by some member of her family which, as we have seen, contained persons enquiring after the true religion and more or less acquainted with Judaism and Christianity. *His early followers.* The friends and some of the relatives of Mahomet listened with reverence to his admonitions, and sought to follow his injunctions as those of a faithful teacher guided haply by the spirit of God. Khadîja his loving wife, Zeid and Ali his adopted sons, and perhaps Abu Bakr his bosom friend, with Waraca who saw in his first teaching the counterpart of his own ideas, were amongst the earliest of his disciples.

Makes no impression on his fellow-citizens. But without this little circle, Superstition and the World held undisputed sway, and expostulation was met by gross ignorance and repellent darkness. The kind and generous Abu Tâlib smiled at the enthusiasm of his nephew. Abu Lahab, another uncle, mocked and insulted him. Abu Jahl and his party sneered. The great body of the Coreish were careless and indifferent. As Mahomet passed by the knots that clustered about the Káaba discussing the events of the day, they would point disdainfully at him as a half-witted creature.

The more susceptible amongst the citizens listened, per-haps at first with attention. But when pressed to practical and decisive steps, they would answer: 'It is well for Jews and Christians to follow the purer faith thou speakest of. *They*, we know, have had prophets bringing them a message of the will of God. Let *us* be content with the light our Maker hath given unto us, and remain as we are. *If a pro-phet had been sent unto us, we should no doubt have followed his directions, and been as devout and spiritual in our worship as the Jews and Christians.*' [1] Mahomet felt the force of such a reply, for it was in unison with hidden thoughts ever present yet undeveloped in his heart. Would the Almighty be unmindful of the appeal thus virtually made to Him for guidance? The appeal might itself be a divine intimation requiring him to furnish the direction so urgently needed, and sincerely desired. And, again, whence the rush of inspiration regarding the unity of God, his power and providence, and a future recompense in heaven and hell? Whence the ecstatic moments, the flow of burning thoughts, the spontaneous burst of eloquence and heavenly speech, which gave form and substance to the long conceived yearnings of his heart, and transformed them as it were into the words of God himself? Could the prophets of old have had a more convincing test of inspiration? What if all this formed a supernatural call, a divine Mission?

Thus we may suppose was Mahomet by degrees led on to believe that God had called him to preach reformation to his countrymen. But was he authorised further to use the name of the Lord, and to recite his warnings, threats, and promises as words of Inspiration? It would surely be to abandon his position if he stood forth as a *Messenger* from God to reclaim

[1] *Sura* xxxv. Mahomet there quotes this reply as showing that his people had at the first declared their willingness to follow a prophet, if only one were sent to them; but now that a Prophet *had been sent*, they disbelieved him, and broke their promise. Such notices are frequent in the Corân, and the pretext assigned in the text was, no doubt, one of the earliest which Mahomet had to answer. Compare *Sura* vi. 155-157: 'And this book WE have sent down,—blessed; wherefore follow it and fear God that ye may find mercy. Lest ye should say: *Verily the Scripture hath been revealed to two Peoples before us, but we are unable to read in their language.* Or lest ye should say: *If the Scripture had been revealed to us, we surely would have followed the direction better than they.* And now verily hath a clear exposition come unto you from your Lord,—a direction and mercy,' &c.

the people of Mecca to himself, and yet brought no message from him that sent him. The work was evidently of God ; why then question that these welling thoughts and living words were intended by God as his commands ? And, ever and anon, the rising doubt would be quelled by a glance at *the end*. For the glorious object of converting his people, could there be anything wrong in the only suitable means? Nay, this strange mental struggle itself seemed but the first bursting forth of inspiration. Would he dare to stay the divine emotion, repress the work within, and fight against the Lord? Why should he hesitate to take the name of God upon his lips, go forth boldly as his Legate, and trust that the same spirit which had guided Jewish and Christian prophets would put words into his mouth? The God that overrules all nature even to its minutest movements, without whom not a leaf falls to the ground, would not suffer these mental longings to miss the aim for which they were destined. Into his hands, then, he would commit himself, and secure in the singleness of his purpose, the glory of God and the good of his fellows, he would go forth speaking his words.

Mental depression and grounds of reassurance.

While absorbed by such reflections, sometimes doubting, sometimes believing, Mahomet at seasons suffered grievous mental distraction. To this period may be attributed the Suras in which, after deep depression, he sought to reassure his soul by remembering the past favours of the Almighty.

Sura xciii.

By the rising sunshine !
By the night when it darkeneth !
Thy Lord hath not removed from thee, neither hath He been dis-
    pleased.
And verily the Future shall be better unto thee than the Past.
Thy Lord shall shortly dispense unto thee a gift ; and thou shalt
    be satisfied,
What ! Did He not find thee an orphan, and give thee a home ?
And found thee astray, and directed thee ?
Now, therefore, as touching the Orphan, do not oppress him ;
And as touching him that asketh of thee, repulse him not ;
And as touching the Favours of thy Lord, rehearse them.

Sura xciv.

What ! Have WE not opened for thee thy breast ?
    And taken off from thee thy burden,—
    That which galled thy back ;
    And exalted the mention of thee ?

Then truly with the difficulty, there shall be ease.
Verily with the difficulty there shall be ease.
And when thou art set at liberty then labour,
And towards thy Lord raise thy desire.

The following Sura refers to the taunts of those who reproached him with the death of his sons as a mark of God's displeasure :—

Surely WE have given unto thee an abundance; Sura cviii.
Wherefore offer unto the Lord thy prayer, and sacrifice unto
    Him.
    Verily, (not thou, but) he that hateth thee shall be childless.

Notwithstanding such consolations, his distress was some- Seeks to commit suicide.
times insupportable, and he repeatedly meditated suicide.
What if all this were but the simulation of divine impulse,
the stirrings of the Evil one and his emissaries? Was any
crime so awful as to forge the name and authority of GOD?
Rather than expose himself to a risk so terrible, he would
anticipate the possibility by casting himself headlong from
one of these wild cliffs. An invisible influence appeared to
hold him back. Was it a divine influence? or might not
even this be also diabolical?

But the old train of reasoning would again revive in his Belief in divine mission revives, mingled with ambition.
heart stronger than ever. And now, when fully surrendered
to it, bright visions of a united people abjuring their gross
idolatry, would rise before him. Thus acknowledged as their
Prophet, why should not he be also their Leader and their
Chief? Faith and piety should yet reign throughout Arabia ;
and the sword should be bared to compel men to enter into
the kingdom of God :—

When the help of the Lord shall come and victory, Sura cx.
And thou shalt see men entering into the faith of God in multi-
    tudes,
Then celebrate His praise, and ask pardon of Him, for He is
    forgiving.

' Moses led forth his people, and so did other Jewish chieftains,
to do battle for the Lord against the idolaters. And why
should not I, as the vicegerent of God, do likewise ; and
bring all Arabia in godly submission prostrate at his feet?
It will be for *his* glory and for the furtherance of *his*
kingdom. Then, what vain abominations are wrought

within the cities of Syria, and the Empire; they have set
up the Queen of Heaven, and burned incense unto her!
They, too, will listen to the voice of reason recalling them to
the worship of God and setting forth his Unity.   They have
a Revelation, and profess to obey it.   I will show to them
from their own Book that they have corrupted and obscured
the Truth.   And Egypt, Persia, Abyssinia, Hîra,—all around,
why should I not dash to the ground the idols, and every
thing that exalts itself against the true God;—if only my
people will be convinced and rally around me to fight the
battles of the Lord.   The whole world, Jew and Christian,
weary of strife and discord, yearns for a Prophet who shall
restore unity and peace.   Will not all, then, flock to my
standard when I proclaim myself that which I surely feel
myself to be,—the Prophet of the Lord?'   Such conceptions at
this time were, it may be, vague and undeveloped, but there
is little doubt that the germ existed in the mind of Mahomet.
It is probable that they formed the evil and delusive element
which, first mingling with the pure aspiration after Truth,
led to the fatal and fearful crime (characterised throughout
the Corân itself as the greatest enormity mortal can commit) of
speaking falsely and without commission in the name of God.
AMBITION, once admitted, opened an easy breach for the
temptations of the world, if not also for the suggestions of the
Evil one.   Yet ambition may have been so subtilely mingled
with spiritual aspirations, that haply it escaped the observation of Mahomet himself.

At this crisis, the fate of Mahomet and of Islâm trembled
in the balance.   It was his hour of trial, and he fell.

Mahomet
in expecta-
tion of a
divine com-
mission.

On the one hand, he was surrounded by a little knot of
believing adherents.   Spiritual truth seemed to shine, clear
and radiant as a sunbeam, upon his own heart; ecstatic
trances impressed a seal, apparently divine, upon his convictions; and (though ambition might be lurking) he was conscious of a sincere desire, and fancied that he perceived a
divine commission, to call forth his people from darkness
into light.   On the other hand, the ungodly laughed him to
scorn; while solemn expostulation and warning were treated,
even by the wise and sober, as the effusion of a fond enthu-
siast.   *Before the* DIVINE COMMISSION *all difficulties would
vanish.*   He would wait, then, for the inspiring influence of

the Holy Spirit to lead him, as it had oftentimes led the prophets before him, in the right way. Gabriel,[1] perhaps, would visit him, as he visited Zacharias and Mary, to announce the advent of a new Dispensation.

He was seated or wandering amidst the peaks of Hîra buried in reveries such as these, when suddenly an apparition rose before him. The heavenly Visitant, whose form had long flitted vaguely before his imagination, stood there close beside him in a vision. It was no other than Gabriel, the Messenger of God, who now appeared in the sky, and, approaching within 'two bows' length' of Mahomet, brought from his Master this memorable behest :—

Vision of Gabriel bringing the commission to 'Recite in the name of God.'

RECITE in the name of the Lord who created,—
Created Man from nought but congealed blood ;—
RECITE ! For thy Lord is beneficent.
It is He who hath taught (to record revelation) with the pen ;—
Hath taught man that which he knoweth not.
Nay, verily, for Man is rebellious ;
Because he seeth himself to abound in wealth.
Verily, unto thy Lord is the return of all.
Hast thou not seen him that holdeth back
The Servant (of God) when he prayeth ?
What thinkest thou ? had he listened to right direction,
And commanded unto piety ?
Dost thou not see that he hath rejected the Truth and turned his
    back ?
What ! Doth he not know that God seeth ?
Nay, verily, if he forbear not, WE shall drag him by the fore-
    lock,—
The lying, sinful forelock !
Then let him call his company of friends, and WE shall call the
    guards of Hell ;
Nay ! submit not unto him ; but worship, and draw nigh unto
    the Lord.

Sura xcvi.

Thus was Mahomet, by whatever deceptive process, led to the high blasphemy of forging the name of God. Thence-

Mahomet thenceforward as-

---

[1] It is clear that at a later period at least, if not the from the first, Mahomet confounded *Gabriel* with the *Holy Ghost*. The idea may have arisen from some such misapprehension as the following. Mary conceived Jesus by the power of the Holy Ghost which overshadowed her. But it was Gabriel who visited Mary to announce the conception of the Saviour. The Holy Ghost was, therefore, another name for Gabriel. We need hardly wonder at this ignorance, when Mahomet seems to have believed that Christians held Mary to be the third Person in the Trinity.

sumes
authority
of God in
his Re-
velations;

forward he spoke literally *in the name of the Lord.* And so scrupulous was he lest there should be in this inspiration even the appearance of human influence, that every sentence of the Corân is prefaced by the divine command, 'SPEAK' or 'SAY;' which, if not expressed, must always be understood. Thus Sura CXII. :—

> SAY:—He is GOD alone : GOD the Eternal !
> He begetteth not, and He is not begotten ;
> And there is not any like unto Him.

and be-
comes his
commis-
sioned pro-
phet.

This commission pervaded throughout the future course of Mahomet, and mingled with every action. He was now the servant, the prophet, the vicegerent of God ; and however much the resulting sphere of action might expand in ever widening circles, the principle on which the commission rested was from the commencement absolute and complete. How far the two ideas of a resolution in his own mind involving spontaneous action, and of a divine inspiration objective and independent of his own will, were at first consciously and simultaneously present, and in what respective degrees, it is difficult to conjecture. But it is certain that the conception of a divine commission soon took entire and undivided possession of his soul; and, however coloured by the events and inducements of the day, or mingled with apparently incongruous motives and desires, retained a paramount influence until the hour of his death. The 96th Sura was, in fact, the starting point of Islâm. Theologians and biographers generally hold it to be the first revealed Sura; and Mahomet himself used to refer to it as the commencement of his inspiration.[1]

---

[1] Several years after he mentions the vision which he believed himself then to have seen, in the following words :—

> ' Verily it is no other than a Revelation that has been inspired :
> One mighty and strong taught it unto him,—
> One endued with wisdom ; and he stood
> In the highest part of the horizon,
> Then he drew near and approached.
> And he reached to the distance of two bows' length, or yet nearer :
> And he revealed unto his servant that which he revealed.
> The heart did not belie in that which he saw.
> What! Will ye then dispute with him concerning that which he
> saw ? '—*Sura* liii.

He then alludes to a *second* vision of Gabriel, which will be referred to hereafter.

But the divine commission was unheeded at Mecca. The commission slighted by the people of Mecca.
Scorn and abuse gathered thicker than ever around him.
He was taunted as a poet carried away by wild fancy ; as a
magician or a soothsayer, for his oaths and rhapsodies resembled in style the oracles of these ; or as one possessed by
genii and demons.

Grieved and dispirited, he fell back upon his commission. The vision, and command to preach.
Was it a warrant and command to *publish* his message even
to a stiff-necked and rebellious people, or not rather a simple
attestation, for himself and his disciples, that the doctrine was
true ?　Engrossed and wearied by these doubts and difficulties,
the Prophet stretched himself on his carpet, and wrapping
his garments about him, fell into a trance or vision.　The
Angel was at hand, and Mahomet was aroused from despondency to energy and action by this animating message :—

Oh thou that art covered! Sura lxxiv.
　　　Arise and preach !
　　　And magnify thy Lord ;
　　　And purify thy clothes ;
　　　And depart from uncleanness.
And show not thy favours, in the hope of self-aggrandisement ;
　And wait patiently for thy Lord.
　　　*　　　*　　　*　　　*　　　*
Leave ME and him whom I have created alone ;
On whom I have bestowed abundant riches,
And sons dwelling before him ;
And disposed his affairs prosperously ;—
Yet he desireth that I should add thereto.
Nay ! Because he is to OUR Signs an adversary,
I will afflict him with fierce calamity ;
For he imagined and devised mischief in his heart,
　May he be damned ! how he devised !
　Again may he be damned ! how he devised !
　Then he looked ;
　Then he frowned and scowled ;
Then he turned his back and looked contemptuously :—
And he said, ' *Verily, this is nothing but Magick that will be*
　　wrought ; [1]
Verily, this is no other than the speech of a mortal.'
　Now, will I cast him into Hell-fire.
And what shall cause thee to know what HELL-FIRE is ?

---

[1] Alluding to the doctrine of the Resurrection.　The revivification of dry
bones and dust was laughed to scorn as mere magic.

It leaveth not, neither doth it suffer to escape,
  Candescent on the skin.

* * * * *

Nay, by the Moon!
By the night when it retireth!
By the morn when it reddeneth!
Verily it is one of the most weighty matters,—
A warning to mankind,—
To him amongst you that desireth to advance, or to remain
  behind.
Every Soul lieth in pledge for that which it hath wrought;—
Excepting the heirs of God's right hand.
In Gardens, they shall enquire concerning the wicked;—
' *What hath cast you into Hell?* '
And they shall reply,—' *We were not of those that prayed;*
  And we did not feed the poor;
  And we babbled vainly with the vain babblers;
  And we were rejecters of the Day of reckoning;
  Until the conviction thereof overtook us.'
And the intercession of the Interceders shall not avail them.
Then what aileth them that they turn aside from the admoni-
  tion;—
As if they were affrighted asses fleeing from a lion?
And every man among them desireth that expanded Pages be
  given unto him.[1]
Nay! they dread not the Life to come.
Nay! this is a warning;
And whoso chooseth is warned thereby.
And there shall none be warned but as the Lord pleaseth.
HE is to be feared, and HE is the Forgiver.

Vindictive abuse of his opponents.

It has been thought expedient to introduce this Sura nearly entire, not only for the remarkable commission in its opening lines *to preach publicly*, which forms a new and marked stage in the mission of Mahomet, but as the best means of conveying some idea of the style of revelation followed by Mahomet about the third or fourth year of his prophetical life. The person so vehemently condemned is supposed to have been Walîd, the honoured chief of Mecca, who was the first to raise his pickaxe on the rebuilding of the Káaba. The heart of Mahomet was vindictive; and he dealt, through his Revelation, reproach and condemnation

---

[1] *i e.* that the divine message recorded upon pages should be miraculously brought from heaven to each objector, in proof of Mahomet's mission.

in severe and crushing terms against his adversaries. It was thus he cursed Abu Lahab his own uncle, and the father-in-law of two of his daughters, on account of his contemptuous bearing :—

> Damned be ABU LAHAB's hands ! and let himself be damned !   Sura cxi.
> His riches shall not profit him, nor that which he hath gained.
> He shall be cast into the fire of flame,[1]
> And his Wife also laden with fuel,
> About her neck shall be a rope of palm-fibre.[2]

I refrain, however, from entering here upon the *consequences* of the public preaching, and the struggle with idolatry. Our present object is simply to trace the growth of the idea of inspiration and of a mission from the Deity in the mind of Mahomet; and this I have attempted to do from the only reliable source,—the revelations of the Prophet himself.

But in order to give a full and perfect view of the progress of Mahomet towards a belief in his own inspiration, it is necessary to place before the reader the statements of Tradition. These, however, are at this point peculiarly untrustworthy. Mahomet himself, from whose lips alone any satisfactory account of the mental process could have been gained, was reserved, if not entirely silent, on the subject. The painful season of perturbation and dubitancy must have recurred ungratefully to his memory; and the grand result, the salient point of his career, namely, the commission to recite and to preach in the name of God, obscured, if it did not entirely hide, the steps which led to it. *Traditional account untrustworthy.* *Mahomet spoke little on the subject.*

Again, the fixed dogma with which every Mahometan sets out, that the Corân contains no Sura, no sentence, not even a single word, which did not emanate by direct communication from God, has precluded enquiry, and misled the early biographers of Mahomet. It would be blasphemy with them to hold that anything of *human* origin—any fragments *Theory of inspiration prevented free enquiry.*

---

[1] A play upon the word *Lahab*, which signifies *flame*, as well as his adversary's name.

[2] The story is that she had strewed Mahomet's path with a bundle of thorns, whence her punishment. Abu Lahab, at an assembly summoned by Mahomet to hear his prophetical message, exclaimed : '*Let him be damned ! Is this all he hath called us together for ?*' Whereupon this passage was revealed, damning Abu Lahab.

of the musings of the Prophet's mind at a period before his revelations were cast in the mould of inspiration—could have found their way into the Corân; and hence they miss the clue which the above or similar speculations may supply for tracing the course of Mahomet's mental and spiritual history.

Miraculous fabrication.

Lastly, whatever facts have been preserved by tradition of Khadija's recollections, are greatly distorted by the miraculous associations cast around them.[1] Mahomet himself was not unwilling to countenance such superstitious belief. And there is no subject which, in the growth of tradition, would imperceptibly acquire more wonderful and mysterious colouring than the communication of divine monitions to the heart of Mahomet, and more especially in their first beginnings. Having thus warned the reader against a too implicit faith in the story of Tradition, I proceed to give it as nearly as possible in the original words.

Traditional statement. Visions and solitude.

The first beginnings of the Prophet's inspiration were '*real visions.*' Every vision that he saw was clear as the breaking forth of the morning. This continued for some time, and caused an unusual love of privacy;—nothing was so pleasing to him as retirement. He used to repair to a cave on mount Hîra, and pass whole days and nights alone before he revisited his family; then he would return to Khadîja, and for a time remain at home through affection for her. This went on until the truth burst upon him, which happened in the cave of Hîra.

Gabriel appears to Mahomet.

About this time, while wandering among the mountains, he saw an angel in the sky calling to him: '*O Mahomet! I am Gabriel!*' and he was terrified, for so often as he raised his head to the heavens he saw the angel. So he returned hastily to Khadîja, and told her all that had happened; and he said: 'O Khadîja! I have never detested anything with greater abhorrence than these idols and soothsayers, and now

[1] It is to be remembered that this period preceded the time when Mahomet assumed the prophetical office and stood forth prominently to public notice. *Then* his system had been fully matured, and the idea of inspiration formed. But before that time he could not have been the object of much observation. Khadîja must have been almost the only witness of his earliest mental struggles. Ali was but a boy; and it is doubtful how far Zeid and Abu Bakr were yet on sufficiently intimate terms with him to be made the confidants of his most secret thoughts.

verily I fear lest I should turn out a soothsayer myself.' He fears becoming a soothsayer.
' Never, my cousin! say not so.   The Lord will not treat thee
thus;' and she proceeded to recount the many virtues on
which she founded this assurance.   Then she repaired to Khadija and Wa- raca re- assure him.
Waraca, and repeated to him what Mahomet had told her.
' By the Lord!' replied the aged man, ' thy uncle's son
speaketh the truth.   This verily is the beginning of prophecy.
And there shall come unto him the *Great law*,[1] like unto the
law of Moses.   Wherefore charge him that he entertain not
any but hopeful thoughts within his heart.   If he should declare himself a prophet while I am yet alive, I will believe
in him and I will stand by him.'

Now the first Sura revealed to Mahomet was the 94th, Inspiration ceases, and he medi- tates suicide.
Recite in the name of the Lord, &c.; and that descended on
him in the cave of Hîra.   After this he waited some time
without seeing Gabriel.   And he became greatly downcast,
so that he went out now to one mountain, and then to another,
seeking to cast himself headlong from thence.   While thus
intent on self-destruction he was suddenly arrested by a voice
from heaven.   He looked up, and behold it was Gabriel upon Gabriel again ap- pears and comforts him.
a throne between the heavens and the earth, who said: ' *O
Mahomet! thou art the Prophet of the Lord, in truth, and I
am Gabriel!*'   Then Mahomet turned to go to his own house;
and the Lord comforted him, and strengthened his heart.
And thereafter revelations began to follow one upon another
with frequency.[2]

[1] *Namûs*, the Arabic form for Nomos, ' the law.'

[2] The above is from Wâckidi, who is here more succinct and rational than
Hishâmi.   Tabari again surpasses Hishâmi in miraculous statements, the
number and variety of which illustrate the rapid fabrication and indiscriminate
reception of marvellous stories in the third century of the Hégira.   Omitting
all such, the following is a brief outline from Hishâmi and Tabari of the
first stirrings of inspiration :—

On the night whereon the Lord was minded to deal graciously with him,
Gabriel came to Mahomet as he slept with his family in the cave of Hîra;
and he held in his hand a piece of silk with writing thereon, and he said *Read!*
Mahomet replied, *I do not* (*i.e.* cannot) *read.*   Whereupon the angel laid hold
of him so tightly that he thought death had come upon him.   Then said
Gabriel a second time, *Read!*   And Mahomet replied, *What shall I read?*
which words he uttered only to escape the previous agony.   Gabriel proceeded:
—*Read* (recite) *in the name of thy Lord*, &c.;—repeating the 96th Sura to the
end of v. 5; and when he had ended, the angel left him; and ' the words,' said
Mahomet, ' were as though they had been graven on my heart.'   Suddenly
the thought occurred to him that he was possessed of evil spirits, and he medi-

Various accounts of stoppage of inspiration.

The period succeeding the revelation of the 96th Sura, during which inspiration was suspended, and Mahomet in despondency contemplated suicide, is generally represented as of longer duration than in the above statement. This interval is variously held to have lasted from six months to three years. At its close, the 74th and 93rd Suras, containing assurance of mercy and the command to preach, were delivered. The accounts, however, are throughout confused, and sometimes contradictory; and we can only gather with certainty that there was a time (corresponding with the deductions which we have drawn from the Corân itself) during which the mind of Mahomet hung in suspense, and doubted the reality of a heavenly mission.

Character of Mahomet's ecstatic periods.

What was the character of Mahomet's ecstatic periods,—whether they were simply reveries of profound meditation, or swoons connected with a morbid excitability of mental or physical constitution, or in fine were connected with any measure of supernatural influence,—it would be difficult to determine. On a subject so closely allied to the supernatural, we must be specially on our guard against the tendency of a credulous and excited imagination to stimulate the production of marvellous tales which would be eagerly adopted and handed down by tradition. With this caution the following particulars may be read :—

tated suicide; but as he rushed forth with the intention of casting himself down a precipice, he was arrested by the appearance of Gabriel, and stood for a long time transfixed by the sight. At last, the vision disappearing, Mahomet returned to Khadîja who, alarmed at his absence, had sent messengers to Mecca in quest of him. In consternation he threw himself into her lap, and told her what had occurred. She reassured him, saying that he would surely be a prophet, and Waraca confirmed her in the belief.

Another story is that Khadîja tested the character of the spirit by making Mahomet sit first on her right knee, then on her left, in both of which positions the apparition continued before him. Then she took him in her lap, and removed her veil, or uncovered her garments, when it disappeared,—thus proving that it was at any rate a modest and virtuous being. Whereupon Khadîja exclaimed: *Rejoice my cousin, for by the Lord! it is an angel, and no devil.*

On another occasion, being terrified, he entreated Khadîja to cover him up, on which was revealed the 74th Sura, beginning, *Oh thou covered!* Again, the Prophet receiving no visits from Gabriel for some time, Khadîja said to him: *Verily I fear that God is displeased with thee*; whereupon was revealed Sura xciii. ;—*Thy Lord hath not removed from thee, neither is He displeased,* &c. But such traditions are simply attempts to explain or illustrate the several passages to which they relate.

At the moment of inspiration, anxiety pressed upon the Traditional account. Prophet, and his countenance was troubled. He fell to the ground like one intoxicated or overcome by sleep; and in the coldest day his forehead would be bedewed with large drops of perspiration. Even his she-camel, if Mahomet chanced to become inspired while he rode upon her, would be affected by a wild excitement, sitting down and rising up, now planting her legs rigidly, then throwing them about as if they would be parted from her. To outward appearance inspiration descended unexpectedly, and without any previous warning even to the Prophet.[1] When questioned on the subject Mahomet Mahomet's own account. replied : ' Inspiration descendeth upon me in one of two ways ; sometimes Gabriel cometh and communicateth the Revelation unto me, as one man unto another, and this is easy ; at other times, it affecteth me like the ringing of a bell, penetrating my very heart, and rending me as it were in pieces; and this it is which grievously afflicteth me.' In the later period of life Mahomet referred his grey hairs to the withering effect produced upon him by the ' *terrific* Suras.' [2]

It will not have escaped observation that Tradition has Mahometan notions regarding devils and genii. represented Mahomet as at one time under serious apprehensions lest the beginnings of inspiration were in reality the promptings of evil spirits or of genii who had taken possession of him. The views entertained by Mahometans regarding the genii are curious, and founded upon traditions

---

[1] Abd al Rahmân relates that on the return from Hodeibia (A.H. 6), he suddenly saw the people urging on their camels ; and every one was enquiring of his neighbour the cause. They replied, *Inspiration hath descended on the Prophet.* So he too urged on his camel, and reached Mahomet, who, seeing that a sufficient number of people had gathered around him, began to recite the 40th Sura. I remember no tradition which represents Mahomet as beforehand aware that inspiration was about to come upon him.

[2] The 'terrific' Suras, as specified in the numerous traditions on this subject, are, 'Sura Hûd, and its Sisters;'—the ' *Sisters*' are variously given as Suras 11, 21, 56, 69, 77, 78, 81, or 101 ;—all revealed at Mecca, and some of them very early. While Abu Bakr and Omar sat in the mosque, at Medîna, Mahomet suddenly came upon them from the door of one of his wives' houses (which opened into the mosque), stroking and lifting up his beard, and looking at it. Now his beard had in it many more white hairs than his head. And Abu Bakr said: 'Ah, thou, for whom I would sacrifice father and mother, white hairs are hastening upon thee !' The Prophet, raising his beard with his hand, gazed at it ; and Abu Bakr's eyes filled with tears. ' Yes,' said Mahomet, ' Hûd ' (Sura xi.) 'and its Sisters have hastened my white hairs.'—' And what,' asked Abu Bakr, ' are its sisters ?' ' The *Inevitable* (Sura 56), and the *Striking* (Sura 101.)'

traced up to the time of Mahomet himself. Before the mission of the Prophet, the devils and genii had access to the outskirts of heaven, and by assiduous eaves-dropping had secured some of the secrets of the upper world, which they communicated to soothsayers and diviners upon the earth. But on the advent of Mahomet they were driven from the skies, and, whenever they dared to approach, flaming bolts were hurled at them, appearing to mankind like falling stars. Hence at this epoch the show of falling stars is said to have been brilliant and uninterrupted; and the Arabs were much alarmed at the portentous phenomenon.[1] Such a belief in the existence and history of the genii, childish as it may appear, is clearly developed in the Corân; and throws a mysterious light upon the inner recesses of the Prophet's mind.[2]

Was Mahomet's belief in his own inspiration the result of Satanic influence?

The early doubts of Mahomet, and his suspicion of being under the influence of genii or evil spirits, suggest the enquiry whether that suspicion rested on any real ground, or was the mere creation of a nervous and excited fancy; whether in short if he was the subject of any supernatural influence, it may not have proceeded from the Evil one. On a subject so mysterious it is not for us to dogmatise; but the teaching of Christianity justifies our alluding to it as *one of the possible causes* of the fall of Mahomet—the once sincere enquirer—into the meshes of deception.[3]

---

[1] It is possible that at the period referred to there may really have been an unusual display of falling stars, which at certain points of the earth's course are known to be specially abundant.

[2] In the Corân the genii are thus represented as conversing one with another: 'And verily we used to pry into the heavens, but we found them to be filled with a strong guard and with flaming darts. And we used to sit in some of the seats thereof to listen; but whoever listeneth now, findeth a flaming bolt in ambush. And we know not whether evil be hereby intended against those upon earth, or whether the Lord be minded to guide them into the right way.' As we shall see below, many of the genii, when they heard Mahomet reciting his revelation, are said to have been converted. The Corân professes to have been revealed for the benefit and salvation *both of Men and Genii*.

[3] Mahomet himself lived under the deep conviction of the personality of Satan and his emissaries, and of his own exposure to their influence. Throughout the Corân the Devil and his angels are represented as possessed of power not only to influence the wicked, but even to suggest sinful thoughts and actions to the good, not excluding Mahomet himself.

We may conceive the nature of such influence, as well as assume its possibility, by turning to the temptation of which our blessed Saviour is related in the Gospels to have been, at the commencement of his ministry, the subject. Let us endeavour briefly to follow out the parallel. *Parallel with the temptation of our Saviour.*

In the first approach, Satan, taking advantage of the cravings of hunger, tempted Jesus to contravene the law of his human existence in supplying his temporal necessities by means of his supernatural powers. He rejected the suggestion, and throughout his life on earth refrained from bringing the divine power which he possessed to the relief of his personal wants. *I. Temptation to minister from supernatural sources to personal wants.*

An analogous temptation lay in wait for Mahomet. He was not, indeed, possessed of any supernatural energy. But, in virtue of his professed inspiration, he arrogated a spiritual power which the records of his life too plainly prove that he misused to subserve his personal necessities and even his erring desires. *Analogy in the case of Mahomet.*

In the second scene our Lord was tempted to seek high and holy ends by unhallowed means; to manifest his Messiahship by a daring display of celestial power. The object was legitimate; but the means would have involved a presumptuous tempting of the divine providence, to which his humanity was subordinate. Jesus was to advance his religion by no such unauthorised expedients. It was the condition of his humanity to deny himself the use of that power, by which he could have summoned legions to work out his plans and blast the machinations of his enemies. *II. Temptation to compass lawful ends by unlawful means.*

What a melancholy contrast does the career of Mahomet present! *He*, it is true, owned no divine power. But, Prometheus-like, he sought to rob the armoury of heaven, and impiously wield a weapon of celestial energy and temper. That instrument was the NAME OF GOD. Jesus discomfited the enemy by opposing to him the revealed Word of God; Mahomet fell by forging it. As his scheme advanced, he did not scruple at other expedients which, though they might be less presumptuous, were not the less unauthorised; and sought by temporal inducements, and by force of arms, to extend the worship of the One God. The subtle temptation was here as in the Evangelists—*to compass a pious end by unlawful means.* *Analogy in the case of Mahomet.*

III. Tempted to compromise with the world.

Again, the Devil tempted Jesus to fall down and worship him by the promise of the kingdoms of the world and the glory of them. Perhaps the Satanic insinuation may be thus conceived. A mortal struggle was at hand between the kingdom of Jesus and the world; in which, through death itself, life was to be won for his people. To the end of time, the power of darkness would be in antagonism to Christianity, impeding its spread, and recapturing its very conquests. Was it possible to compromise the struggle? Would that Power abate the fierceness of its opposition? if even neutral, how would the contest be lightened, and what millions *more* might be brought into the kingdom of heaven! Some compromise with the spirit of the world might avert a struggle of inconceivable anguish and loss, and secure a glorious success not otherwise to be hoped for, all tending to the honour of God. Thus might the worldling have reasoned, and thus decided. But Jesus knew no compromise with sin.

Analogy in the case of Mahomet.

Not so Mahomet. He listened to the suggestion, and was tempted to an alliance between Religion and the World. The result was a politico-religious system, combining the closest union between worldliness and spirituality, between Good and Evil;—barely so much of virtue and spiritual truth retained as to appease the religious principle in man, while passion and indulgence are allowed the utmost license compatible with the appearance of goodness. The spurious imitation of godliness satisfies the Serious; the laxity of its moral code, and the compatibility of its whole ritual with irreligion within, present no barrier to the Sensualist.

Whatever compromise was made by Mahomet on the one hand, the counterpart was well fulfilled; for the kingdoms of this world and the glory of them followed rapidly in the train of Islâm.

If Mahomet was under supernatural influence his course at Medina proves it to have been evil.

Happy would it have been for the memory of the Arabian Prophet if his career had terminated with his flight from Mecca. Then, indeed, the imputation of such a compromise might have been branded as unwarranted and unjust. But the fruits of his principles, as exhibited at Medîna *in connection with his prophetic office*, will not permit the doubt that *if* he acted under a supernatural guidance, such guidance proceeded from no pure and holy source. Ambition, rapine, assassination, lust, are characteristics of his later life, openly sanctioned by the assumed permission, sometimes even by the express command, of the Most High! May we conceive that a diabolical inspiration was permitted to enslave the heart of him who had deliberately yielded to the compromise with evil? May not Satan have beguiled the heart in the habitude of an Angel of light, and, even when insinuating his vilest suggestions, have professed himself a Messenger from the God of purity and holiness? If so, what an assimilation must gradually have been wrought between the promptings of the Evil one, and the subjective perceptions of Mahomet himself, when he could imagine, and with earnestness and sincerity assert, that the Almighty had sanctioned and even encouraged his debased appetites!

It is enough to have suggested the awful possibility. None may venture an unhesitating reply, until there are laid bare to our view, in a more spiritual state, the workings and the manifold agencies of that unseen life which, though unceasingly active both within and around us, is shrouded now from mortal ken.

Such possibilities are suggested, not dogmatised upon.

CHAPTER IV.

EXTENSION OF ISLÂM AND EARLY CONVERTS, FROM THE ASSUMPTION
BY MAHOMET OF THE PROPHETICAL OFFICE TO THE DATE OF
THE FIRST EMIGRATION TO ABYSSINIA.

Ætat. 44–45.

Position of Mahomet in his forty-fourth year.

THE weary region of uncertainty and speculation has been left behind. Towards the forty-fourth year of his age we find Mahomet, now emerged from doubt and obscurity, clearly and unequivocally asserting that he was ordained a prophet with a commission to the people of Arabia, reciting his warnings and exhortations as messages that emanated direct from God, and himself implicitly believing (to all outward appearance) the inspiration and mission to be divine. We find him already surrounded by a little band of followers, all animated by ardent devotion to his person, and earnest belief in God as his guide and inspirer.

Earliest converts.

It is strongly corroborative of Mahomet's sincerity that the earliest converts to Islâm were his bosom friends and the people of his household; who, intimately acquainted with his private life, could not fail otherwise to have detected those discrepancies which more or less invariably exist between the professions of the hypocritical deceiver abroad and his actions at home.

Khadija.

The faithful KHADÎJA has already been made known to the reader, as sharer in the enquiries of her husband, and probably the first convert to his doctrines. 'So Khadîja believed' (runs the simple tradition), 'and attested the truth of that which came to him from God. Thus was the Lord minded to lighten the burden of his Prophet; for he heard nothing that grieved him touching his rejection by the people, but he had recourse unto her, and she comforted, reassured, and supported him.'

ZEID, the former slave, and his wife Omm Ayman (or Baraka) the nurse of Mahomet, have also been noticed. Though Zeid was now a free man, yet being the adopted son and intimate friend of Mahomet, it is probable that he lived in close connection with his family, if not actually a member of it. He, too, was one of the earliest believers. *Zeid.*

His cousin ALI, now thirteen or fourteen years of age, already gave tokens of the wisdom and judgment which distinguished him in after life. Though possessed of indomitable courage, he was meditative and reserved, and lacked the stirring energy which would have rendered him an effective propagator of Islâm. He grew up from a child in the faith of Mahomet, and his earliest associations strengthened the convictions of maturer years. It is said that as Mahomet was once engaged with the lad in prayer, in a glen near Mecca whither they had retired to avoid the jeers of their neighbours, Abu Tâlib chanced to pass by, and said: 'My nephew! what is this new faith I see thee following?' 'O my uncle!' replied Mahomet, 'this is the religion of God, and of his angels, and of his prophets; the religion of Abraham. The Lord hath sent me an Apostle unto his servants; and thou, my uncle, art the most worthy of all that I should address my invitation unto, and the most worthy to assist the Prophet of the Lord.' Abu Tâlib replied: 'I am not able, my nephew, to separate from the religion and the customs of my forefathers, but I swear that so long as I live no one shall dare to trouble thee.' Then, turning to his son, the little Ali, who professed a similar faith and the resolution to follow Mahomet, he said: 'Well, my son, he will not call thee to aught but that which is good; wherefore thou art free to cleave unto him.' *Ali.*

To the family group it is hardly necessary to add the aged cousin of Khadîja, WARACA, whose profession of Christianity and support of Mahomet have been already mentioned, because it is generally agreed that he died before Mahomet had entered upon his *public* ministry. *Waraca.*

In the little circle there was one belonging to another branch of the Coreish, who, after Khadîja, may claim prece- *Abu Bakr.*

dence in the profession of Islâm. ABU BAKR had long been
the familiar friend of Mahomet, and with him probably had la-
mented the gross darkness of Mecca, and sought after a better
faith. He lived in the same quarter of the city as Khadîja.
When Mahomet removed thither the intimacy became closer,
and the attachment of Abu Bakr was soon riveted by
implicit faith in his friend as the apostle of God. Ayesha
his daughter (born about this period, and destined while yet
a girl to be the Prophet's bride) ' could not remember the
time when both her parents were not true believers, and
when Mahomet did not daily visit her father's house morning and evening.' Of Abu Bakr, the Prophet said : ' I never
invited any one to the faith who displayed not hesitation
and perplexity, excepting only Abu Bakr; who, when I
had propounded unto him Islâm, tarried not, neither was
perplexed.

His appear-
ance and
character.

The character and appearance of this chief of Islâm, and
bosom friend of Mahomet, demand detailed description.
Abu Bakr was about two years younger than the Prophet ;
short in stature, and of a small spare frame ; the eyes deeply
seated under a high projecting forehead. His complexion
was fair, and face comely, but thin so that you could see
the veins upon it. Shrewd and intelligent, he yet wanted
the originality of genius ; his nature was mild and sympa-
thetic, but not incapable of firm purpose when important
interests required. Impulse and passion rarely prompted his
actions ; he was guided by reason and calm conviction.
Faithful and unvarying in his attachment to the Prophet, he
was known (and is to the present day familiar throughout the
realms of Islâm) as AL SIDDÎCK, ' the True.' [1] He was also
styled ' the Sighing,' from his tender and compassionate
heart.

His gene-
rosity and
popularity.

Abu Bakr was a diligent and successful merchant, and,
being frugal and simple in his habits, possessed at his conversion about 40,000 dirhems. His generosity was rare and

---

[1] His proper name was Abdallah son of Othmân Abu Cahâfa. It is not
clear when he obtained the name of *Abu Bakr*. If, as appears probable, it was
given him because his daughter Ayesha was Mahomet's only virgin bride, then
it must have been after the emigration to Medîna, when the Prophet, by
marrying many *widows*, had given a distinction and peculiarity to his marriage
with Ayesha.

his charity unwearying. The greater part of his fortune was
now devoted to the purchase of such unfortunate slaves as
were persecuted for their attachment to the new faith; so
that but 5,000 dirhems were left when, ten or twelve years
after, he emigrated with the Prophet to Medîna. Abu Bakr
was unusually familiar with the history of the Coreish, who
often referred to him for genealogical information. His
judgment was sound and impartial, his conversation agreeable,
his demeanour affable and engaging; his society and advice
were much sought after by the Coreish, and he was popular
throughout the city.[1]

To have such a man a staunch adherent of his claims was
for Mahomet a most important step. Abu Bakr's influence
was freely surrendered to the cause of Islâm, and five of the
earliest converts are attributed to his exertions and example.
Three were but striplings. *Sád*, the son of Abu Wackkâs,
converted in his sixteenth or seventeenth year, was the
nephew of Amina.[2] *Zobeir*, probably still younger, was at
once the nephew of Khadîja, and the son of Mahomet's aunt
Safia.[3] About the same age was *Talha*, the renowned warrior
of after days, and related to Abu Bakr himself. The fourth
was *Othmân* son of Affân (successor of Omar in the Caliphate) who, though of the Omeyad stock, was on the mother's
side a grandson of Abd al Muttalib. Mahomet's daughter
Rockeya, being now, or shortly after, free from her connection with Otba (son of the hostile Abu Lahab), the Prophet
gave her in marriage to Othmân, whose wife she continued
until her death some ten or twelve years afterwards. Othmân
was at this period between thirty and forty years of age.
The fifth was *Abd al Rahmân*, ten years younger than the
Prophet, a man of wealth and character. Abd al Rahmân,
Othmân, and Talha were, like Abu Bakr, merchants.

Abu Bakr's influence gains five early converts;

Sád,

Zobeir,

Talha,

Othmân son of Affân, and

Abd al Rahmân.

---

[1] I agree with Sprenger in considering 'the faith of Abu Bakr the greatest
guarantee of the sincerity of Mohammed in the beginning of his career'—
and, indeed, in a modified sense, throughout his life.

[2] The mother of Mahomet. Sád pursued the trade of manufacturing
arrows, and is renowned as the first who shot an arrow on the side of
Islâm.

[3] Zobeir was the grandson of Khuweilid, Khadija's father; and also the
grandson of Abd al Muttalib by his daughter Safia. He was a butcher; and
his father a grain merchant, or, as others have it, a tailor. He became a
distinguished leader and warrior.

Four converts with Abd al Rahmân.

Abd al Rahmân was accompanied on his first visit to the house of Mahomet by four companions, who at the same time embraced Islâm: *Obeida* son of Mahomet's uncle Hârith; *Abu Salma*; [1] *Abu Obeida*, subsequently a warrior of note; and *Othmân* son of Matzûn. The latter had already abandoned wine before his conversion, and was with difficulty persuaded by Mahomet to renounce the asperities of an ascetic life. His family appears to have been well inclined to Islâm, for we find two brothers, a son, and other relatives, in the list of early believers. [2]

Converted slaves. Bilâl.

Of the slaves ransomed by Abu Bakr from persecution, the foremost is BILÂL, the son of an Abyssinian slave-girl. He was tall, dark, and gaunt, with negro features and bushy hair. Mahomet distinguished him as '*the first fruits of Abyssinia*;' and to this day he is known throughout the Moslem world as the first Müadzzin, or crier to prayer. *Amr ibn Foheira*, after being released from severe trial, was employed by Abu Bakr in tending his flocks. [3] *Abdallah ibn Masûd*, 'small in body, but weighty in faith,' the constant attendant who waited upon Mahomet at Medîna; [4] and *Khobâb*, a blacksmith, were also converted at this period.

Meccan slaves susceptible of religious impression.

The slaves of Mecca were peculiarly accessible to the solicitations of the Prophet. As foreigners they were generally familiar either with Judaism or Christianity. Isolated from the influences of hostile partisanship, persecution had alienated them from the Coreish, and misfortune made their hearts susceptible of spiritual impressions.

Thirteen other early believers.

In addition to the twenty persons now noticed as among the first confessors of the new faith, tradition enumerates at least thirteen others as having believed '*before the entry of*

---

[1] Abu Salma was ten years older than Mahomet, and was killed at Bedr. He emigrated twice to Abyssinia with his wife *Omm Salma*. He died of wounds received at Ohod, when Mahomet married his widow.

[2] He wished to renounce the privileges of conjugal life. But Mahomet forbade this, and recommended him to imitate his own practice in this respect, saying that the Lord had not sent his prophet with a monkish faith. The expressions attributed to Mahomet on this occasion are strongly illustrative of his character; but the passage does not admit of further detail.

[3] Amr ibn Foheira was a son (by a former owner) of Omm Rumân, Abu Bakr's wife, the mother of Ayesha.

[4] This Abdallah was once at Medîna climbing up a date tree, and his companions were indulging in pleasantry at the expense of his spare legs, when Mahomet used the expression quoted in the text.

the Prophet into the house of Arcam ;'—by which expression (explained hereafter) the biographers mark the few earliest years of Islâm. Among these thirteen we observe the youthful son *Sáíd* and several relatives of the aged enquirer Zeid, already some time dead, whose remarkable life has been already alluded to as possibly paving the way for Mahomet. The wife of Sáíd belonging to the same family, and her brother, were likewise among the early converts. There were also among the number *Obeidallah*, himself one of the ' Four enquirers,' and two of his brothers. On the persecution becoming hot, he emigrated with his wife, and others of his family, to Abyssinia, where he was converted to Christianity, and died in that faith.[1] It is interesting to note among the converts *Abu Hodzeifa*,[2] son of Otba the father-in-law of Abu Sofiân, a family inveterately opposed to Mahomet. We find also the name of *Arcam*, whose house will shortly be mentioned as memorable in the annals of Islâm.

Besides this little group of three-and-thirty individuals, the wives and daughters of some of the converts are mentioned as faithful and earnest professors of Islâm. Religious movements in every age have found women to take a forward part, if not in direct and public assistance, yet in the encouragement and exhortation which are of even greater value ; and Islâm was no exception. On the other hand, in estimating the number of the early converts, we must not forget that their ranks have been unduly swelled by the traditions of those whose piety or ambition have imagined or invented a priority in the faith for their own ancestors or patrons. Weighing both considerations, we shall not greatly

Several female converts.

[1] Mahomet married Obeidallah's widow. He was Mahomet's cousin by his mother, a daughter of Abd al Muttalib. He was the brother of the famous Zeinab, who was married to Zeid (Mahomet's freedman), and was afterwards divorced by him, that the Prophet himself might take her to wife. The whole of his tribe, the Bani Dúdân, were very favourable to Islâm ; at the Hégira they all emigrated to Medîna, men, women, and children, locking up their houses. It is remarkable that this tribe were *confederates* of Harb and Abu Sofiân, the opponents of Mahomet;—the influence of Islâm thus frequently overleaping and baffling the political combinations of Mecca.

[2] He challenged his father at Badr to single combat. His sister Hind (wife of Abu Sofiân) retorted in satirical verses, taunting him with being squint-eyed, and with the barbarity of offering to fight with his father. He was an ill-favoured man, with projecting teeth.

F

Converts in first four years about forty souls.

err if we conclude that, in the first three or four years after the assumption by Mahomet of his prophetic office, the converts to his faith amounted to nearly forty souls.

Steps by which this success was attained.

By what degrees, under the influence of what motives or arguments, and at what precise periods, these individuals, one by one, gave in their adhesion to the claims of Mahomet, we can scarcely determine, further than has been done in the general outline already before the reader. It is usual in tradition to assign to the Prophet three years of secret preaching and private solicitation, after which an open call was made to the Coreish at large. But we hardly find grounds for this theory in the Corân. It is probable that the preliminary term of doubt and enquiry (which we sought to trace in the preceding chapter) has been confounded by tradition with the actual assumption of the prophetic office. The facts we may conjecture to have been as follows: An interval of pious musing, and probably of expostulation with near relatives and friends, preceded the fortieth year of Mahomet's life. About that time the resolution to 'recite in the name of the Lord' (in other words the *conviction of inspiration*) was fully formed. For some succeeding period his efforts would be naturally directed to individual persuasion and entreaty; but there is nothing to warrant the belief that the prophetic claim, once assumed, was ever confined as esoteric within the limits of a narrow circle. It was after this that the Prophet received (as he imagined) the command to 'preach;'[1] and forthwith his appeal was made to the whole community of Mecca. Gradually his followers increased, and the faith of each (though only the reflection of his own convictions) was accepted by Mahomet as new and independent evidence of his mission, emanating from Him who alone can turn the heart of man. Success made the sphere of Islâm to expand before

---

[1] That is Sura lxxiv. The biographers ordinarily quote another passage as the first command to preach:—

'And preach to thy nearer kinsfolk.
And lower thy wing to the believers that follow thee.
And if they rebel against thee, &c.'—*Sura* xxvi.

But the tradition that this passage was the first call to preach, appears erroneous. It is not only contained in a much later Sura, but itself bears evidence of persecution, and of considerable progress. It was probably revealed while the Prophet with his relatives was shut up in the Quarter of

him ; and that which was primarily intended first for Mecca only, and then for Arabia, soon embraced, in the ever-widening circle of its call, the whole human race.

An important change now occurred in the relations of Mahomet with the citizens of Mecca. Their hostility was aroused, and believers were subjected to persecution and indignity. The main ground of this opposition was a deep-seated attachment to the ancestral idolatry of the Káaba. There was no antagonism of privileged caste, or of a priest-hood supported by the temple ;—no ' craftsmen of Diana ' deriving their livelihood from the shrine. But there was the strong hereditary affection for practices associated from infancy with the daily life of every inhabitant of Mecca, and patriotic devotion to a system which made his city the foremost in Arabia. These advantages he would not lightly abandon.

Persecution caused by attachment to national idolatry.

Whether the idolatry of Mecca would not have succumbed without a struggle before such preaching as Mahomet's, *sustained by reasonable evidence*, may be matter for speculation. That which now imparted to the national faith obstinacy and strength, was the equally weak position of its unexpected antagonist. Amidst the declamation and rhetoric of the Arabian prophet no proof whatever (excepting his own conviction) was advanced in support of the divine commission. Idolatry might be wrong, but what guarantee had the idolater that Islâm was right? This was without doubt the sincere, and for many years the invincible, objection of the Coreish ; and the conviction, though mingled with hatred and jealousy, and degenerating often into intolerance and cruel spite, was the real spring of their long sustained opposition.

Weakness of Mahomet's position.

Persecution, though it may sometimes have deterred the timid from joining his ranks, was eventually of unquestion-

Advantages of opposition

Abu Tâlib, as will be related in the next chapter, and while his preaching was necessarily confined to them. The stories also of the Prophet taking his stand upon Mount Safâ, summoning his relatives, family by family, and . addressing to them the divine message; of the contemptuous reply of Abu Lahab (see *ante*, p 51); of the miraculous dinner at which Mahomet propounded his claim to his relatives, Ali alone standing forth as his champion and 'Vizier,' &c., are all apocryphal. At the miraculous dinner, food was prepared hardly sufficient for one person, but was so multiplied as to suffice for forty.

to Maho-
met. able service to Mahomet. It furnished a plausible excuse for casting aside the garb of toleration ; for opposing force to force against those who ' obstructed the ways of the Lord ;' and last of all for the compulsory conversion of unbelievers. Even before the Hégira it drove the adherents of the Prophet in self-defence into a closer union, and made them stand forth with more resolute aim and a bolder front. The severity and injustice of the Coreish, overshooting the mark, aroused personal and family sympathies ; unbelievers sought to avert or to mitigate the sufferings of the followers of the Prophet ; and in so doing they were sometimes themselves gained over to his side.

Period at
which it com-
menced. It was not, however, till three or four years of his ministry had elapsed, that any general opposition to Mahomet was organised. Even after he had begun publicly to preach, and his followers had multiplied, the people did not gainsay his doctrine. They would only point at him slightingly as he passed, and say : *There goeth the Fellow from among the children of Abd al Muttalib, to speak unto the people about the heavens.* But (adds tradition) when the Prophet began to abuse their idols, and to assert the perdition of their ancestors who had all died in unbelief, then they became displeased and began to treat him with contumely.

Once
formed
it grew
rapidly. Hostility, once excited, soon showed itself in acts of violence. Sáîd, it is related, having retired for prayer with a group of believers to a valley near Mecca, some of his neighbours passed unexpectedly by. A sharp contention arose between them, followed by blows. Sáîd struck one of his opponents with a camel goad ; and this was ' the first blood shed in Islâm.'

Mahomet
occupies,
for his mis-
sion, the
house of
Arcam,
A.D. 613. It was probably about this time—the fourth year of his mission—that, in order to prosecute his endeavours peaceably and without interruption, Mahomet took possession of the house of Arcam (a convert already noticed), situated a short distance from his own dwelling, upon the gentle rise of Safâ. Fronting the Káaba to the east, it was in a frequented position ; and pilgrims, in the prescribed course between Safâ and Marwa, must needs pass often before it. Thither were conducted any who showed a leaning towards Islâm, and there Mahomet expounded to them his way more perfectly. Conversions there. Thus of one and another of the believers, it is recorded that ' he was converted after the entry into the

house of Arcam, and the preaching there ;'—or, that 'he was brought to Mahomet in the house of Arcam, and the Prophet recited the Corân unto him, and explained the doctrines of Islâm, and he was converted and embraced the faith.' So famous was it as the birthplace of believers, that it was in after times styled *the House of Islâm*.[1]

Four sons of Abul Bokeir, a confederate of the family of Khattáb, were the first to believe and '*swear allegiance to Mahomet*'[2] in this house. Hence we may conclude that, although Omar, Khattáb's son, was not yet converted, yet the leaven of the new doctrine was already spreading rapidly among his connections.

Converts among connections of Omar.

The story of *Musáb*, a great-grandson of Háshim, will illustrate the obstacles at this time opposed to the progress of Islâm. His wife was a sister of Obeidallah, the enquirer, and it was probably through the influence of her family that he visited the house of Arcam, listened to the exhortations of Mahomet, and embraced his doctrine. But he feared publicly to confess the change ; for his mother, who doted upon him (and through whose fond attention he was known as the most handsomely dressed youth in Mecca), and the whole tribe were inveterately opposed to Mahomet. His conversion being at last noised abroad, his family seized and kept him in durance ; but he escaped, and proceeded to Abyssinia with the first Moslem emigrants. When he returned, he looked so altered and wretched that his mother had not the heart to abuse him. At a later period, having been deputed by Mahomet to teach the converts at Medîna, he revisited Mecca in company with

Story of Musáb;

[1] There is nothing to show on what footing Mahomet occupied this building; whether continuously with his family, or officially and only as a place of retreat from observation and annoyance. From several incidental notices of converts remaining there concealed during the day, and slipping away in the evening, the latter appears to be the more probable view. Omar, converted at the close of the sixth year of Mahomet's mission, is said to have been the last brought to this house; for his influence enabled them then to dispense with secrecy.

[2] This remarkable expression is the same as that for doing homage, or swearing fealty, to a leader or chief. The 'swearing allegiance to Mahomet' was probably at this time only a general declaration of faith and submission to his teaching. Possibly it may be simply the loose application of a phrase denoting a later practice, to a period when as yet there was no actual *homage* done to Mahomet.

them. His mother, apprised of his arrival, sent to him saying: 'Ah, disobedient son! wilt thou enter a city in which thy mother dwelleth, and not first visit her?' 'Nay, verily,' he replied, 'I shall never visit the house of any one before the Prophet of God.' So, after he had greeted and conferred with Mahomet, he went to his mother, who thus accosted him: 'Well! I suppose thou art still a renegade.' He answered: 'I follow the Prophet of the Lord, and the true faith of Islâm.' 'Art thou then well satisfied with the miserable way thou hast fared in the land of Abyssinia, and now again at Medîna?' But he perceived that she was meditating his imprisonment, and exclaimed: 'What! wilt thou *force* a man from his religion? If ye seek to confine me, I will assuredly slay the first person that layeth hands upon me.' His mother said: 'Then depart from my presence,' and she began to weep. Musáb was moved, and said: 'Oh, my mother! I give thee affectionate counsel. Testify that there is no God but the Lord, and that Mahomet is his servant and messenger.' She replied: 'By the sparkling stars! I shall never make of myself a fool by entering into thy religion. Begone! I wash my hands of thee and thy concerns, and cleave steadfastly unto mine own faith.' [1]

and of
Tuleib.

There were social causes on the other hand to aid the spread of the new doctrine. These may be exemplified by the conversion of Tuleib, a maternal cousin of Mahomet. This young man, having been gained over in the house of Arcam, went to his mother and told her that he now believed in the true God, and followed his Prophet. She replied that he did very right in assisting his cousin; 'And, by the Lord!' she added, 'if I had strength to do that which men do, I would myself defend and protect him.' 'But, my mother! what hindereth thee from believing and following him? And truly thy brother Hamza hath believed.' She replied: 'I wait to see what my sisters do, and will follow them.' 'But, I beseech thee, mother; wilt thou not go unto him and salute him, and testify thy faith?' And she did so; and thenceforward she assisted the cause of Mahomet by her speech, and by stirring up her sons to aid him and to fulfil his commands.

[1] Musáb distinguished himself at Bedr, and was killed at Ohod.

The following tradition will illustrate at once the anxiety of Mahomet to gain over the principal men of the Coreish, and the readiness with which he turned to the poor and uninfluential citizens of Mecca. The Prophet was engaged in deep converse with the chief, Walîd; for he greatly coveted his conversion. Then the blind man Abdallah ibn Omm Maktûm chanced to pass that way, and asked to hear the Corân. Mahomet, displeased at the interruption, spoke roughly to him. Other leading men came up and still further occupied his attention. So he turned from the blind man frowningly and left him. But the heart of Mahomet smote him, because he had thus slighted one whom God perhaps had chosen, and paid court to those whom God had reprobated. As usual, the vivid conception of the moment was framed into a divine revelation, which at once afforded relief to his own mind, and ample amends to the neglected enquirer.

Story of the blind Abdallah ibn Omm Maktûm.

The Prophet frowned and turned aside,
　Because the Blind man came to him.
And what shall cause thee to know whether haply he may not be
　　purified?
Or whether he might not be admonished, and the admonition
　　profit him?
　As for the Man that is rich,
　Him thou receivest graciously;
　And it is not thy concern that he is not purified.
　But he that cometh unto thee earnestly enquiring,
　　　　And trembling anxiously,
　　　　Him dost thou neglect.

Sura lxxx.

This incident shows the tender and ready perception by Mahomet of the slight he had offered, and the magnanimity with which he could confess his fault. Abdallah, though related to Khadija, was at present but of little consideration. Yet he was not an ordinary man. He became remarkable for his knowledge of the Corân, and at Medîna was repeatedly placed in positions of command.

Shortly after Mahomet began to occupy the house of Arcam, several slaves professed themselves his converts. Of these, *Yasâr* and *Jabr* are mentioned as among the persons accused by the Coreish of instructing the Prophet. The latter was the Christian servant of a family from Hadhramaut,

Further slave converts.

and the Prophet is said to have much frequented his cell. The former, better known under the name of Abu Fokeiha, was subjected to great persecution. His daughter Fokeiha was married to Hattâb, a convert, whom we find with others of his family among the subsequent emigrants to Abyssinia. Both these slaves died probably before Mahomet left Mecca.

Yasâr, or Abu Fokeiha.

A more important convert, styled by Mahomet ' the first fruits of Greece,' was *Suheib* son of Sinân. His home was at Mousal or some neighbouring village in Mesopotamia. His father, or his uncle, had been the Persian governor of Obolla. A Grecian band made an incursion into Mesopotamia, and carried him off while yet a boy to Syria, perhaps to Constantinople. Bought afterwards by a party of the Bani Kalb, he was sold at Mecca to Abdallah ibn Jodáân, who gave him freedom and protection. A fair skin and ruddy complexion marked his northern birth, and broken Arabic betrayed a foreign education. By traffic he acquired considerable wealth at Mecca ; but having embraced Islâm, and being left by the death of Abdallah without a patron, he suffered much at the hands of the unbelieving Coreish. It is probable that Mahomet gained some knowledge of Christianity from him, and he may indeed be the person mentioned in the Corân who is accused by the Coreish as the source of his scriptural information ;—*and indeed* WE *know that they say,* VERILY A CERTAIN MAN TEACHETH HIM. *But the tongue of him whom they intend is foreign, whereas this Revelation is in pure Arabic.* At the general emigration to Medîna, the people of Mecca endeavoured to prevent Suheib's departure ; but he bargained to relinquish the whole of his property, if they would let him go free. Mahomet, when he heard of it, exclaimed : ' *Suheib, verily, hath trafficked to profit.*'

Suheib.

Another freed slave, *Ammâr,* used to resort to the house of Arcam, and, simultaneously with Suheib, embraced Islâm. His father, a stranger from Yemen, his mother, and his brother, were also believers.

Ammâr.

The jealousy and enmity of the Coreish were aggravated by the continued success of the new sect, which now numbered more than fifty followers. The brunt of their wrath fell upon the converted slaves and strangers, and the citizens of the lower classes who had no patron or protector. These

Persecution of converted slaves.

were seized and imprisoned ; or they were exposed, in the glare of the mid-day sun, upon the scorching gravel of the valley. The torment was enhanced by intolerable thirst, until the wretched sufferers hardly knew what they said. If under this torture they reviled Mahomet and acknowledged the idols of Mecca, they were refreshed by draughts of water, and then taken to their homes. Bilâl alone escaped the shame of recantation. In the depth of his anguish, the persecutors could force from him but one expression, AHAD ! AHAD ! 'ONE, ONE, only God !' On such an occasion, Abu Bakr passed by, and secured liberty of conscience to the faithful slave by purchasing his freedom. Some of the others retained the scars of sores and wounds now inflicted to the end of their lives. Khobâb and Ammâr used to exhibit with pride and exultation the marks of their suffering and constancy to a wondering generation, in which fortune and glory had well-nigh effaced the very thought of persecution as a possible condition of Islâm.

Towards those who under such trying circumstances renounced their faith, Mahomet showed much commiseration. He even encouraged them to dissemble, in order that they might escape the torment. Happening to pass by Ammâr, as he sobbed and wiped his eyes, Mahomet enquired of him what was the matter. 'Evil ; O Prophet ! They would not let me go until I had abused thee, and spoken well of their gods.' '*But how dost thou find thine own heart ?*' 'Secure and steadfast in the faith.' '*Then,*' replied Mahomet, '*if they repeat their cruelty, repeat thou also thy words.*' A special exemption for such unwilling deniers of Islâm was even provided in the Corân.[1]

Converts permitted to dissemble.

Mahomet himself was safe under the shadow of the respected and now venerable Abu Tâlib, who, although unconvinced by the Prophet, scrupulously acknowledged the claims of the kinsman, and withstood resolutely every approach of the Coreish to detach him from his guardianship.

Mahomet safe with Abu Tâlib.

Abu Bakr, too, and those who could claim affinity with any powerful family of Mecca, though exposed perhaps to

Converts connected with in-

---

[1] *Whoever denieth God after that he hath believed* (EXCEPTING HIM WHO IS FORCIBLY COMPELLED THERETO, HIS HEART REMAINING STEADFAST IN THE FAITH) *on such resteth the wrath of God.*

contumely and reproach, were generally secure from personal injury. The chivalrous feeling which makes common cause among the members and connections of an Arab family, arousing the fierce impetuosity of all against the injurers of a single member, deterred the enemies of Islâm from open and violent persecution. Such immunity, however, depended in part on the goodwill of the convert's family and friends. Where the entire family or tribe was inimical to the new religion, there would always be the risk of insult and injury. Thus, when the Bani Makhzûm were minded to chastise the converts in their tribe, and among them Walîd son of the aged chief of that name, they repaired to his brother Hishâm, a violent opposer of the Prophet, and demanded his permission; this he readily gave, but added : '*Beware of killing him*; *for if ye do, verily I shall slay in his stead the chiefest among you.*'

First emi-
gration to
Abyssinia,
A.D. 615.

To escape these indignities, and the danger of perversion, Mahomet now recommended such of his followers as were without protection, to seek an asylum in a foreign land. '*Yonder,*' pointing to the west, '*lieth a country wherein no one is wronged :—a land of righteousness. Depart thither ; and remain until it pleaseth the Lord to open your way before you.*' Abyssinia was well known at Mecca as a market for the goods of Arabia ; and the Court of the *Najâshy* (Negus, or king) was the ordinary destination of one of their annual caravans. In the seventh month of the fifth year of Mahomet's mission, eleven men, some mounted, some on foot, and four of them accompanied by their wives, set out for the port of Shueiba ;[1] where, finding two vessels about to sail, they embarked in haste, and were conveyed to Abyssinia for half a dinar a-piece. The Coreish pursued them, but they had already left the port. Among the emigrants were Othmân son of Affân, followed by his wife Rockeya the Prophet's daughter, and Abd al Rahmân, both perhaps as merchants already acquainted with the country. The youths Zobeir and Musáb were also of the number. The party was headed by Othmân son of Matzûn, as its leader. They met with a kind reception from the Najâshy and his people. The period of exile was passed in peace and in comfort.

---

[1] The ancient port of Mecca, not far from Jedda.

This is termed the *first* ' Hégira' or flight to Abyssinia, as distinguished from the later and more extensive emigration to the same land.   On this occasion the emigrants were few, but the part they acted was of deep importance in the history of Islâm.   It convinced the Coreish of the sincerity and resolution of the converts, and proved their readiness to undergo any loss and any hardship rather than abjure the faith of Mahomet.   A bright example of self-denial was exhibited to the whole body of believers who were led to regard peril and exile in ' the cause of God,' as a privilege and distinction.   It must also have suggested the possibility that the hostile attitude of their fellow-citizens, combined with the merits of their creed, might secure for them within the limits of Arabia itself a sympathy and hospitality as cordial as that afforded by the Abyssinian king; and thus it gave birth to the idea of a greater ' Hégira,'—the emigration to Medîna.   Finally, it turned the attention of Mahomet more closely and more favourably to the Christian religion.   If an Arab asylum had not at last offered itself at Medîna, the Prophet himself might have emigrated to Abyssinia, and Mahometanism might have dwindled, like Montanism, into an ephemeral Christian heresy.

Bearing and advantages of this emigration.

SUPPLEMENT TO CHAPTER IV.

THE CORÂN, DURING THE PERIOD REVIEWED IN THIS CHAPTER.

The Corân throws light on Mahomet's history.

To complete the history of the period given in this chapter, it is needful to examine the portions of the Corân belonging to it; for their purport, and even their style, will throw an important light upon the inner, as well as the external, struggles of Mahomet.

A change observable during this period.

To the two or three years intervening between the commission to preach and the first emigration to Abyssinia, may be assigned about twenty of the Suras as they now stand in the Corân. During even this short time a marked change may be traced both in the sentiments and the composition of the revelations.

Gradual decline of life and spirit.

At first, like a mountain stream, the current dashes headlong, pure, wild, impetuous. Such are the fragments described in the third chapter. As we advance, the style becomes calmer and more uniform; yet ever and anon, mingled with oaths and wild ejaculations, we come upon a tumultuous rhapsody, like the unexpected cataract, charged with thrilling words of conviction and fervid aspiration. Advancing still, though the dancing stream sometimes sparkles and the foam deceives the eye, we trace a rapid decline in the vivid energy of natural inspiration, and even the mingling with it of grosser elements. There is yet, indeed, a wide difference from the turbid, tame, and sluggish course of later days; but the tendency cannot be mistaken. The decay of life is supplied by artificial expedient. Elaborate periods, and the measured cadence of rhyming prose, convey too often simple truisms and childish fiction. Although we still meet with powerful reasoning against idolatry and with burning words of a living faith, yet the chief substance of the Corân begins to be composed of native legends expanded by the Prophet's imagination; pictures of heaven and hell, the resurrection and the judgment day; and dramatic scenes in which the righteous and the damned, angels, genii and infernal spirits, converse in language framed adroitly as arguments in the cause of Mahomet.

The Suras gradually extend in length. In the preceding stage *The Suras become longer.* a whole Sura seldom exceeds the quarter of an ordinary page. In the present period a Sura occupies one, and sometimes two pages.[1]

The theory of inspiration is more fully developed. The *Theory of inspiration further developed.* Almighty, from whom revelation alone proceeds, is the sole authority also for its collection, recitation, and interpretation. On these points Mahomet must wait for heavenly guidance. He must not be hasty in repeating the Divine words, for ' *the Corân is revealed by a gradual revelation;* ' and it is the pre-rogative of the Lord to prescribe what passages shall be re-membered and what forgotten.[2] How much soever the Prophet may have sincerely believed, or persuaded himself to believe, that this regulating influence was exercised by the Deity, the doctrine offered an irresistible temptation to suit the tenour of his revelations to the varying necessities of the hour. It led eventually to the damaging assertion that where two passages are irreconcilably opposed, the earlier is *abrogated* by the later.

Notwithstanding this apparent fallibility, we begin to trace a *A heavenly original assigned to the Corân.* claim for the Corân not only of divine inspiration, but of a heavenly original. ' *Truly, it is the glorious Corân,* IN THE PRE-SERVED TABLET.'

It is an admonition, in revered pages ; exalted, pure ;   *Sura lxxx.*
Written by scribes (*i.e.* angels) honourable and just.

[1] It is interesting to watch the gradual lengthening of the Suras of which Flügel's beautiful edition forms an excellent standard. The twenty-two Suras first revealed contain an average of only five lines each. The next twenty Suras (those referred to in the present chapter) 16 lines. From this period to the Hégira, the average length of the fifty Suras is about three and a half pages of 22 lines; one being nearly twelve pages long. The average length of the twenty-one Medîna Suras is five pages ; Sura *Bacr* having as many as 22 pages. As before noticed, the arrangement is directly the re-verse of chronological ; the longest and latest Suras coming first, the shortest and earliest last.

At first, the Suras appear to have been produced generally entire at one time, as we now find them. Subsequently it became Mahomet's practice to throw together, according to their subject-matter, passages given forth at various times,—which is one reason why the later Suras are of such great length.

[2] ' We shall cause thee to rehearse (the Revelation), and thou shalt not forget excepting that which the Lord shall please ; for He knoweth both that which is public and that which is hid ; and We shall facilitate unto thee that which is easy.' Again : ' And move not thy tongue in the repetition of the Corân so that thou shouldest be hasty therewith. Verily upon Us devolveth the collection thereof, and the recitation thereof ; and when We shall have recited it unto thee, then follow thou the recitation thereof. Further, upon Us devolveth the explanation thereof.' So in a later Sura : ' And be not hasty in reciting the Corân, before that the revelation thereof hath been completed.'

Sura xcvii.

> Verily WE caused it to descend on the Night of power;
> And what shall make thee to know what the Night of power is?
> The Night of power excelleth a thousand months:
> On that night, the Angels and the Spirit descend by their Lord's command upon every errand.
> It is peace until the breaking of the morn.[1]

The 'holy Spirit' came to signify Gabriel.

It is not clear what ideas Mahomet at first attached to 'the Spirit' here spoken of. They were perhaps indefinite. It was a phrase he had heard used, but with different meanings, both by Jews and Christians. That the 'Holy Ghost' (however interpreted) was originally intended by the term, appears probable from the recurrence in the Corân of the expression—'*God strengthened Him* (Jesus) *by the holy Spirit.*' But eventually there can be no doubt that the 'holy Spirit,' in the acceptation of Mahomet, came to signify the angel Gabriel. He had learned that Jesus was 'born of the Virgin Mary, by the power of the Holy Ghost;' and either knowingly rejecting the divinity of that blessed Person, or imperfectly informed as to His nature, confounded Gabriel announcing the conception, with the Holy Spirit that overshadowed Mary. And so the two expressions became, in the language of the Corân, synonymous.

Visions of Gabriel.

Gabriel, the 'Spirit,' was the messenger who communicated to Mahomet the words of God, and appeared sometimes to him in a corporeal form. The traditional account of the first vision of Gabriel has been noticed in the preceding chapter. It is perhaps to this apparition that the Prophet alludes in an early Sura of the present period :—

Sura lxxxi.

> And I swear by the Star that is retrograde;
> By that which goeth forward, and that which disappeareth;
> > By the Night when it closeth,
> > By the Morn when it breaketh!
> I swear that this verily is the word of an honoured Messenger;
> Powerful; and, in the presence of the Lord of the Throne, of great
> > dignity:
> > Obeyed there and faithful.
> > And your Companion is not mad.
> Truly he hath seen him in the clear Horizon;
> And he entertaineth not any suspicion regarding the Unseen;
> Neither is this the word of a rejected [2] Devil.

---

[1] Thus abruptly does the 97th Sura, a fragment of five verses, open and close. What God is said to have sent down in this night may either signify (with Sale and the commentators) the Corân; or more probably the clear view of divine truth which that night burst upon Mahomet's mind. The 'Night of power' is the famous *Lailat al Cadr*, of which so much has been made in after days.

[2] '*Driven away,*' and so unable to overhear the secrets of Heaven.

Whither then are ye going?
Verily this is no other than an Admonition to all creatures,—
To him amongst you that willeth to walk uprightly.
But ye shall not will unless the Lord willeth—The Lord of Creation!

The concluding verses show that Mahomet already contemplated his ministry as embracing the whole world. But the vivid conviction of his heavenly commission contrasted strangely with the apathy and unbelief around him; and hence is springing up the idea of election and reprobation, which alone could account for these spiritual phenomena;—*Ye shall not will unless the Lord willeth.* Again in the very strength of the asseveration that he was not deceived, and that his inspiration was not that of a 'rejected devil,' may we not trace symptoms of a lurking suspicion thatafter all something possibly was not right?

Growth of the doctrine of predestination.

The teaching of the Corân is, up to this stage, very simple. Belief in the Unity of God, and in Mahomet as his messenger, in the resurrection of the dead, and retribution of the good and evil, are perhaps the sole doctrines insisted upon; and the only duties to be observed, prayer,[1] and charity, honesty in weights and measures, truthfulness in testimony, chastity,[2] and the faithful observance of covenants.

Teaching and precepts.

It is doubtful whether, at this period, Mahomet inculcated the rites of the Káaba as of divine obligation. The absence of allusion to them inclines us to the opinion that, though observed

Renunciation of idolatry.

[1] The *times* of prayer are, up to this time, mentioned only generally as morning, evening, and night.

[2] Among other features of the Believer, his chastity is thus described:—

'And they are continent,
Except as regardeth their Wives, and that which their right hands possess:—
For in respect of them they shall be blameless.
But he that lusteth after more than that, verily they are transgressors.'

Note that even at this early period Mahomet admitted slave-girls to be lawful concubines, besides ordinary wives. Bond-women with whom cohabitation is thus permitted are here specified by the same phrase as was used at Medîna for female slaves taken captive in war, or obtained by purchase, viz. '*that which your right hands possess.*' The liberty was not at this time abused by Mahomet himself, for he was now living chastely with a single wife. Though therefore the license was in after days taken advantage of both for his own indulgence, and as holding out an inducement to his followers to fight in the hope of capturing females who would then be lawful concubines as 'that which their right hand possessed,' yet these were not the original motives for the rule. It was in fact one of the earliest compromises or adaptations, by which Mahomet fitted his system to the usages and wishes of those about him.

by himself and his followers, they formed no part of his positive teaching. There was at any rate a clear and conclusive renunciation of idolatry :—

Sura cix.

SAY, O ye unbelievers !
I worship not that which ye worship,—
And ye do not worship that which I worship.
Never shall I worship that which ye worship,
Neither will ye worship that which I worship.
To you be your Religion ; to me my Religion.

This Sura is said to have been revealed when the aged Walîd pressed Mahomet to the compromise that his God should be worshipped in conjunction with their deities, or alternately every other year. Whatever the occasion, it breathes a spirit of uncompromising hostility to idolatry.

The Paradise of homet.

The vivid pictures of Heaven and Hell, placed to increase their effect in close juxtaposition, are now painted in colours of material joy and torment; which, however to our conceptions absurd and childish, were well calculated to effect a deep impression upon the simple Arab mind. Rest and passive enjoyment; verdant gardens watered by murmuring rivulets, wherein the believers, clothed in green silk brocades and silver ornaments, repose beneath the wide-spreading shade on couches well furnished with cushions and carpets, drink the sweet waters of the fountain, and quaff aromatic wine (such as the Arabian loved) from goblets placed before them, or handed round in silver cups resplendent as glass by beautiful youths ;[1] while clusters of fruit hang close by inviting the hand to gather them ;—such is the Paradise framed to captivate the inhabitant of the thirsty and sterile Mecca.

The Houries of Paradise.

Another element is soon added to complete the Paradise of the pleasure-loving Arab :—

Sura lxxviii.

Verily for the Pious is a blissful abode ;
Gardens and Vineyards,
And damsels with swelling bosoms, of an equal age,
And a full cup.

In the oft-described shady garden 'with fruits and meats, and beakers of wine causing not the head to ache, neither disturbing the reason,' these damsels of Paradise are introduced as '*lovely large-eyed girls* ("Hûries") *resembling pearls hidden in their shells, a reward for that which the faithful have wrought. . . . Verily We have created them of a rare creation; We have made them virgins, fascinating, of an equal age.*'

---

[1] In one passage the wine is spoken of as sealed with musk and spiced with ginger.

The following passages will illustrate the artificial style and gross materialism into which the fire of early inspiration was now rapidly degenerating. The first is taken from a psalm with a fixed alternating versicle throughout, quaintly addressed in the dual number to men and genii. To suit the rhyme the objects are introduced in pairs, excepting the damsels, whose number may not thus be limited.

* * * This is the Hell which the wicked deny ;
  They shall pass to and fro between the same and scalding water.
  Which then of the Signs of your Lord will ye deny ?
But to him that dreadeth the appearing of his Lord, there shall be two
        gardens,
  Which then of the Signs of your Lord will ye deny ?
        Planted with shady trees,
  Which then of the Signs of your Lord will ye deny ?
Through each of them shall two fountains flow,
  Which then of the Signs of your Lord will ye deny ?
And in each shall there be of every fruit two kinds.
  Which then of the Signs of your Lord will ye deny ?
They shall repose on brocaded carpets, the fruits of the two gardens
        hanging close by,
  Which then of the Signs of your Lord will ye deny ?
In them shall be modest damsels, refraining their looks, whom before
        them no man shall have deflowered, neither any genius,
  Which then of the Signs of your Lord will ye deny ?
Like as if they were rubies or pearls.[1]

---

[1] The above is the reward of the *highest* class of believers. Another set of gardens and females follows for the *common* faithful.

'And besides these, there shall be two other gardens,
  Which then of the Signs of your Lord will ye deny ?
        Of a dark green,
  Which then of the Signs of your Lord will ye deny ?
In each, two fountains of welling water.
  Which then of the Signs of your Lord will ye deny ?
In each, fruits and the palm and the pomegranate.
  Which then of the Signs of your Lord will ye deny ?
In them shall be women, amiable, lovely ;
  Which then of the Signs of your Lord will ye deny ?
Large-eyed Houries kept within pavilions ;
  Which then of the Signs of your Lord will ye deny ?
Whom no man shall have deflowered before them, nor any genius.
  Which then of the Signs of your Lord will ye deny ?
The Believers shall recline upon green rugs, and l ovel carpets,
  Which then of the Signs of your Lord will ye deny ?'

So at a somewhat later date : 'And close unto the believers shall be modest damsels refraining their looks, like unto ostrich eggs delicately covered over.' In a passage of the same period, the faithful are said to be '*married*'

The Houries revealed when Mahomet had but one wife.

It is remarkable that the notices in the Corân of this voluptuous Paradise are *almost entirely confined* to a time when, whatever the tendency of his desires, Mahomet was living a chaste and temperate life with a wife threescore years of age.[1] Gibbon characteristically observes that 'Mahomet has not specified the male companions of the female elect, lest he should either alarm the jealousy of the former husbands, or disturb their felicity by the suspicion of an everlasting marriage.' The remark, made in raillery, is pregnant with reason, and aims a fatal blow at the paradise of Islâm. Faithful women will renew their youth in heaven as well as faithful men; why should not their good works merit an equal and analogous reward? But Mahomet shrank from the legitimate conclusion.

The Hell of the Corân.

The Hell of the Corân is no less material and gross than its Heaven. The drink of the damned is described as boiling water and filthy corruption. When cast into the pit, they hear it roar wildly like the braying of an ass. 'Hell boileth over, it almost bursteth with fury: the smoke, rising in three columns, afforded neither shade nor protection, but casteth forth great sparks like castles, or as it were yellow camels.'

Sura lvi.

* * And the companions of the Left hand, how miserable they !
In scorching blasts and scalding water,
    And the shade of smoke,
That is not cold nor is it grateful.
Verily before that, they lived in pleasure;
And they were bent upon great wickedness;
    And they used to say,
What ! after we have died and become dust and bones, shall we be raised ?
Or our Fathers that preceded us ?
Say, Yea, verily, the former and the latter
Shall be gathered at the time of an appointed Day.
    Then shall you, oh ye that err and reject the Truth,
    Eat assuredly of the tree of Zackkûm,

to these 'large-eyed Houries.' In other places of a later date, probably after Khadija's death, the *Wives* of believers (their *proper* wives of this world apparently) are spoken of as entering into Paradise with their husbands. Did Mahomet deem it possible that the earthly wives might still remain united to their husbands in Paradise, in spite of their black-eyed rivals?

[1] It is noteworthy that in the Medîna Suras—that is, in all the voluminous revelations of the ten years following the Hégira—women are only twice referred to as one of the rewards in Paradise; and on both occasions in these simple words,—*and to them* (believers) *there shall be therein pure wives.* Was it that satiety had then left no longings unfulfilled; or that closer contact with Judaism had repressed the budding pruriency of his revelation, and covered with confusion the picture of a sensual Paradise which had been drawn at Mecca?

> Filling your bellies therewith,
> And drinking thereupon boiling water,
> As a thirsty camel drinketh.
> This shall be your entertainment on the Day of reckoning!

The menace of a nearer vengeance in this life begins to loom darkly forth, but as yet mingled mysteriously with the threats of the Judgment-day and Hell, thus :— Threats of temporal judgment.

> * *   The Day of separation!
> And what shall make thee know what the *Day of separation* meaneth?
>   Woe on that day unto the deniers of the Truth!
>   What! Have We not destroyed the former Nations?
> Wherefore We shall cause the latter to follow them.
> Thus shall We deal with the wicked People!
> Woe on that day unto the deniers of the Truth!

Sura lxxvii.

> * *   Verily, We warn you of a Punishment close at hand,—
> The day whereon a man shall see that which his hands have wrought;
> And the unbelievers shall say, *O would that I were dust!*

Sura lxxviii.

> * *   What! are ye secure that He who dwelleth in the Heavens will
>   not cause the Earth to swallow you up, and she shall quake?
> Or that He will not send upon you an overwhelming blast, then ye shall
>   know my warning?
> And verily the Nations that preceded thee, denied the Truth; and how
>   awful was my vengeance!

Sura lxvii.

But the men of Mecca scoffed at the menace, and defied the preacher to bring it into execution. Defiance of the Meccans.

> They say, *When shall this threatened vengeance be, if ye speak the truth?*
> SAY, 'Nay, verily, the knowledge thereof is with God alone; as for
>   me I am but a plain Warner.'
> But when they see it, the countenance of those who disbelieved shall
>   fall;
> And it shall be said, *This is that which ye have been calling for.*
> SAY, 'What think ye? whether the Lord destroy me and those that be
>   with me, or have mercy upon us, who shall deliver the
>   unbelievers from a dreadful punishment?'

Sura lxvii.

We begin also to find embodied in the Corân the arguments used by the Coreish against the Prophet, and the mode in which he replied to them. The progress of incredulity can thus be followed, and some of the very expressions employed by either party traced. Objections of the unbelievers.

The Resurrection of the body was derided by his fellow-citizens as an idle imagination. When the Prophet sought to illustrate the raising of the dead by the analogies of Nature, and the power of God in creation, he was scouted as a sorcerer or magician, who would pretend that a living body could be reproduced from dust and dead men's bones. Resurrection derided.

The Corân impugned.

The Corân was denounced at one time as a bare-faced imposture,—as *Fables of the Ancients* borrowed from foreigners at Mecca, and dressed up to suit the occasion ; at other times, as the effusion of a frenzied poet, or the incoherent drivelling of an insane madman.

Derision.

Jeers and jests were the ordinary weapons by which the believers were assailed :—

Sura lxxxiii.

Verily, the Sinners laugh the Faithful to scorn.
   When they pass by them, they wink at one another.
And when they turn aside unto their own people, they turn aside jesting
   scurrilously.
   And when they see them, they say, *Verily,* THESE *are the erring ones.*
   But they are not sent to be keepers over them.
Wherefore one day the Faithful shall laugh the Unbelievers to scorn,
   Lying upon couches, they shall behold them in Hell.

Patience and stead-fastness inculcated.

Amid the derision and the plots of the Coreish, patience is inculcated on the Prophet. His followers are exhorted to stead-fastness and resignation, and in one passage they are reminded of the constancy of the Christian martyrs in Najrân.

Sura lxxxv

By the Heavens with their Zodiacal signs ;
   By the threatened Day !
By the Witness and the Witnessed !
Damned be the *diggers of the pits* filled with burning fuel, when they
   sat around the same.
   And they were witnesses of that which they did unto the Believers.
And they tormented them no otherwise than because they believed in
   God the Mighty and the Glorious.
   Verily, they who persecute the Believers, male and female, and
   repent them not,
For such the torment of Hell is prepared, and a burning anguish, &c.[1]

Jewish and Christian Scriptures not yet referred to.

There is at this period hardly any allusion to Jewish and Christian Scripture or legend. The Corân did not as yet rest its claim upon the evidence of previous revelation, and the close correspondence therewith of its own contents.

The language of Islâm becomes fixed.

The peculiar phraseology of the new faith was already becoming fixed. The dispensation of Mahomet was distinguished as ISLÂM, that is, the surrender of the soul to God ; his followers as MUSALMÂNS (those who *surrender themselves*), or as Believers ; his opponents as KÂFIRS, that is, *rejecters of the divine message*, or as MUSHRIKÎN, such as *associate* companions or sharers with the Deity. Faith, Repentance, Heaven, Hell, Prayer, Almsgiving, and many other terms of the religion, soon acquired their stereotyped meaning. The naturalisation in Arabia of Judaism and Christianity (chiefly of the former) provided a large and ready fund of

[1] The 'diggers of the pits' were the Jewish persecutors of the Christians of Najrân. See Introduction, Chap. I. p. v.

theological speech, which, if not already in current use, was at least widely known in a sense approaching that in which Mahomet desired to use it.[1]

The reflections contained in this supplement have been suggested by the portion of the Corân produced during the period reviewed in the preceding chapter. By thus connecting the several periods of Mahomet's life with the Suras belonging to them, the enquirer is best able to trace the development of his system, and to observe what bearing external circumstances may have had upon the peculiarities of his creed.

---

[1] See remarks on the prevalence of Jewish legends and expressions, in Introduction, Chap. II. pp. xvi. and xvii. It is difficult to overestimate the advantages which Mahomet thus possessed in the tacit acquiescence of the Coreish in the truth of former Revelations, and in being able to appropriate the apt and ready terms already current as expressive of the spiritual ideas he wished to attach to them, or at least of ideas closely allied.

Thus the phrase, 'the merciful, the compassionate,' affixed by Mahomet to the name of God, though not actually in use, was known among the idolatrous tribes, as we shall see by the treaty of Hodeibia.

CHAPTER V.

FROM THE FIFTH TO THE TENTH YEAR OF THE MISSION OF MAHOMET.

Return of the Abyssinian refugees, 615 A.D.

THREE months had not elapsed from the departure of the little band to Abyssinia, when, notwithstanding their secure retreat and hospitable reception at the Najâshy's Court, the refugees again appeared in Mecca. Their return is linked with one of the strangest episodes in the life of the Prophet. Hishâmi contents himself with saying that they came back because tidings reached them of the conversion of the Coreish. But Wâckidi and Tabari narrate a story, of which the following is an outline.

The lapse of Mahomet.

The aim of Mahomet had been the regeneration of his people. But he had fallen miserably short of it. The conversion of forty or fifty souls ill compensated the bitter alienation of the whole community. His heart was vexed and his spirit chafed by the violent opposition of the most respected and influential chiefs. The prospect was dark; to the human eye, hopeless. Sad and dispirited, the Prophet longed for a reconciliation, and cast about how it could be effected.

Downcast, he desires reconciliation.

Narrative by Wâckidi and Tabari.

On a certain day the chief men of Mecca, assembled in a group beside the Káaba, discussed, as was their custom, the affairs of the city. Mahomet appeared and, seating himself by them in a friendly manner, began to recite in their hearing Sura LIII. The chapter opens with a description of the first visit of Gabriel to Mahomet (already known to the reader);[1] and then unfolds a second vision of that angel, at which certain heavenly mysteries were revealed. The passage is as follows :—

---

[1] See *ante*, p. 47: also p. 78.

* *   He also saw him (Gabriel) at another descent,
By the Lote-tree [1] at the furthest boundary,
Near to which is the Paradise of rest.
When the Lote-tree covered that which it covered,
His sight turned not aside, neither did it wander.
And verily he beheld some of the greatest Signs of his Lord.
And see ye not LÂT and OZZA,
And MANÂT the third besides ?—

When he had reached this verse, the devil suggested to Mahomet an expression of thoughts which had long possessed his soul; and put into his mouth words of reconciliation and compromise such as he had been yearning that God might send unto his people, namely :— *Satan suggests an idolatrous concession.*

These are exalted Females,
And verily their intercession is to be hoped for.

The Coreish were astonished and delighted with this acknowledgment of their deities; and as Mahomet wound up the Sura with these closing words, *The Coreish worship with him.*

Wherefore bow down before God, and serve Him,

the whole assembly prostrated themselves with one accord on the ground and worshipped. Walîd alone, unable from the infirmities of age to bow down, took a handful of earth and worshipped, pressing it to his forehead.

Thus all the people were pleased at that which Mahomet had spoken, and they began to say: *Now we know that it is the Lord alone that giveth life and taketh it away, that createth and supporteth. And as for these our goddesses, they make intercession with Him for us; wherefore, as thou hast conceded unto them a portion, we are content to follow thee.* But their words disquieted Mahomet, and he retired to his house. In the evening Gabriel visited him; and the Prophet (as was his wont) recited the Sura unto him. And Gabriel said: *What is this that thou hast done? thou hast repeated before the people words that I never gave unto thee.* So Mahomet grieved sore, and feared the Lord greatly; and he said, *I have spoken of God that which He hath not said.* But the Lord comforted his Prophet, and restored his *The people pleased.* *Mahomet disowns the whole proceeding.*

[1] The Lote is the wild plum tree, rendered in India by the *Bêr.*

confidence,[1] and cancelled the verse, and revealed the true reading thereof (as it now stands), namely—

> And see ye not LÂT and OZZA,
>   And MANÂT the third beside?
> What! shall there be male progeny unto you, and female unto
>   Him?
> That were indeed an unjust partition!
> They are naught but names, which ye and your fathers have
>   invented, &c.

The Coreish more embittered.

Now when the Coreish heard this, they spoke among themselves, saying: *Mahomet hath repented his favourable mention of the rank of our goddesses with the Lord. He hath changed the same, and brought other words instead.* So the two Satanic verses were in the mouth of every one of the unbelievers, and they increased their malice, and stirred them up to persecute the faithful with still greater severity.

The narrative founded on fact.

Pious Mussulmans of after days, scandalised at the lapse of their Prophet into so flagrant a concession, would reject the whole story. But the authorities are too strong to be impugned. It is hardly possible to conceive how the tale, if not in some shape or other founded in truth, could ever have been invented. The stubborn fact remains, and is by all admitted, that the first refugees did return about this time from Abyssinia; and that they returned in consequence of a rumour that Mecca was converted. To this fact the narratives of Wâckidi and Tabari afford the only intelligible clue. At the same time it is by no means necessary that we should literally adopt the exculpatory version of Mahometan tradition; or seek, in a supernatural interposition, the explanation of actions to be equally accounted for by the natural workings of the Prophet's mind.

The concession neither unpremedi-

It is obvious that the lapse was no sudden event. It was not a concession won by surprise, or an error of the tongue committed unawares, and immediately withdrawn. The

---

[1] Tradition tells us that Mahomet was consoled by the following passage in Sura XXII., which, however (from the reference to former apostles and prophets), must have been revealed at a somewhat later period: *And We have not sent before thee any Apostle, nor any Prophet, but when he longed, Satan cast suggestions into his longing. But God shall cancel that which Satan suggesteth. Then shall God establish His revelations (and God is knowing and wise);—that He may make what Satan hath suggested a trial unto those whose hearts are diseased and hardened, &c.*

hostility of his people had long pressed upon the spirit of tated, nor immediately withdrawn. Mahomet ; and, in his inward musings, it is admitted even by orthodox tradition that he had been meditating the very expression which, as is alleged, the devil prompted him to utter.   Neither can we believe that the concession lasted but for a day.   To outward appearance the reconciliation must have been consolidated and complete ; and it must have continued at the least for some days, probably for several weeks, to allow of the report going forth and reaching the exiles in a shape sufficient to inspire them with confidence.   We are warranted therefore in assuming a far wider basis for the event than is admitted by tradition.

The circumstances may be thus conceived.   Up to this Mahomet tempted by the hope of gaining over his people. point Mahomet's was a spiritual religion, of which faith, and prayer, and the inculcation of virtue, formed the prominent features.   Though the Káaba and its ancient rites were held to have been founded by the patriarch Abraham, yet the worship of idols engrafted thereon, and heretofore consistently rejected by Mahomet, was an integral part of the existing system.   To this superstition, with all its practices, the people were obstinately wedded ; and, unless permission were given to join more or less the time-honoured institutions of Mecca with the true faith, there was little hope of a general conversion.   How far would a strong expediency justify compromise with the prevailing system ; and was it the will of God to admit the concession ?

Was not the worship of the Káaba, after all, a *divine* Considerations by which he may have been influenced. institution ?   The temple was built at the command of God ; the compassing of it symbolised the circling course of the heavenly bodies, and the obedience of all creation to the Deity.   Pious devotion was nurtured by kissing the sacred corner-stone ; the slaying of sacrifices, in commemoration of Abraham's readiness to offer up his son, signified a like submission ; the pilgrimage to Arafât, the shaving of the head, and other popular observances, were innocent, if not directly religious, in their tendency.   But how shall he treat the idols, and the worship rendered to them ?   In their present mind the Coreish would never abandon these.   If, however (as they now professed their readiness), they would acknowledge the one true God as the supreme Lord, and look to the idols only as symbolical of the angels, what harm would result from their bare continuance? Incredible as the concession may appear, and irreconcilable with his first principles of action, Mahomet acceded to it, and consented to maintain the heathen deities as representatives of heavenly beings 'whose intercession was to be hoped for with the Deity.' The imperfect and garbled notices of tradition give no further insight into the compromise. If Mahomet stipulated for any safeguards against the abuses of idolatry, no trace of them can be now discovered. We only know that the arrangements, of whatever nature, gave satisfaction to the chiefs and people, and produced a temporary union.

Error soon discovered; But Mahomet was not long in perceiving the inconsistency into which he had been betrayed. The people still worshipped images, and not God. No reasoning on his part, no assurance from them, could dissemble the galling fact that idolatry was as gross and prevalent as ever.

and remedied by a complete disavowal. His only safety now lay in disowning the concession. The devil had deceived him. The words of compromise were no part of the divine faith received from God through his heavenly messenger. The lapse was thus atoned for. The heretical verses spoken under delusion were cancelled, and others revealed in their stead, denying the existence of female angels such as Lât and Ozza, and denouncing idolatry with a sentence of irrevocable condemnation. Henceforward the Prophet wages mortal strife with images in every shape. His system gathers itself up into a pure and stern theism; and the Corân begins to breathe (though as yet only in the persons of Moses and Abraham) intimations of iconoclastic revenge.

Idols reprobated. Ever after the intercession of idols is scouted as futile and absurd. Angels dare not to intercede with the Almighty; how much less the idols, who

> Have no power over even the husk of a date stone;
> Upon whom if ye call, they hear not your calling,
>   And if they heard they would not answer you;
> And in the Day of judgment, they shall themselves reject your
>   deification of them.

And the government asserted to be God's only. The following passage, produced shortly after his lapse, shows how Mahomet refuted his adversaries, and adroitly turned against them their concession of the supreme divinity of God alone.

And if thou askest them who created the Heavens and the Earth, they will surely answer GOD. SAY, What think ye then? If the Lord be pleased to visit me with affliction, can those upon whom ye call besides God,—what! could *they* remove the visitation? Or if He visit me with mercy, could *they* withhold His mercy? SAY, God sufficeth for me; in Him alone let those that put their trust confide.

Sura xxxix.

However short his fall, Mahomet retained a keen sense of his disgrace, and of the danger which lay in parleying with his adversaries.

The danger of compromise keenly felt.

And truly they were near tempting thee aside from what We revealed unto thee, that thou shouldest fabricate regarding Us a different revelation; and then they would have taken thee for their friend.

Sura xvii.

And if it had not been that We stablished thee, verily thou hadst nearly inclined unto them a little;

Then verily We had caused thee to taste both of the punishment of Life and the punishment of Death;

Then thou shouldest not have found against Us any helper.

And ever and anon the Prophet is cautioned in the Corân to beware lest he should be induced to change the words of inspiration, out of a desire to deal gently with his people; or be deluded by the pomp and numbers of the idolaters, into following after them and deserting the straight and narrow path pointed out to him by God.

But although Mahomet may have completely re-established his own convictions, and regained the confidence of his adherents, there is little doubt that the concession to idolatry, followed by a recantation so sudden and peremptory, seriously weakened his position with the people at large. *They* would not readily credit the excuse, that words of error had been 'cast by the devil into the mouth of Mahomet.' Even supposing it to have been so, what faith could be placed in the revelations of a Prophet liable to such influences? The divine author of a revelation must know beforehand all that he will at any subsequent period reveal. If the Corân were in truth *His* oracle, Mahomet would never be reduced to the petty shift of retracting as a mistake what had once been given forth as a message from heaven. The Coreish laughed to scorn the futile endeavour of the Prophet to effect a compromise which should draw them away from idolatry. They addressed him ironically:—

Mahomet s position injured by the lapse.

Sura xvi.

And when they see thee, they receive thee no otherwise than scoffingly,—*Ah! is this he whom God hath sent as an Apostle? Verily he had nearly seduced us from our gods, unless we had patiently persevered therein.* But they shall know hereafter, when they see the torment, who hath erred most from the right way.

He reiterates his own conviction.

To the accusations thus triumphantly advanced by his adversaries, Mahomet could oppose simply the reiteration of his own assurance :—

Sura xvi.

And when We change one verse in place of another (and God best knoweth that which He revealeth) they say, *Verily thou plainly art a fabricator.* Nay! but the most of them understand not. SAY, The Holy Spirit hath brought it down from thy Lord, &c.

Return of Abyssinian emigrants, A.D. 615.

We have seen that the tidings of reconciliation with the Coreish induced the little band of emigrants, after residing but two months in Abyssinia, to set out for Mecca. Approaching the city, they met a party of travellers who told them that Mahomet had withdrawn his concessions, and that the Coreish had resumed their oppression. After consulting what should now be done, they resolved to go forward and visit their homes. If things came to the worst, they could but again escape to Abyssinia. So they entered Mecca, each under the protection of a relative or friend.

Second emigration to Abyssinia, A.D. 615–616.

The report brought by the emigrants of their kind reception by the Najâshy, following upon the late events, annoyed the Coreish, and the persecution became hotter than ever. Wherefore Mahomet again recommended his followers to take refuge in Abyssinia. The first party of the new expedition set out about the sixth year of the mission; and thereafter at intervals small bodies of converts, accompanied sometimes by their wives and children, joined the exiles, until they reached (without calculating their little ones) the number of 101. Of these, eighty-three were men. Amongst the women, eleven were of the Coreish, and seven belonged to other tribes. Thirty-three of the men, with eight women (including Othmân and his wife Rockeya the daughter of Mahomet), again returned to Mecca, and eventually emigrated to Medîna. The rest of the refugees remained in Abyssinia for several years, and did not rejoin Mahomet until his expedition to Kheibar, in the seventh year of the Hégira.

Although Mahomet himself was not yet forced to quit his native city, he was nevertheless exposed to indignity and insult, while the threatening attitude of his adversaries gave ground for apprehension and anxiety. If, indeed, it had not been for the influence and steadfast protection of Abu Tâlib, it is clear that the hostile intentions of the Coreish would have imperilled the liberty, perhaps the life, of Mahomet. A body of their Elders repaired to the aged chief, and said: *This nephew of thine hath spoken opprobriously of our gods and our religion, and hath upbraided us as fools, and given out that our forefathers were all astray. Now, avenge us thyself of our adversary; or (seeing that thou art in the same case with ourselves) leave him to us that we may take our satisfaction.* But Abu Tâlib answered them softly and in courteous words; so they turned and went away. In process of time, as Mahomet would not change his attitude, they went again to Abu Tâlib in great exasperation; and, reminding him of their former demand that he would restrain his nephew from his offensive conduct, added: *And now verily we cannot have patience any longer with his abuse of us, our ancestors, and our gods; wherefore either do thou hold him back from us, or thyself take part with him that the matter may be decided between us.* Having thus spoken, they departed. And it appeared grievous to Abu Tâlib to break with his people, and be at enmity with them; neither did it please him to desert and surrender his nephew. Thus being in straits, he sent for Mahomet, and having communicated the saying of the Coreish, proceeded earnestly: *Therefore, save thyself and me also; and cast not upon me a burden heavier than I can sustain.* Mahomet was startled and alarmed. He imagined that his uncle, finding himself unequal to the task, had resolved to abandon him. His high resolve did not fail him at this critical moment. *If they brought the sun on my right hand,* he said, *and the moon on my left, to force me from my undertaking, verily I would not desist therefrom until the Lord made manifest my cause, or I should perish in the attempt.* But the thought of desertion by his kind protector overcame him. He burst into tears, and turned to depart. Then Abu Tâlib called aloud: 'Son of my brother! Come back.' So he returned. And Abu Tâlib said, *Depart in*

Endeavour to make Abu Tâlib abandon Mahomet.

Abu Tâlib persists in his protection.

peace, my nephew! and say whatsoever thou desirest. For, by the Lord! I will not, in any wise, give thee up for ever.

A scene at the Káaba. Abu Tâlib awes the Coreish.

Some add the following incident. The same day Mahomet disappeared, and was nowhere to be found. Abu Tâlib, apprehensive of foul play, forthwith made ready a band of Hâshimite youths each armed with a dirk, and set out for the Káaba. On the way he was stopped by the intelligence that Mahomet was safe in a house at Safa; so he returned with his people home. On the morrow the aged chief again made ready his party, and, taking Mahomet with them, repaired to the Káaba. There, standing before the assembly of the Coreish, he desired his young men to uncover that which they had by them; and each drew forth a sharp weapon. Then, turning to the Coreish, he exclaimed: *By the Lord! Had ye killed him, there had not remained one alive amongst you. You should have perished, or We had every one of us been slain.* The bold front of Abu Tâlib awed the Coreish, and repressed their insolence.

Personal indignities sustained by Mahomet.

Though the tendency of tradition is to magnify the insults of the Coreish, yet, apart from invective and abuse, we hardly read of any personal injury or suffering sustained by Mahomet himself. A few of the inveterate enemies of Islâm (Abu Lahab among the number) who lived close by his house, used spitefully to throw unclean and offensive things at the Prophet, or upon his hearth as he cooked his food. Once they flung into his house the entrails of a goat, which Mahomet, putting upon a stick, carried to the door, and called aloud: 'Ye children of Abd Menâf! What sort of good neighbourhood is this?' Then he cast it forth into the street. Two or three centuries afterwards, a little closet, a few feet square, was still shown at the entrance of Khadîja's house where, under the ledge of a projecting stone, the Prophet crouched down when he retired for prayer, to shelter himself from the missiles of his neighbours. There is also a tradition (but ill sustained) of actual violence once offered to Mahomet in public. As he passed through the court of the Káaba, he was suddenly surrounded by the Coreish, who 'leaped upon him as one man,' and seized his mantle. But Abu Bakr stood manfully by him, and called out: 'Woe's me! Will ye slay a man because he saith that *God is my Lord?*' So they departed from him.

In the sixth year of his mission, the cause of Mahomet was strengthened by the accession of two powerful citizens, HAMZA and OMAR. The details of their conversion will be interesting to the reader.

The Prophet was one day seated on the rising ground of Safâ. Abu Jahl, coming up, accosted him with a shower of taunts and reproaches; while Mahomet answered not a word. Both left the place, but a slave-girl had observed the scene. It chanced that, shortly after, Hamza returned that way from the chase, his bow hanging from his shoulder (for he was a hunter of renown); and the maid related to him with indignation the gross abuse of Abu Jahl. Hamza was at once the uncle of Mahomet and his foster-brother. His pride was offended, his rage kindled. He hurried with rapid steps to the Káaba; and there, in the court of the holy House, found Abu Jahl sitting with a company of the Coreish. Hamza rushed upon him, saying: *Ah! hast thou been abusing him, and I follow his religion; there* (raising his bow and striking him violently) *return that if thou darest!* The kinsmen of Abu Jahl started to his succour; but Abu Jahl motioned them away, saying: ' Let him alone, for indeed I did revile his nephew shamefully.' [1] The profession of Islâm, suddenly asserted by Hamza in the passion of the moment, was followed up by the deliberate pledging of himself to Mahomet in the house of Arcam, and by a steady adherence ever after to his faith.

Conversion of Hamza, A.D. 615.

The conversion of Omar took place at the close of the sixth year of Mahomet's mission.[2] He was notorious for his enmity to Islâm, and the harshness and violence with which he treated its professors. His sister Fâtima, and her husband Sáîd (son of the ' enquirer' Zeid), were both converts, but secretly, for fear of the Coreish. While Omar was threatening certain believers, a friend suggested to him that he had better begin at home, and hinted the conversion of his sister and her husband. His wrath was aroused, and he proceeded forthwith

Conversion of Omar, A.D. 615– 616.

[1] Abu Jahl (the ' father of ignorance' or folly) is the butt of tradition as the witless and obstinate opponent of Islâm. He was a nephew of Walîd son of Moghira.

[2] It occurred in Dzul Hajj, the last month in the year. The Believers are said now to have amounted in all to forty men and ten women; or, by other accounts, to forty-five men and eleven women. See *ante*, p. 69, *note*.

to their house. They were listening to the 20th Sura, which the slave Khobâb recited to them from a manuscript. The persecutor drew near, and overheard the low murmur of the reading. At the noise of his steps, Khobâb retired into a closet. *What sound was that I heard just now?* exclaimed Omar, entering angrily. 'There was nothing,' they replied. *Nay*, said he, swearing fiercely, *I hear that ye are renegades!* 'But what, O Omar!' interposed his brother-in-law, 'may there not be truth in another religion than thine?' The question confirmed the suspicions of Omar, and he sprang exasperated upon Sáîd and kicked him. His sister flew to the rescue. In the struggle her face was wounded, and began to bleed. Stung by the insult, she could no longer contain herself, and called aloud: 'Yes, we are converted; we believe in God and in his Prophet; now do thy worst upon us.' When Omar saw her face covered with blood he was softened; and he asked to see the paper they had been reading. But his sister required that he should first cleanse himself, 'for none,' she said, 'but the pure may touch it.' So Omar arose and washed, and took the paper (for he could read), and when he had deciphered a part thereof, he exclaimed: *How excellent is this discourse, and gracious!* Then came forth Khobâb from his hiding-place, and said: 'O Omar! I trust that the Lord hath verily set thee apart for himself, in answer to his Prophet; it was but yesterday I heard him praying thus: *Strengthen Islâm, O God, by Abu Jahl, or by Omar!*' Then said Omar: 'Lead me unto Mahomet, that I may make known unto him my conversion.' And he was directed to the house of Arcam. So Omar knocked at the door, and Hamza with others looked through a crevice, and started back, exclaiming that it was Omar. But Mahomet bade them let him in, and, rising to meet him, seized his skirt and the belt of his sword, saying: 'How long wilt thou not refrain from persecuting, until the Lord send some calamity upon thee?' And Omar replied: '*Verily, I testify that thou are the Prophet of God!*' And Mahomet was filled with joy, and called aloud, GREAT IS THE LORD.[1]

Importance of these conversions.

These conversions were a real triumph to Mahomet. Hamza and Omar both possessed, with great bodily strength,

[1] *Allahu Akbar!* This exclamation is styled the *Takbîr*, and is used on occasions of surprise, or the unexpected occurrence of any great event.

an indomitable courage; which, added to their social position, secured an important influence at Mecca. The heroism of Hamza earned for him the title, familiar to the present day, of *the Lion of God*; but he was prematurely cut off on the field of Ohod. Omar outlived Mahomet and, succeeding Abu Bakr in the Caliphate, left the stamp of his fierce spirit upon Islâm. He was robust in frame, somewhat ruddy in countenance, of a commanding stature; and he towered above his fellows as if he had been mounted. Bold and overbearing, impulsive and precipitate, endowed with a keen glance and steady purpose, he was always ready both in word and deed at the decisive moment. His anger was easily aroused, and the Coreish stood in awe of him, because of his uncertain and impetuous temper. At the period of his conversion he was but six-and-twenty years of age, yet so great and instant was the effect of his accession upon the progress of Islâm, that from this era is dated the commencement of its public and fearless profession at Mecca. Mahomet abandoned the house of Arcam. The Moslems no longer concealed their worship within their own dwellings, but with conscious strength and defiant attitude assembled in companies about the Káaba, and openly performed their rites of worship at the holy House. Their courage rose. Dread and uneasiness seized the Coreish.

Omar described.

The Coreish, indeed, had cause for alarm. They were disquieted by the hospitable reception of the refugees at the Abyssinian Court. An embassy of two chief men from Mecca, laden with costly presents, had made a fruitless attempt to obtain their surrender.[1] What if the Najâshy

Position and fears of the Coreish.

---

[1] The Coreish despatched two envoys with presents of precious leather and other rare articles for the Najâshy (or Negus). They gained over the courtiers, and then presented their gifts to the Christian Prince, saying, that 'certain fools amongst their own people had left their ancestral faith; they had not joined Christianity, but had set up a new religion of their own. They had therefore been deputed by the Coreish to fetch them back.' The courtiers supported their prayer, but the king said he would enquire further into the matter in the presence of the accused. Now the refugees had agreed that they would not garble their doctrine, but, come what might, say nothing more nor less than the teaching of their Prophet. So on the morrow they were summoned into the royal presence, where were also the bishops with their books open before them. The king enquired of the refugees the cause of their secession. Then Jâfar (Mahomet's uncle) answered, in the name of all, 'that they used to worship images, eat the dead, commit lewdness, disregard family ties and the

H

should support them with an armed force, and seek to establish a Christian or reformed faith at Mecca, as one of his predecessors had done in Yemen? Apart even from foreign aid, there was ground for apprehension at home. The Moslem body no longer consisted of oppressed and despised outcasts, struggling for a weak and miserable existence. Rather it was a powerful faction, adding daily to its strength by the accession of influential citizens. It challenged an open hostility. The victory of either party involved the downfall of the other.

Communications with Moslems and their supporters cut off.

Influenced by such fears, the Coreish sought to stay the progress of secession from their ranks, by utterly severing the party of Mahomet from social and friendly communication with themselves. On the other hand, Abu Tâlib was sup-

duties of neighbourhood and hospitality, until Mahomet arose a prophet;' he concluded by describing his system, and the persecutions which had forced them to flee to Abyssinia. On the king asking him to repeat some part of the Prophet's teaching, he recited Sura *Maryam* (regarding the births of John and Jesus, with notices of Abraham, Moses, &c.); whereupon the king wept until his beard became moist; and the bishops also wept so that their tears ran down upon their books, saying: 'Verily, this revelation and that of Moses proceed from one and the same source.' And the Najâshy said to the refugees: 'Depart in peace, for I will never give you up.'

Next day the envoys endeavoured to entrap the refugees into a declaration depreciatory of Jesus, and therefore offensive to the king. But the king fully concurred in their doctrine that Jesus was nothing more than 'a servant of God, and his Apostle; his Spirit and his word, placed in the womb of Mary, the immaculate Virgin.' So the Coreishite embassy departed in bad case.

The above story is no doubt a mere amplification of certain passages in the Corân to the effect that the Jews and Christians wept for joy on hearing the Corân because of its correspondence with their own Scriptures. A similar tale has been invented of the bishops of Najrân; and also regarding an embassy of Christians from Abyssinia, who are said to have visited Mahomet at Mecca, so that not much reliance can be placed on this part of the narrative.

When the Abyssinians rose up against their king on account of the favour he showed to the Mussulman doctrine, the Najâshy put into his pocket a scrap inscribed with the Mahometan creed, and on his people desiring him to say 'that Jesus was the Son of God,' he responded thus (putting his hand upon his pocket): 'Jesus never went beyond *this*'—apparently agreeing in what they said, but inwardly referring to the scrap!—a childish story. Mahomet is said to have regarded him as a convert to Islâm, and to have prayed for him as such at his death. A light is also related to have issued from his tomb.

There is probably a basis of truth for the general outline given in this note; but it would be difficult to draw a probable line between the real and the fictitious parts of it. Had the leaning towards Mahometan doctrine in Abyssinia been as great as is here represented, we should have heard more of its inhabitants in the troublous times immediately following Mahomet's decease.

ported in his defence of Mahomet by all his brothers excepting Abu Lahab, and generally by the descendants of his grandfather Hâshim, whether converts to Islâm or not. Thus the religious struggle merged for a time into a civil feud between the Hâshimites and the rest of the Coreish; and (as we have already seen) there were not wanting long-rooted political associations to add bitterness to the strife.

To secure their purpose, the Coreish entered into a con- *The Ban.* federacy against the Hâshimites—*that they would not marry their women, nor give their own in marriage to them; that they would sell nothing to them, nor buy aught from them; and that dealings with them of every kind should cease.* The ban was carefully committed to writing, and sealed with three seals. When all had bound themselves by it, the record was hung up in the Káaba, and religious sanction thus given to its provisions.

The Hâshimites were unable to withstand the tide of *The Sheb,* public opinion which set in thus violently against them; and *or Quarter* apprehensive perhaps that it might be only the prelude of *of Abu* open attack, or of blows in the dark still more fatal, they *Tálib.* retired into the secluded quarter of the city, known as the *Sheb* of Abu Tâlib. It was formed by one of the defiles or indentations of the mountain, where the projecting rocks of Abu Cobeis pressed upon the eastern outskirts of Mecca. It was entered on the city side by a low gateway, through which a camel passed with difficulty. On all other sides it was detached from the town by cliffs and buildings.[1]

On the first night of the first month of the seventh year *Hâshimites* of the mission of Mahomet, the Hâshimites, including the *with Ma-* Prophet and his family, retired into the quarter of Abu *homet retire into the Sheb,*

[1] The several quarters of Mecca skirting the foot of Abu Cobeis are still distinguished by the name *Sheb*: thus we have the *Sheb Maulad* (quarter in which Mahomet was born); and the *Sheb Ali*, which was probably comprised in the *Sheb* of Abu Tâlib. Burkhardt tells us: 'On the east side, towards the mountain, and partly on its declivity, stands the quarter called Shab Aly, adjoining the Shab el Moled; here is shown the venerated place of Aly's nativity. Both these quarters are among the most ancient parts of the town, where the Koreysh formerly lived; they are even now inhabited principally by Sherifs, and do not contain any shops. The houses are spacious and in an airy situation.' It was into one of these quarters of the city, situated in a defile having behind it the steep ascent of the hill, and so built about as to be inaccessible on all sides, except by a narrow entrance from the city, that the Hâshimites retired.

A.D. 616–
617.
Tâlib; and with them followed also the descendants of Al Muttalib the brother of Hâshim. Abu Lahab alone, moved by hatred of the new religion, went forth to the other party. The ban of separation was put rigorously in force. The Hâshimites soon found themselves cut off from their supplies of corn and other necessaries of life. They were not strong enough to send forth a caravan of their own; if parties of foreign merchants entered the city, the Coreish instigated them to withhold their commodities, except at an exorbitant price; the Coreish themselves would sell them nothing; and a great scarcity ensued. No one ventured forth from the *Sheb* except at the season of pilgrimage, when all enmities were hushed, and Mahomet and his party were free to join securely in the ceremonies. For two or three years the attitude of both parties remained unaltered, and the failing stock of the Hâshimites, replenished only by occasional and surreptitious

*Their dis-
tress.*
ventures, reduced them to want and distress. The citizens could hear the wailing of the famished children within the *Sheb.* Many hearts were softened at the sight of such hardships, and mourned over the hostilities which gave them rise. Among these, and among the relatives of the isolated band, were found some who ventured, in spite of the threats of the Coreish, to introduce from time to time provisions by stealth at night into the quarter of Abu Tâlib. Thus we read of one conducting a camel laden with corn cautiously into the *Sheb,* and making over the burden to the hungry inmates. Hakîm grandson of Khuweilid used also, though the attempt was sometimes perilous, to carry supplies to his aunt Khadîja.

*Unfavour-
able effect
on the
cause of
Mahomet.*
Though the sympathies of many were called forth by the sufferings of the Hâshimites, the cause of Islâm itself did not advance during the period of this weary seclusion; for that seclusion had its full and expected effect in cutting off the mass of the people from the personal influence of Mahomet and his converts. The efforts of the Prophet were of necessity confined to the members of his own noble clan who, though unbelievers in his mission, had resolved to defend his person; and to the strengthening of his previous converts in the faith. Accordingly we find in the portions of the Corân delivered at this time directions from God to

retire from the unbelievers, and confine his preaching to his kinsmen and to the faithful :—

> * * * Verily they are a rebellious people;
> Wherefore turn from them, and thou shalt not be blamed.
> And admonish; for admonition profiteth the believers.

Sura li.

> Invoke with GOD no other god, lest thou be of those consigned to torment.
> And preach unto thy relatives, those that be of nearer kin.
> And conduct thyself gently[1] towards the believers that follow thee.
> And if they disobey thee, SAY, *I am free from that which ye do.*
> And put thy trust in Him that is glorious and merciful.

Sura xxvi.

The exemplary bearing of Mahomet under these trying circumstances, and the spirit of clanship that knit together all who shut themselves up with him and Abu Tâlib, must undoubtedly have secured in some degree for the new religion the general countenance of the Hâshimites, and may perhaps have helped to add some few followers from their ranks. But the weary years of confinement dragged on with no more important result. The time of pilgrimage alone afforded Mahomet a wider field. That interval of universal amnesty was turned (as it had indeed already been before the ban) to careful account in visiting and exhorting the various tribes that flocked to Mecca and the adjacent fairs. Thus the Prophet used to visit the great assemblages at Okâtz and other places, as well as the pilgrim encampments at Mecca and Minâ. On these occasions he warned his countrymen against idolatry; invited them to the worship and service of the one God; and promised them not only

But drawn closer to the Hâshimites.

Mahomet visits the fairs and assemblages of pilgrims.

---

[1] Literally, *Lower thy wings.* So in Sura xv. :—

'Stretch not forth thine eyes unto the provision which We have given unto several of them, neither be covetous thereof.
But behave with gentleness (*lower thy wings*) towards the believers;
And say; Verily, I am a plain preacher.

*   *   *   *   *   *

And publish that which thou art commanded, and withdraw from the idolaters.
Verily, We shall suffice for thee against the scoffers, those that set up with GOD other gods; but they will shortly know;
But do thou praise thy Lord with thanksgiving, and be among the worshippers :—
And serve thy Lord until death (or *the certainty*) overtake thee.'

Paradise hereafter, but prosperity and dominion upon earth, if they would believe.[1]   No one responded to his call.   Abu Lahab would dog his steps crying aloud: *Believe him not, he is a lying renegade!*[2]   And the tribes replied to Mahomet in sore and taunting words, such as these: *Thine own kindred and people should know thee best; wherefore do they not believe and follow thee?*   So the Prophet, repulsed and grieved, would look upwards and make his complaint unto God: *O Lord, if Thou willedst, it would not be thus!*   But the prayer seemed to pass unheeded.

Is repulsed and dispirited.

About this time Mahomet must have found means of communicating freely with the Jews, or at least with some person acquainted with Jewish lore; for his revelation begins now to abound with narratives taken, often at great length, from their scriptures or legends, as will be seen from the following Supplement.

---

[1] Wâckidi says that Mahomet frequented the three great fairs in the neighbourhood *every* year.   There is some foreshadowing of the victories of Islâm in his supposed address, which rather throws doubt upon these traditions.   This was the alleged drift of his preaching: ' *Ye people! Say,* THERE IS NO GOD BUT THE LORD.   *Ye will be benefited thereby.   Ye will gain the rule of all Arabia, and of Ajam* (foreign lands), *and when ye die ye will reign as kings in Paradise.*'

There would be numerous Christians and Jews *at the fairs*, though they did not, of course, attend the Meccan pilgrimage.

[2] 'And behind him there followed a squint-eyed man, fat, having flowing locks on both sides, and clothed in raiment of fine Aden stuff.   And when Mahomet had finished his preaching, this man would begin to address them, saying: *This fellow's only object is to draw you away from your gods and genii, to his fancied revelations; wherefore follow him not, neither listen unto him.*   And who should this be but his uncle Abu Lahab.'

SUPPLEMENT TO CHAPTER V.

THE CORÂN AS REVEALED DURING THIS PERIOD.

ABOUT twenty Suras belong to the period reviewed in this chapter ; they are considerably longer than the early ones, and occupy now each several pages.   The style, though often enlivened by tales from native and (as will be noticed presently) from Jewish legend, has become still more flat and prosaic.   The substance is little changed ; but mingled with instruction for the believers, and denunciation of the scoffers, we begin to have powerful illustrations from nature of the might and wisdom of the Deity, and of the reasonableness of the Resurrection from the dead. The following may be taken as a specimen :— *Analogies of God's power and of the Resurrection.*

Of His signs it is one, that He sendeth the winds bearing good tidings, that He may cause you to taste of His mercy, and that the ships may sail by His command, and ye may seek to enrich yourselves of His bounty ; peradventure ye may be thankful. *Sura xxx.*

And verily We have sent before thee, Apostles unto their nations, and they came unto them with clear proofs ; and We took vengeance on the transgressors ; and it behoved Us to assist the believers.

It is God that sendeth the winds which raise up the clouds ; then He spreadeth the same in the heavens as He pleaseth, and He disposeth them in layers, and thou mayest see the rain issuing from between them.   And when He causeth the same to reach unto such of His servants as He chooseth, behold they are filled with joy ; and before it was sent down unto them, they were already despairing.

Wherefore survey the tokens of God's mercy, how He quickeneth the earth after it hath become dead ; verily, the same will be the Quickener of those who have died ; and He is over all things Mighty.

And if We send a (blasting) wind, and they should see their fields withered, they would, after that, become ungrateful.

Thou canst not make the dead to hear ; neither canst thou make the deaf to hear thy calling, when they turn away from thee backward.   And thou canst not guide the blind out of their error.   Those alone that believe in Our signs thou shalt make to hear, for these are the true Moslems (*i.e.* those that have resigned themselves unto God).

In language which though strange is full of meaning, Mahomet repeatedly affirms that the universe was not made by chance or ' *in play*,' but that God had in creation a sovereign purpose and design :—

Sura xx'. We have not created the heavens and the earth and that which is between them, in sport.

If We had desired to take diversion, verily We had taken it in such wise as beseemeth Us, if We been bent thereon.

Nay, but verily We will oppose the True to the False, and it shall confound the same; and, lo! it shall vanish.

In another passage, but of later date, the doctrine of the responsibility of the human race and consequent liability to punishment, in contrast with those bodies which obey of necessity, is taught thus mystically:—

Sura xxxiii. Verily We offered FAITH unto the heavens and the earth and the mountains; but they refused to undertake the same, and were afraid thereof.

But Man undertook it; for verily he is rash and foolish;—

That God should punish the evil-minded men, and the evil-minded women, and the idolaters and the idolatresses;

And that God may be turned graciously unto the believing men and the believing women; for God is Gracious and Merciful.

Connection with Judaism, and appeal to Jewish Scriptures. A close connection is now springing up between Mahomet and the Jews; and frequent reference to their books, and recital of their legends, forms a new and leading feature of the Corân.[1] The Pentateuch is constantly mentioned as a revelation from God to Moses. The object of the Corân is ' to attest ' its divine origin and that of the succeeding Scriptures. The Jewish books contain ' clear evidence ' of the truth of the Corân, and of the mission of Mahomet. Jewish witnesses are appealed to in proof that the dispensation of Islâm is 'foretold' in their sacred books, and that the Corân is in close conformity with their contents.[1]

Testimony of the Jews in favour of Mahomet. The confidence with which Mahomet thus refers to the testimony of the Jews and their Scriptures is very remarkable. It leaves us no room to doubt that some amongst the Jews, acquainted perhaps but superficially with their own books and traditions, encouraged Mahomet in the idea that he might be, or even affirmed that he was, *that Prophet whom the Lord their God should raise up unto them of their brethren.* His profound veneration for the Jewish Scriptures, to the implicit observance of which he had virtually pledged himself in the Corân, would lull the apprehension of the Israelites, and draw them kindly towards him. 'If this man,' they would say, 'hold firmly by the Law and the Prophets, and seek the guidance of the GOD of our

[1] Sprenger has remarked that about this period the Corân begins to mention a great number of ' prophets,' called by the Jewish term *nabî*; the limited references before being to 'apostles,' or 'messengers,' from God *(rasûl).*

fathers, he will not go astray. Peradventure, the Lord will, through him, lead the heathen Arabs to the truth. Nay; what if we have erred in our interpretation as to the lineage of the coming prophet, and this prove the very Messiah sprung from the seed of Abraham? In anywise let us wait, watching the result; and meanwhile encourage him in the love of the word of God, and the seeking of His face in prayer.' Every Jew must have exulted in the Israelitish tendencies which had possessed his mind. We meet with frequent passages like the following: 'Those unto whom We have given the Book (the Jews) *rejoice* for that which hath been revealed unto thee.' Some going further bore a direct and unequivocal testimony to his mission. Nothing short of such witness could be referred to by Mahomet when he said: *They unto whom We have given the Scripture recognise the Prophet (or the Corân) as they do their own children;* and—

Verily this is a Revelation from the Lord of Creation;   Sura xxvi.
The faithful Spirit hath descended with it
Upon thy heart, that thou mightest be a Warner,
  In the tongue of simple Arabic.
  And verily it is in the former Scriptures;
Hath it not been a Sign unto them that the learned among the Children
    of Israel recognised it?
  And if We had revealed it to a Foreigner,
And he had recited it unto them, they had not believed.

SAY: What think ye, if this Revelation be from God, and ye reject it,   Sura xlvi.
and a Witness from amongst the children of Israel hath witnessed unto the like thereof (*that is, to its conformity with the Old Testament*), and hath believed, and ye turn away scornfully?—Verily, God doth not direct the erring folk.

Whether the 'Witness,' and other Jewish supporters of Mahomet, were among his professed followers, slaves perhaps, at Mecca; or were casual visitors there from the Israelitish tribes; or belonged to the Jewish residents of Medîna (with the inhabitants of which city the Prophet was on the point of establishing friendly relations), we can but conjecture.   Conjectures as to the 'Witness.'

Whoever his Jewish friends may have been, it is evident that they had a knowledge—rude and imperfect, perhaps, but comprehensive—of the outlines of Jewish history and tradition. These, distorted by rabbinical fable, and embellished or travestied by the Prophet's fancy, supplied the material for the scriptural stories which begin to form a chief portion of the Corân. The mixture of truth and fiction, of graphic imagery and of childish fancy, the repetition over and over again of the same tales in stereotyped expression, and the constant elaborate and ill-concealed effort to   The Jews supply Mahomet with materials for the Corân.

draw an analogy between the former prophets and himself, and between their opponents and the Coreish, by putting the speech of his own day into their lips, fatigue and repel the patient reader of the Corân. A bare enumeration of some of the topics will illustrate both the remarkable correspondence of the Corân with the Jewish Scriptures, and the many strange and fanciful deviations from them. The fabulous turn of the stories can often be traced to rabbinical legend.

Illustrations.

God created Adam of clay, and commanded the angels to fall down and worship him; the devil, alleging his nobler formation of fire, refused, and fell; on receiving his sentence, he threatened God that he would seduce his new-created subjects; and, in tempting them to eat of the forbidden tree, he fulfilled the threat. To the facts of Abel's history, is added the Jewish fiction that God, sending a raven to scratch the ground, thus instructed Cain that the corpse should be buried in the earth. It would be an unprofitable task to follow Mahomet through his labyrinth of truth, discrepancy, and fiction. It will suffice if we but allude to the stories of Abraham, who broke in pieces the idols of his people, and miraculously escaped the fire into which the tyrant cast him; of the angel's visit, when 'Sarah laughed' at the promise of a son, and the patriarch, vainly pleading for Sodom, was told that Lot would be saved but that his wife was predestined to destruction; of Abraham's hand being stayed from the sacrifice of his son, who was ransomed by 'a noble victim;' of Joseph, in envy of whose beauty the Egyptian women cut their hands with knives; of Jacob, who, when the garment of Joseph was cast over him by the messengers from Egypt, recovered his long-lost sight; of mount Sinai held above the heads of the terrified Israelites to force their acceptance of the law; of the Seventy who, when struck dead upon the same mount, were quickened to life again; of David, whom the mountains joined in singing the praises of God; and of Solomon, on whose gigantic works the genii and devils were forced to labour at his bidding; of the genii, who brought the throne of the Queen of Sheba to Solomon in 'the twinkling of an eye,' and of the lapwing that flew to her with the royal summons; of the Jews, who broke the sabbath, and were changed into apes; of Ezekiel, who quickened a great multitude of the dead; and of Ezra, who with his ass was raised to life after being dead a hundred years. The following extract may be taken as a fair specimen of the half-scriptural, half-legendary style of these stories:—

Sura vii.

And verily We created you, then fashioned you, then We said unto the Angels, 'Fall down and worship Adam;' and they worshipped all, excepting Eblis who was not one of the worshippers ;—

He said, ' What hindereth thee that thou worshippest not when I command thee ? ' He answered, ' I am better than he : Thou createdst me of fire, and thou createdst him of clay.'

He said, ' Get thee down from Heaven; it shall not be given thee to behave arrogantly therein; get thee hence ; verily, thou shalt be amongst the despicable.'

He said, ' Respite me unto the day when (all) shall be raised.'

God said, ' Verily, thou art of the number respited.'

He said, ' Now, for that Thou hast caused me to fall, I will lie in wait for them in the straight path ;—

Then I will fall upon them from before and from behind, and from their right hand and from their left ; and Thou shalt not find the most part of them thankful.'

He said, ' Depart from hence, despised and driven off: for those of them that shall follow thee—verily, I will fill hell with you together.

And thou, Adam, dwell thou and thy wife in Paradise, and eat from whatsoever quarter ye will, but approach not this tree, lest ye become of the number of the transgressors ! '

And the Devil tempted them both, that he might discover that which was hidden from them of their nakedness.

And he said, ' Your Lord hath only forbidden you this tree, lest ye should become Angels, or become immortal.'

And he sware unto them, ' Verily, I am unto you as one that counselleth good.'

And he caused them to fall through guile ; and when they had tasted of the tree, their nakedness appeared unto them, and they began to join the leaves of Paradise, to cover themselves withal.

And their Lord called unto them, ' What ! did I not forbid you this tree, and say unto you that Satan was your manifest enemy ? '

They said, ' Oh, our Lord ! We have injured our own souls, and if Thou forgivest us not, and are not merciful unto us, we shall be numbered amongst the damned.'

He said, ' Get ye down, the one of you an enemy to the other; and there shall be unto you on the earth an habitation and a provision for a season : '—

He said, ' Therein shall ye live, and therein shall ye die, and from thence shall ye be taken forth.'

Certain favourite passages from the Old Testament are the subject of special amplification and repetition. Such are the history of Moses, the catastrophe of the Flood, and the overthrow of Sodom, through which the Arabian prophet, with a wearisome reiteration, seeks to deal forth exhortation and warning to the citizens of Mecca. An adequate conception of these curious recitals can be gained only from a perusal of the Corân itself; if the reader have patience and interest let him peruse, for an example, the history of Moses in the 20th and 28th Suras.

To acquire so minute a knowledge of considerable portions of Jewish Scripture and legend, to assimilate these to his former

Time spent in study and composition. materials, and to work them up into the elaborate and rhythmical Suras which begin now to extend to a considerable length, much time and careful study, were, no doubt, needed. The revelation is seldom now the spontaneous eloquence of a burning faith; it is rather the tame and laboured result of ordinary composition. For this end many a midnight hour must have been stolen from sleep. Such employment is probably referred to in passages like the following :—

Sura lxxiii.
> Oh thou that are wrapped up?
> Arise during the night, excepting a small portion thereof :—
>   A half of it; or diminish therefrom a little,
> Or add thereto. And recite the Corân with well measured recitation.
>   Verily, We shall inspire thee with weighty words.
> Verily, the hours of night are the best for fervent maceration, and distinct utterance.
>   Truly by day thou hast a protracted labour.
> And commemorate the name of thy Lord, and consecrate thyself wholly unto Him.

Idea of study and inspiration possibly blended together. It is possible that the convictions of Mahomet may have become so blended with his grand object and course of action, that the very study of the Corân and the effort to compose it, were regarded as his best seasons of devotion. But the stealthy and disingenuous manner in which he now availed himself of Jewish information, producing the result, not only as original, but *as evidence of inspiration*, begins to furnish proof of an active, though it may have been unconscious, course of dissimulation and falsehood, to be palliated only by the miserable apology of a pious end.[1]

Imputations of his enemies. On this weak point his enemies were not slow to seize. They accused him of fabrication, and of being assisted therein by others : 'They are fables,' said they, 'of the ancients which he hath had written down; they are dictated unto him morning and evening.' To these imputations Mahomet could only answer:
Sura xxv. 'He hath revealed it who knoweth that which is hidden in heaven and in earth : He is forgiving and merciful.'

Christian Scriptures little mentioned. Up to this period there is little mention of the *Christian* Scriptures; the available sources of information were probably as yet imperfect.

---

[1] The story of Man's creation and the fall of Satan, is thus prefaced: '*I had no knowledge regarding the Heavenly Chiefs when they disputed; verily, it hath been revealed unto me for no other purpose than* (to prove) *that I am a public Preacher.*' So regarding Moses at Mount Sinai. And again, after relating the history of Joseph, it is added : '*This is one of the secret histories, which We have revealed unto thee; thou wast not present with them,*' &c.

CHAPTER VI.

VISIT TO TÂYIF. ISLÂM PLANTED AT MEDÎNA.

A.D. 620–621.

IN the beginning of the tenth year of his mission (the fiftieth of his life), Mahomet and his kinsmen were still shut up in the isolated quarter of Abu Tâlib. The only interval of freedom and relief, as has been already stated, occurred at the annual pilgrimage. Buying and selling, giving and receiving in marriage, in short all the intercourse of social life was totally suspended between them and the rest of the Coreish. The Hâshimites were thus virtually blockaded for the space of two or three years.

Mahomet and his party under the ban from A.D. 617–618 to A.D. 619–620.

At last the sympathies of a numerous section of the Coreish were aroused. They saw in this form of persecution something more than a conscientious struggle against an impostor. The justice of extending the ban to the whole Hâshimite stock was doubtful. Many, especially those related to the clan, began to grieve at the rupture.

Sympathy of their opponents.

It was discovered by some of the friends of Mahomet that the parchment in the Káaba, on which the ban was engrossed, had been almost entirely devoured by insects. The important news was told to Mahomet; and Abu Tâlib resolved to found thereon an effort for the dissolution of the league. The venerable chief, now more than fourscore years of age, issued forth from his closed quarters and proceeded, with a band of followers, to the Káaba. Addressing the chief men of the Coreish, as usual assembled there, he said: ' Intelligence reacheth me that your parchment hath been eaten up of insects. If my words be true, desist from your evil designs; if false, I will deliver up my brother's son unto you that ye may do with him as ye list.' The whole company agreed that it should be thus. Then they sent for the document; and when they had opened it out, they saw

Abu Tâlib acquaints Coreish with deed being eaten of insects; and upbraids them.

that it was even as Abu Tâlib had said; a great part had been devoured by white ants and was no longer legible. Abu Tâlib, perceiving their confusion, bitterly upbraided their inhumanity and breach of social obligations. He then advanced with his band to the Káaba, and, standing behind the curtain, prayed to the Lord of the holy House for deliverance from their machinations. This done, he retired to his secluded abode.

Ban removed, A.D. 619-620.

The murmurs of those who favoured the Hâshimites now found opportunity of effective utterance. The partisans of the Prophet were emboldened. The Coreish had scarce recovered from surprise at the sudden appearance and as sudden departure of Abu Tâlib, when five chief men (probably on a preconcerted plan) rose up from their midst, and, declaring themselves opposed to the league, put on their armour and proceeded to the quarter of Abu Tâlib. Standing by the entrance of the defile, they commanded all that had taken refuge there to go forth to their respective homes in security and peace. So they went forth in the tenth year of the Prophet's mission. The Coreish, confounded by the boldness of the stroke, offered no opposition. They perceived that a strong party had grown up who would resent by arms any attempt to lay violent hands upon the Moslems.

Domestic trials.

Repose and liberty followed the breaking up of the hostile league; but they were not long to be enjoyed without alloy by Mahomet. In a few months he was visited by trials more severe than any that had yet befallen him. The tenth year of his mission (the third before the Hégira) had not yet passed when Khadîja died; and five weeks later he lost his protector Abu Tâlib also.

Death of Khadîja, December, A.D. 619.

The death of his wife was a grievous affliction. For five-and-twenty years she had been his counsellor and support; and now his heart and home were desolate. His family, however, no longer needed maternal care. The youngest daughter, Fâtima, was approaching womanhood, and an attachment was perhaps already forming with Ali, her father's cousin and adopted son. Though Khadîja (at her death threescore and five years old) must long ago have lost the charms of youth, and though the custom of Mecca allowed polygamy, yet Mahomet was during her lifetime restrained from other marriages by affection and gratitude, and perhaps also by the wish to secure more entirely for his cause the influence of her family. His grief at her death at first was inconsolable, liable as he was to violent and deep emotion; but its effects were transient. The place of Khadîja could be filled, though her devotion and virtues might not be rivalled, by numerous successors. Her memory is held in veneration; and her tomb in the ancient burying-ground close by the city is still visited by pilgrims.[1]

The loss of Abu Tâlib, who died as he had lived an unbeliever, was, if possible, a still severer bereavement. We may dismiss the legend that on his deathbed he declared, in reply to the earnest appeal of his nephew, that he was prevented from assenting to the creed of Islâm only because he feared the imputation of fear at the approach of death. Whatever he may have said to comfort Mahomet, his life belies the accusation that apprehended contempt of the Coreish restrained him from avowing his convictions. The sacrifices to which Abu Tâlib exposed himself and his family for the sake of his nephew, while yet incredulous of his mission, stamp his character as singularly noble and unselfish. They afford at the same time strong proof of the sincerity of Mahomet. Abu Tâlib would not have acted thus for an interested deceiver; and he had ample means of scrutiny.

Death of Abu Tâlib, January, A.D. 620.

When the patriarch felt that life was ebbing, he summoned his brethren, the sons of Abd al Muttalib, around his bed; commended his nephew to their protection; and, relieved of the trust, died in peace, and was buried not far from Khadîja's grave. Mahomet wept bitterly for his uncle; and not without reason. For forty years he had been his faithful friend,—the prop of his childhood, the guardian of his youth, and in later life a tower of defence. His very unbelief made his influence the stronger. So long as he survived, Mahomet needed not to fear violence or attack. But there was no strong hand now to protect him from his foes. A second Khadîja might be found, but not a second Abu Tâlib.

The loss of Abu Tâlib severely felt.

---

[1] Sprenger thinks that, but for Khadîja, Mahomet would never have been a prophet, and that by her death Islâm lost in purity and the Corân in dignity. Mahomet is said occasionally to have slaughtered a sheep and distributed it among the poor in remembrance of her.

Abu Lahab for a short time protects Mahomet.

Grieved and dispirited by these bereavements following so closely one upon the other, and dreading the now unchecked insolence of the Coreish, Mahomet seldom went abroad.[1] The dying behest of Abu Tâlib had now an unexpected effect; for Abu Lahab, heretofore the avowed enemy of Mahomet, was softened by his despondency and distress, and spontaneously became his guardian. '*Do*,' he said, '*as thou hast been in the habit of doing, while Abu Tâlib was yet alive. By Lât! no one shall hurt thee while I live.*' But the impulsive and generous pledge was not long observed. Abu Lahab was gained back again by the Coreish, and Mahomet was left to protect himself as he best could.[2]

Critical position of Mahomet.

The position of the Arabian prophet now was critical. He must either gain the ascendency at Mecca, abandon his prophetical claims, or perish in the struggle. Islâm must destroy idolatry, or idolatry must destroy Islâm. Things could not remain stationary. His followers, though devotedly attached, and numbering a few once influential citizens, were but a handful against a host; besides, the greater part of them were now absent in Abyssinia. Open hostilities, notwithstanding every endeavour to prevent them, might any day precipitate the struggle, and irretrievably ruin his cause. The new faith had not recently been gaining ground at Mecca. There had been no conversions, none at least of any note, since those of Omar and Hamza three or four years before. A few more years of similar discouragement, and his chance of success was gone.

He resolves to make trial of Tâyif.

Urged by such reflections, Mahomet began to look around. Mecca knew not the day of its visitation, and

[1] On one occasion the populace cast dirt upon his head; returning home in this plight, one of his daughters rose to wipe it off, and she wept. And Mahomet said: '*My daughter, weep not! for verily the Lord will be thy father's helper.*' It is added that he suffered no such indignity as that while Abu Tâlib lived.

[2] At first, when some one abused Abu Lahab as a renegade for taking the part of Mahomet, the Coreish are said to have excused Abu Lahab, and even praised him for his attempt 'to bind up family differences.' But shortly after Abu Jahl told Abu Lahab to ask Mahomet in what place Abd al Muttalib was, and, on his confessing that he was in hell, Abu Lahab left him in indignation, saying: 'I will not cease to be thine enemy for ever!' Whatever may have been the immediate cause, it is evident that Abu Lahab was soon instigated by the Coreish to abandon his nephew.

its doom was well nigh sealed. It might perchance be the will of the Lord that succour and salvation should come from some other quarter. Tâyif (sixty or seventy miles to the east of Mecca) was the nearest city of importance. God might turn the hearts of its inhabitants, the idolatrous Bani Thackîf, use them as instruments to chastise the reprobate men of Mecca, and establish the true religion on the earth. To them, accordingly, he resolved to deliver his message.

Abu Tâlib had been buried hardly a fortnight when Mahomet, followed only by his faithful attendant Zeid, set out on the adventurous mission. His road (as far as Arafât the pilgrim route) lay over dismal rocks and through barren defiles for about forty miles, when it emerged on the crowning heights of Jebel Kora. Thence, descending through fertile valleys, the smiling fruits and flowers of which suggested perhaps the bright picture of the conversion of the Thackîfites, he advanced to their city. Though connected by frequent intermarriage, the inhabitants of Tâyif were jealous of the Coreish. They had a *Lât*, or chief idol, of their own. It might be possible, by appealing to their national pride as well as to their conscience, to enlist them on the side of Islâm against the people of Mecca. Mahomet went first to the three principal men of the city, who were brothers; and, having explained his mission, invited them to the honour of sustaining the new faith, and supporting him in the face of his hostile tribe. But he failed in producing conviction. They cast in his teeth the common objections of his own people, and advised him to seek protection in some other quarter.

His journey thither, January, A.D. 620.

He fails in gaining over its chief men;

Mahomet remained in Tâyif for about ten days; but, though many of the influential men came at his call, no hopeful impression was made upon them. Thus repulsed, he solicited but one favour, namely, that they would not divulge the object of his visit, for he feared on his return the taunts and aggravated hostility of the Coreish. But this, even if it had been possible, the men of Tâyif were little likely to concede. For the first few days, perhaps, the common people regarded with awe the prophet who had turned Mecca upside down, and whose preaching probably most of them had heard at some of the neighbouring fairs or at the yearly

and is ignominiously expelled the city.

1

pilgrimage. But the neglect manifested by their chiefs, and the disproportion to the outward eye between the magnitude of the prophet's claims and his present solitary helpless condition, turned fear into contempt. Stirred up to hasten the departure of the unwelcome visitor, the people hooted at him in the streets, pelted him with stones, and at last obliged him to flee out of their city pursued by a relentless rabble. Blood flowed from wounds in both his legs; and Zeid, endeavouring to shield him, received a severe injury in his head. The mob did not desist until they had chased him two or three miles across the sandy plain to the foot of the hills that surround the city. There, wearied and mortified, he took refuge in one of the numerous orchards, and rested under a vine. In this the day of his humiliation, little did even his unwavering faith anticipate that in little more than ten years he should stand upon the same spot at the head of a conquering army; and that the great idol of Tâyif, despite the entreaties of its votaries, would be demolished at his command.

Rests at a garden in the outskirts of Tàyif.

Hard by was the garden of two of the Coreish, Otba and Sheyba; for the wealthy Coreish had their pleasure grounds (as they still have) near Tâyif. They watched the flight of Mahomet; and, moved with compassion, sent Addâs their servant with a tray of grapes for his refreshment. The servant, a Christian slave from Nineveh, marvelled at the pious invocation with which the fruit was received by the weary traveller ' in the name of the Lord;' and a conversation ensued in which Mahomet, learning from whence he came, made mention of ' the righteous Jonas son of Mattai of Nineveh,—a brother prophet like himself.' Thereupon Addâs did homage to Mahomet who, we may believe, was solaced more by the humble devotion of the slave than by the grateful shade and welcome grapes.[1] After a little, composed and reassured, he betook himself to prayer, and the following touching petitions are still preserved as those in which his

His prayer. burdened soul gave vent to its distress : 'O Lord! I make my complaint unto thee of the feebleness of my strength, and the poverty of my expedients; and of my insignificance before mankind. O thou most Merciful! thou art the Lord

---

[1] We are told that Addâs fell to kissing the head, hands, and feet of Mahomet, to the astonishment of his masters looking on from a distance; and that he influenced them afterwards in favour of Islâm.

of the weak, and thou art my Lord.   Into whose hands wilt
thou abandon me?   Into the hands of the strangers that
beset me round about? or of the enemy to whom at home
thou hast given the mastery over me?   If thy wrath
be not upon me, I have no concern ; but rather thy favour
is the more wide unto me.   I seek for refuge in the light of
thy gracious countenance, by which darkness is dispersed, and
peace ariseth both for this world and the next, that thy
wrath light not upon me, nor thine indignation.   It is thine
to show anger until thou art pleased ; and there is not any
power or resource but in thee.'

Reinvigorated by the pause, he set forth on his journey *Audience of the genii at Nakhla.* homewards.   About half-way, loth to return to Mecca, he
halted in the valley of Nakhla, where was an idol-temple,
a grove, and a garden.   There, as he arose at night to prayer,
or perhaps as he dreamed, his nervous and excited imagination
pictured crowds of genii pressing forward to hear his exhortations, and ardent to embrace Islâm.   The romantic scene
has been thus perpetuated in the Corân :—

And call to mind when We caused a company of the *Sura xlvi.*
Genii to turn aside unto thee that they might listen to the Corân.
When they were present at the recitation thereof they said, *Give
ear.*   And when it was ended, they returned unto their people,
preaching.   They said,—Oh our People! verily we have been
listening to a Book which hath been sent down since Moses,
attesting the truth of the Scripture preceding it.   It guideth
unto the truth, and into the straight path.   Oh our People!
obey the preacher of God, and believe in him, that he may
forgive you your sins, and save you from an awful punishment.[1]

[1] The scene is again described in Sura lxxii., which opens thus :—

SAY; it hath been revealed to me that a company of Genii listened, and they
    said,—'Verily we have heard a marvellous discourse ;

It guideth to the right direction ; wherefore we believed therein, and we will
    not henceforth associate any with our Lord ;

And as to Him (may the Majesty of our Lord be exalted!)

He hath taken no spouse, neither hath He any offspring.

But verily the foolish people amongst us have spoken of God that which is
    unjust ;

And we verily thought that no one amongst Men or Genii would have uttered
    a lie against God.

And truly there are people amongst men who have sought for refuge unto
    people among the Genii, but they only multiplied their folly.

And they thought, as ye think, that God would not raise any from the dead.

And we tried the Heavens, but found them filled with a powerful guard, and
    with flaming darts ;

After spending some days at Nakhla, he again proceeded towards Mecca. But before entering the city, which he feared to do (now that the object of his visit to Tâyif could not be kept secret) without a protector, he turned aside by a northward path to his ancient haunts in the vicinity of mount Hîra. From thence he sent twice to solicit the guardianship of certain influential chiefs; but without success. At last he bethought him of Mutáim (one of the five who had been instrumental in procuring the removal of the ban); and sent word beseeching that he would bring him into the city under his protection. The chief assented; and having summoned his sons and adherents, bade them buckle on their armour and take their stand by the Káaba. Mahomet and Zeid then entered Mecca; when they had reached the Káaba, Mutáim stood upright on his camel and called aloud: 'O ye Coreish! verily I have given the pledge of protection unto Mahomet; wherefore let not any one amongst you molest him.' Then Mahomet went forward, kissed the corner-stone, and returned to his house guarded by Mutáim and his party. The generosity and faithfulness of this chief have been perpetuated by Hassân the poet of Medîna and friend of the Prophet.[1]

And we sat on some of the Stations to listen, but whoever listeneth now findeth an ambush of flaming darts.
And truly we know not whether evil be intended for them that are on earth, or whether their Lord intendeth for them right direction.
And there are amongst us righteous persons, and amongst us persons of another kind;—we are of various sorts:
And verily we thought that no one could frustrate God on earth, neither could we escape from him by flight;
Wherefore when we heard the right direction, we believed therein '—(and so on, the Genii speaking as true Moslems).   *   *   *
And verily when the servant of God (Mahomet) stood up to call upon Him, they (the Genii) were near jostling him by their numbers, &c.

Notwithstanding the *crowds* of Genii here alluded to, Hishâmi (whose authorities seem to have had a wonderfully intimate acquaintance with their habits and haunts) states that on the present occasion there were *seven* Genii belonging to Nisibîn, who, happening to pass that way, were arrested by hearing Mahomet at his devotions reciting the Corân. Others say they were *nine* in number and came from Yemen, or from Nineveh, and professed the Jewish religion!

[1] The following are the lines. They show how valuable contemporary poetry may be as an auxiliary evidence of tradition:—
Weep, O my eyes! for the chief of men; let tears gush forth; and when they run dry, then pour forth blood!

There is something lofty and heroic in this journey of
Mahomet to Tâyif; a solitary man, despised and rejected by
his own people, going boldly forth in the name of God,
like Jonah to Nineveh, and summoning an idolatrous city
to repent and to support his mission. It sheds a strong
light on the intensity of his belief in the divine origin of
his calling.

Mahomet sought for solace, amidst family bereavement
and public indignities, in a double matrimonial alliance.
Sakrân, with his wife Sawda, both of Coreishite blood (but
of a stock remote from Mahomet), early became converts to
Islâm, and emigrated to Abyssinia. They had lately returned
to Mecca, where Sakrân died. Mahomet now made suit
to Sawda, and the marriage (so far as we know, not one of
mere interest and convenience, but of affection) was celebrated within two months from the death of Khadîja.[1]

Mahomet marries Sawda, February, A.D. 620;

About the same time he contracted a second marriage
with Ayesha, the younger daughter of Abu Bakr; an alliance mainly designed to cement the attachment of his
bosom friend. The yet undeveloped charms of Ayesha could
hardly have swayed the heart of Mahomet. Though her
betrothed husband had reached fifty, she was now but *six* or
seven years of age. Still there may have been something more
than ordinarily interesting and precocious about the child,
for the marriage took place not more than three years
afterwards.

*and is be-
trothed to
Ayesha.*

There is no information as to the terms on which Mahomet
continued to live with the family of his deceased wife,
Khadîja, and whether he retained any part of the property
that had belonged to her. During the troublous years he had

*His private
means.*

If greatness had caused any to survive for ever amongst mankind, then greatness had preserved Mutâim unto this day.
Thou gavest the pledge of protection to the Prophet of God from the Coreish;
  and they became thy servants so long as a pilgrim shall shout 'Labeik!'
  or assume the pilgrim garb.

Mutâim was a chief descended from Abd Shams the brother of Hâshim
(great-grandfather of Mahomet); and, along with Harb, commanded his tribe
in one of the great battles in the Sacrilegious War, A.D. 586.

[1] On the conquest of Kheibar, eight years after, Sawda had her portion
assigned her from its revenues with the Prophet's other wives. In the following year it is said that either on account of her age, or some doubt of her
fidelity, Mahomet wished to put her away, but was afterwards reconciled.
Sprenger, iii. p. 61. She survived Mahomet ten years.

lately encountered, and especially under the ban, it is probable that her wealth had much diminished. Perhaps he shared it with the poorer brethren. It is certain that during his remaining stay at Mecca the Prophet had not much property at his disposal; and there are even indications (as we shall see hereafter) of straitened means. He still continued to live, at least occasionally, in the quarter, if not in the house, of Abu Tâlib.

Light dawns through the darkness.

Repulsed from Tâyif, and utterly hopeless of success at home, the fortunes of Mahomet were enveloped in thick gloom, when hope suddenly dawned from an unexpected quarter.

Mahomet meets a pilgrim party from Medîna, March, A.D. 620;

The season of pilgrimage was at hand; and, as his custom was, the Prophet plied the crowds of pilgrims with solicitations wherever they afforded a likely audience. The ceremonies were nearly at an end; Mahomet had followed the votaries of the Káaba on their procession to the hill of Arafât, and now back again to Minâ; whence, after sacrificing their victims, the multitude would disperse to their homes. Wandering through the busy scene that presented itself in the narrow valley of Minâ, he was attracted by a little group of six or seven persons, whom he recognised as strangers from Medîna. *Of what tribe are ye?* said he, coming up and kindly accosting them. 'Of the tribe of Khazraj,' they replied. *Ah! confederates of the Jews?* 'We are.' *Then, why should we not sit down for a little, and I will speak with you?* The offer was accepted willingly, for the fame of Mahomet had been noised abroad in Medîna, and the strangers were curious to see more of the man who had created such turmoil in Mecca. So he expounded to them his doctrine, asserted the warrant of a divine mission, and, after setting forth the difficulties of his position at home, frankly enquired whether they would

who believe and spread his cause in Medîna.

receive and protect him at Medîna. The listeners were not slow to accept his teaching and embrace the faith of Islâm; 'but as for protecting thee,' said they, 'we have hitherto been at variance among ourselves, and have fought great battles. If thou comest to us thus, we shall be unable to rally around thee. Let us, we pray thee, return unto our people, if haply the Lord will create peace amongst us; and we will come back again unto thee.   Let the season of pilgrimage in the following year be the appointed time.'   Thus they returned to their homes, and invited their people to the faith ; and many believed, so that there‧ remained hardly a family in Medîna in which mention was not made of the Prophet.

As the interest of our story will now in great measure centre in Medîna, it is necessary to make the reader acquainted with its inhabitants and the state of parties there.

State of parties at Medina.

Arab legend peoples northern Arabia in ancient days with Amalekites, in whom we recognise Abrahamic races of other than Israelitish descent.   From time to time, these were supplanted by inroads of the Jews.   The sack of Jerusalem by Nebuchadnezzar, the attack of Pompey sixty-four years before the Christian era, with that of Titus seventy years after it, and the bloody retribution inflicted by Hadrian on Judea, A.D. 136, are some of the later causes which dispersed the Jews and drove large numbers into Arabia.   Such fugitive bodies were the Bani Nadhîr, Coreitza, and Caynocâa, who finding Medîna (the ancient *Yathreb*) peopled by a weak race of Bedouin tribes, took possession of the land and formed settlements in the neighbourhood, where they built for themselves strong castellated houses capable of resisting armed attack.

Settlement of the Jews at Medina.

In the beginning of the fourth century, a branch of those numerous Arab tribes which (as we have seen) had been migrating from Yemen northwards and some of which settling on the Syrian border had founded the Ghassânide dynasty, gained a footing at Medîna.   They were divided into two clans, the Bani Aus and Bani Khazraj.   They soon encroached upon the Jews ; and disputes and enmity sprang up between them.   Aided by their Syrian brethren, and having treacherously massacred the leading Jews assembled at a banquet, they became masters of Medîna, and took possession of the richest lands around it.   Thus established, it was not long before the Bani Aus and Khazraj fell out among themselves ; and in the beginning of the sixth century we find them in a state of chronic enmity, if not engaged in actual warfare with each other.   Four or five years previous to the period of our history, hostilities had reached a crisis between the contending parties.   Each was reinforced by allies from other

Supplanted by the Bani Aus and Khazraj.

Discord between the two clans.

Arab tribes;[1] the Jews were divided, the Coreitza and Nadhîr siding with the Bani Aus, the Caynocâa with the Bani Khazraj. In the year 616 A.D. the forces were marshalled, and there was fought the great battle of Boâth. At first the Ausites were worsted and fled; but their chief in indignation pierced himself and fell; and at the sight, stung by shame, they returned to the charge and fought so bravely that they dispersed the Bani Khazraj with great slaughter. They burned the date groves of the Bani Khazraj with fire, and were scarcely restrained by the cry for mercy from razing their fortified houses to the ground.

Abdallah ibn Obey. The Bani Khazraj were humbled but not reconciled. No open engagement after this took place, but numerous assassinations gave token from time to time of hardly suppressed ill-blood. Wearied with the protracted discord, both parties were inclined to take Abdallah ibn Obey, a distinguished citizen of the Bani Khazraj, as their chief. This man had resented the treacherous murder by his own tribe of their Jewish hostages; he had taken no part in the field of Boâth; and he was respected by both factions. But his bright prospects were destined to be eclipsed by the rising fortunes of the stranger from Mecca.

Medîna prepared for Islâm. From this brief review it will be clear that the success of Islâm at Medîna, though unexpected, was not without perceptible cause. There was, first, the vague expectation, derived from the Jews, of a coming prophet. When the Jews, dividing their allegiance between the Aus and Khazraj clans, used to fight on either side, they would say: *A prophet is about to arise; his time draweth nigh. Him shall we follow; and then we shall slay you with the slaughter of the ungodly nations of old.* So when Mahomet addressed the pilgrims of Medîna at Minâ, they spoke one with another: *Know surely that this is the prophet with whom the Jews are ever threatening us; wherefore let us make haste and be the first to join him.* There is truth, though exaggerated and distorted, in this tradition. In

[1] The Bani Aus sought aid from the Coreish; but they declined to fight against the Bani Khazraj, with whom some (as Mahomet's own family) were allied by marriage. The Prophet is said to have addressed the members of this embassy, and pressed the claims of his mission upon them, but without success.

their close and constant intercourse with the Arabs of Medîna, the expectation of a Messiah must in some measure have been communicated by the Jews to their heathen neighbours. Nor could the idolatrous inhabitants live in daily contact with a race professing the pure theism and practising the stern morality of the Old Testament without realising its practical protest against the errors of Paganism, and its contrast with the spiritual worship of the one true God. Moreover, Medîna was only half the distance of Mecca from the Christian tribes of southern Syria; the poet Hassân, and men of his stamp from Medîna, used to frequent the Christian court of the Ghassânide king; and thus Christianity as well as Judaism had probably wrought a more powerful effect upon the social condition of Medîna than upon any other part of the Peninsula.

Again, the city, as we have seen, had been long torn by internal war. The recent sanguinary conflict of Boâth had weakened and humiliated one of the factions without materially strengthening the other. Assassination succeeded open strife. No one yet appeared bold enough to seize the reins of government; the citizens, both Arab and Jewish, lived in uncertainty and suspense. The advent of a stranger, though likely even to usurp the vacant authority, would excite but little apprehension. Deadly jealousy at home had extinguished the jealousy of influence from abroad. *Internal strife neutralised fear of foreign influence.*

Such was the position of Medîna. A tribe addicted to the superstition of Mecca, yet well acquainted with a purer faith, was in the best state of preparation to join itself to one who aimed at reforming the worship of the Káaba. Idolatrous Arabs impressed with the indefinite anticipation of a Messiah, would readily recognise Mahomet as their prophet. A city wearied with faction and strife would cheerfully admit him to their hospitality as a refugee, if not welcome him to their counsels as a chief. *Medîna prepared to accept Mahomet.*

Again, the politics of Mecca and the history of the Prophet were well known at Medîna. The Syrian caravans of the Coreish not unfrequently halted there. Occasional intermarriages took place between the inhabitants of the two cities. Mahomet himself was descended from a lady of distinguished Khazrajite birth espoused by Hâshim; and a *Its inhabitants familiar with his claims.*

favourable interest, among that tribe at least, was thus secured. Abu Cays, a famous poet of Medîna, had some time before addressed the Coreish in verses intended to dissuade them from interference with Mahomet and his followers.[1] The Jews were already acquainted with the Prophet as a zealous supporter of their Scriptures. Parties from Medîna went up yearly to the solemnities of the Káaba. Many had thus come under the direct influence of his preaching, and all were familiar with the general tenour of his claims. To this was now to be superadded the advocacy of actual converts.[2]

A time of anxiety and suspense, A.D. 620.

To return again to Mecca, the year A.D. 620 was to Mahomet one of expectation and anxiety. Would the handful of Medîna converts remain steady to his cause? Would they be able to extend that cause among their fellow-citizens? If they should prove unfaithful, or fail of success, what resource would then remain? He might be forced to flee to Syria or Abyssinia; and seek refuge with the

[1] The following is an extract :—

'One who is master of his own actions hath chosen a new religion; and there is none other keeper over you than the Lord of the Heavens; '—(that is, it belongs to God alone to call man to account for his religious opinions).

Abu Cays had a Coreishite wife, and had lived some time at Mecca. When Islâm began to spread at Medîna, his adverse influence at first held back his own tribe from joining it. He commanded the Ausites at the battle of Boâth.

[2] We find notices of conversion to Islâm among the citizens of Medîna at an *earlier* period, but none are well substantiated. Thus, before the battle of Boâth, when a deputation visited Mecca to seek for auxiliaries from among the Coreish, we are told that 'they listened to Mahomet; and Ayâs, a youth of their number, declared that this was far better than the errand they had come upon; but their chief cast dust upon him, saying that they had another business than to hear such things.' Ayâs, who was killed shortly after in the intestine struggles at Medîna, is said to have died a true Mussulman.

Similarly, Suweid, a Medîna poet, came to the Prophet at Mecca and repeated the Persian tale of Locmân. Mahomet, saying he had something better than that, recited the Corán to him. The poet was delighted with it; 'he was not far from Islâm, and some said that he died a Moslem.'

And again: 'The first that believed at Medîna were Asád and Dzakwân, who set out for Mecca to contend in rivalry with Otba son of Rabia. On their arrival, Otba said to them: *That praying fellow who fancieth himself to be the Prophet of God, hath occupied us to the exclusion of every other business.* Now Asád and Abul Haytham used to converse at Medîna about the unity of God. When Dzakwân, therefore, heard this saying of Otba, he exclaimed: *Listen, O Asád! this must be thy religion.* So they went straight to Mahomet, who expounded to them Islâm, and they both believed. On their return to Medîna, Asád related to Abul Haytham all that had passed, and he said: *I too am a believer with thee.*'

Ethiopian Negus, or amongst the Christian tribes of the northern desert.

The days of pilgrimage at last came round, and Mahomet sought the appointed spot in a narrow sheltered glen near Minâ. His apprehensions were at once dispelled ; a band of twelve faithful disciples were there ready to acknowledge him as their prophet. Ten were of the Khazraj, and two of the Aus, tribe. They plighted their faith to Mahomet thus : ' *We will not worship any but the one God ; we will not steal, neither will we commit adultery, nor kill our children ; we will not slander in anywise ; nor will we disobey the Prophet in anything that is right.*' This was afterwards called the Pledge of women, because, as not embracing any stipulation to *defend* the Prophet, it was the only oath ever required from the female sex. When the twelve had all taken this engagement, Mahomet replied : ' *If ye fulfil the pledge, Paradise shall be your reward. He that shall fail in any part thereof, to God belongeth his concern either to punish or forgive.*' This memorable proceeding is known in the annals of Islâm as THE FIRST PLEDGE OF ACABA, for that was the name of the little eminence or defile whither Mahomet with the twelve retired from observation. A mosque still marks the spot hard by the pilgrim road.

First pledge of Acaba by the men of Medina, April, A.D. 621.

These twelve men were now committed to the cause of Mahomet. They returned to Medîna the missionaries of Islâm, again to report their success at the following pilgrimage. So prepared was the ground, so zealous the propagation, and so apt the method, that the new faith spread rapidly from house to house and from tribe to tribe. The Jews looked on in amazement at the people whom they had in vain endeavoured for generations to convince of the errors of polytheism and dissuade from the abominations of idolatry, suddenly and of their own accord casting away their idols, and professing belief in one God alone. The secret lay in the adaptation of the instrument. Judaism, foreign in its growth, touched few Arab sympathies ; Islâm, engrafted upon the faith and superstition, the customs and the nationality of the Peninsula, gained ready access to every heart.

Spread of Islâm at Medîna, A.D. 621.

The leaders in the movement soon found themselves unable to keep pace with its rapid progress. So they wrote to

Musáb deputed thither to

instruct the
converts.

Mahomet for a teacher, well versed in the Corân, who might initiate the enquirers in the rudiments of the new faith. The youthful and devoted Musâb, who had lately returned from exile in Abyssinia, was deputed for that purpose. He lodged at Medîna with Asâd ibn Zorâra, who had been already in the habit of gathering the converts together for prayer and the reading of the Corân. The combined devotions of the Aus and Khazraj tribes were now conducted by Musâb; for even in such a matter the rival clans were impatient of a common leader from amongst themselves. Thus speedily, without let or hindrance, did Islâm take firm root at Medîna, and attain to a full and mature growth.[1]

[1] Musâb will be remembered as the youth whose pathetic interview with his mother has been before described. In course of time others were sent to Medîna for the same purpose; and among them is mentioned the blind Abdallah, see *ante*, p. 71.

The following narrative (though of doubtful authority) will illustrate the manner in which Islâm was propagated at Medîna: 'Asâd and Musâb on a certain day went to the quarter of the Bani Aus, and, entering one of their gardens, sat down by a well, where a company of believers gathered around them. Now Sâd ibn Muâdz and Oseid ibn Khuzeir were chief men of the Bani Aus; and they were both idolaters following the old religion. So when they heard of the gathering at the well, Sâd unwilling himself to interfere (being related to Asâd) bade his comrades go and disperse them. Oseid seized his weapons, and hurrying to the spot, began thus to abuse them: *What brings you two men here amongst us, to mislead our youths and silly folk? Begone, if ye have any care for your lives.* Musâb disarmed his wrath by courteously inviting him to sit down and listen to the doctrine. Then Oseid stuck his spear into the ground and seated himself; and as he listened, he was charmed with the new faith, and purified himself and embraced Islâm. And he said: " There is another beside me, even Sâd ibn Muâdz, whom I will send to you; if you can gain him over, there will not be one in his tribe left unconverted." So he departed and sent Sâd, and Musâb persuaded him in like manner. And Sâd returned to his tribe and swore that he would not speak to man or woman who did not acknowledge Mahomet. So great was his influence that *by the evening every one of the tribe was converted.*'

'Such were the exertions of Asâd and Musâb that there remained not a house among the Arabs of Medîna in which there were not believing men and women, excepting the branches of the *Aus Allah* who, owing to the influence of Abu Cays the poet, continued unbelievers till after the siege of Medîna.'

There is a story of an aged chief who, like others at Medîna, had an image in his house. This image the young converts used to cast every night into a filthy well, and the old man as regularly cleansed it; till, one day, they tied it to a dead dog and cast it into the well; whereupon he abandoned his image and believed.

CHAPTER VII.

SPREAD OF ISLÂM AT MEDÎNA. THE HEGIRA, OR FLIGHT TO
THAT CITY.

A.D. 621–622.

THE hopes of Mahomet were now fixed upon Medîna. Visions
of the journey northwards flitted before his imagination.
The musings of the day reappeared in midnight slumbers.
He dreamed to have been swiftly carried by Gabriel on
a winged steed past Medîna to the temple at Jerusalem,
where he was welcomed by the former Prophets assembled
in solemn conclave for his reception. His excited spirit conjured up a still more transcendent scene. From Jerusalem he mounted upwards, ascending from one heaven to
another, till he found himself at last in the awful presence of his Maker, whence he was dismissed with the behest
that his people were to observe the season of prayer five
times in the day. When he awoke next morning in the
house of Abu Tâlib (where he had passed the night), the
vision was still vividly before his eyes ; and he exclaimed to
Omm Hâni, daughter of Abu Tâlib, that during the night
he had performed his devotions in the temple of Jerusalem.
He was going forth to make the vision known, when she
seized him by the mantle, and conjured him not thus to
expose himself to the derision of the unbelievers. But he
persisted. As the story spread abroad, idolaters scoffed,
believers were staggered, and some followers are said even
to have gone back. Abu Bakr supported the Prophet,
and declared his implicit belief in the vision. In the end
the credit of Islâm among its adherents suffered no material
injury.

The tale is one in which tradition revels with congenial
ecstacy. The rein is given loose to a pious and excited ima-

*The mid
night jour-
ney to
Jerusalem
and
Heaven.*

*The vision
embellished
by tradition.*

gination. The journey to the holy city, and the ascent to heaven, are both decked out in the wildest colouring of romance, and in all the gorgeous drapery that fancy could conceive. But the only mention in the Corân of this notable vision is contained in the 17th Sura, which opens thus :—

Only notice of it in the Corân.

Sura xvii.

Praise be to Him who carried His servant by night from the sacred Temple to the farther Temple the environs of which We have blessed, that We might show him some of Our signs. Verily He it is that heareth and seeth.

Mahomet watches struggle between Persia and the Roman empire.

The political events in the north had long engaged the attention of Mahomet. His interest was now quickened by the early prospect of himself approaching so much nearer the scene of action. Almost from the period at which he had assumed the prophetical office, the victorious arms of the Chosroes had been turned against the Grecian frontier. The desert tract, and its Arab Christian tribes who used to oscillate between one dominion and the other according to the fortune of war, were the first to fall into the hands of Persia. The enemy then ravaged the whole of Syria ; Jerusalem was sacked ; Egypt and Asia Minor overrun ; an army advanced upon the Thracian Bosphorus, and (as we read in Gibbon) ' a Persian camp was maintained above ten years in the presence of Constantinople.' In A.D. 621, when the fortunes of the Grecian empire were at the lowest ebb, Heraclius was roused from his inaction, and after several years of arduous conflict, rolled back the invasion, and totally discomfited the Persians.

His sympathies with Heraclius ; foretells victory of Greeks.

In this struggle, the sympathies and hopes of Mahomet were enlisted on the side of the Cæsar. Christianity was a divine faith which, according to his principles, might coalesce with Islâm ; but the fire-worship and superstitions of Persia were utterly repugnant to his views. It was while the career of Persian conquest was yet unchecked, that Mahomet, in the opening of the 30th Sura, uttered this sagacious augury of the eventual issue of the contest :—

The GREEKS have been conquered
In the neighbouring coast ; but, after their defeat, they shall
again be victorious,
In a few years. To GOD belongeth the matter from before,
and after ; and, in that day, the Believers shall rejoice

In the aid of God. He aideth whom He chooseth; and He
    is the Glorious, the Merciful.
It is the promise of God. God changeth not His promise;
    but the greater part of mankind know it not.[1]

About this period, with his increasing interest in the Relations with Christianity.
Roman empire, Mahomet must have gained, either from
some Christian slave at Mecca,[2] or from visitors at the
neighbouring fairs, a closer acquaintance with Christianity.
As will appear in the Supplement to this chapter, he never
showed the same interest in the Christian as in the Jewish
faith, nor indeed had he the same means of learning its
history and doctrines. His treatment of Christianity is
mainly confined to the recitation (in the same legendary
and rhapsodical style as of the Jewish stories) of a few
passages connected with the birth and life of Jesus, whom
he acknowledged as the last and greatest of the Jewish
prophets, but whose Sonship (as well as the doctrine of the
Trinity) he strenuously rejected. At the same time, his
attitude towards Christianity was quite as favourable as it
was towards Judaism; nor was his intercourse with its
professors at any future period embittered by such causes
as led to hostilities with the Jews. But, on the other
hand, his relations with the Christian faith never advanced
materially beyond the point at which we find them now
developed in the Corân; and, in fact, if we except one or
two campaigns against distant Christian tribes, and the reception of embassies from them, he came throughout his
life into little personal contact with the professors of the
faith of Jesus.

There was now a lull at Mecca. Mahomet despaired, by A lull at Mecca.
the simple influence of preaching and persuasion, of effecting
further progress there. His eye was fixed upon Medîna,
and he waited patiently until succour should come from
thence. Meanwhile, at home offensive measures were

---

[1] The commentators add a very convenient story in illustration. Abu
Bakr, on this passage being revealed, laid a wager of ten camels with Obba
ibn Khalf, that the Persians would be beaten within *three* years. Mahomet
desired him to extend the period to *nine* years, and to raise the stake. This
Abu Bakr did, and in due time won one hundred camels from Obba's heirs.

[2] See above in the case of Suheib, p. 72; and Addâs the Christian slave at
Tâyif, p. 114.

abandoned. Islâm was for the present no longer to be aggressive. And the Coreish, congratulating themselves that their enemy had tried his worst and now was harmless, relaxed their vigilance and opposition. For his new course of action, Mahomet, as usual, had divine authority :—

Sura vi. Follow that which hath been revealed unto thee from thy Lord ;—there is no God but he ;—and retire from the Idolaters.

If God had so desired, they had not followed idolatry ; and We have not made thee a keeper over them, neither art thou unto them a guardian.

And revile not those whom they invoke besides God, lest they revile God in enmity from lack of knowledge.

Thus have We rendered attractive unto every people their own doings ; then unto the Lord

Shall be their return, and He shall declare unto them that which they have wrought.[1]

Mahomet's continued assurance of success. But with this cessation of aggressive measures there was no wavering of principle, nor any distrust of eventual success. A calm and lofty front was maintained of superiority, and even of defiance. Eventual success, in spite of present discouragement, was clear and assured. The whole tenour of the Corân at this period is marked by quietness and confidence, and therein for the present lay the Prophet's strength. To all his apostles of old the Lord had given the victory, and he would give the same to Mahomet :—

Sura xxi. We shall hurl the Truth against that which is false and it shall shiver it, and lo, the False shall vanish ;—Wo unto you for that which ye imagine !   *   *   *

Vengeance shall fall suddenly upon them. It shall confound them. They shall not be able to oppose the same, neither shall they be respited.

Sura xiv. Verily, Apostles before thee have been mocked ; but they that laughed them to scorn were encompassed by the vengeance which they mocked at.   *   *   *

The unbelieving (nations) said unto their Apostles—*We will surely expel you from our land, or ye shall return to our religion.* Then their Lord spake by revelation unto them, saying ;—*Verily We shall destroy the unjust.*

[1] The Opposition begin to be termed ' the Confederates' (Sura xi.), and they are thus contrasted with the Moslems: ' The likeness of the two Parties is as the blind and the deaf, compared with him that hath both sight and hearing. What ! are these equal in resemblance ? Ah ! do ye not comprehend ? '

And We shall cause you to inherit the land after them;—this shall
be for him that feareth My appearing and feareth My
threatening.

So they asked assistance of the Lord, and every tyrant and
rebellious one was destroyed.   *   *   *

Verily, they have devised evil devices ; but their devices are in
the hands of God, even if their devices could cause
the mountains to pass away.

Wherefore think not thou that God will work at variance with
his promise which He made unto his Apostles.
Verily the Lord is mighty, and a God of vengeance.

A dearth fell upon Mecca ;—it was a punishment from
God because the people had rejected his messenger.   Relief
at length came ; it was intended to try whether the goodness
of God would not lead them to repentance.   If they still
hardened their hearts, a more fearful fate was denounced.[1]

Judgments threatened against Mecca ;

That tenfold vengeance would overtake the people if
they continued to reject the truth, Mahomet believed surely.
He might not live to see it ; but the decree of God was un-
changeable :—

Which Mahomet might or might not behold.

[1] There are no very credible traditions regarding this visitation ; but the
notices of it in the Corán are so clear and distinct as to allow no doubt that
some affliction of the kind did occur, which was attributed by Mahomet to the
divine vengeance :—

And if We have mercy upon them and withdraw the affliction that befel
them, then they plunge into their wickedness, wandering wildly.

And verily We visited them with affliction, and they humbled not themselves before their Lord, nor made supplication :—

Until, when We open unto them a door of severe punishment, lo! they
are in despair thereat.—*Sura* xxiii.

This punishment the commentators will have to be the battle of Bedr, but
that would be an anachronism.   Again :—

And when We made the people to taste mercy, after the affliction that
befel them, lo! they devise deceit against our Signs.   SAY, God is
more swift than ye are in deceit ; Verily Our messengers write down
that which ye devise.

It is He that causeth you to travel by land and by water, so that when
ye are in ships and sail in them with a pleasant breeze, they rejoice
thereat.

A fierce storm overtaketh them, and the waves come upon them from every
quarter, and they think that verily they are closed in thereby ; then
they call upon God, rendering unto Him pure service, and saying, *If*
Thou savest us from this, we shall verily be amongst the Grateful.

But when He hath saved them, behold! they work evil in the earth un-
righteously.   Oh ye people, verily your evil working is against your
own souls, &c.—*Sura* x.

K

Sura xliii.   What! canst thou make the deaf to hear, or guide the blind, or
him that is wandering widely?

Wherefore, whether We take thee away, verily We will pour our
vengeance upon them,—

Or, whether We cause thee to see that which We have threatened
them with, verily We are all powerful over them.

Therefore hold fast that which hath been revealed unto thee, for
thou art in the straight path.[1]

Sublime
spectacle
here pre-
sented by
Mahomet.

Mahomet thus holding his people at bay; waiting in the
still expectation of victory; to outward appearance defenceless, and with his little band as it were in the lion's mouth;
yet trusting in His almighty power whose Messenger he
believed himself to be, resolute and unmoved; presents a
spectacle of sublimity paralleled only by such scenes in the
Sacred records as that of the prophet of Israel when he complained to his Master, 'I, even I only, am left.' Nay, the
spectacle is in one point of view more amazing; because
the prophets of old were upheld (as we may suppose) by
the prevailing consciousness of a divine inspiration, and
strengthened by the palpable demonstrations of miraculous
power; while with the Arabian prophet, the memory at least
of former doubts, and the confessed inability to work any
miracle, must at times have cast the shadow of uncertainty
across his soul.   It is this which brings if possible into still
bolder prominence the marvellous self-possession and enthusiasm which sustained Mahomet on his course. 'Say unto
the Unbelievers,' such was the reiterated message from on
high, 'Say, *Work ye in your place. Wait in expectation;
We too in expectancy are waiting.*' And again: 'Say, *Each
of us awaits the issue; wait therefore; hereafter ye shall
surely know who they are that have chosen the straight path,
and who hath been guided aright.*'

Authority
assumed
over his
own fol-
lowers.

Mahomet's bearing towards his followers, no less than
towards his opponents, exhibits the assurance of being the
Vicegerent of God and the infallible exponent of his will.
His name is associated with the Deity in the symbol of faith;
and obedience to *God and his Apostle* becomes the watch-

[1] There are many other passages in the Suras of this period to the same
effect; thus: 'Wherefore persevere patiently, for the promise of God is true,
whether We cause thee to see some part of that wherewith We have threatened
them, or cause thee (first) to die; and unto Us shall they return.'—*Sura* xl.

word of Islâm. ' Whosoever disobeyeth GOD AND HIS PRO-
PHET, verily to him shall be the fire of Hell; they shall be
therein alway,—for ever !'[1]

The confidence in his inspiration is sometimes expressed
with imprecations, which one cannot read without a
shudder :—

Impreca-
tions that
his revela-
tion is not
fabricated.

Sura lxix.

> I swear by that which ye see,
>   And by that which ye do not see,
> That this is verily the speech of an honourable Apostle !
> It is not the speech of a Poet ; little is it ye believe !
> And it is not the speech of a Soothsayer ; little is it ye reflect !
>   It is a Revelation from the Lord of creation.
> And if he (Mahomet) had fabricated concerning Us any sayings,
> Verily We had caught him by the right hand ;
> Then had We cut asunder the artery of his neck,[2]
> Nor would there have been among you any to hinder there-
>   from.
> But verily it is an Admonition to the pious,
> And truly We know that there are amongst you those who belie
>   the same ;
> But it shall cause sighing unto the Unbelievers,
>   And it is the TRUTH ;—the CERTAIN !
> Therefore praise the name of thy Lord,—the GLORIOUS !

---

[1] Sura lxxii. The sequel of the passage is singular; God sends a guard to
attend his Prophet to see that the message is duly delivered, as if there were
reason to doubt his fidelity in this respect :—

> When they see that which they were threatened with, then they shall know
>   which side was the weakest in succour, and which the fewest in
>   number.
> SAY I know not whether that which ye are threatened with be near, or
>   whether my Lord shall appoint for it a set time.
> He knoweth the secret thing, and He unveileth not His secrets unto any,—
> Except it be to an Apostle that pleaseth Him ; and He maketh a guard to
>   go before and behind him ;
> That He may know that they have verily delivered the messages of their
>   Lord.
> He encompasseth whatever is beside them,
> And He counteth everything by number.

In further illustration of the text, see Sura lxiv. : ' Wherefore believe in
GOD AND HIS APOSTLE, and the light which WE have sent down.' And again :
' And obey *God and obey the Apostle ;*—but if ye turn back, verily our Apostle
hath only to deliver his message.' Thenceforward the expression becomes
common.

[2] Commentators observe that the allusion is to the mode of execution still
practised in the East ; the executioner seizes the victim by the right hand,
while with a sharp sword he aims a blow at the back of the neck, and detaches
the head at a stroke.

Straitened
means.

It would seem as if the difficulties of the Prophet were at this period increased by straitened means. Though supported probably by help from his relatives and followers, there was yet ground for misgiving and anxiety. The divine promise reassures him in such terms as these:—

Sura xx.

And stretch not forth thine eyes to the provision We have made for divers among them,—the show of this present life, that We may prove them thereby; and the provision of the Lord is better and more lasting.

And command thy Family to observe prayer, and to persevere therein: We ask thee not (to labour) for a provision; We shall provide for thee, and there shall be a successful issue to piety.

Preparations for the Second Pledge of Acaba, March, A.D. 622.

Thus another year passed away in comparative tranquillity, and the month of pilgrimage, when the Medîna converts were again to rally around the Prophet, drew nigh. Written accounts, as well as messages, of the amazing success of Islâm had no doubt reached Mahomet; but he was hardly prepared for the large and enthusiastic band ready to crowd to his standard, and swear allegiance to him as prophet and master. Yet it was necessary to proceed with caution. The Coreish, if aware of this extensive and hostile confederacy,—hostile because pledged to support (though only as yet defensively) a faction in their community,—would have good ground for umbrage; the sword might prematurely be unsheathed, and the cause of Islâm seriously endangered. The movement, therefore, was conducted with the utmost secrecy. Even the other pilgrims from Medîna, in whose company the converts travelled, were unaware of their object.

Musáb reports success to Mahomet.

Musáb, the teacher sent to Medîna, who had also joined the pilgrims' party, immediately on his arrival repaired to Mahomet and related all that had happened at his new scene of labour. The Prophet rejoiced greatly when he heard of the numbers of the converts, and their eagerness in the service of Islâm.

Meeting to be by night at the close of pilgrimage.

To elude the scrutiny of the citizens of Mecca, the meeting between Mahomet and his new adherents was to be by night; and that the strangers might, in case suspicion were aroused, be for as short a time as possible within reach of their enemies, the day was deferred to the very close of the pilgrimage when, the ceremonies and sacrifices being finished, the multitude would on the following morning disperse to their homes. The spot was to be the secluded glen, where the men of Medîna had before met Mahomet, close by the road as the traveller quits the valley of Minâ, and beneath a well-known eminence (Acaba). They were to move cautiously thither, and punctually, when all had retired to rest; 'waking not the sleeper, nor tarrying for the absent.'

An hour or two before midnight, Mahomet repaired to the rendezvous, the first of the party. He was attended only by his uncle Abbâs. To secure the greater secrecy, the assembly was kept private even from his followers at Mecca.[1] Abbâs was the wealthiest of the sons of Abd al Muttalib, but he was weak in character, and ordinarily sailed with wind and tide. He was not a convert; but near relationship, and the close community of interest created by the three years' confinement with Mahomet and his followers in the isolated quarter of Abu-Tâlib, rendered him sufficiently trustworthy on the present occasion.

Mahomet and Abbâs proceed at midnight to the spot.

Mahomet had not long to wait. Soon the converts of Medîna, singly and by twos and threes, were descried through the moonlight moving stealthily along the stony valley and among the barren rocks towards the spot. They were seventy three men (sixty-two of the Bani Khazraj, eleven of the Bani Aus) and two women; and included the earlier converts who had met the Prophet on the two preceding pilgrimages. When they were seated, Abbâs, in a low voice, broke the silence by a speech something to the following effect :—

Joined by the Medîna converts.

'Ye company of the BANI KHAZRAJ![2] This my kinsman dwelleth amongst us in honour and safety. His clan will defend him—both those that are converts, and those who still hold to their ancestral faith. But he preferreth to seek protection from you. Wherefore, ye Khazrajites, consider

Speech of Abbâs;

---

[1] Or if they were admitted to the secret, they were instructed not to be present, the less to excite suspicion. Even Musáb appears not to have accompanied the Medîna converts; for we are told that 'there was no one with Mahomet besides Abbâs.'

[2] The people of Medîna, both of the Aus and Khazraj tribes, used to be addressed collectively as Khazrajites.

well the matter ; and count the cost.   If ye be resolved, and are able, to defend him,—well.   But if ye doubt your ability, at once abandon the design.'

and of Abu Barâ.

Then spoke Abu Barâ, an aged chief: ' We have listened to thy words.   Our resolution is unshaken.   Our lives are at the Prophet's service.   It is now for *him* to speak.'

Address of Mahomet.

Mahomet began, as was his wont, by reciting appropriate passages from the Corân ; he invited all present to the service of God, and dwelt upon the claims and blessings of Islâm ; and then coming to the business of the night, he ended by saying that he should be content if the strangers pledged themselves to defend him as they would their own wives and children.   As he stopped, there arose from every quarter a confused, tumultuous noise ; it was the eager voices of the ' Seventy ' testifying their readiness to take the pledge, and protesting that they would receive the Prophet even at the cost of their property and the lives of their chiefs.   Then Abbâs, who stood by holding his nephew's hand, called aloud : ' Hush !   There are spies about.   Let your men of years stand forth, and let them speak on your behalf.   Of a verity, we are fearful for your safety if our people should discover us.   Then when ye have plighted your faith depart forthwith to your encampment.'   So their chief men stood forth.   Then said Barâ : ' Stretch out thy hand, O Mahomet !' He stretched it out ; and Barâ struck his hand thereon, as the manner was in taking an oath of fealty.   The Seventy came forward one by one, and did the same.[1]   Then Mahomet

Second pledge of Acaba.

named twelve of the chief men, and said : *Moses chose from amongst his people twelve leaders.   Ye shall be the sureties for the rest, even as the apostles of Jesus were ; and I am the surety for my people.*   They answered, ' Be it so.'[2]   At this

[1] The women repeated only the words of the pledge taken by the Twelve at the *first* Acaba.   Mahomet never took women by the hand on such an occasion ; but they used to step forward and recite the prescribed words, and then Mahomet would say, ' Go : for you have pledged yourselves.'

Abu Barâ, who bore so conspicuous a part throughout this transaction, died in the following month.   He is said to have been the first over whose grave Mahomet, when he went to Medîna, prayed in the formula that became usual afterwards : *O Lord, pardon him !   Be merciful unto him !   Be reconciled unto him !   and verily thou art reconciled.*

[2] *Nackîb*, or ' leader,' is the term which was ever after honourably retained by the Twelve.   Four were of the number who met Mahomet here on the two previous pilgrimages.   Three were of the Aus tribes ; the rest, Khazrajites.

moment the voice of one crying aloud, probably a straggler searching for his company, was heard near at hand. Excited fancy conjured up a Coreishite, if not an infernal, spy.[1] Mahomet gave command, and the whole assembly dispersing hurried back to their halting places. Thus passed the memorable night of the SECOND PLEDGE OF ACABA.

So large a gathering could not be held close by Minâ without rumours reaching the Coreish enough to rouse their suspicion. It was notorious that great numbers at Medîna had embraced the doctrines of Mahomet. The clandestine meeting must have been on his behalf; and as such, an unwarrantable interference in the domestic affairs of Mecca; it was virtually a hostile movement. Accordingly, next morning their chief men repaired to the Medîna encampment, stated their suspicions, and complained of unfriendly conduct at the hand of a tribe with whom, of all the tribes in Arabia, they declared, it would grieve them most to be at war. The converts glanced at each other, and held their peace.[2] The rest of the pilgrims from Medîna, ignorant of

Coreish challenge the Medina chiefs.

Several of them, as well as many amongst the Seventy, are mentioned as able to *write* Arabic; and as being *Kâmil* (perfect), *i.e.*, expert in writing, in archery, and in swimming.

[1] 'When the ceremony was ended, the devil called out with a loud voice: *Ye people of Mecca! Have ye no concern for Mahomet and his renegades? They have counselled war against you.*' And another tradition: 'When we had pledged ourselves to the Prophet, Satan called out with a piercing cry, such as I never heard before: *Oh ye that are encamped round about! Have ye no care for* MUDZAMMAM (the "blamed," the antithesis of Mahomet the "praised") *and the renegades that are with him? They have resolved on war with you.* Then said Mahomet: "This is the demon of Acaba; this is the son of the devil. Hearest thou, enemy of God? Verily I will ease me of thee!"' At the battle of Ohod, the voice which cried 'Mahomet is fallen,' was that of 'the demon of Acaba, that is to say the devil;' he is said to have been present at the council of the Coreish to put Mahomet to death; and we have seen that he was represented as having opposed Mahomet at the placing of the corner stone when the Kâaba was rebuilt.

[2] A story is told by Kâb, one of the Seventy, that while this inquisition was going on, in order to divert attention, he pointed to a new pair of shoes which one of the Coreishite chiefs had on, and said to Abu Jâbir, one of his own party: 'Why could'st thou, *our* chief, not wear a pair of new shoes like this Coreishite chief?' The latter taking off the shoes, threw them at Kâb, saying: 'Put them on thyself.' Abu Jâbir said: 'Tush! give back the shoes.' Kâb refused; the Coreishite chief then tried to snatch them from him. A commotion ensued, which was just what Kâb desired, as it served to cover the awkward situation of the Medîna converts. Such tales of service rendered to the cause of Islâm were plentifully fabricated in the earliest times, and

their comrades' proceedings, protested that the people of Mecca had been misinformed, and that the report was utterly without foundation. Their chief, Abdallah ibn Obey, assured the visitors that none of his people would have ventured on such a step without consulting him. The Coreish were satisfied, and took their leave.

They pursue the Medina caravan,

During that day, the vast concourse at Minâ broke up. The numerous caravans prepared for their journey, and took each its homeward course. The party from Medîna had already set out, when the Coreish having strictly enquired into the midnight assembly (which Mahomet hardly cared now to keep secret) found, to their confusion, that not only had it really taken place, but that far larger numbers than they suspected had pledged themselves to the defence of Mahomet. Foiled and exasperated, they pursued the Medîna caravan in the hope that they might lay hands on some of the delinquents; but, though they scoured the roads leading to Medîna, they

and maltreat one of the converts.

fell in with only two. Of these one escaped. The other, Sád ibn Obâda, they seized and, tying his hands behind his back, dragged him by his long hair back to Mecca. There he would no doubt have suffered further maltreatment, had he not been able to claim protection from certain of the Coreishite chiefs to whom he had rendered service at Medîna. He was released, and rejoined the caravan just as his friends were about to return in search of him.

The Coreish, enraged, recommence persecution;

It soon became evident that, in consequence of the covenant entered into at Acaba, Mahomet and his followers contemplated an early emigration to Medîna. The prospect of such a movement, which would remove their opponents entirely out of reach, and plant them in an asylum where they might securely work out their machinations and as opportunity offered take an ample revenge, at first irritated the Coreish. They renewed, after a long cessation, the persecution of the believers; and, wherever they had the power, sought either to make them recant, or by confinement prevent their escape.[1]

deserve little credit; but they are sometimes useful as illustrating passages of history.

[1] The support of the cause at Medîna, and the suspicion of an intended emigration, irritated the Coreish to severity; and this severity forced the Moslems to petition Mahomet for leave to emigrate. The two things would react on one another;—the persecution hastening the departure of the converts, and

Such severities, or the dread of them (for the Moslems were conscious that they had now seriously compromised their loyalty as citizens of Mecca) hastened the crisis. And, indeed, when Mahomet had once resolved upon a general emigration, there was no advantage from a protracted residence among his enemies.

and thus precipitate departure of converts.

It was but a few days after the ' second pledge of Acaba,' that Mahomet gave command to his followers, saying: *Depart unto Medîna; for the Lord hath verily given you brethren in that city, and a home in which ye may find refuge.*[1] So they made preparation, chose companions for the journey, and set out in parties secretly. Such as had the means rode two and two upon camels, and the rest walked.

Mahomet gives command to emigrate to Medîna.

Persecution and artifice caused a few to fall away from the faith. One example will suffice. Omar had arranged a rendezvous with Ayâsh and Hishâm at a spot in the environs of Mecca, whence they were to set out for Medîna. Hishâm was held back by his family, and relapsed for a time into idolatry. ' Thus I, and my brother Ayâsh,' relates Omar, went forward alone, and journeyed to Cobâ in the outskirts of Medîna, where we alighted, and were hospitably received at the house of Rifâa. But Abu Jahl (a uterine brother both of Omar and Ayâsh) followed him to Medîna, and told him that his mother had vowed she would retire beneath no shade, nor suffer a comb or any oil to touch her hair, until she saw his face again. Then I cautioned him

Some fall away through persecution. Story of Ayâsh.

each fresh departure irritating the Coreish to greater cruelty. Tabari says: ' There were two occasions on which persecution raged the hottest; *first*, the period preceding the emigration to Abyssinia; *second*, that following the second covenant at Acaba.' There is good reason, however, to suspect that stronger epithets have been used in tradition regarding this persecution than the facts warrant. Had it been as bad as is spoken of, we should have had abundant instances. Yet, excepting the imprisonment or surveillance of a few waverers, we have no detail of any injuries or sufferings inflicted on this occasion by the Coreish.

[1] We are told that Mahomet was shown in a dream the place of emigration ' a saline plain, with palm trees, between two hills.' He waited some days, uncertain where this might be, and then went forth joyously to his followers, saying: ' Now have I been made acquainted with the place appointed for your emigration. It is *Yathreb*. Whoso desireth let him emigrate thither.' Long before this, however, he had made up his mind where he was going. The story probably grew out of the idea that Mahomet must have had a special and divine command for so important a step as that of emigration to Medîna.

(continues Omar), saying : " By the Lord ! they only desire to tempt thee from thy faith. Thy mother will soon relax her vow. Beware, Ayâsh ! return not nigh to Mecca." But he replied : " Nay, I will not recant. But I have property at Mecca. I will go and fetch it, and it will strengthen me. And I will also release my mother from her vow." Seeing that he was not to be diverted from his purpose, I gave him a swift camel and bade him, if he suspected treachery, to save himself thereon. So when the party alighted at a certain place, his companions seized him suddenly, and bound him with cords ; and, as they carried him into Mecca, they exclaimed : *Even thus, ye men of Mecca, should ye treat your foolish ones!* Then they kept him in durance.'[1]

The emigration, April, A.D. 622, continues for two months.
It was about the beginning of the month Muharram that the emigration commenced. Medîna lies some 250 miles to the north of Mecca. The journey in modern times is accomplished by the pilgrim caravans ' in eleven days, and if pressed for time, in ten.'[2] Within two months nearly all the followers of Mahomet, excepting the few detained in confinement or unable to escape from slavery, had migrated with their families to their new abode. They numbered between one and two hundred souls.[3] They were welcomed with cordial and even eager hospitality by their brethren at Medîna,

---

[1] Both Ayâsh and Hishâm afterwards rejoined Mahomet. Ayâsh as well as Hishâm is said to have relapsed into idolatry. Omar says that until Sura xxxix. v. 53 was revealed, it was thought that no apostate could be saved. When that passage appeared, he wrote it out for Ayâsh, and sent it to him at Mecca ; which when Ayâsh had read, he took courage, and forthwith mounted his camel for Medîna. The verse is as follows : 'Say ;—O my servants who have transgressed against your own souls, despair not of the mercy of God ; for God forgiveth sins wholly : verily He is gracious and merciful.'

[2] *Burkhardt.* The *Tayyara* or ' Flying Caravan ' goes in less time. ' The Rakb is a dromedary caravan, in which each person carries only his saddle bags. It usually descends (from Medîna) by the road called El Khabt, and makes Mecca on the *fifth* day.' The stages by the Nejd, or eastern route, travelled by Burton, are given as eleven, and the distance estimated at 248 miles.

[3] We have no exact statement of the numbers of those who emigrated before Mahomet himself left Mecca. Eighteen months later at the battle of Bedr (when every emigrant but a very few unavoidably detained was present) Mahomet had 314 followers, of whom *eighty-three* were emigrants from Mecca. A few of these may have joined Mahomet after he reached Medîna ; and we shall probably not err far in making the whole number who emigrated *at first*, including women and children, about 150.

who vied with one another for the honour of receiving them into their houses, and supplying them with such things as they had need of.

The Coreish were paralysed by a movement so suddenly planned, and put into such speedy execution. They looked on in amazement, as families silently disappeared, and house after house was abandoned. One or two quarters of the city were entirely deserted, and the doors of the dwelling houses left deliberately locked.[1] There was here a determination and self-sacrifice on which the Coreish had hardly calculated. But even if they had foreseen and resolved to oppose the emigration, it is difficult to perceive what measures they could have adopted. The number of independent clans and separate branches effectually prevented unity of action. Here and there a slave or helpless dependent might be intimidated or held back; but in no other case was there the right to interfere with private judgment or with family counsels; and the least show of violence might have roused a host of champions, who forgetting their antipathy to Islâm would avenge the insulted honour of their tribe.

Coreish paralysed by the sudden movement.

At last Mahomet and Abu Bakr with their families, including Ali, now a youth of about twenty years of age, were the only believers left (excepting those unwillingly detained) at Mecca. Abu Bakr was ambitious of being the companion of the Prophet in his flight; and daily urged him to depart. But Mahomet told him that 'his time was not yet come:— the Lord had not as yet given him the command to emigrate.' Perhaps he was deferring his departure until he could receive assurance from Medîna that the arrangements for his reception were secure, and his adherents there not only ready, but able in the face of the rest of the people, to execute their engagement for his defence.[2] Or, there may have been the

Mahomet, Abu Bakr, and Ali left behind.

---

[1] 'The Bani Ghanam emigrated in a body, men women and children, and left their houses locked: not a soul was to be seen in the quarters of the Bani Ghanam, Abul Bokeir, and Matzûn.'

'Otba, Abbâs, and Abu Jahl passed by the dwelling-place of the Bani Jahsh, and the doors were locked, and the houses deserted. Otba sighed heavily, and said: "Every house, even if its peace be lengthened, at the last a bitter wind will reach it. The quarter of the Bani Jahsh is left without an inhabitant! This is the work of our pestilent Nephew, who hath dispersed our assemblies, ruined our affairs, and made a separation amongst us."'

[2] During the two months elapsing between the second covenant at Acaba

more generous desire to see all his followers safely away from Mecca before he himself fled for refuge to Medîna. Might we conjecture that he was waiting with the undefined expectation that divine retribution, as of old, was about to descend on the unbelieving city, in which peradventure even ten righteous men could not now be found?

Preparations of Abu Bakr.

Meanwhile Abu Bakr made preparations for the journey. In anticipation of the emergency, he had already purchased for 800 dirhems two swift camels, which were now tied up and highly fed in the yard of his house. A guide, accustomed to the devious tracks and byways of the Medîna route, was hired, and the camels were committed to his custody.[1]

Council of the Coreish.

The Coreish were perplexed at the course which Mahomet was taking. They had expected him to emigrate with his people; and perhaps half rejoiced at the prospect of being rid of their enemy. By remaining almost solitary behind, he seemed by his very loneliness to challenge and defy their attack. What might the motive be for this strange procedure? The chief men assembled to discuss their position.

Their deliberations.

Should they imprison him? his followers would come to his rescue. Should they forcibly expel him? he might agitate his cause among the tribes of Arabia, and readily lure adherents by the prospect of supremacy at Mecca. Should they assassinate him? the Bani Hâshim would exact an unrelenting penalty for the blood of their kinsman. But what if representatives from every tribe, including that of Hâshim itself, were each to plunge his sword into the Prophet,—would the Hâshimites dare to wage a mortal feud with the whole body

and Mahomet's emigration, frequent communication was kept up between Mecca and Medîna. Thus after the foremost emigrants had reached Medîna, some of the Medîna converts who had been at the Acaba covenant returned to Mecca, with the view no doubt of making further arrangements with Mahomet. These Medîna converts had thus the merit of being not only 'Ansâr,' *i.e.* allies at Medîna, but 'Muhâjirîn' or Refugees as having in a sense also emigrated from Mecca.

[1] The guide was Abdallah ibn Arcad. He belonged to a tribe affiliated with the Coreish; his mother was pure Coreish. He was still an idolater; and Wâckidi (anticipating the era when war was waged against all idolaters) adds, 'but Mahomet and Abu Bakr had given him quarter, or pledge of protection;' as if he had required any protection then from the fugitives he was guiding! The expression illustrates the proleptic way in which subsequent principles and events were anticipated, insensibly throwing back their light and colour upon the tissue of tradition.

of the Coreish thus implicated in the murder? Even then there would remain the followers at Medîna, whose revenge on account of their master's blood would surely be ruthless and desperate. Assassination by an unknown hand on the road to Medîna might prove the safest course ; but there the chances of escape would preponderate. At last they resolved that a deputation should proceed to the house of Mahomet.

What was the decision as to their future course of action, what the object even of the present deputation, it is impossible amid the one-sided and marvellous tales of tradition to conclude. There is little reason to believe that it was assassination, although tradition asserts that this was determined upon at the instigation of Abu Jahl, supported by the devil who, in the person of an old man from Nejd shrouded in a mantle, joined the council. Mahomet himself, speaking in the Corân of the designs of his enemies, refers to them in these indecisive terms: *And call to mind when the Unbelievers plotted against thee, that they might detain thee, or slay thee, or expel thee. Yea, they plotted; but God plotted likewise. And God is the best of plotters.* Assuredly had assassination been the sentence, and its immediate execution (as pretended by tradition) ordered by the council, Mahomet would not have been slow to indicate the fact in clearer language than these alternative expressions. A resolution so fatal would unquestionably have been dwelt upon at length both in the Corân and in tradition, and have been produced in justification of subsequent hostilities.[1] Had

Chiefs deputed to visit Mahomet.

---

[1] The following is the narrative given by tradition: The Coreish, irritated by hearing of the warm reception the converts experienced at Medîna, held a council. The devil, in the shape of an old man shrouded in a cloak, stood at the door saying that he was a Sheikh from Nejd, who had heard of their weighty consultation, and had come if haply he might help them to a right decision ; so they invited him to enter. One proposed to imprison, another to expel, Mahomet. The old man from Nejd warmly opposed both suggestions. Then said Abu Jahl: 'Let us choose one courageous man from every family of the Coreish, and place in the hands of each a sharp sword, and let the whole slay him with the stroke of one man ; so his blood will be divided amongst all our families, and the relatives of Mahomet will not know how to avenge it.' The old man of Nejd applauded the scheme, saying: 'May God reward this man ; this is the right advice and none other.' So they separated, having agreed thereto. Gabriel forthwith apprised Mahomet of the design, who arose and made Ali to lie down upon his bed. The murderous party came at dusk, and lay in wait about the house. Mahomet went forth, and casting a handful of dust at them, recited

such a resolution really been formed, it *must* sooner or later have reached the ears of Mahomet, and so have found its way into the Corân.

Mahomet and Abu Bakr escape to the cave of Thaur.

Whatever the object of the visit, Mahomet received previous notice of it, and at once anticipated the danger by stealing away from his house. There he left Ali; around whom, that the suspicions of his neighbours might not be aroused, he threw his own red Hadhramaut mantle, and desired him to occupy his bed. He himself went straight to the house of Abu Bakr, and after a short consultation matured the plans for immediate flight. Abu Bakr shed tears of joy; the hour for emigration had at last arrived, and he was to be the companion of the Prophet's journey. After a few hasty preparations, among which Abu Bakr did not forget to secure his remaining funds, they crept in the shade of evening through a back window, and escaped unobserved from the southern suburb. Pursuing their way still south, and clambering in the dark over the bare and rugged rocks of the intervening hills, they reached at last the lofty mountain Thaur (distant about an hour and a half's journey from the city) and took refuge in a cave near its summit.[1] Here they

from the 1st to the 9th verses of Sura xxxvi., ending with the words, *and We have covered them so that they shall not see.* Thus he departed without their knowing what passed; and they continued to watch, some say till morning, thinking that the figure on the bed was Mahomet. As light dawned, they found out their mistake and saw that it was Ali. Others say they watched till some one passed and told them that Mahomet had left, when they arose in confusion and shook from their heads the dust which Mahomet had cast upon them.

[1] The following is from Burkhardt: 'JEBEL THOR. About an hour and a half south of Mecca, to the left of the road to the village of Hosseynye, is a lofty mountain of this name, higher it is said than Djebel Nûr. On the summit of it is a cavern, in which Mohammad and his friend Abu Bekr took refuge from the Mekkawys before he fled to Medîna.' But he did not visit the spot, nor did Ali Bey.

In the Begum of Bhopâl's 'Pilgrimage to Mecca' (1870) the mountain is described. The pathway from Mecca is 'excessively rugged and difficult,' the pilgrim being obliged sometimes to crawl over the great rocks on his hands and knees. The entrance to the cave is still preserved on one side, in what is believed to be its original state; and the pilgrim acquires merit by forcing himself with difficulty, as the Prophet must have done, through the aperture, which is, 'not more than 1½ span in breadth;' but a wide passage has been opened out at the other end of the cave. The hills are wild and bare; huge masses of rock lie scattered about; and nothing green is in sight, save occasionally wild thorny bushes, such as the Indian *gookroo*.

rested in security, for the attention of their adversaries would first be fixed upon the country *north* of Mecca and the route to Medîna, which they knew was Mahomet's destination.

Eight or nine years after, Mahomet thus alludes in the Corân to the position of himself and his friend in the cave of mount Thaur :— *The Cave referred to in the Corân.*

> If ye will not assist the Prophet, verily God assisted him when the Unbelievers cast him forth, in company with a Second only; when they two were in the cave alone; when the Prophet said unto his companion :—*Be not cast down, for verily God is with us.* And God caused to descend tranquillity[1] upon him, and strengthened him with Hosts which ye saw not, and made the word of the Unbelievers to be abased; and the word of the Lord, it is exalted; and God is mighty and wise.—*Sura ix.*

The 'sole companion,' or in Arabic phraseology the *Second of the two*, became one of Abu Bakr's most honoured titles. Hassân, the contemporary poet of Medîna, thus sings of him :— *Abu Bakr 'the Second of the two.'*

> And the Second of the two in the glorious Cave, while the foes were searching around, and they two had ascended the mountain;
> And the Prophet of the Lord, they well knew, loved him,— more than all the world; he held no one equal unto him.[2]

Whatever may have been the real peril, Mahomet and his companion felt it to be a moment of jeopardy. Glancing upward at a crevice whence the morning light broke into the cave, Abu Bakr whispered : 'What if one of them were to look beneath him; he might see us under his very feet.' '*Think not thus, Abu Bakr!*' said the Prophet; 'WE ARE TWO, BUT GOD IS IN THE MIDST A THIRD.'[3] *Their alarm.*

---

[1] The word used is *Sekînah*: borrowed from the 'Shekinah' of the Jews; an expression repeatedly used in the Corân.

[2] Mahomet (we are told) once asked Hassân whether he had composed any poetry regarding Abu Bakr; to which the poet answered that he had, and at Mahomet's request repeated the lines in the text. Mahomet was amused, and laughed so heartily as even to show his back teeth; saying: Thou hast spoken truly, O Hassân! It is just as thou hast said.'

[3] The crowd of miracles that cluster about the cave are so well known as not to need repetition here. It will be interesting, however, to note how far they are related by our early authorities.

Wâckidi says that after Mahomet and Abu Bakr entered, a spider came and wove her webs one over the other at the mouth of the cave. The Coreish

Food and
intelligence
conveyed
to them.

Amir ibn Foheirah, the freed man of Abu Bakr, who in company with the other shepherds of Mecca, tended his master's flock, stole unobserved every evening with a few goats to the cave and furnished its inmates with a plentiful supply of milk. Abdallah, Abu Bakr's son, in the same manner nightly brought them food cooked by his sister Asmâ. It was his business also to watch closely by day the progress of events and of opinion at Mecca, and to report the result at night.

Search
after
Mahomet.

Much excitement prevailed in the city, when the disappearance of Mahomet was first noised abroad. The chief of the Coreish went to his house, and finding Ali there, asked where his uncle was. 'I have no knowledge of him,' replied Ali; 'am I his keeper? Ye bade him to quit the city, and he hath quitted.' Then they repaired to the house of Abu Bakr, and questioned his daughter Asmâ.[1] Failing to elicit from her any information, they despatched scouts in all directions, with the view of gaining a clue to the track and destination of the prophet, if not with less innocent instructions. But the precautions of Mahomet and Abu Bakr rendered it a fruitless search. One by one the emissaries returned with no trace of the fugitives; it was believed that, having gained a fair start, they had outstripped pursuit. The people soon reconciled themselves to the idea. They even breathed more freely now that their troubler was gone. The city again was still.

hotly searched after Mahomet in all directions, till they came close up to the entrance. And when they looked, they said one to another: *Spiders' webs are over it from the birth of Mahomet.* So they turned back.

Again: 'God commanded a tree and a spider to cover the Prophet, and two wild pigeons to perch at the entrance of the cave. Then two men from each branch of the Coreish, armed with swords, issued from Mecca for the pursuit. They were now close to Mahomet, when the foremost saw the pigeons, and returned to his companions, saying that he was sure from this that nobody was in the cave. The Prophet heard his words, and blessed the wild pigeons, and made them sacred in the Holy territory.

There are some miraculous stories, but of somewhat later growth, regarding Abu Bakr putting his hand into the crevices of the cave to remove the snakes that might be lurking there, and being unharmed by their venomous bites.

[1] Asmâ relates that after the Prophet went forth, a company of the Coreish with Abu Jahl, came to her house. As they stood at the door, she went forth to them. 'Where is thy father,' said they. 'Truly I know not where he is,' she replied. Upon which Abu Jahl, who was a bad and impudent man, slapped her on the face with such force that one of her ear-rings dropped.'

On the third night, the tidings brought by Abdallah satisfied the refugees that the search had ceased, and the busy curiosity of the first agitation relaxed. The opportunity was come. They could slip away unobserved now. A longer delay might excite suspicion, and the visits of Abdallah and Amir attract attention to the cave. The roads were clear; they might leave at once fearless of pursuit, and travel without apprehension of arrow or dagger from the wayside assassin.

Mahomet and Abu Bakr resolve to quit the cave.

Abdallah received the commission to have all things in readiness for the following evening. The guide was instructed to wander about with the two camels near the summit of mount Thaur. Asmâ prepared food for the journey, and in the dusk carried it to the cave. In the hurry of the moment, she had forgotten the thong for fastening the wallet. So, tearing up her girdle, with one of the pieces she closed the wallet, and with the other fastened it to the camel's gear. From this incident Asmâ is honourably known in Islâm as 'She of the two shreds.'[1] Abu Bakr, not forgetful of his money, safely secreted among his other property a purse of between five and six thousand dirhems.

Preparations for the journey.

The camels were now ready. Mahomet mounted the swifter of the two, Al Caswâ thenceforward his favourite, with the guide; and Abu Bakr having taken his servant Amir ibn Foheira behind him on the other, they started. Descending mount Thaur, and leaving the lower quarter of Mecca a little to the right, they struck off by a track considerably to the left of the common road to Medîna; and, hurrying westward, soon gained the vicinity of the sea-shore nearly opposite Osfân. The day of the flight was the 4th Rabî I. of the first year of the Hegira,[2] or, by the calculations of M. Caussin de Perceval, June 20, A.D. 622.

They start for Medîna June 20, A.D. 622;

---

[1] There is a curious tradition that Abu Bakr's father, Abu Cuhâfa, now so old that he could hardly see, visited his grand-daughters (Asmâ and Ayesha) after Abu Bakr had departed as he thought with all his money, to condole with them on being left without any means. To comfort the old man, Asmâ placed pebbles in a recess and, covering them with a cloth, put his hands upon them to make him believe that it was his son's money which he had left behind; so the old man went away happy.

[2] *Hégira*, 'emigration.' Though referring *par excellence* to the flight of the Prophet, it is also applicable to all his followers who emigrated to Medîna *prior to the capture of Mecca*; and they are hence called *Muhâjirîn, i.e.*, the

And safely escape pursuit.

By morning they had reached the Bedouin encampment of a party of the Bani Khozâa. An Arab lady sat in the door of her tent ready to give food and drink to any travellers that might chance to pass that way. Mahomet and his followers were fatigued and thirsty (for it was the hottest season of the year); and they gladly refreshed themselves with the milk which she offered them in abundance. During the heat of the day, they rested at Codeid. In the evening, thinking they were now at a safe enough distance, they joined the common road. But they had not proceeded far when they met one of the scouts from Mecca returning on horseback. Surâca (for that was his name), seeing that he had small chance of success single-handed against four opponents, offered no opposition; but on the contrary pledged his word that, if permitted to depart in peace, he would not reveal that he had met them. The party proceeded. The Prophet of Arabia was safe.

Tidings reach Mecca of their flight.

The first tidings that reached Mecca of the course actually taken by Mahomet, were brought, two or three days after his flight from the cave, by a traveller from the Khuzâite camp at which he had rested. It was now certain, from his passing there, that he was bound for Medîna.

Ali quits for Medina.

Ali remained at Mecca three days after the departure of Mahomet, appearing every day in public, for the purpose of restoring the property placed by various persons in trust with his uncle. He met with no opposition or annoyance, and leisurely took his departure for Medîna.

Families of Mahomet and Abu Bakr unmolested at Mecca.

The families of Mahomet and Abu Bakr were equally unmolested. Zeinab continued for a time to dwell at Mecca with her unconverted husband. Rockeya had already emigrated with Othmân to Medîna. The other two daughters of Mahomet, Omm Kolthûm and Fâtima, with his wife Sawda, were for some weeks left behind at Mecca.[1] Ayesha his betrothed bride, with the rest of Abu Bakr's family and several other females, likewise remained in Mecca for a time.

Emigrants, or Refugees. We have seen that they commenced to emigrate from the beginning of Moharram (the first month of the *Hegira era*) two months before.

[1] Omm Kolthûm had been married to one of the sons of Abu Lahab, but was now living in her father's house. Zeinab's husband, Abul Aás, was still an unbeliever, and is said to have kept her back at Mecca in confinement. But subsequent events show that there was a strong mutual attachment.

Mahomet and Abu Bakr trusted their respective clans to protect their families from insult.   But no insult or annoyance of any kind was offered by the Coreish.   Nor was the slightest attempt made to detain them ; although it was not unreasonable that they should have been detained as hostages against any offensive movement from Medîna.   These facts lead us to doubt the intense hatred and cruelty which the strong colouring of tradition at this period attributes to the Coreish.

Thus ends the first great stage of the Prophet's life.   The next scene opens at Medîna.

Forbearance of Coreish.

SUPPLEMENT TO CHAPTER VII.

RELATION OF ISLÂM TO CHRISTIANITY. TEACHING OF MAHOMET
DURING THE LAST THREE YEARS AT MECCA. EFFECT PRODUCED
BY HIS PREACHING THERE.

Suras re-
vealed dur-
ing last
three years
at Mecca.

DURING the last three years of Mahomet's residence at Mecca
about thirty new Suras of the Corân appeared. Some of the
later are very long, extending over as many as fifteen to twenty
pages; and we find in them many passages subsequently revealed
at Medîna, but inserted in the Meccan Suras where they now
stand.[1] Before proceeding to a brief description of these Suras
and the teaching they contain, I propose to pause for a little and
describe

The Relation of Islâm to Christianity.

Relation of
Islâm to
Chris-
tianity.

It has been already said that in the portions of the Corân
revealed before the tenth year of the mission of Mahomet, that is
up to three years preceding his flight to Medîna, we find few
notices of Christianity or the Christian Scriptures. In the Suras,
however, of the period now under consideration, frequent mention
of Christianity begins to appear. Indeed, the approach now
made by Mahomet to our holy faith never afterwards became
closer; nor did his acquaintance with it enlarge, or his views
materially alter. It may, therefore, be not inappropriate here
to review the relation of Islâm to Christianity; and, in so doing,
to extend the enquiry to the entire period of the Prophet's life.

Notices of
Chris-
tianity in
Corân
few and
scattered.

Though Christians and the Messiah are frequently referred
to throughout the Corân by name, yet there are but few sketches
at any length either of the history or doctrines of the Gospel; so
few, indeed, that it will be possible (and I doubt not also interesting) to enumerate them all.

Earliest
and fullest
account of
the Gospel
narrative.

The following, which is the fullest and earliest account of the
Gospel narrative, was produced by Mahomet shortly after his
return from Tâyif. From its subject the Sura is entitled MARY
(Maryam), and opens thus :—

[1] The manner in which the Corân was compiled will be explained in an
Excursus at the close of the volume.

A Commemoration of the mercy of the Lord unto his servant ZACHARIAS;—
When he called upon his Lord with a secret invocation,
He said;—O Lord! as for me, my bones are decrepit, and my head
    white with hoar hair.
And I have never prayed unto thee, O Lord! unheard.
Verily, I fear my kinsmen after me; and my wife is barren.
Wherefore grant unto me from thyself a successor;
Who shall be my heir, and an heir of the family of Jacob; and make him,
    oh Lord! well pleasing.
O ZACHARIAS! We bring thee good tidings of a son, whose name shall
    be John;
We have not made any to be called by that name before.
He said;—O Lord! whence shall there be a son unto me, since my wife
    is barren, and I truly have reached the imbecility of old age?
The Angel said:—So shall it be. Thus saith thy Lord,—It is easy unto
    me; for verily I created thee heretofore when thou wast nothing.
He said;—Lord! give me a sign. The angel said;—This is thy sign; thou
    shalt not speak unto any for three nights, though sound in health.
And he went forth unto his people from the chamber, and he motioned
    unto them that they should praise God in the morning and even-
    ing.
O John! Take the Book (of the Law) with power; and We gave him
    wisdom as a child,
And compassion from us, and purity; and he was virtuous, and dutiful
    unto his parents; he was not overbearing nor rebellious.
Peace be on him the day he was born, and the day he shall die, and the
    day he shall be raised to life!
And make mention in the Book (the Corân) of Mary, when she with-
    drew from her people into an eastern place;
And took a curtain withal to hide herself from them.
And we sent unto her OUR SPIRIT, and he appeared unto her a perfect
    man,
She said;—I seek refuge in the Merciful from thee, if thou fearest God!
He said;—Nay, verily, I am a messenger of thy Lord sent to give unto
    thee a virtuous son.
She said;—How shall there be to me a son, and a man hath not touched
    me, and I am not unchaste.
He said;—So shall it be. Thus saith thy Lord;—It is easy with me;
    and we shall make him a sign unto mankind, and a mercy from
    us, for it is a thing decreed.
And she conceived him, and withdrew with him (*in the womb*) unto a
    distant place.
And the pains of labour came upon her by the trunk of a palm tree;
She said,—Would that I had died before this, and been forgotten out of
    mind!
And there cried one from below her;—Grieve not!—verily thy Lord hath
    provided beneath thee a fountain:—
And shake unto thee the root of the palm tree; it will drop upon thee
    ripe dates, ready plucked.
Wherefore eat and drink, and be comforted; and if thou seest any man,
Say,—Verily I have vowed unto the Merciful a fast, and I will not speak
    to any man this day.

And she came with the child unto her people, carrying him ; they said ;
O MARY ! verily thou hast done a strange thing :
O sister of Aaron ! thy father was not a wicked man, nor was thy
mother unchaste.
And she motioned to the child.   They said ;—How shall we speak with
him that is an infant in the cradle ?
He (*the child*) said ; Verily I am the servant of God; He hath given me
the Book, and made me a Prophet ;
And made me blessed wheresoever I may be, and hath commanded me
(*to observe*) prayer and almsgiving while I remain alive ;
And made me dutiful to my mother, and not overbearing nor wretched :—
Peace be on me the day I was born, and the day I shall die, and the day
I shall be raised alive !
This is JESUS, the Word of truth, concerning whom they are in doubt.
It is not for God to take unto him a Son :—glory be to him !
When he hath decreed a matter, he only saith unto it BE and it
shall be.

Another detailed account of Christ's birth.

The births of John and of Jesus are once again related, as well as the birth of the Virgin Mary, in a passage (Sura iii.) delivered at Medîna only a few years before the death of Mahomet, on the occasion of an embassy (which will be noticed shortly) from the Christian tribe of Najrân.

Statements regarding the life of Christ.

Of the *life* of Christ the statements are fabulous and altogether scant and paltry ; and it is remarkable that they belong solely to the later years of Mahomet's life.   The object of the mission of Jesus to the Jews was to confirm their Scriptures, to modify and lighten some of the burdens of the Mosaical law, and to recall them to the service of God.   His miracles are thus described :—

Sura v.

On a certain day shall God assemble the Apostles, and say ; What answer was made by the people unto you ?   They shall say ;—We know not, verily Thou art the Knower of secrets.

Then shall God say ;—O JESUS ! Son of Mary ! call to mind my grace upon thee and upon thy MOTHER, when I strengthened thee with the HOLY SPIRIT, that thou shouldest speak with men in the cradle, and in mature life ;—and when I taught thee the Scripture and Wisdom, and the Law and the Gospel ;—and when thou formedst of clay like unto the figure of a bird by My permission ;—and thou blewest thereupon and it became a bird by My permission ;   and thou didst heal the blind and the leper by My permission ;—and when thou didst raise the dead by My permission ;[1] and when I held back the children of Israel from thee at the time thou shewedst unto them evident signs, and the unbelievers among them said, Verily this is nought but manifest sorcery.

And remember when I spake by inspiration to the Apostles of JESUS, saying,—Believe on Me, and on my Apostle.   They said,—We believe ; bear thou witness that we are Moslems (*i.e.* surrendered to God).

---

[1] These miracles are repeated in Sura iii., where Jesus is represented as adding: 'And I will tell unto you what ye eat, and what ye store in your houses,' *i.e.* as a proof of his knowledge of the invisible.

When the Apostles of JESUS said,—O JESUS, Son of MARY! is thy Lord able to cause a Table to descend upon us from Heaven? He said,—Fear God; if ye be faithful. They said,—We desire that we may eat therefrom, and that our hearts be set at ease, and that we may know that thou verily hast spoken unto us the truth, and that we may be witnesses thereof. Then spake JESUS, Son of MARY,—O God our Lord! send down unto us a Table from Heaven, that it may be unto us a Feast day [1] unto the first of us and unto the last of us, and a sign from Thee; and nourish us, for Thou art the best of nourishers. And God said,—Verily I will send it down unto you; and whoever after that shall disbelieve amongst you; surely I will torment him with a torment wherewith I shall not torment any other creature.

And when God shall say,—O JESUS, Son of MARY! didst thou speak unto mankind saying,—Take me and my mother for two Gods besides the Lord? He shall say,—Glory be to Thee! it is not for me to say that which I know to be not the Truth; if I had said that, verily Thou wouldest have known it. Thou knowest that which is in me, but I know not what is in Thee; verily Thou art the Knower of secrets. I spake not unto them aught but what Thou commandest me, saying,—Worship God, my Lord and your Lord. And I was a witness unto them whilst I continued amongst them; and since Thou hast taken me away, thou hast Thyself been their keeper, and Thou art a witness over all things. If Thou punish them, verily they are thy servants; and if Thou have mercy upon them, verily Thou art the GLORIOUS, the WISE!

God will answer,—This is a day on which their truthfulness shall profit the truthful. They shall have gardens with rivulets flowing through them, and remain therein for ever. God is well pleased with them, and they are well pleased with Him. That shall be a great felicity!

Allusion to the Lord's Supper.

This passage is remarkable as affording in the supernatural table which descended from heaven, a possible allusion—the only one traceable in the Corân—to the Lord's Supper. The tale is probably founded on some misapprehended tradition regarding 'the *Table* of the Lord.'[2]

Jesus not crucified, but ascended to Heaven.

To complete the miserably deficient and garbled outline, it remains only to add that Jesus escaped the machinations of the Jews, and was taken up alive to heaven. In a passage aimed at his Jewish enemies, Mahomet thus upbraids their rebellious fore-fathers:—

[1] An *Eed* or religious festival recurring periodically, referring apparently to the institution of the Lord's Supper as a feast to be perpetually observed.

[2] The prolific fancy of the Traditionists and Commentators has created a host of miraculous accompaniments to this table:—fruit from the trees of Paradise, bread, meat, with fish which, though broiled, were still alive, and which for the convenience of the guests threw aside their scales and bones! The poor, the lame, and the wretched, were invited to the feast, which lasted forty days. The commentators probably confused the Lord's Supper with the feeding by Jesus of the multitudes.

Sura iv.

And for their unbelief; and for their having spoken against Mary a grievous calumny; and for their saying,—*Verily we have killed the Messiah,* JESUS, son of MARY, the Apostle of God. And they killed him not, neither did they crucify him, but he was simulated (in the person of another) unto them. And verily they that have differed about him, are in doubt concerning this thing. They have no knowledge regarding it, but follow only a conjecture. And they slew him not, certainly. But God raised him up unto Himself; and God is the GLORIOUS, the WISE! And of the People of the Book shall every one believe in him before his death, and in the day of Judgment he will be a witness against them.[1]

Meceans objected that if Jesus was worshipped why not their deities also.

In addressing the idolaters of Mecca, Mahomet appealed to the ministry and preaching of Jesus and his rejection by his people, as he was wont to appeal to the history of other prophets, as an apt analogy to his own case, and in support of his mission. His adversaries retorted that, if Jesus, who appeared in human form, was worshipped by his followers, there could be nothing absurd (as he would insist) in their praying through images, the representatives of heavenly powers, to God; and that thus his whole argument fell to the ground. The reply, as usual, comes from above:—

Mahomet replies that Jesus was but a servant. Sura xliii.

When JESUS, Son of MARY, was proposed as an example, lo, thy people shouted unto thee,
And said, What! Are our own gods better, or he?
They have proposed this unto thee only as a cause of dispute;
Yea, they are a contentious people!
Verily he was no other than a servant, to whom We were gracious, and We made him an example unto the children of Israel:—
(And if We pleased We could make from amongst yourselves Angels to succeed you upon earth:)
And verily he shall be for a sign of the last hour. Wherefore doubt not thereof, and follow Me; this is the right way.
And let not Satan obstruct you, for he is your manifest enemy.

Denies divine Sonship of Jesus; and Trinity.

This was in fact the only position which Mahomet could now consistently fall back upon; and it was ever after carefully maintained. Some terms of veneration, in use among Christians, are indeed applied to Jesus, as 'the WORD of God,' and 'His SPIRIT which he breathed into Mary.' But the divine Sonship is steadfastly denied. The worship of Jesus by the Christians is placed in the same category as the supposed worship of Ezra by the Jews; and, in one place, the doctrine of the Trinity is expressly reprobated. It is a Medîna Sura:—

Sura iv.

Ye people of the Book! Commit not extravagancies in your religion; and speak not of God aught but the truth. For verily the Messiah,

---

[1] 'The people of the Book,' *i.e.*, Jews as well as Christians. There is a passage (Sura iii. 54) which would seem to imply the death of Jesus when on earth, but it is explained away by the commentators.

JESUS, Son of MARY, is an Apostle of God, and his WORD which he placed in Mary, and a Spirit from him. Wherefore believe in God, and in the Apostles; and say not, *There are Three.* Refrain: it will be well for you. Verily the Lord is one God. Glory be to Him! far be it from him, that there should be to Him a Son. To Him belongeth whatsoever is in the Heavens and in the earth; and He is a sufficient patron. The Messiah disdaineth not to be a servant of God; neither the Cherubim that draw nigh unto Him.

It may well be doubted whether Mahomet ever understood the real doctrines of Christianity. The few passing observations regarding our faith to be found in the Corân, commenced at a period when his system was already, in great part, matured; and they were founded on information not only deficient but deceptive. The whole of his historical knowledge[1] (for whatever he knew it was his practice to embody in his Revelation) is contained in the few extracts now before the reader; and this knowledge, whether regarded in its own meagre and apocryphal outlines, or compared with his familiar acquaintance with Jewish scripture and tradition, shows that the sources from which he derived his Christian information were singularly barren and defective. The Sacrament of baptism is not even alluded to; and, if there be an allusion to the Eucharist, we have seen it to be utterly disfigured, and well nigh lost in fable. The great doctrine of redemption through the death of Christ was apparently unknown (for if it had been known and rejected, it would doubtless, like other alleged errors, have been combated in the Corân), and his very crucifixion was denied.

Sources of Christian information imperfect and deceptive.

We do not find a single ceremony or doctrine of Islâm in the smallest degree moulded, or even tinged, by the peculiar tenets of Christianity: while, on the contrary, Judaism has given its colour to the whole system, and lent to it the shape and type, if not the actual substance, of many ordinances.

Christianity had little real influence on Islâm;

But although Christianity is thus so remote from Islâm as to have had practically no influence in the formation of its creed and ritual, yet in the *theory* of Mahomet's system it occupies a place equal, if not superior, to that of Judaism. To understand this we must take a brief review of the development of the system itself.

Yet theoretically stood equal if not superior to Judaism.

[1] The only trace of acquaintance with the period subsequent to the Ascension and the spread of Christianity, is the story (Sura xxxvi.) of the three Apostles (one of whom is supposed to have been Peter) who went to Antioch, and of a convert suffering martyrdom there. The tale of the seven Sleepers, who, with their dog, slumbered 309 years, and then awakening found to their astonishment the whole idolatrous world become Christian, can hardly be classed under this head. It will be found, with abundance of childish romance and fiction, in Sura xviii. Both Suras belong to the late Meccan period.

Growth of
Mahomet's
teaching.

At the outset of his ministry Mahomet professed no distinct relation with any previous religion, except perhaps with the purer element in the national worship said to have been derived from Abraham, though now grievously overlaid with idolatry and superstition. His mission was to recall the Arabs to the service of the true God and belief in ' the day of reckoning.'

Corân at
first held
to be
simply
auxiliary
of previous
Scriptures.

In process of time he gained some acquaintance with the existing Scriptures of the Jews and Christians, and the system founded thereon. The new revelation for Arabia was now announced as concurrent with the previous ' Books.' The Corân was described as being mainly an attestation, in the Arabic tongue and intended for the people of Mecca and its neighbourhood, of the preceding Scriptures. It was strictly auxiliary in its object and local in its action. From the attacks of the idolaters Mahomet took shelter under the authority of the sacred Books of the Jews and Christians,—an authority admitted in some measure even by his adversaries. When his own work was condemned as a ' forgery ' and an ' antiquated tale,' the most common and the most effective retort was : ' Nay, but it is a confirmation of the preceding Revelation, and a warning in simple Arabic to the people of the land.' The number and the solemnity of such asseverations secured the confidence, or at least the neutrality, of both Jews and Christians.

But gradu
ally ac-
quires a
superior
and super-
seding
character ;

But the system of Mahomet could not stop here. Was he not an Apostle, equally inspired with his predecessors ? Was he not foretold, as the prophet that should arise by Moses in the Pentateuch, and in the Gospel by Jesus ? If he was indeed the last of the Apostles would not the catholic faith as now moulded by him remain permanent to the end of time ? These conclusions were fast ripening in the mind of Mahomet ; and their effect was to make the Corân rise superior in authority over both the Old Testament and the New. Not that he ever held it to be superior *in kind* to either. All three—the Corân, the Law, and the Gospel

As the
latest reve-
lation of
God's will.

—are spoken of indifferently as ' the Word of God,' and the belief in them inculcated equally on pain of hell fire.[1] But the Corân was the *latest* revelation ; and, in so far as it pleased the

[1] The New Testament is called in the Corân *Injîl* (Evangelium), and described as a revelation *given by God to Jesus*. It is evident that by ' the Gospel ' Mahomet meant the sacred Scriptures in common use amongst the Christians of the day. His ignorance may have led him to suppose that those Scriptures were ' given ' to Jesus ; or he may perhaps have intended only that the doctrines of the Gospel were revealed by God to Jesus, and by him taught to the Apostles who afterwards recorded them. However this may be, the fact is in nowise affected, that Mahomet, when he enforced observance of ' the Gospel ' on Christians, meant the canon of Scripture at the time being received among them.

Almighty to modify his preceding commands, it must be paramount.

In this latter phase again there are two stages. Mahomet did not at once substitute the Corân for the previous Scriptures. The Jew was still to follow the Law; and in addition he was to believe also in the New Testament and in the mission of Jesus. The Christian was to hold fast by his Gospel. But both Jew and Christian were to admit, as co-ordinate with their own Prophets and Scriptures, the apostleship of Mahomet and the authority of the Corân. The necessity, indeed, of conforming to their respective Revelations is urged upon Jews and Christians in the strongest terms. The Jews of Medîna are repeatedly summoned ' to judge by the Book,' that is by the Old Testament; and are warned against the danger of accepting a part only of God's word, and rejecting a part. The following passages inculcate a similar duty on both Jews and Christians:—

Two stages. 1. Old Testament and Gospel enjoined upon Jews and Christians respectively.

SAY, Oh, ye people of the Book! ye do not stand upon any sure ground until ye set up both the Law [1] and the Gospel, as well as that which hath been sent down unto you from your Lord (*i.e.* the Corân).

Sura v.

And how will they (the Jews of Medîna) make thee (Mahomet) their judge, since they have already by them the Law, wherein is the command of God, and have not obeyed it! They will surely turn their backs after that; and they are not believers.

Verily We have sent down the Old Testament, wherein are direction and light. The Prophets that submitted themselves to God judged thereby the Jews: and the Doctors and Priests did likewise, in accordance with that portion of the Book of God which We committed to their charge; and they were witnesses thereof. Wherefore fear not men, but fear Me; and sell not the signs of God for a small price. AND WHOSOEVER DOTH NOT JUDGE BY THAT WHICH GOD HATH REVEALED, VERILY THEY ARE THE UNBELIEVERS (*Kâfirs*). And We have written therein for them;—Verily life for life, and eye for eye, and nose for nose, and ear for ear, tooth for tooth, and for wounding retaliation: and he that remitteth the same as alms, it is an atonement for him. AND WHOSOEVER JUDGETH NOT BY THAT WHICH GOD HATH REVEALED, THEY ARE THE TRANSGRESSORS.

And We caused JESUS, the Son of MARY, to follow in their footsteps, attesting the Scripture, viz., the Law which preceded him. And We gave him the Gospel wherein are guidance and light, attesting the Law which precedeth it, a direction and an admonition to the pious:—and that the people of the Gospel (Christians) may judge according to that which God hath revealed therein. AND WHOSOEVER DOTH NOT JUDGE ACCORDING TO THAT WHICH GOD HATH REVEALED, THEY ARE THE WICKED ONES.

[1] 'The Towrât,' which, as used in the Corân, sometimes signifies the Pentateuch only, sometimes the entire Scriptures of the Old Testament. According to the context of this and the following passages, the latter meaning is intended.

And We have revealed unto thee the Book (Corân) in truth, attesting the Scripture which precedeth it, and a custodian (or witness) thereof. Wherefore judge between them in accordance with what God hath revealed, and follow not their vain desires away from that which hath been given unto thee.

To every one have We given a law and a way. And if God had pleased, He had made you all one People. But (*He hath done otherwise*) that He might try you in that which he hath severally given unto you. Wherefore press forward in good works. Unto God shall ye all return, and He will declare unto you that concerning which ye disagree.

Judge therefore between them according to what God hath revealed, and follow not their desires, and beware of them lest they tempt thee (*i.e.* Mahomet) aside from a part of that which God hath revealed unto thee.

Thus the former revelations were to be believed in collectively as the word of God by all the faithful of whatever sect. The Old and New Testaments were further to be followed implicitly, the former by the Jews, the latter by the Christians, and both were to be observed by Mahomet himself when determining their respective disputes. In contested and doubtful points, the Corân was to be for all mankind the conclusive oracle.

Grand catholic faith ;—the faith of Abraham.

In conformity with this expansive system, we find that at a period long anterior to the Hegira, Mahomet propounded in the Corân the doctrine that a prophet had been sent to every people, and that a grand catholic faith had pervaded all ages and revelations—a faith which, in its purest form, had been held by the patriarch Abraham. This primitive religion, varying at each dispensation only in accidental rites, comprised, as its essential features, belief in the one true God, rejection of idolatry and of the worship of mediators as sharers in the power and glory of the Deity, and implicit surrender of the will to God. Such surrender is termed ' Islâm ; ' and hence Abraham is called ' the first of Moslems.' To this original Islâm it was now the mission of Mahomet to recall *all mankind*.

Perverted in the course of ages.

Each successive dispensation had been abused by its votaries who had in the course of time turned aside from the catholic element that formed its groundwork. They had magnified or misinterpreted rites intended to be but ancillary and external ; by perverting doctrines, they had turned the gift into a curse. They had fallen into a thousand sects, ' each rejoicing in its own opinions,' and fencing itself round with intolerance and hatred.

Mahomet the final Restorer.

Amidst the contending factions, truth might be discovered by the earnest enquirer, but by steps now difficult and uncertain. The Jew denounced the Christian, and the Christian the Jew. Some worshipped not only Jesus but his mother also ; others held both to be mere creatures. From the labyrinth of confusion and error it pleased the Almighty once again to deliver mankind.

Mahomet was the Apostle of this grand and final mission, and, amid the clash of opposing authorities, his judgment was to be heard unquestioned and supreme. Thus in a passage revealed at Mecca :—

He hath ordained unto you the faith which he commanded unto Noah ; and which We have revealed unto thee, and which We commanded Abraham and Moses and Jesus ; saying, Set up the faith and fall not into dissension.

And they fell not into dissension until after the knowledge (of divine revelation) had come unto them, out of enmity among themselves ; and if the Word from thy Lord had not gone forth (respiting them) unto a set time, the matter had been decided between them. And verily they that have inherited the Book after them are in a perplexing doubt regarding the same.

Wherefore call them thereto (*i.e.* unto the catholic Faith) and be steadfast as thou hast been commanded, and follow not their desires ; and say,—I believe in all the Scriptures which God hath revealed ; and I am commanded to do justice between you. God is our Lord and your Lord. To us will be reckoned our works, and to you your works. There is no ground of difference or contention between us and you.

Sura xlii.

Thus in the growth of Mahomet's opinions there was an intermediate stage in which salvation was not confined to Islâm, but might be obtained by any righteous man, whatever his religion, provided that he was only pure from idolatry.

Salvation not confined to Islâm.

But in the final development of his system, Mahomet makes the Corân to rise triumphant over both the Law and the Gospel, and casts them unheeded into the shade. This, however, was not the result of any express teaching, but rather the necessary though tacit outcome of the system. The popular impression which would attribute to Mahomet either a formal cancelment of the Jewish and Christian Scriptures, or imputations against their genuineness and authority, is entirely mistaken. No expression regarding either the Jewish or Christian Scriptures ever escaped the lips of Mahomet, other than of implicit reverence.[1]

2. Corân entirely supersedes previous Revelation ;

It was the opposition of the Jews and estrangement of the Christians, as well as the martial supremacy of Islâm, that imperceptibly but inevitably led to the universal and exclusive authority of Mahomet and the Corân. The change by which the Prophet dispensed with previous Revelations was made in silence.

Which towards the close of his career is hardly alluded to.

[1] In a treatise by the Author, entitled *The Testimony borne by the Corân to the Jewish and Christian Scriptures*, it is shown that unequivocal testimony is borne by the Corân to the Jewish and Christian Scriptures as current in the time of Mahomet ; that the evidence extends equally to their genuineness and authority ; and that there is not a hint anywhere throughout the Corân of their cancelment or interpolation.

In the concluding as in the earliest days of his mission, Mahomet hardly ever refers to the former Scriptures. His scheme was now complete, and rested upon other pillars. The steps by which he had ascended were left far beneath, forgotten and uncared for.

In its final development Islâm rapidly diverged from the the Bible.

In the later years of the Prophet, Islâm diverged rapidly from all sympathy with the Bible. An appeal to previous revelation would now have proved embarrassing, and silence was perhaps in some degree intentional. Whatever effect the doctrines of Christianity properly understood might have had on Mahomet while yet enquiring and moulding for himself a creed, it is evident that long before the final settlement of Islâm his system had crystallised into a form of which it was impossible that any new influences could produce material alteration. No argument was tolerated now. Mahomet was the Prophet of God, and his word was law. Opposing doctrine must vanish before the divine command.

Hostile declarations against Jews and Christians.

The exclusive and intolerant position finally assumed by Islâm is sufficiently manifest in the ban issued by Mahomet at his last pilgrimage against Jews and Christians, who were for ever debarred the sacred rites and holy precincts of the Káaba; and by the divine command to war against them until, in confession of the supremacy of Islâm, they should consent to the payment of tribute.

Treaties with Christian tribes.

The treatment of Christianity by Mahomet after his acquisition of political power may be illustrated by the engagements which he entered into with Christian tribes. The following relates to the important Christian settlement of Najrân. The Prophet we are told, wrote to the bishop, priests, and monks, saying that everything small and great should continue as it then stood, in their churches, their services, and their monasteries. ' The pledge of God and of his Prophet was given that no bishop should be removed from his bishopric, nor any monk from his monastery, nor any priest from his priesthood; that their authority and rights should not be altered, nor anything that was customary amongst them;—so long as they conducted themselves peaceably and uprightly. They would not be burdened with oppression, neither should they oppress.'

Embassy from the Christians of Najrân.

The embassy of this people to Medîna is in itself curious, and has an additional interest from being referred to in the Corân. A deputation of fourteen chief men from Najrân repaired to Mahomet in the tenth year of the Hegira. Among them was Abd al Masîh of the Bani Kinda, their chief, and Abd al Hârith their bishop. On reaching Medîna, they entered the mosque, and prayed turning towards the east. Then Mahomet called them;

but when they came, the Prophet turned away and would not speak with them, because of their silken attire; for they were clothed in fine raiment lined with silk. So they departed that day. In the morning they came again in their monastic dress, and saluted Mahomet. He now returned their salutation, and invited them to accept Islâm, but they refused; and words and disputation increased between them. Then Mahomet recited to them passages from the Corân, and said: 'If ye deny that which I say unto you, *Come let us curse each the other*;' so they went away to consider the matter. On the morrow Abd al Masîh, with two of the chief men, came to Mahomet and said: ' We have determined that we shall not curse with thee; wherefore command regarding us whatsoever thou wilt, we will give it; and we will enter into treaty with thee.' So he made a treaty with them and they returned to their cities.[1]

Mahomet challenges them to curse.

The incident is thus alluded to in the Corân:—

Affair described in the Corân. Sura iii.

Verily, the analogy of Jesus is, with God, like unto the analogy of Adam. He created him out of the dust; then he said unto him BE, and he was. This is the truth from thy Lord: wherefore be not thou amongst the Doubters.

And whosoever shall dispute with thee therein, after that the true knowledge hath come unto thee; say—*Come let us call out* (the names) *of our sons and your sons, of our wives and your wives, of ourselves and yourselves; then let us curse one the other, and lay the curse of God upon those that lie!*

Verily this is a true exposition. There is no God but the Lord, and verily God is mighty and wise. And if they turn back, verily God is acquainted with the evil doers.

SAY:—Oh ye people of the Book! come unto a just judgment

---

[1] The subsequent history of the Christians of Najrân is thus traced by Wâckidi. They continued in possession of their lands and rights under the above treaty, during the rest of Mahomet's life and the whole of Abu Bakr's Caliphate. Then they were accused of taking usury, and Omar expelled them from the land, and wrote as follows:—

'The despatch of OMAR, the Commander of the Faithful, to the people of Najrân. Whosoever of them emigrates is under the guarantee of God. No Moslem shall injure them;—to fulfil that which Mahomet and Abu Bakr wrote unto them.

'Now to whomsoever of the chiefs of Syria and Irâc they may repair, let such chiefs allot them lands, and whatever they cultivate therefrom shall be theirs; it is an exchange for their own lands. None shall injure or maltreat them; Moslems shall assist them against oppressors. Their tribute is remitted for two years. They will not be troubled except for evil deeds.'

Some of them alighted in Irâc, and settled at Najrânia (so called after them) near to Cufa. That the offence of usury is alleged as the reason of their expulsion disproves the common tradition that a command was given by Mahomet on his death-bed for the Peninsula to be swept clear of all other religions but Islâm.

between us and yourselves, *That we shall not worship aught but God, and that we shall not associate any with Him, nor shall we take any of us the other for lords besides God.* And if they turn back, then bear witness, saying;—Verily, we are the true Believers.

Proof of Mahomet's earnestness.

It was surely a strange manner of settling the question between Islâm and the Christian faith, which the Arabian Prophet here proposed, and we have no reason to be ashamed of the Christian embassy for declining it. Still we cannot but see in this passage the earnestness of Mahomet's belief, and his conviction that a spiritual illumination had been vouchsafed to him, bringing with it knowledge and certainty where to the Christian, as he conceived, all was speculation and conjecture.

Embassy of the Bani Taghlib.

Another Christian embassy was received from the Bani Taghlib. ' It was formed of sixteen men, some Moslems and some Christians. The latter wore crosses of gold. The Prophet made terms with the Christians, stipulating that they might themselves continue in the profession of their religion, but that they *should not baptize their children* in the Christian faith.'

Christianity allowed to exist on sufferance.

These narratives clearly show that the conditions upon which, at the last, Mahomet permitted Christianity to exist were those of sufferance. Christianity, indeed, was less obnoxious to him than Judaism because he did not experience from it such persevering and active hostility. The clergy and monks are even spoken of in expressions of comparative praise.[1] But, not the less, the object of Mahomet was entirely to *supersede* Christianity as well as Judaism, and the professors of both were subjected to an equally humiliating tribute.

Review.

The stealthy progress by which this end was reached has now, I trust, been made apparent. At the beginning Mahomet confirmed the former Scriptures without qualification or reserve. He next asserted for his own Revelation a concurrent authority, and by degrees a superseding and dispensing power. And finally, though he never imputed error to the Bible itself, or (while ceasing to appeal with his former frequency to its evidence) failed to speak of it with veneration, yet he not only himself rejected the dogmas peculiar to Christianity, but demanded their rejection by

[1] ' And We caused Jesus, son of Mary, to succeed them, and We put into the hearts of those that followed him compassion and mercy; and the monastic state,—they framed it for themselves (We did not command it unto them) simply out of a desire to please God.'— *Sura* lvii.

So also Sura v.: ' And thou wilt find the most inclined amongst them to the Believers, those who profess Christianity;—This because there are amongst them Clergy and Monks, and they are not proud; and when they hear that which hath been revealed unto the Prophet, thou shalt see their eyes flow with tears, because of what they recognise therein of the truth,' &c.

his Christian followers, on the simple ground of his own inspiration. Assuming, perhaps, that the former Scriptures could not be at variance with the mind of God as now revealed, he did not care to verify his conclusions by a reference to 'the Book' which he himself admitted to be a 'light and a guide.' Possibly, latent consciousness of the weakness of his position rendered him unwilling to face the difficulty. His course was guided here, as at so many other points, by an inexplicable combination of earnest conviction and uneasy questioning, if not of actual though unperceived self-deception. He was sure as to his object, and the means could not be wrong.

From whence, we may now enquire, did Mahomet gain this meagre and deceptive view of Christianity? *Knowledge whence derived?*

A significant feature in the teaching of the Corân is that Jesus was not crucified; but one resembling Jesus, and mistaken by the Jews for him. This is alleged not in contradiction of the Christians, but *in opposition to the Jews*, who gloried in the assertion that Jesus had been put to death by their nation. Hence it would almost seem that Mahomet believed his teaching on this head to accord with that of the Church; and that he really was ignorant of the fundamental doctrine of the Christian faith, redemption through the death of Christ. *Misleading teaching as to crucifixion.*

The singular correspondence between the allusions to the crucifixion in the Corân and the wild speculations of certain early heretics, has led some to conjecture that Mahomet acquired his notions of Christianity from a Gnostic source. But Gnosticism had disappeared from Egypt before the sixth century, and there is no reason for supposing that it had at any time gained footing in Arabia. Besides, there is no affinity between the supernaturalism of the Gnostics and Docetæ, and the rationalism of the Corân. According to the former, the Deity must be removed far from the gross contact of evil matter; and the æon Christ, which alighted upon Jesus at his baptism, must ascend to its native regions before the crucifixion. With Mahomet, Jesus Christ was a mere man, wonderfully born indeed, but still an ordinary man; a servant of the Almighty, as others had been before him. But although there is no ground for believing that Gnostic doctrines were taught to Mahomet, yet some of the strange fancies of those heretics preserved in Syrian tradition may have come to the ears of his informants (the chief of whom, even on Christian topics, seem to have been Jews, unable probably to distinguish heretical fable from Christian doctrine), and have been by them adopted as a likely and convenient mode of explaining away that which formed the great barrier between Jews and Christians. The *Connection of Mahomet's teaching with Gnosticism.*

Denial of crucifixion a compromise between Jews and Christians. Israelite would have less antipathy to the catholic faith of Islâm and the recognition of the mission of Jesus, if allowed to believe that Christians as well as Jews had been in error; that his people had not, in fact, put Jesus the promised Messiah to a shameful death; but that, like Enoch and Elijah, he had been received up into heaven. 'Christ *crucified*' was still, as in the days of Paul, 'the stumbling-block' of the Jews. But thus the stumbling-block would be removed: and without offence to his national pride, the Jew might confess his belief in an emasculated Christianity. It was a compromise that might readily approve itself to a Jewish mind already unsettled by the prophetic claims of Mahomet.

Apocryphal gospels not accessible to Mahomet. By some again it has been attempted to trace the Christian element in the Corân to certain apocryphal gospels supposed to have been within the reach of Mahomet. But, though some few of its details do coincide with these spurious writings, its statements as a rule in no wise correspond.[1] Whereas, had there been a ready access to such books, we cannot doubt that Mahomet would (as in the case of Jewish history and legend) have borrowed largely from them.

Christian tradition in Arabia insufficient. Others believe that Mahomet acquired his knowledge from no written source, but from Christian tradition as then subsisting among the people of Arabia. As his sole source of information, the indigenous tradition of Arabia is altogether insufficient to account for the knowledge of Mahomet. There is no ground for believing that either at Mecca or Medîna there existed elements of Christian tradition from which could have been framed a narrative agreeing, as that of the Corân does in many particulars and even in several of its expressions, with the Gospels genuine and apocryphal, while in others it follows if not outstrips the popular legend.

Syrian tradition likeliest source of Mahomet's knowledge. But tradition, quite sufficient for this end, survived in the southern confines of Syria, and from thence it no doubt reached Mahomet mainly through a Jewish medium. The general outline of Christian story, as we find it in the Corân, having a few salient points in accordance with the Gospel and the rest filled up with wild marvels, is just such as we might expect an enquiring Jew to learn from the traditions current amongst the ignorant classes in Judea and the Christian tribes of lower Syria. Some-

---

[1] The 'Gospel of Barnabas' is of course excepted, because it is the modern work of a Christian convert to Islâm. 'Aber es ist gewiss, dass diess Evangelium das Werk eines Betrügers ist, der erst lange nach Mahommed, vielleicht in Italien selbst, lebte, und sich bemühte, den Erzählungen des Koran und der Mohammedanischen Schriftsteller durch eine angeblich Christliche Unterlage mehr Ansehen und Glaubwürdigkeit, zu verschaffen.'— *Gerock.*

thing, too, might be learned from the Christian slaves of Mecca; but these had generally been carried off in boyhood, and would remember little more than a few scriptural stories, with perhaps some fragments of their creed. Either the Jew or the Christian may also have heard the opening of the Gospel of Luke, and communicated to Mahomet the outline of the births of John and Jesus, as we find them in the Corân. It is also *possible* that some one may have repeated to Mahomet from memory, or read to him from a manuscript, the verses of the Gospel containing these details;—but this is mere conjecture.[1]

Mahomet's confused notions of the Trinity and of the Holy Ghost, seem most naturally to have been received through a Jewish informant himself imperfectly acquainted with the subject. It is not very apparent, from the few indistinct notices in the Corân, what Mahomet believed the Christian doctrine of the Trinity to be. In a passage already quoted, the Christians are reprobated for 'taking Jesus and his Mother for two Gods besides the Lord.' It is hence concluded that the Trinity of the Corân was composed of the Father, Mary, and Jesus. Such may have been the case, but it is not certain. The service of Mary had long been carried to the pitch nearly of divine worship, and the 'orthodox' party had hotly persecuted those who would not accord to her the title 'Mother of God;' and Mahomet might censure the Christians for this as virtually taking 'Jesus and his Mother for two Gods,' possibly without adverting to the Trinity.

Supported by other considerations.

Trinity of the Corân; and the Virgin Mary.

On the other hand, the assertion that Mahomet believed Mary to be held by the Christians as divine, is supported by his apparent ignorance of the Holy Ghost as a person in the Trinity. The only passage in which the Trinity is specifically mentioned, makes no allusion whatever to the divinity of the Spirit; nor are the expressions 'the Spirit,' and 'the Holy Spirit,' though occurring in numerous texts throughout the Corân, ever used by Mahomet as if in the system of his adversaries they signified a Divine person. Those terms, as has been already shown, commonly meant Gabriel, the messenger of God's revelations to Mahomet. It is probable that a confusion of Gabriel with the Holy Spirit may have arisen in the Prophet's mind from Gabriel having been the medium of the Annunciation, while Christians at the same time hold that Jesus was conceived by the power of the Holy Ghost. The phrase is also re-

Holy Ghost unknown to Mahomet as person in the Trinity.

---

[1] It is very doubtful whether an Arabic translation of the Scriptures, or any part of them, was ever within Mahomet's reach, notwithstanding the traditions regarding Waraca.

peatedly used in a more general sense as signifying *the Spirit of inspiration*. It was the divine 'Spirit' breathed into the clay which gave life to Adam; and Jesus, who like Adam had no earthly father, is also 'a Spirit from God' breathed into Mary. When it is said that God '*strengthened Jesus with the Holy Spirit*,' we may perhaps trace the use of current Christian speech, not inconsistent with Jewish ideas.[1]

Jewish and Christian prophecies and expectations. The assurance with which Mahomet appeals to Jews and Christians as both in expectation of a promised prophet whom, if they but put aside their prejudices, they would at once recognise in Mahomet 'as they recognised their own sons,' is very singular, and must surely have been countenanced by ignorant or designing men of both religions. Mahomet thus seized upon two different and indeed incompatible expectations; and adroitly combined them into a cumulative proof of his own mission. The Jewish anticipation of their Messiah, and the perfectly distinct and even discordant anticipation by the Christians of the second advent of Christ, were by him fused into a common argument for a coming prophet expected by both Jews and Christians and foretold in all the Scriptures, which prophet was himself.

Promise of the Paraclete; That the promise of the Paraclete was capable of perversion we see in the heresy of Montanus; and it is probable that a garbled version of the same promise communicated to Mahomet may have given rise to the following passage:—

Sura lxi. And call to mind when Jesus, son of Mary, said;—Oh Children of Israel! Verily, I am an apostle of God unto you, attesting the Book of the Law revealed before me, and giving good tidings of a prophet that shall come after me, whose name is Ahmad.[2]

And of the Messiah perverted. The prophecy of Moses to the Israelites,' God will raise up unto thee a prophet from the midst of thee, *of thy brethren*, like unto me,' may also plausibly have been adduced by some perverted Jew in favour of the Arabian prophet. And other predictions referring to the Messiah were doubtless forced into a similar service. **Mahomet the Prophet looked for by both people.** That he was the Prophet promised to both Jews and Christians lay indeed at the root of the catholic system so strongly inculcated by Mahomet in the middle stage of his course. He persuaded himself that it was so: and the assumption, once admitted, retained possession of his mind.

[1] Compare Psalm li. 12: 'Uphold me with thy free Spirit.'

[2] *Ahmad* is from the same root as *Muhammed*, signifying, like it, 'the Praised.' See John xvi. 7, where παράκλητος may in some imperfect or garbled translation have been rendered by the equivalent of περικλυτός.

From this review we may conclude that, while some information regarding Christianity may have been drawn from ignorant Christian slaves or Christian Arabs, Mahomet gained his chief knowledge of Christianity from lower Syria, through the same Jewish medium by which, at an earlier period, the more copious details of Jewish history reached him.   His adversaries at Mecca did not conceal their suspicion that the prompting from which the scriptural or legendary tales proceeded, was not solely that of a supernatural inspiration.   They imputed to him the aid of strangers :—

Meccans taunt him with being prompted by others.

From whence shall there be an Admonition for them; for, verily, there hath come unto them an evident Apostle ;—
Then they turn from him and say,—*One taught by others, a Madman!*
And the unbelievers say ; *Verily this is a fraud which he hath fabricated, and other people have assisted him therein.*   But they say that which is unjust and false.   *   *   *

Sura xliv.

They say ; *They are Fables of the ancients which he hath had written down; which are dictated unto him morning and evening.*
SAY :—He hath revealed it who knoweth that which is hidden in Heaven and in Earth.   He is forgiving and merciful.   *   *   *

Sura xxv.

And ;—Verily We know that they say,—*Surely a certain man teacheth him.*   The tongue of him whom they hint at is foreign, but this (Corân) is in the tongue of simple Arabic.

Sura xvi.

Whatever the rough material, its passage through the alembic of 'simple Arabic' converted it into a gem of unearthly water.   The recitations of a credulous and ill-informed Jew reappeared as the inspirations of the Almighty dictated by Gabriel, the noblest of his heavenly messengers.   The wild legend and the garbled Scripture story of yesterday comes forth to-morrow as a portion of the divine and eternal Corân.

Promptings of ignorant Jews transformed into 'divine Corân.'

And, however strange it may appear, the heavenly origin of his Revelations, obtained though they were from such fallible and imperfect sources, appears to have been believed by Mahomet himself.   It would be against the analogy of his life to suppose a conscious and continuing sense that the whole was a fabrication, an imposition upon his followers, and an impious assumption of the name of the Almighty.   Occasional doubts and misgivings, especially when he first submitted to Jewish prompting, there may have been ; but a process similar to that by which he first assured himself of his own inspiration would quickly put them to flight.

Mahomet at first sincere in this belief.

Such was the case at Mecca; but the absence of spiritual light and of opportunities for obtaining it which excused this marvellous self-deception in the early prophetical life of Mahomet, cannot be pleaded for his later years.   Ignorance was then no longer

But ignorance became culpable when voluntary

involuntary. The means of reaching a truer knowledge both of Judaism and Christianity lay plentifully within his reach. But they were not heeded; or rather they were deliberately rejected, because a position had been already taken up from which there could now be no receding without discredit and inconsistency. The living inspiration of God vouchsafed to himself was surely better and more safe than the recorded Revelations of former prophets; it was at any rate incomparably more authoritative than the uncertain doctrines deduced therefrom by their erring and bigoted adherents. Thus did ignorance become wilful. Light was at hand; but Mahomet preferred darkness. He chose to walk 'in the glimmerings of his own fire, and in the sparks which he had kindled.' In the following chapters, frequent and often melancholy illustration will be afforded by the career of the Prophet at Medîna of that unconscious self-deception which can alone explain the mysterious foundation of a faith strong but often descending to subterfuge, never wavering yet always inconsistent.

Teaching of Mahomet during the last three years at Mecca.

Style of Corân during period preceding Flight.

The Corân continues during the last three years of Mahomet's residence at Mecca to be made up, as before, of arguments in refutation of idolatry and the cavillings of his fellow-citizens; of the proofs of God's omnipotence, omniscience, and unity; of vivid picturings of the judgment day and of heaven and hell; and of legendary and scriptural stories. The later Suras contain repeated allusions to the approaching emigration. The great verities of a minute and over-ruling providence and final retribution are sometimes illustrated by passages of exquisite imagery and poetry. The bold impersonation of THUNDER in the following quotation, may be taken as a sample of the better portions of this period :—

Sura xiii.

Verily God changeth not his dealings with a People, until they change that which is in their souls. And when God willeth evil unto a People, there is none that can turn it away, nor have they any protector besides Him.

It is He that showeth you the Lightning to inspire fear and hope; and raised the heavy clouds. The THUNDER doth celebrate His praise; and the Angels also, from awe of Him. And He sendeth forth His bolts; and shivereth therewith whom He pleaseth, while they are wrangling about God :—for He is terrible in might!

He alone is rightly invoked. And those whom they invoke beside Him, they answer them not all, otherwise than as one stretching forth both hands unto the water that it may reach his mouth, and it reacheth it not. So is the invocation of the unbelievers founded only in error. And to God boweth down in worship whatsoever is in the Heavens, and in the Earth, voluntarily and by force; and their shadows likewise in the morning and in the evening.[1]

SAY:—Who is the Lord of the Heavens and of the earth? Say—GOD. Say:—Wherefore, then, do ye take besides him guardians who have no power to do even their ownselves a benefit nor an injury? Say:—What! Are the blind and the seeing equal! What! is the darkness equal with the light? Or do they give unto God partners that have created like unto His creation, so that the creation (of both) should appear alike in their eyes? Say:—GOD is the Creator of all things. He is the ONE; the AVENGER!

He bringeth down from on high the rain, and the valleys flow, each according to its measure; and the flood beareth the swelling froth. And from that which men melt in the furnace to make ornaments or vessels withal, there ariseth a scum, the like thereof. Thus doth God compare the truth with falsehood. As for the scum it passeth away like the froth: but that which benefiteth mankind remaineth on the Earth.

Thus doth God put forth similitudes.

The positive precepts of this period are still very limited. The five times of prayer are said to have been enjoined by God at the period of the Prophet's ascent to heaven one or two years before the Hegira. The flesh of animals was permitted for food *if killed 'in the name of the Lord,'*[2] but the blood, and that which dieth of itself, and the flesh of swine, were strictly prohibited.[3]

Positive precepts.

While some superstitions were denounced, and the practice of compassing the Káaba naked was proscribed as a device of Satan,[4] the rights of pilgrimage were maintained and enjoined as of divine authority and in themselves propitious to piety. It is probable that the Jews strongly objected to this new feature of the reformed faith, and we accordingly find a laboured defence of the innovation :—

Some superstitions discountenanced.

But Meccan pilgrimage and rites maintained.

And call to remembrance when We gave unto Abraham the site of the Temple (at Mecca); saying,—Join not in worship anything with Me, and purify My house for them that compass it, and for them that stand up and bow down to pray.

And proclaim unto Mankind a pilgrimage, that they may come unto

Sura xxii.

---

[1] A conceit Mahomet was fond of. The shadows perform obeisance to God, being long and prostrate in the morning, upright during the day, and again elongated in prostration in the evening.

[2] The reason was the same as that which led to the Apostolical admonition to abstain from 'pollutions of idols,' and 'meats offered to idols,' and points to the Arab practice of slaying their animals as a sacrifice to, or in the name of, their deities.

[3] The influence of Jewish habit and precept is here manifest. It is possible that some of the pieces quoted in this Supplement as Meccan may have been in reality of later date; they may have been given forth at Medina after the emigration, and relegated to passages of corresponding tenor in Meccan Suras.

[4] *Sura vii.* This was connected with the *Homs* : see Introduction, p. xxvii.

thee on foot, and upon every lean camel,[1] flocking from every distant road:—that they may testify to the benefits they have received, and commemorate the name of God, on the appointed days, over the brute beasts which We have given them for a provision:—Wherefore eat thereof and feed the wretched and the poor. Then let them stop the neglect of their persons,[2] fulfil their vows, and compass the ancient House.

This do. And he that honoureth the sacred ordinances of God it is well for him with his Lord. The flesh of cattle is lawful unto you excepting that which hath been read unto you. Wherefore abstain from the pollutions of Idols, and abstain from the false speech, following the Catholic faith respecting God, not associating any with Him; for he that associateth any with God is like that which falleth from the heavens, and the birds snatch it away, and the wind bloweth it into a distant place.

Hearken to this:—whosoever honoureth the Sacrifices of God, verily they proceed from purity of heart. From them (the victims) ye derive benefits until the appointed time: then they are brought for sacrifice unto the ancient House.

And unto every People have We appointed rites, that they may commemorate the name of GOD over the brute beasts with which He hath provided them. And your GOD is ONE GOD; wherefore submit thyself unto him and bear good tidings unto the humble:—Unto those whose hearts, when God is mentioned, tremble thereat;—and unto those that patiently bear what befalleth them and observe prayer, and spend in alms of that We have provided them with.

And the Victims have We made unto you as ordinances of God. From them ye receive benefit. Commemorate therefore the name of God over them as they stand disposed in a line, and when they fall slain upon their sides, eat thereof, and give unto the poor, both to him that is silent and him that beggeth. Thus have We given thee dominion over them that ye may be thankful. Their flesh is not accepted of God, nor yet their blood: but your piety is accepted of Him.

Effect of Mahomet's teaching up to the Hegira.

effect produced by teaching of Mahomet.

Few and simple as were the precepts of Mahomet up to this time, his teaching had wrought a marvellous and a mighty work. Never since the days when primitive Christianity startled the world from its sleep and waged mortal combat with heathenism, had men seen the like arousing of spiritual life, the like faith that suffered sacrifice and took joyfully the spoiling of goods for conscience sake.

Previous dark and torpid state of Mecca and Arabia.

From time beyond memory, Mecca and the whole peninsula had been steeped in spiritual torpor. The slight and transient influences of Judaism, Christianity, or philosophical enquiry upon the Arab mind had been but as the ruffling here and there

---

[1] Lean and famished from the long journey.

[2] *i.e.* they might now again pare their nails, shave their heads, &c., and resume their ordinary dress. See Introduction, p. xii.

of the surface of a quiet lake; all remained still and motionless below. The people were sunk in superstition, cruelty, and vice. It was a common practice for the eldest son to take to wife his father's widows inherited as property with the rest of the estate. Pride and poverty had introduced among them (as they have among the Hindoos) the crime of female infanticide.[1] Their religion was a gross idolatry; and their faith rather the dark superstitious dread of unseen beings whose goodwill they sought to propitiate and whose displeasure to avert, than the belief in an over-ruling Providence. The Life to come and Retribution of good and evil were as motives of action practically unknown.

Thirteen years before the Hegira, Mecca lay lifeless in this debased state. What a change had those thirteen years now produced! A band of several hundred persons had rejected idolatry, adopted the worship of One God, and surrendered themselves implicitly to the guidance of what they believed a revelation from him; praying to the Almighty with frequency and fervour, looking for pardon through his mercy, and striving to follow after good works, alms-giving, chastity, and justice. They now lived under a constant sense of the omnipotent power of God, and of his providential care over the minutest of their concerns. In all the gifts of nature, in every relation of life, at each turn of their affairs individual or public, they saw his hand. And, above all, the new existence in which they exulted was regarded as the mark of his especial grace; while the unbelief of their blinded fellow-citizens was the hardening stamp of reprobation. Mahomet was the minister of life to them, the source under God of their new-born hopes; and to him they yielded an implicit submission.

Effect produced on converts by Mahomet's ministry at Mecca.

In so short a period Mecca had, from this wonderful movement, been rent into two factions which, unmindful of the old landmarks of tribe and family, had arrayed themselves in deadly opposition one against the other. The Believers bore persecution with a patient and tolerant spirit. And though it was their wisdom so to do, the credit of a magnanimous forbearance may be freely accorded. One hundred men and women, rather than abjure their precious faith, had abandoned home and sought refuge, till the storm should be overpast, in Abyssinian exile. And now again a still larger number, with the Prophet himself, were emigrating from their fondly-loved city with its sacred Temple, to them the holiest spot on earth, and fleeing to Medîna. There,

Their sacrifices and abandonment of home.

[1] It is stringently proscribed in the Corân, and disappeared with the progress of Islâm.

the same marvellous charm had within two or three years been preparing for them a brotherhood ready to defend the Prophet and his followers with their blood. Jewish truth had long sounded in the ears of the men of Medîna; but it was not until they heard the spirit-stirring strains of the Arabian prophet that they too awoke from their slumber, and sprang suddenly into a new and earnest life.

Description of his followers by Mahomet.

The virtues of his people may now be described in the words of Mahomet himself:—

Sura xxv.

The servants of the Merciful are they that walk upon the earth softly; and, when the ignorant speak unto them, they reply, PEACE!

They that spend the night worshipping their Lord, prostrate and standing;—

And who say,—'O our Lord! turn away from us the torment of hell; verily, from the torment thereof there is no release. Surely it is an evil abode and resting place!'

Those that when they spend are neither profuse nor niggardly, but take a middle course;—

Those that invoke not with God any other god; and slay not a soul that God hath forbidden, otherwise than by right; and commit not fornication;

(For he who doeth this is involved in sin,—his torment shall be doubled unto him in the day of judgment; therein ignominiously shall he remain for ever,—Excepting him that shall repent and believe and perform righteous works; as for them God shall change their evil things into good things; and God is forgiving and merciful. And whoever repenteth and doeth good works, verily, he turneth unto God with a true repentance).—

They who bear not witness to that which is false; and when they pass by vain sport, they pass it by with dignity:—

They who, when admonished by the Revelations of the Lord, thereupon fall not down as if deaf and blind;—

Who say, 'O our Lord. Grant us of our wives and children such as shall be a comfort unto us, and make us examples unto the pious!'

These shall be rewarded with lofty mansions (in paradise), for that they persevered; and they shall be accosted therein with welcome and salutation:—

For ever therein:—a fair abode and resting place!

Praise not absolute; but in comparison with heathen Arabia.

When I speak, however, with praise of the virtues of the early Mussulmans, it is only in comparison with the state and habits of their heathen countrymen. Neither their tenets nor their practice will in any respect bear to come in competition with Christian or even with Jewish morality. This is plentifully illustrated by the actual working of the system when, shortly after at Medîna, it had a free field for natural development.

Illustrated in matter of chastity.

For instance, we call the Moslems chaste because they abstained from indiscriminate licentiousness, and kept carefully within the bounds prescribed as licit by their Prophet. But those bounds, besides the utmost freedom of divorce and change of wives, admitted an illimitable license of cohabitation with 'all that the right hand of the believer might possess,' or, in other words, with any number of female slaves, purchased, received in gift, or taken captive in war.

The facility of divorce at this period (when even the check of three intervening months before the re-marriage of the divorced wife had not been imposed), may be illustrated by the following incident: Abd al Rahmân, on his first reaching Medîna, was lodged by Sád, a convert of Medîna to whom Mahomet had united him (as will be explained hereafter) in brotherhood. As they sat at meat Sád thus addressed his guest: 'My brother! I have abundance of wealth; I will divide with thee a portion. And behold my two wives! choose which of them thou likest best, and I will divorce her that thou mayest take her to thyself to wife.' And Abd al Rahmân replied: 'The Lord bless thee, my brother, in thy family and in thy property!' So he married one of the wives of Sád.[1]

Facility of divorce.

At the opening scene of the prophetical life of Mahomet, we ventured to fetch an illustration of his position from the temptation of our Saviour. The parallel between the founders of Christianity and Islâm might be continued to the flight of Mahomet, but there it must stop; for it is the only point at all corresponding with the close of Christ's ministry. Beyond that

Comparison of Mahomet's life previous to emigration, with life of Christ.

[1] Mahomet met him in the street with the saffron clothes of nuptial attire upon him, and he said: 'How is this?' And Abd al Rahmân replied: 'I have married me a wife from amongst the people of Medîna.' 'For what dower?' 'For a piece of gold the size of a date stone.' 'And why,' replied Mahomet, 'not with a goat?' The story is intended by tradition to illustrate the poverty of Abd al Rahmân when he reached Medîna, as contrasted with the vast wealth subsequently amassed by him. 'At his death he left gold in such quantities, that it was cut with hatchets till the people's hands bled.' He had 1,000 camels, 3,000 sheep, and 100 horses. He had issue by *sixteen* wives, besides children by concubines. Each of his four widows inherited 100,000 dinars.

Abd al Rahmân was penurious. Mahomet said to him: 'Oh son of Awf! Verily thou art amongst the rich, and thou shalt not enter Paradise but with great difficulty. Lend therefore to thy Lord, so that He may loosen thy steps.' And he departed by Mahomet's advice to give away all his property. But the Prophet sent for him again, and told him by Gabriel's desire that it would suffice if he used hospitality and gave alms.

In perusing the annals of the 'Companions' and first followers of Mahomet, few things so forcibly illustrate the spirit of Islâm as, first, the number of their wives and concubines and the facility of divorce; and, next, the vast riches they amassed; a significant contrast with the early days of Christianity.

term, in the career at Medîna of conquest, rapine, and indulgence, there is absolutely no feature whatever in common with
the life of Jesus.

Apparent-ly greater effect pro-duced by Mahomet.
During the periods thus indicated as possible for comparison,
persecution and rejection were the fate of both. But the
ministry of Mahomet had brought about a far greater change to
the external eye, than did the ministry of Christ. The apostles
fled at the first sound of danger; and, however deep the inner
work may have been in the 500 by whom our Lord was seen,
it had produced as yet but little outward action. There was
amongst them no spontaneous quitting of their homes, no emigration by hundreds, such as distinguished the early Moslems; nor
any rapturous resolution by the converts of a foreign city, such
as that shown by the men of Medîna, to defend the Prophet with
their lives.

Comparison should commence from Pen-tecost.
This is mainly owing to the fact that Christianity did not, as
a fully developed system, begin to assert its claims till after the
personal ministry of Christ had ceased. His life was in fact its
preparation, his death its key-stone. Islâm, on the contrary,
formed a complete and an aggressive faith from the date of the
assumption by Mahomet of his public ministry. To make the
comparison, therefore, equal between the early effects of Christianity and Islâm, the Pentecostal period must be reckoned as
parallel with the beginning of the ministry of Mahomet. And
in this view Christianity will not yield to Islâm in the rapidity
of its first spread, or in the devotion of its early followers.

Condition of Jews widely different from that of Arabs.
But confining, for the moment, our comparison to the lives
of Jesus and of Mahomet, advertence must be had to the different
state of the two people among whom respectively they minis-
tered: Jesus amongst the Jews, whose law he came not to destroy but to fulfil, and in whose *outer* life, therefore, there was no
marked change to be effected: Mahomet amongst a nation of
idolaters sunk in darkness and vice, whose whole system must
be overturned, and from the midst of whom converts to exhibit
any consistency whatever must go forth with a bold and distinctive separation.

System of Jesus spiritual and exclu-sive of worldly means.
There was, moreover, a material difference of aim and
teaching. The spiritual system of Jesus was incompatible with
worldly means and motives. His people though in the world
were to be not 'of the world.' At every step he checked the
Jewish notion of an earthly Messiah's reign. That his followers
should have made him a king, or the citizens of another country
been invited to receive him and support his cause by arms,
would have been at variance with the whole spirit and principles
of his life and doctrine. It was the spirituality of aim and agency

to the exclusion of earthly aids, that (besides the still inchoate nature of the faith) chiefly tended to produce the want of apparent progress during the lifetime of Jesus.

The principles of Mahomet were utterly diverse. His reason for the toleration of his Meccan opponents was present weakness only. Patience *for awhile* was inculcated by God on Mahomet and his followers, but the future breathed of revenge and victory. It is true that in the Corân the instruments as yet lay hid, known to God alone. But not the less were the enemies of the Prophet to be overthrown and perish; and that with a *material* destruction, like the Flood, or the flames of Sodom and Gomorrha. Human agency was moreover diligently sought after. The tribes, as they came up to the yearly solemnities of Mecca, were one by one canvassed and exhorted to rally round 'the cause of God and his Prophet;' the chiefs of Tâyif were tempted by the prospect of sovereignty over the rival city and temple; and, at last, when all nearer aid was despaired of, the converts of Medîna were bound by an oath of fealty to defend the Prophet with the same weapons and the same devotion as they did their wives and children.

It was easy to be foreseen that on the first rise of opposition, arms and warfare, with all the attractive accompaniments of revenge and predatory raids, would decide the struggle. And the prospect had even before the Hegira a marvellous effect upon the imagination of the plunder-loving Arabs.

It was, I believe, with the full anticipation of such a struggle (for he was not long at Medîna before taking the initiative) that Mahomet, alarmed by the council of the Coreish, hid himself in the cave of mount Thaur, and fled from Mecca. Compare with this the peaceful and sublime serenity with which Jesus awaited the machinations of the Jewish council. And contrast with the sword about to be unsheathed by Mahomet, the grand principle for the propagation of his faith pronounced by Jesus before his heathen judge: 'My kingdom is not of this world; if my kingdom were of this world, then would my servants fight that I should not be delivered to the Jews; but now is my kingdom not from hence.' Jesus was 'from above,' and used heavenly weapons; Mahomet, 'of the earth,' and leaned upon earthly props. Islâm is human; Christianity, divine.

Material inducements sought after by Mahomet.

Prospect of warlike struggle.

Sword of Islâm contrasted with expedients of early Christianity.

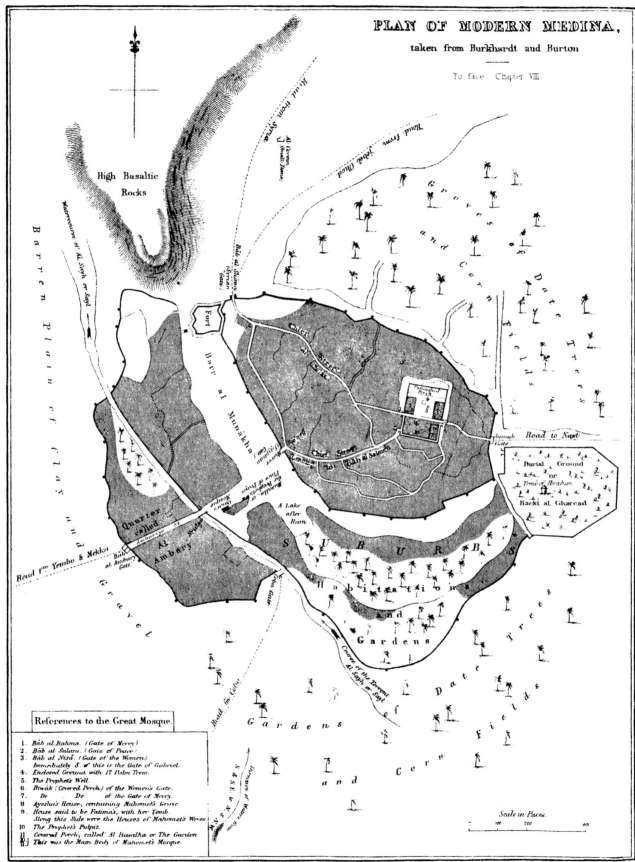

PLAN OF MODERN MEDINA,

taken from Burkhardt and Burton

To face Chapter VIII.

High Basaltic Rocks

Road from Syria

Al Kerun (Small Dome)

Road from Jebel Ohod

Watercourse of Al Seyh or Seyl

Barren Plain of Clay and

Gravel

Road from Yembo & Mekka

Fort

Bab al Shami (Syrian Gate)

Barr al Munakha

Bab al Anbary Gate.

Quarter called Al Ambary

Anbariyye Al.

Musalla or the Prophet's Place of Prayer.

Gate Gate

Road to Koba

Chief Street

Al Sáfa

Leading to Bab al Salam

Chief Street

Jamah Gate

Groves and Corn Fields

Date Trees

Road to Nejd

Burial Ground or Tomb of Ibrahim

Backi al Gharcad

A Lake after Rain

S U B U R B S

Habitations and Gardens

Course of the Torrent Al Seyh or Seyl

Direction of Waters from

Gardens and Corn Fields

Groves of Date Trees and

SSE to NNW

Direction of

References to the Great Mosque.

1. Báb al Rahma. (Gate of Mercy)
2. Báb al Salam. (Gate of Peace)
3. Báb al Nisá. (Gate of the Women)
   Immediately S. of this is the Gate of Gabriel
4. Enclosed Ground with 12 Palm Trees.
5. The Prophet's Well.
6. Riwák (Covered Porch) of the Women's Gate.
7. Do.   Do.   of the Gate of Mercy.
8. Ayesha's House, containing Mahomet's Grave.
9. House said to be Fatima's, with her Tomb.
   Along this Side were the Houses of Mahomet's Wives.
10. The Prophet's Pulpit.
11. Covered Porch, called Al Rawdha or The Garden.
N. This was the Main Body of Mahomet's Mosque.

London, Smith Elder & Co. 15, Waterloo Place

PART SECOND.

MAHOMET AT MEDÎNA.

CHAPTER VIII.

ARRIVAL AT MEDINA. BUILDING OF THE MOSQUE.

A.H. I. *June* A.D. *622 to January* A.D. *623.*

AT the close of the last Chapter we left Mahomet and Abu Bakr, on the second day after their escape from the cave, already beyond the reach of pursuit, and rapidly wending their way towards Medina.

Flight of Mahomet and Abu Bakr to Medina.

They had by this time joined the common road to Syria which runs near the shore of the Red Sea. On the morning of the third day a small caravan was observed in the distance. The apprehensions of the fugitives were soon allayed, for Abu Bakr recognised at the head of the caravan his cousin Talha returning from a mercantile trip to Syria. Warm was the greeting, and loud the congratulations. Talha opened his stores, and producing two changes of fine white Syrian raiment, bestowed them on his kinsman and the Prophet. The present was welcome to the soiled and weary travellers; yet more welcome was the assurance that Talha had left the Moslems at Medîna in eager expectation of their Prophet. So Mahomet and Abu Bakr proceeded on their journey with light hearts and quickened pace; while the merchant resumed his way to Mecca. There Talha disposed of his venture; and so little were the Coreish even now disposed to molest the believers, that, after quietly adjusting his affairs, he set out unopposed some little time afterwards for Medîna with the families of Mahomet and Abu Bakr.

They meet Talha by the way.

Progress towards Medina.

After travelling some way farther by the caravan route, Mahomet and his companion struck off to the right. The valleys which they crossed, the defiles they ascended, the spots on which the fugitive Prophet performed his devotions, have all been preserved in tradition by the pious zeal of his followers. When now within two days' journey of Medîna, one of the camels, worn out by the rapid travelling, was unable to proceed. A chief of the tribe residing in the neighbourhood supplied a fresh camel in its stead, and also furnished a guide.

They approach the city.

At length, on the morning of Monday, eight days after quitting Mecca, the little party reached Al Ackìck, a valley which traverses the mountains four or five miles to the S.W. of Medîna.[1] The heat was intense; for the summer sun, now approaching the meridian, beat fiercely on the bare ridges and stony defiles, the desolation of which was hardly relieved by an occasional clump of the wild acacia. Climbing the opposite ascent, they reached the crest of the mountain. Here a scene opened on them which contrasted strangely with the dark frowning peaks and naked rocks, in the midst of which for hours they had been toiling. It was Medîna surrounded by verdant gardens and groves of the graceful palm. What thoughts must have crowded on the mind of the Prophet and his faithful friend as they gazed on the prospect below them! Wide-spread is the view from the heights on which they stood, and well fitted to stir the heart of any traveller. The vast plain of Nejd stretches

Medina and its environs.

[1] The Wâdi al Ackìck has a north-westerly direction, and discharges its waters into Al Ghâba, the basin in which collects the drainage of the Medîna plain. Burton tells us that the mountains as you approach Medîna are composed of 'inhospitable rocks, pinnacle-shaped, of granite below, and in the upper parts, fine limestone;' but about the Wâdi al Ackìck the surface is 'black scoriaceous basalt.' Burckhardt says that 'all the rocky places' about Medîna, 'as well as the lower ridge of the northern mountainous chain, are covered by a layer of volcanic rock; it is of a bluish black colour, very porous, yet heavy and hard, not glazed like Schlacken, and contains frequently small white substances in its pores of the size of a pin's head, which I never found crystallised. The plain has a completely black colour from this rock, and the pieces with which it is overspread. I met with no lava, although the nature of the ground seemed strongly to indicate the neighbourhood of a volcano.' Burckhardt adds that lava from a volcanic outburst, A.D. 654, passed not far from Medîna, on the east; but he attributes the volcanic substances about the town and the valley Ackìck to some earlier eruption.

away towards the south-east as far as the eye can reach, while on the eastern horizon it is bounded by a low line of dark hills. To the north the prospect is arrested, at the distance of three or four miles, by the granite masses of Ohod, a spur of the great central chain. A well-defined watercourse flowing from the south-east under the nearest side of Medîna is lost among the north-eastern hills, the cliffs of which approach and even touch the city on the north. To the right, Jebel Ayr, a ridge nearly corresponding in distance and height with Ohod, projects into the plain and bounds it on the south-west. Closely embracing the city and in contrast with the rugged rocks around and behind our travellers, are the orchards of palm-trees for which from time immemorial Medîna has been famous. One sheet of gardens extends uninterruptedly to Coba, a suburb little more than two miles to the south, the loveliest and most verdant spot in all the plain. Around the city in every direction date-trees and green fields meet the eye, interspersed here and there with the substantial houses and fortified hamlets of the Jewish tribes, and the suburban residences of the Bani Aus and Khazraj. The tender reminiscence of childhood when he visited Medîna with his mother, was perhaps the first thought to cross the mind of Mahomet. But more pressing considerations were now at hand. How would he be received? Were his adherents powerful enough to secure for him a unanimous welcome? Or would either of the contending factions by whom that peaceful plain had been so often stained with blood, be roused against him? Before putting the friendship of the city to the test, it would be prudent to retire to one of the suburbs, and Coba lay invitingly before them. 'Lead us,' said Mahomet to the guide, Mahomet 'straight to the Bani Amr at Coba, and draw not nigh unto makes for Medîna.' So, leaving the path to Medîna on the left, they Coba. descended at once into the plain and made for Coba.

For several days the city had been in expectation of its People of illustrious visitor. Tidings had been received of Mahomet's Medîna watch for disappearance from Mecca; but no one knew of his three coming of days' withdrawal to the cave. He ought before now to have Mahomet. arrived, even supposing delay in consequence of a devious route. Every morning a large company of the converts of Medîna and the refugees from Mecca had for some days gone forth a mile or two on the road to Mecca and posted themselves on the first rocky ridge to the west of the city. There they watched till the heat of the ascending sun drove them from the unsheltered spot to their homes. On this day they had gone out as usual and after a fruitless watch had retired to the city, when a Jew, catching a glimpse of the three travellers wending their way to Coba, shouted from the top of his house: 'Ho! ye Bani Cayla![1] he has come! he whom ye have been looking for has come at last!' Every one now hurried forth from the city to go to Coba. A shout of joy arose from the Bani Amr (the Ausite tribe which inhabited Coba) when they found that Mahomet had come amongst them. The wearied travellers, amidst the greeting of old friends and the smiles of strange faces, alighted and sat down under the shadow of a tree.[2] It was Monday, June 28, A.D. 622. The journey had been accomplished in eight days. The ordinary time is eleven.[3]

He arrives 12th Rabí I. A.H. I. June 28, A.D. 622.

Is joyfully received.

The joyful news was speedily spread over the city. The very children in the streets cried out with delight: 'Here is the Prophet! He is come! He is come!' The converts from all quarters flocked to Mahomet and made obeisance to him. He received them courteously, and said: 'Ye People! show your joy by giving to your neighbours the salutation of peace; send portions to the poor; bind close the ties of kinsmanship; offer up prayer whilst others sleep. Thus shall ye enter Paradise in peace.'

Lodges with Kolthûm at Coba.

It was shortly arranged that Mahomet should for the present lodge at Coba with Kolthûm, an hospitable chief, who had already received many of the emigrants on their first arrival in Medîna. A great part of every day was also spent in the house of Sád son of Khaithama, one of the Ausite 'Leaders.' There Mahomet received such persons as

---

[1] Cayla was mother of the two patriarchs, of the Bani Aus and Khazraj.

[2] This quarter was called *Aliya*, or upper Medîna, from its more elevated position, and included Coba and some other hamlets with the Jewish settlements of the Bani Coreitza and Nadhîr. When Mahomet arrived, he was on Abu Bakr's camel. Few persons present knew which was the Prophet, till the sun's rays fell upon him, and then Abu Bakr rose to place him in the shade. Out of this, probably, has grown the tradition that the people of Medîna recognised the Prophet from his body *casting no shadow*. Abu Bakr was known to some of the citizens, [as he used to pass through Medîna on his mercantile trips to Syria.

[3] It *can* be travelled by swift dromedaries in five days.

wished to see him, and conferred with his friends on the state of feeling in Medîna.[1]

Abu Bakr was entertained by Khârija, another chief, in the adjoining suburb of Al Sunh. He showed his gratitude by marrying the daughter of Khârija, and permanently took up his residence with the family.[2]

Abu Bakr lodges at Al Sunh.

A day or two after Mahomet's arrival, Ali who, as we have seen, remained only three days at Mecca subsequently to the disappearance of Mahomet and must therefore have set out shortly after him, reached Medîna and was accommodated by Kelthûm in the same house with the Prophet.

Ali joins Mahomet.

It was soon determined in the council of Mahomet that he might with safety enter Medîna. The welcome he had received was warm, and to all appearance unanimous and sincere. Elements of disaffection might be slumbering among the Jews, idolaters, and other yet unconverted citizens; but they were unnoticed amid the universal joy and the first impulses of generous hospitality. Mahomet, therefore, stopped only four days at Coba, from Monday till Friday. During this period, he laid the foundations of a Mosque at Coba, which at a later period was honoured in the Corân with the name of the ' Mosque of godly fear.'[3]

Mahomet remains four days at Coba, and founds a Mosque.

On the morning of Friday, Mahomet mounted his favourite camel Al Caswa, taking Abu Bakr behind him, and surrounded by a crowd of followers proceeded towards the city. He halted at a place of prayer in the vale of the Bani Sâlim a Khazrajite tribe, and there performed his first Friday service with about a hundred Moslems; the spot is still shown to pilgrims, and is marked by a building called

Departure for Medina.

Performs public service by the way.

---

[1] Sâd being a bachelor, the unmarried refugees were accommodated in great numbers in his house, so that it went by the name of the ' bachelors' hostelry.'

[2] That is to say, his wife remained at her father's house, and he used to visit her there when it was her turn to enjoy his society, for he had other wives. Khârija was joined in *brotherhood* (the practice will be explained hereafter) to Abu Bakr.

[3] Sura ix. Mahomet enlarged it after the Kibla was changed, and advanced its foundations and walls ' to their present position.' With his followers he aided in the pious work by carrying the materials. He used to visit it from Medîna every Saturday, and attached to the saying of prayers therein the merit of the *Omra* or lesser pilgrimage to the Kâaba.

in memory of the event the *Masjid al juma*, or 'the Friday Mosque.' On this occasion he added a sermon or oration composed chiefly of religious exhortation and eulogy of the new faith. Friday was thenceforward set apart for the weekly celebration of public worship.

Entry into the city.

When the service was finished Mahomet resumed his progress towards Medîna. He had sent a message to the Bani Najjâr, his relatives through Salma the mother of Abd al Muttalib, to escort him into the city. But there was no need of special invitation. The tribes and families of Medîna came streaming forth, and vied one with another in showing honour to their visitor. It was indeed a triumphal procession. Around the camels of Mahomet and his immediate followers, rode the chief men of the city clad in their best raiment and in glittering armour. The cavalcade pursued its way through the gardens and palm-groves of the southern suburb; and as it now threaded the streets of the city, the heart of Mahomet was gladdened by the incessant call from one and another of the citizens who flocked around: 'Alight here, O Prophet! We have abundance with us; and we have the means of defence and weapons and room. Abide with us.' So urgent was the appeal that sometimes they seized hold of Al Caswa's halter. Mahomet answered them courteously and kindly: 'The decision,' he said, 'rests with the camel; make way for her; let her go free.' It was a stroke of policy. His residence would be hallowed in the eyes of the people as selected supernaturally; while the jealousy which otherwise might arise from the quarter of one tribe being preferred before the quarter of another, would thus receive decisive check.

His camel halts at an open yard.

Onwards Al Caswa moved, with slackened rein; and, leaving the larger portion of the city to the left, entered the eastern quarter inhabited by the Bani Najjâr. There finding a large and open court-yard with a few date-trees, she halted and sat down.[1] The house of Abu Ayûb was close at hand. Mahomet and Abu Bakr, alighting, enquired who the owner

---

[1] To invest the incident with a supernatural air, it is added that Mahomet having left the rein quite loose, Al Caswa got up again and went a little way forward; when she perceived her error, returned straightway to the selfsame spot, knelt down, and, placing her head and neck on the ground, refused to stir.

was. Abu Ayûb stepped forward and invited them to enter. *Mahomet occupies Abu Ayûb's house;* Mahomet became his guest, and occupied the lower story of his house for seven months, until the Mosque and his own apartments were ready. Abu Ayûb offered to resign the upper story in which his family lived, but Mahomet preferred the lower as being more accessible to his visitors.[1]

When Mahomet had alighted, Abu Ayûb lost no time in carrying into his house the saddle and other property of the travellers; while Asád ibn Zorâra, a neighbour, seized Al Caswa's halter and conducted her to his court-yard where he kept her for the Prophet. Dishes of choice viands, bread and meat, butter and milk, presently arrived from various houses; and this hospitality was kept up daily so long as the Prophet resided in the house. *And is treated hospitably.*

The first concern of Mahomet was to secure the plot of land on which Al Caswa halted. It was a neglected spot : on one side was a scanty grove of date-trees ; the other, covered here and there with thorny shrubs, had been used partly as a burial-ground and partly as a yard for tying camels up. It belonged to two orphan boys under the guardianship of Asád, who (they say) had rudely constructed a place of worship there before the arrival of Mahomet, and had already held service within its roofless walls. The Prophet called the two lads before him, and desired to purchase this piece of ground from them that he might build a Mosque upon it. They replied: 'Nay, but we will make a free gift of it to thee.' Mahomet would not accept the land in gift; and so the price was fixed at ten golden dinars, which Abu Bakr by desire of Mahomet paid over to the orphans. *Purchases the yard.*

Arrangements for the construction of a great Mosque, with two houses adjoining,—one for his wife Sauda, the other for his intended bride the precocious maiden Ayesha,—were forthwith set on foot. The date-trees and thorny bushes were cut down. The graves were dug up, and the bones elsewhere deposited. The uneven ground was carefully levelled, and the rubbish cleared. A spring, oozing in the vicinity, rendered the site damp ; it was blocked up and drained, and *Prepares to build Mosque and habitation.*

---

[1] Abu Ayûb used to tell that he and his wife accidentally broke a water-pot in the upper story, and, having wiped up the water as best they could with their clothes, hurried down to Mahomet's apartment in alarm lest any of it should have dropped on him. Abu Ayûb was killed at Constantinople, A.H. 55.

at length quite disappeared. Bricks were prepared, and other materials collected.[1]

Is joined by his family from Mecca.

Having taken up his residence in Abu Ayûb's house Mahomet bethought him of his family, and despatched his freedman Zeid with a slave named Abu Râfi[2] on two camels, with a purse of 500 dirhems, to fetch them from Mecca. They met with no difficulty or opposition, and returned with Sauda the Prophet's wife and his two daughters Fâtima and Omm Kolthûm. The latter had been married into the family of Abu Lahab, but, being separated from her husband, had for some time been living in her father's house. Zeinab, the eldest daughter, remained at Mecca with her husband Ab ul Aás. Rockeya, the second, had already emigrated to Medîna with her husband Othmân. Zeid brought with him his own wife Omm Ayman (Baraka) and their little son Osâma.

And by Abu Bakr's family.

Accompanying the party were Ayesha and her mother Omm Rumân, with other members of the family of Abu Bakr, who had perhaps supplied the purse to Zeid. They were conducted by Abu Bakr's son and Talha.[3] The family of Abu Bakr, including Ayesha, was accommodated in a neighbouring house.

Sauda, Mahomet's wife.

Sauda probably lived with Mahomet in the house of Abu Ayûb. Of this lady we know but little, save that having emigrated with her former husband to Abyssinia, she was more than ordinarily devoted to the cause of Islâm.[4] From the time of her marriage with Mahomet, shortly after the death of Khadija, she continued to be for three or four years his only wife.

Unwholesome climate of Medina.

The climate of Medîna contrasts strongly with that of Mecca. In summer, the days are intensely hot (a more endurable and less sultry heat, however, than at Mecca); but the nights are cool and often chilly. The cold in winter is for the latitude severe, especially after rain which falls

[1] The court-yard in the time of Ibn Jubair contained fifteen date-trees; they are now (according to Burton) reduced to a dozen in a railed-in and watered space, called 'Fâtima's garden;' it also contains the remains of a venerable lote-tree. The 'Prophet's well' is hard by.

[2] He had been a servant of Mahomet's uncle Abbâs, and was given by him to Mahomet, who freed him on his bringing tidings of the conversion of Abbâs.

[3] Talha, it will be remembered, met the Prophet on his way to Medîna. He married Omm Kolthûm, daughter of his cousin Abu Bakr, with whom he always seems to have been on terms of close intimacy.

[4] *Vide supra*, p. 117.

heavily in occasional but not long-continued showers;[1] and even in summer these are not infrequent. Heavy rain always deluges the adjacent country. The drainage is sluggish, and after a storm the water forms a widespread lake in the open space between the city and the southern suburb. The humid exhalations from this and other stagnant pools, and perhaps also the luxuriant vegetation in the neighbourhood, render the stranger liable to attacks of intermittent fever, often followed by swellings and tumours in the legs and stomach, and sometimes fatal. The climate is altogether unfavourable.

Accustomed to the dry air and parched soil of Mecca, the Refugees were severely tried by the dampness of the Medîna summer and the rigour of its winter. Mahomet himself escaped, but most of his followers were prostrated by fever. Abu Bakr and his whole household suffered greatly. Ayesha once related to Mahomet how they all wandered in their speech when struck down by the fever, and how they longed to return to their home at Mecca; on which Mahomet, looking upwards, prayed: 'O Lord! make Medîna dear unto us, even as Mecca, or even dearer. Bless its produce, and banish far from it the pestilence!'[2]

Refugees suffer from Medîna fever.

To raise the spirits of his followers thus home-sick and suffering, and to draw them into nearer relations with the Medîna converts, Mahomet established a new fraternity between the Refugees and the Citizens. 'Become brethren

'Brotherhood' between Refugees and Citizens of Medina.

---

[1] *i.e.* from October till April. The cold in winter is severe; ice and snow are not unknown in the adjoining hills. This is natural if, as Burton says, the city be 6,000 feet above the sea; but this estimate is surely exaggerated. The height, however, must be great, as the rise of the mountains is rapid and continuous on the western side, and the descent insignificant on the eastern. The city is much exposed to storms. We learn from Burton that 'chilly and violent winds from the eastern deserts are much dreaded; and though Ohod screens the town on the N. and N.E., a gap in the mountains to the N.W. fills the air at times with rain and comfortless blasts. The rains begin in October, and last with considerable intervals through the winter; the clouds, gathered by the hill tops and the trees near the town, discharge themselves with violence; and at the equinoxes, thunderstorms are common. At such times the Barr el Munâkhah, or the open space between the town and the suburbs, is a sheet of water, and the land about the S. and S.E. wall of the faubourg, a lake.'

[2] So prevalent was the fever that at one time Mahomet was almost the only person at prayers able to stand up; but he said, 'the prayer of one who sits is worth only half the prayer of him that stands;' so they all made efforts to stand up.

every two and two of you,' he said ; and he set the example by taking Ali, or as others say Othmân, for his brother. Accordingly each of the Refugees selected one of the Citizens as his brother.   The bond was of the closest description, and involved not only a special devotion to each other's interests in the persons thus associated, but in case of death the 'brother' inherited all the property of the deceased.   From forty to fifty Refugees were thus united to as many Citizens of Medîna.   This peculiar custom lasted for about a year and a half, when Mahomet finding it after the victory of Badr to be no longer necessary for the encouragement of his followers, and probably attended with some inconvenience and unpopularity as overriding the ties of nature, abolished the bond and suffered inheritance to take its usual course.

Building of the Mosque ;

During the first half-year of Mahomet's residence at Medîna his own attention and that of his followers was mainly occupied by the construction of the Mosque and of houses for themselves.   In the erection of the Mosque all united with enthusiasm.   Their zeal was stimulated by Mahomet, who himself took an active share in the work, and joined in the song which the labourers chanted as they bore along their burdens :—

O Lord ! there is no happiness but that of futurity.
O Lord ! have mercy on the men of Medîna and the Refugees![1]

The site (on the southern portion of the ground which he had purchased) is the same as that now occupied by the great Mosque and its spacious court ; but the style and dimensions were naturally less ambitious.   It was built four-square, each side being one hundred cubits or somewhat less in length.[2]   The foundations to three cubits above the ground were of stone, the rest of the wall of brick.   The roof was supported by trunks of palm-trees, and covered over with

---

[1] The couplet ran thus :—

Ilâhum lâ áish illâ áish al âkhĭra.
Ilâhum arham al Ansâr w'al Muhâjĭra.

Mahomet joining in the chorus would transpose the last words into *al Muhâjĭra w'al Ansâr*, thus losing the rhyme.   Having been taunted at Mecca with being a mere rhapsodist, he affected to have no ear for poetry, and tradition gives this as an instance.   The fine rhythm of the Corán was thus held to be all the stronger evidence of divine origin.

[2] According to some authorities the breadth was only sixty or seventy cubits.

branches and rafters of the same material. The Kibla, or quarter whither the faithful directed their faces when they prayed, was towards Jerusalem. While leading the public prayers Mahomet stood close to the northern wall looking in that direction ; his back was thus turned upon the congregation, who facing similarly fell into rows behind him. When he preached he turned round with his face towards them. To the south, opposite the Kibla, was a doorway for general entrance.[1] Another opened on the west, called *Bâb Rahmah*, the Gate of Mercy, a name it still retains. A third gate, on the eastern side, was reserved for the use of Mahomet; south of this entrance, and forming part of the eastern wall of the Mosque itself, were the apartments destined for the Prophet's wives. The house of Ayesha was at the extreme S.E. corner, the road into the Mosque passing behind it. That of Sauda was next; and beyond it were the apartments of Rockeya and her husband Othmân, and of the two other daughters of Mahomet. In later years, as Mahomet added to the number of his wives, he provided for each a room or house, on the same side of the Mosque. From these he had private entrances into the Mosque, used only by himself. The eastern gate still bears in its name (*Bâb al Nisa*, 'the *Women's* porch,') the memory of these arrangements. To the north of the Mosque the ground was open, and on that side a place was appropriated for the poorer followers of Mahomet who had no other home. They slept in the Mosque, and had within its courts a sheltered bench or pavement. Mahomet used to send them portions from his table ; and others followed his example. But in a few years victory and the spoil of war caused poverty and distress to disappear, and 'the men of the bench' survived in memory alone. To be near the Prophet, his chief companions by degrees erected houses for themselves in the vicinity of the Mosque ; some of these adjoined upon its court, and had doors opening directly on it.

And apartments for Prophet's wives.

It is to the north of the Mosque, as thus erected by Mahomet, that subsequent additions have been mainly made. The present magnificent buildings occupy probably three or four times the area of the primitive temple. Mahomet, when asked why he did not build a permanent roof to his house of

The Mosque, how used.

---

[1] This was probably closed when the Kibla was turned towards the south. It corresponded with the doorway afterwards opened out to the north.

prayer, replied : 'The thatch is as the thatching of Moses, rafters and small pieces of wood ; man's estate is more fleeting even than this.' But though rude in material, and comparatively insignificant in dimension, the Mosque of Mahomet is glorious in the history of Islâm. Here the Prophet and his companions spent the greater portion of their time : here the daily service, with its oft-recurring prayers, was first publicly established : here the great congregation assembled every week, and trembled often while they listened to the orations of the Prophet and his messages from Heaven. Here he planned victories. From this spot he sent forth envoys to kings and emperors with summons to embrace Islâm. Here he received embassies of contrite and believing tribes ; and from hence issued commands which carried consternation amongst the rebellious to the very outskirts of the Peninsula. Hard by, in the room of Ayesha, he yielded up the ghost ; and there he lies buried.

Type of Saracenic architecture.

The simple building, with its slender and tapering supports, laid the mould for Saracen architecture. It is the type on which buildings for prayer throughout the Moslem world (finding their ideal in the exquisite Mosque at Agra called the Motee Musjid) have been everywhere constructed. The graceful minaret and dome, such as we find them in the Tâj Mehal, may perhaps be traced to the same original. Certainly, if these are the legitimate developments of the Mosque of Medîna, Art owes some of its most signal triumphs to this humble germ.[1]

Houses of Sauda and Ayesha.

The Mosque and the adjoining houses were finished within seven months from Mahomet's arrival. About the middle of winter, he left the house of Abu Ayûb and installed Sauda in her new residence. Shortly afterwards he celebrated his nuptials with Ayesha, who, though she had been three years affianced, was but a girl of ten years. The marriage was completed in her father's house at Al Sunh ; and after that he brought her to the apartments adjoining those of her 'sister' Sauda.

Marriage with Ayesha.

Change wrought in

Thus at the age of fifty-three or fifty-four, a new phase

---

[1] The idea is Sprenger's. He thinks it probable that only the inner part of the temple (that namely next the northern wall, and which formed the 'bachelors' bench,' or hostelry), was originally roofed over ; and that the rest, or about two-thirds of the area, as in modern mosques, was open to the heavens.

commenced in the life of Mahomet. Hitherto, limiting himself to a single wife, he had shunned the indulgences, with
the cares and discord, of polygamy. The unity of his family
was now broken, never again to be restored. Thenceforward
his love was to be claimed, his attentions shared, by a plu-
rality of wives, and his days spent between their houses.
For Mahomet had no separate apartment of his own.

Mahomet's domestic life.

For some time we may suppose that the girl of ten or
eleven years of age would require at the hands of Mahomet
the solicitude of a father, rather than the devotion of a
husband. He conformed to the infantine ideas of his bride
who carried her playthings with her to her new abode; and
at times he even joined in her childish games. But Ayesha
was premature in the development of her charms, as well in
mind as person. Very early she displayed a ready wit with
an arch and playful vivacity of manner. She enthralled the
heart of Mahomet; and, though afterwards exposed to the
frequent competition of fresh rivals, she succeeded in maintaining to the end of his life her supremacy undisputed.

Ayesha's influence over him.

By uniting himself to a second wife Mahomet made a
serious movement away from Christianity, by the tenets and
practice of which he must have known that polygamy was
forbidden. Christianity, however, had little influence over
him; and the step was not repugnant to Judaism, the
authority of which he still recognised, and which in the
example of many illustrious kings and prophets would afford
powerful support to his procedure. But, whatever the bearing of this second marriage, it was planned by Mahomet in a
cool and unimpassioned moment three years before at Mecca.
And it may be doubted whether the propriety of interfering
with the license of Arabian practice, and enforcing between
the sexes the stringent limitations of Christianity, was at any
time even debated in his mind.

Polygamy creates irreconcil-able diver-gence from Christi-anity.

CHAPTER IX.

STATE OF PARTIES AT MEDÎNA. FIRST TWO YEARS OF
MAHOMET'S RESIDENCE THERE.

A.H. II. A.D. 623.

Parties at
Medina.

THE enthusiasm shown by the inhabitants of Medîna at
the reception of Mahomet, by degrees subsided. Various
sentiments began to be entertained towards their visitor by
different sections of the community; and there arose in
consequence a new disposition of parties in the city. Let us
glance for a moment at each of these.

I. *Muhá-
jerín*, or
'Refugees.'

The disciples of Mahomet who had forsaken their homes
and had preceded or followed him in exile, were called by the
title, soon to become illustrious, of MUHÂJERÎN or Refugees.
They are already known to the reader as a devoted band,
forward to acknowledge Mahomet not only as their prophet
but also as their king. Upon them he could depend to the
uttermost.[1]

II. *Ansâr*,
or converts
of Medina.

Next come the converts of Medîna. Bound to Mahomet
by fewer ties of blood or fellowship, they did not yield to the
Refugees in loyalty to his person or enthusiasm for the faith.
They had made less outward sacrifice; but their pledge at
Acaba had involved them in serious risks, as well at home,
should their own countrymen resent or disown the engagement, as from the men of Mecca. In short, they had compromised themselves almost as deeply as the Refugees.

---

[1] The name signifies those who have emigrated, or fled from their home, for
the faith. Among the 'Refugees' are reckoned not only those who having
quitted Mecca were now at Medîna, but also all who subsequently joined Mahomet there (whether coming from Mecca, Abyssinia, or elsewhere) up to the
conquest of Mecca A. H. VIII. The roll of the Refugees was then closed; for
Mecca itself being converted, the merit of emigrating from it ceased.

Bound by their oath only to defend Mahomet in case of attack, they soon practically identified themselves with the Refugees in offensive measures against his enemies at Mecca. Hence they were styled ANSÂR, 'Helpers' or 'Allies.' But as in process of time Medîna was entirely converted, and as Mahomet found many other auxiliaries amongst the Arab tribes, to prevent confusion I ordinarily speak of them simply as Citizens or men of Medîna.[1]

The ancient feuds of the Bani Aus and Khazraj were almost forgotten among the converts from those tribes. Acceptance of the faith required that as Moslems they should acknowledge not only the spiritual but also the temporal authority of Mahomet, and, holding subordinate every distinction of race and kindred, regard each other as brethren. Having surrendered wholly to his will and government, there was little room left for internal rivalry. Still, the memory of long standing jealousies and strife was not always suppressed by the lessons of religion ; and believer was sometimes arrayed against believer in unseemly if not dangerous contention.

Enmity of Aus and Khazraj suppressed by Islâm.

We have no precise data for calculating the proportion of the inhabitants thus actively ranged on the side of Mahomet. The seventy-five adherents who pledged themselves at Acaba were but the representatives of a larger body even then existing at Medîna ; and the cause of Islâm had since that time been daily gaining ground. We may conclude that the professed converts at this time numbered several hundreds.

Converts at Medina numerous.

There was at Medîna one Abu Aámir who had travelled in Syria and other countries, and from his secluded habits was called the *hermit*. This man professed to be a teacher in religion ; and he challenged Mahomet with having superadded doctrines of his own to the 'Faith of Abraham.' Offended at the popularity of the new religion, and sympathising rather with the people who had cast forth the upstart Prophet, Abu Aámir, with about twenty followers, retired to Mecca.[2] Eventually he died an exile in Syria.

Abu Aámir and followers go off to Mecca.

---

[1] Before Mahomet's death, the two terms *Ansâr* and *Citizens* became convertible; that is to say, all the citizens of Medîna were ostensibly converted and so became *Ansârs*.

[2] When Mahomet denied his imputations against Islâm, Abu Aámir abused him as 'a poor solitary outcast.' 'Nay,' replied the Prophet, 'that

Mahomet's
authority
recognised
over his
own ad-
herents. The portion of the Bani Aus and Khazraj remaining un-converted, were neutral, or at least outwardly passive, in their unbelief. There was no active opposition, nor (as at Mecca) any open denial of Mahomet's supernatural claims; neither was his temporal authority over his own adherents denied. The peculiar constitution of Arab society, which admits the residence of several detached bodies at the same place each under its separate independent chief, en-abled Mahomet freely to exercise an absolute and sovereign control over his own people without for the time arrogating any jurisdiction beyond them.

Idolatry
and scepti-
cism sup-
pressed. But although there was nowhere apparent hostility, and the whole body of the citizens, unbelievers as well as con-verts, held themselves bound to fulfil the pledge of pro-tecting the Exile, yet a strong under-current of jealousy and discontent was rapidly setting in against him. We have seen that Abdallah ibn Obey, chief of the Khazrajites and the most powerful citizen in Medîna, was already aspiring to the sovereign power when his hopes were blighted by the arrival of Mahomet.[1] Around Abdallah rallied a numerous party sceptical of the Prophet's claims and unfriendly to the

will be thine own fate, thou liar!' He took a prominent part with fifty followers against Mahomet in the battle of Ohod, in which his own son Hantzala, a devoted Moslem, was killed fighting on the other side. After the conquest of Mecca, he retired to Tâyif. When Tâyif gave in its adhesion to Mahomet, he proceeded to Syria; and there died (in fulfilment of the Prophet's curse) 'a solitary wretched outcast.' He seems to have been an ascetic, and is described by Sprenger as the leader of a party who adhered to the Jews as Proselytes of the Gate.

[1] *Vide* p. 120. The following incident is related of him: One day Ma-homet saddled his ass and went forth to enquire after Sád ibn Obáda, who was sick. By the way he passed Abdallah sitting with a circle of his followers under the shade of his house. Mahomet's courtesy would not permit him to pass without speaking; so he alighted, and saluted him and sat a little while beside him reciting some portion of the Corân, and inviting him to the faith. Abdallah listened quietly till he ended; then he said: 'Nothing could be better than this discourse of thine if it were true. Now, therefore, do thou sit at home in thine own house, and whosoever cometh to thee preach thus unto him, and he that cometh not unto thee refrain from troubling him or intruding into his company with that which he dislikes.' Mahomet went on his way to the house of Sád, downcast at that which Abdallah, the enemy of God, had said unto him. Sád, perceiving him dispirited, enquired the cause. Mahomet told him what Abdallah had said. Then Sád replied: 'Treat him gently, for I swear that when God sent thee unto us, we had already strung pearls to crown him, and he seeth that thou hast snatched the kingdom out of his grasp.'

extension of his rule; but these were unable to check the mysterious influence of the Stranger or stem the tide of his popularity. The circle of his adherents steadily expanded and soon embraced nominally the whole city. Idolatry disappeared, and scepticism, overmatched, was forced to hide its head.

Real belief in Mahomet was not, however, of such rapid growth. Doubts and jealousies possessed the hearts of many; and in private, at a convenient distance from Mahomet, found free expression. They had foolishly espoused a cause which would make them run the gauntlet of all Arabia; and for what return? Only to lose their liberties, and to bring themselves under bondage to a foreign usurper! The class which cherished these sentiments were styled the 'Hypocrites.' But *hypocrisy* and *disaffection* are, in the vocabulary of Islâm, nearly synonymous; and, as the views of this party developed rather into political opposition than religious antagonism, it will be more correct to call them the DISAFFECTED. Such outward conformity, cloaking an ill-concealed antagonism, was more dangerous than open animosity. The class soon became peculiarly obnoxious to Mahomet; he established through his adherents a close watch over their words and conduct; and in due time he followed up his espionage by acts which struck dismay into the hearts of the disaffected.[1]

III. The *Disaffected.*

The JEWISH TRIBES located in the vicinity of Medîna were on an entirely different footing. Mahomet had acknowledged the divine authority of their religion and had even

IV. The *Jews.*

---

[1] Ibn Ishâc thus describes them: 'When the Jewish doctors were filled with hatred and envy of Mahomet, because God had chosen a prophet from amongst the Arabs, there joined them certain men of the Bani Aus and Khazraj, who were in reality little removed from idolatry and unbelief, only that Islâm had by its prevalence overpowered them. So they took the faith as a shield unto them from death; but in secret they were traitors, and their hearts were with the Jews in their rejection of the Prophet.'

Tradition delights to hold up this class to scorn, in stories such as this:— 'Jallâs, the hypocrite, said privately of Mahomet's teaching: "Verily, if this man speak the truth, we are all worse than asses." Omeir, his ward, a believer, overheard the saying and told it to Mahomet; Jallâs went also to Mahomet, and swore by the day of judgment that Omeir lied. Whereupon, a passage of the Coran, convicting Jallâs of falsehood, was revealed."' There are also tales of the 'disaffected' being ignominiously expelled from the Mosque, and even from the clubs or social circles of the citizens; but all such tales are to be received with caution, owing to the strong bias against this class.

rested his claim, in an important degree, upon the evidence of their Scriptures and the testimony of their learned men. One of the objects nearest his heart was a federal union with the Jews. His feasts, fasts, and ceremonies were, up to this time, framed in close correspondence with Jewish custom. His very Kibla, the Holy of holies to which he and his people turned five times a day while they prostrated themselves in prayer, was Jerusalem. No concession, in fact, short of the abandonment of his claim to the prophetic office, was too great to gain the Jews over to his cause.

Mahomet desirous of a combination with them.

It was natural that Mahomet, holding these sentiments, should desire to enter into close association with the Jews. This he did in a formal manner shortly after reaching Medîna. He associated them in a treaty of mutual obligation drawn up in writing, between the Refugees and the Believers of Medîna on the one hand, and the Jews on the other, confirming the latter in the practice of their religion and in the secure possession of their property. The main provisions of this Contract are the following :—

The Treaty of Medina.

'IN THE NAME OF GOD, THE COMPASSIONATE, THE MERCIFUL!

'THE CHARTER of Mahomet the Prophet, unto the Believers of the Coreish and of Medîna, and whosoever else joineth himself unto them and striveth with them for the faith; verily, they are a peculiar people apart from the rest of mankind. The Refugees shall defray the price of blood shed among themselves, and shall ransom honourably their prisoners. The Believers the various tribes of Medîna shall do the same, each according to their several clans. Whosoever is rebellious, or seeketh to spread iniquity, enmity, or sedition amongst the Believers, the hand of every man shall be against him, even if he be the son of one of themselves. No Believer shall be put to death in retaliation for the blood of an infidel; neither shall any infidel be supported against a Believer. Whosoever of the Jews followeth us shall have aid and succour; they shall not be injured, nor shall any enemy be aided against them. No unbeliever shall grant protection to the Coreish of Mecca, either in their persons or their property, nor interpose between the Believers and them.[1] Whosoever killeth a Believer wrongfully shall be liable to retaliation; the Moslems shall join as one man against the murderer. The

---

[1] *Unbeliever* here refers apparently to that portion of the population of Medîna which had not yet submitted to Mahomet's claims, and who are thus brought indirectly within the covenant.

curse of God, and His wrath in the Day of judgment, shall rest
on the man that giveth aid or shelter to the breaker of this
covenant.

'The Jews shall contribute with the Moslems, while at war
with a common enemy. The several branches of the Jews—
those that belong respectively to the various tribes of Medîna—
are one people with the Believers.[1] The Jews will profess their
religion, the Moslems theirs. As with the Jews, so with their
adherents; excepting him who shall transgress and do iniquity,
he alone shall suffer and his family. No one shall go forth (to
war) excepting only with the permission of Mahomet; but this·
shall not hinder any one from seeking his lawful revenge. The
Jews shall be responsible for their expenditure, the Moslems for
theirs; but, if attacked, each shall come to the assistance of the
other. Medîna shall be sacred and inviolable for all that join
this treaty. Strangers, under protection, shall be treated on the
same footing as their protectors; but no female stranger shall be
taken under protection save with consent of her kindred. Controversies and disputes, likely to produce evil and danger, shall
be referred for decision to God and Mahomet His prophet. None
shall join the Coreish or their allies; for verily the engaging
parties are bound together against every one that shall threaten
Medîna. War and Peace shall be made in common. He that
goeth forth shall be secure; and he that sitteth at home in
Medîna shall be secure;—saving him that transgresseth and
committeth wrong. And verily God is the protector of the
righteous and the godly; and Mahomet is the Prophet of God.

'And none but the Evil man and the Oppressor shall change
the conditions of this Charter.'[2]

We are not told when this treaty was entered into, but
it probably was not long after the arrival of Mahomet at
Medîna. For a short time the Jews remained on terms of
cordiality with their new ally; but it soon became apparent
to them that Judaism could not go hand in hand with

Ill-will grows up between Mahomet and Jews.

---

[1] Said to refer to Jewish proselytes from the tribes of Medîna; but the expression may also mean Jews who had attached themselves to those tribes.

[2] The translation is in an abridged form. There is throughout frequent
reiteration that upright and honest dealing shall be observed, and whoever
transgresses shall do so at his own risk, &c. There are also anticipatory
allusions to religious wars, and to the coming crusade against all mankind,
which are evidently additions made at a later time. As there is no reason
to believe that the original or any copy of the treaty was preserved, we can
only regard the version given by tradition as an account transmitted by memory,
admitting much vagueness and looseness of expression; and this will account
for these evidently spurious clauses.

o

Islâm. The position of Mahomet was no longer negative: his religion was not a mere protest against error and superstition. It was daily becoming more positive and more exclusive in its terms. The Prophet rested his claims on the predictions of the Jewish Scriptures; yet he did not profess to be the Messiah of the Jews;—the Messiah, he held, had already appeared in the person of Jesus, and had been rejected by their forefathers. He was himself another, and a greater Prophet, also foretold in their Book. The Jews, he said, knew this: they recognised in Mahomet the promised Prophet, 'as they recognised their own sons;' yet, out of jealousy, spite, and wilful blindness, they rejected him, in like manner as they had rejected their own Messiah. This was the position which Mahomet now held, and to concede it was simply to abandon Judaism. Thus Judaism and Islâm came rapidly into antagonism. In short, a Jew, in joining Mahomet, abandoned of necessity his ancestral faith, and went over to another. With few exceptions, however, the Jews remained steadfast, and fearlessly testified that their Scriptures contained no warrant for the assumptions of the Ishmaelite; — the prophet that was to come, they said, should be not of Arabian, but of Jewish blood, and of the lineage of David. The long cherished and now disappointed hope of the Jews that they would find in Mahomet a supporter of their faith, changed at last into bitter hostility. What availed his oft-repeated professions of respect for their ancient prophets and of allegiance to their Scriptures, when he now so openly contradicted their clearest testimony?

They are inveighed against as blind and stiff-necked.

The few traitors to Judaism, whom Mahomet was able (by what inducements we shall see by-and-by) to gain over, were of the utmost service to his cause. They were constantly referred to as his 'Witnesses.' They bore evidence that the person and character of Mahomet agreed in every particular with the prophetic description in their Books; and they asserted that their brethren, actuated by jealousy, and mortified that the gift of prophecy should pass from them to another people, had concealed the passages which were favourable to his claims. Of such alone the eyes were open. Judicial blindness had seized the rest; a 'thick covering' enveloped their hearts, and rendered them seared and callous. They followed in the footsteps of their forefathers. What but unbelief and rebellion should be looked for from the descendants of those who murmured against Moses, killed their prophets, and rejected their Messiah?

Such was the plausible reasoning by which Mahomet succeeded with his own followers in setting aside the adverse testimony of the Jews. Yet the Jews were a constant cause to him of trouble and anxiety. They plied him with questions of which the point was often difficult to turn aside. The very people to whose corroboration he had appealed over and over again in the Corân, proved a stubborn and standing witness against him.[1] The Jewish tribes were also allied (as we have seen) each with some one or more of the Medîna clans; they had stood by them in trouble, and repeatedly shed blood in their defence. Sympathy in such a direction, especially amongst the doubting and the disaffected citizens, was dangerous to Mahomet. He resolved to rid him of the risk and trouble; and he was not long in finding means to gain his end.

The Jews a standing cause of annoyance to Mahomet.

Meanwhile, his Revelation teemed with invectives against the Israelites. The tales of their forefathers' disobedience, folly, and idolatry were reiterated at wearisome length; and the conclusion continually insinuated that the descendants of so flagitious and incorrigible a race must be equally incorrigible and flagitious.

Notices of them in Corân.

We have somewhat anticipated the narrative; but it was necessary to explain what will be narrated in the following chapter; namely, the early and decisive secession of Mahomet from the customs and institutions of the Jews and the widening breach between the two.

Mahomet's secession from Jewish institutions.

[1] Tradition gives a great variety of tales in illustration, but they are all cast in a mould of ridicule and contempt of the Jew, who is represented as always coming off the worst, humbled and abased. We may be allowed to doubt whether the scales did not oftener turn on the other side. Mahomet evidently smarted at this period under the attacks of the Jews.

CHAPTER X.

RELIGIOUS INSTITUTIONS, AND MISCELLANEOUS EVENTS DURING THE FIRST AND SECOND YEARS OF THE HEGIRA.

A.H. I. & II.—A.D. 623.

The five daily prayers.

THE daily observance of prayer at five stated times (enjoined, it is said, on the Heavenly journey, but nowhere commanded in the Corân) was probably practised by Mahomet and his followers before they left Mecca. At all events, it was now an essential, and perhaps the most noticeable and characteristic, feature of Islâm. The daily prayers were ordinarily said by Mahomet and some of his followers in the adjoining mosque, but might optionally be offered up anywhere. The service was invariably led by Mahomet himself, when present; in his absence, by the chief person in the assembly, or by any one else charged by the Prophet with the duty. The nightly prayers were generally said at home.[1]

Lustration preliminary to prayer.

At what period lustration was introduced as the necessary preliminary of prayer, is not certain. This ceremony, perhaps, was also prescribed at Mecca; but, however that may be, it was evidently borrowed from the Jews, with whose teaching the ordinances established by Mahomet respecting ceremonial impurity and ablutions very closely correspond.

[1] We are told that, when the fast of Ramadhân was appointed, the people in their zeal gathered in the mosque at a late hour for the nightly prayer; and, fancying that the Prophet had fallen asleep, coughed at his door as a sign for him to issue forth. He came out, and said: 'I have observed for some days your coming for the nightly prayer into the mosque, until I feared that it would grow by custom into a binding ordinance; and, verily, if it were so commanded, my people could not fulfil the command. Wherefore, my people, pray ye at even-tide in your own houses. Truly, the best prayer is that which a man offers up in his own house, excepting only the prayers which are commanded to be offered up in the mosque.'

The Believer's life was thus a daily round of religious observances, which, practised at first with zeal and aspiration, soon declined, for the mass, into barren forms.[1] At earliest dawn the Moslem begins the day with lustration, preliminary to the prescribed genuflexions and formularies of prayer; at midday he is called aside from business for the same duty; in the afternoon, and again when the sun has set, the ceremonies are repeated; and the day is closed when darkness has set in by the same rites with which it opened. Saints and sinners join in the stereotyped form; the most heinous crime, just committed or in immediate contemplation, does not interfere with the performance of these devotions; and the neglect to observe them is an abnegation of the faith and an insult to the majesty of Islâm which demand interposition of the temporal arm.

Mahometan prayer a formal service.

The daily prayers are not necessarily congregational. They may be offered up by the worshippers singly or in companies, in the mosque or at home, or by the way. But at mid-day of Friday there was appointed a public service in the mosque, at which the Believers as a body, unless detained by sufficient cause, must attend. The usual prayers were on that occasion followed by an address or sermon pronounced by Mahomet. This weekly oration was skilfully adapted to the circumstances and feelings of the audience. It allowed full scope for the eloquence of the Prophet, and by its frequent recurrence helped to confirm his influence and rivet the claims of Islâm.

Friday, or public service.

Sermon.

No religious antagonism is to be supposed in the selection of Friday for the public service. Because when he fixed upon it, Mahomet was still on friendly terms with the Jews, and inclined to adopt their institutions. In the Christian Sunday he had a precedent for change, and he may have desired in a similar manner to distinguish the sacred day of Islâm from the Jewish Sabbath.[2] Perhaps also he

Motive for selection of Friday.

---

[1] I am far from affirming that with the more devout Moslems, the ceremonial is not often a channel for spiritual worship. I speak of the *general effect*, as gathered from tradition itself, and (as regards modern Mahometans) from personal observation.

[2] There is, moreover, no close analogy between the Jewish Sabbath and the Mussulman Friday. In the latter there is no *hallowing* of the day as one meant for rest or religious worship. After the public service, the people were encouraged to return to their business.

hoped by the choice of another day to secure the attendance of the Jews at his public service, which was composed, like theirs, of prayer, reading of the Scripture, and a sermon. As a Jew (according to the doctrine of Mahomet at this time) might follow all the precepts of Moses and yet be a good Mussulman, it is by no means improbable that some Jews may at the first have attended both the mosque and the synagogue. We have instances of Rabbins being present in the mosque; and the synagogue at Medîna was visited by Mahomet himself, and by his followers.

Jerusalem the first Kibla.

Jerusalem was the first *Kibla* of Mahomet; that is to say, after the fashion of the Jews, he and his followers prayed with their faces turned towards the Temple of Solomon. When there was no longer any hope of gaining over the Jews, or of fusing Judaism and Islâm into one religion, the ceremony lost its value. Rather it opened a vulnerable point: 'This Prophet of yours,' said the Jews tauntingly, 'knew not where to find his Kibla, till we pointed it out to him.' It was now the object of Mahomet to transfer the homage of his people from Jerusalem, and to concentrate it upon Mecca. His system would receive a fresh accession of strength and local influence if he were thus to magnify the Káaba and make it the Kibla of his people.

The Kibla changed to Mecca. A.H. II. Nov. A.D. 623.

Mahomet, we are told, and some of his followers also, greatly desired the change.[1] How it was effected is thus related with the usual supernatural colouring. It was sixteen or seventeen months after his arrival in Medîna that Mahomet, longing for the Kibla to be transferred from Jerusalem to the Káaba, thus addressed his guardian angel: 'O Gabriel! would that the Lord might change the direction of my face at prayer away from the Kibla of the Jews!' 'I am but a servant,' replied Gabriel; 'address thy prayer to God.' Then Mahomet made his petition to the Lord. So it came to pass, on a certain day, that as he was praying in the assembly towards the Temple of Jerusalem, and was raising his face upwards in that direction, unexpectedly the following divine revelation was made to him: '*Verily We have seen thee turning about thy face towards the Heavens; where- fore We shall cause thee to turn towards a Kibla that*

---

[1] Sprenger thinks that it was advised by Omar.

shall please thee. Turn now thy face toward the Holy Temple of Mecca. Wheresoever ye are, when ye pray, turn toward it.' The Prophet had already performed two prostrations in the direction of Jerusalem, when suddenly, reciting this behest, he turned towards the south, and the congregation (which followed closely all his movements) turned round also. Thenceforward Jerusalem was abandoned, and the Káaba became the Kibla of Islâm.[1] The Jews, knowing full well the motives for the change, were mortified and still further estranged. Mahomet had broken, as it were, the last outward link that bound him to their creed. They charged him with fickleness, and with worshipping towards an idolatrous Temple, and these charges he endeavoured to meet in the Corân.[2] But it required the victory at Bedr, and the subsequent hostilities against the Jews themselves, to silence their objections. From this time forward Islâm cast aside the trammels of Judaism, and became indissolubly bound up with the worship of the Káaba.

[1] About three miles to the N.W. of the town lies the mosque called the 'Mosque of the *double Kibla.'* Some give this title also to the mosque at Koba. The change of the Kibla has elicited a great mass of discrepant tradition. Many spots are mentioned as the scene of its occurrence, and many different companies claim the honour of being its witnesses. Tradition delights to tell how, as the rumour spread abroad, one and another was startled by the strange intelligence. The most probable account gives the Great mosque as the scene, and the time that of the mid-day prayer.

[2] The passage in which Mahomet sought to refute the charge is highly illustrative of our subject. The context relates to the Jews: —

'The Fools from amongst the people will say, *What hath turned them* Sura ii. *from their Kiblah, towards which they used to pray?* SAY, Unto God belongeth the East and the West: He guideth whom He chooseth into the right way. Thus have We made you an intermediate People, that ye should be Witnesses for mankind; and the Prophet shall be Witness for you. We appointed the Kiblah towards which thou usedst to pray, only that We might know him who followeth the Apostle from him that turneth back on his heels, although it be a stumbling block, excepting unto those whom God hath directed.' [*Here follows the verse quoted in the text; after which the passage proceeds:*—] 'And verily, if thou wert to show unto those who have received the Scriptures every kind of sign, they would not follow thy Kiblah; and thou shalt not follow their Kiblah. Neither doth one part of them follow the Kiblah of the other part.[1] And if thou wert to follow their desires after the knowledge that hath reached thee, then verily thou shouldest be amongst the Transgressors. They to whom We have given the Scriptures know this,[2] even as they know their own children; but verily, a party amongst

[1] Christians turn towards the East, and Jews towards Jerusalem: whence Mahomet would argue a propriety in having a peculiar and distinctive Kibla for Islâm.

[2] Either the rightness of the change; or 'this *Apostle,' i.e.* recognise Mahomet.

Circum-
cision.

The rite of circumcision is hardly to be mentioned as an institution of Islâm. It was current among the Arabs as an Abrahamic ceremony,[1] and continued (without any command in the Corân) to be practised by the followers of Mahomet.

Mahomet
at first
observes
Fast of
Atone-
ment.
A.H. II.
Sept. A.D.
622.
Fast of
Rama-
dhân sub-
stituted.
A.H. II.
Dec. A.D.
623.

Two or three months after his arrival in Medîna, Mahomet saw the Jews keeping the great Fast of the Atonement;[2] and he readily adopted it for his own people. Prior to this, fasting does not appear to have been a prescribed ordinance of Islâm. It was established at a period when the great object of Mahomet was to bring his religion into harmony with the Jewish rites and ceremonies. But when he began to cast off Judaism and its customs, this fast was to be superseded by another. Accordingly about a year and a half after his arrival in Medîna, Mahomet promulgated, as a divine command, that the following month of Ramadhân was to be thenceforward observed as an annual fast. Although the new ordinance was expressly ordained as similar in principle to

them hideth the truth designedly. . . . And every (people) hath a direction to which it turneth (in prayer). Wherefore press forward in good works; wheresoever ye may be, God will bring you back together; surely God's power is over all things. Now, therefore, from whatsoever place thou comest forth, turn thy face towards the Holy Temple; for it is the truth from thy Lord, and God is not regardless of that which ye are doing. . . . . That men may have no cause of dispute against you, excepting them that transgress. Fear them not therefore; but fear Me, that I may fulfil My grace upon you, and that ye may be rightly directed.'

Shortly after occurs the following passage (addressed probably also to the Jews) in justification of the pilgrim ceremony at *Safa* and *Marwa*, alleged to be, or to have been, the sites where two idols stood: 'Verily *Safa* and *Marwa* are of the monuments of God. Whosoever, therefore, performeth the greater pilgrimage, of the holy House, or the lesser, it shall be no crime in him if he perform the circuit of them both. And whosoever performeth that which is good of a willing heart, verily God is grateful and knowing.'

[1] The practice is incumbent on Mahometans as a part of the *Sunnat* (custom or example of the Prophet), but it is curious that we have no authentic account of Mahomet's own circumcision.

[2] *Ashôr*, or the 'Fast of the Tenth,' *i.e.* tenth day of the seventh month. *Lev.* xxiii. 27. It was a day of affliction and atonement; but popular tradition at Medîna assigned to it another origin. 'When Mahomet asked the Jews what was the origin of the Fast, they said that it was in memory of the delivery of Moses out the hands of Pharaoh, and the destruction of the tyrant in the Red Sea: "*We* have a greater right in Moses than they," said Mahomet; so he fasted like the Jews, and commanded his people to fast also. And when the Mussulman Fast of Ramadhân was imposed, Mahomet did not command the Fast of Ashôr (*i.e.* of the Tenth) to be observed, neither did he forbid it;' *i.e.* he left it optional to keep it up as well as the other.

that of the Jews, yet the mode of its observance was entirely different. At first the Moslems (following the Jews who fasted for four-and-twenty hours from sunset to sunset) thought themselves bound to abstain from all enjoyments night and day throughout the month. But Mahomet checked this ascetic spirit. His followers were to fast rigorously by day, but from sunset till dawn they might eat and drink and indulge in pleasures that were otherwise lawful.[1]

It was winter when this fast was ordained, and Mahomet probably then contemplated its being always kept at the same season, in which case the prohibition to eat or drink during the day would not have involved any extreme hardship.[2] In the course of time, however, by the introduction of the lunar year, the month of Ramadhân gradually shifted till it reached the summer season; and then the prohibition to taste water from morning till evening became a burden heavy to bear. The strictness of the fast, as thus instituted by Mahomet,

Its unequal pressure and rigour.

---

[1] 'O ye that believe! A Fast is ordained for you, as it was ordained for those before you, that haply ye may follow Piety :—   *Sura ii.*

'For the computed number of days. The sick amongst you, and the traveller, (shall fast) an equal number of other days; but he that is able to keep it (and neglecteth) shall make atonement by the feeding of a poor man. And whoever performeth that which is good, of a willing heart, it shall be well for him. And if ye fast it shall be well for you, if ye comprehend :—

'In the month of Ramadhân; wherein the Corân was sent down. . . . Wherefore let him that is present in this month fast during the same; but he that is sick, or on a journey, shall fast an equal number of other days. God willeth that which is easy for you: He willeth not for you that which is difficult; and that ye may fulfil the number of days, and magnify God, for that He hath directed you, and may give thanks. . . . It is lawful unto you, during the nights of the Fast, to consort with your wives. They are a garment unto you, and ye are a garment unto them. God knoweth that ye are defrauding yourselves, wherefore He hath turned unto you, and forgiven you. Now, therefore, sleep with them, and earnestly desire that which God hath ordained for you; and eat and drink until ye can distinguish a white thread from a black thread, by the daybreak. Then keep the fast again until night, and consort not with them (during the day); but be in attendance in the places of worship. These are the limits prescribed by God: wherefore draw not near unto them. Thus God declareth His signs unto mankind, that they may follow Piety.'

[2] The Jewish intercalary year, which was probably in use at this time, would have prevented any change of season for a very long series of years (see *ante*, p. 29). But when Mahomet introduced the lunar year, that which might have been 'easy' at the first, came by the change of seasons to be often a grievous burden to his followers.

has nevertheless been maintained unrelaxed at whatsoever season it may fall; and to this day, in the parched plains of India, during the month of Ramadhân, however burning the sun and scorching the wind, the follower of Mahomet may not suffer a drop of water, during the long summer day, to pass his lips ; and he looks forward with indescribable longing for the sunset when, without compromising his faith, he may slake his thirst and refresh with food his drooping frame. The trial, though thus unequally severe in different climes and at different terms of the lunar cycle, is no doubt a wholesome exercise of faith and self-denial. But in so far as the fast was intended to be a restraint upon licentiousness, its limitation to the daytime must defeat the object.

Eed al Fitr, or Festival of ' breaking the fast.'
A.H. II. Feb. A.D. 624.

At the conclusion of the fast, a festival was appointed, called the EED AL FITR, or ' breaking of the fast.' A day or two before the expiration of the month Ramadhân, Mahomet assembled the people, and instructed them in the ceremonies to be observed at the conclusion of the fast. On the first day of the following month they were early in the morning to bring together their offerings for the poor ; each one—young or old, bond or free, male or female—a measure of dates, of barley, or of raisins, or a smaller measure of wheat.[1] ' See,' said he, ' that ye give plenty to the poor this day, so that they need not to go about and beg.' Having presented their alms, all went forth with the Prophet who was clad in festive garments to the *Musalla*, or place of prayer, outside the city on the road to Mecca.[2] A short spear or iron-shod staff (brought by Zobeir from Abyssinia) was carried before him by Bilâl and planted on the spot. Taking his stand there, the Prophet recited certain prayers appropriate to the occasion, and then addressed the assembled multitude. The service over, they returned to their homes, and Mahomet made a great feast at the Great mosque, and distributed the accumulated alms amongst the poor.

---

[1] Tradition takes care to note that this was before the imposition of regular almsgiving, or Zakât, which will be noticed hereafter.

[2] Speaking of ' Mahomet's mosque in the Munâka' (or open space between the city and its western suburb), Burton writes : ' Others believed it to be founded upon the Musalla el Nabi, a place where the Prophet recited the first Festival prayers after his arrival at El Medinah, and used frequently to pray, and to address those of his followers who lived far from the Haram' (or Great mosque).—ii. 192.

Another great festival was established by Mahomet ;—the Eed al Zoha, or 'day of sacrifice.' The slaying of victims formed the concluding scene in the pilgrimage at Mecca, and in that ceremony the new festival was eventually merged. In the first year of the Prophet's residence at Medîna the season of pilgrimage passed unnoticed. In its stead, as mentioned above, Mahomet kept the great Day of Atonement with its sacrifice of victims, in conformity with the practice of the Jews ; and had he continued on a friendly footing with them, he would probably have maintained this rite. In the following year, however, it was in keeping with his altered relations to abandon altogether the Jewish ritual of sacrifice, and to substitute for it another somewhat similar in character, but grounded on the ceremonies of the Káaba. It was accordingly after having waged war against one of the Jewish tribes settled in the suburbs of Medîna, and having expatriated them from the country, that Mahomet resolved upon the change. On the tenth day of Dzul Hijj, while the votaries of the Káaba, after making the circuit of mount Arafât, were engaged in the closing solemnities of the pilgrimage at Minâ, Mahomet preceded by Bilâl with the Abyssinian lance, and followed by his people, went forth to the place of prayer without the city. After a service resembling that of the breaking of the Fast, two fatted sucking kids, with budding horns, were placed before the Prophet. Seizing a knife, he sacrificed the first, saying : ' O Lord ! I offer this for my people, all those that bear testimony to thy Unity and to my Mission.' Then he called for the other, and slaying it likewise, said : ' O Lord ! this is for Mahomet, and for the family of Mahomet.' Of the latter kid both he and his family partook, and that which was over he gave to the poor. The double sacrifice seems in its main features to have been founded on the practice of the Jewish High-priest at the Day of the Atonement, when he sacrificed ' first for his own sins, and then for the people's.' [1] This ceremony was repeated by Mahomet every year when present at Medîna ; and it was kept up there after his decease.[2]

Eed al Zoha combined with Fast of Atonement. Dzul Hijj, A.H. I. March, A.D. 623.

But subsequently shifted to correspond with Meccan pilgrimage. A.H. II. April, A.D. 624.

---

[1] *Heb.* vii. 27 ; *Lev.* xvi. Aaron offered a sacrifice ' for himself and for his house,' besides ' the goat of the sin-offering that is for the people.'

[2] The short lance, used at the two Festivals by the Prophet, was still in the keeping of the Mueddzin at Medîna, in the second or third century. It used to

The summons to prayer was at first the simple cry, 'To public prayer!' After the Kibla was changed, Mahomet bethought himself of a more formal call. Some suggested the Jewish trumpet, others the Christian bell; but neither was grateful to the Prophet's ear.[1] The ADZÂN, or call to prayer, was then established. Tradition claims for it a supernatural origin. 'While the matter was under discussion, a citizen of Medîna dreamed that he met a man clad in green raiment carrying a bell, and he sought to buy it, saying that it would do well for assembling the faithful to prayer. "I will show thee," replied the stranger, "a better way than that; let a crier call aloud, GREAT IS THE LORD! GREAT IS THE LORD! *I bear witness that there is no God but the Lord: I bear witness that Mahomet is the Prophet of God. Come unto Prayer: Come unto Salvation. God is Great! God is Great! There is no God but the Lord!*" Awaking from sleep, the citizen went straightway to Mahomet, and told him his dream. The Prophet perceived that it was a vision from the Lord, and forthwith commanded Bilâl, his negro servant, to carry out the divine behest.' Ascending the top of a lofty house beside the mosque while it was yet dark, Bilâl watched for the break of day, and on the first glimmer of light, with his far-sounding voice, aroused all around from their slumbers, adding to the divinely-appointed call these words, 'Prayer is better than Sleep! Prayer is better than Sleep!' Every day, at the five appointed times, the well-known cry summoned the people to their devotions. For twelve centuries the same call has continually been sounded forth by the successors of Bilâl from a myriad minarets; and the traveller in the East is still startled in his sleep at early dawn by Mueddzins crying aloud from their various mosques the self-same words used by Bilâl.[2]

be carried in state before the Governor of Medîna when he went forth to celebrate these Festivals.

[1] Hishâmi says that he had actually given orders for a trumpet to be made, which was probable enough during his first relations with the Jews. Afterwards disliking the idea, he ordered a wooden bell or 'gong' to be constructed; and it was already hewn out, when the dream settled the question in favour of the *Adzân*.

[2] After crying the Adzân, Bilâl used to come to the door of Mahomet and rouse him thus: 'To prayer, oh Apostle of God! to Salvation!' Then Bilâl would take his stand in the front row of the worshippers, who used strictly to

The old cry, 'To public prayer,' was still maintained Call used for convening a general assembly. whenever an assembly was summoned for the announcement of important intelligence, as of a victory; or for the proclamation of a general order, as the going forth to war. The people hurried to the mosque at the call, but it had no longer any connection with their devotions.

On the spot where Mahomet used to stand in the Great The pulpit. mosque at public prayers, the branch of a date-tree was planted as a post for him to hold by. When the Kibla was changed, the post was taken up from the northern end of the Mosque and fixed near the southern wall. In process of time Mahomet, now beyond the prime of life, began to feel fatigue at standing throughout the long Friday service. So he consulted with his followers; and one said: 'Shall I make for thee a pulpit such as I have seen them make in Syria?' The suggestion pleased Mahomet, both as a relief to himself, and with the view of being better seen and heard at public worship. Accordingly one or two tamarisk trees were felled and fashioned into a pulpit, having a place to sit on, and three steps leading up to it. It was placed near the southern wall on the spot which the pulpit of the Great mosque still occupies at the present day.

Mahomet ascended the pulpit for the first time on a Friday. Manner of the daily service. As he mounted the steps, he turned towards the Káaba, and uttered a loud *Takbîr*, ' Great is the Lord!' and the whole assembly from behind burst forth into the same exclamation. Then he bowed himself in prayer, still standing in the pulpit with his face toward the south, and averted from the people; after which he descended walking backwards, and at the foot of the pulpit prostrated himself towards the Káaba. This he did twice, using appropriate verses and ejaculations; and then the prayers being ended, he turned to the congregation and told them he had done this that they might know and imitate his manner of worship. Such was the form of daily prayer;

---

follow his example in the prayers and genuflexions. There were two other Mueddzins employed by Mahomet, but they acted only in case of Bilâl's absence. As the Prophet's treasurer, Bilâl also kept the money and the gifts presented to Mahomet. He was held in much esteem by the Moslems; and by his influence obtained a free-born Arab wife for his negro brother. Bilâl, like many other Moslem warriors, was granted landed property at Damascus, where he died A.H. 20, aged sixty, and where his tomb is still shown.

and, handed down from generation to generation, such to the minutest point it has continued ever since. Worshippers drawn up now as then by rows in the mosques, the wayfarer who overtaken by the hour of prayer spreads his carpet for his devotions at the road-side, the prince and the peasant, all equally follow with exactest scrupulosity the practice of their Prophet in his forms of obeisance and prostration.[1]

And of the Friday service.

The fashion of the Friday service is thus described. As the Prophet mounted the steps of the pulpit he greeted the assembly with the salutation of peace. Then he sat down, and Bilâl sounded forth the call to prayer. After the prescribed obeisances and prayers with recitation from the Corân, he was wont to deliver two discourses sitting down twice; and he used at times to point with his fingers, enforcing his instructions; the people raised their faces towards him, listening attentively, and fixing their eyes upon him; and when he had ended they joined in a universal *Amen*. As he discoursed he leant upon a staff. His dress on these occasions was a mantle of striped Yemen stuff, six cubits in length, thrown over his shoulders; the lower garment was a girdle of fine cloth from Omân, but of smaller dimensions than the other. These robes were worn only on Friday, and on the two great Festivals; at the conclusion of each service, they were folded up and carefully put away.

Extraordinary sanctity of the pulpit.

The pulpit was invested by Mahomet with great sanctity. Oaths regarding disputed rights were to be taken close beside it. Any one who should swear falsely by it, ' even if the subject of the oath were as insignificant as a tooth-pick,' was doomed to hell. The blessedness of the spot was shadowed forth by the saying of the Prophet that the space between his house and the pulpit was ' as one of the gardens of Paradise.' Credulous tradition holds that it is literally so; and the fond conceit has been perpetuated by a wretched endeavour to adorn the place with painted figures of shrubs and flowers. ' It is a space,' says Burton, ' of about eighty feet in length, tawdrily decorated, so as to resemble a garden.

---

[1] A series of two obeisances followed by prostration, with appropriate ejaculations and prayers, is called a *Rakàat*. It is said that Mahomet, a month after his arrival at Medîna, prescribed two such Rakáats for each time of prayer, but subsequently increased them to four, excepting for persons on a journey.

The carpets are flowered, and the pediments of the columns are cased with bright green tiles, and adorned to the height of a man with gaudy and unnatural vegetation in arabesque.' [1]

When Mahomet took possession of the pulpit, he expressed his regret at parting with the post by which he had so long prayed, in affectionate terms, and commanded it to be buried under the pulpit. Traditionists have coloured this incident with the romantic addition that the post moaned loudly at its desertion, and would not cease until the Prophet placed his hand upon it, and soothed its grief. [2]

The moaning post.

During the first year of his residence at Medîna Mahomet lost two of his chief adherents among the men of Medîna. Kolthûm, with whom he lodged at Cobâ, died shortly after his arrival. And the Mosque was hardly completed, when Asád son of Zorâra was seized with a virulent sore-throat. Asád was one of the earliest converts of Medîna. He belonged to the famous Six who first met Mahomet, three or four years before, at Mina. He was elected the 'Leader' of the Bani Najjâr, when they pledged their faith to the Prophet at the 'second Acaba,' and he had ever since taken a prominent part in the spread of Islâm. Musáb, when sent from Mecca to instruct the enquirers at Medîna, lodged with him, and together they had openly established Mussulman prayers in the city. His house was hard by the Great mosque, where, as we have seen, he welcomed Mahomet on his arrival, and took charge of his favourite camel. The Prophet was deeply grieved at his illness ; but, most of all, was he troubled by the insinuations of the Jews and the disaffected citizens. ' If this man were a prophet,' they said, ' could he not ward off sickness from his friend ? ' ' And yet,' said Mahomet, ' I

Death of Kolthûm and Asád ibn Zorâra.

---

[1] Similarly, Mahomet said that his pulpit was ' over one of the Fountains of Paradise ;'—as a church might be called ' the gate of Heaven.' The sanctity of the pulpit was so great that at times other than the public assembly, worshippers used to come, and, catching the knob of the pulpit, pray, holding it with their hands.

[2] It is a congenial subject for tradition. The people were terrified at the noise, for the groanings of the post were 'like those of a she-camel ten months gone with young.' On Mahomet stroking it with his hand, it ceased. It was then either buried under the pulpit, or put away among the rafters of the roof.

According to another tradition, Mahomet *embraced* the post, and then it stopped moaning ; on which the Prophet said, that ' had he not done so, it would not have ceased to moan till the Day of judgment.'

have no power from my Lord over even mine own life, or over that of any of my followers. The Lord destroy the Jews that speak thus!' He visited his sick friend frequently, and twice caused his neck to be cauterised all round. But the remedies were of no avail; he sank rapidly and died. Mahomet preceded the funeral procession to the spot which had been selected for a burial-ground. It was a large enclosure, studded with thorny shrubs, without the city, on its eastern side. Asád was the first of the illustrious band of early heroes who were buried in the cemetery, and whose tombs are still visited by the pilgrim.

Barrenness of the Moslem women.

For many months after the arrival of Mahomet, it so happened that no children were born to the Moslem women; and the rumour began to spread abroad that their barrenness was occasioned by Jewish sorcery and enchantments. More than a year of the Hegira had elapsed when the first infant was born to the Refugees,—the wife of Zobeir presenting him with a son; and shortly after, the same good fortune happened to one of the Medîna citizens. These births, dispelling their apprehensions, caused great joy among the Believers. It may possibly have been with reference to such supposed enchantments, that Mahomet composed one or other of the two short Suras which now stand at the close of the Corân and which are used as spells to counteract mischief designed by enemies. A later occasion, which will be hereafter mentioned, is, however, assigned to them by tradition.

Mahomet superstitious.

The Prophet was in many respects superstitious. So afraid was he of darkness, that on entering a room at night, he would not sit down till a lamp had been lighted for him.[1] When cupped, he used to have the operation performed an *odd* number of times, believing that the virtue was greater than with an even number. He also fancied that cupping on any Tuesday which fell on the 17th of the month was peculiarly efficacious, and proved a remedy for all the disorders of the coming year. If the heavens were overcast with heavy clouds, he would change colour, and betray a mysterious apprehension till they cleared away. He was also supersti-

[1] He is said to have had such a repugnance to the form of the cross that he broke everything brought into his house with its figure upon it. The tradition may, however, have been only symbolical of his extreme aversion to the doctrine of the Crucifixion.

tiously anxious about the effect of the winds.[1] Such traditions, which, from their number and agreement, must be more
or less founded on fact, illustrate the weakness, nervous sensi-
bility, and apprehension of unseen and supernatural influences
for good or for evil, which affected the mind of Mahomet.

Mahomet lived in great simplicity. His wives' apart- Simplicity
ments, in which he dwelt by turns, were cabins built of sun- of Maho-
burnt brick and thatched with palm-branches, in area little met's life.
more than twelve feet square, and in height so mean that the
roof might be reached by the hand. The doorway was protected by a screen of goat and camel hair; but Ayesha's
apartment had a wooden door. Some of the houses (in course
of time nine, one for each of his wives) had an outer room or
verandah formed by a second wall, but in others by a mere
partition of palm-twigs daubed with mud. Entering the
court of the Mosque from Ayesha's door was a small ante-
chamber into which Mahomet used to retire for his evening
devotions.

The furnishing of the apartments corresponded with their
low exterior. A leathern mattress stuffed with palm-fibre
served for a bed, and the pillows were of the same material.
The Prophet himself sometimes used a cot of teak-wood
strung with coarse cords of the palm;[2] but ordinarily the
mattresses were spread for repose upon the ground. The
walls of the rooms were hung with skins or leathern bottles
used to hold water, milk, or honey; but when empty, blown
out and thus suspended.

The constant attendant of Mahomet was Abdallah ibn

[1] 'When the wind blew (Ayesha tells us) the Prophet would say: "O
Lord! verily I supplicate Thee for good from this wind, and good from its
nature, and good for that thing for which it is sent; and I seek protection with
Thee from the bad effects of this wind, and its baneful influence, and the harm
which it was sent to do." And when clouds appeared, he used to change
colour; and he would come out, go in, walk forwards and backwards; and
when they rained, and passed away without doing harm, his alarm would
cease. On Ayesha asking him the reason, he said: "O Ayesha! peradventure
these clouds and winds might be like those which are mentioned in the history
of the tribe of Ad. For when they saw a cloud overshadowing the heavens,
they said, *This is a cloud bringing rain for us;* but it was not so, but a
punishment to them, in calling for it impatiently; and there was in it a
destroying wind."'

[2] The cot is said to have been a gift from Asád ibn Zorára. After the
Prophet's death it was used as a bier at funerals, and was eventually sold for
a great price.

Masûd, whose mother, once a slave like her son, performed the same menial office for the Prophet's wives. Both were now free. Abdallah was secretary to Mahomet as well as body-servant, and attended him in his campaigns. He took charge of his bed, his shoes or sandals, his toothpicks, and his washing gear. When bathing he screened him; when sleeping he watched him; and he accompanied him abroad. If the Prophet went forth upon a visit, Abdallah would bring his shoes for him to put on, and taking charge of his staff precede him on the way. Arrived at his destination, Abdallah again took charge of his shoes and gave the staff into his hand; returning, he did as before and re-entered his house in advance of him. Abdallah resided close by the Mosque, and was always ready at the call of Mahomet. From him much of the tradition regarding the life and habits of the Prophet has been derived; and his known intelligence and veracity have secured for his narrations special weight.[1] Anas also attended the Prophet, and above a dozen other persons are named as having served him at various times: but Abdallah was his favourite.

Contrast
between
Mahomet's
simple life
and the
luxury
of his
followers.

Comparing the sumptuous luxury which rapidly sprang up throughout the Moslem world with the homeliness of Mahomet's life, tradition would draw therefrom for his degenerate followers a lesson of frugality and self-denial, and even imply that the Prophet suffered hardship. But want and discomfort lay only in the contrast. Bred in the primitive simplicity of Arab life, Mahomet could not have appreciated, probably would not have tolerated, the artificial comforts which his followers soon learned to hold as necessary to their existence. The Prophet was happier with his wives each in her small and rudely furnished cabin, than if he had been surrounded by the luxuries of a palace.

Our story will now lead us to more stirring scenes.

---

[1] If one may judge by the style of his traditions, he was particularly careful and conscientious in the statement of his recollections; though, like the other Companions of the Prophet, he used to be surrounded by crowds of curious enquirers, and thus had every temptation to exaggerate. He was settled by Omar at Cûfa with great distinction, and survived Mahomet twenty years.

CHAPTER XI.

HOSTILITIES BETWEEN MEDÎNA AND MECCA.

A.H. I. & II.—A.D. 623.

THE first six months of Mahomet's residence at Medîna were undisturbed either by alarms from without or by hostile counsels at home. No vindictive measures were planned by the citizens of Mecca. He who had for more than ten years kept the city in continual excitement, broken up old parties, and introduced a new faction of his own, was now gone forth with all his adherents, and his absence afforded immediate relief. The current of society, long troubled and diverted by his designs, now returned, to flow peaceably for a while in its ancient channel. *Repose at Medina for the first six months.*

The thoughts of Mahomet, indeed, from the day of his flight, were not thoughts of peace. He had threatened in the Corân that vengeance should overtake the enemies of his mission,—a vengeance not postponed to a future life, but immediate and overwhelming even in the present world. He now occupied a position where he might become the agent for executing the divine sentence, and at the same time triumphantly impose the true religion on those who had rejected it. Hostility to the Coreish lay as a seed germinating in his heart; it wanted but a favourable opportunity to spring up. *Hostilities contemplated by Mahomet from the first;*

The opportunity did not at once present itself. The people of Medîna were pledged only to defend the Prophet from attack, not to join him in aggressive steps against the Coreish. He must take time to gain their affections, and to secure their co-operation in offensive measures against his enemies. His followers from Mecca were too few to measure arms alone with the Coreish. They were also, like *But deferred from motives of policy.*

himself, at present occupied by the duty of providing dwelling-places for their families. In fulfilling this domestic obligation, in establishing friendly relations with the citizens of Medîna and at first also with the Jewish tribes, in organising civil and religious institutions for his followers now fast assuming the position of an independent society, and in riveting the hold of his theocratic government upon them, the autumn of the first year passed away.

Extent and value of the caravan trade of Mecca with Syria.

But in their caravan traffic with the north (the beaten path of which passed between Medîna and the sea-coast), the Coreish offered a point for attack too vulnerable, and the prospect of a booty too tempting, for this inaction long to last. The trade of Mecca was large and profitable. From thence, and from its sister city Tâyif, caravans proceeded in the autumn to Yemen and Abyssinia, and in spring to Syria. Leather, gums, frankincense, the precious metals, and other products of Arabia, formed the staples of export. The leather of Mecca, Tâyif, and Yemen was in much request both in Syria and Persia, and fetched a high price. Piece-goods, silk, and articles of luxury were received in exchange at Gaza and other Syrian marts, and carried back to Mecca. We read of at least six such expeditions during the year A.D. 623, and there were no doubt several more. Some of the caravans were very large and very rich. One, we are told, consisted of 2,000 camels, whose freight was valued at 50,000 (golden) dinârs. The annual export trade of Mecca has been estimated by Dr. Sprenger at not less than 250,000 dinârs, and the return merchandise at the same amount.[1] The ordinary profit being 50 per cent., it is easy to see how

---

[1] These figures must be taken as conjectural; but as each camel carried about two cwt. of costly goods, the value must no doubt have been very considerable.

The dinâr (or *Mithcâl*) was a golden coin corresponding with the Byzantine *aureus*; the dirhem (drachma) a silver coin. Sprenger, by elaborate calculation, estimates the dinâr at about 15 francs,—or say about two-thirds of a Pound sterling. The silver dirhem he rates at 72 centimes, say 6*d.* to 8*d.* Considering the high value in that age of the precious metals, the caravans at the figures mentioned in the text must have been rich indeed. By the Byzantine system, gold stood to silver in the ratio of 14⅔ to 1; among the Moslems, strange to say, the ratio was as low as 8 or 9, and even 7, to 1; at which rate the legal demands were commuted; subsequently the ratio rose to 10 or 12. Gold was the currency in the Byzantine provinces, as Syria and Western Mesopotamia; silver in Persia and Babylonia.

lucrative was the traffic; and to understand how the merchants of Mecca must have been dismayed at any contingency that might threaten its safety.

Moreover the whole city of Mecca was devoted to the trade. While the leading merchants embarked great sums in these expeditions, almost every citizen who could spare a dinâr or two invested in them his little capital. A caravan was ordinarily under the conduct of but one or two of the chief men who owned the bulk of the merchandise; but these, for a consideration of half the profit, readily took charge also of the smaller ventures, as commissions to be accounted for on their return. It thus happened that in some of the larger caravans, almost every citizen of Mecca, man and woman, having any means at command, owned a share however small; and when such a caravan was threatened the whole city was thrown into alarm.

The whole city devoted to the traffic.

The caravans, indeed, had always been subject to a certain risk from the attack of Arab bandits. Halting by day and travelling by night, the long strings of camels, with but a slender escort, were at once thrown into confusion, especially in ravines or narrow passes, by the onset of a few determined brigands, who in the turmoil could secure their plunder and effect an easy retreat. The danger from such desultory attack was ordinarily met by extreme caution on the part of the leader, whose scouts gave timely notice of any risk, and who was able accordingly, either by retiring or by a hurried movement forward, to avoid it. But the Coreish were not slow to perceive that their position must be very different now with an enemy situated as Mahomet at Medîna, who, like an eagle from his eyrie ever on the watch, was ready to swoop down unawares upon their caravans. During the first six months, however, it was not the period for traffic northwards, and Mahomet was otherwise engaged at home. But the season was now approaching; and the Coreish watched with anxiety the attitude of the Prophet and his exiled band towards the first caravans which they were now despatching to Syria.

This trade a vulnerable point of attack from Medîna.

The earliest indications of hostility were of a petty and marauding character. Seven months after his arrival Mahomet despatched his uncle Hamza, at the head of thirty Refugees, to surprise a Meccan caravan returning from Syria

Expeditions against Coreishite caravans.

First:
Hamza.
Ramadhân,
A.H. I.
Dec. A.D.
622.[1]
under the guidance of Abu Jahl. This caravan, guarded by some 300 of the Coreish, was overtaken near the sea-shore, between Mecca and Medîna, in the territory of the Bani Joheina. A chief of that tribe, confederate of both, interposed between the parties already drawn up for an encounter. Hamza retired to Medîna, and Abu Jahl proceeded onwards to Mecca.

Second:
Obeida ibn
al Hârith.
A.H. I.
Jan. A.D.
623.
About a month later a body, double the strength of the first, was sent by Mahomet under command of his cousin Obeida son of Hârith, in pursuit of another caravan protected by Abu Sofiân with an escort of 200 men. The Coreish were surprised while their camels were grazing by a fountain in the valley of Râbigh; but the Moslems found the caravan too strong for them, and, beyond the discharge of arrows from a distance, no hostilities were attempted. Obeida is distinguished in tradition as he who upon this occasion 'shot the first arrow for Islâm.' We are told that among the Coreishite convoy there were two followers of Mahomet, who, finding an opportunity, fled from the caravan and joined the party of Obeida.

Third:
Sád, son
of Abu
Wackkâs.
After the lapse of another month, a third expedition started, under the youthful Sád with twenty followers, in the same direction. He was desired to proceed as far as a certain valley on the road to Mecca, and to lie in wait for a caravan expected to pass that way. Like most of the subsequent marauding parties intended to effect a surprise, they marched by night and lay in concealment during the day. Notwithstanding this precaution, when they reached their destination on the fifth morning, they found that the caravan had passed a day before, and they returned empty-handed to Medîna.

A standard
presented
by Maho-
met to each
leader.
These excursions occurred in the winter and spring of the year A.D. 623. On each occasion, Mahomet mounted a white banner on a staff or lance, and presented it to the leader on his departure. In these and all other expeditions of any importance the names of the leaders, and also of those who carried the standard, are carefully recorded by tradition.[2]

---

[1] I follow the chronology of M. C. de Perceval. Sprenger makes the date fall about two and a half months later.

[2] These small night attacks are called *Sariya*; the larger expeditions, those especially in which Mahomet himself was leader, *Ghazia*—a term still in use.

In the summer and autumn of the same year, Mahomet led in person three somewhat larger, though equally unsuccessful, parties. The first set out in Safar, nearly twelve months after his arrival, and was directed to Abwâ (the spot where his mother was buried) in pursuit of a Coreishite caravan. The prey was missed; but something was gained in a friendly treaty concluded with the Bani Dhamra, a tribe hitherto connected with Mecca, but now detached from their alliance. The treaty was committed to writing, and was the first that Mahomet entered into with any foreign tribe. He returned, after fifteen days' absence, to Medîna.

Three expeditions conducted by Mahomet himself:— Abwâ: A.H. II. June, A.D. 623.

In the succeeding month, the Prophet again marched, at the head of 200 followers, including a large number of the citizens of Medîna,[1] to Bowât on the caravan route four stages south-west of Medîna. A rich burden laden on 2,500 camels, under the escort of one of Mahomet's chief opponents, Omeya ibn Khalf, with 100 armed men, was to proceed by that road. But it eluded pursuit, and passed on in safety. The presence of so many citizens of Medîna shows the advancing influence of Mahomet; they were no doubt tempted by the hope of so great a prize; but whether or no, they had now crossed the Rubicon and identified themselves with Mahomet in hostilities against the Coreish. Shortly after their return, some of the camels and flocks of Medîna, while feeding in a plain a few miles from the city, were fallen upon by Kurz ibn Jâbir, a marauding Bedouin chieftain, and carried off. Mahomet pursued him nearly to Bedr, but he made good his escape. We find him not long afterwards converted to Islâm, and leading a Moslem expedition against a Bedouin robber like himself.

Bowât: A.H. II. July, A.D 623.

(Kurz ibn Jâbir commits a raid near Medîna.)

Two or three months elapsed before Mahomet set out on his third expedition. Volunteers were invited, and from 150 to 200 followers joined the party. They had between them only thirty camels, on which they rode by turns. At Osheira, distant nine stages in the direction of Yenbo, they expected to waylay another rich caravan which Abu Sofiân was conducting towards Syria, and of the departure of which from Mecca tidings had been received. But it had passed

And Osheira. A.H. II. Oct. A.D. 623.

---

[1] More than half must have been Medîna men: for at the battle of Bedr, when every follower from Mecca was mustered, there were but 83 Refugees present.

several days before they reached the spot. This is the same caravan which, on its return from Syria, gave occasion to the famous action of Bedr.

Mahomet concludes an alliance with two tribes.

In this excursion, the Prophet entered into an alliance with the Bani Mudlij, a tribe inhabiting the vicinity of Osheira, and with another branch of the Bani Dhamra, their adherents. He was thus gradually extending his political connections, and thus still further hedging the passage of the Meccan caravans.

Mahomet calls Ali, Abu Torâb.

An instance of the pleasantry in which the Prophet sometimes indulged, is here recorded. Ali had fallen asleep on the dusty ground under the shade of a palm-grove. Mahomet espied him lying thus, all soiled with the dust; and, pushing him with his foot, called out, 'Ho! Abu Torâb! (*Father of the dust!*) is it thou? Abu Torâb, sit up!' Ali, half-ashamed, sat up; and the sobriquet ever after clung to him.

His standard-bearers.

On each of these expeditions Mahomet appointed a standard-bearer to carry his white banner. Hamza, Sád, and Ali successively had this honour.

During his absence, Mahomet leaves a representative or governor at Medina.

Whenever the Prophet left Medîna to proceed to any distance, he named a representative to exercise authority over those who were left behind, and to lead the public prayers during his absence. The first person selected for the office was one of the twelve 'leaders,' Sád ibn Obâda, of the Khazraj tribe. The next who received the token of confidence was Sád ibn Muâdz, of the Bani Aus; so carefully was Mahomet minded to distribute his favours between these two jealous tribes. On the third occasion his friend Zeid was honoured with the post.

Affair of Nakhla. Rajab: A.H. II. Nov. A.D. 623.

In November and December, Mahomet did not himself quit Medîna; but he sent forth Abdallah ibn Jahsh, with seven other Refugees, on an expedition which was attended with more serious results than any of the preceding. As he bade farewell to Abdallah, the Prophet placed in his hands a closed packet of instructions, and charged him not to open it till he entered a certain valley two days' march on the road to Mecca. On reaching the appointed spot, Abdallâh broke open the letter, and read it aloud to his comrades as follows: *Go forward to Nakhla, in the name of the Lord, and with His blessing! Yet force not any of thy followers against his inclination. Proceed with those that accompany thee willingly. And when thou hast arrived at the valley of Nakhla, there lie in wait for the caravans of the Coreish.* Nakhla is a valley to the east of Mecca, about half-way to Tâyif; and the southern trade all passed that way. Watched and pursued in their commerce with Syria, the traffic towards the south would be more securely and more busily prosecuted by the merchants of Mecca; for the route lay far removed from the vicinity of their enemy. Mahomet had, no doubt, intimation that some rich venture, lightly guarded, was shortly expected at Mecca by this route; and by his sealed instructions he effectually provided against intelligence and alarm being conveyed to the Coreish.

Having read the order, Abdallah told his comrades that any one who wished was at liberty to go back: 'As for myself,' he said, 'I will go forward and fulfil the command of the Prophet.' All joined in the same determination, and proceeded onwards. Two of them fell behind in search of their camel which had strayed, and lost their party.[1] The remaining six, having reached Nakhla, waited there. In a short time a caravan laden with wine, raisins, and leather, came up. It was guarded by four of the Coreish, who, seeing the strangers, were alarmed, and halted. To disarm their apprehensions, one of Abdallah's party shaved his head, in token that they were returning from the Lesser pilgrimage; for this was one of the months in which that ceremony was ordinarily performed. The men of the caravan seeing his shaven head were at once reassured, and turning the camels adrift to pasture, began to cook their food. Meanwhile, Abdallah and his comrades debated the propriety of an attack during the sacred month of Rajab, and thus they spoke one to another: 'If we should defer the attack this night, they will surely move off, and, entering the holy territory, thus escape us; and if we should fight against them now, it is unlawful, for we shall be transgressing the sacred month.' They were thus fixed on the horns of a dilemma. At last they overcame their scruples. Wâckid,

A Coreishite killed, and caravan, with two of the escort, carried off.

---

[1] By some accounts they took advantage of the option to go back, and turned aside. The straying of their camel may have been invented to cover what in after days must have appeared discreditable lukewarmness.

one of their number, advanced covertly; and discharging an arrow, killed a man of the convoy, Amr ibn al Hadhrami, on the spot. All then rushed upon the caravan, and securing two of the Coreish, Othmân and Al Hakam, carried them off prisoners, with the spoil, to Medîna. Nowfal, the brother of Othmân, leaped on his horse and escaped to Mecca; but too late to give the alarm for a pursuit.

Mahomet at first disclaims responsibility for the attack:

On Abdallah reaching Medîna, he acquainted Mahomet with what had passed. The Prophet, who had probably not expected the party to reach Nakhla or the attack to be made till after the close of Rajab, appeared displeased, and said: 'I never commanded thee to fight in the sacred month.' So he put the booty aside, pending further orders, and kept the prisoners in bonds. Abdallah and his comrades were ashamed and grieved; the people also reproached them with what they had done. But Mahomet was unwilling to discourage his followers; and soon after, a revelation was given forth, justifying hostilities even during the sacred months as a lesser evil than idolatry and opposition to Islâm:—

Then promulgates a revelation approving it.

Sura ii.

They will ask thee concerning the Sacred months, whether they may war therein. SAY:—Warring therein is grievous; but to obstruct the way of God, and to deny Him, and hinder men from the Holy temple, and expel His people from thence, is more grievous with God. Tempting (to idolatry) is more grievous than killing.

Having promulgated this verse, Mahomet gave over the booty to the captors, who (anticipating the subsequent practice) presented a fifth of it to Mahomet, and divided the remainder among themselves.

Prisoners ransomed.

The relatives of the two prisoners now sent a deputation from Mecca for their ransom. Sád and Otba, the two Refugees who had wandered from Abdallah's party, were not yet returned. Mahomet, apprehensive for their safety, refused to ransom the captives till he was assured that no foul play had been used towards them: 'If ye have killed my two men,' he said, 'verily, I will put yours also to death.' But, soon after, they made their appearance, and Mahomet accepted the proffered ransom—forty ounces of silver for each.[1] Al

[1] The silver *owckea*, or ounce, is said to have been equal to forty dirhems. For the value of the dirhem see note *ante*, p. 212.

Hakam, however, continued at Medîna, and eventually embraced Islâm.

The Arabian writers rightly attach much importance to this expedition. 'This was,' says Ibn Hishâm, 'the first booty that the Mussulmans obtained; the first captives they seized; the first life they took.' Abdallah is said to have been called in this expedition *Amîr al Mominîn*,—an appellation—'Commander of the Faithful'—assumed in after days by the Caliphs.

Importance of this expedition.

It was now a year and a half since Mahomet and his followers had taken refuge in Medîna. Their attitude towards Mecca was becoming daily more hostile. Latterly, no opportunity had been lost of threatening the numerous caravans which passed through the Hejâz. On the regular and uninterrupted march of these to Syria depended, as we have seen, the prosperity of Mecca; for the traffic with Yemen and Abyssinia was of a subordinate character. Even towards Yemen and Tâyif, as it now appeared, their enemy would allow them no security. This last attack had also shown that Mahomet and his followers, in the combat on which they were entering, would respect neither life nor the inviolability of the sacred months. Blood had been shed foully and sacrilegiously, and was yet unavenged.

Growing hostility of Mahomet and his followers towards the Coreish.

Still there came no hostile response from Mecca. Though followers of the Prophet were known to be in the city, no cruelties were perpetrated on them, nor any reprisals attempted by the Coreish. But the breach was widening, and the enmity becoming deeper seated: blood could be washed out by blood alone.

Forbearance of the Coreish.

At Medîna, on the other hand, the prospect of a mortal conflict with their enemies was steadily contemplated, and openly spoken of by Mahomet and his adherents. At what period the divine command to fight against the Unbelievers of Mecca was promulgated, is uncertain. Repeated attacks on the caravans of the Coreish had been gradually paving the way for it; and when given forth, it was no more than the embodiment of a resolution which the desire of Mahomet for revenge, and of his followers for the plunder of the rich merchandise which passed to and fro in tempting proximity to their city, had long ago given birth to. The following are the earliest passages on the subject:—

Divine command to fight against the Coreish.

Sura xxii. ' Bear good tidings unto the Righteous. Truly the Lord will keep back the Enemy from those who believe, for God loveth not the perfidious Unbeliever. Permission is granted unto those who take up arms for that they have been injuriously entreated; and verily the Lord is mighty for the assistance of those who have been driven from their homes without just cause,—for no other reason than because they said, *God is our Lord.* And truly if it were not that God holdeth back mankind, one part of them by means of another part, Monasteries and Churches and Places of prayer and of worship, wherein the name of the Lord is frequently commemorated, would be demolished. And God will surely assist them that assist Him. For God is Mighty and Glorious.'

Sura ii. ' And fight in the way of God with them that fight against you : but transgress not, for God loveth not the Transgressors. Kill them wheresoever ye find them ; and expel them from that out of which they have expelled you : for temptation (to idolatry) is more grievous than killing. Yet fight not against them beside the Holy temple, until they fight with you thereat. * * *

' Fight, therefore, until there be no temptation (to idolatry) and the Religion be God's. And if they leave off, then let there be no hostility, excepting against the Oppressors.

' War is ordained for you, even though it be irksome unto you. Perchance ye dislike that which is good for you, and love that which is evil for you. But God knoweth, and ye know not.'

Fighting prescribed on religious grounds.

Thus war, upon grounds professedly religious, was established as an ordinance of Islâm. Hostilities, indeed, were justified by the 'expulsion' of the Believers from Mecca. But the main and undisguised issue which Mahomet in this warfare set before him was the victory of Islâm. They were to fight *until the religion became the Lord's alone.*

The fearful reproved.

Although the general bearing of the Believers was, like that of their Prophet, defiant and daring, yet there were timorous brethren amongst them, who needed reproof and encouragement. They were thus addressed : —

Sura xlvii. The Believers say,—*If a Sura were revealed (commanding war), we would fight;* and now when a plain Sura is revealed, and fighting is mentioned therein, thou seest those in whose heart is an infirmity, looking towards thee with the look of one overshadowed with death. But obedience had been better for them, and propriety of speech. Wherefore, when the command is established, if they give credit unto God, it shall be better for them.

For those that fall in battle, the promise of Paradise is given :—

They who have gone into Exile for the cause of God, and then have been slain, or have died, We shall certainly nourish these with an excellent provision : For God is the best Provider. He will surely grant unto them an entrance such as they will approve : For God is knowing and gracious.

Paradise promised to the slain.

Yet the Believer was not to imagine that the success of Islâm was dependent on his feeble efforts. God could accomplish the work equally well without him. Thus after the fierce exhortation to ' strike off the heads of the Unbelievers, to make great slaughter amongst them, and bind them fast in bonds,' the Prophet adds :—

The cause not dependent on their efforts.

This do. If the Lord willed, He could surely Himself take vengeance on them : but (He hath ordained fighting for the faith) in order that He may prove some of you by others. They that are killed in the way of God, He will not suffer their works to perish. He will guide them, and dispose their hearts aright. He will lead them into the Paradise whereof He hath told them.

Sura xlvii.

Furthermore, the true Believer was expected not only to fight : he was to contribute of his substance towards the charges of war :—

Believers to contribute towards war expenditure.

What hath befallen you that ye contribute not (of your substance) in the cause of God ? and to God belongeth the inheritance of the Heavens and of the Earth. Those of you that contribute before the victory,[1] and fight, shall not be placed on the same level, but shall have a rank superior over those who contribute after it and fight. Who is he that lendeth unto the Lord a goodly loan ? He shall double the same, and he shall have an honourable recompense.

He doth not ask you for (all) your substance. Had He asked you for (the whole of) it, and importunately pressed you, ye had become grudging, and it had stirred up your ill-will. But ye are they who are called on to contribute a part of the same in the cause of God, and there be some of you that grudge; but whosoever grudgeth, he verily grudgeth against his own soul. God

---

[1] *Al Fath ;* the 'decision' of God against the idolaters, and the victory of Islâm. The term came subsequently to be applied *par excellence* to the taking of Mecca—the great crisis, prior to which there was a peculiar merit in fighting for and supporting Islâm. But the word had of course at this moment no such distinct anticipative sense.

needeth nothing, but ye are needy. If ye turn back, He will substitute in your room a people other than you, and they shall not be like unto you.

And somewhat later :—

Prepare against them what force ye can, of your ability, and troops of horse, that ye may thereby strike terror into the enemy of God and your enemy, and into others beside them; ye know them not, but God knoweth them. And what thing soever ye contribute in the cause of God, it shall be made good unto you, and ye shall not be treated unjustly.

These commands addressed to the citizens of Medína also.

These passages were all promulgated within two or three years after Mahomet's arrival in Medîna. They are no longer addressed to the Refugees only, but to all believers including the men of Medîna. We have seen that some of these latter had already joined in expeditions against the caravans of Mecca; but the first occasion on which they came forward in any considerable number to the aid of Mahomet, was on the field of Bedr;—and there, probably more from the hope of sharing in the spoils of a richly-laden caravan, than with any idea of fighting for the faith, or of avenging the wrongs of the Moslems. The result was, nevertheless, equally important to Mahomet.

But the battle of Bedr, deserving separate notice, will be reserved for another chapter.

CHAPTER XII.

A.H. I. & II.—A.D. 623.

Ramadhân, A.H. II.—*January,* A.D. 624.

WITH the battle of Bedr opens a new era in Islâm. The biographers of Mahomet have shown their appreciation of the influence which it exercised on his future fortunes, by the disproportionate space allotted to this chapter of their story. The minutest circumstances, and most trifling details, even to the name of each person engaged in it, have been carefully treasured up. From this vast mass of undigested tradition it will be my endeavour to draw forth the important facts and frame them into a consistent narrative.

> Great detail with which campaign of Bedr is related.

The caravan of Abu Sofiân, which, on its passage through the Hejâz, had escaped the pursuit of Mahomet in the autumn, was now, after the lapse of about three months, returning to Mecca. Mahomet was resolved that it should not this time elude his grasp. His first step was to secure the neutrality, if not the co-operation, of the tribes through whose territory the caravan must pass. In the beginning of January, A.D. 624, he despatched two Refugees as scouts to Haura, a caravan station on the sea-shore west of Medîna, to bring early intelligence of the approach of Abu Sofiân. They were hospitably lodged and concealed by an aged chief of the Joheina tribe, whose family was subsequently rewarded by the grant of Yenbo. When the caravan appeared, they were to hasten back and apprise Mahomet of its approach.

> Scouts sent for intelligence of Abu Sofiân's approach. A.H. II. Jan. A.D. 624.

The Prophet had not yet learned to mask his projected campaigns. His intention of attacking the caravan was noised abroad. The rumour reached Abu Sofiân while yet on the confines of Syria. He was warned, perhaps by the

> Abu Sofiân, warned, sends to Mecca for succour.

treachery of some disaffected citizen of Medîna, to be on his guard, as Mahomet had entered into confederacy with the tribes upon the road to surprise the caravan. The party was greatly alarmed. Abu Sofiân forthwith despatched to Mecca a messenger, named Dhamdham, bidding the Coreish hasten with an army to his rescue. The caravan then moved rapidly, yet with caution, along the route which lay closest to the shore of the Red Sea.

Mahomet gives command for the campaign.

Mahomet, becoming impatient, and apprehensive lest the caravan by such rapid movement should, as on previous occasions, be beforehand with him, resolved not to wait for the return of the spies. So he called upon his followers at once to make ready: 'Here,' said he, 'is a caravan of the Coreish in which they have embarked much wealth. Come! perchance the Lord will enrich you with the same.' The love of booty and of adventure, so passionate in the Arab, induced not only all the Refugees, but a large body of the Citizens also, to respond with alacrity to his call. Of the former, Othmân alone remained behind to tend the sick bed of his wife Rockeya, the Prophet's daughter.' [1]

Marches from Medîna.

On Sunday, the 12th of Ramadhân, A.H. II., Mahomet set out upon his march. He left Abu Lubâba, one of the Citizens,

---

[1] The motive which prompted most of Mahomet's followers to accompany the force, as well as tempted many to join Islâm itself, is illustrated by the following anecdote, which bears the stamp at least of verisimilitude. Two citizens of Medîna, still heathens, were noticed by Mahomet among the troops. He called them near his camel, and asked them what had brought them there. 'Thou art our kinsman,' they replied, 'to whom our city hath given protection; and we go forth with our people in the hope of plunder.' 'None shall go forth with me,' said Mahomet, 'but he who is of our Faith.' They tried to pass, saying that they were great warriors, and would fight bravely by his side, requiring nothing beyond their share of the plunder; but Mahomet was firm. 'Ye shall not go thus. *Believe and fight!*' Seeing no alternative they 'believed,' and confessed that Mahomet was the Prophet of God. 'Now,' said Mahomet, 'go forth and fight!' So they accompanied the army, and became noted spoilers both at Bedr and in other expeditions. On Mahomet's return to Medîna, one of the Citizens exclaimed: 'Would that I had gone forth with the Prophet! Then I had surely secured large booty!'

Eight persons who remained behind are popularly counted in the number of the veterans of Bedr—the nobility of Islâm; *three* Refugees, viz. Othmân and the two spies; and *five* Citizens, viz. the two left in command of Upper and Lower Medîna, a messenger sent back to the Bani Amr at Coba, and two men, who having received a hurt on the road, were left behind. The names of the famous Three hundred and five were recorded in a Register at Medîna, called *Sadr al Kitâb*.

in charge of Medîna; and, for some special reason not fully A.H. II. explained, he appointed another over Coba and Upper Jan. 8, Medîna.[1] At a short distance from the city on the Mecca A.D. 623. road, he halted to review his little army, and send back the striplings unfit for action.   The number that remained, and with which he proceeded onwards, was three hundred and five.   Eighty were Refugees; of the remainder, about one fourth belonged to the Bani Aus, and the rest to the Bani Khazraj.   They had but two horses; and there were seventy camels, on which by turns they mounted.

For two days they travelled by the road to Mecca.   At Spies sent Safra, thirty-four hours' journey from Medîna, the way forward by divides into two branches; the left leads southward to Mahomet to Bedr. Mecca, falling, after one or two days' march, into the great Syrian road by the sea-shore; the right runs west in the direction of Yenbo, and at the distance of about fifteen hours meets the caravan track at a point called Bedr, which was (and still is) a halting place on the route to Syria, and where a fair was also held. While on the march, Mahomet de-spatched two spies to find out whether any preparations were making for the reception of Abu Sofiân at Bedr; for it was there that he hoped to waylay the caravan.[2] At the foun-tain of Bedr, the spies overheard some women who had come to draw water talking among themselves ' of the caravan expected on the morrow or the day after,' and they returned in haste with the intelligence to Mahomet.

Let us now turn to Abu Sofiân.   As he approached Bedr, Abu his apprehensions were quickened by the vicinity of Medîna, Sofiân, dis- covering and, hastening in advance of the caravan, he resolved himself traces of to reconnoitre the spot.   At Bedr, he was told by a chief of the scouts, hastens for- the Bani Joheina that no strangers had been seen, excepting ward and two men, who, after resting their camels for a little by the escapes.

---

[1] It is said that he did this because he heard something suspicious regarding the Bani Amr ibn Auf who lived there.   He also sent back Hârith from his camp with a message to the same tribe. The two persons left in charge, as well as this messenger, belonged to the Bani Aus.

[2] This was probably on the Monday. It is somewhat difficult to find time for all the events that crowd in between Sunday and Thursday evening. The spies were of the Joheina tribe which dwelt on the sea-shore; they were acquainted with the vicinity, and better fitted than either the Refugees or the Citizens of Medîna to gain the information Mahomet required.

well, and drinking water, went off again. Proceeding to the spot, he carefully scrutinised it all around. 'Camels from Yathreb!' he exclaimed, as among the litter of the camels' dung, his practised eye discerned the small stones peculiar to the dates of Medîna;—'these are the spies of Mahomet!' So saying, he hurried back to the caravan; and forthwith diverting its course to the right, so as to keep close by the sea-shore, pressed forward, halting neither day nor night, and was soon beyond the reach of danger. Then hearing that an army of the Coreish had marched from Mecca to his aid, he sent a courier to them saying that all was safe, and that they should now return to their homes.

Alarm at Mecca. Coreish resolve to rescue caravan.

Ten or twelve days before this, Mecca had been thrown into great alarm by the sudden appearance of Dhamdham, the first messenger of Abu Sofiân. Urging his camel at full speed along the valley and up the main street of Mecca, he made it kneel down in the open space before the Káaba, hastily reversed its saddle, cut off its ears and nose, and rent his shirt before and behind. Having signified by these acts the alarming import of his mission, he cried at the pitch of his voice to the people crowding around: 'Coreish! Coreish! your caravan is pursued by Mahomet. Help! O help!' Immediately the city was in commotion; for the caravan was the chief annual one to Syria, in which every Coreishite of any substance had a venture; and the value of the whole was 50,000 golden dinârs. It was at once determined to march in great force, repel the marauding troops, and rescue the caravan. 'Doth Mahomet, indeed, imagine,' said they among themselves, 'that it will be this time as in the affair of the Hadhramite!' alluding to the treacherous surprise at Nakhla where, two months before, Amr the Hadhramite had been slain. 'Never! He shall know it otherwise.'

Meccan army marches and meets Abu Sofiân's messenger at Johfa.

Preparations were hurried forward on every side. The resolve, at any sacrifice, to chastise and crush the Moslems was universal. Every man of consequence prepared to join the army. A few, unable themselves to go, sent substitutes; among these was Abu Lahab, the uncle of Mahomet.[1] One

---

[1] Some say that Abu Lahab neither went himself nor sent a substitute; others, that he sent in his stead the grandson of Mughîra, in consideration of the remission of a debt of 400 dirhems. It is said that he refused to accom-

fear there was that Mecca might, during their absence, be surprised by the Bani Bakr, an adjacent tribe, with which there was a present feud. But this was obviated by the guarantee of a powerful chief allied to both tribes. So great was the alacrity, that in two or three days after the alarm by Dhamdham, and probably about the very time that Mahomet was marching from Medîna, the army was in motion. They then despatched a messenger to apprise Abu Sofiân of their approach, but he missed the caravan which (as we have seen) had left the ordinary route. The army marched in haste, but not without some display of rude pomp; for singing women, with their tabrets, followed and sang by the fountains at which they halted. At Johfa, the second courier of Abu Sofiân (who himself shortly after, with the caravan, passed them unobserved by a route closer to the sea) reached the army with intelligence of his safety, and the message that they were to return.

On receiving this welcome intimation, the question of going forward or of turning back was warmly debated by the leading chiefs. On the one hand, it was argued that the object for which they had set out having been secured, they should at once retrace their steps; and that being so closely related to the army of Mahomet, they should abstain from fatal extremities. 'When we have fought and spilled the blood of our brethren and our kinsmen,' said the advocates of peace, 'of what use will life be to us any longer? Let us now go back, and we will be responsible for the blood-money of Amr, killed at Nakhla.' Many persons, and among them Hakîm the nephew of Khadîja (who supplied food to Mahomet's party when shut up with Abu Tâlib) were urgent with this advice. Others, and Abu Jahl at their head, demanded that the army should advance. 'If we turn back now,' they said, 'it will surely be imputed to cowardice. Let us go forward to Bedr; and there, by the fountain,

Coreishite army debates whether to return or go forward.

They resolve to

pany the army in consequence of a dream of his sister Atika. I have omitted any allusion to this dream, as well as to other dreams and prodigies seen by the Coreish, anticipatory of the disasters at Bedr, because I believe them all to be fictitious. The tinge of horror in after days reflected back on the 'sacrilegious' battle, the anxiety to excuse certain families, and the wish to invest others with a species of merit in having, even while in infidelity, served Islâm by dreams or prophecies, combined to give rise to them.

advance on Bedr.

spend three days eating and making merry. All Arabia shall hear of it, and ever after stand in awe of us.' The affair of Nakhla, and the slaughter of the Hadhramite, still rankled in the heart of the Coreish, and they listened willingly to the warlike counsel. Two tribes alone, the Bani Zohra and Adi, returned to Mecca.[1] The rest marched onwards.[2] Leaving the Medîna branch to the right, they kept along the Syrian road, and made straight for Bedr.

Mahomet receives intelligence of Coreishite army. Thursday.

We now return to Mahomet. He, too, was advancing rapidly on Bedr; for there he expected, from the report of his spies, to find the caravan. On Tuesday night, he reached Rûha; as he drank from the well there, he blessed the valley in terms of which the pious traveller is reminded to the present day. On Wednesday he proceeded onwards. Next day, while on the last march to Bedr, the startling news was brought by some wayfarers that the enemy was in full march upon him. This was the first intimation to the Moslems that the Coreish had heard of the danger of the caravan, and were on their way to defend it. A council of war was summoned,

Mahomet's council of war enthusiastically decides on onward march.

and Mahomet invited his chief men to offer their advice. There was but one opinion, and each delivered it more enthusiastically than another. Abu Bakr and Omar advised an immediate advance. The Prophet turned to the men of Medîna, for their pledge did not bind them to offensive action, or even to fight for him away from their city. Sád ibn Muâdz, their spokesman, replied: 'Prophet of the Lord! march whither thou listest: encamp wheresoever thou mayest choose: make war or conclude peace with whom thou wilt. For I swear by him who hath sent thee with

---

[1] The reason is not given; the Bani Zohra (of whom 100 men were present) was the tribe of Mahomet's mother; the Bani Adi, that of Omar.

[2] But they sent back the singing girls. The messenger, who carried the intelligence to Abu Sofiân that the Coreish refused to turn back, reached him near Mecca; and Abu Sofiân is represented as lamenting the folly of his countrymen. All this seems apocryphal. Till viewed in the light of its disastrous issue, the advance on Bedr must have appeared a politic and reasonable measure. It was not *an attack on Medîna*, for Bedr was on the road to Syria, so that the Coreish left Medîna far on the right. If therefore they met the Medîna forces at Bedr, it could only be because the latter had come forth gratuitously to attack the Meccan caravan,—a fair and sufficient *casus belli*; for what security could there any longer be if the men of Medîna were allowed thus with impunity to attack the convoys and plunder the caravans of Mecca?

the Truth, that if thou wert to march till our camels fell down dead, we should go forward with thee to the world's end. Not one of us would be left behind.' Then said Mahomet: ' Go forward, with the blessing of God! For, verily, He hath promised one of the two,—the army or the caravan, that He will deliver it into my hands.[1] Methinks, by the Lord, I even now see the battle-field strewn with their dead.'[2]

It is remarkable, in comparing this council with that of the Coreish at Johfa, that in the minds of the Mussulmans there was no trace whatever of compunction at the prospect of mortal combat with their kinsmen. The Coreish, goaded as they had been by repeated attacks upon their caravans and the blood shed at Nakhla, were yet staggered by the prospect of an internecine war, and nearly persuaded by their better feelings to return. The Moslems, though the aggressors, were hardened by memory of former injuries, by the dogma that their faith had severed all earthly ties without the pale of Islâm, and by a fierce fanaticism for their Prophet's cause. At one of the stages, where he halted to lead the public devotions, Mahomet, after rising from his knees, thus called down the curse of God upon the infidels, and prayed: ' O Lord! Let not Abu Jahl escape, the Pharaoh of his people! Lord, let not Zamáa escape; rather let the eyes of his father run sore for him with weeping, and become blind!' The Prophet's hate was unrelenting, and his followers imbibed from him the same inexorable spirit.

Moslems more implacable than Coreish.

In the afternoon of Thursday, on reaching the neighbourhood of Bedr, Mahomet sent forward Ali, with a few

Mahomet learns from Coreishite

[1] This point is alluded to in the Corân, which henceforth becomes often the vehicle of the ' general orders' of Mahomet, as of a military commander. 'And when the Lord promised one of the two parties that it should be given over unto you; and ye desired that it should be the party unarmed for war (*i.e.* that ye should fall upon the caravan, and not upon the Coreishite army), whereas the Lord willed to established the Truth by His words, and to cut away the foundation from the Unbelievers;—that He might establish the Truth, and abolish Falsehood, even though the transgressors be averse thereto.'—*Sura* viii.

[2] The latter clause may be apocryphal. In later traditions it is worked out to a fabulous extent. Mahomet, for example, points out what was to be the death spot, as seen in the vision, of each of his chief opponents; 'and,' it is added, 'the people were by this apprised for the first time that it was the Coreishite army they were about to encounter, and not the caravan.'

others, to reconnoitre the rising ground about the springs.
There they surprised three water-carriers of the enemy, as
they were about to fill their sheepskins. One escaped to
the Coreish; the other two were captured and taken to
the Moslem army. The chiefs questioned them about the
caravan, imagining that they belonged to it; and, receiving
no satisfactory answer, had begun to beat them, when
Mahomet interfered, and soon discovered the proximity of
his enemy. The camp, they replied to his enquiries, lay just
beyond the sand-hills, which they pointed to as skirting the
south-western side of the valley. As they could not tell the
strength of the force, the Prophet asked how many camels
they slaughtered for their daily food. 'Nine,' they answered,
'one day, and ten the next, alternately.' 'Then,' said Mahomet, 'they are between 900 and 1,000 strong.' The estimate was correct. There were 950 men;—more than three-
fold the number of the Moslem force. They were mounted
on 700 camels and 100 horses, the horsemen all clad in
mail.

The followers of Mahomet were deeply chagrined at
finding their expectation of an easy prey thus changed into
the prospect of a bloody battle. They seem to have advanced even to the field of action with the hope that they
might still, as conquerors, pursue and seize the caravan.
But it was, in truth, a fortunate event for Mahomet that
Abu Sofiân had already passed. The continuing jeopardy of
the caravan would have bound the Coreish together by a
unity and determination which the knowledge of its safety
had already dissipated. The prize of victory on the field of
Bedr was of incomparably greater consequence to Mahomet
than any spoil however costly.

The valley of Bedr consists of a plain, with steep hills
to the north and east; on the south is a low rocky range;
and on the west rise a succession of sandy hillocks. A
rivulet, rising in the inland mountains, runs through the
valley, producing along its course numerous springs, which
here and there were dug into cisterns for the accommodation
of travellers. At the nearest of these springs, the army of
Mahomet halted. Hobâb, a citizen of Medîna, advised him
to proceed onwards: 'Let us go,' he said, 'to the farthest
spring on the side of the enemy. I know a never-failing

water-
carriers
proximity
and
strength
of enemy.

Escape of
caravan a
benefit to
Mahomet.

Mahomet's
position at
Bedr.

fountain of sweet water there ; let us make that our reservoir, and destroy the other wells.' The advice was good. It was at once adopted, and the command of the water thus secured.

The night was drawing on. So they hastily constructed near the well, a hut of palm branches in which Mahomet and Abu Bakr slept. Sád ibn Muâdz kept watch by the entrance with his drawn sword. It rained during the night, but more heavily towards the camp of the Coreish.[1] The Moslem army, wearied with its long march, enjoyed sound and refreshing sleep. The dreams of Mahomet turned upon his enemies, and they were pictured to his imagination as a weak and contemptible force.[2]

Mahomet sleeps in a hut of palm branches.

In the morning he drew up his little army, and, pointing with an arrow which he held in his hand, arranged the ranks. The previous day, he had placed the chief banner, that of the Refugees, in the hands of Musáb, who nobly proved his right to the distinction. The Khazrajite ensign was committed to Hobâb ; that of the Bani Aus, to Sád ibn Muâdz.[3]

Mahomet draws up his army.

Meanwhile dissension again broke out in the camp of the Coreish on the policy of fighting against their kinsmen. Shaiba and Otba, two chiefs of rank, influenced it is said by their slave Addâs (the same who comforted the Prophet on his flight from Tâyif), strongly urged that the attack should be abandoned. Just then, Omeir, a diviner by arrows, having ridden hastily round the valley, returned to report the result of his reconnaissance. 'Ye Coreish,' he said after telling them his estimate of the enemy's number, 'calamities approach you, fraught with destruction. Inevitable death rideth upon the camels of Yathreb. It is a people

Coreish, after further dissensions, move forward.

[1] The rain is thus alluded to in the Corán: 'When He overshadowed you with a deep sleep, as a security, from Himself; and caused to descend upon you Rain from the heavens, that He might purify you therewith, and take from you the uncleanness of Satan ; and that He might strengthen your hearts, and establish your steps thereby.'—*Sura* viii. As a foil to this picture, the Coreish are represented apprehensive and restless till morning broke.

[2] 'And when God caused them to appear before thee in thy sleep, few in number ; and if He had caused them to appear unto thee a great multitude, ye would have been affrighted, and have disputed in the matter (of their attack). But truly God preserved thee, for He knoweth the heart of man.'

[3] The name given is *Liwâ*, a white ensign. The *Râya*, Mahomet's black banner, is said to have been first unfurled on the expedition to Kheibar.

that hath neither defence nor refuge but in their swords. They are dumb as the grave; their tongues they put forth with the serpent's deadly aim.　Not a man of them shall we kill, but in his stead one of ourselves also will be slain; and when there shall have been slaughtered amongst us a number equal unto them, of what avail will life be to us after that!' These words began to produce a pacific effect, when Abu Jahl, as before, loudly opposed the proposals for peace. Turning to Amir the Hadhramite, he bade him call to mind the blood of his brother slain at Nakhla. The flame was rekindled. Amir threw off his clothes, cast dust upon his body, and began frantically to cry aloud his brother's name. The deceased had been a confederate of the family of Shaiba and Otba. Their pride and honour were affected. They saw that thoughts of peace must now be scattered to the winds; and they resolved signally to vindicate themselves from the imputation of cowardice cast on them by Abu Jahl. The army was drawn up in line. The three standards, for the centre and wings, were borne, according to ancient privilege, by members of the house of Abd al Dâr. They moved forward but slowly over the intervening sand-hills, which the rain had made heavy and fatiguing. The same cause, acting with less intensity, had rendered the ground in front of Mahomet lighter and more firm to walk upon. The Coreish laboured under another disadvantage; they had the rising sun before them, while the army of Medîna faced the west.

Mahomet awaits battle anxiously. His earnest prayer.

Mahomet had barely arrayed his line of battle, when the advanced column of the enemy was discerned over the rising sands in front. Their greatly superior numbers were concealed by the fall of the ground behind; and this imparted confidence to the Moslems.[1]　But Mahomet was

[1] Represented in the Corân as the result of divine interposition. After mentioning Mahomet's dream, the passage (Sura viii.) proceeds: 'And when He caused them to appear in your eyes, at the time ye met, to be few in number, and diminished you in their eyes, that God might accomplish the thing that was to be;' i.e. by this ocular deception the Mussulmans were encouraged in their advance to victory, and the Coreish lured on to their fate. So again: 'When ye were on the hither side, and they on the farther side (of the valley), and the caravan below you;[1] and if ye had made a mutual appointment to fight, ye would surely have declined the appointment; but (the Lord ordered otherwise) that he might bring to pass the thing that was to be ―that he who perisheth might perish by a manifest interposition, and he that

[1] i.e. on the plain, by the sea-shore, passing on towards Mecca.

fully alive to the critical position. The fate of Islâm hung upon the issue of the approaching battle. Followed by Abu Bakr, he hastened for a moment into the little hut, and, raising his hands, poured forth these earnest petitions: 'O Lord! I beseech thee, forget not thy promise of assistance and of victory. O Lord! if this little band be vanquished, Idolatry will prevail, and the pure worship of thee cease from off the earth!' 'The Lord,' said Abu Bakr, comforting him, 'will surely come to thine aid, and will lighten thy countenance with the joy of victory.'[1]

The time for action had arrived. Mahomet again came forth. The enemy was already close; but the army of Medîna remained still. Mahomet had no cavalry to cover an advance; and before superior numbers he must keep close his ranks. Accordingly the Prophet had strictly forbidden his followers to stir till he should give the order for advance; only they were to check any flank movement of the Coreish by the discharge of arrows. The cistern was guarded as their palladium. Certain desperate warriors of the Coreish swore that they would drink water from it, destroy it, or perish in the attempt. Scarcely one returned from the rash enterprise. With signal gallantry, Aswad advanced close to the brink, when a blow from Hamza's sword fell upon his leg and nearly severed it from his body. Still defending himself, he crawled onwards and made good his vow; for he drank of the water, and with his remaining leg demolished part of the cistern before the sword of Hamza put an end to his life.

Fierce combat by the reservoir.

Already, after the fashion of Arabian warfare, single combats had been fought at various points, when the two brothers Shaiba and Otba, and Walîd the son of Otba, still

Three Coreish challenge Moslems to

liveth might live by a manifest interposition;' that is, each army advanced to the field of battle, without knowing of the approach of the other; an unseen hand led them on.

In a later passage, the interposition of God is represented as *doubling* the army of Medîna in the eyes of the Coreish. The discrepancy is thus explained by the commentators: The Coreish were at first drawn on by fancying Mahomet's army to be a mere handful; when they had actually closed in battle, they were terrified by the exaggerated appearance of the Moslems, who now seemed a great multitude.

[1] Sprenger (iii. 122) says that outside the hut a swift dromedary was tied up to carry Mahomet off in case of defeat; but I do not remember seeing this in any early authority.

single combat.

smarting from the words of Abu Jahl, advanced into the space between the armies, and defied three champions from the army of Mahomet to meet them singly. Three citizens of Medîna stepped forward; but Mahomet, unwilling either that the glory or the burden of the opening conflict should rest with his allies, called them back; and, turning to his kinsmen, said: 'Ye sons of Hâshim! arise and fight, according to your right.' Then Obeida, Hamza, and Ali, the uncle and cousins of the Prophet, went forth. Hamza wore an ostrich feather in his breast, and a white plume distinguished the helmet of Ali. But their features were hid by their armour. Otba, therefore, not knowing who his opponents might be, cried aloud: 'Speak, that we may recognise you! If ye be equals, we shall fight with you.' Hamza answered: 'I am the son of Abd al Muttalib—Hamza, *the Lion of God, and the Lion of His Prophet.*' 'A worthy foe,' exclaimed Otba; 'but who are these others with thee?' Hamza repeated their names. Otba replied: 'Meet foes, every one!'

Coreishite champions slain.

Then Otba called to his son Walîd, 'Arise and fight:' So Walîd stepped forth and Ali came out against him. They were the youngest of the six. The combat was short; Walîd fell mortally wounded by the sword of Ali. Eager to avenge his son's death, Otba hastened forward, and Hamza advanced to meet him. The swords gleamed quick, and again the Coreishite warrior was slain by the Moslem lion. Shaiba alone remained of the three champions of Mecca; and Obeida, the veteran of the Moslems, threescore years and five, now drew near to fight with him. Both being well advanced in years, the conflict was less decisive than before. At last, Shaiba dealt a sword-cut on the leg of Obeida with such force as to sever the tendon, and bring him to the ground. Seeing this, Hamza and Ali both rushed on Shaiba and despatched him. Obeida survived but for a few days, and was buried on the march back at Safra.

The armies close.

The fate of their champions was ominous for the Coreish, and their spirits sank. The ranks began to close, with the battle-cry on the Moslem side of *Yâ Mansur Amit,* 'Ye conquerors, strike!' and the fighting became general. But there were still many of those scenes of individual bravery which characterise the irregular warfare of Asiatic armies, and often impart to them a Homeric interest. Prodigies of valour were exhibited on both sides; but the army of the Faithful was borne forward by an enthusiasm which the half-hearted Coreish were unable to withstand.

What part Mahomet himself took in the battle is not clear. Some traditions represent him moving along the ranks with a drawn sword. It is more likely (according to others) that he contented himself with inciting his followers by the promise of divine assistance, and by holding out the prospect of Paradise to those who fell. The spirit of Omeir, a lad of but sixteen years, was kindled within him as he listened to the Prophet's words. Tradition delights to tell of the ardour with which the stripling threw away a handful of dates which he was eating. ' Is it these,' he exclaimed, ' that hold me back from Paradise? Verily I will taste no more of them until I meet my Lord!' With such words, he drew his sword, and, casting himself upon the enemy, soon obtained the fate he coveted. *Mahomet incites his followers.*

It was a stormy wintry day. A piercing blast swept across the valley. *That*, said Mahomet, *is Gabriel with a thousand angels flying as a whirlwind at our foe.* Another, and yet another blast:—it was Michael, and after him, Seraphîl, each with a like angelic troop. The battle raged. The Prophet stooped, and lifting a handful of gravel, cast it towards the Coreish, and cried, *Confusion seize their faces!* The action was well timed. The line of the Coreish began to waver. Their movements were impeded by the heavy sands on which they stood ; and, when the ranks gave way, their numbers added but confusion. The Moslems followed eagerly on their retreating steps, slaying or taking captive all that fell within their reach. Retreat soon turned into ignominious flight. The Coreish, in their haste to escape, cast away their armour and abandoned their beasts of burden with the camp and equipage. Forty-nine were killed, and about the same number taken prisoners. Mahomet lost only fourteen, of whom eight were Citizens of Medîna, and six Refugees. *Moslems put the Coreish to flight.*

Many of the principal men of the Coreish, and some of Mahomet's bitterest opponents, were slain. Chief amongst these was Abu Jahl. Muâdz brought him to the ground by a blow which cut his leg in two. Muâdz, in his turn, was *Slaughter of Mahomet's chief opponents. Abu Jahl.*

attacked ly Ikrima, the son of Abu Jah¹, and his arm nearly severed from his shoulder. As the mutilated limb hanging by the skin impeded his action, Muâdz put his foot upon it, pulled it off, and went on his way fighting. Such were the heroes of Bedr. Abu Jahl was yet breathing when Abdallah, Mahomet's servant, ran up, and cutting off his head, carried it to his master. 'The head of the enemy of God!' exclaimed Mahomet,—'God! there is none other God but he!' 'There is no other!' responded Abdallah, as he cast the bloody head at the Prophet's feet. 'It is more acceptable to me,' cried Mahomet, ' than the choicest camel in all Arabia.'

Abul Bokhtari, whom Mahomet had desired to spare, is slain. But there were others whose death caused no gratification to Mahomet. Abul Bokhtari had shown him special kindness at the time when he was shut up in the quarter of Abu Tâlib; Mahomet, mindful of this favour, had commanded that he should not be harmed. Abul Bokhtari had a companion seated on his camel behind him. A warrior, riding up, told him of the quarter given by Mahomet; but added, ' I cannot spare the man behind thee.' 'The women of Mecca,' Abul Bokhtari exclaimed, ' shall never say that I abandoned my comrade through love of life. Do thy work upon us.' So they were killed, both he and his companion.

Savage slaughter of some of the prisoners.

After the battle was over, some of the prisoners were cruelly put to death. The following incident illustrates the savage spirit already characteristic of the faith. Omeya ibn Khalf and his son were unable to escape with the fugitive Coreish, and, seeing Abd al Rahmân pass, implored that he would make them his prisoners. Abd al Rahmân, mindful of an ancient friendship, cast away the plunder he was carrying, and, making both his prisoners, was proceeding with them to the Moslem camp. As the party passed, Bilâl espied his old enemy,—for Omeya had used to persecute him; and he screamed aloud, ' Slay him. This man is the head of the Unbelievers. I am lost, I am lost, if he lives!' From all sides the infuriated soldiers, hearing Bilâl's appeal, poured in upon the wretched captives; and Abd al Rahmân, finding resistance impossible, bade them save their lives as best they could. Defence was vain; and the two prisoners were immediately cut in pieces.¹

¹ Two other prisoners are mentioned by Wâckidi as having been slaughtered in cold blood. The first was Nowfal, for whose death it is said that Ali

When the enemy had disappeared, the army of Medîna Booty is collected. was for some time engaged in gathering the spoil. Every man was allowed to retain the plunder of any one whom he himself had slain. The rest was thrown into a common stock. The booty consisted of one hundred and fifteen camels, fourteen horses, carpets and other articles of fine leather, vestments, and much equipage and armour. A diversity of opinion arose about the distribution. Those who had hotly pursued the enemy and exposed their lives in securing the spoil, claimed the whole, or at the least a superior portion ; while such as had remained behind upon the field of battle for the safety of the Prophet and of the camp, urged that they had equally with the others fulfilled the part assigned to them, and that, having been restrained by duty from the pursuit, they were entitled to a full share of the prey. The Contention about its division decided by revelation. contention was so sharp that Mahomet interposed with a message from Heaven, and assumed possession of the whole booty. It was God who had given the victory, and to God the spoil belonged : 'They will ask thee concerning the Prey. Sura viii. Say, the Prey is God's and his Prophet's. Wherefore, fear God, and dispose of the matter rightly among yourselves ; and be obedient unto God and his Prophet, if ye be true Believers ;'—and soon in the same strain. Shortly afterwards, the following ordinance, which the Mussulman law of prize recognises to the present day, was given forth : 'And know that whatsoever thing ye plunder, verily one Fifth thereof is for God and the Prophet, and for him that is of kin (unto the Prophet), and for the Orphans, and the Poor, and the Wayfarer,—if ye be they that believe in God, and in that which We sent down to our Servant on the day of Discrimination, the day on which the two armies met : and God is over all things powerful.'

In accordance with the divine command, the booty was Spoil divided near Safra. gathered together on the field, and placed under a special officer, a citizen of Medîna. The next day it was divided,

---

overheard Mahomet praying ; so, when he saw him being led off a prisoner, he fell upon him and killed him. Mahomet uttered a *takbîr* of joy when told of it, and said that it had happened in answer to his prayer. The other was Mábad. Omar met one of his comrades carrying him off, and taunted him : 'Well, ye are beaten now!' 'Nay, by Lât and Ozza!' said the prisoner. 'Is that the manner of speech for a captive Infidel towards a Believer?' cried Omar, as he cut off the wretched man's head by one blow of his scimitar.

near Safra, in equal allotments, among the whole army, after the Prophet's fifth had been set apart. All shared alike, excepting that the horsemen received each two extra portions for their horses. To the lot of every man fell a camel, with its gear; or two camels unaccoutred; or a leathern couch, or some such equivalent. Mahomet obtained the famous camel of Abu Jahl, and a sword known by the name of Dzul Ficâr. The sword was selected by him beyond his share, according to a custom which allowed him, in virtue of the prophetic dignity, to choose from the booty, before division, whatever thing might please him most.

Enemy's dead cast into a pit. The sun was now declining, so they hastily dug a pit on the battle-field, and cast the enemy's dead into it. Mahomet looked on, as the bodies were brought up and cast in. Abu Bakr too stood by, and, examining their features, called aloud *Colloquy of Mahomet with the dead.* their names. 'Otba!—Shaiba!—Omeyya!—Abu Jahl!' exclaimed Mahomet, as one by one the corpses were, without ceremony, thrown into the common grave. 'Have ye now found that which your Lord promised you true? What my Lord promised me, that verily have I found to be true. Woe unto this people! Ye have rejected me, your Prophet! Ye cast me forth, and others gave me refuge; ye fought against me, and others came to my help!' 'O Prophet!' said the bystanders, 'dost thou speak unto the dead?' 'Yea, verily,' replied Mahomet, 'for they well know that the promise of their Lord unto them hath fully come to pass.'

Abu Hodzeifa's grief for his father. At the moment when the corpse of Otba was tossed into the pit, a look of distress overcast the countenance of his son, Abu Hodzeifa. Mahomet turned kindly to him, and said: 'Perhaps thou art distressed for thy father's fate?' 'Not so, O Prophet of the Lord! I do not doubt the justice of my father's fate; but I knew well his wise and generous heart, and I had trusted that the Lord would have led him to the faith. But now that I see him slain, and my hope destroyed! it is for that I grieve.' So the Prophet comforted Abu Hodzeifa, and blessed him; and said, 'It is well.'[1]

---

[1] On the other hand, we are told that when Otba came forth to challenge the Moslem army, Abu Hodzeifa arose to combat with his father, but Mahomet bade him sit down. It is said that he aided Hamza in giving his father the *coup de grâce* Tradition gloats over such savage passages; and it is all the more pleasing to light upon the outburst of natural affection in the text.

The army of Medîna, carrying their dead and wounded, retired in the evening to the valley of Otheil, several miles from Bedr; and there Mahomet passed the night. On the morrow, the prisoners were brought up before him. As he scrutinised each, his eye fell fiercely on Nadhr son of Hârith. ' There was death in that glance,' whispered Nadhr trembling, to a bystander. ' Not so,' replied the other; ' it is but thine own imagination.' The unfortunate prisoner thought otherwise, and besought Musâb to intercede for him. Musâb reminded him that he had denied the faith and persecuted Believers. ' Ah!' said Nadhr, ' had the Coreish made thee a prisoner, they would never have put thee to death!' ' Even were it so,' Musâb scornfully replied, ' I am not as thou art; Islâm hath rent all bonds asunder.' Micdâd, the captor, fearing lest the prisoner, and with him the chance of a rich ransom, was about to slip from his hands, cried out: ' The prisoner is mine!' But at this moment, the command to ' strike off his head!' was interposed by Mahomet, who had been watching what passed. ' And, O Lord!' he added, ' do thou of thy bounty grant unto Micdâd a better prey than this.' Nadhr was forthwith beheaded by Ali.[1]

A prisoner put to death by Mahomet.

Two days afterwards, about half-way to Medîna, Ocba, another prisoner, was ordered out for execution. He ventured to expostulate, and demand why he should be treated more rigorously than the other captives. ' Because of thy enmity to God and to his Prophet,' replied Mahomet. ' *And my little girl!* ' cried Ocba, in the bitterness of his soul,—' *who will take care of her?* ' ' Hell-fire!' exclaimed the heartless conqueror; and on the instant his victim was hewn to the ground. ' Wretch that thou wast!' continued Mahomet, ' and persecutor! unbeliever in God, in his Prophet, and in his Book! I give thanks unto the Lord that hath slain thee, and comforted mine eyes thereby.'

Ocba, another prisoner, executed.

It would even seem to have been contemplated at the close of the battle to kill all the prisoners. Mahomet is represented by tradition as himself directing this course.[2] Abu

Mahomet said to have been reprimanded

---

[1] The phrase, *Strike his neck*, is always used for beheading. The executioner, by a dexterous stroke of the sword on the back of the neck, generally severs the head at one blow. It is still the mode of capital punishment in Mahometan countries.

[2] Thus Mahomet said: ' Tell not Sáîd of his brother Mábad's death' (see

for saving
prisoners
alive.
Bakr, always on the side of mercy, pleaded for them. Omar, the personification of stern justice, urged Mahomet vehemently to put them all to death. At this juncture (tradition tells us) Gabriel brought a message from heaven, leaving it at the Prophet's option either to slay the captives or demand a ransom for them; but to the latter alternative was annexed the condition, that an equal number of the Believers should be killed in battle the ensuing year.[1] Mahomet consulted his followers; and they said: 'Let us save the prisoners alive, and take their ransom; hereafter, they that are killed in lieu thereof will inherit Paradise and the crown of martyrdom;'—which counsel was adopted. These traditions em-

Teaching
of Corân
on the
subject.
body the popular belief on the subject. But the only mention of it in the Corân is in the following verse; which, though produced by Mahomet rather to justify the slaughter of the few prisoners put to death by himself and his followers, and to gain the character of having, against the divine commission, erred on the side of mercy, has no doubt given rise to this mass of fiction :—

Sura viii.
It is not for a prophet to take prisoners until he hath inflicted a grievous wound upon his enemies on the Earth. Ye seek after the good things of this Life: but God seeketh after the Life to come; and God is glorious and wise. Unless an order from the Lord had interposed, surely a grievous punishment had overtaken you. Now, therefore, of the spoil which ye have taken, eat that which is lawful and desirable; and fear God, for God is gracious and merciful.

'O thou Prophet! say unto the prisoners in thine hands,—If God knoweth anything in your hearts which is good, He will give unto you better than that (freedom) which is taken from you; and He will forgive you, for the Lord is forgiving and merciful. But if they seek to act unfaithfully towards thee—verily they

---

ante, p. 237 note); but kill ye every man his prisoner.' Again: 'Take not any man his brother prisoner, but rather kill him.' I would not, however, lay much stress on these traditions. I am inclined rather to view them as called into existence by the passage I have quoted from the Corân. Mahomet (they say) likened Abu Bakr to Michael, Abraham, and Jesus, all advocates of mercy; and Omar to Gabriel, Noah, and Moses, the ministers of justice. He added that if the sin of Bedr in sparing the prisoners had been punished rigorously, none would have escaped but Omar and Sád ibn Muâdz (another sanguinary Believer, as we shall have full proof hereafter), who both urged the slaughter of all the prisoners.

[1] 'Which thing' (tradition adds) 'came to pass at Ohod.'

have acted unfaithfully towards God already, and God is knowing and wise.

It will be remarked that Mahomet already contemplated *Mahomet hopes to convert prisoners.*
the possibility of converting the prisoners to his cause; and
in some instances, as we shall see, he was successful.

From Otheil, Mahomet had despatched Zeid and Abdal- *Tidings of victory made known in Medîna.*
lah the poet to make known his victory at Medîna. From
the valley of Ackîck, Abdallah struck off to the right, and
spread the good tidings throughout Coba and Upper Medîna.
Zeid, mounted on Al Caswa, proceeded straightway to the city.
The enemies of Mahomet had passed the time in hopes of his
defeat: and now, seeing his favourite camel approach without her master, they prognosticated that he had been slain.
But they were soon undeceived and crestfallen; for Zeid,
stopping at the place of prayer, near the entrance of the city,
cried aloud that the Coreish had been overthrown; and then
he enumerated by name the chief men of Mecca who had
been killed or taken prisoner. The joy of the Prophet's adherents was unbounded; and, as the news ran from door to
door, even the little children caused the streets to resound
with the cry, *Abu Jahl, the sinner, is slain!*

The next day, Mahomet himself arrived. His gladness *Mahomet's return; death of his daughter Rockeya.*
was damped by finding that his daughter Rockeya had died
and been buried during his absence. They had just
smoothed the earth over her tomb in the graveyard of Backî,
as Zeid entered Medîna. Othmân had watched tenderly
over her death-bed; and Mahomet sought to solace him by
uniting him in marriage, a few months later, to his remaining single daughter, Omm Kolthûm. Like Rockeya, she
had been married to a cousin, the son of Abu Lahab, but had
for some time been separated from him. She died a year or
two before Mahomet, who used, after her death, to say he so
dearly loved Othmân, that had there been a third daughter,
he would have given her also in marriage to him.

In the evening, the prisoners were brought in. Sauda, *Prisoners brought into Medîna.*
the Prophet's wife, had gone out to join in lamentation with
the family of Afra, a citizen, who had lost two sons at Bedr.
On her return, she found, standing by her house, Suheil, one of
the prisoners, with his hands tied behind his neck.[1] Surprised

---

[1] Perhaps greater stringency than usual was used in his restraint, as he

R

at the sight, she suddenly offered to loose his hands, when she was startled by the voice of Mahomet, calling loudly from within: 'By the Lord and his Prophet! O Sauda, what art thou doing?' She replied that she had addressed Suheil from an involuntary impulse. Yet Mahomet was far from intending to treat the prisoners whose lives he had spared, with harshness. He rather hoped, by a kind and courteous demeanour, to win their affections and draw them over to the Faith. Thus, when Omm Salmâ was, like Sauda, lamenting at the house of Afra, news was brought that some of the prisoners had been quartered at her house. She first proceeded to Mahomet, whom she found in the apartment of Ayesha, and thus addressed him: 'O Prophet! my uncle's sons desire that I should entertain certain of the prisoners, anoint their heads, and comb their dishevelled hair; but I did not venture to do so until I had first obtained thine ords.' Mahomet replied that he did not at all object to these marks of hospitality, and desired her to do to them as she was minded.[1]

Prisoners treated kindly;

In pursuance of Mahomet's commands, the citizens of Medîna, and such of the Refugees as already had houses of their own, received the prisoners, and treated them with much consideration. 'Blessings be on the men of Medîna!' said one of these prisoners in later days: 'they made us ride, while they themselves walked: they gave us wheaten bread to eat when there was little of it, contenting themselves with dates.' It is not surprising that when, some time afterwards, their friends came to ransom them, several of the prisoners who had been thus received declared themselves adherents of Islâm; and to such the Prophet granted liberty without ransom. It was long before the Coreish could reconcile themselves to the humiliation of visiting Medîna to arrange for the liberation of their relatives. Their kindly treatment was thus prolonged, and left a favourable impression on the minds even of those who did not at once

---

had nearly escaped on the road. Mahomet gave orders to chase and kill him. Coming up with him, he spared his life, but bound his hands behind his neck, and tied him with a rope to his camel. Usâma met Mahomet entering Medîna with Suheil following in this condition, and exclaimed: 'What! Abu Yazid!' (Suheil's name). 'Yes,' said Mahomet, 'it is the same; the Chief who used to feed the people with bread at Mecca.'

[1] One or two years afterwards, on her husband's death, Mahomet married this lady.

go over to Islâm. Eventually the army of Bedr was en- And ransomed from Mecca. riched by the large payments made for the prisoners; for they were redeemed according to their several means,— some paying a thousand, and others as much as four thousand dirhems. Such as had nothing to give were liberated without any payment; but a service was required of them which shows how far Mecca was in advance of Medîna in learning. To each prisoner were allotted ten boys, who were to be taught the art of writing; and their tuition, when completed, was accepted as full ransom.

The importance of the field of Bedr is marked, as I have Importance of the battle of Bedr, and rank assigned to those engaged in it. already said, by the marvellous labour with which every incident relating to it has been treasured up, so that the narrative far exceeds in profusion of detail that of probably any other of the great battles that have turned the destinies of the world. Its significance is also stamped by the exalted rank assigned to each one of the famous Three Hundred. After the death of Mahomet their names were enrolled as recipients of princely dotations in the great 'Register of Bedr.' These were the peerage of Islâm. 'Bring me here the garment in which I went forth to Bedr; for this end have I kept it laid up unto this day.' So spake Sád, the youthful convert of Mecca, now about to die at fourscore years of age. Crowned with renown as the conqueror of Persia, the founder of Cûfa, and the Viceroy of Irâc, his honours were all cast into the shade by the glory of having shared in the battle of Bedr. In his eyes the 'garment of Bedr' was the highest badge of nobility, and in it would he be carried to his grave.[1]

The battle of Bedr was indeed a critical point in the The victory represented as a divine declaration in favour of Islâm. career of Mahomet. However skilful in turning every incident, whether favourable or not, into a proof of the divine interposition for the furtherance of Islâm, the Prophet would have found it difficult on the present occasion to maintain his position at Medîna in the face of a reverse. The victory now supplied him with new and cogent arguments. He did not hesitate to ascribe his success to the miraculous assistance of God; and this was the easier in

[1] He had amassed great wealth in his various commands, and, avoiding the civil wars which followed the death of the Caliph Othmân, had retired to his castle at Al Ackîck near Medîna, where he died A.H. 55.

consequence of the superior numbers of the Coreish.   I
have already quoted some passages from the Corân to this

effect, and the following are equally conclusive.   The presence of an Angelic host, a thousand strong, was actively
engaged against the enemy :—

When ye sought assistance from your Lord; and He answered,
*Verily, I will assist you with a thousand Angels, following one
upon another :*—this the Lord did as good tidings for you, and
that your hearts might be thereby reassured.   As for victory,
it is from none other than God : for God is glorious and
wise.

Verily there hath been given unto you a Sign in the two
armies which fought.   One army fought in the way of God.
The other was unbelieving, and saw their enemy double of themselves by the sight of the eye.   And God strengtheneth with His
aid whom He pleaseth.   Verily, therein is a lesson unto the discerning people.

And ye slew them not, but God slew them.   And thou (O
Prophet) didst not cast (the gravel); but God cast it; that He
might prove the Believers by a gracious probation from Himself.
Verily, God heareth and knoweth.   It was even so.   And God
weakeneth the devices of the Infidels.

If ye desire a Decision, truly the Decision (or Victory) hath
already come unto you.   If ye hold back, it will be better for
you; but if ye return, We also shall return.   And your troops
will not avail you anything, even though they be many in number,
for surely God is with the Believers.

Furthermore, not only was divine aid afforded to the
army of Medîna, but the help which Satan had designed for
the army of Mecca was signally frustrated :—

Be not like unto those who went forth from their habitations
vain-gloriously to be seen of men, and who turned aside from the
way of God : and God compasseth about that which they do.

And (remember) when Satan bedecked their works for them,
and said,—*None shall prevail this day against you ; for I verily am
your Confederate.*   But when the two armies came within sight
of each other, he turned back upon his heels, and said,—*Verily I
am clear of you.   Truly I see that which ye do not see.   I fear God,
for God is terrible in vengeance.*[1]

---

[1] As may be imagined, these passages have given rise to endless legends.
The Devil appeared in the favourite form of Surâca.   This man was seen running
away from the field of battle, and was taxed with it by the Coreish—while all
the time it was the Devil !   We have gravely given to us the circumstantial
evidence of a witness regarding the Devil's words and behaviour on this

The cause of Mahomet, it was distinctly admitted, must stand or fall by the result of the armed struggle with his native city on which he had now fairly entered : difficult and dangerous ground, no doubt, for a fallible mortal to stand upon; but the die was cast, and the battle must be fought out to the death. The scabbard having been cast away, little additional risk was incurred by the founder of Islâm when he made success in arms the criterion of his prophetical claim. However strong his position otherwise, it could not possibly be maintained in the face of a final and conclusive defeat; however otherwise weak, a succession of victories would establish it triumphantly.

Mahomet now stands or falls by success in the field.

There was much in the battle of Bedr which Mahomet could plausibly represent as a special interposition of the Deity in his behalf. Not only was a most decisive victory gained over a force three times his own in number, but the slain on the enemy's side included in a remarkable manner many of his most influential opponents. In addition to the chief men killed or made prisoners, Abu Lahab, who was not present in the battle, died a few days after the return of the fugitive army,—as if the decree marking out the enemies of the Prophet was inevitable.[1]

Number of chief Coreish killed at Bedr.

At Mecca itself, the news of the defeat was received with consternation. Shame and burning desire for revenge stifled the expression of grief. ' Weep not for your slain,' such was the counsel of Abu Sofiân, ' bewail not their loss, neither let the bard mourn for them. Show that ye are men and heroes. If ye wail and lament and mourn over them with elegies, it will ease your wrath and diminish your enmity towards Mahomet and his fellows. Moreover, if that reach our enemies' ears, and they laugh at us, will not their scorn be worse than all? Perchance ye may yet ob-

Consternation and thirst for revenge at Mecca.

occasion, his jumping into the sea, &c. As to the angels, we have pages filled with accounts of them :—such as that one of the enemy suddenly perceived a tall white figure in the air, mounted on a piebald horse : it was an angel who bound him, and left him on the spot a prisoner, and this was the cause of his conversion. But it would be endless and unprofitable to multiply such tales.

[1] Abasside traditions add that his death was caused by malignant and infectious ulcers; that he remained two days unburied, as no one would approach the offensive corpse; that he was not washed, but that water was cast from a distance on his body, which was then carried forth and cast into a well in Upper Mecca, and stones heaped over the well. The bias is palpable.

tain your revenge. As for me, I will touch no oil, neither approach any woman, until I go forth to war against Mahomet.' It was this savage pride which so long prevented their sending to Medîna for the ransom of their captive kinsmen.[1]

A month elapsed thus ; and they could refrain no longer. The wild demonstrations of Asiatic grief burst forth at last from the whole city. In almost every house there were cries and wailings for the captive or the dead. And this lasted an entire month.[2] There was one exception : 'Why sheddest thou no tears,' said they to Hind, the wife of Abu Sofiân ; 'why weep not for thy father Otba, for thy brother, and thine uncle ?' 'Nay,' replied Hind, 'I will not weep until ye again wage war with Mahomet and his fellows. If weeping would wash away grief from my heart, I would weep even as ye ; but it is not thus with me.' To mark her sullen sorrow, she forswore to use oil for her hair, or to go near the bed of Abu Sofiân, until an army should march forth against Medîna.

[1] Abu Sofiân declared that he would not send to ransom his own son, even if Mahomet kept him a whole year. His son was eventually exchanged for a Moslem who incautiously visited Mecca for the Lesser pilgrimage.

[2] A plaintive illustration of the force of pent-up grief is given by Wâckidi with all the pathos of Arab feeling. The blind and aged Aswad had lost two sons and a grandson in the battle. Like the rest of the Coreish, he sternly repressed his grief; but as days rolled on he longed to give vent to his feelings. One night he heard the wild notes of a female wailing, and he said to his servant: 'Go see! it may be that the Coreish have begun to wail for their dead : perchance I, too, may wail for Zamâa, my son ; for grief consumeth me within.' The servant returned, saying, that it was but the voice of a woman lamenting for her strayed camel. On this the old man gave way to a burst of beautiful and impassioned poetry. 'Doth she weep for her camel, and for it banish sleep from her eyes? Nay, if ye will weep, let us weep over Bedr :— Weep for Ockeil, and for Hârith the lion of lions !' &c.

CHAPTER XIII.

THE YEAR FOLLOWING THE BATTLE OF BEDR.

(*Ramadhân*, A.H. II., *to Shabân*, A.H. III.—A.D. 624.)

Ætat. 56.

THE triumph of Bedr was not less important in its effect upon the inhabitants of Medîna than it was upon the Coreish at Mecca. It was, indeed, more important. It consolidated the power of Mahomet over the wavering, and it struck alarm into the hearts of the Disaffected. The issue had been put not on political, but upon religious grounds. It was for their unbelief that the Coreish were overthrown. The victory, the 'Decision,' was vouchsafed by God to vindicate the Faith. The Lord had ' frustrated the devices of the Infidels ;—for surely God is with the Believers.' The conclusion applied with equal force to the Unbelievers of Medîna. ' Verily,' said the Prophet in his revelation,—' verily herein is a lesson unto the discerning people ; ' and the citizens of Medîna were not slow to learn it. Abdallah ibn Obey still possessed great influence in the city, and was the head of those who had not yet gone over to the new faith and tendered allegiance to the stranger. Mahomet on his first arrival had been counselled to deal tenderly with this Chief, and he had followed the advice. Abdallah, on his side, either saw no opportunity for a successful rupture, or found his own power too insecure, or the attitude of his people too weak and wavering, for an open conflict with the fierce fanaticism of Mahomet's followers. The stranger's power was daily undermining his authority and rising rapidly on its ruins.

Important effect of victory on Mahomet's position at Medîna.

Still there were clans as well as individuals who declined to go over to the new faith ; and there were the Jewish tribes, and their Arab converts or adherents, whose reliion

Disaffected Jews a thorn in Mahomet's side.

Mahomet, having already recognised, was obliged at first to respect. These were a thorn in the Prophet's side. They spoke covertly against him, and they ridiculed him in satires which passed readily into the mouths of the Disaffected, but they had not calculated on the craft and power of Mahomet to crush them. The unquestioning devotion of Mahomet's followers made them ready instruments not only of an all-pervading espionage from which no family was secure, but also for ridding him of those whose opposition was dangerous to his cause. Even secret conversations were reported to the Prophet, and on such information he based proceedings that were sometimes both cruel and unscrupulous. It was the strength gained at Bedr which enabled him fearlessly to enter on this course.

Assassination of Asma. Ramadhân, A.H. II. January, A.D. 624.

The first blood shed at Medîna with the countenance of Mahomet was that of a woman. Asma, daughter of Marwân, belonged to a disaffected tribe, the Bani Aus, and to a family which had not as yet thrown off their ancestral faith. She made no secret of her dislike to Islâm; and, being a poetess, composed some couplets, after the battle of Bedr, on the folly of her fellow citizens in receiving and trusting one who had slain the chief men amongst his own people. The verses spread from mouth to mouth (for such was one of the few means possessed by the Arabs of giving expression to public opinion), and at last reached the ears of the Mussulmans. They were offended; and Omeir, a blind man of the same tribe (and according to some a former husband of Asma) vowed that he would kill the author. It was but a few days after the return of Mahomet from Bedr, that this man, in the dead of night, crept into the apartment where, surrounded by her little ones, Asma lay asleep. Feeling stealthily with his hand, he removed her infant from her breast, and plunged his sword into her bosom with such force that it passed through her back. Next morning, being present in the Mosque at prayers, Mahomet, who was aware of the bloody design, said to Omeir: ' Hast thou slain the daughter of Marwân ? ' ' Yes,' he answered ; ' but tell me now is there any cause of apprehension for what I have done ? ' ' None,' said Mahomet ; ' a couple of goats will not knock their heads together for it.' Then turning to the people assembled in the Mosque, he said : ' If ye desire to see a man that hath assisted the Lord and his Prophet, look ye here!' 'What!' Omar exclaimed, 'the blind Omeir!' 'Nay,' replied the Prophet, 'call him not blind; rather call him *Omeir the Seeing.*'

As the assassin returned to his home in Upper Medîna, he passed the sons of Asma burying their mother; they accused him of the murder, which without compunction he avowed, and added that if they dared to repeat things such as she had uttered, he would slay the whole clan of them. The bloody threat had the desired effect. Those of the family who had secretly espoused the cause of Mahomet, now openly professed their adherence, and the whole tribe soon succumbed before the fierce determination and growing influence of the Prophet's followers. Indeed, as Sprenger remarks, the only course by which they could now preserve their honour without entering on a hopeless blood-feud, was the adoption of Islâm.

Many weeks did not elapse before another foul murder was committed by the express command of Mahomet. Abu Afak belonged to the Bani Amr (whose doubtful loyalty is marked by the message sent to them by Mahomet on his march to Bedr); he had embraced Judaism, but still lived with his tribe in Upper Medîna. Though (as is said) above a hundred years of age he was active in his opposition to the new religion. He, too, composed some stinging and disloyal verses which annoyed the Mussulmans. The Prophet signified his wish for his assassination by saying: 'Who will rid me of this pestilent fellow?' A convert from amongst the Bani Amr watched his opportunity, and falling unawares upon the aged man, as he slept in the court-yard outside his house, despatched him with his sword. The death shriek of the Jew drew the neighbours to the spot; but though they vowed vengeance against the murderer, he escaped unrecognised.

And of Abu Afak. A.H. II. February, A.D. 624.

These lawless and perfidious acts alarmed all that party at Medîna which still regarded the strangers and the new faith with suspicion and dislike. Terror crept over the hearts of the Jews. There was good reason for it.

Alarm of Jews.

The Bani Cainucâa, who followed the trade of goldsmiths and lived in a strongly built suburb, were the first of the Jewish tribes to bear the brunt of the Prophet's displeasure. It is asserted that the Jews rebelled and broke

Bani Cainucâa threatened by Mahomet

their treaty. How the breach first occurred is not altogether certain. Mahomet, we are told, went to their chief place of resort, shortly after his return from Bedr; and, having assembled the chief men, summoned them to acknowledge him as their Prophet. 'By the Lord!' he said, 'ye know full well that I am the Apostle of God. Believe, therefore, before that happen to you which has befallen the Coreish!' They refused, and defied him to do his worst. An incident soon occurred which afforded the pretext for an attack. An Arab girl, married to a convert of Medîna, went to a gold-smith's shop in the market-place of the Cainucâa, and, while waiting for some ornaments, sat down. A silly neighbour, unperceived, pinned the lower hem of her skirt behind to the upper dress. When she arose, the awkward exposure excited laughter, and she screamed with shame. A Mussulman, being apprised of the affront, slew the offending Jew; the brethren of the Jew, in their turn, fell upon the Mussulman and killed him. The family of the murdered Mussulman appealed to the converts of Medîna, who espoused their cause. Though bound by a friendly treaty, Mahomet made no attempt to compose the quarrel, nor any demand that the guilty should be singled out and brought to justice. Without further communication, he marshalled his followers, and, placing the great white banner in the hands of Hamza, marched forth to attack the offending tribe. Their settlement was sufficiently fortified to resist assault. It was therefore invested, and a strict blockade maintained. This happened within one month from the battle of Bedr.

The Bani Cainucâa were besieged closely by Mahomet for fifteen days. They had expected that Abdallah ibn Obey and the Bani Khazraj, with whom they had long been in close bonds of defensive alliance, would have interfered in their behalf; but no one dared to stir. At last, despairing of the looked-for aid, they surrendered at discretion. As, one by one, they issued from the stronghold, their hands were tied behind their backs, and preparations made for execution. But Abdallah, fallen as he was from his high estate, could not endure to see his faithful allies led thus away to be massacred in cold blood. Approaching Mahomet, he begged for mercy to be shown them; but Mahomet turned his face away. Abdallah persisted in his suit, and seizing the Prophet by

Quarrel between Jews and citizens of Medina.

Bani Cainucâa are besieged. A H. II. February, A.D. 624.

Surrender at discretion, and are sent into exile.

the side, as he stood armed in his coat of mail, reiterated the petition. 'Let me alone!' cried Mahomet; but Abdallah did not relax his hold. The marks of anger mantled in the Prophet's face, and again he exclaimed loudly: 'Wretch, let me go!' 'Nay!' said Abdallah, 'I will not let thee go until thou hast compassion on my friends; 300 soldiers armed in mail, and 400 unequipped,—they defended me on the fields of Hadâick and Boâth from every foe.[1] Wilt thou cut them down in one day, O Mahomet? As for me, I am one verily that feareth the vicissitudes of fortune.' Abdallah was yet too strong for Mahomet with safety to neglect the appeal so urgently preferred. 'Let them go!' the Prophet said, reluctantly; 'God curse them, and God curse him also!' So Mahomet released them from death, and commanded that they should be sent into exile. They were led forth some distance by Obâda, one of the Khazrajite 'leaders;' thence they proceeded to the Jewish settlement of Wâdi al Cora, and, being assisted there with carriage, reached Adzrâât, a territory on the confines of Syria.

The spoil consisted mainly of armour and goldsmiths' tools, for that was the chief occupation of the tribe: they possessed no agricultural property, nor any fields. Mahomet took his choice of the arms,—three bows, three swords, and two coats of mail. The royal fifth was then set aside, and the remainder distributed amongst the army.

The spoil.

The Jews might now see clearly the designs of Mahomet. It was no petty question of an affronted female. Blood had no doubt been shed in the quarrel; but it was shed equally on both sides. And had there not been a deadly enmity, and a predetermination to root out the Israelites, the difference might easily have been composed. Moreover Mahomet was bound by treaty to deal justly and amicably with the tribe: the murderer alone was 'liable to retaliation.'[2] Indeed, of such minor importance was the quarrel, that some biographers do not mention it at all, but justify the attack by a divine revelation of Jewish treachery. The violent proceedings of Mahomet widened also to some extent the breach between his followers and the disaffected citizens. Abdallah thus upbraided Obâda (they were both principals in the confederacy with the Bani

Effect on the Jews and Disaffected.

Cainucâa) for the part he had taken in abandoning their allies, and aiding in their exile: 'What! art thou free from the oath with which we ratified their alliance? Hast thou forgotten how they stood by us, and shed for us their blood, on such and such a field?'—and he began enumerating the engagements in which they had fought together. Obâda cut him short with the decisive answer: 'Hearts have changed. Islâm hath blotted all treaties out.'

Affair of the *Meal bags*, a petty attack by Abu Sofiân. A.H. II. April, A.D. 624.

After the expulsion of the Bani Cainucâa, Medîna enjoyed a month of repose. It was then thrown into alarm by a petty inroad of the Coreish. Abu Sofiân, smarting under the defeat at Bedr, and still bound by his oath of abstinence, resolved, by way of revenge, to beard his enemies at their very doors. Setting out with two hundred mounted followers, he took the eastern road skirting the table land of Nejd, and arrived by night at the settlement of the Bani Nadhîr, a Jewish tribe living close to Medîna. Refused admittance by their chief, Huwey, Abu Sofiân repaired to another leading man of the same tribe, who furnished him with intelligence regarding Medîna, and hospitably entertained his party during the night. When the dawn was about to break, the Coreish moved stealthily forward, and fell upon the corn fields and palm gardens of a valley two or three miles north-east of Medîna. Some of these, with their farm-houses, they burned to the ground, and killed two of the cultivators. Then, holding his vow to be fulfilled, Abu Sofiân hurried back to Mecca. Meanwhile, the alarm was raised in Medîna, and Mahomet hastened, at the head of the citizens, in pursuit. To accelerate their flight, the Coreish cast away their wallets filled with meal (whence the name of the expedition) which were picked up by the pursuers. After an absence of five days, Mahomet returned from the fruitless chase. And shortly after, he celebrated the first festival of the *Eed al Zoha*, which I have already described.

Expedition to Carcarat al Cadr, against the Bani Ghatafân and Suleim. A.H. III. May, A.D. 624.

During the summer and autumn, two or three expeditions were undertaken against the tribes inhabiting the table land to the east of Medîna. These were of minor interest in their immediate results, but they are significant of the widening circle of the struggle. The Joheina and other tribes on the sea-coast being in the interest of Mahomet, the Syrian trade by that route was now absolutely barred. There remained the eastern route to Babylonia. This passed through the territories of two powerful nomad tribes, the Bani Suleim and Ghatafân, both allied to the Coreish and employed by them as carriers. They inhabited that part of the great table-land of Nejd lying to the east of Medîna. There the Bani Suleim had their head-quarters in a fruitful plain, the seventh station from Mecca on the caravan route which lay diagonally across the table land. The Coreish now turned their eyes towards this territory, and entered into closer bonds with the tribes inhabiting it. Henceforth the attitude of the Bani Suleim and Ghatafân, especially of the former, became actively hostile towards Mahomet. Incited by the Coreish, and by the example of Abu Sofiân, they now projected a plundering attack upon Medîna, a task in itself congenial with their predatory habits. Timely intelligence reached Medîna that they had begun to assemble at Carcarat al Cadr; Mahomet, anticipating their design, hastened to surprise them, at the head of two hundred men. On reaching the spot he found it deserted; but a herd of five hundred camels, securely feeding under charge of a single boy, fell into his hands, and was divided as spoil of war. The boy was made captive, but afterwards released on his professing belief in Mahomet.

A month later, the Bani Ghatafân were reported to be again collecting troops in Nejd. Having assembled a strong force of four hundred and fifty men, some mounted on horses, Mahomet proceeded to disperse them. In three or four marches he reached the spot; but the enemy, having notice of his approach, had retired to the hills, and secured in the fastnesses their families and cattle. One of them, who was met on the road, and employed as a guide, embraced Islâm and was spared. In effecting this demonstration Mahomet was absent eleven days.

Second expedition against Bani Ghatafân, to Dzu Amr. June.

In the autumn Mahomet led another attack, at the head of three hundred followers, against the Bani Suleim, who still maintained a threatening attitude. Arrived at their rendezvous, he found that the force had broken up. So after staying unavailingly for some time to watch the autumn caravans of the Coreish proceeding northwards, he returned without meeting the enemy.

And against Bani Suleim, to Bohrân. August.

The following month was marked by a more successful

Zeid plunders

Coreishite
caravan
at al
Carada.
September.

affair. The Coreish (as we have seen), finding the sea-shore
closely watched by Mahomet, dared not expose their merchandise to the perils of that route. They were reduced to
great straits. 'If we sit still at home,' they said, 'we shall be
eating up our capital; how can we live, unless we maintain
uninterrupted our winter and our summer caravans? We are
shut out from the coast; let us try the eastern road by Irâc.'
Water is scarce upon this route, but the summer was now
past, and moreover water could be carried on their camels
between the distant wells. Accordingly they equipped a
caravan to traverse the table land of the central desert. It
was headed by Safwân, and the Coreish sent much property
with him for barter, chiefly in vessels and bars of silver. An
Arab guide promised to lead them by a way unknown to the
followers of Mahomet; but intelligence of the rich venture,
and of the road which it was to take, reached the Prophet
through an Arab who chanced to visit the Jews at Medîna;
whereupon Zeid, the son of Hârith, was immediately despatched in pursuit, with one hundred picked and well-
mounted men. He came up with the caravan, and fell suddenly upon it. The leaders of the Coreish fled, the rest were
overpowered, and all the merchandise and silver were carried
off, with one or two prisoners, by Zeid, to Medîna. The booty
was valued at one hundred thousand dirhems; so that, after
appropriation of the Prophet's fifth, eight hundred dirhems fell
to the lot of each soldier. The guide was brought to Mahomet, who promised him liberty without ransom, if he would
believe. He embraced Islâm, and was set free. This was the
first occasion on which the Moslems secured the rich plunder
of a caravan. Zeid obtained great distinction in consequence, and thenceforward became a favourite commander.

Assassina-
tion of
Káb son of
Ashraf.
A.H. III.
July, A.D.
624.

No further expedition was undertaken during this year;
but I must not omit to notice another of those dastardly assassinations which darken the pages of this history. Káb ibn
Ashraf was the son of a Jewess of the Bani Nadhîr, and with
that tribe he appears to have identified himself. He was a
'proselyte of the gate,' and is said to have followed Mahomet
till he abandoned Jerusalem as his Kibla. The victory of
Bedr deeply mortified him, in common with other ill-wishers
of the Prophet. He made no attempt to conceal his discontent; and soon after proceeded to Mecca, where, being a

poet, he stirred up the Coreish to avenge their heroes buried in the pit of Bedr, by elegies lamenting their hard fate. On his return to Medîna he was further accused of disquieting the Mussulmans by the publication of amatory sonnets addressed to certain of their women,—a curious and favourite mode of annoyance amongst the Arabs.[1] Mahomet, apprehensive that the free expression of hostile feeling by persons of such influence would sap his authority at Medîna, made no secret of his animosity towards Káb. He prayed aloud: '*O Lord, deliver me from the son of Ashraf, in whatsoever way it seemeth good unto thee, because of his open sedition and his verses.*' But instead of adopting a fair and straightforward course, he prompted his followers, as on previous occasions, to assassination, by saying to them: 'Who will ease me of the son of Ashraf? for he troubleth me.' Mohammad son of Maslama, replied: 'Here am I;—I will slay him.' Mahomet, signifying his approval, desired him to take counsel with Sád ibn Moâdz, the chief man of his tribe the Bani Aus. By the advice of Sád, the conspirator chose four other men from the same tribe as accomplices, and taking them to Mahomet, obtained his sanction to their plan of throwing the victim off his guard by fair words and the pretence of unfriendliness to the Prophet's rule. Abu Naila, foster-brother of Káb, being deputed to pave the way, complained to him of the calamities and poverty which the advent of Mahomet had brought upon them, and begged that he would

---

[1] The following couplets by Káb are quoted by the biographers in support of the accusation :—

Alas my heart! Wilt thou pass on? Wilt thou not tarry to praise her?
    Wilt thou leave Omm al Fadhl deserted?

Of saffron colour is she: so full of charms, that if thou wert to clasp her, there
    would be pressed forth Wine, Henna, and Katam;[1]

So slim that her figure, from ankle to shoulder, bends as she desires to stand
    upright, and cannot.

When we met she caused me to forget (my own wife) Omm Hâlim, although
    the cord that bindeth me to her is not to be broken.

Sprung of the Bani Aámir, my heart is mad with the love of her; and if she
    chose she could cure Káb of his sickness.

She is the Princess of women; and her father is the Prince of his tribe, the
    Entertainer of strangers, the Fulfiller of promises.

I never saw the Sun come forth by night, but one dark evening when she
    appeared unto me in her splendour.

[1] The elements of beauty; red, yellow, and black.

advance corn and dates for the sustenance of himself and a party like-minded with him. Káb, taken in the snare, demanded security; Abu Naila agreed that they should pledge their arms, and appointed a late hour of meeting at the house of Káb, when the bargain would be completed. Towards evening the band of conspirators assembled at the house of Mahomet. It was a bright moonlight night, and the Prophet accompanied them to the outskirts of the town. As they emerged from the low shrubs of the Moslem burying ground, he bade them god-speed: 'Go!' said he; 'the blessing of God be with you, and assistance from on high!' The house of Káb was near one of the Jewish suburbs, two or three miles from the city. When they reached it, he had retired to rest. Abu Naila called aloud for him to come down, and Káb started from his couch. His bride (for he had been lately married, and the biographers delight to record every circumstance which adds to the heartlessness of the affair) caught him by the skirt, and warned him not to go. 'It is but my brother Abu Naila,' he said; and, as he pulled the garment from her, gaily added the verse: 'Shall a warrior be challenged and not respond?' Descending, he was not alarmed to find the party armed, as the weapons were to be left with him in pledge. They wandered along, conversing on the misfortunes of Medîna, till they reached a waterfall, and upon its bank they proposed to pass some part of the moonlight night. Meanwhile, his foster-brother, having thrown his arm around Káb, was familiarly drawing his hand through his long locks, and praising their sweet scent, which Káb said was that of his bride. Suddenly the traitor seized his hair, and dragging him to the ground, shouted: '*Slay him! slay the enemy of God!*' All drew their swords, and fell upon their victim. The wretched man clung so close to his foster-brother that he was with difficulty put to death. As he received the fatal wound he uttered a fearful scream, which resounded far and near amongst the strongholds of the Jews, and lights were seen at the windows of the affrighted inhabitants. The assassins, fearful of pursuit, retired in haste, carrying in their arms one of their number who had received two deep sword-cuts aimed at Káb. As they regained the burying ground, they shouted the well-known *takbîr*, 'Great is the Lord;' which Mahomet hearing knew that their work had been successfully accomplished. At the gate of the Mosque he met them, saying: 'Welcome; for your countenances beam with the joy of victory.' 'And thine also, O Prophet,' they exclaimed, as they threw before him the ghastly head of their victim. Then Mahomet praised God for what had been done, and comforted the wounded man.

I have been thus minute in transcribing the record of the murder of Káb, because it faithfully illustrates the ruthless fanaticism into which Mahomet was fast drifting. It was a spirit too congenial with the passions of the Arabs not to be immediately caught up by his followers. The strong religious impulse under which they acted, untempered by the divine graces and heaven-born morality of the Christian faith, hurried them into excesses of barbarous treachery, and justified that treachery by the interests of Islâm and the direct approval of the Deity. I am far from asserting that every detail in the foregoing narrative, either of instigation by Mahomet, or of deception by the assassins, is beyond suspicion. The actors in such scenes were not slow to magnify and embellish their own services at the expense of truth. There may also have been the desire to justify an act of perfidy, that startled even the loose morality of the day, by casting the burden of it on the infallible Prophet. But, after allowing due weight to both considerations, enough remains to prove the worst features of assassination, and the fact that they were countenanced, in some instances directly prompted, by Mahomet himself.[1]

Reflections on Káb's assassination.

[1] There can be little doubt that the faith even of some Moslems was at times scandalised by crimes like this; though it was not in the nature of one-sided tradition to preserve the record of what they said. The present is one of the few occasions on which the murmurs of the aggrieved parties have come to light. When Merwán was Governor of Medîna, he one day asked Benjamin, a convert from the Bani Nadhîr (Káb's tribe), in what manner Káb met his death. 'By guile and perfidy,' said Benjamin. Now Muhammad son of Maslama (the assassin), by this time a very aged man, was sitting by. He exclaimed: 'What, O Merwân! could the Prophet of the Lord, thinkest thou, be guilty of perfidy? By the Lord! we did not kill him but by command of the Prophet. I swear that no roof, save that of the Mosque, shall hereafter cover thee and me.' Then, turning to Benjamin, he swore that if he had had a sword in his hand, he would have cut off his head. The unfortunate Benjamin could not thenceforward quit his house without first sending a messenger to see that Muhammad was out of the way. His enemy caught him one day at a funeral, and seizing a bundle of date branches from a woman passing by, broke them every one over the face and back of Benjamin. Thus

s

Murder
of Ibn
Sanîna, a
Jew,

On the morning after the murder of Káb, Mahomet, exasperated at the opposition (or, as tradition would represent, the treachery) of the Jews, is said to have given a general permission to his followers to slay them indiscriminately wherever met. Accordingly, Muheiasa, a Moslem, having encountered Ibn Sanîna, a Jewish merchant, slew him. The occurrence is alluded to by the biographers rather for the purpose of explaining the sudden conversion of the assassin's brother Huweisa, than to record the murder of a petty

Causes conversion of the murderer's brother.

Jewish trader. When Huweisa upbraided Muheiasa for killing his confederate the Jew, and appropriating his wealth : ' By the Lord!' replied Muheiasa, 'if he that commanded me to kill him had commanded to kill thee also, I would have done it.' 'What!' Huweisa cried; 'wouldst thou have slain thine own brother at Mahomet's bidding?' 'Even so,' answered the fanatic. 'Strange indeed!' Huweisa responded; 'hath the new religion reached to this? Verily, it is a wonderful faith.' And Huweisa was converted from that very hour. The progress of Islâm begins to stand out in unenviable contrast with that of early Christianity. Converts were gained to the faith of Jesus by witnessing the constancy with which its confessors *suffered* death ; they were gained to Islâm by the spectacle of the readiness with which its adherents *inflicted* death. In the one case conversion often imperilled the believer's life ; in the other, it was for the most part the only means of saving it.

New treaty
with the
Jews.

The Jews were now in extreme alarm. None ventured abroad. Every family lived in the fear of a night attack ; every individual dreaded the fate of Káb and Ibn Sanîna. A deputation of their principal men waited upon Mahomet, and complained that he had treacherously cut off one of their chiefs without fault or apparent cause. 'Had Káb conducted himself,' replied Mahomet, 'as ye have done, he would not have been cut off. But he offended me by his seditious speeches and his evil poetry. And if any one amongst you,' he added, 'doeth the same, verily the sword shall be again unsheathed.' At the same time he invited them to enter into a fresh compact with him, such as he might deem sufficient for the interests of Islâm. So a new

were murmurers against the infallibility of the Prophet silenced in the early days of Islâm.

treaty was written out and deposited with Ali. Nevertheless, adds Wâckidi, the Jews thenceforward lived (as well they might) in a state of depression and disquietude.

The winter months of the year 624 closed without any incident of political importance. But during this period the Prophet took to himself a third wife, Haphsa, the daughter of Omar, now eighteen to twenty years of age. She was the widow of Khoneis, an early convert, who had died six or seven months previously. By marrying this widow, Mahomet not only gratified the passion for fresh espousals, a leading feature of his advancing years, but bound himself closer in friendship to her father Omar. Abu Bakr and Omar were now connected equally with the Prophet, and through their daughters had access to his ear. There was much rivalry between Ayesha and Haphsa; but the youth, vivacity, and beauty of Ayesha maintained the supremacy.

Mahome marries Haphsa. A.H. III. November, A.D. 624.

The marriages contracted by Mahomet at Medîna were all unfruitful. But meanwhile his house was built up in the female line of Khadîja's progeny. We hear of no issue, certainly of none that survived, by his daughters Zeinab and Omm Kolthûm, though the name of the latter would imply maternity.[1] Rockeya bore Othmân a son, two or three years before the Flight, but his eyes were pecked out at Medîna by a fowl, and he died still a child.[2] It was through Fâtima alone that the Prophet's race, the famous *Syads* or nobility of Islâm, was to be perpetuated. Ali was now five-and-twenty years of age. Though not above middle stature, he was broad and powerful in make, with a ruddy complexion, and a thick and comely beard. He had already given proof of daring gallantry and prowess on the field of Bedr. Endowed with a clear intellect, warm in affection, and confiding in friendship, he was from boyhood devoted heart and soul to the Prophet. But he was simple, unpretending, and unambitious; and in after days when he obtained the rule of half the Moslem world, it was rather

Marriage of Fâtima with Ali, A.D. 624, and birth of Hasan and Hosein.

---

[1] Omm Kolthûm, *i.e.* 'mother of Kolthûm.'

[2] Rockeya, as we have seen, died immediately after the battle of Bedr. Zeinab and Omm Kolthûm died two or three years before Mahomet, and Fâtima a few months after him. Ali survived the Prophet about thirty years. Besides the issue by Fâtima, he had twelve sons and seventeen daughters by nine wives besides concubines.

thrust upon him than sought. Shortly after the field of
Bedr (some authorities say before it) Mahomet gave him
the hand of Fâtima his youngest daughter, now seventeen or eighteen years of age, in marriage. Within the next
twelve months she gave birth to Hasan, the first grandson
born to Mahomet that survived, and in the following year
to Hosein, his brother.

CHAPTER XIV.

THE BATTLE OF OHOD.

Shawwâl, A.H. III.—*January,* A.D. 625.

Ætat. 56.

THE year A.D. 625, the third of the Hegira, opened stormily on Mahomet. Twelve months had elapsed since the battle of Bedr. The cry of revenge had ever since resounded in the valley of Mecca; and the long suspended threat was now put into execution.

Coreish resolve to avenge defeat at Bedr.

Rumours of preparation by the Coreish for a grand attack upon Medîna had for some time been reaching Mahomet: but the first authentic notice of the impending invasion was a sealed letter placed in his hands, while at the Mosque in Coba, by a messenger from Mecca. It was from his uncle Abbâs, who, as usual holding with both sides, had engaged the courier, by a high reward, to deliver it in three days. Obey son of Káb, who was standing by, read the despatch aloud; it contained the startling intelligence that the Coreish, three thousand strong, were on the point of marching. Mahomet enjoined secrecy; but the tidings could not be suppressed. The Prophet communicated the news privately to Sád son of Rabî, 'Leader' of the Bani Khazraj, and his wife overheard the conversation. Whether thus, or otherwise, the coming attack was soon noised abroad, and caused great excitement, especially among the Jews and those who sympathised with them.

Mahomet receives intimation from Abbâs.

The movement at Mecca did, indeed, justify alarm. The Coreish had unanimously agreed to devote the profits of the caravan, whose precious freight was still retained in the Council-hall as it were in bond, and for which so much blood had been shed at Bedr, towards avenging their defeat. These

Coreish march from Mecca. A.H. III. January, A.D. 625.

profits amply sufficed for the equipment and provisioning of a great army. Emissaries were despatched throughout the Bedouin tribes, connected with the Coreish by alliance or descent, inviting them to join the enterprise. At length, near the close of Shawwâl or beginning of Ramadhân, they commenced their march, three thousand in number; seven hundred were mailed warriors, and two hundred well-mounted cavalry; the remainder rode on camels. The Bani Zohra (who had, on the previous occasion, retired before reaching Bedr) remained behind; but the army was reinforced by one hundred men of the Bani Thackîf from Tâyif. The chiefs of the Coreish all joined the force. After a sharp discussion, women were allowed to accompany them; and fifteen, including the two wives of Abu Sofiân, availed themselves of the permission. These enkindled the fury of the army by verses chanted to the stirring cadence of the timbrel, and invoked vengeance on the Moslems for friends and kinsmen slain at Bedr. Foremost was Hind the wife of Abu Sofiân, who, thirsting for the blood of Hamza, had engaged an Ethiopian, with his deadly javelin, to make sure of her victim. There was also with the army a band of Medîna citizens under Abu Aámir 'the Monk,' who, it will be remembered, went over to Mecca in disgust at the enthusiastic reception of Mahomet, and now boasted that his presence in the ranks of the Coreish would of itself produce an immediate reaction and disarm the opposition of his fellow-citizens.

And encamp near Medína.

Thursday.

Friday.

The army took the ordinary route by the sea-shore, and, after a march of ten days, reached Dzul Huleifa, a halting place in the valley of Ackîck, about five miles west of Medîna. It was Thursday morning; and the same day, striking off by a valley to the left, they marched northward for a few miles, and encamped in an extensive and fertile plain to the west of the hill of Ohod. The luxuriant corn was cut down as forage for the horses; and the camels, set loose to graze, trampled the fields in all directions. Friday was passed by the Coreish inactively. Between this plain and Medîna were several rocky ridges, which, closing down upon the city on the north, rendered it secure from any direct attack on that side; but the road, sweeping eastward under Ohod, and then south, reached the northern suburbs by an easy circuit.

The Coreish feared to advance by this route upon the city as the houses on the road would have afforded their enemy a strong position. They hoped rather to draw them to the outskirts and overpower them, upon equal ground, by their superior numbers. Perhaps also it was expected that, by delay, the party unfavourable to Mahomet might have time to gain heart, and create in the city itself a dangerous diversion.

Meanwhile Mahomet, by his spies, was kept apprised of the enemy's movements. Hobâb reconnoitred their camp and brought back an alarming estimate of its strength, which the Prophet desired him to keep secret. The farmers of the plain had withdrawn in time their labourers, cattle, and implements of husbandry; but the complete destruction of their fields was severely felt. The hold which Mahomet had already attained over the people of Medîna is remarkable. There was no ebullition of resentment against him as the cause of their losses; and, amidst all the elements of disaffection, he was at once recognised as the leader and director of every defensive measure. Several chief men, both of the Aus and Khazraj, with a strong party of armed adherents, posted themselves at the great Mosque, and kept watch over the Prophet's door throughout the night of Thursday. The sleep of Mahomet was troubled. He dreamed, tradition tells us, that he was securely clad in mail, that his sword was broken at its point, that a cow was being slaughtered, and that he rode upon a ram.

Proceedings in Medina.

Thursday.

The next day, Friday, the people came together, and Mahomet discussed with them the course to be pursued. He told them of his dream. 'The fracture in my sword portendeth some injury to my own person,' he said; 'and the slaughtering of the cow, damage to my people; riding upon the ram signifieth carnage amongst the enemy; and the being covered with a coat of mail is a type of Medîna fortified and secure. Within the city then,' he argued, 'we are safe : without it, loss and disaster may await us.' In this opinion coincided the men of years and wisdom, both Citizens and Refugees. Abdallah ibn Obey, who, notwithstanding his jealousy of Mahomet, was equally concerned in the protection of Medîna from insult and violence, strongly supported the views of Mahomet : 'O Prophet!' he said, ' our city is a virgin, inviolate. We have never gone forth

Resolution to remain within city;

Friday.

to our enemies but we have suffered loss: remaining within our walls, we have beaten them off with slaughter. Leave the Coreish alone. If they remain, it will be in evil case; when they retire, it will be frustrated in their designs.' So it was determined that the women and children of the suburbs and surrounding hamlets should be brought within the city, and that the enemy, if they approached, should be met with arrows, stones, and other missiles from the house-tops, and pursued in confusion through the streets and narrow passages of the town.

Set aside by ardour of younger converts.

The decision was displeasing to the younger and more impetuous citizens. 'Shall we sit quietly here,' they asked indignantly, 'and see our possessions ravaged all around? Disgrace will cleave to us irretrievably, and the Arab tribes, emboldened, will repeat the insult. Let us go forth and smite our foes, even as we did at Bedr?' There were not wanting men even among the Refugees who sided with this party, and their ardour was so great that Mahomet at last gave way.[1] He announced his resolution to give battle to the Coreish. Ascending the pulpit for the weekly service, he stirred up the people, in his discourse, to fight

[1] As usual, we are overwhelmed with anecdotes of Believers bent on martyrdom, and dreams and pious anticipations of the rewards to be shortly enjoyed in Paradise. These are the growth of after years; the halo, in fact, pictured by tradition around the martyr's head. There were nevertheless worldly motives enough to justify this party in their desire to go forth. The citizens were grieved at the occupation of their fields; the barley crops were being destroyed, and the season for sowing was passing away. Even Hamza joined them, on political considerations. 'We fear,' he said, 'lest the Coreish should attribute our backwardness to cowardice, and that it will embolden them ever after. We were but three hundred at Bedr, and we are many now. Verily, this is the day we have longed and prayed to the Lord for; and now He hath driven the enemy as a prey into the midst of our habitations.'

Some specimens of the martyr spirit may interest the reader. One said, to Mahomet: 'The slaughtered cow which thou sawest was an emblem of the dead amongst thy followers, and verily I shall be of the number; wherefore, hinder me not from Paradise. Let us go forth; surely, by the one God! I shall quickly enter therein.' Again, Khaithama told Mahomet that his son, whom he had lost at Bedr, appeared to him in his sleep: 'A goodly appearance truly he had: he described to me the blessedness of Paradise; all is true that our Lord hath promised; and he besought me to come quickly, and be his companion there. And now, verily, I am old, and long for the meeting with my Lord. Pray, therefore, that God would grant me martyrdom, and reunite me with my son.' So Mahomet prayed; and Khaithama was slain at Ohod. Such are the tales which tradition delights to embellish or to create.

courageously: 'If ye be steadfast,' he said, 'the Lord will grant you victory.' Then he commanded them to make ready for the battle. The most part rejoiced greatly, but some were grieved that the first decision had been set aside.

By the time the afternoon prayer was ended, the people had assembled in the court of the Mosque, armed for battle. Mahomet then retired with Abu Bakr and Omar, to make ready. In a little while he issued from his chamber clad in mail and helmet, his sword hanging from a leathern girdle,[1] and shield slung over his shoulder. His followers now repented that they had importuned him to go forth, and prayed that he would even now do as seemed good to him. But it was too late: 'I invited you to this,' he said, 'and ye would not. It doth not become a prophet, when once he hath put on his helmet, to lay it down again until the Lord hath decided betwixt him and his enemies. Wait, therefore, on the Lord. Only be steadfast, and He will send you victory.'

Mahomet puts on his armour;

Then he called for three lances, and fixed banners upon them. One for the Refugees he gave to Musáb, the second to a leader of the Bani Aus, the third to a leader of the Bani Khazraj. Abdallah ibn Omm Maktûm (the blind man of whom we read at Mecca) was appointed to command the city, and lead the public prayers, during his absence. Just then the bier of a citizen was brought, according to custom, into the Mosque. Mahomet pronounced over it the usual service; then mounting his horse, and surrounded by his followers, he took the road to Ohod. There was but one other horse with the Moslem army. Arrived at an eminence, the Prophet turned round and saw following, amid the palm plantations on the right, a rude and disorderly band of men. Being told that they were the Jewish confederates of Abdallah ibn Obey, he commanded that they should go back; 'for,' said he, 'ye shall not seek the aid of idolaters to fight against idolaters.' He then passed onwards to a place called Al Shaikhain,[2] where he reviewed the force, and, having sent

Marches from Medina, and halts; Friday night.

[1] This girdle was preserved and handed down in the family of Abu Râfi, Mahomet's servant.

[2] Burckhardt notices it as 'a ruined edifice of stones or bricks,' a mile from the town, 'where Mahomet put on his coat of mail;' *i.e.* on the following morning. 'Farther on' is a stone where the Prophet 'leaned for a few minutes on his way to Ohod.'

back some striplings unequal to the contest, halted for the night. Abdallah ibn Obey, with his followers, encamped near at hand; but, displeased at the rejection of his advice and the unfriendly treatment of his Jewish adherents, kept sullenly aloof. Mahomet passed the night in the encampment of the Bani Najjâr, and a guard of faithful followers was stationed over him. Muhammad son of Maslama patrolled the camp with fifty men. A similar duty was performed for the Coreish by Ikrima with a troop of horse; these approached close enough to alarm the Moslems by their neighing, but did not venture over the volcanic ridge which separated the two armies.

Mahomet advances to Ohod, and draws up line of battle. Saturday, A.H. III. January, A.D. 624.

By the first dawn, the army of Medîna was in motion advancing upon Ohod. In the dim light of early morning a guide led Mahomet, by the nearest path, through the fields and gardens which occupied the intervening space.[1] The vicinity owes its verdure to a watercourse, which carries off the drainage of the country lying to the south and east. The hill of Ohod, three miles distant from Medîna, is a rugged and almost insulated offshoot of the great mountain range, projecting for three or four miles eastward into the plain. The torrent, sometimes swollen so as quite to inundate the adjacent tract, sweeps along its southern and western face, and discharges its flood into the *Ghâba*, or low basin lying beyond. It was now dry, and its course marked only by deep sand and scattered stones. On the farther bank, upon a slightly sloping plain, bare and stony, over which, as Burton tells us, 'the seared and jagged flanks of Ohod rise like masses of iron,' Mahomet halted his army. By this time it was daylight, and, although the columns of the enemy were in sight, the cry for morning prayers was raised by Bilâl, and the whole army, led by the Prophet, prostrated itself in worship. Abdallah ibn Obey at

---

[1] As he passed through one of these gardens, its owner, a blind man, murmured at the injury to his property, and cast dust at Mahomet. One of the Bani Aus sprang up and beat him. A chief of the Bani Khazraj resented the affront, and a fierce contention arose. It was ended by a savage threat from Oseid, the Ausite 'Leader,' who said that had he not known that it would be displeasing to Mahomet, he would have cut off the blind man's head.

There must, no doubt, have been difficulty in keeping down these intestine quarrels and jealousies, though, in the hands of a skilful administrator like Mahomet, they were really elements of power.

this moment wheeled suddenly round, and, deserting the army with his three hundred followers, took the road back to the city. Mahomet was thus left with but seven hundred followers, only one hundred of whom were clad in mail; but they were all true men, and, fighting in what they believed to be the cause of God, they boldly faced an enemy four times their number. Advancing they occupied the rising ground in front; their rear was thus protected by the frowning heights of Ohod, excepting on the left, where the rocks receded and afforded the enemy an opening, the more dangerous because suited to the movements of the Coreishite horse. Mahomet, therefore, posted on an adjoining eminence the flower of his archery, and gave their leader an absolute injunction to hold fast, and steadily check the attempts which he expected the Coreish would here make to turn his flank: 'Guard our rear,' he said, 'and stir not from this spot: if ye see us pursuing and plundering the enemy, join not with us: even if we be pursued and worsted, do not venture to our aid.' Then he drew out his line, facing towards Medîna ;— Musáb, with the Refugee standard, being in the centre, and the Aus and Khazraj allies forming either wing. He forbad his followers to engage the enemy till he gave command; for he knew that the strength of his position would be sacrificed by a premature advance. Having thus disposed his force, Mahomet put on a second coat of mail, and calmly awaited the enemy's approach.

Meanwhile Abu Sofiân, as hereditary leader, brought up the Meccan army; and, facing Ohod, marshalled it in front of Mahomet. The banner, which had been duly mounted on its standard in the Council-hall at Mecca, was borne by Talha son of Abd al Ozza.[1] The right wing was commanded by Khâlid; the left by Ikrima son of Abu Jahl. Amr ibn

Army of Mecca advances.

---

[1] This Talha is to be distinguished from Talha son of Obeidallah, who stood by Mahomet in the battle. The Talha in the text was of the family of Abd al Dâr, which retained the right of carrying the Coreishite standard. Abu Sofiân desired not only to lead the army, but to carry the standard, or at least to raise a second banner; but the descendants of Abd al Dâr would hear of no encroachment on their ancestral privilege. There is a tradition that, as the enemy drew near, Mahomet enquired who bore their standard. On being told that it was one of the house of Abd al Dâr, he exclaimed: 'Our side is more worthy of the honour;' and, calling for Musáb (who was of the same lineage), he placed the standard in his hands.

al Aás (the famous Amru) was over the Coreishite horse. The women at first kept to the front, sounding their timbrels and singing martial verses; but as the line advanced, they fell to the rear.

Battle opens with single combats. The battle opened by the inglorious advance of Abu Aámir, 'the Monk,' who vainly expected his fellow-citizens of Medîna to fraternise with him. He was received with a shower of stones, and forced to retire. Talha cried out indignantly to him and his followers: ' Get to the rear, ye slaves! Guard the camp,—a fitting employment for you!' Flourishing the Coreishite banner, Talha now advanced alone, and challenged the enemy to single combat, shouting these words :—

> The standard-bearer hath the right
> To dye its shaft in blood,
> Till it be broken in his hand.

Ali stepped forth, and, rushing on him, with one blow of his sword brought him to the ground.[1] Mahomet, who had intently watched the rapid combat, exclaimed with a loud voice: *Great is the Lord!* and the cry, repeated, arose in an overwhelming shout from the whole Moslem army. Talha's brother, Othmân, who was in charge of the women, then ran forward and seized the banner which lay by the lifeless body. The women beat their timbrels loudly, as they sang :—

> Daughters of the Brave are we,
> On carpets step we delicately;
> Boldly advance, and we embrace you!
> Turn your backs and we will shun you,
> Shun you with disdain.

Hamza responded to Othmân's challenge, and, after a brief encounter, brought him lifeless to the ground. Then as he strode proudly back to the Moslem ranks, Hamza shouted: ' I am the son of him who gave drink to the pilgrims,'— meaning of Abd al Muttalib, who had held that office. One after another, the family of Talha, two brothers and three sons, seized the standard; one after another, they fell in single combat.[2]

---

[1] Mahomet declared that thus was fulfilled that part of his vision in which he appeared to ride upon a ram. Talha was the ram.

[2] One of the sons was wounded by an arrow, shot by Aásim. The

The Arab custom of single combats put the two armies on an equality for a time. So long as these combats went on, the Coreish derived no advantage from their superior numbers; and the rapid destruction of their standard-bearers carried dismay into their ranks. A general engagement ensued; and, pressed by the fierce ardour of the Mussulmans, the Meccan army began to waver. Their horse sought repeatedly to turn the left flank of Mahomet; but they were each time forced back by the galling archery of the little band posted on the neighbouring height. The same daring contempt of danger was displayed as at Bedr. The Meccan ranks might be seen to quiver as Abu Dujâna, distinguished by the red kerchief wound round his helmet, swept along and, with a sword given him by Mahomet, dealt death on every side.[1] Hamza, conspicuous from his waving ostrich feather; Ali, marked by his long white plume; and Zobeir, known by his bright yellow turban,—like heroes of the Iliad,—carried confusion wherever they appeared. Such were the scenes in which were reared the great leaders of the Moslem conquests.[2]

But the advance was pressed too hotly by the army of Mahomet. Their own line became irregular and confused; and a portion, piercing the ranks of the enemy, fell to plundering his camp and baggage. The archers, from their eminence, perceiving this, could not resist the temptation; casting to the winds the injunction of the Prophet and the earnest expostulation of their leader, they hurried to the

---

wounded lad was carried to his mother Sulâfa, at the rear. She asked him, as he was breathing his last, who killed him. He said that as his foe shot the arrow, he heard him cry: 'Take that from me, the son of Al Aclah!' 'By the Lord!' Sulâfa said, 'it was Aâsim, one of our own kin;' and she vowed she would yet drink wine out of Aâsim's skull. The savage vow was nearly being fulfilled, as we shall see hereafter.

[1] There is a mass of tradition about the prodigies of bravery shown by Abu Dujâna with this sword of Mahomet. At the commencement of the action Mahomet held up his sword, and said: 'Who will take this sword, and give to it its due?' Omar, Zobeir, &c., one after another, came forward and were rejected; last of all Abu Dujâna offered, and Mahomet gave it to him; 'And he clave therewith the heads of the Unbelievers.'

After the battle, Ali, giving his bloody sword to Fâtima to wash, said: 'Take this sword, for it is not a despicable one,' alluding to his own acts of prowess that day. Mahomet added: 'If thou hast done well, O, Ali! verily Hârith and Abu Dujâna have done well also.'

[2] For example, in this battle we have the famous Sâd and Abu Obeida on the side of Mahomet, and Khâlid and Amru on the side of the Coreish.

Day changed by charge of Khâlid, and army of Medîna routed.

spoil. The ready eye of Khâlid saw the opportunity, and he hastened to retrieve the day. Gathering the Coreishite horse at his extreme right, he wheeled round the enemy's left wing, now uncovered, swept off the few remaining archers from the rising ground, and, appearing suddenly in rear of the Moslems, charged down into their ranks. The surprise was fatal, the discomfiture complete. Musâb was slain, and the standard of the Refugees disappeared.[1] Hind's wild negro, Wahshî, watched for Hamza, and, swinging his javelin with unerring aim, brought him lifeless to the ground. The Coreish now raised their war cries of OZZA and HOBAL, and advanced with rapid step. The Moslem army, pressed on every side, broke, and fled in dismay. They did not stop till they had found refuge on the heights of Ohod.

Mahomet wounded.

It was a moment of peril for Mahomet. At the first success he had kept behind, watching the advance of his troops; and, remaining in that position, he narrowly escaped the sweeping charge of Khâlid's cavalry.[2] Some marvellous but improbable stories are told of his prowess, as well as of his signal escapes. With the staff of followers who surrounded him, he joined in discharging arrows till his bow was broken; and then he betook himself to casting stones. At one period, he is said to have inflicted a deadly wound on one of the Coreish, who pressed madly forward to cut him down. When the Moslem ranks were broken and forced back, he tried to stay their flight, crying aloud: *Whither away? Come back! I am the Apostle of God! Return!* But the call was not heeded; the retreat went on unchecked. The enemy soon bore down in force upon the Prophet himself; and if a party of devoted followers (seven Citizens and seven Refugees) had not rallied round his person, escape had been impossible. The Coreish scoured the field in special quest of their arch enemy. Suddenly, Ibn Camia, the hero who had just slain Musâb, and others, came upon the little group. Stones and arrows flew thick around. A stone wounded the Prophet's under lip and broke one of his

---

[1] Tradition tells it was seized by an angel. 'The angels,' it is added, 'though present, did not fight that day; but had the Believers stood fast they would have fought.'

[2] The spot of Mahomet's misfortunes is marked by a Cupola, *Cubbat al Sanâya*, the dome of the teeth, 'nearer the foot of the mountain' than the graves of Hamza, &c. The print of a tooth is still shown there.

front teeth.   Another severe blow upon the face drove the
rings of the helmet deep into his cheek, and made a gash in
his forehead.   The sword of Ibn Camia was barely warded
from the head of Mahomet by the naked hand of Talha son
of Obeidallah, whose fingers were thereby disabled.   Mahomet
fell to the ground, and Ibn Camia returned to his comrades
exclaiming that he had killed him.   The cry was taken up
all around, and resounded from the rocks of Ohod.[1]   It spread
consternation among the Prophet's followers.   ' Where now,'
they asked, ' is the promise of his Lord ? '   But at the same
time, the rumour checked the ardour of the enemy's pursuit.   Their controversy was with Mahomet rather than with
Medîna.   If he were killed, their object was accomplished,
their revenge fulfilled.

Cry that Mahomet is slain.

But Mahomet was only stunned.   The cliffs of Ohod
were close behind.   Talha (himself in several places severely
wounded) raised him gently, and, with one or two others
affording support, hastened to make him climb the defile
where the greater part of his army had already found
secure retreat.   The joy of his followers was unbounded at
finding their Prophet still alive.   Káb met him on the way,
and began to call aloud the good news; but Mahomet,
feeling that he was not yet beyond the reach of danger,
motioned him to be silent.   When they were sheltered
behind the rocks,[2] the first care of his followers was to
remove the helmet from his head.   Two of its rings were so
firmly imbedded in his cheek, that Abu Obeida, who extracted
them with his mouth, lost two teeth in the operation.   The
blood flowed copiously from the Prophet's wounds.   Ali ran
to a hollow in the rock, and brought some water in his
shield.   Mahomet could not drink of it, but only rinsed his
mouth.   As the blood was being washed off his face, he
exclaimed : *How shall the people prosper that have treated
thus their Prophet who calleth them unto their Lord !   Let*

Mahomet takes refuge behind rocks of Ohod.

---

[1] As usual, it is the devil who is accused of this piece of malice.   In the
shape of Ibn Surâca (see *ante*, p. 244 note), he screamed aloud that Mahomet
was dead.

[2] The very ' cave ' is professed to be shown to the pilgrims in which
Mahomet hid himself.   *Burton*, ii. 248.   There are some stories of Mahomet's
party having been pursued up the hill.   Also that they were in danger of
being shot upon by their own people, who mistook them for the enemy.   But
they seem embellishments.

the wrath of God burn against the men that have besprinkled the face of His Apostle with his own blood![1] He then put on the yellow helm of Káb, in place of his own broken one; and, joining the rest of his followers, watched the movements of the Coreish in the plains below. Many of the Moslem warriors, wearied with the struggle, fell thus asleep. In this manner, mid-day passed away.

Colloquy between Abu Sofiân and Omar. Coreish retire.

The leaders of the Coreish were now busy on the field of battle. They sought for the body of Mahomet, and, not finding it, began to doubt his death. Many acts of barbarous mutilation were committed on the slain. Hind gloated over the body of her victim Hamza. She tore out his liver and chewed it; she strung his nails and pieces of his skin together to bedeck her arms and legs.[2] When the Coreish had spent some time thus, and had leisurely disposed of their own dead, Abu Sofiân drew near to the foot of the hill, and, raising his voice, called aloud the names successively of *Mahomet, Abu Bakr, Omar.* Receiving no reply (for the Prophet enjoined silence) he cried again: 'Then all these are slain, and ye are rid of them!' Omar could contain himself no longer: 'Thou liest!' he exclaimed; 'they are all alive, thou enemy of God, and will requite thee, yet.' 'Then,' continued Abu Sofiân, 'this day shall be a return for Bedr. Fortune alternates, even as the bucket. Hearken! ye will find amongst the dead some that are mutilated: this was not by my counsel; but neither am I displeased thereat. Glory to Ozza! Glory to Hobal! Ozza is ours; it is not yours!'[3] At the bidding of Mahomet, Omar replied: '*God is ours; He is not yours.*' Abu Sofiân said: 'We shall meet again; let it be after a year, at Bedr.' 'Be it so,' answered Omar. On this Abu Sofiân turned to go, and the Meccan army began its homeward march.

Number of slain.

As soon as the enemy was out of sight, Mahomet and his followers descended into the field of battle. The full extent of their ignominious overthrow was now apparent. Seventy-

---

[1] 'He cursed those that inflicted the wounds, saying: *Let not the year pass over them alive;* and it came to pass that not one of those that shot at the Prophet survived beyond the year.' Compare Luke xxiii. 34.

[2] But tradition delights to abuse Hind, as it did Abu Jahl; and we must beware of the patent tendency to exaggerate.

[3] A play on the word, which signifies *glory* as well as the Idol Ozza.

four corpses were strewn upon the plain : four of these were Refugees,[1] whilst threescore and ten were citizens of Medîna. Indeed, it was evident that the destruction of the whole force was only averted by the foresight of Mahomet in keeping a secure place of refuge in his rear. On the enemy's side the loss was but twenty. The news of the discomfiture soon reached Medîna, with rumours of the death of Mahomet; and the road was covered with men and women hastening towards the scene of action, to nurse the wounded, or search for the dead. The disaffected citizens did not conceal their satisfaction, and some even talked of an embassy to Abu Sofiân.

The news reaches Medina.

Arrived at the field of battle, Fâtima helped to dress the gash on her father's temple, the bleeding from which could only be staunched by applying the cinder of a piece of burned matting. This added to the ghastly appearance of the wound, which was deep, and did not fully heal for above a month. Safia, the Prophet's aunt, now came up. She was fondly attached to her brother Hamza; and Mahomet, fearful of the effect which the sight of his mangled remains might have upon her, desired Zobeir, her son, to keep her aside till the corpse was buried; but she insisted on going forward to the spot. 'Where is my brother?' she eagerly enquired of Mahomet. 'Among the people,' he replied. 'I will not go back,' she said, 'until I see him.' So he led her to the body, saying : 'Leave her to her grief alone.' She sat down by it and wept : then she sobbed aloud, and Mahomet wept also. Fâtima, too, sat by sobbing. Mahomet's spirit was stirred within him at the sight of Safia's anguish, and the disfigured corpse of his noble uncle; pulling his beard angrily, as when grieved and agitated he was wont to do, he swore that he would mutilate the bodies of thirty of the Coreish in the stead of Hamza.[2] To comfort Safia, he told her that her brother's name was

Dressing of Mahomet's wounds.

Safia mourns over her brother Hamza.

[1] One of the Refugees, being mortally wounded, was carried to Upper Medina, where he died ; but his body, by desire of Mahomet, was carried back to Ohod, and buried there. The tombs of the four Refugees are still maintained in repair.

[2] But he afterwards affected to receive a revelation forbidding the savage practice. The verse quoted for this order is at the end of Sura xvi., which, however, is a Meccan one; and the passage itself does not bear very plainly on the occasion here referred to. However this may be, there is no doubt that Mahomet abolished the practice of mutilation altogether, and it is to the credit of his humanity that he did so.

T

recorded, among the dwellers in the highest Paradise, as the *Lion of God and the Lion of His Apostle.* He spoke kindly also to the women of Medîna, who were wailing over their dead. When the graves were ready, and the bodies laid out in order, he prayed over them, and commanded that they should be buried by twos and threes in each grave.[1] He then mounted his horse, and the whole company, turning sadly from Ohod, began their homeward march.

Mahomet returns to Medina.

The Meccan army, though withdrawn from the field of battle, might still have fallen by another route upon Medîna, uncovered as it was by the absence of the Moslem army. Mahomet and his followers trembled for the safety of their families. Immediately after descending the hill, the Prophet had despatched Sád son of Abu Wackkâs to watch the movements of the enemy. When they reached the valley of Ackîck, the Coreish paused there awhile. Their counsels were divided. Some urged to follow up the defeat by a blow on the defenceless city. Others pointed to the danger of entanglement and loss in the outskirts and narrow streets, and contended that they should rest content with their signal victory. The opinions of the latter prevailed; mounting their camels, and leading their horses,[2] they slowly wended their way through the defiles that led towards the road to Mecca. Sád, hurrying back to Mahomet, called aloud the joyful news. ' Gently,' said Mahomet; ' let us not appear before the people to rejoice at the departure of the enemy ! ' The intelligence, nevertheless, brought intense relief both to Mahomet and his people ; for the crestfallen, crippled army of Medîna could ill have ventured on a second struggle.

Coreish, after hesitation, take route to Mecca.

As Mahomet and his followers reached the foot of the intervening ridge, the whole company, at his command, fell into two lines, with the women ranged behind, and there offered up prayer and thanksgiving to God. Drawing

Night of distress and insecurity at Medina.

---

[1] They were not washed. ' Wind them,' said the Prophet, ' as they are, in their wounds and in their blood. I will be surety for them ;' alluding to the necessity for legal ablution. Hence the angels are said to have washed Hamza and Hantzala. Some of the traditions, to the effect that the latter was in a state of legal impurity, are too indelicate to be quoted.

[2] This was the sign given by Mahomet to Sád : ' If they mount their horses,' said he, ' and lead their camels, then they meditate an advance on Medîna ; if they mount the camels, and lead the horses, then they are going home.' The camel was their working animal.

near to Medîna, they passed the habitations of the Bani
Ashal, whose females were wailing loudly for their dead:
'And Hamza!' cried Mahomet, 'alas, who is there to
weep for him!' The numerous wounded here received permission to go to their homes. The rest followed Mahomet
to the great Mosque, which they reached in time for the
sunset prayer. It was a night of mourning at Medîna. A
sense of insecurity still pervaded the city; the chief men
again kept watch over the Prophet's door, for fear of a night
attack from the Coreish. Some of the wounded remained
near the Mosque, and the fires kindled for them cast a fitful
and lurid light around its courts. Mahomet slept heavily,
and did not answer the call of Bilâl for the second evening
prayer. Shortly afterwards he awoke, and, walking forth,
asked who it was that wailed so loudly near the Mosque. It
was the women of Medîna, who had heard his plaintive words
regarding Hamza, and came to mourn for him. Mahomet
blessed them, and sent them to their homes. Ever after, it
was the custom at Medîna for the women, when they mourned
for their dead, first to wail for Hamza.

On the morrow, Mahomet commanded Bilâl to pro- Mahomet
claim through the city that he was about to start in pursuit makes de-
of the Coreish, but that none should accompany him except- tion in
ing those who had been present at the battle of Ohod. The Coreish.
pursuit of
movement was intended to raise the spirits of his followers,
to remove the impression of defeat, and to show the Coreish
that an attack upon the city would have been vigorously
repelled. As the warriors in their armour began to assemble
at the Mosque, Talha came up: 'What thinkest thou,' enquired Mahomet of him; 'how far have the Coreish by this
time reached on their journey homewards?' 'To the valley of
Sayyala,' he answered, which is one long march from Medîna.
'So was I thinking also,' rejoined Mahomet; 'but, Talha!
they will never again inflict upon us such a disaster as we
suffered yesterday,—no, not till we wrest Mecca from them.'
The great white flag of the Refugees was not recovered from
the field of battle; but one of the other banners stood in the
mosque yet unfurled, and the Prophet placed it in the hands
of Abu Bakr. Stiff and disfigured as he was from the wounds of
the previous day, he then mounted his horse, and set out on
the Meccan road. Two scouts, whom he had sent in advance,

fell into the enemy's hands, and were put to death at Hamrâ al Asád. The army of Mahomet, which advanced by forced marches, reached this spot the day after it was evacuated by the Coreish, and found the two dead bodies there. At Hamrà al Asád (a little way short of Safra) Mahomet spent three days, and regaled himself and his followers with fresh dates, a plentiful harvest of which had just been gathered. He commanded five hundred fires to be kindled on the adjoining lofty heights, to make the Coreish believe that the pursuing force was very large. And, contenting himself with this demonstration, he returned to Medîna, after an absence of five or six days.

Abu Ozza, a prisoner, put to death.

At Hamrâ al Asád Mahomet made prisoner one of the enemy, the poet Abu Ozza, who had loitered behind the rest. He had been taken prisoner at Bedr, and, having five daughters dependent on him, had been freely released on the promise that he would not again bear arms in the war against the Prophet. He now sought for mercy: 'O Mahomet!' he prayed, 'forgive me of thy clemency!' 'Nay, verily,' said the Prophet, 'a Believer may not twice be bitten from the same hole. Thou shalt never return to Mecca, stroke thy beard, and say, *I have again deceived Mahomet*. Lead him forth to execution!' So saying, he motioned to a bystander, who with his sword struck off the captive's head.

Othmân ibn Mughîra, after three days' truce, pursued and killed.

Another Coreishite, Othmân son of Mughîra, perished by a too great confidence in the generosity of his enemy. When quitting Ohod, he missed his way, and passed the night near Medîna. Next morning he ventured to the house of Othmân the Prophet's son-in-law, who procured for him a three days' truce, and, having found him a camel and provisions for the way, departed with Mahomet for Hamrâ al Asád. The Coreishite incautiously lingered at Medîna till the last day of his term of grace, when he set out for Mecca. In the endeavour to avoid the returning Moslem force, he again lost his way; and Mahomet, hearing of his delay, sent men upon his track, who came up with him, and put him to death.

Halo of glory around

The field of Ohod was ever after invested for the Moslems with a peculiar interest. Mahomet used to visit it

once a year, and to bless the martyrs buried there. ' *Peace* the mar-
tyrs of
Ohod.
be on you !' he would say; '*for all that ye endured,—
and a blessed Futurity !*' The citizens, as they passed to
and fro, visiting their fields at Al Ghâba, would invoke peace
upon the souls of the warriors who lay buried by the way,
and their imagination conjure up the audible response, ' And
on you be peace !' from the lips of the dead. There is
also a strange story that, nearly half a century after, a great
flood having ploughed up the banks of the torrent and
uncovered the graves, the bodies of the martyrs were seen
reclining in the attitude of sleep, fresh as the day of their
interment, and blood still trickling from their wounds.

The victories of Islâm reflect back upon the heroes of But Ma-
homet's
prestige
affected at
the time
by the
defeat.
Ohod a halo of glory. But at this time their memories
were far from receiving at Medîna universal homage.
Murmurs at the inglorious retreat were rife throughout the city. Tradition passes lightly over this uncongenial subject, and dwells complacently on the ignominious
manner in which Abdallah ibn Obey, and the Jews who
hazarded remarks disparaging to the Prophet, were treated,
and on the boastful threats of Omar against them. But the
Corân tells a different story. We there find that even
the adherents of Mahomet were staggered by the reverse.
It was natural that they should. The success at Bedr
had been assumed as a proof of divine support ; and, by
parity of reasoning, the defeat at Ohod was subversive of
the prophetic claim. The Jews broadly advanced this stubborn argument.[1] It required all the address of Mahomet to
avert the dangerous imputation, sustain the credit of his
cause, and reanimate his followers. This he did mainly by
means of that portion of the Corân which appears in the
latter half of the Third Sura.[2] A lofty tone of assurance Line of
argument
by which
Mahomet
pervades the studied explanation and remonstrance of the
Prophet, which, like the rest of the Corân, are in the form of

---

[1] 'How can Mahomet pretend now,' they asked, 'to be anything more
than an aspirant to the *kingly* office ? No true claimant of the *prophetic*
dignity hath ever been beaten in the field, or suffered loss in his own person,
and that of his followers, as Mahomet hath.'

[2] The Third Sura is a collection of passages given forth at various periods.
We have in it portions revealed shortly after Bedr, A.H. II. ; after Ohod, A.H.
III. ; after the second Bedr, A.H. IV. ; also after the interview with the
Najrân Christians, A.H. IX.

a direct address from the Deity. Much stress is adroitly laid
on the marvellous interposition which brought victory at
Bedr. The reverse at Ohod was necessary to sift the true
Believers from those who were infidels at heart. The light
afflictions there sustained were a meet prelude to the eternal
glories of Paradise. The faithful had coveted the happy
state of the martyrs at Bedr, and had longed for the same
blessed fortune ; now, when death presented itself, they fled
before its terrors ! The slaughter, anywise, could not have
been averted by following the counsels of those who stayed
at home ; for the hour of death is fixed for every one, and is
inevitable. Future success was largely promised, if the Believers would but remain steadfast and be courageous. The
Lord had already at Ohod placed victory within their reach,
when by cowardice and disobedience they drew defeat upon
themselves. Even if Mahomet had been killed in battle,
what then ? he was but the Messenger of God like other
Apostles who had died before him. The cause itself was
immortal and divine. Such is the line of argument, mingled with comfort, reproof, and exhortation. It had its full
effect in reassuring the true adherents of the Prophet ; and,
so long as these were heart and soul on Mahomet's side, his
position at Medîna was secure.

The style and tenor of these passages so fully and curiously
illustrate the situation of Mahomet at this time, that the
reader will not, I think, object to peruse the following extracts from them :—

> Remember when thou wentest forth from thy family in the
> early morning to secure for the Faithful an encampment for
> the battle ; and God heareth and knoweth ;—And when two
> companies of you became anxious, so that ye lost heart ; and God
> is the Patron of both, and in God let the Believers put their
> trust. And, truly, God helped you at Bedr, when ye were
> fewer in number ; fear God, therefore, that haply ye may be
> thankful.
>
> When thou saidst to the Believers : *What ! doth it not suffice
> you that your Lord should aid you with 3,000 Angels sent down ?*
> Nay, if ye persevere, and fear God, and this Enemy were to come
> suddenly upon you, your Lord would help you with five thou-
> sand Angels attired for battle ;—And God made this (promise)
> none otherwise than as glad tidings for you, and that your
> hearts might be stayed. Victory cometh from God alone, the

Glorious, the Wise, that He may cut off the uttermost part of Sura iii.
the unbelievers.   *   *   *   *   *

Be not cast down, neither be ye grieved. Ye shall be victorious, if ye are true Believers. If a wound hath befallen you, verily a wound like unto it hath befallen your enemy. This various success We cause to alternate among men, that God may know those that believe, and may have witnesses amongst you (God loveth not the transgressors) ;—that God might prove them that believe, and annihilate the Infidels. What! did ye think to enter Paradise, while as yet God knew not those that fight for Him, and knew not the persevering amongst you ? And truly ye were longing for death before ye faced it. And verily ye saw it and looked on. Mahomet is no more than an Apostle, as other Apostles that have gone before him. What! if he were to die or be killed, must ye needs turn back upon your heels ? He that turneth back upon his heels injureth not God in the least degree ; but God will reward the thankful. Furthermore, no soul dieth but by the permission of God, as it is written and predestined.   *   *   *   *

How many Prophets have fought against those that had multitudes on their side. And they were not cast down at that which befell them fighting in the way of God, neither did they become weak, nor make themselves abject ; and God loveth the persevering.   *   *   *   *

We will surely cast terror into the hearts of the Infidels, because they have associated with God that which He hath nowise authorised. Their resting-place shall be the Fire : wretched is the abode of the transgressors ! And truly the Lord had already made good unto you His promise at what time ye were, by His permission, cutting them to pieces ;—until ye lost heart and fell to variance in the matter, and disobeyed, after that He had showed unto you that which ye longed for. Amongst you were those that desired the present Life, and amongst you those that desired the Life to come. Then He caused you to flee from before them, that He might prove you (but now He hath pardoned you, for God is gracious unto the Believers), when ye made for the Mountain, and looked not back on any one, though the Apostle was calling unto you,—even unto those of you that were behind. Wherefore He caused grief to overtake you upon grief, that ye may not be afflicted hereafter at that which ye lose, nor at that which shall befall you : for God knoweth what ye do. Then He caused to descend upon you after the grief, Security, even slumber which covered a part of you ; and a part of you were troubled in your own souls,—questioning about God that

Sura iii.

which is not the truth,—a questioning of ignorance ;—In that ye said, *What! Is there any reality in this matter unto us?* [1] SAY :— Verily the matter belongeth wholly unto God. They concealed in their hearts that which they did not open unto thee. They say,—*Had there been any reality in the matter, we had not been slain here.* Say,—If ye had been in your own houses, verily those would have gone forth for whom fighting was decreed, unto the places of their death ;—and (so it came to pass) that the Lord might prove what is in your hearts, for God knoweth the breast of Man. Verily they amongst you who turned their backs in the day when the two armies met, Satan caused them to slip for some part of that which they had wrought : but God hath forgiven them, for God is Forgiving and Merciful.

Blessedness of the Martyrs. Sura iii.

The blessed state of the Martyrs is thus described :—

Think not in anywise of those killed in the way of the Lord, as if they were dead. Yea, they are alive, and are nourished with their Lord,—exulting in that which God hath given them of His favour, and rejoicing on behalf of those who have not yet joined them, but are following after. No terror afflicteth them, neither are they grieved.[2]

Mahomet addressing people in Mosque.

The reader may picture to himself the now venerable Prophet delivering, as the spokesman of the Almighty, these pregnant messages. He is about to issue from one of the apartments which, built for his increasing harem, form the eastern side of the Mosque. Under its rude but spacious roof of palm-branches, the Citizens and Refugees assemble

---

[1] *i.e.* questioning the truth of Mahomet's mission, and his promise of divine interposition and victory.

[2] To secure the crown of martyrdom, it sufficed to make at the very last moment the simplest and most formal profession of faith in God and Mahomet. Thus Amr ibn Thâbit had, up to the day of Ohod, been an open unbeliever. He accompanied the Moslem army and was mortally wounded on the field. His comrades asked him regarding his creed ; with his dying breath he whispered in reply that it was for Islâm he had fought, and that he believed in God and in his Prophet. When this was told to Mahomet, he blessed his memory, and said that he was already an inheritor of Paradise. On the other hand, any amount of bravery without such formal profession was of no avail. Thus Cozmân, who was numbered among the Disaffected, showed incredible valour at Ohod, killing with his own hands seven or eight of the Coreish. When, expiring on the field, and being congratulated on the prospect of Paradise, he said, with his last breath, that he had been fighting not for the faith, but for his people, and in defence of his native city. Mahomet, when told of it, declared that in spite of his services he was ' a child of hell-fire.'

at mid-day for the weekly service, throng around the pulpit, and occupy the long space in front of it. As Mahomet appears, the hum and bustle cease (for it was the hall of business and politics, as well as the house of worship), and the whole congregation fall into their ranks for prayer. Mahomet advances to the foot of the pulpit, and with his face turned toward the holy temple of Mecca, and his back to the people, goes through the stated ritual. The assembly, arrayed in rows behind, follow every motion of their leader, just as a Moslem congregation at the present day follow the genuflexions and prostrations of their Imâm. The prayers ended, the Prophet, with grave step, ascends the slightly elevated pulpit, and in a solemn voice, and accents suited to the measured cadence of the revelation, delivers to the audience the message which he says that he has received from above. Fear creeps over the heart. It is as if the Deity were present by some visible token, like the cloud overshadowing the Tabernacle. The Disaffected may scoff elsewhere, and the Jew in his own assembly curse the upstart Prophet; but at this moment, disaffection and treason vanish, for the dread sense of immediate communication with the Almighty overwhelms all other feelings. And now the rhetoric of Mahomet comes into play. In his oration are mingled rebuke, exhortation, encouragement, in pure and nervous eloquence, such as no Arab could hear without emotion. Hell with its flaming gates, and the gardens and joys of Paradise, are conjured up as vivid and close realities before the hearer; for the hour, the present life fades into insignificance, excepting as the means of escaping the one, and of winning the other. Thus did Mahomet wield at his will the awe-stricken assembly; and wind the enchantments of faith or superstition in inextricable folds around them. It was thus that he moulded to his purpose the various elements about him, and even under adversity and misfortune maintained his influence supreme.

In close connection with the field of Ohod was the execution of a stern judicial sentence. Mujaddzir, a stranger naturalised at Medîna, had, some years previously, slain Suweid, a chief of the Bani Khazraj. The battle of Boâth ensued; but the blood there shed did not efface the memory of the murder. Hârith, son of Suweid, had long sought to avenge his father's

Execution of Hârith for the murder of Mujaddzir.

death; at last, he found his opportunity at Ohod. In the confusion of that reverse, he treacherously drew near to Mujaddzir, and killed him. A comrade, who was witness to the deed, reported it to Mahomet. An investigation was held, and the crime brought home to Hârith. Shortly after his return from Hamrâ al Asâd, the Prophet called for his ass, and rode forth to Coba. It was not one of the days (Saturday and Monday) on which he ordinarily repaired to that suburb, and the men of Upper Medîna boded no good from his unusual visit. He entered the Mosque and received the salutation of the chief inhabitants of the vicinity. At length the culprit himself, clothed in a yellow dress, and little anticipating the event, came up. Perceiving him approach, Mahomet called aloud to Oweim, a chief of the Bani Aus: *Take Hârith the son of Suweid unto the gate of the Mosque, and there strike off his head, because of Mujaddzir son of Dziâd; for verily he slew him on the day of Ohod.* Oweim prepared to obey the command, when Hârith desired leave to speak, and hastening towards Mahomet laid hold of his stirrup as he was about to mount his ass. He begged for mercy, and promised to expiate the crime by any sacrifice the Prophet might direct. Mahomet turned from him, and reiterated the order of execution. Seeing the decree to be irrevocable, Oweim dragged Hârith back to the gate, and there beheaded him, in the presence of Mahomet, the sons of Mujaddzir, and the assembled chiefs. The assumption of supreme authority was unquestioned, and it is indicative of the absolute command now exercised by the Prophet over the whole city.

Widow of Sád entertains Mahomet at a feast.

Another scene which occurred shortly after the battle of Ohod illustrates the manner in which the oracles of Mahomet were given forth, and the incidental way in which the political and social code that still rules the Moslem world grew up. Among the slain was Sád son of Rabî, a leader of the Bani Khazraj.[1] He left a widow and two daughters; but his brother, according to the practice of the times, took possession of the whole inheritance. The widow was grieved at this; and, being a discreet and prudent person, pondered how she might obtain redress. She in-

---

[1] This is the same person who allowed Abd al Rahmân, when he lodged with him on his arrival from Mecca, to choose one of his two wives.

vited Mahomet to a feast, with about twenty of his chief
companions. He agreed to go. A retired spot among the
palm-trees of her garden was well sprinkled with water, and
the repast spread. Mahomet arrived, and with his followers
seated himself upon the carpets prepared for them. He
spoke kindly to the widow of her husband's memory, so that
all the women wept, and the eyes of the Prophet also filled
with tears. The supper was then eaten, and a feast of fresh
dates followed. When the repast was over, the widow arose,
and thus disclosed her grief: 'Sád, as thou well knowest,
was slain at Ohod. His brother hath seized the inheritance.
There is nothing left for the two daughters; and how shall
they be married without a portion?' Mahomet, moved by
the simple tale, replied: 'The Lord shall decide regarding   Origin of
the inheritance; for no command hath been yet revealed to   the law of
                                                                female in-
me in this matter. Come again unto me when I shall have   heritance.
returned home.' So he departed. Shortly after, as he sate
with his companions at the door of his own house, symptoms
of inspiration came upon him;—he was oppressed, and the
drops of sweat fell like pearls from his forehead. Then
he commanded that the widow of Sád and his brother
should be summoned. When they were brought before him,
he thus addressed the brother: 'Restore unto the daughters
of Sád two-thirds of that which he hath left behind him,
and one-eighth part unto his widow: the remainder is for
thee.' The widow was overjoyed and uttered the *Takbír*:
'Great is the Lord!' Such was the origin of one of the
main provisions of the Mahometan law of inheritance.[1]

[1] See Sura iv. v. 10, *et seq*. Supplementary rules are added at the close of
the Sura. These *administrative* parts of Mahomet's Revelation were not, I
conceive, originally used for recitation on devotional occasions, though the
record of them was placed together with the leaves on which the rest of the
Corân was transcribed.

CHAPTER XV.

FROM THE BATTLE OF OHOD TO THE EXPULSION OF THE BANI NADHÎR.

A.H. IV. — A.D. 625.

Ætat. 57.

Satisfaction of Coreish at the victory of Ohod.

THE people of Mecca were satisfied with the loss they had inflicted upon Mahomet. Abu Sofiân, on his return home, went straight to the Káaba, where he rendered thanks to HOBAL for the victory, and shaved his head. Those who had taken vows of abstinence were now absolved. Medîna enjoyed a long exemption from the threat of another attack on the part of the Coreish. But the disaster weakened the prestige of Mahomet among the Arab tribes; and these, either stirred up by the Coreish or encouraged by the defeat at Ohod, from time to time gave Mahomet trouble and anxiety.

Hostile designs in other quarters.

The two next months, including the festival of Dzul Hijj, were passed in tranquillity; but with the opening of the fourth year of the Hegira, rumours reached Mahomet from various quarters of gatherings being organised against him, and he hastened to take the initiative.

Bani Asád dispersed by a force from Medîna. A.H. IV. April, A.D. 625.

The Bani Asád, a powerful tribe connected with the Coreish, ranged over an extensive territory in the central desert of Nejd. Intelligence was received that Tuleiha, one of their chiefs, had assembled a force of cavalry and rapid camel-riders to make a raid upon Medîna. Mahomet forthwith despatched a hundred and fifty men, Citizens and Refugees indifferently, under Abu Salma, with instructions to march at night by an unfrequented route, and conceal themselves by day, so as to take the camp of the Bani Asád by surprise. They were so far successful as to fall unexpectedly upon a large herd of camels, which, with three of the herdsmen, they captured, and, having ravaged the country far and wide, returned after eleven days with their booty to Medîna. One of the prisoners and the usual share of the plunder having been set apart for Mahomet, the remainder was divided amongst the soldiers. The Bani Asád were effectually dispersed for the present; but they reserved their hostility for a future occasion. This Tuleiha is the same who at a later period set himself up as a prophet in antagonism to Mahomet. Abu Salma had signalised himself at Bedr, and there received a deep wound. It broke out afresh on this expedition, and in the end proved fatal, as we shall see hereafter.

Another gathering about the same time had taken place at a spot between Mecca and Tâyif. The Bani Lahyân, a branch of the Hodzeil (which inhabited, as they still do, a territory two days east of Mecca), and other tribes of the neighbourhood, rallied round their chief, Sofiân son of Khâlid, at Orna, with the avowed intention of following up the late victory at Ohod. Mahomet, knowing that their movements depended solely upon Sofiân, despatched Abdallah ibn Oneis, with instructions to assassinate him. Abdallah went forth alone, and joined himself as a volunteer to Sofiân, fell upon him unawares while no one was near, cut off his head, and carried it with him. He eluded pursuit, and, reaching Medîna in safety, presented himself before Mahomet in the Mosque. The Prophet welcomed him, and asked the issue of his adventure. Abdallah replied by displaying the head of his victim. Mahomet, in token of his gratification, presented the assassin with his own staff: ‘ *This,*’ said he, ‘ *shall be a token betwixt thee and me on the day of resurrection. Verily, few on that day shall have wherewithal to lean upon.*’ Abdallah joined the precious memorial to his sword, and wore it by his side till the day of his death, when it was buried with him. The murder of Sofiân broke up the assemblage at Orna; and probably, from the laxity of Arab morals, the outrage did not much affect the reputation of the Prophet; but, in forming *our* estimation of his character, it must be numbered against him as a fresh proof of treacherous cruelty. Mahomet had no right to complain, when he shortly afterwards paid the penalty

Bani Lahyân broken up by assassination of their chief. A.H. IV. May, A.D. 625.

of his treachery in the loss of several of his followers by an act of guile and inhumanity no greater than his own.

Mishap at Raji.
A.H. IV.
May, A.D
625.

In the succeeding month, Mahomet despatched six of his followers in the direction of Mecca. The object is variously stated. The most likely is that they were simply spies sent to gain information of the intentions of the Coreish. But the tradition most generally received is, that they were deputed for the instruction of two small tribes, which, at the instigation of the Bani Lahyân, pretended a desire to embrace Islâm. The party were, with one exception, citizens of Medîna. When they had journeyed as far as Rajî, a stage or two from Mecca, they were treacherously surrounded and overpowered by an armed band of the Bani Lahyân, who thirsted to avenge the assassination of their chief. Three died fighting bravely:[1] the other three were seized and bound as prisoners to be sold at Mecca. One of these succeeded in loosening his bands, and had nearly escaped when he was crushed by pieces of rock hurled down upon him; his tomb is preserved and visited to the present day at Marr al Tzahrân. The only survivors, Zeid and Khobeib, were purchased by the heirs of two chiefs of the Coreish slain at Bedr. They were kept till the sacred month of Safar had expired. They were then taken to Tanîm beyond the limits of the holy territory, and, in presence of a large concourse from Mecca, put to death.

Martyrdom of Zeid and Khobeib.

Zeid and Khobeib are glorified in the annals of Islâm as Martyrs. And if the traditions related of their refusal to recant even on the promise of life and liberty, and their constancy to Mahomet and his faith when thus standing alone amidst his enemies, be in any degree true, they are entitled to the name.[2] But it is a kind of martyrdom which, in its

---

[1] One of these was Aâsim, who, it will be remembered, killed a son of Talha at Ohod, and out of whose skull Sulâfa, the mother of the slain man, swore that she would drink wine. See *ante*, p. 269, note. The Bani Lahyân were about to cut off the head of Aâsim and carry it to Sulâfa, but a swarm of bees interposed, and when the people went to seek for it afterwards, the Lord had swept it away with a flood, and thus frustrated the vow of Sulâfa!

[2] I see no reason to doubt the main facts of the story, although in the details much of the marvellous has been superadded. Thus Khobeib, when in confinement, was supplied by supernatural visitants with large bunches of grapes, not a single grape being at the season to be had elsewhere. At his execution he bade his salutation to be sent to Mahomet, and there being none

motives and antecedents, will not bear comparison with corresponding scenes in the history of the Christian faith. Zeid and Khobeib were avowedly either *spies* or *prisoners of war*, and their execution was hardly less excusable (some may be inclined to think it more excusable) than many similar acts of Mahomet himself. It was a meet accompaniment of an internecine war, waged with almost equal ferocity on either side. The curse of Khobeib was not easily forgotten by the spectators of that day. After praying briefly, while they bound him to the stake, he called out with a loud voice: '*O Lord! number these men one by one, and destroy them utterly. Let not one escape!*' At this imprecation, the Coreish cast themselves and their children flat upon the ground,—a superstitious act to escape the potency of the dying man's curse. Spears were then placed in the hands of the children of the warriors who had fallen at Bedr; grasping these weapons, which were still kept partially in the children's hands,[1] the Coreish stabbed the bodies of their victims. And thus ended the wretched tragedy.

In the same month another and more serious catastrophe took place. The Bani Aámir, inhabiting territory in Nejd that adjoined the Bani Suleim, belonged to the great Hawázin tribe, which some time before had fought against the Coreish. They were under the leadership of two chiefs, Abu Berá and Aámir ibn Tofail. The former, who was now very aged and had retired from active command, paid a

Moslem party cut to pieces at Bîr Maûna. A.H. IV. May, A.D. 625.

---

to take it, Gabriel himself carried it to the Prophet, who returned the salutation in the hearing of his companions. When imprisoned, the only requests made by Khobeib were to be furnished with sweet water, to have no food that had been offered to idols, and to be told beforehand of the time of his execution. The day before he was put to death, he desired a razor to shave himself with, which a female attendant sent by her little boy. He asked the child whether he did not fear that he would kill him with it, out of revenge. The mother was alarmed, and then Khobeib said: 'Nay, fear not. I would never kill your son; *for treachery is not allowable in our religion.*' When they had bound him to the stake, they said: 'Now abjure Islâm, and we will let thee go.' 'Not so,' he said; 'I would not abjure Islâm if it were to get me the whole world in return.' 'Wouldst thou not that Mahomet were in thy place, and thou sitting in security at home?' 'I would not,' he replied, 'that I should have deliverance, and Mahomet suffer the pain even of a thorn.' Similar stories are told of Zeid. They embraced each other when they came to the place of execution.

[1] To keep up the fiction that it was *the children* who slew the victims in retaliation for their parents' death.

friendly visit to Mahomet about this time.[1] He came with a
present of two horses and two riding-camels. These the
Prophet declined to receive, unless Abu Berâ would embrace
Islâm. The chief did not comply with the invitation to join
the new faith; but he said: 'If thou wilt send a company
of thy followers to my tribe, I have hopes that they will
accept thy call. Mahomet replied, that he feared for the
safety of his people among the treacherous tribes of Nejd,
some of whom were in immediate alliance with the Coreish.
But Abu Berâ declared that he would himself be responsible
for their safety. Trusting to this pledge, Mahomet despatched forty (by some accounts seventy) of his followers,
mostly citizens of Medîna, with a letter to the Bani Aámir.[2]
After four days' marching, they reached a fountain called Bîr
Maûna, lying between the Bani Aámir and Suleim. Here
they halted, and despatched a messenger with the letter to
Aámir ibn Tofail. This chief, without reading the letter,
put the messenger to death, and called upon his tribe to
attack the rest of the party. They refused to break the pledge
of Abu Berâ, who happened to be absent. Aámir then
sought the aid of the Bani Suleim, who, having lost some of
their kinsmen at Bedr, were bitterly hostile to Mahomet.
Joined by a large body of these, he proceeded to Bîr Maûna
and fell upon the Mussulmans, who were waiting for the return
of their messenger. They were all cut to pieces, excepting
two men, one who was left for dead on the field, and another,
Amr ibn Omeya, who, having been absent with the camels
at the time of the slaughter, was spared on his return by
the chief, in fulfilment of a vow made at his mother's
grave.[3]

[1] Abu Berâ (called also Amr ibn Mâlik) at a later period consulted Mahomet regarding an internal disease from which, in his old age, he was suffering. It is possible that this visit also may have had a similar object.

[2] They are described as chiefly citizens who spent the day in hewing wood
and drawing water for Mahomet's family, and at night slept in the Mosque.
But there were several Refugees; and among them Amr ibn Foheira, the
freedman of Abu Bakr who accompanied his master and the Prophet in their
flight from Mecca. The number *seventy* is a favourite one; Wâckidi remarks
that seventy men of Medîna were killed at Ohod; seventy at Bîr Maûna;
seventy at Yemâma; and seventy at Yasr Abu Obeid, or the battle of the
Bridge.

[3] Mundzir, the leader, escaped the massacre and was offered quarter, which
he refused. Mahomet, on hearing this, declared that *he embraced death*; which

The news of this disaster reached Mahomet simultaneously with that of Rajî, and greatly afflicted him. Next day, after the morning prayer was concluded, he invoked the Divine vengeance on the perpetrators of both these massacres, saying : ' *O Lord! trample under foot in thine indignation the Bani Lahyân, Bani Rîl, Bani Dzakwân*' (and so on, naming the several tribes in succession); ' *make their years like unto the years of Joseph,*[1] *for that they have rebelled against God, and rebelled against His Prophet!* ' This commination was offered up with the daily prayers in public for a month. The Prophet professed also to have received through Gabriel the following message from the martyrs of Maûna : ' Acquaint our People that we have met our Lord. He is well pleased with us, and we are well pleased with Him.'[2]

Mahomet's grief, and revengeful prayer.

Amr ibn Omeya, one of the survivors, on his way back to Medîna, fell in with two men belonging to a branch of the Bani Aámir, and slew them while asleep as a reprisal for the massacre at Bîr Maûna. But it turned out that these men were returning from Mahomet, with whom they had just entered into terms. When Amr, therefore, reported what he had done, instead of being praised, he was rebuked by Mahomet, who declared his intention of paying the full blood-money for the two murdered men. The act, indeed,

Mahomet pays blood-money for two men, wrongly killed as reprisals.

expression has been magnified into meaning that he went on the expedition with a sure presentiment of his end. When Amr ibn Tofail went over the battle-field, he asked his prisoner to identify the dead bodies. This he did, but the corpse of Amr ibn Foheira was nowhere to be seen ; whereupon one of the tribe declared that when Ibn Foheira was stabbed, he heard him call out, '*I have gained Paradise,*' and saw him straightway ascend in the air to heaven. There is a multitude of such traditions.

[1] Alluding to the seven bad years in Pharaoh's dream. The tribes named after the Bani Lahyân were the clans of the Bani Suleim who joined in the attack.

[2] This formed a verse of the Corân; but, for some reason not apparent, it was 'cancelled' and removed. On receiving the message Mahomet prayed: 'O Lord! guide the Bani Aámir to the truth. I seek unto Thee for protection from Aámir ibn Tofail!' The visit of Abu Berâ, and what immediately follows, show that there had been some friendly communication between Mahomet and the tribe. Perhaps there were divided opinions in the tribe as to receiving the Moslem teachers. The mode in which tradition treats the massacre, and Mahomet's almost immediately after entering into communication with Aámir ibn Tofail on the subject of a claim for blood-money, look as if the attack was not so gratuitous as it is made to appear. Mahomet at first attributed it to Abu Berâ; but Abu Berâ cleared himself; his son attacked Aámir, and struck him with a spear, to show that his father disowned the transaction.

being a breach of truce, was so contrary to the international code of the Arabs, that Aámir ibn Tofail himself sent a despatch to Mahomet, complaining of it. Accordingly, the full compensation in money for the lives of the two men was transmitted to the tribe, together with the booty taken from them.

Bani Nadhîr ordered into exile. A.H. IV. June, A.D. 625.

The Bani Nadhîr, one of the Jewish tribes inhabiting the vicinity of Medîna, were confederate with the Bani Aámir. Mahomet thought it right, perhaps on account of the ill treatment he had received from their allies, that the Bani Nadhîr should aid him in defraying the price of blood for the two men murdered by Amr. Attended by a few followers, he visited their village, which was beyond Coba two or three miles distant, and laid his request before their chiefs. They answered courteously, promised assistance, and invited him to sit down while they made ready a repast. After sitting thus for a little while, he suddenly arose, and, without saying a word to any one, walked out of the assembly. His followers waited long, expecting his return. But they waited in vain; at length they also arose, and went back to Medîna. They found, to their astonishment, that Mahomet had returned straightway to his home, and had given out that his hasty departure from the assembly was caused by a divine intimation that the chiefs of the Bani Nadhîr were seeking treacherously to take his life. It is asserted that they had formed a plot to ascend the roof under which he sat, and roll down great stones upon him. But as his own followers saw nothing to excite suspicion, and as the chapter of the Corân specially devoted to the subject does not hint at any such perfidy, we must receive the narrative with distrust. However this may be, Mahomet resolved that the Bani Nadhîr should no longer remain in the neighbourhood of Medîna. Muhammad son of Maslama (the assassin of Káb) was immediately sent for and commissioned to deliver the command: '*Thus saith the Prophet of the Lord, Ye shall go forth out of my country within the space of ten days : whosoever remaineth behind after that shall be put to death.*' 'O Muhammad!' said they, on receiving this cruel order, 'we did not think that thou, or any other of the Bani Aus, would ever consent to be the bearer of a message such as this.' '*Hearts are changed now,*' was the reply, as he turned his back and left them startled and dismayed.

At first they began to make their preparations for departure. But it was a grievous prospect for them to be exiled from the home of their fathers, from their fertile fields, and their choice date-groves. Abdallah ibn Obey, and the party whose adherence to Mahomet had not yet made them forget the close and ancient obligations which bound them to the Jews, were displeased at the order for their banishment. Abdallah at first strove to bring about a reconciliation.[1] Failing in this, he is accused of openly attributing to Mahomet's duplicity the charge of treachery against the Bani Nadhîr, and of instigating them to resistance by a promise to stand by them with his own people and with his allies from Nejd. Reassured by this hope, and trusting to the strength of their fortress, they at last resolved to hold fast. So they sent to Mahomet, saying: 'We shall not depart from our possessions; do what thou wilt against us.' When Mahomet heard this, he cried out with delight: '*The Jews have resolved to fight! Great is the Lord!*' a cry which, taken up by his companions, re-echoed exultingly throughout the courts of the Mosque. Arming at once, they made ready for the campaign, and marched forth, Ali carrying the standard, to invest the stronghold of the rebellious tribe. The besiegers were kept at a distance by arrows and stones; but the Banî Nadhîr looked in vain for succour either from Medîna or from the tribes of Nejd. The Bani Coreitza, their Jewish brethren, either swayed by ancient jealousies or fearful of incurring the wrath of the vindictive Prophet, pretended that they could not break their treaty with him, and held aloof. Two years did not elapse before they rued the day on which they made this fatal mistake. Notwithstanding these disappointments, the Bani Nadhîr held out gallantly, and defied all the attempts of their enemy. Ma-

They refuse, and are besieged.

---

[1] The part taken by Abdallah was natural. That he really broke faith with the Jews in promising them aid, and then holding back, is questionable; for tradition delights to cast contempt and abuse upon Abdallah as the impersonation of disaffection and hypocrisy. The accusation is, however, made by Mahomet himself in the Corân, as will be seen hereafter. The position of Abdallah was very trying. The new faith had penetrated into every branch of the Medîna tribes, and rendered any combined opposition to Mahomet impossible. He probably found it impracticable to fulfil his promise.

homet, at last, to hasten their surrender, had recourse to an expedient, unusual, if not wholly unwarranted, according to the laws of Arab warfare. He cut down the surrounding date-trees, and burned the choicest of them to the roots with fire. The Jews remonstrated against this proceeding as barbarous and opposed to the law of Moses; and Mahomet (who for treachery and assassination needed no such justification) felt that his reputation demanded a special order from the Almighty, sanctioning the destruction of his enemy's palm-trees.[1]

Their date-trees are burned.

They submit to expatriation.

After the siege had lasted thus fifteen or twenty days, the Bani Nadhîr, seeing no prospect of relief, sent to say that they were now ready to abandon the lands which had already to them lost their chief value. Mahomet was glad to accede to the offer; for the siege might still have been indefinitely prolonged, and there were dangerous elements around him. They submitted, moreover, to the stipulation that they should leave their arms behind them. Upon this, Mahomet retired; and the Bani Nadhîr having laden the whole of their property, even to their doors and lintels, upon camels, set out, with tabrets and music, on the road to Syria. Some of them, with their chiefs Hoyei, Sallâm, and Kinâna, turned aside at Kheibar. The rest went on to Jericho and the highlands south of Syria.

Two renegades.

Two of their number only abandoned their ancestral faith, and, having embraced Islâm, were maintained in the possession of their fields and property. Thus early were the inducements of this life brought to bear on the advancement of the creed of Mahomet.

Fields of the Bani Nadhîr divided among Refugees.

The spoil consisted of fifty coats of mail, fifty stand of armour complete, and three hundred and forty swords. But of greater importance was the fertile tract now at the disposal of Mahomet. This he claimed as exempt from the usual law of distribution, because it had been gained without actual fighting; and he divided it at his discretion. With the exception of two indigent Citizens who had distinguished

---

[1] The Bani Nadhîr, on their palm-trees being cut down, called out from their ramparts: 'O Mahomet! thou wert heretofore wont to forbid injustice on the earth, and to rebuke him that committed it. Wherefore, then, hast thou cut down our palm-trees, and burned them with fire?' The prohibition against cutting down trees at a siege is in Deut. xx. 19.

themselves in the field, the whole of the confiscated lands were apportioned among the Refugees, who were now enabled to dispense with the bounty of the men of Medîna, and promoted to a position of independence and affluence. Abu Bakr, Omar, Zobeir, and other chief Companions of the Prophet, are named among the persons endowed thus with valuable estates.

The expulsion of the Bani Nadhîr was a material triumph for Mahomet. One by one he was breaking up the adjoining Jewish settlements, and weakening the cause of disaffection; for a combination at any time, between the Jews and the other enemies of Islâm, would have proved critical to his safety at Medîna. A whole Sura is devoted to the victory over the Bani Nadhîr, which is ascribed to the terror struck by the Almighty into their hearts. The following are extracts :—

Importance of victory over the Bani Nadhîr.

Notices of it in Corân.

All that is in the Heavens and in the Earth praiseth God— the Mighty and the Wise. He it is that hath driven forth the unbelieving Jews from their habitations to join the former Exiles. Ye thought not that they would go forth; and they themselves thought that their Fortresses would defend them against God. But God visited them from a quarter on which they counted not, and cast terror into their hearts. They destroyed their houses with their own hands, and with the hands of the Believers. Take warning, therefore, ye that have eyes. And if God had not decreed against them expatriation, He had verily punished them (otherwise) in this World, and in the World to come there is prepared for them the punishment of Fire. This because they set themselves up against God and His Prophet; and whosoever setteth himself up against God,—verily God is strong in Vengeance. That which thou didst cut down of the Date-trees, or left of them standing upon their roots, it was by the command of God,—that He might abase the evil-doers. And that which God gave unto his Prophet as booty from them;—ye did not march any horses or camels against the same; but God giveth unto His Prophet dominion over whom He pleaseth; and God is over all things Powerful. That which God hath given unto His Prophet from the inhabitants of the Villages (thus surrendering), is for God and the Prophet, and his Kindred, and the Orphan, and the Destitute, and the Wayfarer, that the turn (of booty) be not confined unto the Rich amongst you. That therefore which the Prophet giveth unto you, receive it: and that which he withholdeth from you, with-

Sura lix.

hold yourselves from the same; and fear God; for God is strong in vengeance. It is for the poor of the Refugees,—those who have been driven forth from their homes and from their properties, desiring the grace of God and His favour, and assisting God and His Apostle. These are the sincere ones. They that were before them in possession of the City and the faith, love those that have taken refuge with them, and find not in their breasts any want of the booty:[1] they prefer (their Guests) before themselves, even if they themselves be destitute. * * * *

Hast thou not observed the Disaffected? They say unto their Brethren,—the unbelieving People of the Book: '*If ye be driven forth, we will surely go forth with you. We will never submit concerning you unto any one: and if ye be attacked we shall certainly aid you.*' But God is witness that they are liars. If they are driven forth, these will not go forth with them; and if they be attacked, they will not assist them; and if they were to assist them, they would surely turn their backs, and then they would be bereft of aid. Verily ye are the stronger, because of the terror cast into their breasts from God;—this, because they are a People devoid of understanding. They shall never fight against you unitedly, excepting in fenced towns, or from behind walls. Their warlike strength is mighty among themselves; ye think they are united, but their hearts are divided, because they are a people that doth not comprehend.

They are like unto those that shortly preceded them (*i.e.* the Bani Cainocâa); they have tasted the grievous punishment of their undertaking. They are like unto Satan when he said unto Man: '*Become an Infidel;*' and when he had become an Infidel, the Tempter said: '*Verily, I am clear of thee! Verily I fear the Lord of all Worlds.*' Wherefore the end of them both is that they are cast into the Fire, dwelling for ever therein! That is the reward of the transgressors.'[2]

Mahomet had hitherto trusted Jewish amanuenses with

---

[1] That is, the Citizens of Medîna have no grudge against the Refugees because the booty was appropriated to them.

[2] The Sura ends with a few more verses in the ordinary style. In the peroration Mahomet catches (as every here and there he does to the last) some of his ancient fire: 'He is the Lord! There is no God besides: knowing both the Visible and the Invisible; He is the All Merciful and Compassionate. He is the Lord! there is no God but He:—The King, the Holy, the Giver of peace, the Faithful, the Guardian, the Glorious, the Omnipotent, the Most High. Far exalted is God above that which they associate with Him! He is God, the Creator, the Maker, the Former! Most goodly are His names. All that is in the Heavens and in the Earth praiseth Him. The Glorious and the Wise is He!'

the transcription of such despatches as required to be written in the Jewish or Syriac tongues. But his relations were gradually expanding northwards, and he could not trust documents of political importance in the hands of any one belonging to a people who regarded him now, with good reason, as the enemy of their race. About this time therefore he desired a youth of Medîna, Zeid the son of Thâbit, to learn the Hebrew or Syriac language. He had already been taught Arabic by one of the prisoners of Bedr. Mahomet now made use of him as a Secretary, both for his vernacular and his foreign despatches. This is the same Zeid, afterwards so famous as the collector of the Corân into one volume in the Caliphate of Abu Bakr, and the controller of the recension of the same under the Caliph Othmân.[1]

Zeid qualifies himself as secretary by learning Hebrew and Syriac.

[1] He was eleven years old when Mahomet arrived in Medîna, and was now therefore fifteen or sixteen. He learned Hebrew (or Syriac) in *half a month*, it is said. Mahomet used to tell him to stick his pen behind his ear, 'for this will bring to remembrance that which the distracted mind is seeking after.'

Mahomet employed another Citizen, Obey ibn Mâlik, as Secretary; and he also assisted in the compilation of the Corân.

CHAPTER XVI.

THE FOURTH AND FIFTH YEARS OF THE HEGIRA;

OR, FROM THE MIDDLE OF A.D. 635 TO THE END OF A.D. 626.

Ætat. 57, 58.

FOR about a year and a half after the expulsion of the Bani Nadhîr, Medîna was little disturbed by war either of aggression or defence.

Bedr the Second.
Mahomet marches to Bedr. Coreish remain at home.
A.H. IV.
February, March,
A.D. 625.

The summer and autumn of the fourth year of the Hegira passed in peace. At last the time came round when, by the appointment of Ohod, the forces of Mecca and Medîna were again to meet at Bedr. The year was one of great drought, and Abu Sofiân was desirous that the expedition should be deferred to a more plentiful season. Accordingly, the Coreish engaged Nueim, an Arab of a neutral tribe, to repair to Medîna, and there give forth an exaggerated account of the preparations at Mecca, in the hope that, with the field of Ohod yet fresh in memory, it might deter them from setting out. The Coreish eventually marched from Mecca with two thousand foot and fifty horse; but after one or two days, the scarcity of provender forced them to retrace their steps. The report of Nueim alarmed the inhabitants of Medîna, and a disinclination appeared in some quarters again to meet the enemy. But Mahomet, indignant at the cowardly spirit, or it may be better informed of the real counsels of the Coreish, declared with an oath that he would go forth to Bedr, even if he went alone. His bold front inspired such confidence that fifteen hundred men, a force more than double of any he had ever yet led to battle, rallied round his standard; and they carried with them a great store of wares and merchandise for the annual fair.

They maintained a standing camp at Bedr for eight days, in defiance of the Coreish, and, having bartered their goods to advantage, returned to Medîna.   Mahomet was much pleased at the result of the campaign, and signified the divine approbation in the following revelation :— *Mahomet gratified at the result.*

Those that responded to the call of God and His Prophet, after the wound which they had received—to such of them as are virtuous and fear God, there shall be a great reward.   Certain men said unto them,—' *Verily the people have gathered themselves against you ; wherefore be afraid of them.*'   But it increased their faith, and they said,—' *God sufficeth for us : He is the best Patron.*' Therefore they returned with a blessing from God, and favour. No evil touched them.   They followed after that which is well-pleasing unto God : and God is possessed of boundless grace. *Sura iii.*

Verily this devil[1] would cause you to fear his friends ; but fear Me if ye be Believers.

The Coreish, mortified at this triumph, began to project another grand attack against Mahomet.   But a year elapsed before the design was carried into execution : meanwhile Medîna enjoyed a respite. *Coreish mortified.*

In the beginning of the fifth year of the Hegira, Mahomet set out with four hundred men, to disperse certain tribes of the Bani Ghatafân, which were assembled with suspicious purpose at Dzât al Ricâ.   They fled to the mountains at his approach.   Mahomet advanced unexpectedly upon their habitations, and carried off some of their women. After an absence of fifteen days the party returned to Medîna.[2] *Expedition to Dzât al Ricâ. A.H. V. May, A.D. 626.*

[1] Applied by some commentators to Abu Sofiân ; by others, with more likelihood, to Nueim.

[2] A story illustrative of the kind and unbending manner by which Mahomet engaged the affections of his followers, may be briefly recounted here, as it relates to the present expedition.   Jâbir, a poor Citizen, son of a man slain at Ohod, was mounted on a wretched camel, which Mahomet (after miraculously transforming from a slow into a very rapid walker) said he would buy from him.   He spoke to Jâbir kindly concerning his father, and five-and-twenty times invoked mercy on him.   Then in a livelier strain : ' Hast thou married lately ?'   Jâbir replied, ' Yes.'   ' A maiden, or one that had before been married ?'   ' The latter,' said Jâbir.   ' And why not a young damsel, who would have sported with thee, and thou with her ?'   ' My father,' he explained, ' left seven daughters, so I married a woman of experience, able to guide them.'   ' Thou hast done well,' rejoined Mahomet ; (he might here himself have learned a lesson from his humble follower)—' Now when we reach thy home at Sarâr, we shall kill a camel and rest there, and thy wife will hear of it and will spread carpets for us.'   ' But, O Prophet ! I have not any

'Service of Danger.'

It was in this short campaign that the 'Service of Danger' was introduced. Fearing that the enemy, who held the fastnesses above the Moslem army, would attempt a surprise and rescue their women, a part of the force was kept constantly under arms. The public prayers were therefore repeated twice,—one division watching while the other prayed. The revelation sanctioning this practice is quoted less for its own interest, than to illustrate the tendency of the Corân now to become the vehicle of military commands. In the Corân, victories are announced, success promised, actions recounted; failure is explained, bravery applauded, cowardice or disobedience chided; military or political movements are directed;—and all this as an immediate communication from the Deity. The passage resembles what one might expect to find in the 'General Orders' of some Puritan leader, or Commander of a crusade in the Holy Land :—

Corân, a vehicle for 'General Orders.'

Sura iv.

When ye march abroad in the earth, it shall be no crime unto you that ye shorten your prayers, if ye fear that the Unbelievers may attack you; for the Unbelievers are an open enemy unto you. And when thou art amongst them, and leadest their prayers, let one Division of them arise to prayer with thee, taking their weapons with them, and when they have worshipped, let them remove behind you. Then let the other Division come up that hath not prayed, and let them pray with thee, and let them take their due precaution and their weapons. The Unbelievers would that ye should neglect your weapons and your baggage; then would they fall upon you with one onset. It shall be no crime unto you, if ye be incommoded by rain, or if ye be sick, that ye lay down your weapons; but take your due precaution. Verily God hath prepared for the Unbelievers an ignominious punishment.

Campaign to Dûmah al Jandal. A.H. V. July, A.D. 626.

During the summer, another campaign was undertaken by Mahomet. It was in the direction of Dûmah al Jandal, an Oasis and entrepôt on the borders of Syria midway between the Red Sea and the Gulf of Persia, where marauding bands, driven to violence by the prevailing famine, were plundering travellers, and even threatened a

carpets.' 'We shall get them for thee: do therefore as I have said.' So they had the entertainment at Sarâr. On Mahomet's returning home, Jâbir took his camel to Mahomet, who not only gave him its full price, but also returned the camel itself. Jâbir, thus set up in life, prospered greatly.

raid upon Medîna. Mahomet stopped short a march or two from Dûmah, and contented himself with capturing the herds which grazed in the neighbourhood. The robbers fled without offering any opposition. This expedition is touched very lightly upon by tradition, being disposed of in a brief notice of two or three lines; but it was in reality most important. Mahomet, followed by a thousand men, reached the confines of Syria; distant tribes learned the terror of his name; the political horizon was extended; the lust of plunder in the hearts of the Moslems acquired a wider range; while they were inured, at the hottest season of the year, to long and fatiguing marches. The army was absent for nearly a month. On his way back Mahomet entered into a treaty with Oyeina, a powerful chieftain of the Fezâra, and gave him the right to graze on certain tracts of table land to the east of Medîna, where, notwithstanding the drought, forage was still procurable.

It is necessary now to turn to what was passing within the home of Mahomet. The reader has already been made acquainted with his three wives, Sauda, Ayesha, and Haphsa. After his marriage with Haphsa, in the middle of the third year of the Hegira, he contracted no new nuptials for some time. But in the ninth month of the fourth year, he espoused Zeinab daughter of Khozeima, the widow of his cousin Obeida, who had been killed at Bedr. She was called 'the Mother of the Poor,' from her care of the destitute converts. Zeinab lived but a year and a half after the marriage, and was the only one of the Prophet's wives (excepting always Khadîja) who died before him.[1]

Mahomet marries a fourth wife, Zeinab bint Khozeima. A.H. IV. January, 626.

Within another month he sought the hand of a fifth wife. Omm Salma was the widow of Abu Salma, to whom she had borne several children. Both had been exiles to Abyssinia, from whence they returned to Medîna. At Ohod Abu Salma was wounded, but he had recovered so much as to take the command of the expedition to Catan, when the wound broke out afresh. Mahomet visited his death-bed. He was breathing his last, and the women wailed loudly. 'Hush!' said the Prophet as he entered. 'Invoke not on yourselves aught but what is good; for

And a fifth, Omm Salma. A.H. IV. February, 626.

---

[1] Rihâna, the Jewess, died a year before him; but it is doubtful whether she was ever more than his concubine.

Prayer at
death-bed
oɪ her
previous
husband.

verily the angels are present with the dying man, and say *Amen* to that which ye pray. *O Lord! give unto him width and comfort in his grave: Lighten his darkness: Pardon his sins: Raise him to Paradise: Exalt his rank among the Blessed; and raise up faithful followers from his seed!* Ye indeed are looking at the fixed eyes, but the sight itself hath already followed the dead.' So saying he drew the palm of his hand over the eyes of his departed friend, and closed them. It was eight months after the battle of Ohod, when Abu Salma died; and four months afterwards Mahomet made proposals of marriage to his widow, who though not young was very beautiful. She at first excused herself on the score of her family and her own mature age; but the Prophet removed her objection by saying that he too was well advanced in years, and that her children should be his care. Atter the marriage he remained three days with his bride,--an example ever after followed by Believers when adding fresh inmates to their harems. Her son Omar was brought up by Mahomet.

Mahomet
marries
*Zeinab bint
Jahsh,*
divorced
by his
adopted
son, Zeid.
A.H. V.
June, A.D.
626.

The numerous marriages of Mahomet failed to confine his inclinations within the ample circuit of his harem. Rather its multiplied attractions weakened restraint, and stimulated desire after new and varied charms. We have already made acquaintance with Zeid, the Prophet's freedman and adopted son. His wife Zeinab, now over thirty years of age, was fair to look upon. On a certain day, the Prophet visited, as he often did, their house. Zeid being absent, Zeinab invited him to enter, and, starting up in her loose and scanty dress, made haste to array herself for his reception. But the beauties of her figure through the half-opened door had already unveiled themselves too freely before the licentious gaze of Mahomet. He was smitten by the sight: '*Gracious God Almighty!*' he exclaimed; '*Gracious God! how Thou turnest the hearts of mankind!*' These rapturous words were repeated, as he turned to depart, in a low voice; but they were uttered distinctly enough to be heard by Zeinab, who perceived the flame she had kindled, and, proud of her conquest, was nothing loth to tell her husband of it. Zeid went straightway to Mahomet, and declared his readiness to divorce Zeinab for him. This Mahomet declined: 'Keep thy wife to thyself,' he said, 'and fear God.' But Zeid saw probably that these words proceeded from unwilling lips, and that the Prophet had still a longing eye for Zeinab. Perhaps he did not care to keep her, when he found that she desired to leave him, and was ambitious of the new and distinguished alliance. Accordingly he completed the divorce. Mahomet still hesitated. There might be little scandal according to Arab morals in seeking the hand of a married woman whose husband had no wish to retain her; but the husband in the present case was Mahomet's adopted son, and even in Arabia such a union was unlawful. Still the passion for Zeinab could not be smothered; it continued to burn within the heart of Mahomet, and at last, bursting forth, scattered his scruples to the winds. Sitting one day with Ayesha, the prophetic ecstasy appeared to come over him. As he recovered, he smiled joyfully and said: 'Who will go and congratulate Zeinab, and say that the Lord hath joined her unto me in marriage?' His maid Solma made haste to carry the glad news to Zeinab, who showed her delight by bestowing on the messenger all the jewels she had upon her person. Mahomet delayed not to fulfil the divine behest, and, having made a great feast in the court of the Mosque, took Zeinab to be his wife.[1]

The marriage caused much obloquy, and, to save his reputation, Mahomet had the effrontery to promulgate a special Revelation in which the Almighty is represented as formally recording a divine warrant for the union, dis-

And supports the marriage by divine command.

---

[1] Zeid was short and not well favoured, having a pug-nose; but he was ten years younger than the Prophet.

Zeinab was industrious, and could tan leather and make shoes. What she made in this way, even (it is said) after her marriage with the Prophet, she gave to the poor. She survived Mahomet ten or eleven years.

Tabari is the fullest of the earliest authorities on this passage, and in the text I have followed him closely. He gives a second narrative, differing only in this that, as Mahomet waited at Zeid's door, the wind blew aside the curtain of Zeinab's chamber and disclosed her in a scanty undress. After Zeid had divorced her, Mahomet asked him whether he had seen anything to dislike in her. 'Nothing,' he replied, 'only good.' Ayesha relates that strange misgivings arose in her heart when she heard the divine message commanding the marriage, and, mindful of the beauty of Zeinab, feared lest she should glory over the other wives of Mahomet as his divinely appointed bride. We learn from tradition that Zeinab did thus vaunt herself, saying, that *God had given her in marriage to His Prophet, whereas his other wives were given to him by their relatives.*

allowing objections raised on the score of adoptive affinity, and even reprehending the Prophet for his hesitation and fear of men :—

God hath not given to a man two hearts within him. * * * Nor hath He made your adopted sons your (real) sons. This your speech proceedeth from your mouths; but God speaketh the Truth ; and He directeth in the right way. Let your adopted sons go by their own fathers' names. This is more just with God. * * *

And when thou saidst to him on whom God hath bestowed favour, and upon whom thou too hast bestowed favours :[1] 'Keep thy Wife to thyself, and fear God ;' and thou concealedst in thy mind what God was about to make known, and thou fearedst man—whereas God is more worthy that thou shouldst fear Him. And when Zeid had fulfilled her divorce, We joined thee in marriage unto her, that there might be no offence chargeable to Believers in marrying the Wives of their adopted sons, when they have fulfilled their divorce ; and the command of God is to be fulfilled. There is no offence chargeable to the Prophet in that which God hath enjoined upon him according to the ordinance of God regarding those that preceded him (and the command of God is a predestined decree) :—those who conveyed the messages of God, and feared Him, and feared none but God, and God is a sufficient accountant. Mahomet is not the father of any man amongst you. Rather he is the Apostle of God, and the Seal of the Prophets ; and God knoweth all things.

The scandal of the marriage was removed by this extraordinary Revelation, and Zeid was thenceforward called not 'the son of Mahomet,' as heretofore, but by his proper name, 'Zeid, the son of Hârith.' Our only matter of wonder is, that the Revelations of Mahomet continued after this to be respected by the people as inspired communications from the Almighty, when they were so palpably formed to secure his own objects, and pander even to his evil desires. We hear of no doubts or questionings ; and we can only attribute the confiding and credulous spirit of his followers to the absolute ascendency of his powerful mind over all who came within its influence.

The seclusion of the Veil or curtain was at this time

---

[1] Meaning Zeid, whom Mahomet, after freeing, had adopted. In the following verse he is mentioned by name, a singular instance; no other follower or contemporary is mentioned in the Corân by name.

enjoined upon the wives of Mahomet. Himself well stricken posed on Mahomet's wives. in years, surrounded by six wives, some of whom were sprightly, young, and beautiful, and living as he did with his family in the midst of a continual concourse of courtiers and visitors, worshippers and suitors, such a restriction was not unneeded. Indeed, he had himself proved, in the case of Zeinab, the danger arising from a free admission of friends or strangers; and his followers could hardly expect to be freer from temptation than their Prophet. The command to take the veil, as usual, comes from heaven; and the jealousy of Mahomet's heart is further allayed by the divine prohibition that his wives shall never marry again, even after his death. Henceforward, they are to be called '*the Mothers of the Faithful.*' The following is the passage. How has the fine gold become dim!—

O ye that believe ! Enter not the Habitations of the Prophet, Sura xxxiii except it be permitted you to eat bread therein, without waiting his convenient time. But when ye are bidden, then enter; and when ye have eaten, then disperse. And be not familiar in discourse,—for verily that giveth uneasiness to the Prophet. It shameth him (to speak thus) to you: but God is not ashamed of the Truth. And when ye ask anything of his women, ask it of them from behind a curtain (or veil), that will be more pure for your hearts and for their hearts. It is not fitting for you that ye give uneasiness to the Apostle of God, nor that ye should marry his Wives after him at any time :—Verily that would be an enormity in the sight of God. * * * The Prophet is nearer unto the Believers than their own souls, and his Wives are their Mothers.

Certain restrictions, but of a less stringent nature, were Moslem women to be partly veiled when walking abroad. about this time placed upon the dress and demeanour of all believing women. These were exposed in their walks abroad to the rude remarks of disaffected and licentious citizens; they were therefore commanded to throw their garments around them so as partially to veil their persons, and conceal their ornaments. The men who thus troubled the Moslem females were threatened with expulsion and with a general slaughter.

O Prophet! Speak unto thy wives and thy daughters, and Sura xxxiii. the wives of the Believers, that they throw around them a part of their mantles. This will be more seemly, that they may be recognised (*i.e.* as women of reputation) and may not be subject to annoyance; for God is gracious and merciful. And truly, if the Disaffected, and they in whose hearts is a disease (*i.e.* of incontinency), and the propagators of falsehoods in the city, hold not back, We shall surely stir thee up against them. Then they shall not be permitted to live near unto thee therein but for a little. Accursed! wherever they are found, they shall be taken and killed with a great slaughter. It is the wont of God concerning those that have gone before. And these shall not find in the wont of God any variation.

And elsewhere :—

Sura xxiv.

Speak unto the Believing women that they restrain their eyes, and preserve their chastity; and display not their ornaments, except what appeareth thereof; and let them throw their veils over their bosoms; and let them not display their ornaments except to their husbands, fathers (and so on, enumerating a number of relations, and ending with slaves, eunuchs, and children). And let them not shake their feet that their hidden ornaments be discovered.

Rules for entering houses, &c. of neighbours.

Rules and precautions were also prescribed to regulate the visits of strangers to their neighbours' houses, and to prevent the privacy of Believers being intruded upon without due warning.[1]

Restrictions rendered necessary by loose code of Corân.

The truth is that the extreme license of Polygamy and Divorce permitted to his followers by Mahomet, rendered some safeguards of this nature necessary. Such license would not, without opening a door to flagrant immorality, be compatible with the free and open intercourse of civilised society. It would not in any nation be tolerable, unless guarded by restrictions that must fetter and degrade the female sex.[2]

[1] Sura xxiv. Believers are forbidden to enter any house but their own (even if there be no one inside) until they have first asked leave and saluted the family. During three periods of the day—*i.e.* before morning prayer, at the time of the siesta, and after evening prayer—even slaves and young children (who are otherwise excepted) must ask permission before entering an apartment. Women past child-bearing may alone dispense with the outer garment. The sick, and certain near relatives, are exempted from the prohibition of dining familiarly in each other's inner apartments.

[2] On this account the introduction of European manners and customs into Mahometan society, is altogether to be deprecated. The licentious tendency of the *system* without its present checks, cruel and unnatural as they are, would certainly create in Mussulman countries an utter dissolution of morality. Let the state of things be conceived, if with unrestricted social intercourse between the sexes, there existed also the practice of polygamy, and an unbounded

A goodly row of houses now formed the eastern side of the Mosque; these were the Prophet's ' habitations,' one of which was erected on every fresh marriage for the accommodation of his new spouse. Mahomet professed to share his time equally amongst his wives, passing a day and night in the house of each successively. Thus their turn was

facility of divorce and remarriage, under the sanction of divine revelation; if the marriage bond were simply at the discretion of the husband to hold or to break; if, the husband consenting, any man might look upon any married woman (near relatives excepted) as within his reach by marriage; and if every married woman felt like Zeinab, that she might become the lawful wife of any other man whom she might captivate, and who could persuade her husband to pronounce a divorce! The foundations of society would be broken up.

As legitimate results of the system, take one or two instances. Of the Malays of Penang it is said: ' A man observes the neglect of his wife, knows how easily she may be separated from him, broods over the result, and may be led into that state of mind' (*i.e.* the tendency to *run a muck*). He 'views with jealousy any attention of another man to his wife, and a fancied reciprocation on the woman's part leads to the direst results. * * * Divorces are so easily accomplished that the most abominable licentiousness is promoted, and the fine feelings that characterise the union of the sexes under the Christian dispensation are unknown. * * * Young men of thirty to thirty-five years of age may be met with who have had from fifteen to twenty wives, and children by several of them. These women have been divorced, married others, and had families by them.'

Burckhardt tells us of an Arab, forty-five years old, who had had fifty wives; so that he must have divorced two wives and married two fresh ones on the average nearly every year. And if we would know what is the present state of morality in the sacred city itself, we have the evidence of a keen observer, the late reigning Begum of Bhopâl, herself an orthodox follower of the Prophet. After making the pilgrimage a few years ago, her Highness wrote thus of Mecca: 'The women frequently contract as many as ten marriages, and those who have been only married twice are few in number. If a woman sees her husband growing old, or if she happen to admire any one else, she goes to the Shereef, and, after having settled the matter with him, she puts away her husband, and takes to herself another, who is perhaps young, good-looking, and rich. In this way, a marriage seldom lasts more than a year or two.' It may be remarked that the *wife* (excepting under a few rare conditions) has not legally the power of divorce; but the impression on the Begum's mind from personal intercourse with the upper society of Mecca sufficiently proves the great laxity of morals prevailing there.

Wherever in Mahometan society polygamy and divorce are discouraged, it is owing to the accident of position or custom. The natural propriety and *humanity* of Monogamy and of the indissolubility of the marriage tie, has with many individuals and many classes (as among the Puthans of Upper India) to some extent introduced a purer practice in supersession of that allowed by the Corân, and notwithstanding its temptations. But this abstinence cannot be carried to the credit of the system introduced by Mahomet; it is owing, *in spite of that system*, to the remedial tendencies in human nature.

known as 'the day of Sauda,'—'the day of Zeinab,' and so on. Yet Ayesha maintained her pre-eminence in this as in all other respects; and, however much there may have been a formal circuit of the harem reducing nominally her portion to one day in six, still hers was the most frequented of the apartments of all his wives, and best deserved the name of the Prophet's *home*. The irregularity of his attentions at length provoked a natural discontent; and Mahomet did not scruple to release himself from the obligation of consorting with his wives equally and in undeviating order, by a command from heaven. 'Postpone any of them thou mayest wish; and admit unto thyself her whom thou choosest, as well as her whom thou mayest desire of those whom thou hadst put aside; it will be no offence in thee. This will be easier, that they may be satisfied, and not repine, but be all content with that thou givest unto them.'[1] The burlesque on inspiration could hardly be carried further. Yet the command was gravely incorporated in the Corân (whether Mahomet intended that it should be we have no means of judging); and to this day it is recited in its course, as part of the Word of God, in the worship of every Mussulman, and of every Mosque!

It is a relief to turn for a time from these unworthy passages, to other scenes in the life of Mahomet.

Sura xxxiii.

Mahomet attacks and takes captive the Bani Mustalick.

Three or four months after his return from Dûma, rumours reached the Prophet of new projects against him in the direction of Mecca. The Bani Mustalick, a branch of the Khozâa, hitherto friendly to his cause, were now

---

[1] A passage follows which was probably given forth at a later stage, for in this Sura are collected a variety of precepts, of different periods, all relating to the treatment of women: 'No more Women are lawful unto thee after this: nor that thou shouldest exchange any of thy wives for them, even though their beauty fascinate thee, excepting those (*i.e.* slaves) that thy right hand may possess, and God observeth all things.' Some commentators think that this prohibition was abrogated by a preceding verse, which makes lawful to the Prophet in marriage any of his maternal or paternal cousins, and any believing woman who might willingly surrender herself to him. Others say that the passage was revealed after his number of nine wives was completed. In the latter case, it is to be noted that cohabitation with slaves as concubines, in addition to his regular wives, is still permitted *ad libitum*. The interpretation implying *abrogation* seems gratuitously to impute a fraud, for the 'prohibition' was in the manner of a guarantee to his existing wives, which he had no right to abrogate.

raising forces with the view of joining the Coreish in the A.H. V. December, A.D. 626. threatened attack on Medîna. Having ascertained the truth of these reports through a Bedouin spy who ingratiated himself with the hostile chief, Mahomet at once resolved by a bold inroad to prevent their design. All the fighting men of Medîna rallied round him; and a great multitude of those hitherto lukewarm in the interests of Islâm, with Abdallah ibn Obey at their head, desirous to maintain a friendly appearance, or allured by the hope of plunder, joined his standard. Mahomet could now muster thirty well appointed horse.[1] After a march of eight days he encamped at the wells of Moraisî, near the sea-shore, some marches short of Mecca. Here he had a tent of leather pitched for himself and for Ayesha and Omm Salma, who accompanied him. The tidings of his approach carried dismay into the ranks of the Bani Mustalick, and caused all their allies to fall away from them. The overpowering force advanced; and, after a brisk discharge of archery, closed so rapidly on the enemy, that the whole were surrounded and taken prisoners with their families, their herds and flocks. Of the enemy ten were killed, while Mahomet lost but one man, and that from an erring shot by a Moslem. Two hundred families, two thousand camels, and five thousand sheep and goats, besides much household goods, formed the booty. It was divided in the usual manner.[2]

The army remained encamped for several days at the wells of Moraisî. In this interval an altercation sprang up between a Citizen and a Refugee the servant of Omar. The latter struck the Citizen a blow, and the men of Medîna rushing in to avenge their comrade's insult, the Refugee cried loudly on his fellows for aid. High words and threats passed on both sides, swords were drawn, and the result might have been serious, had not the Citizen been

Altercation between the Citizens and Refugees.

---

[1] At the second Bedr he had but ten. Of the thirty horse, twenty belonged to Citizens and ten to Refugees. The standard of the Refugees was held by Abu Bakr, that of the Citizens by Sád ibn Obâda.

[2] The household stuff was sold to the highest bidder, on the spot. In the division of the spoil a camel was reckoned equal to ten sheep or goats. On this occasion the law was introduced which gives each horseman *three* times the share of a footman, two shares being reckoned for the horse. Mahomet desired thus to encourage the development of cavalry in his army.

persuaded to withdraw his complaint and forgive the injury. During the quarrel, the disaffected party gave free expression to murmurs at the insolence of the Refugees: 'This,' said Abdallah ibn Obey plainly, ' ye have brought upon yourselves, by inviting these strangers to dwell amongst us. When we return to Medîna, the Mightier shall surely expel the Meaner!'

Mahomet no sooner heard of the strife, and of the violent language of Abdallah, than he gave orders for an immediate march. The discontent of the Citizens and the momentary antagonism betwixt them and the Refugees, if allowed to spread, would have been dangerous to his safety. By breaking up the camp, and at once ordering a long and wearisome march, he hoped to divert men's minds from the events of the morning and make the quarrel to die away. Therefore, though the hour was still early and unseasonable, and although amity had apparently been re-established, Mahomet started without delay, and kept the army marching the whole of that day and night and the following day, till the sun was high. Then he halted, and the force, overpowered with fatigue, was soon asleep. From thence they proceeded onwards to Medîna by regular marches.

Before the army moved, Abdallah protested to Mahomet that he had not made use of the expressions attributed to him; and Mahomet, although some of his followers counselled severe and decisive measures, received his excuse with civility. When Abdallah was being hardly handled by his fanatical son, who tried to extort from him the confession that *he* was the *Meaner*, and Mahomet the *Mightier*,[1] the Prophet, chancing to pass by, interfered and said:

Mahomet orders immediate march.

Abdallah and disaffected citizens reprimanded in Corân.

---

[1] There are worse actions than this attributed to Abdallah's son. He offered to bring his father's head, if Mahomet desired it; saying: 'If he is to be killed, I will do it myself. If any other man commits the deed, the Devil will tempt me to avenge my father's blood: and by killing a Believer for an Unbeliever, I shall go to hell. Suffer me to kill him myself!'

Omar also is said to have counselled Mahomet at Moraisî to put Abdallah to death. But Mahomet replied: 'Omar! How will it be if men should say that Mahomet killeth his own followers? nay, but let us give orders for an immediate march.' In after days when Abdallah's authority waned, and he was treated without reverence even by his own people, Mahomet reminded Omar of his advice on this occasion, and asked whether it was not far better to have reserved him for this fate, than to have put him to death. Omar confessed the wisdom of the Prophet.

'Leave him alone!   For, by my life! so long as he remaineth with us, we shall make our companionship pleasant
unto him.'   Still, when he returned to Medîna, and found
himself again firmly fixed in the affections of the citizens,
Mahomet deemed it necessary to administer to Abdallah and
his followers a public reprimand, and his bitter feelings
found expression in the 63rd Sura.   The heavenly message
thus revealed, contains a curse against the insincere and
disaffected professors of Islâm; while the quotation of the
very words attributed to Abdallah, fixes the point of the
divine reprimand against him, and shows significantly that
Mahomet did not credit his denial.[1]

The captives of the Bani Mustalick having been carried
to Medîna with the rest of the booty, men from their tribe
soon arrived to make terms for their release.   One of them
was Juweiria a damsel about twenty years of age, full of
grace and beauty, the daughter of a chief, and married
to one of her own tribe.   She fell to the lot of a citizen,
who, taking advantage of her rank and comeliness, fixed the
ransom at nine ounces of gold.[2]   Despairing to raise so
large a sum, she ventured into the presence of the Prophet
while seated in the apartment of Ayesha, and pleaded for

Mahomet marries the captive Juweiria, his seventh wife.

---

[1] The following is the passage :—' When the Disaffected come unto thee,
they say : *We testify that thou art the Prophet of God :* and God knoweth
that thou art his Prophet, and God testifieth that the Disaffected are liars.
They take their oaths as a shield, and they turn men aside from the way
of God; verily it is evil, that which they do:—This because they believed,
and afterwards disbelieved ; Wherefore, their hearts are sealed, and they
understand not.   When thou seest them, thou admirest their outward man ;
but when they speak, thou listenest to their words, as if they were logs set up
(against the wall); they fancy every cry is against themselves.   They are
enemies.   Beware of them!   God curse them!   How are they turned unto
lies!

' And when it is said unto them : *Come! let the Prophet of God ask
pardon for you,* they avert their heads, and ye see them turn aside, puffed up
with pride.   It is the same for them whether thou askest pardon for them, or
dost not ask pardon for them.   God will not pardon them.   God doth not
guide wicked men unto the truth.   These are they which say: *Do not expend
your Wealth upon those who are with the Prophet of God, and so they will
disperse :*—Whereas unto God belong the treasures of the Heavens and of the
Earth : but the Disaffected understand not.   They say: *When we return unto
Medina, verily the Mightier shall expel from thence the Meaner :*—Whereas
Might belongeth to God and His Prophet, and to the Believers : but the
Disaffected do not comprehend.'

[2] The ordinary ransom of a woman or child was ten camels.

some remission of the heavy price demanded for her freedom. Ayesha no sooner saw that she was fair to look upon and of a sprightly winning carriage, than her jealousy prognosticated what was about to come to pass. Mahomet listened to her supplication, and the conqueror was soon the captive of his prisoner. 'Wilt thou hearken,' he said, 'to something better than what thou askest of me?' Surprised by his gentle accents, she enquired what that might be: 'Even that I should pay thy ransom, and marry thee myself!' The damsel forthwith expressed her consent; the ransom was paid; and Mahomet, taking her at once to wife, built a seventh house for her reception. As soon as the marriage was noised abroad, the people said that the Bani Mustalick having now become their relatives, they would let the rest of the prisoners go free as Juweiria's dower;—'and thus no woman,' said Ayesha, telling the story in after days, 'was ever a greater blessing to her people than this Juweiria.'

Ayesha falls into trouble.

But a severer trial than the advent of a new rival hung over Ayesha. Her honour was about to be called in question.

Her mis-adventure with Safwân.

The wives of Mahomet, when they marched with him, travelled each in a litter carried by a camel. Since the order for the veil, this litter had been carefully shrouded from the public gaze. It was placed before the door of the tent, and at the hour of marching the lady entered it in seclusion and adjusted the curtains; the servants then approached and lifted it upon the camel: when alighting the same privacy was observed. On the day on which the army returned to Medîna from the expedition against the Bani Mustalick, the camel of Ayesha at the end of the journey was set down at the door of her house near the Mosque; but when the litter was opened it was found to be empty. Some time after Safwân, one of the Refugees, appeared leading his camel, with Ayesha seated upon it. Ayesha explained that at night just before the time of marching, she had occasion to go to some little distance from her tent, when she dropped her necklace of Yemen beads. On returning to mount her litter, she missed the necklace, and went back to seek for it. Meanwhile the bearers came up, and, imagining Ayesha to be within (for she was yet light and of slender figure), lifted the litter according to custom, and led the camel away. On her return, Ayesha was astonished to find the place deserted, and no one left anywhere in sight.[1] So, expecting that the mistake would be soon discovered, and the litter brought back, she wrapped her clothes around her, sat patiently on the ground and fell fast asleep. Towards morning, Safwân, who had been also accidentally detained, passed by, and, recognising Ayesha, expressed surprise at finding one of the Prophet's wives in this predicament. She did not answer him. No other words (so Ayesha declared) passed between them; but Safwân brought his camel near her, and, modestly turning his face in the opposite direction, desired her to mount. When she was seated, he approached, and, taking hold of the halter, led the camel towards Medîna. Though he made every haste, he could not overtake the army; and thus they entered before the gaze of the people, and some time after the others had alighted and pitched their camp outside the city.

The scandal-loving Arabs were not slow in drawing sinister conclusions from this inopportune occurrence. The reports soon reached the ears of Mahomet and caused him great uneasiness. Ayesha felt the change of his manner towards her, and (though professing to have been ignorant till some time after of the cause) it preyed upon her mind. She fell sick for several weeks; and at last, finding his indifference to be still maintained, and learning at length from a friend the rumours affecting her character, she obtained permission of Mahomet to return to her father's house. Mahomet's estrangement from Ayesha.

The estrangement of Mahomet from his favourite wife strengthened the grounds of defamation. Her fall was gloried over by those who bore no love to the Prophet, and became a topic of malicious conversation even among some of his staunch adherents. At the head of the former was Abdallah ibn Obey; and foremost among the latter were Mistah (a relative and dependent of Abu Bakr), the poet Hassân, and Hamna daughter of Jahsh, who rejoiced over the dishonour of her sister Zeinab's rival.[2] Scandal occasioned in Medina.

---

[1] Her tent must have been light, easily taken down, and carried off immediately she was supposed to have entered the litter.

[2] Ayesha says: 'Now Hamna took up the scandal, because she was sister of Zeinab daughter of Jahsh (the former wife of Zeid); and there was none that dared to put herself in competition with me, but Zeinab only. She herself said nothing bad; but her sister did so, envying me because of my superiority to Zeinab.'

Mahomet chides his followers for meddling in the matter.

When matters had gone on thus for a month, Mahomet resolved to put an end to the scandal. So he mounted the pulpit, and sharply reprimanded his followers: 'O ye people!' he said, 'what concern is it of others that they should disquiet me in affairs touching my family, and that they should unjustly blame them! Whereas, I myself know concerning my family naught but that which is good. And moreover ye have traduced a man, regarding whom likewise I know not aught but what is good.' Then Oseid, a leader of the Bani Aus, arose and swore that he would punish the delinquents, even to the death, if Mahomet would but give permission. On this an altercation sprang up between him and the Bani Khazraj, to whom the chief offenders amongst the citizens belonged. The quarrel was with some difficulty appeased by Mahomet, who then left the Mosque and proceeded to the house of Abu Bakr.

He consults Osâma and Ali.

There, having called to him Osâma [1] and Ali, he asked counsel of them. Osâma declared his utter disbelief of the slanderous report. Ali, with greater caution, recommended the examination of Ayesha's maid; and the maid when called could give them nothing but her testimony to the innocence of her mistress. [2]

Ayesha cleared by revelation from heaven.

Mahomet then went to Ayesha herself. From the time when she had first learned the damaging nature of the reports about her character, she had abandoned herself to excessive grief. Her mother exhorted her to patience: 'Assuage thy sorrow, my daughter!' she said; 'it is seldom that a beautiful woman is married to a man who loves her, and who has other wives besides, but the latter multiply scandal against her; and so do men likewise.' But she refused to be comforted, and continued to pine away. Now when Mahomet entered, he sat down beside her, with her father and mother; and he said: 'Ayesha! thou knowest

---

[1] Son of Baraka (Omm Ayman) the Prophet's nurse and her husband Zeid.

[2] Ali answered Mahomet: 'O Prophet! there is no lack of women, and thou canst without difficulty supply her place. Ask this servant girl about her, perchance she may tell the truth.' So Mahoment called the maid. Ali arose and struck her, saying: 'Tell the truth unto the Prophet.' 'I know nothing,' said she, 'of Ayesha but what is good:—excepting this, indeed, that one day I was kneading corn, and I asked her to watch it, and she went asleep, and the goats came and ate thereof.' We must not forget, however, that all this is from Ayesha, who had a strong antipathy to Ali.

what men have spoken of thee. Fear God. If indeed thou hast been guilty of that which they accuse thee of, then repent towards God, for the Lord accepteth the repentance of His servants.' Ayesha held her peace, expecting (as she tells us) that her parents would reply for her;—but they too were silent. At last she burst into a passionate flood of tears, and exclaimed: ' By the Lord! I say that I will never repent towards God of that which ye speak of. I am helpless. If I confess, God knoweth that I am not guilty. If I deny, no one believeth me. All I can say is that which Joseph's father said,—*Patience becometh me: God is my helper!* '[1] Then, as all sat silent, Mahomet appeared to fall into a prophetic trance. They covered him over, and placed a pillow under his head. Thus he lay seemingly unconscious. Ayesha assures us that her mind was perfectly tranquil at this critical moment, confident that her innocence would be vindicated from heaven. In a little while he recovered himself, cast off the clothes, and sat up. Wiping away the great drops of sweat from his forehead, he exclaimed: ' *Ayesha! rejoice! Verily the Lord hath revealed thine innocence.*' Her mother bade her embrace the Prophet; but to ejaculate ' *Praise be to God!*' was all that Ayesha could do.

Then Mahomet went forth to the people, and recited before them the commands which he had received in this matter from heaven. They are contained in the 24th Sura, which opens with declaring one hundred stripes[2] to be the punishment for harlotry, and proceeds thus :—

Passages of Corân revealed on the occasion.

They that slander married women, and thereafter do not bring forward four witnesses, scourge them with four-score stripes : and ye shall never again receive their testimony; for they are infamous,—Unless they repent after that, and amend, for God is forgiving and merciful.[3] * * * Verily as for them,—a

Sura xxiv.

---

[1] Ayesha says that the name of *Jacob* having gone from her memory at the moment, she substituted the words *Joseph's father*.

[2] This penalty is made by the Moslem divines to apply to fornication only, and not to adultery. For the latter no punishment is mentioned *in the Corân*, but the Sonna awards death by stoning, for it.

[3] Here intervenes the ordinance prescribed for a husband charging his wife with adultery. If he have no witnesses, the charge, sworn to four times, with a fifth oath imprecating the wrath of God upon himself if swearing falsely, is accepted without witnesses. The wife may avert the punishment by similar

party amongst you,—that have fabricated lies, think it not to be an evil unto you. To every man amongst them shall be (dealt out according to) the crime which he hath wrought; and he that hath been forward amongst them in aggravating the same, his punishment shall be grievous.[1] Wherefore, when they heard it, did not the Believers, men and women, imagine in their minds that which is good, and say,—*This is a manifest lie?* Have they brought four witnesses thereof? Wherefore, since they have not produced the witnesses, they are liars, these men, in the sight of God. If it were not for the favour of God upon you, and His mercy in this world and in the next, verily for that which ye have spread abroad, a grievous punishment had overtaken you;—when ye published it with your tongues, and said with your mouths that of which ye had no knowledge: and ye counted it light, but with God it is weighty. Why, when ye heard it, did ye not say: *It belongeth not to us that we should speak of this;—Gracious God! This is a monstrous calumny!*

God admonisheth you that ye return not again to the like thereof for ever. And God manifesteth unto you His signs, for God is knowing and wise. Verily, they who love that infamy should be published regarding the Believers: to them shall be a grievous torment in this world and in the next. And God knoweth, but ye do not know. And if it had not been for the grace of God upon you, and His mercy,—Verily, God is merciful and forgiving.

Calumniators of Ayesha scourged.

After some further denunciations of the wrath and curse of God against the traducers of innocent females, Mahomet stopped short; and, in accordance with the divine command, ordered the calumniators of Ayesha to receive the punishment ordained for them. Mistah and Hassân received each four-score stripes; and even Hamna, the sister of the favourite Zeinab, did not escape. But against Abdallah, Mahomet did not venture to enforce the sentence. It was fortunate that he refrained from doing so, for a time of trial was at hand when the alienation of this powerful citizen and his adherents might have proved fatal to his cause.

Hassân conciliated

Satisfied with the infliction of these punishments,

oaths and a similar imprecation. No corresponding privilege is conceded to the wife who accuses her husband of adultery.

[1] The expression is so strong that some take it to mean hell, and apply it to Abdallah. Others refer it to Hassân, who shortly after became blind. But the natural meaning is the punishment of stripes, severe enough certainly for the honourable class of persons on whom it was inflicted.

Mahomet, instead of keeping up the grudge, sought rather by present of an estate.
to conciliate the slanderers of Ayesha. Safwân (the hero of
the misadventure), smarting under the satires of the poet
Hassân, drew his sword upon him and inflicted a deep wound.
Hassân and his friends seized and bound Safwân, and carried
him before Mahomet. The Prophet first rebuked Hassân
for troubling the citizens with his lampoons; and then,
having composed the difference, more than compensated the
Poet for his wound and the disgrace of the stripes, by con-
ferring on him a valuable estate and mansion in the vicinity
of Medîna. He also commanded Abu Bakr not to withdraw
from Mistah, his indigent relative, the support he had
hitherto given him.[1]

Ayesha, again received back to the home and heart of Hassân reconciles Ayesha by an ode in her praise.
Mahomet, re-established herself, perhaps more firmly than
before, in the paramount influence which she exercised there.
Her praises were sung by Hassân himself,—her purity, her
grace, her wit, and (what Ayesha piqued herself more than
all upon) her slender and elegant figure,—in glowing verse,
which entirely reconciled her to the Poet.[2] But she never
forgave Ali for having doubted her integrity.

Little remark is needed regarding the character of Guilt or innocence of Ayesha.
Ayesha, and the alleged message from above to which
it gave occasion. There are not materials sufficient for
deciding upon the charges brought against her, and the
question is immaterial. That there were grounds of grave
suspicion, Mahomet, by his behaviour towards her, himself
admitted. The reason subsequently assigned for her innocence and the punishment of the slanderers, namely, the
absence of four witnesses, is inconclusive. It might have Law of slander established by Ma-homet.
been necessary that Mahomet should caution his followers,
and even punish them, for lightly or maliciously damaging
a reputation hitherto untarnished; but to prohibit, on pain
of stripes, all comment on suspicious morality unless attested

---

[1] This injunction was not thought too small a matter for a special *Revelation*. See verse 23. Of Hassân, we learn that though by far the first
poet in Medîna, his character was not such as to inspire respect. He
was foul-mouthed and cowardly, and never went into battle. Combing his
hair over his forehead and eyes, and dyeing his moustache a bright red while
the rest of his hair was black, he affected the wild appearance of a wolf.

[2] When he came to the passage referring to her *slimness*, she archly interrupted him by a piece of raillery at his own corpulence.

by four witnesses, is to cast a veil over conduct which the interests of society might imperatively require to be canvassed and held up to reprobation.[1]

Although admitting so decisively the innocence of Ayesha, Mahomet did not deem the character of his wives above the necessity of caution, and the threat of a double punishment if they erred. They were not as other women; far more than others they were bound to abstain from every word and action that might encourage those 'whose hearts are diseased.' The passage, in which the jealousy of the Prophet thus betrays itself through the transparent veil of a *Revelation*, is too curious to be curtailed, even at the risk of the reader's patience.

O Prophet, say unto thy wives,—*If ye seek after this present Life and the fashion thereof, come, I will make provision for you and dismiss you with a fair dismission.* But if ye seek after God and His Apostle, and the Life to come, then verily God hath prepared for the excellent amongst you a great reward. O Women of the Prophet! If any amongst you should be guilty of incontinence, the punishment shall be doubled unto her twofold; and that were easy with God. But she that amongst you devoteth herself to God and His Apostle, and worketh righteousness, We shall give unto her her reward twice told, and We have prepared for her a gracious maintenance.

O ye Women of the Prophet! Ye are not like unto any one amongst (other) Women. If ye fear the Lord, be not bland in your speech, lest he indulge desire in whose heart is a disease. Yet speak the speech that is suitable. And abide within your houses; and array not yourselves as ye used to do in the days of Ignorance gone by. And observe the times of Prayer; and give Alms: and obey God and His Apostle. Verily the Lord desireth only to purge away from you impurity, ye that are of (his) household, and to purify you wholly. And keep in memory that which is recited in your houses, of the Word of God, and Wisdom: for God pierceth that which is hidden, and is acquainted with all things.

[1] It is true that an exception is made in favour of the husband whose simple oath five times repeated may be substituted, so far as his own interests are concerned, for that of the four witnesses. But this would not touch the case of unmarried women, or widows, or of a blind or conniving husband; and yet the interests of public morals might justify society in taking cognisance of strongly suspected immorality even under such circumstances. The practical result of Mahomet's rule is that the Mahometan husband immures or secludes his wife, or watches her at every turn; and with such a system is it to be wondered at?

CHAPTER XVII.

SIEGE OF MEDÎNA, AND MASSACRE OF THE BANI COREITZA.

Dzul Câda, A.H. V.—*February, March*, A.D. 627.

WHILE Mahomet thus occupied himself with the cares of his increasing harem, and, by messages addressed to them from heaven, enjoined upon his wives virtue and propriety of life, more weighty and stirring scenes suddenly opened out before him.

Stirring scenes open upon Mahomet.

The winter season was again come round at which it had now become customary with the Coreish to prepare for hostilities against Mahomet. Their enmity was at this time further stimulated by Huwey and other Jewish chiefs exiled from Medîna, who undertook the duty of rousing the Bedouin tribes bound by alliance or sympathy in the same cause. Among these were several clans of the great Ghatafân family, between whom and Mahomet there had already been some warlike passages. The Bani Ashja and Murra, each brought four hundred warriors; and the Bani Fezâra, a large force, with one thousand camels, under Oyeina; the Bani Suleim, who had been concerned in the massacre at Maûna, joined the army on the way, with seven hundred men. The Bani Sád and Bani Asád also swelled the force, the latter still smarting from the attack made on them by Mahomet about two years before. The Coreish themselves brought into the field four thousand soldiers, including three hundred horse, and one thousand five hundred riders upon camels. The banner was mounted in the hall of Council and delivered to Othmân, son of Talha the standard-bearer who was killed at Ohod. The entire

Coreish, joined by Bedouin tribes, march against Medina.

force was estimated at ten thousand men. They marched in three separate camps; all were under the general leadership of Abu Sofiân, but, when the time for action came, the several chiefs each for a day commanded in succession.

Mahomet defends Medina by digging a trench.
A.H. V.
February, A.D. 627.

Mahomet was apprised by the Bani Khozâa of their approach, but barely in time to prepare for their reception. The unfortunate issue of the affair at Ohod against numbers much inferior, put it out of the question to offer battle; and great alarm prevailed throughout the city. A happy suggestion was made by Salmân 'the Persian,' who was familiar with the mode in which camps and cities were defended in other countries.[1] Following his advice, Mahomet at once adopted the stratagem, hitherto unknown in Arabia, of entrenching the town. The stone houses of Medîna were built so compactly together that, for a considerable distance, they presented a high and nearly unbroken wall, of itself a sufficient protection. But it was necessary to connect this barrier by a line of defence with the rugged mass of rocks which on the north-west approach the city, and to carry it round the other unsheltered quarters on the east and south.[2] The work, consisting of a deep ditch and rude earthen dyke, was portioned out amongst the various clans. Shovels, pickaxes, and baskets were borrowed from the Jews of the Coreitza tribe. Mahomet stimulated the enthusiasm of his followers by himself taking a basket and carrying the excavated earth; and by joining in their song, as at the building of the Mosque:—

O Lord! there is no happiness but the happiness of Futurity.
O Lord! have mercy on the Citizens and the Refugees!

He also frequently repeated the following verses, covered as he was, like the rest, with earth and dust:—

---

[1] He is said to have been a Christian captive of Mesopotamia, bought by a Jew from the Bani Kalb, and ransomed on his profession of Islâm. This is the first occasion on which he comes to notice.

[2] The fortress or castle of Medîna is now built on this 'out-cropping mass of rock.'—*Burton.* Burckhardt calls it a small rocky elevation. Speaking of the great Syrian chain, he also says: 'The last undulations of these mountains touch the town on the north side.' This is apparently what, in tradition, is called *Silâ,* though Burckhardt gives that name, 'Jebel Sila,' to the *Monâkh* (or encamping ground) lying immediately south of it. I gather that the part of modern Medîna immediately to the east of the fort was in ancient times open and unbuilt upon.

O Lord! without Thee, we had not been guided!
We should not have given alms, neither should we have prayed!
Send down upon us tranquillity, and in battle stablish our
    steps!
For they have risen up against us, and sought to pervert us,
    but we refused!—Yea, WE REFUSED.

And as he repeated the last two words, he raised his voice
high and loud.

In six days the trench was finished, deep and wide
throughout almost the whole length of the defence; and
great stones were heaped along the inner side to be used
against the enemy. The dwellings outside the town were
evacuated, and the women and children placed for security
on the tops of the double-storied houses within the entrench-
ment. These arrangements were hardly completed when
the enemy was reported to be advancing by Ohod. The
army of Medîna, three thousand strong, was immediately
marshalled and posted across the road leading to Ohod,
having the trench in front, and their rear resting upon the
north-eastern quarter of the city and the rising ground of
Silá. The northern face was the point most vulnerable to
the enemy, the approaches from the east being covered by
walls and palm enclosures. A tent of red leather was
pitched for Mahomet on the ground, in which Ayesha, Omm
Salma, and Zeinab visited him by turns.

Army of Medina posted within trench. A.H. V. March 2, A.D. 626.

The Coreish, with their allies, encamped at first upon
their old ground at Jorf and al Ghâba, near Ohod. Then
passing unopposed by the scene of their former victory, and
finding the country deserted, they swept rapidly up the road
to Medîna. The enemy formed their several camps in front
of the Moslem army, the picquets of which were now posted
closely along the trench. The Coreish were astonished and
disconcerted at the new tactics of Mahomet. Unable to
come to close quarters, they contented themselves for some
time with a distant discharge of archery.

Coreish encamp opposite them,

Meanwhile, Abu Sofiân succeeded in detaching the
Jewish tribe of Coreitza from their allegiance to Mahomet.
Huwey, the Jewish ally of the Coreish, deputed by him to
their fortress, was at first refused admittance. But, persevering in his solicitations, dwelling upon the ill-concealed
enmity of Mahomet towards the Jews, and representing the

And de-tach Bani Coreitza from allegi-ance to Mahomet.

overwhelming numbers of the confederate army as 'a surging sea,' he at last persuaded Káb their chief to relent. It was agreed that the Coreitza would assist the Coreish, and that Huwey should retire into their fortress in case the allies marched back without inflicting a fatal blow upon Medîna. Rumours of this defection reaching Mahomet, he sent the two Sáds, chiefs of the Aus and Khazraj, to ascertain the truth of the report; and he strictly charged them, if the result of their enquiry should prove unfavourable, to divulge it to none other but himself. They found the Coreitza in a sullen mood. 'Who is Mahomet,' said they, 'and who is the Apostle of God, that we should obey him? There is no bond or compact betwixt us and him.' After high words and threats, the messengers took their leave, and reported to Mahomet that the temper of the Jews was worse even than he had feared.[1]

[1] It is not easy to determine what the compact was, at this time existing between Mahomet and the Coreitza, and what part the Coreitza actually took in assisting the Allies. The evidence is altogether *ex parte*, and is of course as adverse to the Coreitza as possible. The Corân, our surest guide, says simply that they 'assisted' the Allies; and the best traditions confine themselves to this general expression. Had any active hostilities been entered upon, they would, according to Mahomet's habit, have been more distinctly specified in the Corân. On the other hand, a tradition from Ayesha states that, when the Allies broke up, the Coreitza 'returned' to their fort; and some traditions, though not of much weight, speak of them as part of the besieging force *before Medîna*. There is also a weak tradition that Hodzeifa, sent by Mahomet as a spy to the enemy's camp, overheard Abu Sofiân telling his comrades the good news that the Coreitza had agreed to join him, *after ten days' preparation*, provided he sent seventy warriors to hold their fortress while they were absent in the field; and that Hodzeifa's report was the first intelligence Mahomet had of the defection.

On the whole, my impression is that the Coreitza entered into a league with Huwey, making common cause with him, and promising to take part in following up any success on the part of the Coreish,—a promise which they were in the best position to fulfil,—their fortress being, though at some distance from the city, on its undefended side. But, before any opportunity offered, they saw the likelihood of the siege failing, and then distrust and disunion broke out.

It is to be noticed that the compact existing betwixt them and Mahomet is admitted by Wâckidi to have been a '*slight*' one. Al Jowhari says that this term means a treaty entered into without forecast or design, or 'infirm.' 'Fœdus vel pactum forte initum, vel haud firmum.'

Sprenger notes these alternatives. *First*, that, as at Ohod, the Coreitza were forbidden by Mahomet to take part in the fight; *second*, that of their own free-will they remained neutral. He decides in favour of the first;—that they resisted the temptation and remained faithful, and that even the Jews of Kheibar kept aloof from the Coreish for fear of compromising their brethren at Medîna.

The question is important as bearing on the sentence executed against the Coreitza after the Coreish retired.

This news alarmed Mahomet. He justly apprehended that his previous treatment of the Jewish tribes might now drive the Coreitza to desperate measures. The south-eastern quarter of the city, which lay on their side, was the least capable of defence. The Jews had still many friends and adherents among the citizens. His tactics, being offensive, embraced the whole population, including the disloyal, who had joined the Moslem army on the battle ground. Disaffection lurked everywhere. Even amongst the professed followers of the Prophet, some began to talk already of deserting. To protect the families of his adherents throughout the town, and to guard against surprise or treachery, Mahomet was obliged to detach from his force, already barely adequate to man the long trench, two parties, each composed of two or three hundred soldiers, which night and day patrolled the streets. For this purpose a body of three hundred was placed under Zeid, Mahomet's freedman, and another of two hundred under a citizen of Medîna. A strong guard was also kept over his own tent.

Danger to Medina from this defection, and measures for its safety

The enemy, notwithstanding their numbers, were paralysed by the vigilance of the Moslem outposts. They professed to regard the trench as an unworthy subterfuge: 'Truly,' they said in their chagrin, 'this ditch is a foreign artifice, to which no Arabs have ever yet descended.' But it was nevertheless the safety of Medîna. The confederate army resolved if possible to storm it, and, having discovered a certain narrow and weakly-guarded part, a general attack was made upon it. The cavalry spurred their horses forward, and a few of them, led by Ikrima son of Abu Jahl, cleared the ditch, and galloped vauntingly in front of the enemy. No sooner was this perceived than Ali with a body of picked men moved out against them. These, by a rapid manœuvre, gained the rear of Ikrima, and, occupying the narrow point which he had crossed, cut off his retreat. At this moment Amr son of Abd Wudd, an aged chief in the train of Ikrima, challenged his adversaries to single combat. Ali forthwith accepted the challenge, and the two stood alone in the open plain. Amr, dismounting, maimed his horse, in token of his resolve to conquer or to die. They closed, and for a short time were hidden in a cloud of dust. But it was not long before the well-known *Takbîr*, 'Great is

Party of enemy's horse clear the trench, but are driven back by Ali.

the Lord!' from the lips of Ali, made known that he was the victor.[1] The rest, taking advantage of the diversion, again spurred their horses, and all gained the opposite side of the trench, excepting Nowfal, who, failing in the leap, was despatched by Zobeir.

General attack upon line of defence successfully repelled.

Nothing further was attempted that day. But great preparations were made during the night; and next morning, Mahomet found the whole force of the Allies drawn out against him. It required the utmost activity and an unceasing vigilance on his side to frustrate the manœuvres of the enemy. Now they would threaten a general assault; then breaking up into divisions they would attack various posts in rapid and distracting succession; and at last, watching their opportunity, they would mass their troops on the least protected point, and, under cover of a sustained and galling discharge of arrows, attempt to force the trench. Over and again a gallant dash was made at the city, and at the tent of Mahomet, by such leaders of renown as Khâlid and Amru; and these were only repelled by constant counter-marches and unremitting archery. This continued throughout the day; and, as the army of Mahomet was but just sufficient to guard the long line, there could be no relief. Even at night Khâlid, with a strong party of horse, kept up the alarm, and, still threatening the line of defence, rendered outposts at frequent intervals necessary. But all the endeavours of the enemy were without effect. The trench was not crossed; and during the whole affair Mahomet lost only five men. Sád ibn Muâdz, chief of the Bani Aus, was wounded severely by an arrow in the shoulder. The archer, as he shot it, cried aloud: 'There, take that from the son of Arca.' Whereupon Mahomet exclaimed, with a savage play upon the name: '*Arrack!* the Lord cause thy face to sweat in hell fire!' The Confederates had but three men killed.

Prayers repeated in the evening for those omitted during day.

No prayers had been said that day: the duty at the trench was too heavy and incessant. When it was dark, therefore, and the greater part of the the enemy had retired to their camp, the Moslem troops assembled, and a separate service was repeated for each prayer which had been omitted.

---

[1] The Coreish, it is said, offered a great sum for the body; but Mahomet returned the 'worthless carcase' (as he termed it) free.

Mahomet on this occasion cursed the allied army, and said: 'They have kept us from our daily prayers: God fill with fire their bellies and their graves!'

Though the loss of life had been trifling, yet the army of Medîna was harassed and wearied with the unceasing watch and duty. The enemy had a great advantage in the overwhelming superiority of his numbers; and, though the Moslems at last formed two sets of parties one of which slept while the other patrolled, they had no other respite day or night. They were moreover dispirited by finding themselves hemmed in, and by seeing no prospect of the siege being raised. Mahomet himself was in constant alarm lest the trench should be forced, and his rear be threatened by the Jews or other disaffected citizens. Many of his followers, whose habitations and possessions lay outside the city, afraid or pretending to fear that they would be plundered, begged leave to go and protect them. Mahomet appeared in the eyes of his people weak and helpless. 'Where,' it was asked, 'were now the Prophet's hopes, and where his promises of divine assistance?' It was indeed a day of grievous trial. In the vivid language of the Corân, *'the enemy came upon them from above and from beneath; and the Sight became confused; and Hearts reached to the throat; and the people imagined concerning God strange imaginations.'* In this state of alarm, when the siege had now lasted ten or twelve days, Mahomet bethought him of a stratagem for buying off the least hostile portion of his foe. He sent secretly to Oyeina chief of the Fezâra, and sounded him as to whether he would engage to withdraw the Ghatafân tribes, and thus break up the confederate army, on condition of receiving one third of the produce of the date-trees of Medîna. Oyeina signified his readiness, if one half were guaranteed to him. But Mahomet had over-estimated his own authority. On sending for the two Sáds, as representatives of the Bani Aus and Khazraj, they spurned the compromise. But, still maintaining their subordination to the Prophet, they added: 'If thou hast received a command from God for this, then do thou act according to the same.' 'Nay,' said Mahomet, 'if I had received a command, I would not have consulted you; I ask only your advice as to that which is the most expedient.' 'Then our counsel is,'

Distress at Medina.

Secret negotiation to buy off Bani Ghatafân,

they replied, 'to give nothing unto them but the Sword.'
And so the project dropped.

Mutual
distrust
between
Coreish
and Jews
excited by
an emissary
from Ma-
homet.

Another and more artful device was now tried. There
was a man of the allied army, who possessed the ear of both
sides,—the same Nueim who had been employed in the
previous year to prevent Mahomet from advancing on Bedr,
by exaggerated accounts of the preparations at Mecca. He
is now represented as an exemplary believer, but secretly for
fear of his tribe the Bani Ashjá. This man offered his
services to the Prophet and they were gladly accepted. 'See
now,' said Mahomet to him, 'whether thou canst not break
up this confederacy against us: for War verily is a game of
deception.' Nueim went first to the Bani Coreitza and, representing himself as a true friend, artfully insinuated that the
interests of the Allies were diverse from theirs; and that,
before the Coreitza compromised themselves irretrievably
with Mahomet by joining in the impending general attack on
Medîna, they ought to demand from the Coreish hostages, as
a guarantee against being deserted by them and left in the
enemy's power.[1] Suspecting no harm, they agreed to act on
his advice. Next he went to the allied chiefs and cautioned
them against the Jews: 'I have heard,' said he, 'that the
Coreitza intend to ask for hostages; beware how ye give
them, for they have already repented of their compact with
you, and promised Mahomet to give up the hostages to be
slain, and then to join in the battle against you.' The insidious plot immediately took effect. When the Coreish
sent to demand of the Coreitza the fulfilment of their engagement to join in a general attack on the following day,
they pleaded their Sabbath as a pretext against fighting
then, and their fear of being deserted as a ground for demand-
ing hostages. The Allies, regarding this as a confirmation
of Nueim's intelligence, were so fully persuaded of the
treachery of the Coreitza that they began even to fear an
attack upon themselves from that quarter.

The confederate chiefs were already disheartened. After

[1] The tenor of Nueim's advice, as given uniformly by tradition, is opposed
to the supposition that the Coreitza had as yet joined in active hostilities
against Mahomet, or committed any such overt act as would have prevented
them rejoining his cause. Sprenger says that, at this stage, Huwey made
a last attempt to persuade the Coreitza to fall upon the rear of the Moslems
at the time of a general attack, but did not succeed.

the two days of vigorous but unsuccessful fighting, they had not again attempted any general assault. Perhaps the system by which the chiefs commanded each on successive days had paralysed their energies. The hope entertained from another engagement, during which the Coreitza were to have fallen upon the city in the rear of Mahomet, was now changed into the fear of hostilities from the treacherous Coreitza themselves. Forage was obtained with the utmost difficulty; provisions were now running short; and the camels and horses were dying daily in great numbers. Wearied and damped in spirit, the night set in upon them cold and tempestuous. Wind and rain beat mercilessly on the unprotected camp. The storm rose to a hurricane. Fires were extinguished, tents blown down, cooking vessels and other equipage overthrown. Cold and comfortless, Abu Sofiân suddenly resolved on an immediate march. Hastily summoning the chiefs, he made known his decision: 'Break up the camp,' he said, 'and march; as for myself, I am gone.' With these words he leaped on his camel (so great was his impatience) while its fore leg was yet untied, and led the way. Khâlid with two hundred horse brought up the rear, as a guard against pursuit. The Coreish took the road by Ohod for Mecca, and the Bani Ghatafân retired to their haunts in the desert.

A tempest: Abu Sofiân orders allied force to break up.

Enemy retires:

The grateful intelligence soon reached Mahomet, who had sent a follower in the dark to spy out the enemy's movements. In the morning not one of them was left in sight. The Prophet was not slow in attributing this happy issue to divine interposition. It was an answer, he said, to the earnest prayer which he had for some days been offering up: '*O Lord! Revealer of the sacred Book, who art swift in taking account! turn to flight the confederate Host! Turn them to flight, O Lord, and make them to quake!*' It was God who, hearing these petitions, had sent the tempestuous wind; and the armies of heaven had fought likewise, striking terror into the enemy.

Mahomet attributes relief to divine interposition.

The army of Medîna, thus unexpectedly relieved, joyfully broke up their camp, in which they had been besieged now for fifteen days, and returned to their homes in the city. Mahomet had no thoughts of a pursuit: it would have been affording the Coreish that which they perhaps

Moslem army breaks up.

still desired,—an action in the open country. His thought was of a surer and more important blow nearer home.

But imme diately formed again, to chastise Bani Coreitza.

He had just begun to cleanse himself from the dust of the campaign, when suddenly Gabriel brought him command to proceed immediately against the Bani Coreitza. 'What!' said the heavenly visitant, in the language of reproach, 'hast thou laid aside thine armour, while as yet the Angels have not laid theirs aside! Arise and go forth against the Coreitza. Behold I go before thee to shake the foundations of their walls.'[1] Instantly Bilâl was sent to make procla-

Siege of Coreitza fortress. A.H. V. March, A.D. 626

mation throughout the town. An immediate march was ordered; all were to be present at the evening prayer in the camp pitched before the fortress of the Coreitza, two or three miles to the south-east of Medîna. The stand-ard raised to oppose the Coreish stood yet unfurled in the Mosque: it was now placed in the hands of Ali. Mahomet mounted his ass, and the army (as before three thousand strong, with thirty-six horse) followed him. The for-tress of the Coreitza was at once invested, and a discharge of archery kept up steadily, but without effect. One man, approaching incautiously near, was killed by a Jewess, who cast down a millstone on him. But the improvident Jews, whom the fate of their brethren should have taught to better purpose, had not calculated on the chances and necessities of a siege; they were soon reduced to great distress, and sought to capitulate on condition of quitting the neighbourhood even empty-handed. But Mahomet, having no longer other Jewish neighbours to alarm or alienate by his severity, was bent on a bloody revenge, and he refused to listen. In their extremity, the Coreitza appealed to their ancient friendship with the Bani Aus, and the services rendered to them in by-gone days. They begged that Abu Lubâba, a friend and

---

[1] Tradition abounds with stories of Gabriel on this occasion. He was seen to go before the Mussulman army in the appearance of Dihya the Kalbite, who 'resembled Gabriel in his beard and face.' Again, Mahomet desired to postpone the campaign a few days as his people were fatigued; but Gabriel would not admit of a moment's delay, and galloped off with his troop of angels, raising a great dust. Gabriel's dress is particularised: he rode on a mule with a silken saddle, a silken turban, &c. Mahomet was washing his face after his return from the campaign of the Ditch, when Gabriel appeared; he had washed the right cheek and was beginning to wash the left, when he received the order to march to the siege of the Coreitza; and, leaving thus his face half washed, obeyed at once!

ally belonging to that tribe, might be allowed to visit and counsel them.   He came, and, overcome by the wailing of the children and the cries of the women, he had no heart to speak; but, symbolically drawing his hand across his throat, intimated that they must fight to the last, as death was all they had to hope for.   On retiring, he felt that he had been too plain and honest in his advice; for 'war,' as the Prophet had said, 'is a game of deception.'   Therefore he went to Mahomet, and, confessing his guilt, said : 'I repent; for verily I have dealt treacherously with the Lord, and with his Prophet.'   Mahomet vouchsafed no reply; and Abu Lubâba, the more strongly to mark his contrition, went straightway to the Mosque and bound himself to one of its posts.   In this position he remained for several days, till at last Mahomet relented, and sent to pardon and release him.   The 'Pillar of repentance' is still pointed out in the Mosque to the pious pilgrim.

At last the wretched Jews, brought now to the last verge of starvation, offered to surrender, on condition that their fate would be decided by their allies the Bani Aus.   To this Mahomet agreed; and, after a siege of fourteen days (according to others of twenty-five), the whole tribe, men, women and children, came forth from their stronghold.   The men, handcuffed behind their backs, were placed on one side, under charge of Muhammad son of Maslama, the assassin of Káb; the women and children, torn from their fathers and husbands, were put under the care of Abdallah, a renegade Jew.   As the women passed before the conqueror, his eye marked the lovely features of Rîhâna, and he destined her to be his own.   The household stuff of the captives, their clothes and armour,[1] their camels and flocks, were all brought forth to await the arbiter's award.   The wine and fermented liquors were poured forth, the use of such being now forbidden to Believers.

The Bani Aus were importunate that their ancient allies should be spared.   'These were *our* confederates,' they urged; 'we pray thee that the same consideration may be shown to them as aforetime, at the suit of the Bani Khazraj, thou didst show to *their* allies the Bani Nadhîr.'   'Are ye

---

[1] There were fifteen hundred swords, one thousand lances, five hundred shields, and three hundred coats of mail.

then content,' replied Mahomet, 'that their fate be committed to one of yourselves?' They expressed satisfaction, and Mahomet forthwith nominated Sád ibn Muâdz to be the judge.

Sád still suffered from the severe wound received at the trench. From the field of battle he had been carried to a tent pitched by Mahomet in the court-yard of the Mosque, where the wounded men were waited on by Rufeida an experienced nurse. His wound had begun apparently to heal. But the sense of the injury still rankled in his heart; and Mahomet knew well the bitter hate into which his former friendship had been turned by the treachery of the Coreitza.[1] He was now summoned. His figure was large and corpulent. Having been mounted with some difficulty on a well-padded ass, he was conducted to the camp. The men of his tribe who thronged about him by the way continually reminded him of the friendship and services of the Coreitza, and urged him as their own representative to deal gently with the prisoners. He answered not a word till he approached the scene; and then he replied: 'Verily, this grace is given to Sád, that he careth not, in the affairs of God, for any blame the Blamers may cast upon him.' As he drew near, Mahomet called aloud to those around him: 'Stand up to meet your master, and assist him to alight.'[2] Then he commanded that Sád should pronounce his judgment on the Coreitza. It was a scene well worthy the pencil of a painter. In the background, the army of Medîna watch with deep interest this show of justice, regarding eagerly the booty, the household stuff and armour, the camels and flocks, the date-groves, and the deserted town, all, by the expected decree of confiscation, about to become their own. On the right, with hands pinioned behind their backs, are the captive men, seven or eight hundred in number, dejection and despair at the ominous rigour of their treatment stamped upon their

---

[1] On his being wounded, Sád had cursed the Coreitza and prayed: 'O Lord! suffer me not to die until my heart hath had its revenge against them.'

[2] The Refugees held with much pertinacity that this order was only addressed to the citizens of Medîna, as Sád was their chief. The Citizens, on the contrary, regarded the words as addressed to all then present, including the Refugees, and as significant of the honourable and commanding post of judge, assigned to Sád.

faces. On the left, are the women and the little children, pale with terror, or frantic with grief and alarm for themselves and for the fate of their husbands and fathers, from whom they have been just now so rudely dragged. In front is Mahomet, with his chief Companions by his side, and a crowd of followers thronging behind. Before him stands Sád, supported by his friends, weak and jaded with the journey, yet distinguished above all around by his portly and commanding figure. 'Proceed with thy judgment!' repeated the Prophet. Sád turned himself to his people, who were still urging mercy upon him, and said: 'Will ye, then, bind yourselves by the covenant of God that whatsoever I shall decide, ye will accept it?' There was a general murmur of assent. Then he proceeded: '*This verily is my judgment, that the male captives shall be put to death, that the female captives and the children shall be sold into slavery, and the spoil be divided amongst the army.*' Many a heart quailed, besides the hearts of the wretched prisoners, at this bloody decree. But all questionings were forthwith stopped by Mahomet, who sternly adopted the verdict as his own, nay, declared it to be the solemn judgment of the Almighty;—cold and unmoved he said: '*Truly thou hast decided according to the judgment of God pronounced on high from beyond the seven heavens.*'

No sooner was the sentence passed and ratified than the camp broke up, and the people wended their way back to Medîna. The captives, still under charge of Muhammad the assassin, were dragged roughly along; one alone was treated with tenderness and care,—it was Rîhâna the beautiful Jewess, set apart for Mahomet. The men and women were penned up for the night in separate yards; they were supplied with dates and spent the night in prayer, repeating passages from their Scriptures and exhorting one another to constancy. During the night graves or trenches sufficient to contain the dead bodies of the men were dug in the chief market-place of the city. When these were ready in the morning, Mahomet, himself a spectator of the tragedy, gave command that the captives should be brought forth in companies of five or six at a time. Each company was made to sit down by the brink of the trench destined for its grave, and there beheaded. Party after party were led out and butchered in

Butchery of the Bani Coreitza.

cold blood, till the whole were slain.[1] One woman alone was put to death ; it was she who threw the millstone from the battlements. When she heard that her husband had been slain, she loudly avowed what she had done, and demanded to be led to execution also,—a request which Mahomet granted in more mercy perhaps than he intended ; and she met her death with a cheerful countenance.[2] For Zoheir, an aged Jew, who had saved some of the Bani Aus in the battle of Boâth, Thâbit interceded and procured a pardon, including the freedom of his family and restoration of his property. 'But what hath become of all our chiefs,—of Káb, of Huwey, of Ozzâl the son of Samuel?' asked the old man. As one after another he named the leading chiefs of his tribe, he received to each inquiry the same reply ;—they had all been slain already. 'Then of what use is life to me any longer? Leave me not to that bloodthirsty man who has killed all that are dear to me in cold blood. But slay me also, I entreat thee. Here, take my sword, it is sharp ; strike high and hard.' Thâbit refused, and gave him over to another who, under Ali's orders, beheaded the aged man, but attended to his last request in obtaining freedom for his family. When Mahomet was told of his saying,—'Slay me also, that I may go to my home and join those that have preceded me ;' he answered: '*Yea, he shall join them in the fire of Hell !*'

Mahomet takes the captive Rîhâna for his concubine.

The murderous work begun in the morning, lasted all day, and was concluded by torchlight in the evening. Having sated his revenge, and drenched the market-place with the blood of eight hundred victims,[3] and having given command for the earth to be smoothed over their remains,

[1] As the messenger went to bring up each successive party, the miserable prisoners, not conceiving a wholesale butchery possible, asked what was about to be done with them. 'What! will ye never understand?' said the hard-hearted keeper; 'will ye always remain blind? See ye not that each company goeth and returneth not hither again? What is this but death?'

[2] Ayesha relates that this woman, whose heart perhaps was sustained by faith in the God of her fathers, went smiling and fearlessly to her fate. Ayesha said that she could never get this woman out of her imagination.

[3] The numbers are variously given as six hundred, seven hundred, eight hundred, and even nine hundred. If the number of the arms enumerated among the spoil in a former note be correct, nine hundred would seem to be a moderate calculation for the adult males : but I have taken eight hundred as the number more commonly given.

Mahomet returned from the horrid spectacle to solace himself with the charms of Rîhâna, whose husband and all her male relatives had just perished in the massacre. He invited her to be his wife ; but she declined, and chose to remain (as indeed, having refused marriage, she had no alternative) his slave or concubine.[1] She also declined the summons to conversion, and continued in the Jewish faith, at which the Prophet was much concerned. It is said, however, that she afterwards embraced Islâm. She lived with Mahomet till her death.

The booty was divided into four classes—lands, chattels, cattle, and slaves ; and Mahomet took a fifth of each. There were (besides little children who counted with their mothers) a thousand captives ; from his share of these, Mahomet made certain presents to his friends of slave girls and female servants. The rest of the women and children he sent to be sold among the Bedouin tribes of Nejd, in exchange for horses and arms ; for he kept steadily in view the advantage of raising a body of efficient horse. The remaining property was divided amongst the three thousand soldiers of Medîna, to the highest bidders among whom the women also were sold.[2]

The women and children sold as slaves in Nejd.

We are told that three or four men of the doomed tribe saved their lives, their families, and property by embracing Islâm, probably before the siege began. No doubt the whole tribe might have, on the same terms, bought their safety. But they remained firm, and may be counted as martyrs to their faith.

Notice of these events in Corân.

[1] She is represented as saying, when he offered her marriage and the same privileges as his other wives : ' Nay, O Prophet ! But let me remain as thy slave ; this will be easier both for me and for thee.' By this is probably meant that she would have felt the strict seclusion as a married wife irksome to her. That she refused to abandon the faith of her fathers shows a more than usual independence of mind ; and there may have been scenes of sorrow in her poor widowed heart, and aversion from her licentious conqueror, which tradition is too one-sided to hand down, or which indeed tradition may never have known. She died A.H. 632, a year before Mahomet himself.

[2] Muhammad (Kâb's assassin) said that, being mounted, his share was three females with their children, worth forty-five golden dinârs ; the whole booty at the prize valuation would thus be 40,000 dinârs. Mahomet sold a number of the state slaves to Othmân and Abd al Rahman, who made a good speculation therefrom. They divided them into old and young. Othmân took the old, and found as he expected much money on their persons. Large sums were obtained from the Jews of Kheibar and other places for the ransom of the women and children they were interested in.

The siege of Medîna, and the massacre of the Bani Coreitza, are noticed, and the Disaffected bitterly reproached for their cowardice before the besieging army, in a passage of the Corân revealed shortly after, and recited by Mahomet, as was customary, from the pulpit :—

Sura
xxxiii.

O ye that believe! Call to mind the favour of God towards you, when Hosts came upon you, and We sent against them a Tempest and Hosts which ye saw not; and God beholdeth that which ye do. When they came at you from above you, and from beneath you, and when the Sight was confused, and the Hearts reached to the throat, and ye imagined of God (strange) imaginations. There were the Faithful tried and made to tremble violently. And when the Disaffected said, and they in whose hearts is a disease said, *God and His Prophet have promised only a delusion :—*And when a Party amongst them said :—*O men of Yathreb* (Medîna), *there is no security for you, wherefore retire;* and a part of them asked leave of the Prophet to depart, saying, *Our houses are without protection;* and they were not without protection, but they desired only to escape :—And if an entrance had been effected amongst them (by the enemy) from some adjacent quarter, and they had been invited to desert, they had surely consented thereto; then they had not remained in the same, but for a little. And verily they had heretofore covenanted with God, that they would not turn their backs; and the covenant of God will surely be enquired after. Say,—Flight will not profit you, were ye to flee from death or slaughter; and if ye did, ye would enjoy this life but for a little. Say,—Who is he that shall defend you from God, if He intend Evil for you, or if He intend Mercy for you: and they shall not find for themselves besides God any patron or any helper. Verily God knoweth those amongst you that turn (others) aside, and those that say to their brethren,— *Come hither to us;* and they go not to the battle excepting for a little. Covetous are they towards you. But when fear cometh, thou mayest see them looking towards thee, their eyes rolling about, like unto him that is overshadowed with death. Then, when the fear hath gone, they attack thee with sharp tongues, being covetous of the best part (of the booty). These do not believe; wherefore God hath made their works of no avail; and with God that is easy. They thought that the Confederates[1] would not depart. And if the Confederates should come (again), they would wish themselves amongst the Arabs of the desert, asking tidings of you. And if they were amongst you, they would not fight, excepting a little. Verily, ye have in the Apostle of God

[1] The Coreish and their allies.

an excellent example, to him that hopeth in the Lord and in the last Day, and remembereth God frequently. And when the Believers saw the Confederates, they said,—*This is what God and His Apostle promised us, and God and His Apostle have spoken the Truth.* And it only increased their faith and submission. Of those that believe, some men have fulfilled that which they covenanted with God; and some of them have finished their course, and some of them are waiting; and they have not changed their covenant in anywise. That God may reward those that fulfil (their covenant) on account of their fidelity; and may chastise the Disaffected, if He pleaseth, or may be turned unto them. Verily God is forgiving and merciful. And God drave back the Infidels in their wrath. They obtained no advantage. And God sufficeth for the Believers in battle. God is strong and mighty.

And He hath caused to descend from their strongholds the Jews who assisted them; and He struck terror into their hearts. A part ye slaughtered, and ye made captive a part. And He hath made you inherit their land, and their habitations, and their wealth, and a land which ye had not trodden upon; and God is over all things powerful.

In reviewing these transactions, it is evident that the position of Mahomet was now greatly improved in strength and influence. The whole weight of the Coreish and of the Ghatafânide tribes, with all their mighty preparations, had been successfully repelled, and that with hardly any loss. The entire defence of Medîna, by tacit consent, had been conducted by Mahomet as its Chief; notwithstanding the ill-concealed disaffection of some of the inhabitants, he was now the acknowledged Ruler, as well as Prophet, of the city. The negotiation with Oyeina was no doubt a proof of weakness at the moment, and distrust in his own cause; but, fortunately for him, it was hardly entered upon when, by the firmness of the two Sáds, it was broken off; and the episode was lost sight of afterwards in the signal success of the defence. We cannot, indeed, approve the employment of Nueim to break up the confederacy by falsehood and deception, but this perhaps would hardly affect his character in Arab estimation.

Mahomet's position greatly improved.

The sanguinary fate of the Coreitza removed the last remnant of open opposition, political or religious, from the immediate neighbourhood of Medîna; and though the deed

Effect of massacre of the Coreitza.

did not at the time escape criticism, yet it struck so great
a terror into the hearts of all, and the authority of the Prophet was already invested with so mysterious and supernatural a sanction, that no one dared openly impugn it: and,
moreover, the links which bound that ill-fated tribe to the
citizens of Medîna had already grown obsolete and feeble.

Bearing on Mahomet's character.

That the massacre was barbarous and inhuman requires
no comment to prove. The ostensible grounds upon which
Mahomet proceeded were purely political, for as yet he did
not profess to *force* men to join Islâm, or to punish them for
not embracing it.   It may be admitted that a sufficient
casus belli had arisen. The compact with the Coreitza was
indeed weak and precarious. Mahomet's policy towards the
Jews, from a period shortly after his arrival at Medîna, had
been harsh and oppressive; he had attacked and expatriated
two whole tribes on very doubtful grounds; he had caused
the assassination of several Jews in so perfidious a manner
as to create universal distrust and alarm; after the murder
of Káb and the incautious permission then given to slaughter
the Jews indiscriminately, he himself felt that the existing
treaty had been practically set aside, and, to restore confidence, he had entered into a new compact.[1]   All these circumstances must plead against the strength of obligation
which bound the Coreitza to his cause. They had, moreover,
stood by the second contract at a time when they might
fairly have set it aside and joined the Bani Nadhîr. That
they now hearkened to the overtures of the Coreish, though
proof of want of a singular prudence and foresight, was no
more than Mahomet might have expected, as the result of his
own hostile and treacherous conduct. Still the Coreitza had
joined his enemies at a critical period, and he had now a
good cause for warring against them. He had, furthermore,
fair grounds of political necessity for requiring them perhaps to quit altogether a vicinity where they must have
continued to form a dangerous nucleus of disaffection, and
possibly an encouragement for renewed attack. We might
even concede that the conduct of their leaders amounted to
treason against the city, and warranted a severe retribution.
But the indiscriminate slaughter of eight hundred men, and
the subjugation of the women and children of the whole

[1] See p. 258.

tribe to slavery, can be recognised by no civilised people otherwise than as an act of enormous cruelty. The plea of divine ratification or command may allay the scruples of the credulous Moslem; but it will be summarily rejected by others, who call to mind that the same authority was now habitually produced for personal ends, and for the justification even of unhallowed actions. However much Mahomet may have deluded himself into the belief that he had the divine sanction for that which he did, a candid and severe examination of his heart must have shown him that these so-called revelations were but the counterpart of his own will, that they followed the course of his own longings and desires, and that he was himself responsible for their shape and colour. The butchery of the Coreitza casts an indelible blot upon the character of Mahomet.

Before closing this chapter, I will follow to its end the career of Sád ibn Muâdz. After delivering himself of the bloody decree, he was conducted back upon his ass to Rufeida's tent. But the excitement was fatal to him; the wound burst forth anew. Mahomet hastened to the side of his bed: embracing him, he placed the dying man's head upon his knee and prayed thus: '*O Lord! Verily Sád hath laboured in thy service. He hath believed in thy Prophet, and hath fulfilled his covenant. Wherefore do thou, O Lord, receive his spirit with the best reception wherewith thou receivest a departing soul!*' Sád heard the words, and in faltering accents whispered: 'Peace be on thee, O Apostle of God!—Verily I testify that thou art the Prophet of the Lord.' When he had breathed his last, they carried home the corpse.[1] After the forenoon prayer, Mahomet pro-

Death-bed of Sád ibn Muâdz.

---

[1] The tale of Sád is surrounded with supernatural associations. For instance, when Mahomet went to be present at the washing of the body, he walked so rapidly that the people could scarcely keep up with him; 'you would have thought the thongs of their sandals would have broken, and their mantles fallen from their shoulders, they hurried so fast.' When they asked why he hastened so, he replied: 'Verily, I fear lest the Angels should reach his house before us, as they got before us unto Hantzala;'—alluding to the burial of the latter, and the supposed washing of his corpse by the angels. Then there are numerous legends about the angels crowding into the room where the corpse was laid out, and one of them spreading out his wing for Mahomet to sit upon. These traditions have grown out of the reply of Mahomet to the Disaffected, viz. that the bier was light, *because supported by a crowd of Angels.*

ceeded to join the burial. He reached the house as they were washing the body. The mother of Sád, weeping loudly, gave vent to her grief in plaintive Arab verse. They chided her for reciting poetry on such an occasion; but Mahomet interposed, saying: 'Leave her thus alone; all other poets lie but

His burial she.' The bier was then carried forth, and Mahomet helped to bear it for the first thirty or forty yards. Notwithstanding that Sád was so large and corpulent a man, the bier was reported to be marvellously light. The Disaffected said: 'We have never heard of a corpse lighter in the bier than that of Sád: know ye why this is? It is because of his judgment against the Bani Coreitza.'[1] Mahomet, hearing the rash remark, turned aside its point by a mysterious explanation, which was eagerly caught up by his followers: 'The angels are carrying the bier,' he said, 'therefore it is light in your hands. Verily the throne on high doth vibrate for Sád, and the portals of heaven are opened, and he is attended by seventy thousand angels that never trod the earth before.' The long procession, with Mahomet leading, wended its way slowly to the burial-ground of the Mussulmans. When they reached the spot, four men descended into the grave, and lowered the body into its place. Just then Mahomet changed colour, and his countenance betrayed strong emotion. But he immediately recovered himself, and gave praise to God. Then he three times uttered the *Takbîr*, 'Great is the Lord!' and the whole concourse, which filled the burial-ground to overflowing, took up the words, until the place re-echoed with the shout. Some of the people asked him concerning his change of colour, and he explained it to them thus: 'At that moment the grave had become strait for your comrade, and the sides

[1] The death of Sád followed so immediately on his sanguinary judgment, that the Disaffected could hardly avoid coupling the two together. To avert this inference, it is pretended in tradition that Sád had prayed thus: 'O Lord! If thou hast in store any further fighting with the Coreish, then preserve me to take part in it: but if thou hast put an end to their warring against thy Prophet, then take me unto thyself!' which when he prayed, he was to all appearance well, the wound presenting only a cicatrised ring. But shortly after he was carried to the tent, and died.

Although, in fact, it may be said with truth that there was hardly any more fighting with the Coreish after this date, yet the prayer is evidently an afterthought. It was at the time quite uncertain whether Medîna might not again be besieged by the Coreish, in proof of which see Sura xxxiii. 20.

thereof closed in upon him.   Verily, if any one could have
escaped the straitening of the tomb it had been Sád.   Then
the Lord gave him expansion therein.'   The mother of Sád
drew near, desiring to look into the grave, and they forbade
her.   But Mahomet said: 'Suffer her to look.'   So she
looked in, before the body was covered over.   As she gazed
on the remains of her son, she said: 'I commit thee unto the
Lord;' and Mahomet comforted her.   Then he went aside
and sat down near the grave, while they built it over with
bricks, and filled in the earth.   When the whole was levelled,
and the tomb sprinkled with water, the Prophet again drew
near, and, standing over the grave, prayed once more for the
departed chief.   Then he turned, and retired to his home.

SUPPLEMENT TO THE SEVENTEENTH AND
PRECEDING CHAPTERS.

SURAS REVEALED DURING THE FIRST FIVE YEARS OF MAHOMET'S
RESIDENCE AT MEDÎNA.

Review of
portions of
Corân re-
vealed at
Medîna.

WE have now reached a stage at which it may be useful once more to pause, to review the character of the Revelations of Mahomet during the early years of his sojourn at Medîna, and to consider the points in which they illustrate his life and the principles of Islâm.

Mahomet
at first en-
deavours to
prevail on
Jews to
bear evi-
dence in his
favour.

The people most prominently addressed in the earlier Medîna Suras are the Jews. Like the closing Suras at Mecca, these abound in Jewish fable and legend, based upon the Old Testament and upon rabbinical tradition. The marvellous interpositions of the Almighty in behalf of His people of old, are recounted with the avowed object of stirring up the Jews of Medîna to gratitude, and of inciting them to publish unreservedly the evidence which (as Mahomet still continued to assert) their Scriptures contained in substantiation of his claims. They were appealed to in language such as this :—

Sura ii.

Ye Children of Israel! Remember my favour wherewith I have favoured you, and have preferred you above all the world. And fear the day whereon no soul shall at all make satisfaction for another soul ; nor shall intercession be accepted therefrom : neither shall compensation be received from it,—and they shall not be helped. * * * O Children of Israel! Remember the favour wherewith I have favoured you. And fulfil my Covenant : so will I fulfil your Covenant. And let Me be your dread. And believe in that (Corân) which I reveal attesting the Revelation which is with you ; and be not the first unbelievers therein ; and sell not my signs for a small price : and let Me be your fear. And clothe not the Truth with falsehood ; neither conceal the Truth while ye know it. Set ye up prayer, and give alms ; and bow down with them that bow themselves down. What! will ye command men to do justice, and forget your own selves, while yet ye read the Scripture ? What! do ye not understand ?

On their
refusal he
changes

But, excepting a few, the Jews, as we have seen, refused to acknowledge the Arabian prophet. He had none of the signs of the Messiah, who was to come of the seed of Jacob and David, and not from amongst a strange people the progeny of Ishmael. They did not object to enter into a treaty with Mahomet of amity and good neighbourhood, but they scorned to bow to his spiritual pretensions. Their refusal was set down to envy and malice. The Jews (thus argued Mahomet) could not brook that the prophetic dignity should pass from themselves to another people; they well knew the prophecies regarding Islâm; but they stifled their convictions, suppressed the plain declarations of their Scriptures, and perverted their meaning by 'dislocating' the context, or by producing false glosses of the rabbins. Their hearts were hardened, and every avenue to conviction closed. It was in vain to seek for their conversion through the Corân, for they had already shown themselves proof against the Word of God as revealed in the Old Testament. They were following in the steps of their stiff-necked forefathers who slew the prophets, departed from the worship of the true God, and sought out inventions of their own creation. As an example:—

style of address to rebuke and reproach.

And verily We gave Moses the Scriptures, and We made Apostles to follow after him, and We gave JESUS son of Mary evident miracles, and We strengthened him with the Holy Spirit. Wherefore is it that so often as an Apostle cometh unto you with that which ye desire not, ye are puffed up; and some ye reject as liars, and some ye put to death? * * * And when a book (the Corân) cometh unto them from God, attesting that Scripture which is with them,—and truly they had aforetime been praying for assistance against the Unbelievers,—yet when there came unto them that which they recognised, they disbelieved the same. Wherefore the curse of God is on the Unbelievers. Evil is that for which they have sold themselves, to reject what God hath revealed, out of rebellion against God for sending down a portion of His favour upon such of His servants as He pleaseth. Wherefore they have incurred wrath upon wrath; and for the Unbelievers there is prepared an ignominious punishment.

Sura ii.

And when it is said unto them, *Believe in that which is sent down,* they say, *We believe in that which God hath sent down to us;* and they disbelieve in that which came after it, although it be the Truth attesting that Scripture which is with them. Say,—Why, therefore, have ye killed the Prophets of God aforetime, if ye are Believers?

And verily Moses came with evident Signs; then ye took the Calf thereupon, and became transgressors, &c.

This denunciation of the Jews' malice, unbelief, and perversion of the truth, naturally aroused their hatred. They no longer put any faith in the trite asseveration of Mahomet that he was a prophet come to 'attest their Scripture,' and re-establish the divine doctrines it contained. The hope, once fondly cherished, that, through the influence of their holy oracles which he thus professed to revere and follow, Mahomet would be guided towards

Jews thus stirred up to hatred of Mahomet.

the Truth, was now seen to be fallacious. Their political inferiority, indeed, compelled them to disguise their hatred; but their real feelings transpired in various ways, and among others in expressions of double meaning, which greatly displeased and affronted Mahomet:—

Sura iv Of the Jews there are that pervert words from their places, saying, *We have heard and disobeyed,* and *Hear without hearing,* and (RÂINÂ) *Look upon us,* twisting their tongues and reviling the Faith. But if they had said, *We have heard and obeyed,* and *Hearken,* and (ANTZORNÂ) *Look upon us,* it had been better for them; but God hath cursed them for their Unbelief; wherefore they shall not believe, excepting a few.

O ye to whom the Scripture hath been given, believe in what We have sent down, attesting that (Revelation) which is with you,—before We deface your countenances, turning the front backwards; or curse them as We cursed those that broke the Sabbath.

And two or three years later:—

Sura v. O ye that believe! Take not as your friends those who make a laughing-stock and a sport of your Religion, from amongst the people of the previous Scripture and the Infidels: and fear God, if ye be Believers. Say, —Ye people of the Book! Do ye keep aloof from us otherwise than because we believe in God, and in that which hath been sent down to us, and in that which hath been sent down before, and because the greater part of you are evil? Say,—Shall I announce unto you what is worse than that, as to the reward which is with God? He whom God hath cursed, and against whom He is wroth, and hath made of them Monkeys and Swine,[1] these, and the worshippers of Idols, are in an evil case. * * * Thou shalt see multitudes of them running greedily after wickedness and injustice, and eating what is forbidden. Alas for that which they work! Wherefore do their Rabbins and their Priests restrain them not from uttering wickedness, and eating that which is forbidden? Alas for that which they commit! The Jews say, *The hand of God is tied up.* Their own hands are tied up, and they are cursed for what they say. Nay, but His hands are both stretched out. He bestoweth as He pleaseth. That which hath been revealed to thee from thy Lord, shall increase rebellion and impiety in many of them. We have cast among them enmity and hatred, until the day of Judgment. So often as they shall kindle the fire of war, God shall extinguish the same; and they shall set themselves to do wickedness in the Earth. And God loveth not the wicked doers.

Jews accused of encouraging idolatry at Mecca. *Sura iv.* In one passage the Jews are even accused of encouraging the Coreish to continue in idolatry by representing that it was preferable to the doctrine of Mahomet:—

Hast thou not seen those to whom a portion of the Scripture hath been given? They believe in false gods and idols. They say to the Unbelievers, —These are better directed in the right way than those that believe.

---

[1] Alluding to the legendary punishment inflicted on the Israelites who broke the Sabbath day.

These are they whom God hath cursed; and for him that God curseth, thou shalt find no helper. Shall *they*, indeed, have any portion in the Kingdom, since, if they had, they would not part unto men with the least iota thereof? Do they envy men that which God hath given them of His bounty? And verily We gave unto the house of Abraham the Scripture, and Wisdom; and We gave them a great Kingdom. And there is of them that believeth in him: and there is that turneth aside from him. But the raging fire of hell will suffice for such. Verily, they that reject our Signs, We will surely cast them into the fire. So often as their skins are burned, We will change for them other skins, that they may fully taste the torment. For God is mighty and wise. They that believe and do good works, We shall introduce them into gardens with rivers running beneath them; they shall abide therein for ever. And there shall they have pure Wives: and We shall lead them into grateful shades.

Eventually, as we have seen, Mahomet did not confine his communications with the Jewish tribes of Medîna to simple threats of the divine wrath. He himself inflicted condign punishment upon them, till by exile and slaughter they were all removed from the scene. Such was the spirit of Islâm. Judaism would not yield to its pretensions. And Mahomet, notwithstanding his liberal professions of respect for other creeds, the still reiterated assurance that 'he was only a public preacher,' and his express guarantee that 'there should be no constraint in Religion,' could not brook the profession of any tenets whatever that were opposed to his claims. The first step had now been taken for sweeping away from the Peninsula every creed but that of the Corân. *Removal of Jews from the scene.*

The disappearance of the Jews is followed by a corresponding change in the material of the Corân. The Revelations of Mahomet formed in no respect an abstract and systematic compilation. The Corân is purely concrete in its origin and progress. It grew up and formed itself, with all the peculiarities of the religious system and social code of Islâm, out of the circumstances and sentiments of the day. Hence, the necessity for referring to Jewish Scripture and history having passed away with the disappearance of the Jews themselves, we have no longer in the later Suras those constant allusions to the Old Testament and repetition of biblical stories and legends which are so prominent a feature in the middle stage of the Corân. The few notices which hereafter occur bear as much upon the Christian as upon the Jewish record. Both are still spoken of, though with extreme infrequency, yet with veneration and respect. And, as I have already stated, there is nowhere to be found throughout the Corân any imputation against the authority or genuineness of either. The occasion for their mention having now died away, they pass into oblivion. *Followed by discontinuance in Corân of Jewish legends and reference to Scriptures. But Scriptures still referred to with reverence.*

I have drawn attention to the Corân as a medium for the

Corân
depository
of orders
and com-
ments
in all de-
partments
of the theo-
cratic go-
vernment.

publication of 'general orders' on victory or defeat, in rebuke of backwardness or cowardice, in applause of constancy and courage. But it was not merely in respect of military affairs, as the reader will have observed, that the Revelation contains comments and commands. Scattered throughout its Suras, we have, to some extent, the archives of a theocratic government in all its depart-ments. The conduct of the Disaffected, the treatment of allies, the formation of treaties, the acceptance of terms, and other poli-tical matters, not infrequently found a place among the divine messages. Liberality in contributing towards the expenses of war —the only object as yet requiring a public purse—is continually inculcated. The elements of a code both civil and criminal are also introduced. Punishments for certain offences are specified, and a mass of legislation laid down for the tutelage of orphans, for marriage, divorce, sales, bargains, wills, evidence, usury, and other similar concerns. Further, there are copious instructions for the guidance of the Believer in his private life; and special provisions, some of which I have quoted at length, regulating the intercourse of Mahomet with his people, and with his own family. These all partake of the essential character of the Corân, being in the form of a revelation direct from heaven; and they ordinarily end with some such trite expression as, 'God is knowing and wise'—'God is forgiving and merciful'—'Evil is the fate of the Transgressors,' &c., thus completing the rhythm, and investing the record with an inspired and oracular character. Throughout this, which may be styled the *administrative*, portion of the Corân are interspersed as heretofore passages inculcating piety and virtue, denouncing infidelity and vice, and containing directions for social duties and religious ceremonies. In the exhortations and denunciations, the main change is that at first the Jews, and sub-sequently the Disaffected, now usurp almost entirely the place before occupied by the Idolaters of Mecca.

Though
simple in
habits,
Mahomet
assumed
regal power
and dignity.

The advancing power and dignity of Mahomet may be traced in the reverence and submission exacted by command of the Corân from all his followers. A kingly court was not in ac-cordance with the customs of the people, nor with the tastes and habits of Mahomet himself. The artless life and simple dress and surroundings of an Arab chieftain were not departed from at Medîna; and it is this which, in vivid contrast with the state and luxury of the Caliphs his successors, induced tradition to cast around the Prophet's life an air of hardship and privation.[1] The

[1] The following traditions will illustrate the supposed hardships. Mahomet on a certain occasion having hurt his hand, his attendants carried him into his house, and placed him on a bed plaited with ropes of palm-fibre,

delusion is manifest; for Mahomet and his Companions enjoyed all that the resources of the land and the plunder of their enemies could yield; and if they maintained plain and frugal habits, it was not from necessity, but because magnificence and pomp were foreign and distasteful to their habits. A row of modest houses, built of sun-dried brick, and covered in with rough palm-branches, the inner walls hung about with bags of ill-tanned leather for domestic use, formed a habitation for the Prophet and his wives far more desirable than the most splendid seraglio 'ceiled with cedar and painted with vermilion.' A mattress of date-fibre covered with leather was a luxury to the Arab incomparably greater than a stately 'bed of the wood of Lebanon, decked with tapestry.' The trappings of a royal camp would have ill comported with the grave simplicity of Mahomet, while an ordinary tent of leather afforded him ample accommodation; and his bag, containing an ivory comb, a tooth-pick, oil for his hair, and antimony for his eyes, supplied all the comforts within the compass of an Arab's imagination. The luxurious

and put under his head a pillow of leather stuffed with the same material. Omar, seeing the marks of the corded bedding on his side, wept aloud. On Mahomet asking why he wept, he replied: 'Verily, I called to mind how the Chosroes and the Kaiser (the Emperors of the East and of the West) sit upon thrones of gold, and wear garments of silk and brocade; and thou art in this sad condition!' 'What, Omar!' said the Prophet, 'art thou not content that *thou* shouldest have the portion of Futurity, and *they* the portion of this Life?' On another occasion, Mahomet having risen from sleep with the marks of the matting on his side, Abdallah, his attendant, rubbed the place, and said: 'Let me, I pray thee, spread a soft covering for thee over this mat.' 'Not so,' replied Mahomet. 'What have I to do with the comforts of this life? The world and I, what connection is there between us? Verily, the world is no otherwise than as a tree unto me; when the traveller hath rested under its shade, he passeth on.'

Notwithstanding incidents like these, exaggerated by strong contrast with the subsequent luxury of the Moslems, it is evident that Mahomet had everything in abundance which he really desired, and which wealth or authority could procure. He sometimes gave a large price for his clothes: once he exchanged nineteen (others say seventeen) camels for a single dress, and he bought a mantle for eight golden dinars. He had a collyrium-box, from which at bedtime he used to apply antimony to his eyelids, saying that it made the sight more piercing, and caused the hair to grow. The Governor of Egypt sent him a crystal goblet; and either this, or another jug from which he drank, was set in silver. He had also a copper vase, which he used in bathing. He was very fond of perfumes, and indulged, as Ayesha tells us, in 'men's scents,' *i.e.* in musk and ambergris; he used also to burn camphor on odoriferous wood, and enjoy the fragrant smell. Anis, his servant, says: 'We always used to know when Mahomet had issued forth from his chamber by the odoriferous perfume that filled the air.'

These, and such like, were perhaps the only luxuries which Mahomet, from his previous habits, was able to appreciate.

and pampered courtiers of Baghdad and Damascus wondered at the tales of their Prophet having mended his sandals, and of their first Caliph having tended his own flock of goats, not reflecting that a more artificial state would have been at variance with everything around, and that the habits of three-score years had become a second life.

Honour and reverence paid to Mahomet. His prerogatives.

Nevertheless, in whatever constitutes real dignity and power, —that which satisfies the cravings of pride and ambition,— Mahomet was not behind the most absolute Dictator, or the most pompous Sovereign. To him every difference or dispute must be referred, and his word was law. On his appearance the assembly rose, and gave place to him and his chief Companions; the people were required to approach him reverently, to speak softly in his presence, and not to crowd around, or throng him. They were not to visit his house unasked; and even when invited they must not linger long, or indulge familiarly in discourse with him. 'The calling of the Apostle was not to be esteemed as the calling of one Believer to the other;' it was to be implicitly and promptly obeyed. Those in attendance upon him were not to leave without permission first received. His wives were withdrawn from the vulgar gaze; none might communicate directly or familiarly with them, excepting their near relatives and domestic servants. The Prophet was the favourite of Heaven; the true Believer but followed the example of the heavenly hosts and of God himself when he invoked blessings upon Mahomet :—

Sura xxxiii.

Verily, God and His angels invoke blessings upon the Prophet. O ye that believe ! do ye also invoke blessings upon him, and salute him with a (reverential) salutation. Verily, they that trouble God and His Apostle, God hath cursed them in this world, and in that which is to come: He hath prepared for them an ignominious punishment.

Conceit of being favourite of heaven, key to special prerogatives.

This vain conceit, that he was *the Favourite of Heaven*, once admitted into his heart, may peradventure be the key to those strange Revelations which secured for the Prophet peculiar privileges, especially in his conjugal relations. In the self-complacency of these fatal and impious pretensions, he brought himself to believe that no immunity or indulgence could be withheld from him; but that every wish and desire of his heart would be gratified, and that even by the direct interposition of the Almighty !

But no supernatural character asserted.

Still, no supernatural character was claimed by Mahomet. He did not differ in the nature of his office from the former Prophets. Like other men he was mortal; and equally with them needed to pray to God for the pardon of his sins.

Irreverent manner in which

I have before observed that Mahomet did not contemplate the consecration of any day, like the Sabbath, to religious Worship.

On Friday, the day appointed for general public prayer, business and merchandise might be transacted as much as on any other day. The weekly service, indeed, appears at first to have been treated with little respect. On a certain Friday, while Mahomet discoursed from the Pulpit to a crowded assembly in the Mosque, the sound of drums announced the arrival of a Syrian caravan, upon which the greater part of his audience hurried forth to meet it, and left Mahomet standing in the Pulpit nearly alone :— *weekly service at first observed.*

O ye that believe! When the call to Prayer is raised on the day of Assembly, then hasten to the commemoration of God, and leave off trafficking—that will be better for you, if ye knew it. *Sura lxii.*

And when the Prayers are ended, then disperse over the land, and seek (gain) from the favour of God, and make frequent mention of God, that ye may prosper.

When they see Merchandising or Sport, they break away, flocking thereto, and leave thee standing; say, That which is with God is better than Sport or Merchandise; and God is the best Supporter.'

In another passage we find Mahomet forbidding his followers to be present at prayer in a state of drunkenness: ' O ye that believe; draw not nigh unto Prayers, while ye are drunken, until ye can understand that which ye say.' This injunction, being connected with another of a general nature, may be viewed as additional evidence of the lax manner in which the devotions of the Moslems were at first performed, as well as of the prevalence of intemperance. In a previous passage the use of Wine had been discouraged, though not prohibited, on the ground that it was productive of greater injury than good :— *Drunkenness common, till wine was forbidden.*

They will ask thee concerning Wine, and Casting of lots. Say,—In both there is great evil, and (also) advantages, to Mankind; but the evil of them is greater than the advantages of them. *Sura ii.*

But Mahomet at last perceived that the sanctions of his Religion were too weak to enforce a middle course, and that the imposition of entire abstinence was the only means by which he could check intemperance. The command against the use of wine was issued in the Fourth year of the Hegira, during the siege (it is said) of the Bani Nadhîr :—

O ye that believe! Verily Wine, and the Casting of lots, and Images, and Divining-arrows, are an abomination from amongst the works of Satan: Shun them, therefore, that ye may prosper. *Sura v.*

Verily, Satan seeketh that he may cast amongst you enmity and hatred through Wine and Games of chance, and hinder you from the remembrance of God and from Prayer. Will ye not, then, refrain? Obey God, and obey the Apostle; and beware! For if ye turn back,—Verily, our Apostle's duty is but to deliver his Message publicly.

Influence of Judaism still maintained in moulding institutions.

The influence of the Jewish law and ritual may still be traced in moulding the institutions of Mahomet. Usury is absolutely forbidden. The criminal code follows largely the Law of retaliation. Ceremonial purification before prayer is strictly enjoined, and in the absence of water sand may be used as a substitute. An oath something resembling the curse of jealousy is permitted to a wife suspected by her husband of infidelity. And generally in the relations established between the Sexes, a considerable degree of similarity may be traced to the injunctions of the Pentateuch.

Coarseness of instructions regarding marriage and divorce.

As in all other matters, so in those referring to Marriage and Divorce, instead of laying down general principles, and leaving their application to each man's conscience and sense of propriety, Mahomet ventured upon particular and detailed instruction. Apart altogether from the tenor of these precepts, the coarse language in which they are expressed, and the indelicacy of the ideas conveyed, are a serious reproach to the Corân. Making every reasonable allowance for the rudeness of speech and sentiment current in Arabia, much remains that must be set down to the pruriency of Mahomet's own mind, much that is offensive to purity of thought, and which has no doubt freely contributed toward laxity of morals in the Mahometan world.

Corruption engendered thereby in Moslem literature.

Further than this, the legislation of the Corân on these subjects has given birth to endless volumes, by Jurists and Theologians, of interpretation, illustration, construction, corollary, supplement,—a mass of corruption poisoning the mind and morals of the Mahometan student. To define the line between the forbidden and the lawful, ingenuity and labour have been expended lavishly in describing and solving cases the very mention of which is repugnant to modesty, in drawing elaborate distinctions and in demonstrating points of casuistry within a domain of thought which cannot even be approached without moral injury and contamination. The Arabic language, as moulded by the system which grew out of the precepts of Islâm, is itself evidence of this defilement.[1] For these evils the Corân is responsible; and, if there were no other indictment against

[1] This will be painfully evident from a cursory glance into any Arabic dictionary. The fault is not in the language, but in the uses to which it has been turned by a licentious people, driven by the Corân to distinguish in repulsive detail the licit from the illicit; and it can hardly be the duty of a Lexicographer to perpetuate impurities of the kind. As to the 'Hadees,' I altogether fail to understand how any translator can justify himself in rendering into English much that is contained in the Sections on marriage, divorce, and female slavery.

its author, that alone would go far towards a verdict of condemnation.

I have before adverted to the laxity of morals and manners encouraged by the precepts of the Corân on the relations between the Sexes. The number of lawful wives is restricted to four; but any one of these may at any moment be divorced at the caprice and by the simple word of the husband, and another substituted in her stead. As to the number of female slaves with whom (irrespective of his four wives) a Moslem may, without any antecedent ceremony or any guarantee of continuance, cohabit, there is no limit. Female slavery, being a condition necessary to the legality of this coveted indulgence, will never be put down, with a willing or hearty co-operation, by any Mussulman community.[1]

Four wives allowed, and any number of slaves.

It has often been asserted that the institutions of Mahomet have tended to elevate and improve the state of Woman. Yet, excepting in so far as she necessarily shares in the general elevation and improvement introduced by a purer religion, and more spiritual worship,[2] it is to me very doubtful whether, in married life, her position has not been rendered by Islâm more dependent and degrading than before. I do not speak of unmarried and widowed females; for, if we put aside the depressing influence which the constraint and thraldom of the married state has exercised upon *the sex at large*, the unmarried free woman has nothing to complain of. And, in one particular, viz., the inheritance by the son of his father's wives, she was delivered by Mahomet from a gross and intolerable abuse. No free woman can be forced, under the code of Islâm, to marry against her will; and, so long as single, she is mistress of her actions.

Unmarried women, how affected by his system.

But in respect of the married state (which in the East

---

[1] On the laxity of morals in connection with female slavery, I will quote again from the Mahometan Princess who lately visited Mecca. Speaking of the great numbers of African and Georgian slaves, the ruling Begum of Bhopâl wrote: 'Some of the women are taken in marriage, and after that on being sold again they receive from their masters a divorce, and are sold in their houses; that is to say, they are sent to the purchaser from their master's house on receipt of payment, and are not exposed for sale in the Dakkah (slave market); they are only *married* when purchased for the first time. * * * When the poorer people buy slaves, they keep them for themselves, and change them every year as one would replace old things by new.' (*Pilgrimage to Mecca.* Translated by Mrs. W. Osborne, 1870.) Such, according to a shrewd observer, are the results of female slavery in the holiest city of Islâm.

[2] The notion that the female sex is overlooked in the rewards of the future life arose, apparently, from their not having been provided with indulgences similar to those promised to the other sex. Not only is the idea of their exclusion from Paradise at variance with the whole tenor of the Corân, but it is contradicted by express passages.

Married women and female slaves occupy inferior and debased position.

embraces practically the whole sex during the greater part of their lives), the condition fixed by Mahomet for woman is that of a dependent inferior creature, destined only for the service of her lord, liable to be cast off without the assignment of any reason and without the notice of a single hour. While the husband possesses the power of divorce, absolute, immediate, unquestioned, no privilege of a corresponding nature has been reserved for the Wife.[1] She hangs on, however unwilling, neglected, or superseded, the perpetual slave of her lord,—if such be his will. When actually divorced, she can, indeed, claim her dower,—her *hire*, as it is called, in the too plain language of the Corân; but the knowledge that a wife can make this claim is at the best a miserable security against capricious taste; and in the case of female slaves, even that imperfect check is wanting. The power of divorce is not the only power that may be arbitrarily exercised by the tyrannical husband : authority to confine and to beat his wives is distinctly vested in his discretion.

Sura iv.

'Men stand above Women, because of the superiority which God hath conferred on one of them over the other, and because of that which they expend of their wealth. Wherefore let the good Women be obedient, preserving their purity in secret, in that wherein God preserveth them. But such as ye may fear disobedience (or provocation) from, rebuke them, and put them away in separate apartments, and chastise (or beat) them. But, if they be obedient unto you, seek not against them an excuse (for severity) ; verily God is lofty and great.' The 'exchanging of one wife for another'—that is, the divorcing of one in order to marry another—is recognised in the Corân, with only this caution, that the dower stipulated at marriage be given in full to her that is put away.[2] Thus restrained, secluded, degraded, the mere minister of enjoyment, liable at the caprice or passion of the moment to be turned adrift, it would be hard to say that the position of a wife was improved by the code of Mahomet. I do not hesitate to decide that she was possessed of more freedom, and exercised a greater, a healthier, and

Position of married women impaired by Islâm.

[1] The Corân has not contemplated anywhere the contingency of divorce being claimed by the wife. The idea of any independent rights of the kind was entirely foreign to Mahomet's notions of the position of the sex. The Mahometan doctors have, indeed, determined that under a few rare contingencies divorce may be demanded; but they are so exceptional as hardly to deserve notice.

[2] 'And if ye be desirous to exchange (*or substitute*) one wife in place of another wife, and ye have given one of them a talent, then take not away anything therefrom. What! will ye take it away falsely, and commit an open sin? And how can ye take it away, seeing that one of you hath gone in unto the other, and they have received from you a firm covenant ?'—*Sura* iv.

more legitimate influence, under the pre-existing institutions of Arabia.[1]

As regards female slaves under the thraldom of Mahometan masters, it is difficult to conceive more signal degradation of the human species. They are treated as an inferior class of beings. Equally restricted as under the marriage contract, they are expressly excluded from any title to conjugal rights.[2] The female slave is at the absolute disposal of her master, to be toyed and sported with purely at his pleasure. The only redeeming feature is that when once a slave has borne a child to her master, she cannot be sold, and at his death obtains her freedom.[3] The children of slave-girls are also as legitimate as those of married wives.

Wretched condition of female slaves.

In the rules regarding Divorce, there is one which (much as I might desire) cannot be passed over in silence. A husband may twice divorce his wife, and each time receive her back again. But when the words of separation have been thrice repeated, the divorce is irreversible. However unjust or injurious the action, how much soever the result of passion or of caprice, however it may affect the interests not only of an innocent wife, but also of her innocent children, however desirous the husband may be of undoing the wrong,—the decision cannot be recalled; the divorced wife can return to her husband but on one condition, and that is that she shall first be married to another, and after cohabitation be again divorced.[4] The tone of Mahometan

Divorce thrice repeated irrevocable. Revolting condition on which alone original marriage can be reverted to.

[1] It would be a gratuitous dishonour to Christian marriage to compare it with marriage under the Corân. Excepting where (from custom, or chance, and in spite of the Corân and the example of Mahomet) a husband may confine himself *for life* to one wife, there is little common to the two institutions. The idea of conjugal *unity* is utterly unknown to Mahometans, excepting when the Christian example happens to be followed; and even there, the continuance of the bond is purely dependent on the will of the husband. The wives have a *separate interest*, not only each in regard to her sister-wives, but even in regard to her husband; so much so, that, on the death of a son, the father and mother receive separate shares from the inheritance. In this respect I believe the *morale* of Hindoo society, in which polygamy is far less encouraged, and divorce practically unknown, to be sounder, in a very marked degree, than that of Mahometan society.

[2] The subject is not one which I can explain or illustrate further without offence to decency. The reader must believe at second hand that the whole system is vile and revolting.

[3] This is not provided for in the Corân, but rests on the precedent of Mahomet, who freed his own slave-girl Mary, on her bearing a son to him. Such a slave is called *Omm al Walad*, or 'Mother of the child.'

[4] 'And if he (a third time) divorce her, she shall not be lawful unto him after that, until she shall have married a husband other than he; and if the latter divorce her, then there shall be no sin in the two that they again return

manners may be imagined from the functions of the *temporary* husband hired to legalise re-marriage with a thrice-divorced wife, having passed into a proverb.[1] Such flagrant breach of decency, such cruel violation of the modesty of an unoffending wife, may be an abuse the full extent of which was not at the time contemplated by Mahomet; but it is not the less an abuse for which, as a direct result of the unnatural and revolting provision framed by him, Mahomet is justly responsible.[2]

The fierce and warlike spirit of the Suras of this period has

to each other, if they think that they can observe the limits appointed by God. These are the ordinances of God, which He manifesteth to people that understand.'—*Sura* ii.

[1] '*A thousand lovers, rather than one Mostahil;* many lovers or gallants cause less shame to a woman than one Mostahil (*i.e.* husband procured for the occasion). According to the Moslem law, a person who has (thrice) divorced his wife cannot re-marry her until she has been married to some other man, who becomes her legitimate husband, cohabits with her for one night, and divorces her next morning; after which the first husband may again possess her as his wife. Such cases are of frequent occurrence—as men in the haste of anger often divorce their wives by the simple expression (*I divorce thee*), which (thrice repeated) cannot be retracted. In order to re-gain his wife a man hires (at no inconsiderable rate) some peasant, whom he chooses from the ugliest that can be found in the streets. A temporary husband of this kind is called Mostahil, and is generally most disgusting to the wife,' &c. (Burckhardt's *Arabic Proverbs*, p. 21.) Tradition and law books abound with fetid commentaries illustrative of this subject, and with checks against the intermediate marriage and cohabitation being merely nominal.

Some commentators hold the practice as described by Burckhardt to be illegal; whether legal or not, I gladly believe that it is far from being so frequent as he represents it. But its existence is undoubted; and it has existed, in a more or less revolting form, ever since the verse which I have quoted was revealed. A case is mentioned by tradition in which Mahomet himself insisted on the fulfilment of the condition of cohabitation with another husband, before the original union could be returned to, in language which it is probable that prurient tradition has fabricated for him.

It must not be forgotten that all the immorality of speech and action connected with this shameful institution, and the outrage done to female virtue (not necessarily for any fault of the wretched wife, but the passion and thoughtlessness of the husband himself), is chargeable solely and exclusively to the verse of the Corân quoted above. It is a sorry excuse that Mahomet wished thereby to check inconsiderate divorce: a good object is not to be sought for through such abominable means.

[2] The severe epithets in the text are justified by the 24th chapter of Numbers, at the beginning of which the case above supposed is described exactly, and the following judgment given: 'Her former husband, which sent her away, may not take her again to be his wife after that she is defiled; *for that is an abomination before the Lord;* and thou shalt not cause the land to sin, which the Lord thy God giveth thee for an inheritance.'

Warlike spirit of Corân.

been perhaps sufficiently illustrated in the preceding chapters. I may here just refer to one passage which appears to me peculiarly demonstrative of the eager desire after plunder which Mahomet had stirred up, and which (so natural was it to the Arab) he soon found it difficult to restrain within expedient bounds. Only those, according to Mahomet's own principles, could be lawfully slain and plundered, who were *disbelievers* in his mission ; but so insatiable had the thirst for spoil become, that cases now occurred of Moslems slaying persons, even after they had made profession of the Mahometan faith, on the pretext that they were insincere believers. Stringent prohibition was required to guard against this abuse. Whoever trifled with the life of one professing Islâm, did so at the peril of his soul. After prescribing the penalty or penance for killing a Moslem unintentionally, the ordinance proceeds :—

Sura iv.

But whosoever killeth a Believer wilfully, his reward shall be Hell,— for ever therein. God shall be wroth with him, and shall curse him : He hath prepared for him a great punishment. O ye that believe! When ye go forth (fighting) in the way of God, rightly discriminate, and say not to him that saluteth you,' *Thou art not a Believer*,—seeking the transitory things of this present life,—whilst with God there is great spoil. And such were ye yourselves aforetime, but God had favour towards you. Wherefore carefully discriminate, for God is attentive to that which ye do.

References to Coreish and to idolatry.

Though Mecca with its Idolaters has now faded in the distance, and the Coreish are referred to chiefly for their hostile inroads only, yet we still find occasional passages, after the old Meccan style, in reprobation of Idolatry, and menace of the city 'which had cast its Prophet out.' Polytheism and Idolatry are denounced as the only unpardonable sins. The tone of defiance becomes bolder and at times even exulting. Mahomet and his people are 'to fight till opposition shall cease, and the Religion becometh God's alone.' Until this glorious consummation is secured, 'they are not to faint, neither invite to peace.' A complete and speedy victory is promised. God is the stronger, and will prevail : Islâm shall shortly be established triumphantly.

Waverers threatened.

Such as withdraw from Mecca, and rally around the standard of Mahomet while the struggle is yet undecided, shall have a merit superior far to the merit of those who may join it after opposition shall have been beaten down. The waverers, who, though persuaded of the truth of the new Faith, cannot make up their minds to abandon Mecca, are told that their excuse of

---

¹ *i.e.* with the salutation peculiar to Islâm (*salâm alei kûm*), which was held equivalent to professing oneself a Moslem.

inability will not be accepted of God,—'their habitation shall be Hell,—an evil journey is it thither!' But a word of comfort is added for those who though believers were amongst 'the weak,' and were withheld by real helplessness from leaving Mecca. The rescue of such from their unhappy position is adduced as a powerful motive why their more fortunate brethren at Medîna should fight bravely in the cause :—

Weak believers at Mecca comforted.

Sura iv.

Fight in the way of God, ye that sell the present Life for that which is to come. Whosoever fighteth in the way of God, whether he be slain or be victorious, We shall surely give him a great Reward.

And what aileth you that ye fight not in the way of God, and for the Weak amongst the men and women and children, who say, 'O Lord! Deliver us out of this City, whose people are oppressors ; and grant us from thyself a Protector, and grant us from thyself a Defender.'

Style tame, but with occasional touches of poetic fire.

From the numerous examples I have given (so numerous, I fear, as to have been irksome to the reader) it will be evident that the style of the Corân, though varying greatly in force and vigour, has for the most part lost altogether the marks of vivid imagination and poetic fire which characterise the earlier Suras. It becomes tame and ordinary both in thought and language. Occasionally, indeed, we still find traces of the former spirit. Here for instance the Deity is described in a passage of which the followers of Mahomet are justly proud :—

Sura ii.

God! There is no God but He : the Living, the Eternal. Slumber doth not overtake Him, neither Sleep. To Him belongeth all that is in the Heavens and in the Earth. Who is he that shall intercede before Him, excepting by His permission? He knoweth that which is before them, and that which is behind them, and they shall not comprehend anything of His knowledge, saving in so far as He pleaseth. His throne stretcheth over Heaven and Earth, and the protection of them both is no burden unto Him. He is the Lofty and the Great.

In the following extract, the verses in which Infidelity is compared to a tempestuous Sea, of which the crested waves below mingle with the lowering clouds above,—a scene of impenetrable darkness and despair,—are to my apprehension amongst the grandest and most powerful in the whole Corân. The Sura belongs to the Fifth year of the Hegira; but part of it is in the best style of the Meccan period.

Sura xxiv.

God is the Light of the Heavens and the Earth. The likeness of His light is as the niche wherein is a Lamp (enclosed) in glass ;—the glass is a refulgent Star. It is lighted from a blessed tree,—an Olive neither of the East nor of the West. Its Oil is near unto giving light, even if the fire did not touch it,—light upon light. God directeth unto His light whom He pleaseth.

[Here intervenes a description of the worship, and good works, of believers].

And those that disbelieve,—their works are as the *Serâb* in the plain; the thirsty man thinketh it to be water, until, when he cometh thereto, he doth not find it anything.—But he findeth God to be about him, and He will fulfil unto him his account.   God is swift in taking account :—

Or as the Darkness in a bottomless Sea :—Wave covereth it from above, wave upon wave.   Above them are Clouds; darkness of one kind over another kind.   When one stretcheth forth his hand, he hardly seeth it.   And to whomsoever God doth not grant light, he shall have no light.

What! seest thou not that unto God giveth praise everything that is in the Heavens and in the Earth, and the Birds in a well-ordered line,— truly every one knoweth his prayer and his hymn of praise; and God knoweth whatsoever ye do.   .   .   .

Seest thou not that God driveth the clouds along, then gathereth them together, then setteth them in layers; and thou seest the rain issuing forth from between them.   And He sendeth down from the heavens (as it were) mountains wherein is hail; and He striketh therewith whom He pleaseth, and averteth the same from whom He pleaseth.   The brightness of His lightning well-nigh taketh the sight away.

God converteth the Night and the Day; verily herein is a Monition unto those that are endowed with sight.   And God hath created every beast out of water.   Of them there is that goeth upon his belly; and of them there is that goeth upon two legs; and of them there is that goeth upon four.   God createth that which He pleaseth.   Verily God is over all things powerful.

CHAPTER XVIII.

SIXTH YEAR OF THE HEGIRA.

A.D. 627, 628.

Ætat. 59.

Numerous minor expeditions in Sixth year of the Hegira.

THE Sixth year of the Hegira was one of considerable activity at Medîna. No important battle indeed was fought, nor any grand expedition undertaken. But small parties were almost incessantly in motion, either for the chastisement of hostile tribes, for the capture of caravans, or for the repulse of robbers and marauders. We read of as many as sixteen or seventeen such expeditions during the year. They generally resulted in the dispersion of the enemy and the capture of flocks and herds, which greatly enriched the followers of Mahomet, and stimulated their zeal for active service. They also maintained and increased the name and terror of the new potentate. But few of them were otherwise attended with marked results; and it will not therefore be necessary to give a narrative of them all.[1]

Expedition by Mahomet against Bani Lahyân. A.H. VI. June, A.D. 627.

Two of the expeditions were led by Mahomet himself. One was against the Bani Lahyân, whom he had long been desirous of chastising for their treacherous attack, two years before, on the little band of his followers at Rajî. In the early part of the year he set out with a selected body of two hundred men on camels, and twenty horse. That he might the more surely fall upon his enemy unawares, he first took

---

[1] Weil regards the comparative insignificance of these expeditions, and especially the smallness of Mahomet's following on the pilgrimage to Hodeibia, as a proof how low his authority had sunk. I see no grounds for this conclusion. There was no object on these occasions for any great exertion or any extensive following. The authority of Mahomet, which had been materially increased by his successful resistance to the grand confederation at the siege of Medîna, was steadily advancing.

the road N.W. towards Syria. After two or three marches
in that direction, he suddenly turned south, and travelled
rapidly along the seashore by the road to Mecca. But the
stratagem was of no avail, for the Bani Lahyân had notice of
his approach, and, taking their cattle with them, retired to
heights where they were safe from attack. At the spot
where his followers had been slaughtered, he halted, and invoked pardon and mercy on them. Small parties were then,
for one or two days, sent to scour the vicinity, but no traces
of the tribe were anywhere to be found. Mahomet, being now
within two marches of Mecca, advanced to Osfân with the
view of alarming the Coreish. From thence he sent Abu
Bakr with ten horsemen, as it were his vanguard, to approach
still nearer. Satisfied with this demonstration, the force retraced its steps to Medîna. On his way back from this
unsuccessful journey, Mahomet, who had been greatly incommoded by the heat, is said to have prayed thus: ‘ *Returning
and repentant, yet if it please the Lord, praising His name
and serving Him, I seek refuge in God from the troubles
of the way, the vexation of return, and the evil eye which
affecteth family and wealth.*’

Not many days after his return, Medîna was early one
morning startled by a cry of alarm from the adjoining
height of Sila. Oyeina, chief of the Bani Fezâra, came down
during the night, with a troop of forty horse, upon the plain
of Al Ghâba, within a few miles of Medîna, fell upon the
milch camels of Mahomet which were grazing there, and
drove off the whole herd, killing the keeper, and carrying
away his wife a prisoner. A citizen, early on his way to the
pasture lands, saw the marauding band and gave the alarm.
The call to arms was ordered by Mahomet. A troop of horse
was immediately at the gate of the Mosque.[1] A flag having

Pursuit of
Oyeina,
who had
fallen upon
Mahomet's
camels near
Medina.
A.H. VI.
July, A.D.
627.

---

[1] Micdâd was the first to come up to the Mosque on Mahomet's call;
and, Mahomet having mounted a flag on his spear, some say that he was the
leader of the whole expedition, while that honour belonged in reality to Sâd
ibn Zeid. There is a curious anecdote on this point, which shows that Hassân's poetry sometimes *originated* errors in tradition. In his piece on this
expedition, the poet speaks of *the horsemen of Micdâd*, as if he had been the
leader. On hearing the poetry recited, Sâd repaired in great wrath to Hassân,
and required amends for the misrepresentation. The poet quietly replied that
his name did not suit the rhythm so well as Micdâd's. And yet, says Wâckidi,
the verses remained in circulation and gave rise to the erroneous tradition that
Micdâd was leader.

been mounted for them, they were despatched at once in pursuit, and Mahomet himself, with five or six hundred men, followed shortly after. Sád ibn Obâda, with three hundred followers, remained behind, to guard the city. The advanced party hung daringly upon the rear of the marauders, slew several of them, and recovered half of the plundered camels. On the side of the Mussulmans only one man was killed. Mahomet, with the main body, marched onwards as far as Dzu Carad, in the direction of Kheibar; but by this time the robbers were safe in the desert among the Bani Ghatafân. The captive female effected her escape on one of the plundered camels, which she vowed if she reached Medîna in safety to offer up as a sacrifice of thanksgiving. On acquainting Mahomet with her vow, he rallied her on the ingratitude of seeking to slay the animal which had saved her life, and which moreover was not hers to offer up. He bade her go to her home in peace. The army having left without provisions, Sád ibn Obâda despatched from Medîna a convoy of camels laden with dates for their consumption; the camels too were slaughtered by Mahomet, one for every hundred men. Finding that hostile tribes were gathering in dangerous numbers, the force returned, having been five days absent from Medîna.

Affair at Dzul Cassa: party of Moslems cut up. A.H. VI. August, A.D. 627.

Scarcity still prevailed in Nejd, and, rain having fallen plentifully towards Medîna, the Ghatafân tribes were tempted, in their search for pasture, to advance beyond their usual limits. The herds of camels belonging to the Moslems, greatly increased by the plunder of late years, had been sent out to graze in the same direction. They offered a tempting prize for a foray, and the neighbouring tribes were suspected to be gathering for the purpose. Mohammad ibn Maslama was deputed with ten followers to visit the locality and ascertain how matters stood. At Dzul Cassa, a place two or three days' distance from Medina,[1] he was surrounded in the night-time by overpowering numbers. After a short resistance, all his men were slain, and he himself, severely wounded, left on the field as dead. An adherent of Mahomet, happening to pass that way, assisted him on his journey back to Medîna. Immediately a body of forty well-mounted soldiers

[1] Twenty-four Arabian miles from Medîna, on the road to Rabadza.

was despatched to chastise the offenders; but these had dispersed among the neighbouring heights, and, excepting the plunder of some flocks and household stuff, no reprisals were effected.

During the autumn of this year, a force of one hundred and seventy men was despatched toward Al îs, to intercept, on its return, a rich caravan, which the Coreish had ventured rashly to despatch by the route of the sea-shore to Syria. The attack was completely successful. The whole caravan, including a large store of silver belonging to Safwân, was plundered, and some of those who guarded it taken prisoners.

A Meccan caravan plundered at Al îs. A. H. VI. September, A.D. 627.

Among the prisoners was Abul Aás, son-in-law of Mahomet. His romantic story deserves recital, as well for its own interest, as for the share which the Prophet himself bore therein. The reader will remember that Mahomet, at Khadîja's desire, had married his daughter Zeinab to her nephew Abul Aás, a prosperous trader in Mecca. On the assumption of the prophetic office by his father-in-law, Abul Aás declined to embrace Islâm. But he listened with equal unwillingness to the Coreish who bade him abandon Zeinab, and offered him the choice of their own daughters in her stead: 'I will not separate from my wife,' he said,—'neither do I desire any other woman from amongst your daughters.' Mahomet was much pleased at the faithfulness of Abul Aás to his daughter. The attachment was mutual, for when Mahomet and the rest of his family emigrated to Medîna, Zeinab remained behind at Mecca with her husband.

Abul Aás, and Zeinab Mahomet's daughter.

In the battle of Bedr, Abul Aás was taken captive. When the Coreish deputed men to ransom their prisoners, Zeinab sent by their hands such property as she had for her husband's freedom. Among other things was a necklace, which Khadîja had given her on her marriage. When the Prophet saw this touching memorial of his former wife, he was greatly overcome and said to the people: 'If it seem right in your eyes, let my daughter's husband go free, and send back these things unto her.' All agreed; and, as the sole condition of his freedom, Mahomet required of Abul Aás that he should send Zeinab to Medîna. Accordingly, on his return to Mecca, Abul Aás, having made arrangements for his wife's departure, sent her away mounted on a camel-litter, under the charge of his brother Kinâna. Cer-

Abul Aás, when taken prisoner at Bedr, freed on condition of sending Zeinab to Medina.

tain of the baser sort from amongst the Coreish, hearing of her departure, went in pursuit, determined to bring her back. The first that appeared was Habbâr, who struck the camel with his spear, and so affrighted Zeinab as to cause her a miscarriage. Kinâna at once made the camel sit down and, by the mere sight of his bow and well-filled quiver, kept the pursuers at bay. Just then Abu Sofiân came up and held a parley with Kinâna: 'Ye should not,' he said, ' have gone forth thus publicly, knowing the disaster we have so lately sustained at the hands of Mahomet. The open departure of his daughter would be accounted a proof of our weakness and humiliation. But it is no object of ours to keep back this woman from her father, or to retaliate our wrongs on her. Return, therefore, for a little while to Mecca, and when this excitement shall have died away, then set out secretly.' They followed his advice, and some days after, Zeinab, escorted by Zeid son of Hârith, who had been sent to fetch her, reached Mahomet in safety.

Abul Aás, taken prisoner at Al îs, is converted. A.H. VI.
It was between three and four years after this that Abul Aás was again made prisoner at Al îs. As the party approached Medîna, he contrived by night to have an interview with Zeinab, who granted the protection which he sought. He then rejoined the other prisoners. In the morning, the people being assembled for prayers in the Mosque, Zeinab called aloud from her apartment that she had given to Abul Aás her guarantee of protection. When the prayers were ended, Mahomet thus addressed the assembly: 'Ye have heard, as I have, the voice of my daughter. I swear by Him in whose hands is my life, that I knew nothing of her guarantee until this moment. But the pledge even of the least of my followers must be respected.' Thus saying, he retired to his daughter, and desired her to treat Abul Aás with honour, as a guest, but not to recognise him as her husband. Then he sent for the captors of the caravan, and, reminding them of his close connection with Abul Aás, said: 'If ye treat him well, and return his property unto him, it would be pleasing to me; but if not, the booty is yours which the Lord hath given into your hands, and it is your right to keep the same.' They all with one consent agreed to let the prisoner go free, and to return the whole of his property. This generosity, and the continued attach-

ment of Zeinab, so wrought upon Abul Aás, that, when he had adjusted his affairs at Mecca, he made profession of Islâm and joined his wife at Medîna.   Their domestic happiness, thus renewed, was not of long continuance; for Zeinab died the following year from disease, said to have originated in the miscarriage caused by the attack of Habbâr at Mecca.[1]

The treatment of his daughter on that occasion, and especially the unmanly and barbarous conduct of Habbâr, greatly incensed Mahomet.   Once, when a party was setting out on an expedition towards Mecca, he commanded that if Habbâr, and another who had joined him in the pursuit of Zeinab, fell into their hands, they should both be burned alive.   But during the night he reconsidered the order, and sent to countermand it in these words: ' It is not fitting for any to punish by fire but God only; wherefore if ye find the culprits, ye shall put them to death in the ordinary way.'[2]

Mahomet commands that the pursuers of his daughter be put to death, if caught.

The following incidents are connected with the first communication held by Mahomet with the Roman Empire.   Dihya, one of his followers, was sent on a mission to the Emperor, or perhaps to one of the Governors of Syria.   He was graciously received, and presented with a dress of honour.   On his way home, he was plundered of everything at a place beyond Wâdi al Corâ, by the Bani Judzâm.   A neighbouring tribe, however, which was under treaty with Mahomet and to which Dihya at once complained, attacked the robbers, recovered the spoil, and restored it to him uninjured.   On the robbery reaching the ears of Mahomet, he despatched Zeid (now a favourite commander) with five hundred men, to chastise the delinquents.   Marching by night, and concealing themselves by day, they fell unexpectedly on the Bani Judzâm, killed several of them, including their leader, and carried off a hundred of their women and children, with a great collection of herds and flocks.   Un-

Bani Judzâm chastised for robbing Dihya, sent by Mahomet on an embassy to Syria. A.H. VI. October, A.D. 627.

---

[1] They had two children, a son who died in infancy, and a daughter whom Ali married after the death of Fâtima.

[2] It is satisfactory to find that at Mecca, the cruelty of Habbâr was scouted as unmanly.   Even Hind, wife of Abu Sofiân, gave vent to her indignation; meeting the party as it returned, she extemporised some severe verses against them: ' Ah! in time of peace ye are very brave and fierce against the weak and unprotected, but in battle ye are like women with gentle speeches,' &c.

fortunately, the branch thus punished had previously tendered its submission to Mahomet; its chief therefore hastened to Medîna and appealed against these proceedings. He produced the letter of terms which Mahomet had made with his people, and demanded justice. 'But,' said Mahomet, 'how can I compensate thee for those that have been slain?' 'Release to us the living,' was the chief's reply; 'as for the dead, they are beneath our feet.' Mahomet acknowledged the justice of the demand, and despatched Ali to order restoration. He met Zeid returning to Medîna, and the prisoners and booty were immediately surrendered to the chief.

Second expedition to Dûma. A.H. V. November, 627.

Soon after, Abd al Rahmân set out with seven hundred men, on a second expedition to Dûmat al Jandal. Mahomet bound a black turban, in token of command, about his head. He was to endeavour first to gain over the people of Dûma, and to fight only in the last resort:—'but in no case,' continued the Prophet, 'shalt thou use deceit or perfidy, nor shalt thou kill any child.' On reaching Dûma, he summoned the tribes to embrace Islâm, and allowed them three days' grace. Within that period, Asbagh, a Christian chief of the Bani Kalb, gave in his adhesion, and many followed his example. Others preferred to be tributaries, with the condition of being allowed to retain the profession of Christianity. Abd al Rahmân communicated these tidings by a messenger to Mahomet, who, in reply, desired him to marry Tamâdhir, daughter of the chief. Abd al Rahmân accordingly brought this lady with him to Medîna, where she bore him Abu Salma (the famous jurisconsult of after days) and amid many rivals, maintained her position as one of his wives, till her husband's death.[1]

Bani Fezâra chastised for waylaying Medîna caravan. A.H. VI. December, A.D. 627.

After several warlike raids of inferior importance, Zeid set out upon a mercantile expedition to Syria, carrying with him ventures for barter from many of the citizens. The caravan was waylaid near Wâdi al Corâ, seven marches from Medîna, and maltreated and plundered by the Bani Fezâra. This occasioned much exasperation at Medîna. When Zeid was sufficiently recovered from the injuries

[1] For some account of Abd al Rahmân's conjugal relations, see *ante*, p. 171. Besides slave-girls, he *had issue by sixteen wives*, and may have married many others who bore him no children. As he could have no more than *four* wives at a time, the frequent changes and divorces may be imagined.

inflicted by the robbers, he was sent forth with a strong
force to execute vengeance upon them. He approached
stealthily, and, effecting a complete surprise, captured the
marauders' stronghold. Omm Kirfa, aunt of Oyeina, a lady
who had gained celebrity as the mistress of this nest of
robbers, was taken prisoner with her daughter. Neither the
sex, nor the great age of Omm Kirfa, saved her from a death
of extreme barbarity. Her legs were tied each to a separate
camel. The camels were driven in different directions, and
thus she was torn in sunder. Two young brothers of the
same family were also put to death. Zeid, on his return,
hastened to visit Mahomet, who, eager to learn the intelligence, hurried forth to meet him with his dress ungirded;
and, learning the success of the expedition, embraced and
kissed him. We read of no disapprobation expressed by
the Prophet at the inhuman treatment of Omm Kirfa, and
are therefore warranted in holding him accessory to the fero-
cious act. The daughter was given as a slave to Mahomet,
who presented her to one of his followers.

His old enemies, the Jews, were still the cause of annoyance to Mahomet. A party of the Bani Nadhîr, with their
chief, Abul Huckeick, after being expelled from Medîna, had
settled among their brethren at Kheibar. Abul Huckeick
(called also Abu Râfi) had taken a prominent part among the
confederates who besieged Medîna, and he was now suspected
of inciting the Bani Fezâra and other Bedouin tribes in their
depredations. An expedition was undertaken by Ali, with
one hundred men, against a combination of the Bani Sád ibn
Bakr with the Jews of Kheibar; but besides a rich booty of
camels and flocks, it produced no other result. As a surer
means of putting a stop to these machinations Mahomet
resolved on ridding himself of their supposed author, the
Jewish chief. The Bani Khazraj, emulous of the distinction
which the Bani Aus gained some years before by the assassination of Káb, had long declared themselves ready to
perform like service. Mahomet therefore chose five men
from amongst that tribe, and gave them command to
make away with Abul Huckeick. On approaching Kheibar, they concealed themselves till nightfall, when they
repaired to the house of their victim. The leader of the
party, who was familiar with the Bani Nadhîr, and spoke

their language fluently, addressed the wife of the chief who came at his summons to the door, and thus gained admittance on a false pretext. When she perceived that the men were armed, she screamed aloud; but they pointed their weapons at her, and forced her to be silent, at the peril of her life. Then they rushed into the inner chamber, and despatched Abul Huckeick with their swords. They hastily withdrew, and hid themselves in some adjacent caves till the pursuit was over. Then they returned to Medîna. When Mahomet saw them approaching, he exclaimed: ' Success attend you!' ' And thee, O Prophet!' they replied. They recounted to him all that had happened; and, as each one claimed the honour of the deed, Mahomet examined their weapons, and, from the marks on the sword of Abdallah ibn Oneis, assigned to him the merit of the fatal blow.[1]

Oseir and party of Jews slain. A.H. VI. January, A.D. 628.

The assassination of Abul Huckeick did not relieve Mahomet of his apprehensions from the Jews of Kheibar; for Oseir, elected chief in his room, maintained the same relations with the Bani Ghatafân, and was reported to be designing fresh movements against Medîna. Mahomet deputed Abdallah ibn Rawâha, a leader of the Bani Khazraj, to Kheibar, with three followers, to make enquiries as to how Oseir also might be taken unawares. But Abdallah found the Jews too much on the alert to admit of a second successful attempt. On his return, therefore, a new stratagem was devised. Abdallah was sent openly with thirty men mounted on camels, to persuade Oseir to visit Medîna. They assured him that Mahomet would make him ruler over Kheibar, and would treat him with great distinction; and they gave him a solemn guarantee of safety. Oseir consented, and set out with thirty followers, each Moslem taking one of the Jewish party behind him on his camel. The unfortunate chief was mounted on the camel of Abdallah, who relates that, after they had travelled some distance, he perceived Oseir stretching forth his hand towards his sword. Urging forward his camel till he was well beyond the rest of the party, Abdallah called out: ' Enemy of the Lord! Treachery! Twice hath he done this thing.' As he spoke, he leaped from the camel, and aimed a deadly blow at Oseir, which took

---

[1] It is the same Abdallah ibn Oneis who had assassinated Sofiân, chief of the Bani Lahyân. See *ante*, p. 285.

effect on the hip joint. The chief fell mortally wounded from the camel; but in his descent he succeeded in wounding Abdallah's head with the camel staff, the only weapon within his reach. At this signal, each of the Mussulmans turned upon the man behind him, and the Jews were all murdered, excepting one who eluded pursuit. The party continued their journey to Medîna, and reported the tragedy to Mahomet, who gave thanks and said: ' Verily, the Lord hath delivered you from an unrighteous people.'

The reader will not fail to remark that we have the evidence only of the practised assassin, Abdallah ibn Oneis, for the treachery of Oseir. This man knew that Abdallah ibn Rawâha had already been despatched on a secret errand with the view of getting rid of the Jewish Chief; and, from his previous history, it is too evident that he scrupled little as to the means employed for taking the life of any one proscribed by the Prophet. Abdallah alleges that Oseir suddenly repented of his determination to go to Medîna, and meditated treachery. On which side the treachery lay may be gathered from the result. Oseir was unarmed, and so apparently were all his followers: for excepting the wound inflicted with the camel-staff upon Abdallah, no injury was sustained by any of the Moslems. The probabilities are entirely opposed to the charge of Abdallah; and even supposing the suspicions against Oseir well founded, they will hardly be viewed as a sufficient justification of the cold-blooded massacre of his unoffending companions.

A treacherous proceeding.

A party of eight Bedouin Arabs had some time previously come to Medîna and embraced Islâm. The damp of the climate disagreed with them, and they pined away from disease of the spleen. Mahomet bade them, for a cure, to join themselves to one of his herds of milch camels which grazed in the plain south of Coba, under the hill of Ayr, and drink of their milk. Following his advice they soon recovered; but with returning strength, there revived also the innate love of plunder. They drove off the camels, and attempted to escape with them. The herdsman, joined by a few others, pursued the plunderers, but was repulsed and barbarously handled; for they cut off his hands and legs, and stuck thorny spikes into his tongue and eyes,

Certain robbers executed barbarously, for plunder and murder.

till he died. When tidings of this outrage reached Mahomet, he despatched twenty horsemen in pursuit.[1] They surrounded and seized the robbers, and recovered all the camels but one, which had been slaughtered and eaten. The captives were conducted to Mahomet, who was justly exasperated at their ingratitude and savage treatment of his servant. They had merited death; but the mode in which he inflicted it was barbarous and inhuman. The arms and legs of the eight men were cut off, and their eyes put out. The shapeless sightless trunks of these wretched Bedouins were then impaled upon the plain of Al Ghâba, until life was extinct.

On reflection, Mahomet appears to have felt that this punishment exceeded the bounds of humanity. He accordingly promulgated a Revelation, in which capital sentence is limited to simple death or crucifixion. Amputation of the hands and feet is, however, sanctioned as a penal measure; and amputation of the hands is even enjoined as the proper penalty for theft, whether the criminal be male or female. This barbarous custom has accordingly been perpetuated throughout the Mahometan world. But putting out of the eyes is not recognised among the legal punishments. The following is the passage referred to:—

Mutilation recognised as a legal punishment.

Sura v.

Verily the recompense of those that fight against God and his Prophet, and haste to commit wickedness in the land, is that they shall be slain or crucified; or that their hands and feet of the opposite sides be cut off; or that they be banished from the land. That shall be their punishment in this life, and in the life to come they shall have great torment. * * *

As regards the robber, and the female robber, cut off the hands of both.[2]

Attempt, under orders of Mahomet, to assassinate Abu Sofiân.

The Secretary of Wâckidi assigns to this period an attempt made, under the orders of Mahomet, to assassinate Abu Sofiân. As its cause, he states that a Bedouin Arab had been sent by Abu Sofiân to Medîna, on a similar errand against Mahomet; but that the emissary was discovered, and

---

[1] They were commanded by Kurz ibn Jâbir, whom we have seen *ante*, p. 215, as engaged in one of the first raids against Medîna. At what period he was converted and came to Medîna is not mentioned.

[2] For repeated robberies, a second, third, and fourth hand and foot may be cut off, rendering the criminal a helpless shapeless cripple.

confessed the object of his mission. According to Hishâmi (who makes no mention of this latter circumstance) the attempted assassination was ordered by Mahomet in the *Fourth* year of the Hegira, in immediate revenge for the execution of the two captives taken at Rajî. Whatever the inciting cause, there is no reasonable doubt that a commission was given by the Prophet to Amr ibn Omeya, a practised assassin,[1] to proceed to Mecca, and murder his opponent Abu Sofiân. Amr was recognised, as he lurked near the Káaba before he could carry his design into effect, and he was obliged to flee for his life. True, however, to his profession, he claims the credit of having assassinated three of the Coreish by the way, and a fourth he brought prisoner to Medîna.

During this year and the following, Mahomet made an important advance in gaining over some of the Bedouin tribes in the direction of Mecca. These did not, indeed, as yet make profession of Islâm, but they entered into friendly relations; and Mahomet could now count on the assistance, or at least the neutrality, of all the tribes between Mecca and Medîna.

Some Bedouin tribes gained over.

About this time, ten men of the Bani Abs, a small but warlike tribe in Nejd, joined the faith and settled at Medîna. They distinguished themselves in battle under the title of 'the ten,' and Mahomet gave them a banner, which in the Syrian conquests became famous as the Absite ensign.

'The ten' of the Bani Abs.

Thus steadily did the influence of Mahomet, partly through religious motives, and partly from motives of rapine and conquest, extend and become consolidated.

---

[1] He is the same who, escaping from the massacre at Bîr Maûna, assassinated the two travellers for whom Mahomet paid compensation (p. 289). He is stated by the Secretary to have been before Islâm a '*professional* assassin;' so that the people of Mecca, recognising him, immediately understood what his errand was.

CHAPTER XIX.

PILGRIMAGE TO AL HODEIBIA.

Dzul Cáda, A.H. VI.—*March,* A.D. 628.

Mahomet
and his
followers
anxious to
perform
pilgrimage
to Mecca.

SIX years had now passed away since Mahomet, and those who emigrated with him, had seen their native city; had worshipped at the Holy house, and the sacred places around it; or had joined in the yearly pilgrimage, which from childhood they had grown up to regard as an essential part of their social and religious life. They longed to revisit these scenes, and once more to unite in the solemn rites of the Káaba.

Political
considera-
tions added
force to the
desire.

No one shared in these feelings more earnestly than Mahomet. It was, moreover, of great importance to his cause that he should show practically his attachment to the ancient faith of Mecca. He had, indeed, in the Corân, insisted upon that faith as an indispensable element of the new religion; he had upbraided the Coreish for obstructing the approach of pious worshippers to the Temple of God; and had denounced them, because of their idolatrous practices, as not its rightful guardians. Thus he had threatened the citizens of Mecca :—

Sura viii.

And what have they to urge that God should not chastise them, seeing that they have hindered His servants from the sacred Temple; and they are not the Guardians thereof,—verily, none are its Guardians but the pious. But the greater part of them do not consider. And their prayers at the Temple are nought but whistling through the fingers, and clapping of the hands. Taste, therefore, the punishment of your unbelief.

Yet something more than this was needed to exhibit his

attachment to the ancestral creed and observances of the Coreish. If he made no effort to visit the holy places, and fulfil the sacred rites, he would lay himself justly open to the charge of lukewarmness and neglect. His precept must be supported by example.

Meditating thus, Mahomet had a vision in the night. Followed by his people, he dreamed that he entered Mecca in peaceful security, and that having made the circuit of the Káaba, and slain the victims, he completed all the ceremonies of the pilgrimage. The dream was communicated to his followers, and every one longed for its realisation. It foretold nothing of fighting or contest; the entrance was to be quiet and unopposed. Now the sacred month of Dzul Cáda was at hand, in which the *Omra*, or Lesser pilgrimage, might with much propriety and merit be performed. There would be less chance of collision with hostile tribes, than at the Greater pilgrimage in the succeeding month. Furthermore, in the month of Dzul Cáda, war was unlawful throughout Arabia, much more within the inviolate precincts of Mecca. If Mahomet and his followers, therefore, should at this time approach the Káaba in the peaceful garb of pilgrims, the Coreish would be bound by every pledge of national faith to leave them unmolested. On the other hand, should their advance be opposed, the opprobrium would rest with the Coreish; and even in that case, the strength of the pilgrim band would secure its safety—if not a decisive victory.

Inducements for making Lesser pilgrimage in Dzul Cáda, A.D. VI.

So soon as this course was resolved upon, the people of Medîna were invited to join the Prophet in the Lesser pilgrimage, and all made haste to prepare themselves. To swell the camp and render it more imposing, the Arab tribes around, who had entered into friendly relations with Mahomet, were also summoned. But few of them responded to the call; there was little inducement on the score of booty, and the most part alleged that their occupations and families prevented them from leaving home.[1]

Surrounding tribes invited to join, but most of them decline.

Early in the month of Dzul Cáda, in the Sixth year of the Hegira, arrangements for the pilgrimage being completed, Mahomet entered his house, bathed himself, and put

Mahomet and his followers set out from Medina.

---

[1] A few of the Bani Aslam joined, and they are consequently reckoned among the 'Refugees.'

on the two pieces of cloth which constitute the pilgrim garb. He then mounted his camel, Al Caswa, and led the cavalcade, numbering about fifteen hundred men, across the valley Al Ackîck, to Dzul Huleifa, the first stage on the road to Mecca. There they halted, and Mahomet with the rest entered the pilgrim state by repeatedly uttering the cry, *Labbeik! Labbeik!* which signifies, 'Here am I, O Lord!' 'I am entering, Lord, upon thy service!' The victims were then consecrated for sacrifice; their heads having been turned towards Mecca, the customary ornaments were hung about their necks, and a mark affixed upon their right sides. Seventy camels were thus devoted; amongst them was the famous camel of Abu Jahl, taken on the field of Bedr. This done, the pilgrims moved forward by the ordinary stages. A troop of twenty horse marched in advance to give notice of danger. The pilgrims carried no arms but such as were allowed by custom to the traveller, namely, each a sheathed sword, with perhaps a bow and quiver filled with arrows. The Prophet took one of his wives, Omm Salma, with him.

Tidings of Mahomet's approach soon reached Mecca; and, notwithstanding the pious object and unwarlike attitude of the pilgrims, filled the Coreish with apprehension. They did not credit their peaceful professions; and, perhaps not without reason, suspected treachery. The citizens of Mecca, with their allies from the surrounding tribes, were soon under arms, and occupied a position on the Medina road, resolved to perish rather than allow Mahomet to enter. A body of two hundred horsemen, under Khâlid and Ikrima son of Abu Jahl, was pushed forward in advance.

Mahomet had nearly reached Osfân, the second stage from Mecca, when a spy returned with this intelligence: 'The Coreish,' he said, 'are encamped at Dzu Towa, clothed in panthers' skins;[1] their wives and little ones are with them; and they have sworn to die rather than let thee pass.' Shortly after, the Meccan cavalry came in sight, and Mahomet's horse went forward to hold them in check. Further advance on the high road was now impossible without a battle, and for this Mahomet was not yet prepared. Having

---

[1] Expressive symbolically of the fixed resolution of the Coreish to fight to the last, like beasts of prey.

therefore halted and procured a guide, he turned off in the evening towards the right by a route safe from the enemy's horse, and, after a fatiguing march through rugged and difficult defiles, reached the open space called Hodeibia, on the verge of the sacred territory which encircles Mecca. Here his camel stopped, and, planting her fore legs firmly on the ground, refused to advance another step. 'She is wearied,' said the people, as they urged her forward. 'Nay,' exclaimed Mahomet, 'Al Caswa is not weary; but the same hand restraineth her that aforetime held back the Elephant,'—alluding to the preservation of Mecca from the invasion of Abraha. 'By the Lord!' he continued, 'no request of the Coreish this day, which they shall make for the honour of the Holy place, shall be denied by me.' So he alighted, and all the people with him, at Hodeibia. Some wells were on the spot, but, having been choked by sand, there was little or no water in them. Mahomet, accordingly, taking an arrow from his quiver (the only implement at hand), desired one of his followers to descend a well, and with it dig and scrape away the obstructing sand. Abundance of water soon accumulated.[1]

The road from Hodeibia led by a circuitous route to Lower Mecca.[2] The Coreish no sooner learned that the pilgrims had taken this direction, than they fell back on the city for its defence, and began sending deputations to ascertain the real intentions of Mahomet. Hodeibia being only a short stage distant, the communications were rapid and frequent. Bodeil, a chief of the Bani Khozâa, with a party of his tribe, was the first to approach. He acquainted Mahomet with the excited state of the Coreish, and their resolve to defend the city to the last extremity. The Prophet replied, that it was not for war he had come forth: 'I have no other design,' he said, 'but to perform the pilgrimage of the Holy house: and whosoever hindereth us therefrom, we

Negotiations between Coreish and Mahomet.

---

[1] This has been magnified into a miracle. As soon as the arrow was *planted* in the hitherto empty well, the fountain gushed up, so rapidly that the people sitting on the brink could draw water at ease. By another account, Mahomet spat into the well, on which a spring immediately bubbled up. According to a third tradition, he thrust his hand into a vessel, on which the water poured forth as it were from between his fingers, and all drank therefrom: 'The stream would have sufficed for a hundred thousand people.'

[2] It probably joined the Jedda road, some little distance from Mecca.

shall fight against them.' The report of Bodeil to the
Coreish was favourable. Orwa, a chief from Tâyif, and son-
in-law of Abu Sofiân, was the next ambassador. He came,
saying 'that the people of Mecca were desperate. They will
not suffer this rabble of thine to approach the city; I swear
that even now I see thee as it were, by the morrow, deserted by
them all.' At this Abu Bakr started up and warmly resented
the imputation. Orwa, not heeding him, became still more
earnest in his speech, and (according to the familiar Bedouin
custom) stretched forth his hand to take hold of Mahomet's
beard. 'Back!' cried a bystander, striking his arm. 'Hold
off thy hands from the Prophet of God!' 'And who is this?'
said Orwa, surprised at the interposition of a red-haired
ungainly youth. 'It is thy brother's son, Moghîra.' 'O
ungrateful!' he exclaimed (alluding to his having paid compensation for certain murders committed by his nephew), 'it
is but as yesterday that I redeemed thy life.' These and other
circumstances which transpired at the interview, struck Orwa
with a deep sense of the reverence and devotion of the Moslems towards their Prophet; and this he endeavoured to
impress upon the Coreish, when he carried back to them a
message similar to that of Bodeil. But the Coreish were firm.
Whatever his intentions, Mahomet should not approach the
city with the show of force, and thus humble them in the
eyes of all Arabia. 'Tell him,' they said, 'that this year he
must go back; but in the year following, he may enter
Mecca and perform the pilgrimage.' One of their messengers
was the chief of the Bedouin tribes that dwelt around Mecca.
The goodly row of victims, with their sacrificial ornaments,
and the marks upon their necks of having been many days
tied up for this pious object, at once convinced him of the
sincerity of Mahomet's peaceful professions. But the Coreish,
on his return, refused to listen to him. 'Thou art a simple
Arab of the desert,' they said, 'and knowest not the devices
of other men.' The Bedouin chief was enraged at this
slight, and swore that if they continued to oppose the advance
of Mahomet to the Káaba, he would retire with all his
Arabs. The threat alarmed the Coreish. 'Have patience
for a little while,' they said, 'until we can make such terms
as are needful for our security.' Negotiations were then
opened in greater earnest.

The first messenger sent from the Moslem camp to Mecca, the Coreish had seized and treated roughly; they maimed the Prophet's camel which he rode, and even threatened his life. But the feeling was now more pacific, and Mahomet desired Omar to proceed to Mecca as his ambassador. Omar excused himself on account of the personal enmity of the Coreish; he had, moreover, no influential relatives in the city who could shield him from danger; and he pointed to Othmân, who belonged to one of the most powerful families in Mecca, as a fitter envoy. Othmân consented, and was at once despatched. On entering the city, he received the protection of a cousin, and went straightway to Abu Sofiân and the other chiefs of the Coreish. 'We come,' said Othmân, 'to visit the Holy house, to honour it, and to perform worship there. We have brought victims with us, and after slaying them we shall then depart in peace.' They replied that Othmân, if he chose, might visit the Káaba and worship there; but as for Mahomet, they had sworn that this year he should not enter the precincts of their city. Othmân declined the offer, and retired carrying their message to the camp.

Deputation of Othmân to Coreish.

During the absence of Othmân, there was great excitement at Hodeibia. Some considerable delay having occurred in his return, a report, meanwhile, gained currency that he had been murdered at Mecca. Anxiety and alarm overspread the camp. Mahomet himself began to suspect treachery: he summoned the whole body of the pilgrims around him, and, taking his stand under the thick shade of an Acacia, required a pledge from all of faithful service to the death. When they had taken the solemn oath, striking one by one their hand upon the hand of Mahomet, the Prophet struck his own left hand upon his right as a pledge that he would stand by his absent son-in-law. While war and revenge thus breathed throughout the pilgrim camp, their fears were suddenly relieved by the reappearance of Othmân. But 'the pledge of the Tree' is a scene to which Mahomet, and all who were then present, ever after loved to revert; for here the strong feelings of devotion and sympathy between the Prophet and his followers had found fitting and ardent expression. Their martial spirit and religious fervour had

The Pledge of the Tree, on report of Othmân's murder.

been excited to the highest pitch; and they were prepared to rush upon the enemy with a resistless onset. It was one of those romantic occasions so congenial to an Arab's spirit, and which survives ever in his memory.

Treaty
between
Mahomet
and Co-
reish.

After some further interchange of messages, the Coreish deputed one of their chiefs, Soheil ibn Amr, and other representatives, with full power to conclude a treaty of peace. The conference was long, and the discussion, especially on the part of Omar, warm. But at last the terms were settled. A ten years' truce secured, on the one hand, the safety of the Syrian caravans; while, on the other, it gave free liberty to converts passing over to the Moslem side. Mahomet summoned Ali to write from his dictation. And thus he began :—

'IN THE NAME OF GOD, MOST GRACIOUS AND MERCIFUL!' —'Stop!' said Soheil. 'As for God, we know Him; but this new title of the Deity, we know it not. Say, as we have always said, *In thy name, O God!*' Mahomet yielded. 'Write,' he said—

'IN THY NAME, O GOD! *These are the conditions of peace between Mahomet the Prophet of God and*'—'Stop again!' interposed Soheil. 'If I acknowledged thee to be the Prophet of God, I had not taken up arms against thee. Write, as the custom is, thine own name and the name of thy father.' 'Write, then,' continued Mahomet, calmly, —'*between Mahomet son of Abdallah, and Soheil son of Amr.* War shall be suspended for ten years. Neither side shall attack the other. Perfect amity shall prevail betwixt us. Whosoever wisheth to join Mahomet, and enter into treaty with him, shall have liberty to do so; and whosoever wisheth to join the Coreish, and enter into treaty with them, shall have liberty so to do. If any one goeth over to Mahomet without the permission of his guardian, he shall be sent back to his guardian. If any one from amongst the followers of Mahomet return to the Coreish, the same shall not be sent back. Provided (on the part of the Coreish) that Mahomet and his followers shall retire from us this year without entering our city. In the coming year, he may visit Mecca, he and his followers, for three days, when we shall retire therefrom. But they may not enter it with any weapons, save those of the traveller, namely, to each a sheathed sword. *The witnesses hereof are Abu Bakr,*' &c.[1]

A copy of this important document, duly attested, was made over to Soheil and his comrades, who, taking it, departed. The original was kept by Mahomet himself.

Deputies of Coreish depart.

Though unable to enter Mecca, Mahomet resolved to complete such ceremonies of the pilgrimage as the nature of the spot admitted. So he sacrificed the victims, and concluded the solemnities by shaving his head. The rest of the pilgrims having followed his example,[2] the whole assembly broke up, and, after a stay at Hodeibia of ten or fifteen days, began their march homewards.

Mahomet and his followers sacrifice their victims.

The people, led by the Vision to anticipate an unopposed visit to the Káaba, were disappointed at this imperfect fulfilment of the Pilgrimage, and crestfallen at the abortive result of their long journey. But, in truth, a great step had been gained by Mahomet. His political status, as an equal and independent Power, was acknowledged by the treaty: the ten years' truce would afford opportunity and time for the new Religion to expand, and to force its claims upon the conviction of the Coreish; while conquest, political and spiritual, might be pursued unshackled in other directions. The stipulation that no one under the protection of a guardian should leave the Coreish without his guardian's consent, though unpopular at Medîna, was in accordance with the settled principles of Arabian society; and the Prophet had sufficient confidence in the loyalty of his people and the superior attractions of his cause, to fear no ill effect from the counter clause that none should be delivered up who might desert his own standard. Above all, the great and patent success in the negotiation was the free permission accorded

Although people disappointed, treaty gave Mahomet great advantages.

[1] Here follow eight other names, viz.—Omar, Abd al Rahmân, Sád ibn Abi Wackkâs, Othmân, Abu Obeida, Muhammad ibn Maslama, Huweitib ibn Abd al Ozza, and Mukriz ibn Hafaz (the last two belonged to the Coreishite party), and below the signatures followed these words: 'The upper part of this was written by Ali' (meaning probably the text of the treaty above the signatures).

[2] Some *cut* their hair instead of shaving it. There is a great array of tradition to prove that Mahomet blessed the 'Cutters,' as well as the 'Shavers,' of their hair. Among the miracles mentioned on the occasion is this, 'that the Lord sent a strong wind and swept the hair of the Pilgrims into the sacred Territory,' which was within a stone's throw of the camp;— thus signifying acceptance of the rite, notwithstanding its performance on common ground.

to Mahomet and his people to visit Mecca in the following
year, and for three days to occupy the city undisturbed. A
Revelation was accordingly produced, to place in a clear
light this view of the treaty, and to raise the drooping

*In Corân
it is styled
a Victory.*

spirits of the pilgrims. At the close of the first march, the
people might be seen hurrying across the plain, urging their
camels from all directions, and crowding round the Prophet.
' Inspiration hath descended on him,' passed from mouth to
mouth throughout the camp. Standing on his camel, Mahomet thus opened his address :—

Sura xlviii.

Verily We have given unto thee an evident Victory ;—
That God may pardon thee the Sin that is past and that
which is to come, and fulfil His favour upon thee, and lead thee
in the right way ;—
And that God may assist thee with a glorious assistance.

*Nature and
effects
of the
' Victory.'*

This *Victory* has puzzled many of the commentators, who
seek to apply it to other occasions ; but all their applications
are far-fetched and untenable. When the passage was ended,
it is said that a bystander enquired: ' What ! is *this* the
Victory ? ' ' Yea,' Mahomet replied, ' by Him that holdeth
in His hand my breath, it is a Victory.' Another reminded
him of the promise that they should enter into Mecca unmolested. ' True ; the Lord hath promised that indeed,'
said the Prophet ; ' but when did He promise that it should
be in the present year ? ' The comments of the biographer
Zohri, though somewhat exaggerated, are very much to the
purpose. ' There was no previous Victory,' he says, ' in
Islâm, greater than this. On all other occasions there was
fighting : but here war was laid aside, tranquillity and peace
restored ; the one party henceforward met and conversed
freely with the other, and there was no man of sense or judgment amongst the idolaters who was not led thereby to join
Islâm. And truly in the two years that followed, as many
persons entered the Faith as there belonged to it altogether
before, or even a greater number.' ' And the proof of this,'
adds Ibn Hishâm, ' is that, whereas Mahomet went forth to
Hodeibia with only fourteen hundred (or fifteen hundred)
men, he was followed two years later, in the attack on Mecca,
by ten thousand.' [1]

[1] The truth is, that tradition depreciates the treaty in the light of subsequent events. It appeared strange that he, who in less than two years was

After this opening pæan, and a reference to the future recompense of heaven and hell, Mahomet went on to reprimand severely the Arab tribes which neglected the summons to the pilgrimage; their professions should hereafter be tested in battle with ' a people of great might in war;'[1] and meanwhile (the severest punishment for a Bedouin) they are forbidden to join the true believers in any marauding excursion whatever :— Bedouins denounced for not joining pilgrimage.

The Arabs who stayed behind will say to thee,—*Our Possessions and our Families engaged us ; wherefore ask thou Pardon for us.* They say that with their tongues which is not in their hearts ;—Say ;—And who could procure for you any (other) thing from God, if He intended against you Evil,—or if He intended for you Good. Verily God is acquainted with that which ye do. Truly ye thought that the Apostle and the Believers would not return to their Families again for ever; this thought was decked out in your hearts; ye imagined an evil Imagination ; and ye are a corrupt people. * * * Sura xlviii.

Those that stayed behind will say when ye go forth to seize the Spoil, *Suffer us to follow you.* They seek to change the word of God. Say ;—*Ye shall not follow us !* for thus hath God already spoken. And they will say ;—*Nay but ye grudge us* (a share in the booty). By no means. They are a People that understandeth little. Say unto the Arabs that stayed behind, Ye shall hereafter be called out against a People of great might in war, with whom ye shall fight, or else they shall profess Islâm. Then if ye obey, God will give you a fair reward ; but if ye turn back as ye have turned back heretofore, He shall chastise you with a grievous chastisement.

The pilgrims who took the solemn oath under the Tree Further notices of

supreme dictator at Mecca, could now be suing for permission to enter that city, and that he was not only satisfied with these scanty terms, but could even call them a 'Victory.' His present weakness was overlooked in the consideration of later triumphs. Hence the vaunting speech at Hodeibia put into Omar's mouth, that ' had these terms been settled by any other than by Mahomet himself,—even by a commander of his appointment,—he would have scorned to listen to them ;' and the indignant conversation he is said to have held with Abu Bakr: 'What! Is not Mahomet the Prophet of God ? Are we not Moslems ? Are not they Infidels ? Why then is our divine religion to be thus lowered ?' Hence also the alleged unwillingness of the people to kill their victims at Hodeibia ; for, says Hishâmi, they were like men dying of vexation.

[1] The meaning apparently is that these Arabs would first have to prove themselves in real and severe fighting (perhaps in Syria or elsewhere) before they were again allowed to join in easy expeditions for booty.

are then applauded for their faithfulness. It was the hand of God himself, not the hand of His Apostle merely, which was placed upon each of theirs when the pledge was given: Victory and great spoil should be their reward :—

Sura xlviii.

Verily God was well pleased with the Believers, when they pledged themselves to Thee under the Tree. He knew what was in their hearts, and He caused Tranquillity [1] to descend upon them, and granted them a speedy Victory ;—And Spoils in abundance, which they shall take ; [2] and God is glorious and wise. God hath promised you great Spoil, which ye shall seize ; and He hath sent this (truce) beforehand. He hath restrained the hands of men from you, that it may be a sign unto the Believers, and that He may guide you into the right way. And yet other (Spoils are prepared for you), over which ye have (now) no power. But God hath encompassed them ; for God is over all things powerful. If the Unbelievers had fought against you, verily they had turned their backs. * * *

It is God that restrained their hands from you, and your hands from them, in the valley of Mecca, after that He had already made you superior to them ; and God observed that which ye did. These are they which disbelieve, which hindered you from visiting the holy Temple ; and (hindered) the Victims also, which were kept back, so that they reached not their destination.

And had it not been for believing men, and believing women, whom ye know not, and whom ye might have trampled upon, and blame might on their account unwittingly have fallen upon you, (God had not held thee back from entering Mecca ; but he did so) that God might cause such as He pleaseth to enter into His Mercy. If these had been separable, verily We had punished those of them (the inhabitants of Mecca) that disbelieve, [3] with a grievous punishment. When the Unbelievers raised scruples in their own hearts,—the scruples of Ignorance,— then God sent down Tranquillity upon His Apostle, and upon the

---

[1] Sekîna (Shechina), divine influence overshadowing the heart. Sprenger remarks that the tree having been mentioned in the Corân, Omar had it cut down, lest it should become an object of worship.

[2] Mahomet had no doubt Kheibar, and other expeditions northward, in his mind's eye at the moment : the prospect is also intended to aggravate the chagrin of the Bedouins at the loss of so fine a prize.

[3] That is, the unbelieving Coreish Mahomet would make it appear that there were numerous believers in his mission at Mecca unknown to him, and that God had held him back from attacking Mecca lest these should have been involved in the common destruction.

Believers, and fixed in them the word of Piety; [1] and they were the best entitled to it, and worthy of the same ;—for God comprehendeth all things.

Now hath God verified unto His Apostle the Vision in truth ;—Ye shall surely enter the Holy Temple, if it please God, in security, having your heads shaven and your hair cut. Fear ye not: for He knoweth that which ye know not. And He hath appointed for you after this a speedy Victory besides.

It is He who hath sent His Apostle with Guidance, and the true Religion,—that He may exalt it above every other.

One of the first political effects of the treaty was that the Bani Khozâa, who had long shown favour to the new faith, entered immediately into open alliance with Mahomet. The Bani Bakr, another tribe resident in the vicinity of Mecca, adhered to the Coreish.

Bani Khozâa enter into alliance with Mahomet.

The stipulation for the surrender of converts at the instance of their guardians, was soon illustrated by one or two peculiar incidents. The son of Soheil, himself the representative of the Coreish, rushed into the camp at Hodeibia, just as the treaty was concluded, and desired to follow Mahomet. But his father claimed him under the compact already ratified, and, although the lad earnestly remonstrated, the claim was admitted. 'Have patience, Abu Jandal!' said Mahomet to him as he was dragged away,—'put thy trust in the Lord. He will work out for thee, and for others like-minded with thee, a way of deliverance.' [2]

Soheil's son given up by Mahomet.

Some little time after the return of Mahomet, Abu Basîr, a young convert, effected his escape from Mecca, and appeared at Medîna. His guardians sent two servants with a letter to Mahomet and instructions to bring the deserter back to his home. The obligation of surrender was at once admitted by

Abu Basîr gathers band of marauders, and harasses Coreish.

---

[1] That is, the right profession of faith, which should otherwise have been embodied in the treaty. All this is a sort of apology for having yielded to Soheil in respect of the epithets used at the beginning of the treaty.

[2] The story is told with much over-colouring. Abu Jandal came up just as the treaty was completed, having escaped from Mecca *in his chains.* His father beat him and dragged him away. He screamed aloud to the Moslems to save him: but Mahomet said that he could not diverge from the terms of the treaty just concluded. Omar walked by the lad as he was being led back, and comforted him with such words as these: 'The blood of these infidels is no better than the blood of dogs.' The whole story is so exaggerated, that it is difficult to say what degree of truth there is in it. But it must have had *some* foundation in fact.

Mahomet, and Abu Basîr was led away towards Mecca. But he had travelled only a few miles, when he treacherously seized the sword of one of his conductors, and slew him. The other servant fled back to Medîna; Abu Basîr himself followed, the naked sword in his hand still reeking with blood. Both soon reached the presence of Mahomet; the servant to complain of the murder, Abu Basîr to plead for his freedom. The youth contended that as the Prophet had once for all fulfilled the letter of the treaty in delivering him up, he was now free to remain behind. Mahomet gave no direct reply. His answer was enigmatical: after an exclamation in praise of his bravery,[1] he added in a voice of admiration: '*What a kindler of war, if he had but with him a body of adherents!*' Thus encouraged, Abu Basîr quitted Medîna and, accompanied by five other Meccan youths, went to Al îs by the sea-shore, on the caravan road to Syria. The words of Mahomet were not long in becoming known at Mecca, and the restless youth of the Coreish, receiving them as a suggestion to follow the same example, set out to join Abu Basîr, who was soon surrounded with about seventy followers desperate as himself. They waylaid every caravan from Mecca (for since the truce, traffic with Syria had again sprung up) and spared the life of no one. The Coreish were at length so harassed by these attacks, that they solicited the interference of Mahomet; and, on condition that the outrages were stopped, they waived their right to have the deserters delivered up. Mahomet acceded to the request, and summoned the marauders to desist. Abu Basîr was on his death-bed when he received the order; but the rest returned and took up their abode at Medîna.

Mahomet's support of him in contravention of spirit of treaty.

It seems obvious to remark that, however much Mahomet may have been within the letter of the truce in this proceeding, the encouragement held out by him to Abu Basîr and his comrades in their hostility to the Coreish, was a breach of its spirit. Abu Basîr professed himself an adherent of Islâm, and, as such, implicitly subservient to the commands of the Prophet. To incite him, therefore, to a course of plunder and rapine, was in contravention of the engagement to promote amity and peace.

---

[1] 'Alas for his mother!' signifying that his bravery would surely lead him to be killed in some daring conflict.

XIX. WOMEN NOT SURRENDERED UNDER THE TRUCE.

The stipulation for the surrender of deserters made no express distinction as to sex. A female having fled to Medîna whose guardians were at Mecca, her brothers followed her and demanded her restoration under the terms of truce. Mahomet demurred. The Divine oracle was called in, and it gave judgment in favour of the woman. All women who came over to Medîna were to be 'tried,' and, if their profession was found sincere, they were to be retained. The unbelief of their husbands dissolved the previous marriage; they now might legally contract fresh nuptials with believers, provided only that restitution were made of any sums expended by their former husbands as dower upon them. The marriage bond was similarly annulled between believers and their unbelieving wives who had remained behind at Mecca;— and their dowers might be reckoned in adjusting the payments due to the Coreish on account of the women retained at Medîna. Though the rule is thus laid down at length in the Corân, but few cases of the kind are cited by tradition.[1]

Rule as to women who fled from Mecca to Medina.

[1] The woman here mentioned as coming over to Medîna was daughter of Ocba, so cruelly executed by Mahomet after Bedr. Another similar refugee is noticed by C. de Perceval as married to Omar. On the other hand, Omar divorced Coreina, his wife, who remained at Mecca, and who was then married by Abu Sofiân. Another similar case is cited by Hishâmi.

The rule is given in the 60th Sura, which opens with strong remonstrances against making friends of unbelievers. Mahomet probably found that his people were, since the truce, becoming too intimate with the Meccans, and he feared lest the tendency of such friendships would relax the discipline and *esprit de corps* of Islâm. Then follows the passage regarding women :—

'O ye that believe! When believing women come over unto you as refugees, then try them; God well knoweth their faith. And if ye know them to be believers, return them not again unto the infidels; they are not lawful (as wives) unto the infidels; neither are the infidels lawful (as husbands) unto them. But give unto them (the infidels) what they may have expended (on their dowers). It is no sin for you that ye marry them, after that ye shall have given them (the women) their dowers. And retain not the patronage of the unbelieving women; but demand back that which ye have spent (in their dowers); and let the infidels demand back what they have spent (on the women which come over to you). This is the judgment of God, which He establisheth between you; and God is knowing and wise.

'And if any of your wives escape from you unto the infidels, and ye have your turn (by the elopement of their wives unto you), then give to those whose wives have gone (out of the dowers of the latter) a sum equal to that which they have expended (on the dowers of the former); and fear God in whom ye believe. O Prophet! When believing Women come unto thee, and plight their faith unto thee that they will not associate any with God, that they will not steal, neither commit adultery, that they will not kill their children, nor

Mahomet's dream of universal submission to Islâm.

The pilgrimage to Hodeibia is the last event of importance which occurred in the Sixth year of Mahomet's residence at Medîna. But towards its close a new and singular project occupied his attention. It was nothing less than to summon the sovereigns of the surrounding States and Empires to his allegiance! The principles of Mahomet had been slowly but surely tending towards the universal imposition of his faith. Wherever his arms had reached, the recognition of his Mission, and of his spiritual authority as the Apostle of God, had been peremptorily demanded. An exception indeed was made in favour of Jews and Christians; but even these, if they retained their faith, must pay tribute, as an admission of inferiority. It may seem a chimerical and wild design in the Prophet of Medîna,—scarcely able as he was to maintain his own position, helplessly besieged twelve months before, and forced but lately to retire from Mecca with his purpose of pilgrimage unaccomplished,—that he should dream of supremacy, either spiritual or political, over Egypt, Abyssinia, and Syria, nay over the Roman and Persian Empires. But so it was. Apart from the steadfast and lofty conviction which he had of his duty and mission as the Apostle of God, it is not to be supposed that a person so sagacious and discerning should have failed to perceive in the signs of the times a grand opportunity of success. The Roman Empire was broken and wearied by successive shocks of barbarous invasion, and together with the Kingdom of Persia had been wasted by a long and devastating war. Schism had rent and paralysed the Christian Church. The Melchites and the Jacobites, the Monothelites and the Nestorians, regarded each other with a deadly hatred, and

promulgate a calumny forged between their hands and their feet, and that they will not be disobedient unto thee in that which is reasonable,—then pledge thy faith unto them, and seek pardon of God for them. For God is gracious and merciful.'

Stanley (on 1 Cor. vii. 1-40) quotes the above passage, and says that the rule it contains 'resembles that of the Apostle.' But there is really no analogy between them; the Christian inculcation differs *toto cœlo* from that of Mahomet: 'If any brother hath a wife that believeth not, and she be pleased to dwell with him, let him not put her away.' And similarly the case of a believing wife with an unbelieving husband (1 Cor. vii. 12-16). Whereas Mahomet declares the marriage bond *ipso facto* annulled by the unbelief of either party, which indeed was only to be expected from his loose ideas regarding the marriage contract.

were ready to welcome any intruder who would rid them of their adversaries. The new faith would sweep away all the sophistries about which they vainly contended : holding fast the groundwork of previous Revelations, it would substitute a reformed and universal religion for the effete and erring systems which man had introduced. It was perhaps in anticipation of this project, that Mahomet had already told the Bedouin tribes 'that they should hereafter be called out against a people of great might in war, against whom they should fight unless they professed Islâm.' The claims of truth, enforced thus by the army of God, would surely conquer. Such no doubt were the thoughts of Mahomet, when he determined to send embassies to the Kaiser and the Chosroes, to Abyssinia, Egypt, Syria, and Yemâma.

It was suggested by one of his followers that the kings of the earth did not receive despatches, unless they were attested by a seal. Accordingly Mahomet had a seal made of silver, and engraved with the words MAHOMET THE APOSTLE OF GOD.[1] Letters were written and sealed, and the six messengers simultaneously despatched to their various destinations on the opening of the new year, as shall be further related in the following chapter.

Seal engraved ; and despatches prepared for foreign princes.

[1] It is pretended that his messengers, 'like the Apostles of Jesus,' were immediately endowed with the faculty of speaking the language of the country to which they were deputed, But Mahomet evidently selected for the purpose men who, as travellers, merchants, or otherwise, had before visited the respective countries. So Dihya was sent to Syria. (See *ante*, p. 359.) Less trustworthy authorities make these embassies to have started from Medîna, on various dates. But Wâckidi's secretary states distinctly that all set out *on the same day*, in Moharram, A.H. VII.

CHAPTER XX.

EMBASSIES TO VARIOUS SOVEREIGNS AND PRINCES.

A.H. VII.—A.D. 627.

State of Roman and Persian empires.

A BRIEF glance at the state of the Roman and Persian Empires will enable us the better to connect the salient points of external history with the career of Mahomet.

Struggle between the two empires, A.D. 609–627.

From a period as far back as the assumption by Mahomet of the prophetic office, the two kingdoms had been waging with each other a ceaseless and deadly warfare. Until the year A.D. 621 unvarying success attended the Persian arms. Syria, Egypt, Asia Minor, were overrun. Constantinople itself was threatened. At last, Heraclius awoke from his inglorious lethargy; and about the time of Mahomet's flight

A.H. I.
A.D. 622.

from Mecca, he was driving his invaders forth from their

A.H. II.–IV.
A.D. 623–625.

fastnesses in Asia Minor. In the second campaign he carried the war into the heart of Persia. During the three years in which by this brilliant stroke the Kaiser was retrieving the fortunes of the Empire, Mahomet was engaged in his

July, A.D. 626.

doubtful struggle with the Coreish. Then came the critical siege of Constantinople by the Avars and Persians which preceded, by little more than half a year, the siege of Medîna

March, A.D. 627.

known as the battle of the Ditch. It is curious to remark that while the Moslems attributed the sudden departure of Abu Sofiân and his Arab hosts to the special interposition of the Almighty, the Romans equally ascribed their signal deliverance from the hordes of the Chagan to the favour of the Virgin. In the third campaign, Heraclius followed up his

A.H. VI.
A.D. 627.

previous success, and at the close of 627 achieved the decisive victory of Nineveh. In this action the forces of Persia were irretrievably broken, and shortly after the Chrosroes fled

from his capital.   Early in the following year, he was mur-   February, March. A.D. 628.
dered by his son Siroes, who ascended the throne and con-
cluded a treaty of peace with the Emperor.   About the same
period Mahomet was at Hodeibia, ratifying his truce with
the chiefs of Mecca.

In the autumn of this year, Heraclius fulfilled his vow of   I. Despatch of Ma- homet to Heraclius. A.H. VII. A.D. 628.
thanksgiving for the splendid success which had crowned
his arms; he performed on foot the pilgrimage from Edessa
to Jerusalem, where the 'true cross,' recovered from the Persians, was with solemnity and pomp restored to the Holy
sepulchre.   While preparing for this journey, or during the
journey itself, an uncouth despatch, in the Arabic character,
was laid before Heraclius.   It was forwarded by the Governor
of Bostra, into whose hands it had been delivered by an
Arab chief.   The epistle was addressed to the Emperor himself, from 'Mahomet the Apostle of God,' the rude impression of whose seal could be deciphered at the foot.   In
strange and simple accents, like those of the Prophets of old,
it summoned Heraclius to acknowledge the mission of Mahomet, to cast aside the idolatrous worship of Jesus and his
Mother, and to return to the Catholic faith of the one only
God.[1]   The letter was probably cast aside, or preserved, it
may be, as a strange curiosity, the effusion of some harmless
fanatic.[2]

[1] The terms of the several despatches are quite uncertain.   The drafts of
them given by tradition, with the replies, are apocryphal.   The ordinary copy
of the letter to Heraclius contains a passage from the Corân which, as shown
by Weil, was not given forth till the ninth year of the Hegira.   Dihya, the
bearer of this despatch, was desired by Mahomet to forward it through the
Governor of Bostra.

[2] Tradition has another story.   'Now the Emperor was at this time at
Hims, performing a pedestrian journey, in fulfilment of the vow which he had
made that, if the Romans overcame the Persians, he would travel on foot from
Constantinople to Ælia (Jerusalem).   So having read the letter, he commanded his chief men to meet him in the royal camp at Hims.   And thus he
addressed them: 'Ye chiefs of Rome!   Do ye desire safety and guidance, so
that your kingdom shall be firmly established, and that ye may follow the
commands of Jesus son of Mary?'   'And what, O King! shall secure us
this?'   'Even that ye follow the Arabian Prophet,' said Heraclius.   Hearing
this they all started aside like wild asses of the desert, each raising his cross
and waving it aloft in the air.   Whereupon, Heraclius, despairing of their
conversion, and unwilling to lose his kingdom, desisted, saying that he had
only wished to test their constancy and faith, and that he was now satisfied
by this display of firmness and devotion.   The courtiers bowed their heads;
and so the Prophet's despatch was rejected.'

II. Despatch to Ghassânide Prince.

Not long after, another despatch, bearing the same seal, and couched in similar terms, reached the court of Heraclius. It was addressed to Hârith VII., Prince of the Bani Ghassân, who forwarded it to the Emperor, with an address from himself, soliciting permission to chastise the audacious impostor.[1] But Heraclius, regarding the ominous voice from Arabia beneath his notice, forbade the expedition, and desired that Hârith should be in attendance at Jerusalem, to swell the imperial train at the approaching visitation of the Temple. Little did the Emperor imagine that the kingdom which, unperceived by the world, this obscure Pretender was founding in Arabia, would in a few short years wrest from his grasp that Holy City, and the fair provinces which, with so much toil and so much glory, he had just recovered from the Persians!

III. Despatch to King of Persia.

The despatch for the King of Persia reached the court probably some months after the accession of Siroes. It was delivered to the Monarch, who, on hearing the contents, tore it in pieces. When this was reported to Mahomet, he prayed and said: 'Even thus, O Lord! rend thou his kingdom from him!'

Conversion of Bâdzân, Governor of Yemen.
A.H. VI.
A.D. 628.

Connected with the court of Persia, but of date somewhat earlier than the despatch sent to it, is a remarkable incident, which was followed by results of considerable importance. A few months before his overthrow, the Chosroes, receiving strange reports of the prophetical claims of Mahomet, and of

[1] See Introd. p. xxii. In the traditional account of these events, it is difficult to say whether any grains of truth mingle with the fiction. We are told that the messenger of Mahomet found Hârith in the gardens of Damascus, busied with preparations for the reception of the Emperor who was shortly expected on his way to Jerusalem. He waited at the gate of Hârith three or four days, as audience was granted only at certain intervals. During this delay, he taught the Porter about Mahomet and his doctrine. The Porter wept and said: 'I read the Gospel, and I find therein the description of this Prophet exactly as thou tellest me:' thereupon he embraced Islâm, and desired his salutation to be given to the Prophet. On a set day, Hârith, sitting in state, called for the messenger, and had the despatch read. Then he cast it aside and said: 'Who is he that will snatch my kingdom from me? I will march against him, were he even in Yemen.' He became very angry, and, having called out his army in battle array, said to the messenger: 'Go, tell thy Master that which thou seest.' The messenger, however, was afterwards permitted to wait for the reply of Heraclius: on its receipt, Hârith dismissed him with a present of one hundred mithcals of gold. When the messenger reported what had passed, the Prophet said that the kingdom had departed from Hârith; and so Hârith died the following year.

the depredations committed on the Syrian border by his marauding bands, sent orders to Bâdzân, the Persian Governor
of Yemen, to despatch two trusty men to Medîna, and procure
for him certain information regarding the Pretender. Bâdzân
obeyed, and with the messengers sent a courteous despatch to
Mahomet. By the time they arrived at Medîna, tidings had
reached the Prophet of the deposition and death of the Persian
Monarch. When the despatch, therefore, was read before him,
he smiled at its contents, and summoned the ambassadors to
embrace Islâm. He then apprised them of the murder of the
Chosroes, and accession of his son: ' Go,' said he, ' inform
your master of this, and require him to tender his submission
to the Prophet of the Lord.' The glory of Persia had now
departed. She had long ago relaxed her grasp upon Arabia;
and the Governor of Yemen was free to choose a protectorate
more congenial to his people. Bâdzân therefore gladly
recognised the rising fortunes of Islâm, and signified his adhesion to the Prophet. From the distance of this Province,
its allegiance was at the first little more than nominal; but
the accession served as a point for further action, and meanwhile added new prestige to the Prophet's name.

The embassy to Egypt was received with courtesy by
Muckoukas, the Roman Governor. While refusing to admit
the claims of the Prophet, he gave substantial proof of
friendly feeling in valuable presents which he forwarded to
him with this reply: ' I am aware that a Prophet is yet to
arise; but I am of opinion that he will appear in Syria. Thy
messenger hath been received with honour. I send for thine
acceptance two sisters, highly valued among the Copts, a
present of raiment, and a mule for thee to ride upon.'
Though Mahomet ascribed the unbelief of Muckoukas to
sordid fear lest the government of Egypt should slip from his
hands, yet he willingly accepted the gifts which, indeed, were
well adapted to his tastes. Mary, the fairest of the two damsels, was retained for his own harem; Shirîn, the other, was
presented to Hassân the Poet who, since his reconciliation
with Ayesha, had regained the Prophet's favour. The mule
was white,—a rarity in Arabia; it was greatly prized, and
was constantly ridden by Mahomet.[1]

IV. De-
spatch to
Governor
of Egypt.

[1] The Egyptian Governor must have shrewdly apprehended the weakness of
Mahomet, when he sent him these two slave girls;—a strange present, how-

V. De-
spatch to
King of
Abyssinia.

The court of Abyssinia stood in a different relation to Mahomet from that of the other courts to which he addressed his apostolic summons. There his followers had long ago found a secure and hospitable retreat from the persecutions of the Coreish; and although about forty of these exiles had rejoined the Prophet after his flight to Medîna, there remained fifty or sixty who still enjoyed the protection of the Abyssinian Prince. Amr ibn Omeya was now the bearer of two despatches to him.[1] One was couched in language like that addressed to the other Christian kings; and to this the Negûs is said to have replied in terms of humble acquiescence,—embracing the new faith, and mourning over his inability to join in person the standard of the Prophet.[2] The answer was entrusted to the care of Jáfar son of Abu Tâlib, Mahomet's cousin, who was still an exile at the Abyssinian court. In the second despatch, the Prophet begged that his remaining followers might now be sent to Medîna; and the singular request was added that, before their departure, the Prince would betroth to him Omm Habîba, daughter of Abu Sofiân, now five-and-thirty years of age, but whose early charms still held a place in his imagination. The former husband of Omm Habîba was Obeidallah, one of the 'Four Enquirers,' who, after emigrating as a Mussulman to Abyssinia, had embraced Christianity, and died there in the profession of the Christian faith. By this alliance Mahomet at once gratified his passion for fresh nuptials (he had been now a whole year without adding any new inmate to his harem); and, perhaps, further hoped to make Abu Sofiân, the father of Omm Habîba, more favourable to his cause.[3] The Prince performed with readiness the part

Omm
Habîba
betrothed
to Ma-
homet.

Abyssinian
refugees

ever, for a *Christian* governor to make. The messenger was treated kindly: he was not kept waiting at the gate, and was not detained more than five days.

[1] Mentioned above as a noted assassin, p. 365.

[2] I have before, p. 98, given grounds for doubting the conversion of the Negûs. It was quite possible for a Christian Prince, more especially if he belonged to an Arian or Nestorian sect, and had seen or heard only certain portions of the Corân, (those for example containing strong attestations of the Jewish and Christian Scriptures, and exhortations against idolatry) to have expressed an assent to the vague terms of Mahomet's epistle. For the efforts of the various Christian sects to gain over the Abyssinians, see Gibbon, chapter xlvii.

[3] Sprenger questions this view and thinks that, with the Arab sentiments

allotted to him in the ceremony.   He also provided two ships   reach
for the exiles, in which they all embarked ; and during the   Medina.
August,
autumn they reached Medîna safely.   A.D. 628.

The sixth messenger of Mahomet was sent to Haudza,   VI. De-
the chief of a Christian tribe, the Bani Hanîfa, of Yemâma.   spatch to
Chief of
The messenger was hospitably entertained ; and the chief,   Yemâma.
having presented him with changes of raiment and provisions for the journey home, dismissed him with this reply for
his master : ' How excellent is that Revelation to which thou
invitest me, and how beautiful !   Know that I am the Poet
of my tribe, and their Orator.   The Arabs revere my dignity.
Grant unto me, therefore, a share in the rule, and I will
follow thee.'   When Mahomet had read the answer, he
said : ' Had this man stipulated for an unripe date only, as
his share in the land, I would not have consented.   Let him
perish, and his vainglory with him ! '   And so Haudza died,
the tradition adds, in the following year.

regarding women, Mahomet's marriage with Abu Sofiân's daughter must rather,
so long as he was unconverted, have been a mortification to him. Omm
Habîba survived Mahomet some thirty years, and died during the Caliphate
of her brother Muâvia.

CHAPTER XXI.

THE CONQUEST OF KHEIBAR.

A.H. VII.—*August and September,* A.D. 628.

Ætat. 60.

Mahomet resolves on attacking Jews of Kheibar.

On his return from Hodeibia, in the spring of the year 628, Mahomet had promised to those who accompanied him in that pilgrimage the early prospect of a rich and extensive plunder. The summer passed without any enterprise whatever; and his followers began to be impatient for the fulfilment of their expectations. But quiet and peace still prevailed around. Mahomet probably waited for some act of aggression on the part of the Jews of Kheibar, whose fertile lands and villages he had destined for his followers, or on the part of their allies the Bani Ghatafân, to furnish the excuse for an attack. But, no such opportunity offering, he resolved, in the autumn of this year, on a sudden and unprovoked invasion of their territory.

Army marches.
A.H. VII.
August,
A.D. 628.

The army marched from Medîna, sixteen hundred strong; being about the same number as had followed the Prophet on his pilgrimage to Hodeibia. But the force was greatly more powerful in cavalry :—the number on the present occasion being variously estimated at from one hundred to two hundred. The Mussulman horse had never before exceeded thirty. Many of the inhabitants of Medîna and the Bedouin tribes who had neglected the Prophet's former summons, would gladly now have joined the tempting expedition; but, according to the divine injunction, they were not permitted, and their mortification was great at being left behind. Omm Salma, the same wife who accompanied the Prophet to Hodeibia, was again his companion on the present journey.

The distance, perhaps one hundred miles, was accom- Kheibar
plished in three forced marches. So quick was the movement surprised.
and the surprise so complete, that the cultivators of Kheibar,
issuing forth in the morning to their fields, suddenly found
themselves confronted by a great army, and rushed back to
the city in dismay. The rapidity of the approach cut off all
hope of timely aid from the Bani Ghatafân.[1]

The rich vale of Kheibar was studded with villages and The for-
fortresses rudely built but posted strongly on the rocks or tresses one
                                                              by one fall
eminences which here and there rose from amidst the luxu- before
riant date-groves and fields of corn. One by one, before any Mahomet.
general opposition could be organised, these forts were
attacked and carried. ' *Kheibar is undone*,' exclaimed Mahomet, with a play upon the word,[2] as he passed from one
stronghold triumphantly to another: ' *Great is the Lord!*
Truly when I light upon the coasts of any People, wretched
for them is that day!' From the villages in the valleys
first attacked, which were gained with little loss, Mahomet
proceeded to the region of Kuteiba. Here the Jews, who
now had time to rally round their chief Kinâna (the successor of his grandfather Abul Huckeick, who had been assas- General
sinated several months before), posted themselves in front of action be-
                                                               fore the
the citadel Camuss, resolved on a desperate struggle. After fort of
some vain attempts to dislodge them, Mahomet planned a Camuss.
grand attack: ' I will give the Eagle,' he said,—' the great
black Flag,—into the hands of one that loveth the Lord and
His Apostle, even as he is beloved of them; he shall gain the
victory.'[3] Next morning the flag was placed in Ali's hands,

---

[1] Hishâmi says that Mahomet took up a position so as to cut off their
assistance, and adds that the Bani Ghatafân did go forth to aid their allies, but
returned on a rumour that their own homes were being attacked. The fact is,
that Mahomet's advent was totally unexpected. ' When the Moslem army
alighted before Kheibar, they did not stir that night, nor did a fowl cackle at
them, till the sun arose. Then the Kheibarites opened their fortresses as
usual, and went forth to their labours with their cattle, their spades, hoes, and
other instruments of husbandry; suddenly they perceived the army in front of
them, and fled back into their forts, screaming out: " *It is Mahomet and his*
hosts!" '

[2] By inversion, *Kharrabat Kheibar.*

[3] There had been no great standard like this before. It is said to have
been made out of a black shawl or mantle worn by Ayesha,—a gallant device,
—and was called *ucâb*, the ' Black Eagle.' There were two other smaller banners of white, held, one by Hobâb, the other by Sâd ibn Obâda, both Citizens.

and the troops advanced.   At this moment, a soldier stepped forth from the Jewish line, and challenged his adversaries to single combat: 'I am Marhab,' he cried, 'as all Kheibar knows, a warrior bristling with arms, when the war fiercely burns.' The first Moslem who answered the challenge, aimed a blow at the Jewish champion with deadly force, but the sword recoiled upon himself, and he fell fatally wounded.[1] Marhab repeated his vainglorious challenge, and then Ali himself advanced saying: ' I am he whom my mother named *the Lion;* like a lion of the howling wilderness, I weigh my foes in a giant's balance.' The combatants closed, and Ali cleft the head of Marhab in two.   Marhab's brother having rashly renewed the challenge, Zobeir went forth and slew him.[2]

Jews beaten back with loss.

The Moslem line now made a general advance, and, after a sharp conflict, drove back the enemy.   In this battle, Ali performed great feats of prowess.   Having lost his shield, he seized the lintel of a door, which he wielded effectually in its stead.   Tradition, in its expansive process, has transformed this extemporised shield into a gigantic beam, and magnified the hero into a second Samson.[3] The victory was decisive, for the Jews lost ninety-three men ; while of the Moslems, only nineteen were killed throughout the whole campaign.

Kinâna tortured and put to death.

After this defeat, the fortress of Camuss surrendered, on condition that the inhabitants were free to leave the country, but that they should give up all their property to the con-

[1] The people cried out 'He hath killed himself: his works are vain' (because of his suicidal death). 'Nay,' said Mahomet, 'he shall have a double reward !' On the road to Kheibar, this man had recited some martial verses before Mahomet, who thanked him, saying: ' The Lord have mercy on thee !' It is pretended that this mode of blessing from Mahomet, invariably portended impending martyrdom. The verses, by the way, are the same as those ascribed to Mahomet at the battle of the Ditch.

[2] As Zobeir walked forth to the combat, his mother Safia ran up to Mahomet in alarm, crying out that her son would be killed: 'Not so, my Aunt!' replied Mahomet; 'he will slay his fellow, if the Lord will!' Many women went from Medina on this campaign to minister to the wounded. A story, very illustrative of the combined simplicity and coarseness of Arab manners, is given in the conversation of Mahomet with a young woman of the Bani Ghifâr, who rode on the same camel, and confided to him certain of her ailments.

[3] The story is in the ordinary cast of exaggerated tradition. Abu Râfi, Mahomet's servant, went after the battle to see the beam, in company with seven others, who together tried to *turn it over,* and were unable !

queror. With the rest, came forth Kinâna, chief of the
Jews of Kheibar, and his cousin. Mahomet accused them
both of keeping back, in contravention of the compact, a
portion of their riches, especially the treasures of the Bani
Nadhîr which Kinâna had obtained as a marriage portion
with his wife Safia, the daughter of Huwey who perished
in the slaughter of the Bani Coreitza. 'Where are the
vessels of gold,' he asked, 'which ye used to lend to the
people of Mecca?' They protested that they no longer
possessed them. 'If ye conceal anything from me,' said
Mahomet, 'and I should gain knowledge of it, then your
lives and the lives of your families shall be at my disposal.'
They answered that it should be so. A traitorous Jew, having
divulged to Mahomet the place in which a part of their
wealth was deposited, he sent and fetched it. On the discovery of this attempt at imposition, Kinâna was subjected
to cruel torture,—'fire being placed upon his breast till his
breath had almost departed,'—in the hope that he would
confess where the rest of his treasures were concealed. Mahomet then gave command, and the heads of the chief and
his cousin were severed from their bodies.

The scene of torture and bloodshed was hardly ended,
when Mahomet sent his negro servant Bilâl to fetch the bride
of Kinâna, a damsel seventeen or eighteen years of age,
whose beauty was probably well known at Medîna.[1] Bilâl
speedily performed his errand. Finding with Safia another
lady, her cousin, he brought them both straight across the
battlefield strewed with the dead, and close by the corpses
of Kinâna and his cousin. At the ghastly sight of their
headless trunks, the companion of Safia screamed wildly,
beating her face, and casting dust upon her head. 'Take
that she-devil hence,' said Mahomet, angrily: but aside he
chided Bilâl for his want of consideration in bringing the
women so near the bodies of their relatives. 'Truly,' said
Bilâl, 'I did it designedly; I wished to see their grief and
anger stirred up.' But Mahomet was moved by tenderer

Marriage of Mahomet with Safia, Kinâna's bride,

---

[1] No doubt this was the case, because (1) she was the daughter of a chief
who had long lived at Medîna, and was well known there; and (2), because
Mahomet, immediately upon Kinâna's execution, sent for her and cast his
mantle over her. Indeed he is not free from the suspicion of being influenced
in the destruction of Kinâna by the desire of obtaining his wife.

emotions; turning complacently towards Safia, he cast his mantle around her, in token that she was to be his own, and then made her over to the care of Bilâl. One of his followers had also coveted this Jewish beauty; but Mahomet made him content with the present of her cousin.

Consummated at Kheibar.

Mahomet did not long postpone his nuptials with Safia.[1] The wedding feast was celebrated by an abundant feast of dates, curdled milk, and butter. Earth was heaped up into the shape of tables; on these the viands were spread, and the guests ate and made merry. Meanwhile the Prophet had charged a female attendant with the duty of suitably arraying the bride, and making her ready for him. When the repast was ended, the people prepared for the march; and they watched Mahomet, saying : ' We shall see now whether he hath taken her for his wife or for a slave girl.' So when he called for a screen to hide her from public gaze, they knew from thence that she was to be his wife. Mahomet then lowered his knee to help her to ascend the camel: after some coy demur, she placed her foot upon his bended knee, and Mahomet (a bridegroom now of sixty years of age) raising her into the litter, and taking his seat before her on the camel, conducted her to the bridal tent. In the morning he heard the noise of one rustling against the curtain of the tent. It was Abu Ayûb, who had there kept watch all night with his drawn sword. ' What has brought thee here ? ' asked Mahomet, surprised at the inopportune presence of his friend : ' O Prophet! ' he replied, ' I bethought me that the damsel is young; it is but as yesterday that she was married to Kinâna, whom thou hast slain. And thus, distrusting her, I said to myself, *I will watch by the tent and be close at hand, in case she attempt anything against thee.*' Mahomet

---

[1] The interval is not stated anywhere, but it could not have been of long duration. Hishâmi says the marriage took place at Kheibar, or on the way returning from it, and other traditions imply no delay whatever. I find no credible tradition intimating Safia's conversion, as is commonly supposed, before her marriage. Under any circumstances, it is clear that the period prescribed as necessary to intervene before marrying a woman who had previously been the wife of another, was not on this occasion observed by Mahomet. Either such ordinance had not yet been imposed, or Mahomet exempted himself from its operation.

Omm Suleim (mother of the Prophet's servant Anis) bathed Safia, dressed her hair, and, having arrayed her in bridal attire, carried her to Mahomet. Safia's dower was her freedom.

blessed him for his careful vigilance, and desired him to withdraw in peace.

The precaution was unnecessary; for (if tradition speak truly) while Mahomet doted on his bride, she not the less readily accommodated herself to the new alliance. It is related that she bore the mark of a bruise upon her eye; when the Prophet asked her tenderly the cause, she told him that, being yet Kinâna's bride, she saw in a dream as if the moon had fallen from the heavens into her lap; and that when she told Kinâna, he struck her violently, saying: 'What is this thy dream but that thou covetest the new king of the Hejâz, the Prophet, for thy husband!' The mark of the blow was the same which Mahomet saw.[1]

Safia's dream.

But all the women of Kheibar were not equally fickle and faithless. The nuptials of Mahomet were damped by the revenge of Zeinab, sister of the warrior Marhab, who had lost her husband, father, brothers, and other relatives in the battle. She dressed a kid, and, having steeped it in deadly poison, placed the dish with fair words before Mahomet at the hour of his evening repast. Graciously accepting the gift, he took the shoulder (the part he loved to eat, and which Zeinab had therefore impregnated the most strongly) for himself, tore off a choice bone for Bishr a follower who sat next him, and distributed portions to Abu Bakr and his other friends around. Scarcely had he swallowed a mouthful, when he exclaimed: 'Hold! surely this shoulder hath been poisoned;' and he spat forth what was in his mouth.[2] Bishr, who had eaten more than Mahomet, at once changed colour, and stirred neither hand nor foot until he died. Mahomet was seized with excruciating pain, and caused himself, and all those who had with him partaken of the dish, to be freely cupped between the shoulders. Zeinab was then summoned, and interrogated as to the motive of her offence. 'Thou hast inflicted,' she replied, boldly, 'these grievous injuries on my people; thou hast slain my father, and my uncle, and my husband. Therefore I said within

Mahomet partakes a poisoned kid.

---

[1] Safia survived Mahomet forty years, and died A.H. 52.

[2] It is a favourite tradition, that Mahomet said, 'the shoulder *tells* me,' or '*lets me know* that it is poisoned.' But, however this story may have grown up, the tradition is clear that he 'swallowed' the first mouthful before he perceived the evil taste.

myself, if he is a Prophet he will be aware that the shoulder of the kid is poisoned; but if he be a mere pretender, then we shall be rid of him, and the Jews again will prosper.' She was put to death.[1] The effect of the poison was felt by Mahomet to his dying day.[2]

Remaining fortresses, with Fadak, capitulate.

After the victory of Camuss, the only remaining strong-holds of Kheibar, namely, Watîh and Salâlim, were invested, and, seeing no prospect of relief, they capitulated. Both were thus saved from being sacked; but, like the rest of Kheibar, their lands were subjected to a tax of half the produce. Fadak, a Jewish town, not far from Kheibar, profited by the example, and, having tendered a timely submission, was admitted on the same terms.

Siege of Wadi al Cora.
A.H. VII. September, A.D. 628.

On his march homeward from Kheibar, Mahomet laid siege to the Jewish settlement of Wadi al Cora, which, after a resistance of one or two days, surrendered upon like conditions. The authority of Mahomet was thus established over all the Jewish tribes north of Medîna.

Division of the rich plunder.

The plunder of Kheibar was rich beyond all previous experience. Besides vast stores of dates, oil, honey and barley, flocks of sheep and herds of camels, the spoil in treasure and jewels was very large.[3] A fifth of the whole was as usual set apart for the use of the Prophet, and for distribution at will among his family and the destitute poor. The remaining four-fifths were sold by outcry, and the proceeds, according to the prescribed rule, divided into one thousand eight hundred shares, being one share for a foot soldier, and three for a horseman.

[1] Some say that she was set free upon making this exculpatory statement. But the balance of tradition is according to the text. Certain traditions state that she was made over to the relatives of Bishr, to be put to death judicially for having poisoned him. The woman's speech in justification is cast in a rather common traditional type. Still, under the circumstances, it is not so unnatural as the ordinary speeches of this kind are; and if true it is a specimen (such as has not often been preserved by servile tradition) of undaunted opposition to the Conqueror,—a contrast to the fickle heartlessness of Safia.

[2] Hence, the traditionists delight in the conceit that Mahomet had the merit of a 'martyr;' and the same is also said of Abu Bakr, one of those who also partook of the kid.

[3] Hishâmi says, that from the time of Kheibar, *slaves* became very plentiful among the Moslems. I do not find that, excepting the family of Kinâna, any mention is made of slaves taken at Kheibar. But money, which the victors obtained plentifully at Kheibar, could purchase them cheaply in any part of Arabia.

The villages and lands were disposed of upon another principle. One half, embracing all the places which surrendered without fighting, was reserved for Mahomet, and constituted thereafter a species of Crown domain. The other moiety was divided into one thousand eight hundred portions, and allotted by the same rule as the personal booty. A large and permanent reward was thus secured for all those who had given proof of their faith and loyalty by accompanying Mahomet to Hodeibia, and the promise made on that expedition was fully redeemed. The Prophet had now an ample revenue at his disposal. From this he made a liberal assignment for his wives' maintenance in so many measures to each annually of dates and barley. The poor also were not forgotten. The remainder formed a large reserve for the entertainment of visitors, the support of auxiliaries, and other purposes of State. Thus the dominion of Mahomet no longer rested now on spiritual resources alone, but also on the more substantial basis of the thews and sinews of war.

Even of those portions of Kheibar which, having been gained by storm, were apportioned as private property, it was found expedient, in the absence of other cultivators, to leave the Jewish inhabitants in possession, on the same condition as of the public lands, namely, surrendering half the produce. An appraiser was deputed yearly to assess the amount, to realise the rents, and transmit them to Medîna.[1] This arrangement continued till the Caliphate of Omar, when, there being no scarcity of Moslem husbandmen, the Jews were expatriated, and entire possession taken of their lands.[2]

Territory, how disposed of.

Jewish cultivators left in occupation.

[1] Abdallah ibn Rawâha first performed this duty, being a sort of arbiter between the Jewish cultivators and the Moslem proprietors. Whenever the former charged him with exceeding in his estimate, he would say: 'If it seem good unto you, take ye the estimated sum and give us the crop, or give us the estimated sum, and keep ye the crop.' The Jews greatly esteemed his justice. He was killed the year following at Mûta.

[2] This is the plain and consistent statement of Wâckidi. Advantage was naturally taken by Omar, when he decided on the expatriation of the Jews, of the fact that his son Abdallah had been wounded in his possessions at Kheibar; but it is distinctly admitted that there was no proof as to who committed the outrage. Omar concluded that it must have been the Jews, simply because it was the second case of the kind. The previous case was one of murder; but the perpetrator was not discovered, and therefore Mahomet justly paid the blood-money himself.

Two other grounds to justify Omar's expulsion of the Jews are given by tradition, (1) Mahomet had stipulated that the Jews were to hold possession, pending his pleasure,—they were mere tenants-at-will. (2) Mahomet said on

Special
ordinances
promul-
gated at
Kheibar.

Some special ordinances were promulgated in this campaign. The flesh of the domestic ass (which the army on
their first approach to Kheibar were driven by want of other
food to eat) was forbidden, as well as that of all carnivorous
animals.[1] Some restrictions were laid upon the immediate
liberty of cohabitation heretofore enjoyed in respect of
female captives; but, of whatever nature they were, it is
clear that they did not fetter Mahomet in the marriage contracted with his female captive Safia.[2] The most stringent
rules were issued to prevent fraudulent appropriation from
the common stock of booty. 'No Believer shall sell aught
of the spoil, until it has been divided; nor shall he take a
beast therefrom and, after riding upon it until it become
lean, return it to the common stock; nor shall he take and
wear a garment, and then send it back threadbare.' A follower was convicted of plundering two sandal-straps; the
articles in themselves were insignificant; yet, said the Prophet
to the thief: 'Verily there shall be cut out for thee hereafter
two thongs like unto them of fire.' When the army alighted
before Wadi al Cora, one of Mahomet's servants was shot by
an arrow while in the act of taking the litter down from one
of the camels. 'Welcome to Paradise!' exclaimed the by-

his death-bed that no religion but Islâm was to be permitted throughout the
peninsula. I doubt both grounds, and believe that they have been adduced
simply from the desire to justify Omar's cruel expulsion of the Jews. (On the
parallel case of the Christians of Najrân, vide *supra*, p. 159.) According to
Sprenger, Omar paid the Jews of Kheibar half the value of their lands as
compensation.

[1] See the similar prohibitions in the Corân (Sura v.), including what is
torn, or dieth of itself, &c. There are some curious traditions on this part of
the narrative; the soldiers were everywhere boiling asses' flesh in their pots
throughout the camp, when the order was given, and forthwith they all overturned their pots. Horseflesh is allowed.

[2] The subject is one into which, from its nature, I cannot enter with much
detail; but as it partly affects the character of Mahomet, in not having himself conformed to a law imposed upon his followers, I may remark that some
traditions hold that Mahomet now prescribed that the 'istibra,' or interval
required of a woman between divorce and re-marriage, was to be equally observed in the case of women taken in war as in all other cases. The Sonna has
fixed this period for female slaves at half the interval required for free women,
—that is, two months (or possibly a month and a half), before the lapse of
which, consorting with slave girls so captured is unlawful. Mahomet did
not himself conform to this rule in the case of Safia, as before explained.
Some traditions make the prohibition delivered on the present occasion to
apply to pregnant women only; but, if so, it is not apparent at what later
period the further and more general restriction was introduced.

standers. 'Never!' said Mahomet; 'by Him in whose hand my life is! Even now his vestment is burning upon him in the fire of Hell; for he pilfered it before Kheibar from amongst the booty.'[1]

As a counterpart to this incident, and showing the certainty of Paradise secured by the mere *profession* of Islâm, I may transcribe the following tradition. Al Aswad, the shepherd of one of the Jews of Kheibar, came over to Mahomet, and declared himself a believer. Abandoning his flock, he straightway joined the Moslem army and fought in its ranks.[2] He was struck by a stone and killed, before he had yet as a Moslem offered up a single prayer. But he died fighting for the faith, and therefore had secured the Martyr's crown. Surrounded by a company of his followers, Mahomet visited the corpse, which had been laid out for him to pray over. When he drew close to the spot, he abruptly stopped and looked away from the dead body. 'Why dost thou thus avert thy face?' asked those about him. 'Because,' said Mahomet, 'two black-eyed houries of Paradise, his wives,

A martyr gains Paradise who had never prayed.

---

[1] The story is very possibly exaggerated, it being an object among the Mussulmans to make the general right of the army in all the booty taken by it as sacred as possible. But it shows the tendency and spirit of the system, under which a tradition of this nature could be put into the mouth of the Prophet, and, as such, gain currency.

[2] It is said that he asked Mahomet what he was to do with his flock. On the principle that a believer must discharge all his trusts and obligations, even those contracted with idolaters, before joining the standard of Islâm, the Prophet desired him to throw a handful of gravel in the faces of the sheep and goats, whereupon they all ran off forthwith to their owner in the fortress.

On the same principle, it is said that Ali and other converts first scrupulously discharged the trusts which the Coreish had committed to them, before leaving Mecca to join Mahomet at Medîna. And a like principle has been applied by many strict Mahometans in decisive condemnation of the perfidy of the Sepoys in the late Indian rebellion;—they were the servants of the British Government; and (even if there had been grounds for a religious war) ought first, like Ali and Al Aswad, to have discharged their trusts in full, and *e.g.* rendered up, instead of plundering, the arsenals and treasures in their custody.

As a counterpoise to Al Aswad's integrity, I may mention the artifice by which Al Hajâj is said to have recovered his debts. With Mahomet's permission he went to Mecca, and told the Coreish that Mahomet had been vanquished at Kheibar, and, with all his followers, taken prisoner. The Coreish, in ecstasies at the intelligence, paid off all his claims. Before leaving Mecca, he made known to Abbâs, on condition of his keeping it secret for three days, that he had told a lie,—for that Mahomet had vanquished Kheibar, and married the king's daughter. The story is doubtful, however.

are with the Martyr now; they wipe the dust from off his face, and fondly solace him.'[1]

Mahomet welcomes Jáfar and other Abyssinian exiles. Autumn. A.H. VII. A.D. 628.

About this period, Mahomet had the pleasure to welcome back his cousin Jáfar, Ali's brother, who, with some of the exiles just returned from Abyssinia, went out to meet the army as it came back from Kheibar. 'I know not,' Mahomet said, 'which of the two delighteth me the most— Jáfar's arrival, or the conquest of Kheibar.' The army cheerfully acceded to his proposal that Jáfar and his comrades should be admitted to share in the spoil.

And marries Omm Habîba.

On the return of Mahomet to Medîna, he completed the marriage with Omm Habîba, daughter of Abu Sofiân, which the Negûs had contracted for him in Abyssinia. There were now nine wives, besides two female slaves, in the harem of the Prophet.

Mahomet bewitched by Jews.

Before closing this chapter, which contains the last notice of the Jews of Arabia, I ought to mention the tale of Mahomet's having been bewitched by a Jewish spell. On his return from Hodeibia, the Jews who still remained at Medîna (ostensibly converted but hypocrites at heart) bribed a sorcerer named Labîd and his daughters to bewitch Mahomet. This they did by secretly procuring hairs combed from the Prophet's head, and tying eleven knots with them on a palm-branch, which was then sunk at the bottom of a well with a large stone over it. The enchantment took effect: Mahomet began to pine away—to fancy he had done things which in reality he never had done, to lose his appetite, and to neglect his wives. At last, Gabriel told him the secret of his ailment. The well was emptied, and the knots untied. Immediately the spell broke, and the Prophet was relieved.

Suras cxiii. and cxiv.

I must confess myself unable to decide what portion of the tale is true, or whether it has any foundation at all in fact. The common tradition is, that the last two Suras in the Corân were revealed on this occasion, containing a charm against all spells and incantations; and, that during the

---

[1] Neither can I vouch for this story; but, like that in the last note, it illustrates the spirit of Islâm, and the teaching of Mahomet, under the influence of which such tales grew up. 'Whenever a martyr is slain in battle,' so runs the tradition, 'his two black-eyed wives, the houries, draw near unto him, wipe the dust from off his face, and say,—" *The Lord cast dust on the face of him who hath cast dust on thine, and slay him who slew thee!*"'

recitation of the eleven verses which they contain, the knots unravelled themselves one by one till the whole were unloosed, and the charm dissolved.   One of the Suras is as follows :—

Say ;—I flee for Refuge to the Lord of the Daybreak,—from the evil of that which he hath created ; and from the evil of the darkness when it overshadoweth ; and from the evil of the Women that blow upon the knots ; and from the evil of the Envious man when he envieth.

Sura cxiii.

The story may possibly have grown out of the penultimate verse of this Sura, in which Mahomet prays to be delivered ' from the evil of women blowing upon knots.'   Or, on the other hand, it may be founded on suspicions actually entertained by Mahomet against the Jews, of sorcery by the tying of knots and other forms of incantation ; and these suspicions may have led to the composition of the Sura.

Considerations as to credibility of the tale.

The latter alternative is supported by the consideration that Mahomet was by nature superstitious, and that he had already suspected the Jews of bewitching the Moslem women into barrenness.[1]   On the present occasion, he is said to have caused the well into which the mysterious knots had been cast to be dug up, and another sunk in its place.   On his return from visiting the spot, he told Ayesha that ' the date-trees in the garden were like devils' heads, and the water of the well dark as a decoction of Henna.'   She enquired whether the incident might with propriety be spoken of ; he replied that it would be better that she should not divulge it, lest it might cause the evil of witchcraft to spread amongst his people.

Its credibility partly sustained.

Some traditions say that the sorcerer was put to death ; but the more reliable account is, that Mahomet let him go free, but turned with aversion from him.

The sorcerer allowed to escape.

[1] Vide *supra,* p. 208.

CHAPTER XXII.

PILGRIMAGE TO MECCA.

A.H. VII.—*February*, A.D. 629.

Expedi-
tions in
autumn
and winter
A.H. VII.
A.D. 628.

AFTER returning from Kheibar, Mahomet passed the rest of the autumn and the winter at Medîna. Five or six expeditions were, during this period, despatched, under command of different Moslem chiefs, in various directions. Beyond the chastisement and plunder of some offending tribes, and an occasional reverse, they were not attended by any political results. But they show that the influence of Mahomet was fast expanding and bringing him gradually into relations, hostile or friendly, with even distant tribes.[1]

Mahomet
sets out on
Lesser Pil-
grimage.
A.H. VII.
February,
A.D. 629.

The time had now come round when Mahomet, according to the treaty of Hodeibia, might visit Mecca and fulfil undisturbed the Omra, or Lesser Pilgrimage, from the rites of which he had been in the previous year debarred. Besides those who had made the unsuccessful pilgrimage to Hodeibia, many others now accompanied him, so that the cavalcade numbered about two thousand men. Each was armed, according to the stipulation, only with a sword; but, as a precaution against treachery, a large reserve of armour and

[1] Abu Bakr and Omar were among the commanders, and the expeditions were to distant parts; one beyond Mecca towards Najrân, the others to Nejd in the east, and towards Kheibar in the north. One of the parties consisting of thirty men was cut to pieces, the leader only escaping. In another, many prisoners were taken, and among them (according to Sprenger) a female of great beauty who was sent to Mecca in ransom for certain prisoners; it seems doubtful, however, whether there were any prisoners there at this time. In another expedition, Mahomet chided Osâma son of Zeid for killing an antagonist who shouted aloud the Moslem creed: 'What! didst thou split open his breast to see whether he told the truth or not?' Osâma promised not to do the like again.

lances was carried separately.   Muhammad, son of Maslama, with a hundred horse, marched one stage in advance of the pilgrims.   Sixty camels for sacrifice were also driven in front.

At Marr al Tzahrân, one stage from Mecca, Mahomet sent forward the store of armour to the valley of Yajâj outside the sacred territory, where it remained guarded by two hundred well-appointed soldiers, while the rest of the pilgrims advanced to the Káaba.   The victims were also sent forward to a spot in the immediate vicinity of Mecca. *Precautionary arrangements before entering Mecca.*

Meanwhile, the Coreish, apprised of Mahomet's near approach, according to agreement evacuated the city in a body; and, ascending the adjacent hills, watched with curious eye for the appearance of the Exile so long the troubler of their city.   At last the cavalcade was seen emerging from the northern valley.   At its head was Mahomet, seated on Al Caswa; Abdallah ibn Rawâha, walking in front, held the bridle; around the Prophet crowded his chief Companions; and behind, in a long extended line, followed. the rest of the pilgrims on camels and on foot. Seven eventful years had passed since Mahomet and the Refugees last saw their native valley and its Holy temple. They hastened forward with the eagerness of long repressed desire, shouting the pilgrim cry, *Labbeik! Labbeik!*   Still mounted on his camel, the pilgrim's mantle drawn under his right arm and thrown over the left shoulder, Mahomet approached the Káaba, touched the Black stone reverentially with his staff, and then accomplished the seven prescribed circuits of the Holy house.   The people followed, and, at the bidding of Mahomet, to show the Meccans that they were not weakened (as their enemies pretended) by the fever of Medîna, they ran the first three circuits at a rapid pace. Abdallah, as he led the Prophet's camel, shouted at the pitch of his voice some warlike and defiant verses.   But Omar checked him. And Mahomet said: ' Gently! son of Rawâha! Recite not this; but say instead, *There is no God but the Lord alone!   It is He that hath upholden His servant, and exalted His army!   Alone hath He discomfited the Confederated hosts.*'   Abdallah proclaimed this accordingly : and all the people taking up his words shouted them aloud as they ran round the Káaba, till the sound reverberated throughout the valley. *Mahomet enters Mecca; performs circuit of Káaba;*

D D

And slays the victims.

The circuits completed, Mahomet, still upon his camel, proceeded to the adjoining eminence of Safa, and rode from thence to the opposite rising ground of Marwa and back again, seven times, according to the ancient custom. The victims having then been brought and placed in order at Marwa, were sacrificed; Mahomet calling aloud: 'This is the place of sacrifice, and so is every open valley of Mecca.' Then he shaved his head, and thus ended the ceremonies of the Lesser pilgrimage.

Guard over weapons do the same.

His next care was to relieve the soldiers on guard over the weapons at Yajâj, who then visited Mecca and fulfilled their pilgrimage after the same example.

Public prayer performed at the Káaba

On the morrow, Mahomet entered the Káaba and remained there till the hour of mid-day prayer. At the appointed time, Bilâl ascended the Holy house, and from its summit vociferated the Moslem call to Prayer. The pilgrims assembled at the cry, and under the shadow of the Temple the service was led by the Prophet in the same form as in the great Mosque of Medîna.

Singular sight presented by Mecca.

It was surely a strange sight which at this time presented itself in the vale of Mecca,—a sight unique in the history of the world. The ancient city is for three days evacuated by all its inhabitants, high and low, every house deserted; and, as they retire, the exiled converts, many years banished from their birthplace, approach in a great body, accompanied by their allies, revisit the empty homes of their childhood, and within the short allotted space fulfil the rites of pilgrimage. The ousted inhabitants, climbing the heights around, take refuge under tents or other shelter amongst the hills and glens; and, clustering on the overhanging peak of Abu Cobeis, thence watch the movements of the visitors beneath, as with the Prophet at their head they make the circuit of the Káaba and the rapid procession between Safa and Marwa; and anxiously scan every figure if perchance they may recognise among the worshippers some long-lost friend or relative.[1] It was a scene rendered possible only by the throes which gave birth to Islâm.

[1] Her Highness the Begum of Bhopâl thus describes the hill Abu Cobeis: 'The ascent of this hill is only about one mile from the base. The view from its summit of the house of God, its enclosure and of the whole district comprised within the sacred boundary is very distinct and picturesque. It is possible even to see distinctly the worshippers employed at their devotions within the holy shrine.'—*Pilgrimage to Mecca,* p. 204.

While at Mecca, Mahomet entered none of the houses there. He lived in a tent of leather pitched for him in the open space south of the Káaba. But he held friendly communication with several of the citizens. And, during this interval, he was not deterred either by the sacred object of his visit, his advanced age (now exceeding threescore years), or the recollection that within the present year he had already welcomed three new inmates to his harem, from negotiating another marriage. Meimûna, the favoured lady, was sister to Omm al Fadhl wife of Abbâs, into whose keeping since her widowhood she had committed the disposal of her hand. Mahomet listened to the overtures of his uncle that she should be added to the number of his wives, the more readily perhaps as two of her sisters were already allied to his family, one being the wife of Jáfar, and another the widow of Hamza.

Mahomet takes Meimûna to wife.

Mahomet endeavoured to turn the present opportunity for conciliating the citizens of Mecca to the best effect, and, as the sequel will show, not without success. But the time was short. Already the stipulated term of three days was ended, and he had entered on a fourth, when Suheil and Huweitib, chief men of the Coreish, appeared before him and said: 'The period allowed thee hath elapsed: depart now therefore from amongst us.' To which the Prophet replied courteously: 'And what harm if ye allowed me to remain and celebrate my nuptials in your midst, and make you a feast at which ye might all sit down?' 'Nay,' roughly answered the chiefs, ' we have no need of thy viands: retire!' Mahomet gave immediate orders for departure: it was proclaimed among the pilgrims that by the evening not one should be left behind at Mecca. Placing his bride in charge of his servant Abu Râfi, he himself proceeded at once to Sarif, distant from the city eight or ten Arabian miles.[1] In the evening Abu Râfi, carrying Meimûna with him, reached the same place, and there the marriage was consummated. Early next morning, the march was resumed, and the *cortége* returned to Medîna.

Mahomet warned to leave Mecca.

Consummates his marriage with Meimûna.

Meimûna is said to have been at this time six-and-twenty years of age. She survived the Prophet fifty years, and was

Number of his harem now complete.

[1] She died A.H. 61, aged eighty. Burton states that her tomb is still visited at this place in the Wady Fâtima.

buried on the spot on which she had celebrated her marriage with him.[1] The harem of Mahomet had reached its limit; for this was the last marriage contracted by him. He now had ten wives, besides two slaves or concubines. But Zeinab bint Khozeima died before him; the number consequently was then reduced to nine, or, including concubines, to eleven.[2]

Sister and niece of his bride accompany him to Medina.

Mahomet brought with him to Medîna his bride's sister, Salma the widow of Hamza (who, it would seem, had not accompanied her husband in his exile) and Omârah, her unmarried daughter. Jáfar, Ali, and Zeid ibn Hârith, each contending for the honour of receiving Omârah into his family, Mahomet decided in favour of Jáfar, because he was married to her aunt.

Khâlid, Amru, and Othmân ibn Talha, go over to Mahomet.

Another sister of Meimûna was the mother of Khâlid, the famous warrior who had turned the tide of the battle at Ohod against the Moslems. Not long after the marriage of his aunt to the Prophet, Khâlid repaired to Medîna, and gave in his adhesion to the cause of Islâm. Two others followed him. One, his friend the equally famous Amru, whose poetic talents had often been used for the annoyance and injury of Mahomet. He was a man of weight in the councils of the Coreish, and had been employed by them in their embassy to Abyssinia.[3] The other was Othmân son of

---

[1] Mahomet's jealousy of his wives may be illustrated by the following anecdote: A deputation from a certain tribe came to Medîna, asking Mahomet for help to discharge a debt which he promised to give when the tithes came in. A nephew of Meimûna, being with this party, went to see his aunt. Mahomet coming suddenly into the place was disconcerted at the sight of the young man in such a position; his visage showed marks of wrath, and he turned to go away. 'It is only my sister's son,' cried Meimûna after him. So he returned. Then he took the young man into the Mosque for the mid-day prayer; and dismissed him with a blessing, placing both hands upon his head, and drawing them over his nose.

[2] I have not thought it necessary to mention two or three other women whose intended marriage with Mahomet was broken off at various stages before consummation; more especially as doubt attaches to the narratives. The families of these women would naturally try to suppress the tradition of such abortive negotiations as not creditable to them; but, whatever the cause, little credence is, I think, to be placed in the not very edifying details connected with them.

[3] His name is properly Amr, the u at its close being added by Arab scribes to distinguish it from that of Omar, which it otherwise resembles, when written. But Amru (or Amrou), the conqueror of Egypt, is a name familiar to the European reader, and the confusion from changing it would not be counterbalanced by the benefits of orthography. He was one of the envoys sent by the Coreish to Abyssinia; vide supra, p. 97.

Talha, a chief of some note, and custodian of the Káaba.   He had, no doubt, in that capacity, attended with the keys of his office to give Mahomet admittance to the Holy house; and, perhaps, like many others, who gazed from a respectful distance on that memorable scene, was gained over by the earnest devotion of Mahomet to the national shrine, and by the elevation and beauty of the services which he there performed.

The position of Mahomet at Mecca was greatly strengthened by the accession of such leading men.   The balance was already wavering : it required little now to throw it entirely on the side of Islâm.   To what extent persons of less note and influence about this time came over to Medîna, or remaining at Mecca declared in favour of Mahomet, is not told to us.   But there can be no doubt that the movement was not confined to Khâlid, Amru, and Othmân, but was wide and general ; and that the cause of Islâm was every day gaining popularity.

Mahomet's position at Mecca improving.

His visit to Mecca enabled Mahomet to see and estimate the growth of his own influence there, upon the one hand, and the waning power and spirit of the Coreish, upon the other.   The citizens of Mecca were weary of intestine war and bloodshed.   The advocates of peace and compromise were growing in numbers and in confidence.   Among the Coreish there were no chiefs of marked ability or commanding influence.   A bold and rapid stroke of policy might put an end to the struggle which for so many years had depressed and agitated Mecca.   A *coup d'état* was now becoming possible.

Coup d'état becoming possible.

CHAPTER XXIII.

BATTLE OF MÛTA, AND OTHER EVENTS IN THE FIRST EIGHT
MONTHS OF A.H. VIII.—A.D. 629.

Ætat. 61.

Unfortunate expedition against Bani Suleim. A.H. VII. April, A.D. 629.

DURING the summer, several military excursions were undertaken. Some of these ended disastrously. About a month after the return of Mahomet from pilgrimage, he despatched a party of fifty men to the Bani Suleim, under a converted chief of their own, with the view apparently of winning them over to the faith of Islâm. But the tribe, suspicious of their designs, received the strangers with a cloud of arrows. Most of them were slain, and the leader with difficulty escaped to Medîna. The Bani Suleim must have seen cause shortly after to change their views, for we find them amongst the tribes which in the following year sent embassies of submission to the Prophet, and they contributed an important contingent to the attack on Mecca.

Marauding party sent against Bani Leith. A.H. VIII. June, A.D. 629.

Two or three months later an expedition was planned against a petty branch of the Bani Leith, near Cudeid, on the road to Mecca, the object of which is not stated. The encampment of the tribe was surprised, and their camels plundered. But the marauders were in their turn pursued, and were only saved by a rapid flight back to Medîna.

Bani Murra chastised.

In the preceding winter, a small party, sent by Mahomet towards Fadak, had been cut to pieces by the Bani Murra. A detachment of two hundred men was now despatched to inflict chastisement upon them : ' If the Lord deliver them into thy hands,' said Mahomet to the leader, ' let not a soul of them escape.' The commission was executed with complete success. All who fell within reach of the avenging force were slain, and the camels of the tribe were carried off in triumph to Medîna.

Soon after this, a party of fifteen men was sent to Dzât Atlâh, a place on the borders of Syria. There they found a great assemblage of people, who were called upon to embrace Islâm. A shower of arrows was the decisive answer. The Mussulmans fought desperately : one man alone survived to tell the tale. Mahomet was much afflicted by this calamity, and planned an expedition to avenge the death of his followers. But tidings reached him that the place had been deserted, and he relinquished the idea for the moment. Like similar mishaps, this reverse is described by tradition with such enigmatical brevity that it is difficult to determine with what object the little band was sent forth. It may have been an embassy to certain tribes ; or a secret mission to spy out the cause of some rumoured gathering and uneasiness on the Syrian frontier. However this may be, the disaster not improbably paved the way for the great inroad directed by Mahomet about two months afterwards against the border-districts of Syria.

Mishap at Dzât Atlâh. A.H. VIII. July, A.D. 629.

Perhaps the cause of the attack on Mûta.

The cause ordinarily assigned for this invasion of the Roman territory was the murder by Sharahbîl, chief of Maâb or Mûta, of a messenger despatched by Mahomet to the Ghassânide Prince at Bostra. It was immediately resolved to attack and punish the offending chief. A general assembly of the fighting men was called, and a camp of three thousand soldiers formed outside the city at Jorf. A white banner was mounted ; and the Prophet, placing it in the hands of Zeid son of Hârith as commander, bade him march to the spot where his messenger had been slain, summon the inhabitants to embrace Islâm, and, should they refuse, in the name of the Lord to fight against them. If Zeid were cut down, then Jáfar was to command ; if Jáfar, then Abdallah ibn Rawâha ; and if he too were disabled, then the army should choose their own commander. Mahomet accompanied them as far as the *Mount of Farewell*, a rising ground some little distance from Medîna ; and, as they passed onwards, blessed them thus : 'The Lord shield you from every evil, and bring you back in peace, laden with spoil !'

A large army marches from Medîna upon Mûta. A.H. VIII. September, A.D. 629.

Tidings of the approach of this formidable army reached Sharahbîl, who summoned to his assistance all the tribes of the

Preparations made by Syrian

tribes for
its repulse.

vicinity. The hostile incursions which Mahomet had from time to time directed against the Syrian border, the repeated attacks on Dûma, the conquest of Kheibar, and his generally aggressive attitude towards the north, had no doubt led to precautionary measures of alliance among the people of the frontier. Upon the alarm of invasion, therefore, there quickly rallied round Sharahbîl a large and (compared with the troops of Medîna) a well-appointed army.[1] On reaching

Council of
war held by
Moslems at
Maân.

Maân, Zeid first received the startling intelligence of these preparations. The enemy, he heard, was encamped at Maâb, in the territory of Belcâa; and his apprehension was increased by the rumour that it was composed of Roman troops, and that the Kaiser was himself at their head.[2] He halted, and for two whole days the Moslem chiefs discussed the difficulties of their position. Many advised that a letter should be sent to Mahomet. He had not contemplated, they said, an encounter with the Imperial forces; they were sent only to avenge the treachery of a petty chief, and ought not to risk an encounter with an enemy so vastly their superior : at least, the Prophet should be apprised of the new aspect of affairs, and solicited for fresh instructions. Abdallah, on the contrary, urged an immediate advance: 'What have we marched thus far for,' he cried out indignantly, ' but for this? Is it our numbers, or the help of the Lord, in which we trust? Victory or martyrdom—one or the other—is surely ours! *Then forward!*' Overcome by this fervid appeal, they all responded: ' By the Lord! The son of Rowâha speaketh the truth. Let us hasten onwards!' So the camp advanced.

Battle of
Mûta.

On entering the confines of Belcâa, on the southern shore of the Dead Sea, they suddenly found themselves confronted by an enemy in numbers and equipment far surpassing anything they had ever seen. Alarmed at the glittering array, they fell back, notwithstanding the enthusiastic aspirations which had just pervaded their ranks, on the village of Mûta.

---

[1] M. C. de Perceval quotes Theophanes to show that this great army was probably brought together by Theodorus brother of Heraclius, which he thinks may account for the rumour reaching the Moslem camp that the Kaiser himself was in the field with two hundred thousand men.

[2] The Syrian army was composed partly of Romans, partly of the semi-Christian tribes of the desert,—the Bani Bahrâ, Balî, Wâil, Bakr, Lakhm, and Judzâm.

There, finding advantageous ground, they halted, and forming
front resolved to offer battle. The Roman phalanx, with its
cloud of Arabs upon either flank, moved steadily down upon
them. Zeid, seizing the white flag, led his columns forward,
and fought manfully at their head till pierced by the spears
of the enemy he fell to the ground. Then Jáfar leaped from
his horse, and, maiming it in token that he would either
conquer or die, raised aloft the banner, and urged forward
the attack. His body was soon covered with wounds, yet
he fought on till a Roman soldier closed with him, and dealt
him a fatal blow.[1] Seeing Jáfar fall, Abdallah seized the
standard, but he, too, speedily met the same fate. Then a
Citizen rescuing the ensign planted it in the ground, and
cried aloud,—*Hither, hither, ye Moslems!* and there was a
temporary rally. Meanwhile, following the instructions of
Mahomet, the chief men assembled in hasty council, and
with one consent fixed on Khâlid, who forthwith assumed the
command. But the chance of victory had passed away. The
ranks were already broken ; and the Romans in full pursuit
made great havoc amongst the fugitives. It remained for
Khâlid but to save the scattered and retreating columns from
destruction, and even this taxed to the utmost his great skill
and prowess. By a series of ingenious and rapid movements,
he succeeded in deceiving or eluding the enemy, and drew
off the shattered remains of his army from the field, with
little further loss. He dared not linger in the dangerous
vicinity, but marched back straightway to Medîna. As he
drew near to the city, the people came out to meet the returning army, and reproachfully cast dust at them, crying
out : ' Ah ye runaways! Do ye indeed flee before the enemy
when fighting for the Lord ? ' But Mahomet, who also had
ridden out, carrying on the mule in front of him the little
son of Jáfar, put a stop to these reproaches, and reassured
the downcast troops by saying : ' Nay, they are not runaways ; but they are men who will yet again return to battle,
if the Lord will.'

Khâlid saves the broken force.

[1] The song with which Jáfar led the attack is no doubt apocryphal, but it
strongly illustrates the fanatical feeling now rapidly growing up : ' *Paradise!* '
he cried, amid the glare and heat of the dusty battlefield,—'*Oh Paradise!
how fair a resting-place! Cold is the water there, and sweet the shade. Rome,
Rome! thine hour of tribulation draweth nigh. When I close with her, I will
hurl her to the ground.*'

Mahomet's grief at death of Jáfar and Zeid.

The loss of his cousin Jáfar the brother of Ali, and of Zeid the faithful and beloved friend of five-and-thirty years, affected Mahomet deeply. On the first intelligence of the reverse, and of the death of these dear friends, which he received early through a confidential messenger, he proceeded to the house of Jáfar. His widow Asma tells us that she had just bathed and dressed her little ones when the Prophet entered, embraced the children tenderly, and burst into tears. Asma guessed the truth, and wailed loudly. A crowd of women soon gathering around her, Mahomet silently left the place, and returning to his own family desired them to send provisions to Jáfar's house. 'No food,' he said, 'will be prepared there this day; for they are overwhelmed with grief at the loss of their master.'[1] He then went to the house of Zeid; and Zeid's little daughter rushed into his arms, crying bitterly. Mahomet was overcome, and wept until he sobbed aloud. A bystander, thinking to check his grief, said to him: 'Why is this, O Prophet?' 'This,' he replied, 'is but the fond yearning in the heart of friend for friend.'[2]

Martyrdom of Farwa.

In connection with the battle of Mûta, I may mention here the story of Farwa, an Arab of the Bani Judzâm, and Governor of Ammân, who is represented by tradition (though upon imperfect evidence) as one of the early martyrs. He sent a despatch announcing his conversion to Mahomet, with several presents,—a white mule, a horse, an ass, and raiment inwrought with gold. The presents were graciously acknowledged in a letter from the Prophet, which contained directions for the spiritual guidance of the new convert. The Roman government heard of his defection, and sought to bribe the renegade, by offers of promotion, to return to the Christian faith. He refused, and was put to death.[3]

---

[1] Asma afterwards married Abu Bakr, and on his death Ali, and bore sons to both.

[2] Next morning, he entered smiling into the Mosque, and when the people accosted him he said: 'That which ye saw in me yesterday was because of sorrow for the slaughter of my Companions, until I saw them in Paradise, seated as brethren, opposite one another, upon couches. And in some I perceived marks, as it were wounds of the sword. And I saw Jáfar as an angel with two wings, covered with blood,—his limbs stained therewith.' Hence Jáfar is known as 'the winged Martyr.'

[3] The tradition is surrounded by much that is marvellous; but there must have been some foundation of fact. Theophanes mentions about this period

The repulse of his army from Mûta affected dangerously the prestige of Mahomet among the tribes of the Syrian frontier. There were rumours that the Bedouin tribes of that neighbourhood had assembled in great force, and were even threatening a descent upon Medîna. Amru, the new convert, was therefore placed at the head of three hundred men, including thirty horse, with instructions to subjugate the hostile tribes and incite those whom he found friendly to harass the Syrian border. The name and ability of Amru justified the selection; being, moreover, connected with the Bani Balî, a powerful community in the vicinity of the field of operations, he was possessed of personal influence which would aid in effecting the objects of the campaign. In the event of serious opposition, he was to call upon those Arabs who had already tendered their submission, to come to his aid. After a march of ten days he encamped at a spring near the Syrian confines. There he found that the enemy were assembled in great numbers, and that he could look for little aid from the local tribes. He halted and despatched a messenger for reinforcements. Mahomet at once complied, and sent two hundred men (among whom were both Abu Bakr and Omar) under command of Abu Obeida. On joining Amru, Abu Obeida wished to assume the leadership of the whole force, or at the least to retain the chief authority over his own detachment; but Amru, giving promise of the decision and firmness which characterised him in after days, insisted on retaining the sole command. Abu Obeida, a man of mild and pliant temper, succumbed. 'If thou refusest to acknowledge my authority,' he said, 'I have no resource but to obey thee; for the Prophet strictly charged me to suffer no altercation, nor any division of command.' Amru replied imperiously: 'I am the chief over thee. Thou hast only brought a reinforcement to my army.' 'Be it so,' said Abu Obeida. Amru then assumed command of the united troops, and led their prayers; for thus early were the spiritual functions in Islâm blended with the political and military.

Amru, reinforced by Abu Obeida, restores Mahomet's prestige on Syrian border.
A.H. VIII.
October, A.D. 629.

the secession of the Arabs employed in guarding the Syrian frontier, as occasioned by the insolent refusal of a Roman officer to pay them their perquisites. On this they are said to have organised an attack on Ghaza. Such a movement may have occurred in connection with the numerous accessions to Mahomet's cause about this time, and the expedition to Tabûk next year.

Strengthened by this addition to his forces, Amru went forward. He passed through the territories of the Bani Odzra and Balî, receiving their allegiance : when he reached their farther limits, the enemy which had assembled to oppose him fled in alarm. Thus Amru had the satisfaction of despatching a messenger to announce to Mahomet the complete success of his first campaign, and the re-establishment of the Prophet's influence on the frontier of Syria. He then returned to Medîna.

Expedition of the Fish. A.H. VIII. November, A.D. 629.

In the month following, to compensate Abu Obeida for his disappointment in giving up the command to Amru, Mahomet sent him at the head of three hundred men to chastise a refractory branch of the Bani Joheina on the sea-coast. There was no fighting in this expedition, but it has become famous from the occurrence of a curious incident. Provisions failed, and the troops were already well nigh famished, when to their joy a prodigious fish was cast opportunely on the shore, so large that it sufficed amply to relieve their hunger.[1]

Raid in Nejd. December, A.D. 629.

There was one other petty expedition during the winter against a tribe of the Bani Ghatafân in Nejd, which yielded large plunder in camels, flocks, and prisoners. The object is not stated. A fair damsel fell to the lot of the leader. He presented her to Mahomet, who again gave her to one of his followers.

Various tribes tender their submission.

Besides the Bedouin tribes in the direction of Syria gained over by the success of Amru, several others now gave in their adhesion to Mahomet. Among these were the Bani Abs, Murr, and Dzobian ; and the Bani Fezâra with their chief Oyeina, who had so long caused anxiety and alarm at Medîna, at last tendered their submission. The Bani Suleim, which, like the Fezâra, had taken part in the siege of Medîna, also joined the cause of Islâm about this time, and engaged to bring, when called upon, one thousand men into the field. Most of the tribes in the vicinity of Medîna had already recognised the supremacy of Mahomet.[2] The courteous

[1] So Wâckidi ; but Hishâmi deals in extravagancies. The whole army, which had been reduced to a famishing state, fed for twenty days upon it, and from being lean and famished became strong and fat. One of its bones, being set up as an arch, a camel with its rider passed under without touching it, &c.

[2] The Bani Ashjâ, who had joined in the siege of Medîna, gave in their adhesion shortly after the massacre of the Coreitza ; they told Mahomet that

treatment which the deputations of these various clans experienced from the Prophet, his ready attention to their grievances, the wisdom with which he composed their disputes, and the politic assignments of territory by which he rewarded an early declaration in favour of Islâm, made his name to be popular, and spread his fame as a great and generous Prince throughout the Peninsula.   And, moreover, the accession of so many tribes enabled him, whenever occasion might require, to call into the field a far more imposing force than he had ever before aspired to command.

they were so pressed by his warring against them, that they could stand out no longer.   In the Secretary's chapter of 'Deputations from the Tribes,' &c., we learn that the Bani Ashár from Jedda, the Bani Khushain, and the Bani Dous, came to Mahomet at Kheibar, the latter with sixty or seventy followers, to all of whom were assigned shares in the booty.   The Bani Sád ibn Bakr came over, A.H. V.; and the Bani Thalaba, A. H. VIII.   The Bani Abd al Keis (partly at least Christian) from Bahrein, in the same year.   The Bani Judzâm (see *ante*, p. 359) also in that year.   The chief of the latter tribe carried back a letter from Mahomet, of this tenor: 'Whoever accepteth the call to Islâm, he is amongst the confederates of the Lord: whoever refuseth the same, a truce of two months is allowed him for consideration.'   All the tribes of the vicinity accepted the invitation.

CHAPTER XXIV.

THE CONQUEST OF MECCA.

Ramadhân, A.H. VIII.—*January,* A.D. 630.

Ætat 61.

Pretext arises for advance upon Mecca.

THE truce of Hodeibia had been now nearly two years in force, when the alleged infraction of its terms by the Coreish afforded Mahomet a fair pretext for the grand object of his ambition, the conquest of Mecca.

Bani Bakr attack Bani Khozâa. A.H. VIII. December, A.D. 629.

The Bani Khozâa, as before noticed, acting on the discretion allowed by the treaty, had declared themselves the partisans of Mahomet; while the Bani Bakr had ranged themselves on the side of the Coreish. Both tribes inhabited Mecca and its adjoining valleys. There had been sanguinary feuds of old standing between them, and, though these paled before the excitement of the war with Mahomet, the murders which had been committed on either side still rankled in their breasts. The peace of Hodeibia allowed the Bani Bakr again to brood over their wrongs, and they sought opportunity to make reprisals. Aided by some of the chief men of the Coreish, who disguised themselves, they attacked by night an unsuspecting encampment of the Khozâa, and slew several of them.

Khozâa appeal to Mahomet, who promises aid.

A deputation of forty men from the injured tribe, mounted on camels, hastened to Medîna, spread their wrongs before the Prophet, and pleaded that the treacherous murders might be avenged. Entreaty was little needed. The opportunity long expected had at last arrived. Starting up, with his raiment yet ungirded, he fervently pledged himself to the suppliants: 'If I assist you not with the same aid as if the cause were mine own, then let me never more be assisted by

the Lord!'   A cloud at the moment chanced to overshadow
the heavens; accepting the augury, Mahomet added: 'As
the rain poureth down from yonder cloud, even so shall
succour descend upon the Bani Khozâa from above.'

The Coreish, aware of this deputation, were thrown into
great alarm.   They despatched Abu Sofiân to Medîna in the
hope of renewing and extending the compact of peace.   On
his way, he met Bodeil, a chief of the Bani Khozâa, who was
returning from Medîna after an interview with Mahomet.[1]
The mission of Abu Sofiân was not followed by any satisfactory result.   He could gain from Mahomet no promise,
nor any assurance of pacific designs.   Foiled in his endeavours, he took the only course open to him of expressing the
friendly relations which the Coreish desired to maintain.
He stood up in the court of the great Mosque, and cried
aloud: 'Hearken unto me, ye people!   Peace and protection I guarantee for all.'   To which Mahomet answered:
'It is thou that sayest this, not any one of us, O Abu Sofiân!'
Thereupon he departed home, and reported the affair to the
Coreish.   They perceived that they were in an evil plight;
but they did not suspect that Mahomet had any immediate
designs against them.[2]

[1] But it will be seen hereafter that that there are reasons for suspecting
collusion between Abu Sofiân and Bodeil.   Whether the collusion began at
this interview, or upon Abu Sofiân's return to Mecca, I cannot say.

[2] Abbasside tradition delights to cast contumely on Abu Sofiân.   On the
present occasion it turns him into a laughing-stock.   But, from passages that
follow, there will be seen ground for conjecturing that communications of a
less unfriendly character than those here represented, passed between him and
the Prophet.

The following narrative is strongly tinged with Alyite tendencies: 'Arrived at Medîna, Abu Sofiân entered the house of his daughter Omm Habîba
Mahomet's wife.   He was about to seat himself on the carpet or rug spread
upon the floor, when she hastily drew it away and folded it up.   'My
daughter!' he said, 'whether is it that thou thinkest the carpet is too good for
me, or that I am too good for the carpet?'   'Nay, but it is the carpet of the
Prophet,' she replied; 'and I choose not that thou, an impure idolater, shouldst
sit upon the Prophet's carpet.'   'Truly, my daughter, thou art changed for the
worse since thou leftest me.'   So saying, he went straight to Mahomet, but
could get no reply from his lips.   Omar, to whom he next addressed himself,
received him with indignation.   Ali was more cordial: 'Let me not go back
unsuccessful as I came,' urged Abu Sofiân; 'intercede for me with the
Prophet.'   'Alas for thee!' said Ali; 'truly, the Prophet hath resolved on a
thing concerning which we may not speak with thee.'   Then Abu Sofiân adjured

Prepara-
tions for
attacking
Mecca.

Mahomet had already resolved to make a grand attack upon his native city. But he kept his counsel secret even from his closest friends as long as it was possible.[1] To divert attention, he despatched a small body of men in another direction. Meanwhile he summoned his allies amongst the Bedouin tribes to join him at Medîna, or to meet him at certain convenient points, which he indicated to them, on the road to Mecca. At the last moment he ordered his followers in the city to arm themselves, announced his intentions, and enjoined on all the urgent command that no hint regarding his hostile designs should in any way reach Mecca. To this effect he prayed publicly: '*O Lord! Let not any spy draw near with tidings unto the Coreish: take away their sight, that they see me not until I come suddenly upon them and seize them unawares!*'

Hâtib's en-
deavour to
communi-
cate intel-
ligence
frustrated.

Notwithstanding this injunction, Hâtib, one of Mahomet's most trusted followers, despatched privately a female messenger with a letter to his friends in Mecca, containing intimation of the intended assault. Information of this soon came to the ears of the Prophet, and he sent Ali with Zobeir in pursuit of the messenger. They overtook her, and after a long search discovered the letter carefully hidden in her locks. Hâtib excused himself by the natural desire he had to save his unprotected family at Mecca; and the plea, in view of his former services, was graciously accepted.

Army
marches.
A.H. VIII.
January,
A.D. 630.

On January 1, A.D. 630, the army commenced its march. It was the largest force Medîna had ever seen. The tents of the Bedouin auxiliaries darkened the plain for miles

Fâtima (Ali's wife) to let her little son Hasan take him under his protection, 'and he will be the lord of the Arabs till the end of time.' But she told him that no one could be his protector against Mahomet. On this, he besought Ali for his advice. Ali said that he saw no other course for him, but to arise and call aloud that he took all parties under the guarantee of his protection: 'But will this benefit me at all?' 'Nay, I do not say so, but I see nothing else for thee.' Having followed this advice, Abu Sofiân returned to Mecca, and told the Coreish what he had done. 'But did Mahomet sanction thy guarantee?' asked they. He replied in the negative. 'Out upon thee!' they cried; 'this will not benefit us at all; the man meant only to make sport of thee.' 'I know it,' said Abu Sofiân, 'but I could think of nothing else that I could do.'

[1] Even Abu Bakr was kept in ignorance of it. Entering Ayesha's house, he found her busy preparing the accoutrements of the Prophet; and, enquiring the cause, was told that an expedition had been resolved on, but she did not know in what direction.

around, and several important tribes fell in with Mahomet on the line of march. Two of these, the Mozeina and Suleim, contributed each a thousand soldiers. Mahomet now found himself at the head of between eight and ten thousand men. Two of his wives, Zeinab and Omm Salmâ, accompanied him.[1] Zobeir with two hundred men led the van. The march was made with such rapidity that the army encamped at Marr al Tzahrân, one stage from Mecca, on the seventh or eighth day.

Meanwhile, Abbâs had joined Mahomet on the road. The traditions of the Abbassides claim him as having been long a true believer, and class him among the exiles from Mecca, the Refugees, whose favoured number was now about to close. But Abbâs was only worldly wise. He had waited till the supremacy of his nephew was beyond a doubt; and now, at the last moment, when there was no merit in the act, openly espoused his cause. Nevertheless, he was welcomed by the Prophet with favour and affection.[2]

Abbâs joins Mahomet.

And now we come to a curious and somewhat mysterious passage in the campaign. Mahomet commanded his followers that every one should kindle a fire that night on the heights above the camp. Ten thousand fires soon blazed on the mountain tops of Marr al Tzahrân. The Prophet trusted that this first intimation of his approach would burst upon the city with alarming grandeur, and prove the hopelessness of opposition. No certain information of the march of Ma-

Abu Sofiân visits camp of Mahomet.

---

[1] Omm Salmâ seems to have been the favourite companion of Mahomet on his marches. Ayesha is not mentioned as accompanying him after the affair in the expedition against the Bani Mustalick.

[2] He is said to have joined Mahomet near Râbigh, about half way between Medîna and Mecca. It is highly probable that he came by previous appointment. Abbasside tradition naturally makes everything as favourable to Abbâs as possible. The truth is that he always sailed with wind and tide. It is quite possible that ever since the treaty, and especially since the Pilgrimage, he may have been in collusion with Mahomet, and secretly forwarding his cause at Mecca.

Two other persons of some note also tendered allegiance to Mahomet on the march: Abu Sofiân, son of Mahomet's uncle Hârith; and Abdallah, brother of his wife Omm Salmâ. Omm Salmâ interceded for them; but Mahomet at first refused to receive them Both had incurred his severe displeasure,—the former having greatly annoyed him with his satires; and the latter having also been a keen opponent. Abu Sofiân, being repulsed, declared that he would go forth into the desert with his little son, and that there they would both die of hunger; whereat Mahomet relented.

homet from Medîna had yet reached the Coreish ; the enemy
had cut off carefully all sources of intelligence, and within
Mecca itself there may possibly have been traitors who
sought to lull suspicion. At last the chief men became
uneasy at the portentous calm, broken only by vague reports
of a coming storm ; and they sent forth Abu Sofiân to reconnoitre. In the evening, accompanied by Hakîm (the nephew
of Khadîja, who had shown kindness to Mahomet when shut
up with Abu Tâlib) and Bodeil the Khozâite chief, Abu
Sofiân sallied forth on the Medîna road. The fires on the
mountain tops began to appear in full sight and to engage
their speculations, when suddenly, in the dark, a stranger
approaching thus accosted Abu Sofiân : 'Abu Hantzala ![1]
is that thy voice I hear ?' 'Yes, I am he,' said Abu Sofiân,
'but what hast thou left behind thee ?' 'Yonder,' replied
the stranger, 'is Mahomet encamped with ten thousand
followers. See ye not the myriad fires which they have
kindled in their camp ? Believe and cast in thy lot with us,
else thy mother and thy house shall weep for thee !' It was
Abbâs who spoke. Mounted on the Prophet's white mule,
he had issued forth (tradition tells us), hoping that he might
meet some wayfarer on the road, and send him to the Coreish,
if haply they might come and sue for peace, and thus save
Mecca from destruction. 'Seat thee upon the mule behind
me,' continued Abbâs ; 'I will conduct thee to the Prophet,
and thou shalt seek for quarter from him.' They were soon
at the tent of Mahomet. Abbâs entered, and announced
the welcome news of the arrival of his distinguished friend :
'Take him to thy tent, Abbâs,' replied the Prophet ; 'and in
the morning come to me with him again.' In the morning
accordingly they sought the Prophet's tent : '*Out upon
thee, Abu Sofiân !*' cried Mahomet as the Coreishite chief
drew near ; '*hast thou not yet discovered that there is no God
but the Lord alone ?*' 'Noble and generous Sire ! Had there
been any God beside, verily he had been of some avail to
me.' '*And dost thou not acknowledge that I am the Prophet
of the Lord ?*' continued Mahomet. 'Noble Sire ! As to
this thing, there is yet in my heart some hesitancy.' 'Woe
is thee !' exclaimed Abbâs ; 'it is no time for hesitancy,
this. Believe and testify forthwith the creed of Islâm, or else

---

[1] Abu Sofiân, so called after his son, Hantzala.

thy neck shall be in danger!' It was, indeed, no time for
idle pride or scruple; and so Abu Sofiân, finding no alternative left him, repeated the formula of belief in God and in his
Prophet. What a moment of exultation it must have been
for Mahomet when he saw his great antagonist a suppliant
believer at his feet! 'Haste thee to Mecca!' he said; for
he knew well when to show forbearance and generosity;—
'haste thee to the city: no one that taketh refuge in the
house of Abu Sofiân shall be harmed this day. And hearken!
speak unto the people, that whoever closeth the door of his
house, the inmates thereof shall escape in safety.' Abu
Sofiân hastened to retire. But before he could quit the camp,
the forces were already under arms, and were being marshalled
in their respective columns. Standing by Abbâs, he watched
amazed the various tribes, each defiling with the banner
given to it by Mahomet, into its proper place. One by
one, the different clans were pointed out by name, and recognised. 'And what is that black mass,' asked Abu Sofiân,
'with dark mail and shining lances?' 'It is the flower of
the chivalry of Mecca and Medîna,' replied Abbâs—'the
favoured band that guards the person of the Prophet.'
'Truly,' exclaimed the astonished chief, 'this kingdom of thine
Uncle's is a mighty kingdom.' 'Nay, Abu Sofiân! he is more
than a King—he is a mighty Prophet!' 'Yes, thou sayest
truly; now let me go.' 'Away!' said Abbâs; 'speed thee to
thy people!'

Abu Sofiân hurried back to Mecca, and, as he entered the
city, he shouted at the pitch of his voice: 'Ye Coreish!
Mahomet is close upon us. He hath an army which ye are
not able to withstand. Whoever entereth the house of Abu
Sofiân shall be safe this day; and whoever shutteth his door
upon him shall be safe; and whosoever entereth the Holy
house shall be safe!' So the people fled in all directions to
their houses, and to the Káaba.

Abu Sofiân
carries mes-
sage of
quarter to
Mecca.

Such is the account given by tradition. But, beneath the
narrative, I find symptoms of a previous understanding between Mahomet and Abu Sofiân. Whether there was any
collusion so early as the visit of Abu Sofiân to Medîna,
whether Abbâs was charged by the chiefs of Mecca with the
conduct of negotiations with the Prophet, and from which
side the overtures first came, can be matter for conjecture

Was there
collusion
between
Abu Sofiân
and Ma-
homet?

only. But there seems strong reason to believe that the meeting by night of Abu Sofiân with Abbâs was a concerted measure, and not the result of mere accident. That Abu Sofiân, wearied with the long protracted struggle between the Prophet and his people,—a struggle now about to be renewed with all the prospects of internecine strife ; assured, from what he saw and heard at Medîna, that the chances of victory lay on Mahomet's side; and anxious to avert a bloody battle,—conspired to lull alarm and prevent a timely and a general rising at Mecca against the invader, seems perhaps hardly less evident. As hereditary leader of the Coreish he possessed more influence to effect that object than any other chief at Mecca, and of his influence Mahomet willingly availed himself. To the treason, or the patriotism, of Abu Sofiân, it is mainly due that the submission of Mecca was secured with scarcely any bloodshed. Such at least is the conclusion which I draw from the garbled tale of tradition.

The army moves forward upon Mecca.

To return to the camp of Mahomet. The army was now in full march on Mecca. It was an hour of anxiety for the Prophet. But when he reached the plain of Dzu Towa near the city, it became evident that his precautions had been effectual. Had any general opposition been organised to check his farther progress, this was the place where a stand would have been made ; yet no army appeared in sight. In token of his gratitude, he bowed himself low upon his camel, and offered up to God thanksgiving. The troops were told off in four divisions, and to each was assigned a different road, by which they were simultaneously to advance upon the city. They now separated to perform their several parts, with strict injunctions from Mahomet not to fight excepting in the last extremity, nor offer violence to any one. Zobeir, leading the left battalion, was to enter from the north. Khâlid, with the Bedouin tribes, was marshalled on the right : passing the city on the west he was to make his way into the southern or lower suburbs. The men of Medîna under Sád ibn Obâda were to force their way into the western quarter. The mild but vigilant Abu Obeida, commanding the flower of the force with the Refugees and followed by Mahomet himself, took the nearest road skirting Jebel Hind. This disposition of his forces was wisely made : if opposition were offered to any column, one of the other divisions would be at hand to take the enemy in the rear. As Sád led on the citizens of Medîna, he sang : 'To-day is the day of slaughter ; there is no security this day for Mecca!' Hearing these martial and vindictive words, and apprehending evil from the fiery temper of Sád, Mahomet took the Medîna banner from his hands, and gave it to Cays, his son,—a person of towering stature, but of gentler disposition than his father.

About this time, an old man, blind and decrepit, might be seen climbing, with the help of his daughter, one of the heights of Abu Cobeis which overhang the city. It was Abu Cuhâfa, the aged parent of Abu Bakr. To his frequent enquiry whether anything was yet in sight, the maiden at last replied : 'A dark moving mass has just emerged from yonder valley.' 'It is the army!' said the aged man. 'And now I see a figure hasting to and fro amid the columns of that mass.' 'This is the leader marshalling the force.' 'But the blackness is dispersing rapidly. It spreads'— continued the girl. 'Ah! then the army is advancing!' exclaimed Abu Cuhâfa ;—haste thee, my daughter, and lead me home.' It was full time to do so, for the troops were already sweeping along the approaches to the town on every side ; and a rude assailant snatched the maiden's silver necklace from her neck while she was yet guiding her father's tottering steps toward their house.

Abu Cuhâfa watches advance of Moslem army.

The several columns entered peaceably, excepting that of Khâlid. On the road by which he was to approach, the bitterest of Mahomet's enemies and those most deeply implicated in the attack upon the Bani Khozâa, had taken up a defensive position, or perhaps in despair they were preparing for a hasty flight towards the sea-shore. They were led by Safwân, Suheil, and Ikrima son of Abu Jahl. As the battalion of Khâlid appeared in view, it was saluted by a discharge of arrows. But Khâlid was ready to receive his opponents, and soon put them all to flight. Flushed with success, and unmindful of the Prophet's order, he pursued with his wild Bedouins the fugitive Coreish into the streets of Mecca. The leaders escaped ; but eight-and-twenty citizens were killed in the conflict. Khâlid lost only two men, and those because they missed their way.

Khâlid encounters opposition.

Mahomet's concern at the encounter.

While this encounter was going forward, Mahomet, following the column of the Refugees, crossed an eminence from whence the full view of the vale and city burst upon him. But his pleasure at the grateful prospect was at once turned into concern as his eye caught the gleaming of swords on the farther side of the city, and the troops of Khâlid in pursuit. 'What!' he cried in surprise and anger, 'did I not strictly command that there should not be any fighting?' The cause was soon explained, and Mahomet said: 'That which the Lord decreeth is the best.'

Mahomet reposes in his tent.

From the pass, Mahomet descended into the valley at a spot not far from the tombs of Abu Tâlib and Khadîja. He was there joined by the division of Zobeir, and, having assured himself that Mecca was now wholly at his will, he directed his tent of leather to be pitched in the open space to the north of the city.[1] 'Wilt thou not alight at thine own house?' enquired his followers. 'Not so,' he said, 'for have they left me yet any house within the city?' The great banner was planted at the door of his tent, and Mahomet retired to repose therein, and to reflect on the accomplishment of his life's dream. The abused, rejected, exiled Prophet now had the rebellious city at his feet. Mahomet was lord of Mecca.

Worships at the Káaba, and destroys its idols.

But Mahomet did not long repose. Again mounted on Al Caswa, he proceeded to the Káaba, reverently saluted with his staff the sacred stone, and made the seven circuits of the temple. Then, pointing with the staff one by one to the numerous idols placed around, he commanded that they should be hewn down. The great image of Hobal, reared as the tutelary deity of Mecca in front of the Káaba, shared the common fate. 'Truth hath come,' exclaimed Mahomet, in

---

[1] See the map facing Chapter I. The pathway north of Jebel Mind brought him into the valley near the burying ground; a little below this he pitched his tent, and in the same vicinity the two northern divisions of the army encamped. The two other divisions probably occupied ground to the south of the city. The tradition of the Prophet's route is still retained, though in a loose and inaccurate form. 'Mounting our animals,' says Burton, 'we followed the road to the Jannat al Maala, the sacred cemetery of Mecca. A rough wall, with a poor gateway, encloses a patch of barren and grim-looking ground, at the foot of the chain which bounds the city's western suburb; and below Al Akaba, the gap through which Khâlid entered Mecca with the triumphant Prophet.' As regards Khâlid, this is a mistake.

words of the Corân, as it fell with a crash to the ground, 'and falsehood hath vanished; for falsehood is but evanescent.'[1] Advancing now to the *Station of Abraham*, twenty or thirty paces from the Káaba, he bowed himself in worship; and, sitting down, he sent Bilâl to summon Othmân ibn Talha with the key of the temple. When Othmân appeared, he took from him the key, and, opening therewith the door of the Káaba, he entered and again performed devout prostrations. He then returned to the doorway, and, standing upon the elevated step, seized hold of the two rings attached to the door, and gazed around on the multitude that thronged below. 'Othmân ibn Talha!' he called aloud,—'here, take back the key to be kept in custody by thee and thy posterity, an hereditary and perpetual office. No one shall take it from thee save the unjust. And thou Abbâs,' turning to his uncle, 'I confirm thee in the office of giving drink unto the pilgrims: it is no mean privilege this that I give now unto thee.'

Having destroyed the images and obliterated the pictures of Abraham and of the angels which (it is said) covered the walls of the Káaba, Mahomet desired Bilâl to sound the call for prayer from the top of the Káaba, and worship was performed, and has been daily ever since, at the holy Shrine according to the ritual of the great Mosque of Medîna. Mahomet then sent a crier through the streets of Mecca with this proclamation: 'Whoever believeth in God and in the day of Judgment, let him not leave in his house any image whatever that he doth not break in pieces.' He likewise deputed a party of the Bani Khozâa to repair the boundary pillars around the sacred territory.[2] Thus he gave practical proof that, while determined to root out idolatry from the land, he was equally resolved to cherish and per-

Mahomet's attachment to Mecca.

[1] Sura xvii. 82. Tradition says that there were three hundred and sixty idols ranged round the Káaba, and that as Mahomet pointed to each in succession with his staff, reciting this verse, the idol of its own accord fell forwards on its face. The use of metaphorical language in describing the actual scene would easily give rise to such tales.

[2] Pillars were then, as at the present day, placed at the limits of the sacred territory on either side of all the main roads leading to Mecca. They had probably become neglected or injured, as Mahomet observed in passing. The distance of these landmarks from Mecca varies in different directions. On the Jedda road they are nine miles from Mecca; towards Al Omra, only three.

petuate the sanctity of Mecca. He won the hearts of the inhabitants by his passionate declaration of attachment to their city: 'Thou art the choicest portion of the earth unto me,' he said, 'and the most lovable thereof. If I had not been cast forth from thy borders I never had forsaken thee!' The men of Medîna now began to fear that, as the Lord had given him the victory over his native city and country, he would return to it as his home. Mahomet overheard them conversing thus and, calling them around him, assured them all that he would never quit Medìna: ' God forbid it,' he said; 'where ye live there I shall live, and there too shall I die.'

Abu Bakr brings his father to visit Mahomet. Mahomet now retired again to his tent. Soon after, Abu Bakr approached the door leading his father, Abu Cuhâfa, who was bowed down with great age, and his locks 'white as the flower of the mountain grass.'[1] Mahomet accosted him kindly: ' Why didst thou not leave thine aged father in his house, Abu Bakr? and I would have gone and seen him there.' ' It was more fitting that he should visit thee, O Prophet, than that thou shouldst visit him.' Mahomet seated Abu Cuhâfa beside him, and, affectionately pressing his hand upon the old man's breast, invited him to make profession of the Moslem faith, which he readily did.

Citizens proscribed. From the general amnesty extended to the citizens of Mecca, Mahomet excluded ten or twelve persons. Of these, however, only four were actually put to death.

Huweirith and Habbâr: the former executed. Huweirith and Habbâr were proscribed in consequence of their barbarous conduct in pursuing Zeinab, Mahomet's daughter, when she escaped from Mecca. The former was put to death by Ali. The latter concealed himself; and some months later, appearing at Medîna, a repentant convert, he was forgiven.

Two murderers and a singing girl put to death. The next two were renegade Moslems who, having shed blood at Medîna, had fled to Mecca and abjured Islâm. They were both slain, and also a singing girl belonging to one of them, who had been in the habit of annoying the Prophet by abusive verses.[2]

---

[1] The fine image is spoiled by the addition that Mahomet desired him to dye his snow-white hair. He lived to see his son Caliph, and died A.H. 14, aged ninety-seven.

[2] One was killed clinging to the curtain of the Káaba. The execution of the singing girl appears to have been the most questionable act committed by Mahomet on the occupation of Mecca.

The rest escaped. Among them was another apostate, Abdallah, an apostate, escapes.
Abdallah, whom Mahomet had employed at Medina in
writing out passages of the Corân from his dictation. His
foster brother sheltered him till quiet was restored, then
brought him forward and implored forgiveness for him. The
Prophet, unwilling to pardon so great an offender, for some
time held his peace; but at last granted him quarter. When
Abdallah retired, Mahomet thus addressed his Companions
who were seated about him: 'Why did not one of you arise
and smite Abdallah on the neck. I remained silent expecting
this.' 'But thou gavest no sign unto us,' replied one of
them. 'To give signs,' said Mahomet, 'is treachery; it is
not fitting for a Prophet in such fashion to ordain the death
of any.'

Safwân and Ikrima, after eluding the pursuit of Khâlid, Safwân, Ikrima, Hind, and Sârah escape.
fled towards the sea-shore; they were on the point of em-
barking, when the assurance of forgiveness reached them and
they were persuaded to return.[1] Hind the wife of Abu
Sofiân, and Sârah a singing girl who had in the discharge of
her profession given offence to Mahomet, escaped the sentence of death by opportune submission.[2]

The proscriptions were thus comparatively few in number; Treatment of Mecca by Mahomet magnanimous and forbearing.
and capital sentence, where actually carried into effect, was
probably (with the single exception of the singing girl)
justified by other crimes than mere political antagonism.
The conduct of Mahomet on the conquest of Mecca was
marked by singular magnanimity and moderation. It was
indeed for his own interest to forgive the past, and to cast into

---

[1] Ikrima was brought back by his wife, who had obtained a pardon from
Mahomet, and hurried after him to Jedda. M. C. de Perceval tells a romantic
story of her reaching the shore just as he had embarked, and waving her scarf
to bring him back. Omeir, a Meccan chief, went after Safwân, taking as a
pledge the red striped turban worn by Mahomet around his head as he entered
Mecca. He asked for two months' quarter; Mahomet gave him four.

[2] Wahshî, the Abyssinian slave who slew Hamza, fled to Tâyif, and eventually obtained pardon in company with its inhabitants.

Omm Hâni, daughter of Abu Tâlib, gave refuge to two men of her
husband's tribe whom her brother Ali wished to kill. She asked quarter for
them of Mahomet, who received her graciously, saying: 'I give protection to
whomsoever thou dost give protection.' A curious scene is here described of
Mahomet's camp life; the Prophet, wearied and covered with dust, had retired
to a corner of the tent across which Fâtima held a screen; thus veiled, he
bathed himself, and then came forth to meet the persons waiting for him.

oblivion all its slights and injuries. But to do this did not the less require a large and generous heart.[1] And Mahomet had his reward, for the whole population of his native city at once gave in their adhesion, and espoused his cause with alacrity and apparent devotion. Whatever the strength or weakness of spiritual conviction, there were no 'disaffected' inhabitants at Mecca, as there had been at Medîna. Within a few weeks we find two thousand of the citizens fighting faithfully by his side.

Bloodshed prohibited.

On the night after the occupation of Mecca, some men of the Bani Khozâa, to gratify an old-standing enmity, rose upon a neighbouring tribe, and put one of them to death. The day following, Mahomet took advantage of the incident, and in these words addressed the congregation assembled in front of the Káaba for the mid-day prayer: 'Verily the Lord hallowed Mecca in the day that He created the heavens and the earth. Nor was it common unto me but for a single watch of the day; then it returned to its sacredness as before. Neither was the plunder thereof lawful unto me. Let him that is present tell it unto him that is absent. Ye Bani Khozâa! withdraw your hands from shedding blood. The man whom ye have killed, I will myself pay compensation for him; but whoso slayeth any man after this, verily the blood of him that is murdered shall be required at his hands.'

Parties sent out to destroy images.

During the succeeding fortnight, which was occupied in the arrangement of public affairs at Mecca, Mahomet sent forth several armed parties to destroy the idolatrous shrines in the vicinity, and secure the submission of the surrounding tribes. Khâlid demolished the fane of Al Ozza at Nakhla, the famous goddess of the Meccan tribes; Amru broke in pieces Suwâ, an image adored by the Bani Hodzeil; and Manât, the divinity worshipped at Cudeid, was destroyed by a band of the citizens of Medîna who had formerly been especially devoted to its service.[2]

---

[1] Mahomet is said to have compared himself in his treatment of Mecca to Joseph forgiving the injuries of his brethren.

[2] Curious stories are told about these deities. When Khâlid returned from Nakhla, Mahomet asked him what he had seen. He replied, Nothing. 'Then thou hast not yet destroyed the goddess? Return and do so.' On his going back, a naked female, black, and with dishevelled hair, rushed out, and

On his return from Nakhla, Khâlid was sent with a large detachment to require the adhesion of the Bani Jadzîma, who dwelt a day's march south of Mecca. They tendered an immediate submission, professed themselves converts, and, at the bidding of Khâlid, laid down their arms. But Khâlid, actuated by an ancient enmity, and thus giving early proof of the cruelty which marked his subsequent career and gained for him the title of *The Sword of God*, made them all prisoners and gave command for their execution. A portion were put to death by his Bedouin followers, but fortunately there were also present some citizens of Medîna and Refugees, who interposed and saved the rest. Mahomet, displeased and grieved at the intelligence, raised up his hands to heaven, and said: 'O Lord! I am innocent in thy sight of that which Khâlid hath done.' To prove the sincerity of his displeasure, he sent forth Ali with money to make compensation for the slain, and for the plunder.

Cruelty of Khâlid to Bani Jadzîma.

Khâlid cut her in pieces. '*That* was Ozza,' said the Prophet, when it was reported to him. A similar tale is told of Manât.

The servitor of one of these images, after suspending his sword about its neck, retired to an adjoining hill, and cried out to the image to wield the sword and save itself.

CHAPTER XXV.

THE BATTLE OF HONEIN AND SIEGE OF TÂYIF.

Bani Ha-
wâzin as-
semble
against
Mahomet:

THE great Bedouin stock of the Bani Hawâzin occupied (as they still occupy) the ranges and slopes of the hill country to the south and east of Mecca; and, with their numerous branches and affiliated clans, spread themselves over the wide steppes east and north of Tâyif. That city, inhabited by the Bani Thackîf of the same descent, was the centre of the tribe. The people of Tâyif, devoted to idol worship, and closely connected with Mecca, feared not unnaturally that the iconoclastic conqueror would strike his next blow at their faith and liberties. They felt that the only chance of safety lay in an early offensive movement, and they sent an urgent summons to all the branches of the Hawâzin race to assemble, in order effectively to check the arrogant assumptions of Mahomet, now too plainly developing his scheme of conquest and universal supremacy. They appointed a rendezvous at Autâs, a valley in the mountain range north-east of Tâyif, where they began rapidly to assemble.

Who is
therefore
obliged
to leave
Mecca.

This movement obliged Mahomet to cut short his stay at Mecca. Although the city had cheerfully accepted his authority, all its inhabitants had not yet embraced the new religion, nor formally acknowledged his prophetical claim. Perhaps he intended to follow the course he had pursued at Medîna, and leave the conversion of the people to be gradually accomplished without compulsion. However this may have been, the threatening intelligence called him away from Mecca after little more than a fortnight's stay. Moâdz ibn Jabal, a young citizen of Medîna, well skilled in the Corân and in all questions of religious practice, was left behind to instruct the citizens of Mecca in the tenets and requirements of Islâm; and Attâb, a youthful Coreishite, of the house of Abd Shams, was placed over the secular administration of the city.

Four weeks had just elapsed since he quitted Medîna, when Mahomet marched forth from Mecca at the head of all his forces, swelled now, by the addition of two thousand auxiliaries from Mecca, to the large number of twelve thousand men. Safwân, at his request, made over to him one hundred suits of mail and stand of arms complete, and as many camels. The array of tribes, each with a banner waving at its head, was so imposing, that Abu Bakr broke forth, as the marshalled forces passed, with the exclamation: 'We shall not this day be worsted by reason of the smallness of our numbers!' Mahomet smiled with a complacent assent. The vainglorious boast was remembered by the Prophet afterwards with self-reproach. In three or four marches the army arrived near the entrance of the valley of Honein.

Mahomet sets out to disperse the enemy. A.H. VIII. January 28, A.D. 630;—

And reaches Honein.

The Bani Hawâzin, assembled in great force at Autâs under their chief Mâlik, had meanwhile also been advancing upon the valley of Honein. The women and children of the tribe, their property, and their herds and flocks, followed in the rear. Mâlik hoped, by the presence of their families, and consciousness of the disastrous results of a defeat, to nerve his troops to victory. Doreid, a very aged warrior who accompanied the army in his litter, protested against the fatal measure. But the youthful leader derided his advice. During the night, after Mahomet's arrival in the vicinity of Honein, Mâlik drew up his men in a masked position, commanding a steep and narrow defile which formed the entrance to the valley, and awaited in silence the approach of the enemy.[1]

Bani Hawâzin also advance upon Honein.

---

[1] Mâlik was only thirty years of age. Doreid was a famous chief in his day. After the battle, he was cruelly put to death by a youth of the Bani Suleim, who captured him as he was endeavouring to escape in his camel-litter. The first cut of the youth's sword took no effect. 'How badly has thy mother furnished thee!' said the old man, cold and unmoved at the prospect of death. 'There, take that sword hung up behind my litter, and strike just between the spine and the head. It was thus I used to slay the adversary in my day. Then go and tell thy mother that thou hast killed Doreid. Many are the days in which I have saved the lives of the women of thy tribe.' He had, in fact, saved the lad's mother, and his two grandmothers. The skin of his legs resembled paper, from constant riding on the bare backs of horses.

Battle of
Honein,
February 1,
A.D. 630.

Very early in the morning, while the dawn was yet gray, and the sky overcast with clouds, the army of Mahomet was in motion. Clad in full panoply, as on the day of Ohod, he rode on his white mule Duldul in the rear of the forces. The vanguard, formed of the Bani Suleim and led by Khâlid, were defiling leisurely up the steep and narrow pass, when on a sudden the Hawâzin sprang forth from their ambuscade, and charged them with impetuosity. Staggered by the unexpected onslaught, the Bani Suleim broke and fell back. The shock was communicated from column to column. Aggravated by the obscurity of the hour, and the straitness and ruggedness of the road, panic seized the whole army ; all turned and fled.

Mahomet's
army sur-
prised and
driven
back, but
eventually
rallied.

As troop by troop they hurried past him, Mahomet called out: 'Whither away? The Prophet of the Lord is here! Return! return!'—but his words had no effect, excepting that a band of devoted friends and followers gathered round him.[1] The confusion increased, the multitude of camels jostled wildly one against another; all was noise and clamour, and the voice of Mahomet was lost amid the din. At last, seeing the column of Medîna troops bearing down in the common flight, he bade his uncle Abbâs, who held his mule, to cry aloud: 'O citizens of Medîna! O men of the Tree of Fealty! Ye of the Sura *Bacr!*'[2] Abbâs had a stentorian voice, and as he shouted these words over and over again at the pitch of his voice, they were heard far and near. At once they touched a chord in the hearts of the men of Medîna. They were arrested in their flight, and 'like she camels when their bowels are stirred towards their young,' hastened to Mahomet, crying aloud, '*Yâ Labeik!* Here we are, ready at thy call!' One hundred of these devoted followers, disengaged with difficulty from the camels that jammed the narrow pass, threw themselves upon the advancing enemy and checked his progress. Relieved from the pressure, the army rallied gradually, and returned to the battle. The conflict was severe : and the issue, from

[1] The following are among those who stood firm by Mahomet:—Abbâs and his son Fadhl, Ali, Abu Bakr, Omar, Osâma, Ayman, &c.

[2] Alluding to those who took the oath of fealty under the Acacia tree at Hodeibia; and to Sura Bacr, the first chapter of the Corân revealed at Medîna. The double allusion would thus remind them at once of their conversion, and of their oath to defend Mahomet to the death.

the adverse nature of the ground and the impetuosity of the wild Bedouins, remained for some time doubtful. Mahomet ascended an eminence and watched the struggle. Excited by the spectacle, he began loudly to exclaim: '*Now is the furnace heated: I am the Prophet that lieth not. I am the offspring of Abd al Muttalib!*' Then bidding Abbâs to pick up for him a handful of gravel, he cast it towards the enemy, saying, '*Ruin seize them!*' They had indeed already wavered. 'They are discomfited,' he cried out eagerly; 'I swear by the Lord of the Káaba, they yield! God hath cast fear into their hearts.' The steadiness of the Medîna band, and the enthusiasm of the rest when once recalled, had won the day. The enemy fled, and the rout was complete. Many were slain, and so fiercely did the Moslems pursue the charge, that they killed among the rest some of the little children—an atrocity which Mahomet had strictly forbidden.

The Bani Hawâzin beaten back.

Mâlik, taking his stand, with the flower of his army, upon a height at the farther end of the valley, covered the escape of his broken forces; but he was unable to rescue the women and children. They fell into the hands of Mahomet, with the camp and all that it contained. Six thousand prisoners were taken; and the spoil included twenty-four thousand camels, forty thousand sheep and goats, and four thousand ounces of silver. The prisoners and the booty were removed to the neighbouring valley of Jierrâna, and kept there in the shelter of huts and enclosures, awaiting the return of the army from Tâyif. Mahomet knew that the Bani Hawâzin would seek to regain their families, and an opportunity thus was skilfully left open for negotiation.

Their families and camp captured.

The fugitive army was pursued with slaughter as far as Nakhla; from thence part fled back to Autâs, and part to Tâyif. The former entrenched themselves in their previous camp. A strong detachment was sent to dislodge them, which they accomplished after severe fighting, and the loss of their leader struck by an arrow. The dispersed fragments of the enemy found refuge in the surrounding hills.

Pursuit of fugitive columns.

The victory was thus complete, but not without some considerable loss on the part of Mahomet. Only five of his immediate followers are named among the slain. But some of the auxiliaries, who being in the van bore the brunt of the

Loss on Mahomet's side.

enemy's onset, must have suffered greatly; and two tribes are spoken of as almost annihilated. For these Mahomet offered up a special prayer, and said: 'O Lord! recompense them because of their calamities!'

Victory
ascribed to
angelic
aid.
The reverse sustained at the opening of the day was attributed by the Prophet to the vainglorious confidence with which the Believers looked upon their great army; and the subsequent success, to the aid of invisible hosts which fought against the enemy. The engagement is thus alluded to in the Corân:—

Sura ix.
Verily God hath assisted you in many battlefields; and on the day of Honein, when indeed ye rejoiced in the multitude of your host. But their great number did not in any wise benefit you: the earth became too strait for you with all its spaciousness.[1] Then ye turned your backs and fled.

Afterwards the Lord sent down His peace upon His Prophet and upon the Believers, and sent down Hosts which ye saw not, and punished them that disbelieved; and that is the end of the Unbelievers.

Then God will be turned hereafter unto whom He pleaseth; for God is gracious and merciful.[2]

Siege of
Tâyif.
February,
A.D. 630.
As soon as the detachment had returned from Autâs, Mahomet pushed forward his army by way of Nakhla, and laid siege to Tâyif. But the city was surrounded by strong battlements; it was provisioned for many months, and there was a plentiful supply of water within the walls. The besiegers were received with showers of arrows, so thick and well sustained that they are described as darkening the sky like a flight of locusts. It was soon discovered that the camp was pitched too near the city. Twelve men were killed, and many wounded, among whom was a son of Abu Bakr. The encampment was speedily withdrawn beyond the range of the enemy's archery. A tent of red leather was erected for Omm Salmâ, and another for Zeinab. Both had followed

---

[1] That is to say, in the narrow and precipitous pass, their great numbers, of which they had been vaingloriously proud, only added to the difficulty.

[2] The last verse is generally construed as referring to the mercy afterwards shown to the Bani Hawâzin; but it more probably means forgiveness for the vainglory and cowardice just described. As usual, the angels are a favourite subject of tradition. On this occasion they wore *red uniform*. A cloud was seen to fill the valley like ants: this was the angelic troop.

their lord through all the dangers of the way. Between these tents Mahomet performed the daily prayers; and on this spot the great Mosque of Tâyif was afterwards erected.

The siege did not advance, for no one dared to expose himself before the galling archery from the walls. This had been anticipated, and a remedy already sought. The Bani Dous, who lived one or two days' journey south of Mecca, were famous for their acquaintance with the use of the testudo and catapult. Tufeil, one of their chiefs, had joined Mahomet at Kheibar with a party of his tribe.[1] He had lately been despatched from Mecca or Honein to secure the allegiance of his people, and to seek their aid in the reduction of Tâyif. They accepted the summons; and Tufeil, having burned their famous tutelary image, joined Mahomet four days after siege had been laid to Tâyif. The besieging engines were speedily prepared, and parties pushed forward under cover of them to undermine the walls. But the citizens were prepared for the stratagem. They cast down balls of heated iron from the battlements, and set the machines on fire. The soldiers labouring under their shelter fled in alarm. A discharge of arrows opened upon them; some were killed and many wounded before they got beyond their range. The testudo and catapult were not tried again.

Testudos and catapults tried without success.

Seeing no other way of bringing the city to terms, Mahomet gave command to cut down and burn the far-famed vineyards which surrounded it.[2] This order was being carried into effect, as the unfortunate citizens from the wall could descry, with merciless vigour, when they succeeded in conveying to Mahomet an earnest expostulation; they besought, 'for the sake of mercy and of God,' that he would desist. He listened to the appeal, and stayed further destruction. But he caused a proclamation to reach the garrison which grievously displeased them, that if any slaves came forth from the city, they would receive their freedom. About twenty were able to avail themselves of the offer, and became eventually valiant followers of their liberator.

Vineyards cut down and liberty offered to slaves of garrison.

[1] Tradition gives him the credit of having been converted at Mecca, before the Hegira; but this is apocryphal.

[2] These charming gardens, with their rills of running water, lie at the foot of the low mountains encircling the sandy plain in the middle of which Tâyif stands. They are still as famous as they were 1,200 years ago. The nearest is ' now about a half or three quarters of an hour from the city.' Vide *supra*, pp. 113, 114.

Siege
raised, and
army re-
turns to
Jierrâna,
end of Feb-
ruary,
A.D. 630.

The siege had now been protracted for half a month without producing the slightest effect. The army was beginning to exhibit symptoms of impatience, and of anxiety for the distribution of the spoil at Jierrâna. Mahomet took counsel with the principal men. 'What thinkest thou,' said he to a Bedouin leader;—'what thinkest thou of this stubborn city?' 'A fox in its hole,' replied the astute and sententious chief;—'remain long enough and you will catch it: leave it alone, and it will not harm you.' A dream was seen by the Prophet which ratified this view.[1] It was not the divine will that operations should be continued. The siege was therefore raised, and the army marched back to Jierrâna, which it reached about the end of February.

Scene
between
Mahomet
and his
foster
sister.

Here occurred an interesting incident, already described in the opening chapter. An aged female among the captives, being roughly treated like the rest, warned the rude soldiery to beware,—'For,' said she, 'I am the foster sister of your chief.' Hearing this, they carried her to Mahomet, who recognised in the complainant the little girl, Shîma, who used, when he was nurtured by Halîma among the Bani Sád, to tend and carry him. He seated her affectionately beside him, and offered to take her to Medîna. But as she preferred remaining with her tribe, he dismissed her with a handsome present.[2]

Prisoners
of Bani Ha-
wâzin
given up.

Encouraged by the kind treatment of their kinswoman, a deputation from the various tribes of the Hawâzin presented themselves before the Prophet. Among them was an aged man who claimed to be his foster uncle. They professed their submission to the authority of their conqueror,

---

[1] Mahomet dreamed that a bowl of cream was presented to him, which a hen pecked at and spilled. Abu Bakr interpreted the dream to mean that he would not at this time obtain his desire against Tâyif, and Mahomet thought so too.

A story told of Oyeina, chief of the Fezâra, illustrates the feelings and motives of Mahomet's Bedouin auxiliaries. Oyeina was lauding the garrison of Tâyif for their brave and determined resistance. 'Out upon thee, Oyeina!' said his neighbour; 'dost thou praise the enemies of the Prophet,—the very people whom thou hast come to aid him in destroying?' 'Verily,' said the Bedouin chief, 'I had another object in coming hither. I hoped that, if Mahomet gained the victory, I should obtain one of the damsels of Tâyif; then should I have had worthy issue; for truly the tribe of Thackîf are a warlike, noble race.'

[2] See ante, p. 8. The mark of the bite, recognised by Mahomet as having been inflicted by himself when a child on Shîma's back, is probably a traditional embellishment.

recounted the calamities which had befallen them, and thus urged their special claims upon his favour. 'There, in these huts among the prisoners, are thy foster mothers and foster sisters,—they that have nursed thee and fondled thee in their bosoms. We have known thee a suckling, a weaned child, a youth generous and noble : and now thou hast risen to this dignity. Be gracious therefore unto us, even as the Lord hath been gracious unto thee !' Mahomet could not withstand the appeal. Turning kindly to them, he said: 'Whether of the two, your families or your property, is the dearer to you ?' 'Our women and our children,' they replied ; 'we would not take anything in exchange for them.' 'Then,' continued the Prophet, 'whatsoever prisoners fall to my portion and that of my family, I give them up unto you ; and I will presently speak unto the people concerning the rest. Come again unto me at the mid-day prayer when the congregation is assembled, and beg publicly of me to make intercession with them for you.' At the appointed time they appeared and made their petition. The men of Medina and of Mecca cheerfully followed the example of Mahomet. But some of the allied tribes as the Bani Fazâra, with Oyeina at their head, declined to do so. Mahomet urged the claims of his new converts, and promised that such of the allies as were unwilling to part with their share of the prisoners should be recompensed hereafter from the first booty the Lord might give into their hands, at the rate of six camels for every captive. To this they agreed, and the prisoners were all released.

I ought not here to omit a curious illustration of the Prophet's mode of life. Among the captives were three beautiful women, who were brought to Mahomet. One was presented by him to Ali, the second to Othmân, and the third to Omar. Omar transferred the one allotted him to his son Abdallah, who returned her uninjured to the tribe, when the rest of the prisoners were given up.[1] Whether the other two were restored likewise is not stated : but, be this as it may, it throws certainly a strange light on the domestic history of Mahomet, that he should have presented such gifts as captive damsels to the father of one of his wives, and to the husbands of two of his own daughters.

Mahomet presents female slaves to Ali, Othmân, and Omar.

[1] Abdallah had sent the girl to be kept in readiness for him after he had visited the Káaba ; but meanwhile the prisoners were surrendered.

Having arranged for the restoration of the prisoners, Mahomet had already mounted his camel and was proceeding to his tent, when the people, fearing lest the spoil, as well as the prisoners, should slip from their grasp, crowded round him with loud cries : ' Distribute to us the booty, the camels and the flocks ! ' The crowd thronged him so closely and so rudely, that he was driven to seek refuge under a tree. While thus pressed on every side, his mantle was torn from his shoulders. ' Return to me my mantle, O man ! ' cried Mahomet, who had now secured a more free position ; ' return my mantle : for I swear by the Lord that if the sheep and the camels were as many as the trees of the Tihâma in number, I would divide them all amongst you. Ye have not heretofore found me niggardly or false.' Then he plucked a hair from his camel's hump, and holding it aloft said : ' Even to a hair like this, I shall not keep back aught but the fifth ; and that, too, I will give up unto you.' The people were pacified, and Mahomet went on his way.

He took an early opportunity of making good his promise, and at the same time of gaining, by a princely liberality, the hearts of the leading chiefs of Mecca and of the Bedouin tribes. To those of the greatest influence he presented each one hundred camels. Among them we find Abu Sofiân, with his two sons, Yazîd and Muâvia; Hakîm ibn Hizâm, Safwân, Suheil, Huweitib, Oyeina, and several others, who but a few weeks before were the Prophet's deadly enemies. To the lesser chiefs he gave fifty camels each. And so liberal was he that, in some instances where discontent was expressed with the amount, the gift was without hesitation doubled.

Although the largesses were taken from the Prophet's fifth, yet the favour and honour lavished on these recent and doubtful adherents, gave great umbrage to the old and faithful followers of Mahomet. Thus one complained that such Bedouin chieftains as Acra and Oyeina received each one hundred camels, while a faithful believer like Jueil got nothing at all. ' And what of that ? ' replied the Prophet ; ' I swear that Jueil is the best man that ever stepped on earth, were it filled never so full of Acras and Oyeinas ; but I wished to gain over the hearts of these men to Islâm, while Jueil hath no need of any such inducement.' A

Bedouin follower, who watched the proceeding, openly impugned its equity. Mahomet became angry, and said: 'Out upon thee! If justice and equity be not with me, where will ye find them?' But what concerned Mahomet the most, were the murmurs of the citizens of Medîna. 'Truly (thus they spake among themselves) he hath now joined his own people and forsaken us.' The discontent proceeded so far that Sâd ibn Obáda thought right to represent it to the Prophet, who bade him call the murmurers together. He then addressed them in these words: 'Ye men of Medîna,[1] it hath been reported to me that ye are disconcerted, because I have given unto these chiefs largesses, and have given nothing unto you. Now speak unto me. Did I not come unto you whilst ye were wandering, and the Lord gave you the right direction?—needy, and He enriched you;—at enmity amongst yourselves, and He hath filled your hearts with love and unity?' He paused for a reply. 'Indeed, it is even as thou sayest,' they answered; 'to the Lord and to his Prophet belong benevolence and grace.' 'Nay, by the Lord!' continued Mahomet; 'but ye might have answered (and answered truly, for I would have vouched for it myself,) —*Thou camest to Medîna rejected as an impostor, and we bore witness to thy veracity: thou camest a helpless fugitive and we assisted thee; an outcast, and we gave thee an asylum; destitute, and we solaced thee.* Why are ye disturbed in mind because of the things of this life wherewith I have sought to incline the hearts of these men unto Islâm, whereas ye are already steadfast in the faith? Are ye not satisfied that others should obtain the flocks and the camels, while ye carry back the Prophet of the Lord unto your homes? Nay, I will not leave you for ever. If all mankind went one way, and the men of Medîna went another way, verily I would go the way of the men of Medîna. The Lord be favourable unto them, and bless them, and their sons and their sons' sons for ever!' At these words they all wept, till the tears ran down upon their beards; and they called out with one voice: 'Yea, we are well satisfied, O Prophet, with our lot!'

It will be seen that Mahomet made no attempt to hide the motive which dictated these munificent gifts. The chiefs

Subject noticed in Corân.

---

[1] *Ansâr*, 'helpers,' as before explained; and so throughout this address.

who received them are referred to in the Corân as 'those *whose hearts have been gained over*;' and they retained the appellation ever after. The passage is as follows :—

Sura ix.

There are that blame thee in the (distribution of the) alms;[1] if they receive therefrom they are well pleased, but if they do not receive a part they are indignant. Now, if they had been well pleased with whatever God and his Apostle gave unto them, and had said,—' God will suffice for us; God will give unto us of his bounty, and his Prophet also,—verily unto God is our desire,'— (it had been better for them). Verily, Alms are for the poor and the needy, and for the collectors of the same, and for them whose hearts are to be gained over, and for captives, and for debtors, and for the service of God, and for the wayfarer. It is an ordinance from God; and God is knowing and wise.

Mâlik, the Hawâzinite chief, gained over.

Mâlik, the chief who had led the Bani Hawâzin, was still in Tâyif. Mahomet desired to gain him over also. So he directed his tribe to make known to him that if he embraced Islâm, his family and all his property would be restored, and a present of one hundred camels bestowed upon him. He soon joined Mahomet and became an exemplary believer. Being confirmed in his chiefship, he engaged to maintain a constant warfare with the citizens of Tâyif. He cut off their cattle whenever they were sent beyond the precincts of the city to graze, and reduced them to great straits.

Booty distributed, February, March, 630.

Mahomet spent about a fortnight at Jierrâna, during which period the booty captured at Honein was all distributed. Four camels, and forty sheep or goats, fell to the lot of each foot soldier, and three times that amount to each horseman.

Mahomet performs Lesser pilgrimage.

The distribution being ended, Mahomet took upon him the pilgrim vows, and fulfilled the Lesser pilgrimage at Mecca. But he made no stay there. He returned to Jierrâna that same night; and the following day, striking through the valleys by a direct route that joined the main road, marched homewards to Medîna.

Attâb left in the govern-

The youthful Attâb was confirmed in the government of Mecca, and an allowance assigned him of one dirhem a day.[2]

---

[1] That is, they complained that the Prophet's fifth destined for charity, &c., along with the tithes, had been diverted by Mahomet from its proper use.

[2] Attâb was quite content with this moderate allowance. He said: 'Let the Lord make hungry that man's liver, who is hungry upon a dirhem a day.

He also presided over the Annual pilgrimage, which took place in less than a month after Mahomet's departure. Believers and Idolaters were still permitted to join promiscuously in its ceremonies. Moâdz was left behind by the Prophet to complete the spiritual instruction of the city. ment of Mecca.

On his return to Medîna, Mahomet despatched letters to the Chiefs of Bahrein, Omân, and Yemen, the result of which, however, belongs to the narrative of the following year. Despatches to Bahrein, &c.

The Prophet hath appointed that as my sustenance. I have no further claim upon any one.'

CHAPTER XXVI.

MARY, THE COPTIC MAID, AND HER SON IBRAHÎM.

A.H. VIII., IX.—A.D. 630, 631.

Ætat. 61, 62.

Death of
Zeinab,
Mahomet's
daughter.

In the ninth year of the Hegira, Mahomet lost his daughter Zeinab, who had never recovered the barbarous treatment of the Coreish on her escape from Mecca. Omm Kolthûm (whom Othmân married after he lost Rockeya) had already died, so that of his daughters Fâtima alone was left. But his heart was now to be solaced by the birth of another child.

Mary, the
Coptic
maid,

I have before related that Muckouckas, the Governor of Egypt, sent two Coptic maids, Shirîn and Mary, as a gift to Mahomet. They were both comely; but it was not lawful, according to his own strict precept, for the Prophet to place two sisters in his harem. The beauty of Mary, whose fair complexion and delicate features were adorned by a profusion of black curling hair, fascinated Mahomet. So he kept Mary, and gave her sister to another. Omm Salim, the wife of his servant Abu Râfi (the same that adorned Safia for him at Kheibar) was entrusted with the new charge. Mary was not at once placed in the harem at the Mosque, but a garden house was prepared for her in Upper Medîna, where, in the heat of the summer and the date harvest, she used to receive the visits of the Prophet.[1]

[1] Burton tells us that the place is shown to the present day. It lies in the quarter called Ambariya, on the S.E. side of the city, where the road emerges to Yenbo and Mecca; it is separated from the rest of the town by the stream and low intervening land. A Mosque called Masjid Mashrabat Omm Ibrahîm, 'the Mosque of the summer house of the mother of Ibrahîm,' still marks the spot. At what period Mahomet provided this garden for her is not certain: possibly *after* the birth of Ibrahîm, or on her becoming *enceinte*.

A singular fortune elevated Mary to a dignity which the charms of her person alone could not have secured. Shortly after the return of her master from Jierrâna, she gave birth to a son. Salma, who had long ago attended at the birth of Khadîja's children, now performed the same office for Mary. And Omm Burda was selected from amongst many candidates to be the infant's nurse. His name was called Ibrahîm.[1] More than five-and-twenty years had elapsed since the birth of Mahomet's last child, and his numerous marriages at Medîna had given no promise of any progeny. His joy, therefore, at the birth of a son in his old age was very great. On the seventh day, following the example of Khadîja, he sacrificed a kid; and, having shaved his head, he distributed silver among the poor to the weight of the hair, which then was buried.[2] He used daily to visit the house of the nurse (where according to custom Ibrahîm was brought up), and calling for the little child would embrace him in his arms and kiss him fondly.

Presents Mahomet with a son. A.H. VIII. April, A.D. 630.

The wives of Mahomet were envious of Mary, who as the mother of Ibrahîm was advanced beyond the position of a slave, and enjoyed peculiar favour. As the infant grew and throve, Mahomet one day carried him to Ayesha, and with pride exclaimed: 'Look, what a likeness his countenance shows to me!' 'I cannot see any likeness,' said Ayesha, who would gladly have put Mahomet out of conceit with the child. 'What!' repeated Mahomet; 'seest thou not how closely he resembleth me, and how fair and fat he is?' 'Yes,' she replied; 'and any child that drank as much goats' milk would be, like him, both fat and fair.' A flock of goats was kept for the especial service of the child.

Jealousy of Mahomet's wives.

But the jealousy of Mary's 'sisters' showed itself in a more practical manner, and led to an incident in the Prophet's

Certainly it was an honour one would not have expected to be conferred on a slave girl without some special cause. Sprenger thinks that Mahomet kept her in a neighbour's house at first, and transferred her to the garden only after the affair of Haphsa.

[1] The name, I need hardly inform the reader, is the Arabian form of *Abraham*. Another tradition says that the child was given to be nursed by the wife of a blacksmith, who used to be blowing his forge when Mahomet came to see the child, and the house was consequently full of smoke.

[2] The weight must have been trifling, as he had only shaved his head a month or six weeks before, at the Lesser pilgrimage.

life surpassed in scandal only by his amour with Zeinab. The biographers pass over the scene in decent silence, and I should gladly have followed their example if the Corân itself had not accredited the facts and stamped them with unavoidable notoriety.

Affair with Mary creates scandal in Mahomet's harem.

It once happened that Haphsa paid a visit to her father on the day which, in due course, Mahomet was passing in her house.[1] Returning unexpectedly, she surprised the Prophet in her own private room with Mary. She was indignant at the wrong. The affront was the more intolerable from the servile position of her rival. She reproached her lord bitterly, and threatened to make the occurrence known to all his wives. Afraid of the exposure, and anxious to appease his offended wife, Mahomet begged of her to keep the matter quiet, and promised to forego the society of Mary altogether. Haphsa, however, did not care to keep the secret to herself. She told it all to Ayesha, who equally boiled with indignation. The scandal spread apace over the harem, and Mahomet soon found himself received by his wives with coldness and with slight.

Mahomet's displeasure with his wives.

As in the case of Zeinab, Mahomet produced a message from Heaven which disallowed his promise of separation from Mary, chided Haphsa and Ayesha for their insubordination, and hinted at the possibility of all his wives being divorced for demeanour so disloyal towards himself. He then withdrew from their society, and for a whole month lived alone with Mary. Omar and Abu Bakr were greatly mortified at the desertion of their daughters for a menial concubine, and grieved at the scandal of the whole proceeding. At length Mahomet, unwilling longer to continue the disgrace of his wives, or impatient at his self-imposed seclusion from them, listened to their prayer. Gabriel, he said, had spoken in praise of Haphsa, the chief offender, and desired him to take her back again. Accordingly, he pardoned them all and returned to their apartments as before.

Notice of affair in Corân.

The narrative may well be left without comment. I will only draw attention to the marvellous fact that this exhibition

---

[1] I have before explained how Mahomet used to divide his time among his wives. He would say : '*This*' (*i.e.* living in rotation with each) 'I have power to do ; but Thou, O Lord, art the master over that in respect of which I have no power' (meaning love in the heart).

of frailty and petulance, supported as it was asserted to be by the direct interposition of the Almighty, did not in any perceptible degree affect either the reputation and influence of the Prophet, or the credit and divine character of the Revelation, among his followers.   The passage in the Corân relating to the affair is as follows :—

O Prophet !   Why hast thou forbidden thyself that which God hath made lawful unto thee, out of desire to please thy Wives; for God is forgiving and merciful?   Verily God hath sanctioned the revocation of your oaths; and God is your Master.   He is knowing and wise. Sura lxvi.

The Prophet had entrusted as a secret to one of his wives a certain affair ; and when she disclosed it (to another), and God made known the same unto him, he acquainted (her) with a part thereof, and withheld a part.[1]   And when he had acquainted her (Haphsa) therewith, she said, *Who told thee this ?*   He replied, *He told it to me, the Knowing and the Wise.*

If ye both turn with repentance unto God (for verily the hearts of you both have swerved)—Well.   But if ye combine with each other against him, surely God is his Master ; and Gabriel and (every) good man of the Believers, and the Angels, will thereafter be his supporters.

Haply, his Lord, if he divorce you,[2] will give him in your stead Wives better than ye are, submissive unto God, believers, pious, repentant, devout, fasting ;—both Women married previously, and Virgins.[3]

---

[1] The passage is enigmatical.   The meaning is apparently this : Mahomet told a part,—that is, a part of what he had supernaturally learned that Haphsa had said to Ayesha ; and withheld a part, *i.e.* refrained from upbraiding her with a part of what he had thus learned :—the one part perhaps relating to Mahomet's misdemeanor in Haphsa's room ; the other, to his promise that he would not consort with Mary again.   According to another tradition, Mahomet, with the view of appeasing Haphsa, told her that Abu Bakr, and after him her father Omar, were to succeed him ; this being the part which, from fear of its getting abroad, he did not mention ; but such an interpretation is altogether unlikely.

[2] 'You' in the plural, not as before in the dual number,—implying that all his wives were involved in his displeasure.

[3] The Sura is a short one of only thirteen verses.   After the passage quoted, there follow admonitions to obedience and repentance, addressed to Believers generally, with references to Heaven and Hell.   The Sura closes with a pregnant allusion to two wicked women, who, although the wives of two good men, Noah and Lot, were yet condemned to hell,—signifying that his own wives, unless they repented, might possibly find themselves in the same category ; and to two good women, the wife of Pharaoh, and Mary mother of Jesus, examples propounded for their imitation.

I turn gladly to a more edifying and inviting scene. A year and more had passed; and the child Ibrahîm was now advanced to an age at which the innocent prattle and winning ways of infancy stole upon the heart of Mahomet. His hopes and affections centred for a while in his little son. There is, indeed, no ground for supposing that Mahomet ever contemplated the building up of a kingdom to be perpetuated in his own family. The prophetical office was personal, and his political authority was exercised solely in virtue of that office. But he regarded his children with a loving and partial eye; and no doubt rejoiced in the prospect, dear to every Arab, of having his name and memory perpetuated by male issue; and he might also naturally expect that his son would be cherished and honoured by all the followers of Islâm. But his expectations, of whatever nature, were doomed to be prematurely blighted. When aged but fifteeen or sixteen months, Ibrahîm fell sick, and it was soon apparent that he would not survive. The child lay in a palm-

His death,
A.H. X.
June or
July, A.D.
631.
grove near the house of his nurse. There his mother Mary, with her sister Shirîn, tended his dying bed. And there too was Mahomet in deep and bitter grief. Seeing that the child was soon to breathe his last, he took him up in his arms and sobbed aloud. The bystanders tried to comfort him. They reminded him of his exhortations to others that they should not wail. ' Nay,' said Mahomet, calming himself by an effort as he hung over the expiring infant; ' it is not this that I forbade, but loud wailing and false laudation of the dead. This that ye see in me is but the working of pity in the heart: he that showeth no pity, unto him no pity shall be shown. We grieve for the child: the eye runneth down with tears, and the heart swelleth inwardly; yet we say not aught that would offend our Lord. Ibrahîm! O Ibrahîm! if it were not that the promise is faithful, and the hope of resurrection sure, if it were not that this is the way to be trodden by all, and the last of us shall join the first, I would grieve for thee with a grief deeper even than this!' But the spirit had already passed away, and the last fond words of Mahomet fell on ears that could no longer hear them. So he laid down the infant's body, saying: ' The remainder of the days of his nursing shall be fulfilled in Paradise.'[1] Then

[1] Mahomet held *two years* as the proper period for suckling a child.

he comforted Mary and Shirîn, and bade them, now that the child was gone, to be silent and resigned.

Mahomet, with his uncle Abbâs, sat by while Fadhl, the son of the latter, washed and laid out the body. It was then carried forth upon a little bier. The Prophet prayed according to his usual practice over it, and then followed the procession to the grave-yard. He lingered over the grave after it was filled up; and calling for a skin of water, caused it to be sprinkled upon the spot. Then, observing some unevenness, he smoothed it over with his hand, saying to the bystanders: 'When ye do this thing, do it carefully, for it giveth ease to the afflicted heart. It cannot injure the dead, neither can it profit him; but it giveth comfort to the living.' *Burial of the child.*

An eclipse of the sun occurred on the same day, and the people spoke of it as a tribute to the death of the Prophet's son. A vulgar impostor would have accepted and confirmed the delusion; but Mahomet rejected the idea. 'The sun and the moon,' he taught them, 'are amongst the signs appointed by the Lord. They are not eclipsed on the death of any one. Whensoever ye see an eclipse, then betake yourselves to prayer until it passeth away.' *Eclipse.*

In gratitude for the services of Omm Burda, the nurse of his little boy, he presented her with a piece of ground planted as an orchard with palm-trees. *The nurse rewarded.*

In this chapter I have anticipated the march of events by about a year, in order to bring under one view the circumstances connected with Mary, the Coptic maid. *General history anticipated.*

CHAPTER XXVII.

EMBASSIES TO MEDÎNA.

FIRST HALF OF THE NINTH YEAR OF THE HEGIRA.—*April 20 to September*, A.D. 630.

Political
supremacy
attained by
conquest of
Mecca.

THE conquest of Mecca opens a new era in the progress of Islâm. It practically decided the struggle for supremacy in Arabia. Followed by the victory of Honein, it not only removed the apprehension of future attack upon Medîna, but elevated Mahomet to a position in which it was natural for him to assert authority as paramount over the whole Peninsula. It is true that no such authority had ever been vested in the chiefs of Mecca. The Byzantine empire had never pretended to the exercise of any influence beyond the tribes of the Syrian desert. The suzerainty of Arabia, enjoyed in remote times by the Kings of Himyar, had indeed been transferred to the dynasty of Hîra representing the court of Persia. But Hîra had now fallen to the rank of an ordinary Satrapy; and the Chosroes, who some time before had been discomfited in a decisive battle, by the Arabs themselves,[1] and more lately humbled by the Roman arms, no longer commanded respect. There was actually at the moment no political power paramount in Arabia. Besides Mahomet himself, no one had ever claimed the dignity, or dreamed of aspiring to it. The possession of Mecca now imparted a colour of right to his pretensions; for Mecca was the spiritual centre of the Peninsula, and to Mecca the tribes from every quarter yielded a reverential homage. The conduct of the

---

[1] The battle of Dzu Câr, fought A.D. 611, just before Mahomet assumed the prophetic office. The Persians were completely routed by the great tribe of the Bani Bakr, inhabiting the N.E. of the Peninsula; and thereafter Hîra sank in importance. See Introd. pp. iv. and viii.

Annual pilgrimage, the custody of the Holy house, the inter-calation of the year, the commutation at will of the sacred months,—institutions affecting all Arabia,—belonged by an-cient privilege to the Coreish, and were now in the hands of Mahomet. Throughout Arabia, who could advance preten-sions to the paramount authority, but Mahomet the Prophet of Medîna and the conqueror of Mecca?

Moreover, it had been the special care of Mahomet art-fully to interweave with the reformed faith all essential parts of the ancient ceremonial. The one was made an in-separable portion of the other. It was not, indeed, till the expiry of another year that Mahomet ventured to take full advantage of his position, by admitting none but the adhe-rents of Islâm to the Káaba and its rites. Yet the spiritual power which the author of the new faith had gained by combining that faith with the Pilgrimage, was universally felt from the moment that Mecca submitted to his arms. There remained but one religion for Arabia, and that was Islâm.

Possession of Mecca increased Mahomet's spiritual power;

Again, the new religion was so closely bound together with the civil polity, that the recognition of Mahomet's spiritual power necessarily involved a simultaneous submis-sion to his secular jurisdiction. It was an essential tenet of Islâm, that the convert should not only submit to its teaching, and adopt its ritual and code of ethics, but also that he should render an implicit obedience in all things 'to the Lord and *to his Prophet*,' and that he should pay tithes annually (not indeed as a tribute, but as a religious offering, which sancti-fied the rest of his wealth) towards the charities and expenses of Mahomet and his growing empire.[1] It was the privilege of believing tribes alone, to pay the tithe : from conquered Jews, Christians, and heathen tribes, tribute was prescribed in token of their servitude.

Which, in its turn, involved absolute secular authority.

It was under these circumstances that, on his return

Collectors deputed to

[1] Tithes and voluntary almsgiving are called by two names of Jewish derivation, *Zakât* and *Sadakât*; the former signifying purification (see Luke xi. 41), the latter righteousness as in Matt. vi. 1. The tax on unbelievers is called *Khirâj*.

For the purposes to which Mahomet applied the tithes, see the passage quoted at p. 438. Mahomet assisted debtors from the fund. A debtor once applied for aid : 'Wait,' said Mahomet, 'till the tithes come in, and then I will help thee.'

gather
tithes.
A.H. IX.
April 20,
A.D. 630.

from Jierrâna, at the opening of the ninth year of the Hegira, the Prophet demanded from the tribes which had tendered their adhesion, the prescribed offerings or tithes. Collectors were deputed by him in every direction to assess a tenth part of the increase, and bring it to Medîna.[1] They were well received, and accomplished their mission without obstruction, excepting only the following instance.

Bani Ta-
mim
attacked
for driving
away tax-
gatherer,
and pri-
soners
taken.

A branch of the Bani Tamîm chanced to be encamped close at hand when the tax-gatherer arrived to gather the tithes of an adjoining tribe. While the herds and flocks of their neighbours were being collected in order that the tenth might be taken from them, the Bani Tamîm, anticipating a like demand upon themselves, came forward armed with bows and swords and drove the tax-gatherer away. Mahomet resolved on making a prompt example of the offenders. Oyeina, with fifty of his Arab horsemen, travelling with haste and secrecy, fell unexpectedly upon them, and making above fifty prisoners,—men, women, and children,—carried them off to Medîna, where they were kept by Mahomet in confinement.

Bani Ta-
mim send
deputation
for release
of prison-
ers.

The Bani Tamîm, some of whom had fought by the side of Mahomet at Mecca and Honein, and been munificently rewarded at Jierrâna, lost no time in sending a deputation, consisting of eighty or ninety persons headed by their chief men, to beg for the prisoners' release. As these passed through the streets of Medîna, the captive women and children recognising their friends raised a loud cry of distress. Moved by the sight, the chiefs hastened onwards to obtain their liberty. They reached the Mosque, and, after waiting impatiently for some time in its spacious court, at last called out (for they were rude children of the desert) in a loud and familiar voice to Mahomet, who was in one of the female apartments adjoining the hall of audience: 'O Mahomet, come forth unto us!' The Prophet was displeased at their roughness and importunity, for he loved to be addressed in low and submissive accents. But, as the mid-day prayer was at hand, he came forth; and while Bilâl was summoning the

---

[1] Nine such parties are mentioned as having started on the first day of the new year, to various tribes. They were instructed to take the best and unblemished part of the property, but not to interfere with the capital or source of increase.

people, he entered into discourse with the strangers and listened to their application.

The prayers being ended, Mahomet seated himself in the court of the Mosque, when a scene occurred illustrative at once of Arab manners, and of the successful readiness with which Mahomet adapted himself to the circumstances of the moment. The chiefs sought leave to contend for victory in rhetoric and poetry with the orators and poets of Medîna.[1] It was hardly the proper issue for Mahomet on which to place his cause; but to have refused would have injured him in the eyes of these wild Bedouins; and the Prophet was confident in the superior eloquence of his followers. So he gave permission. First arose Otârid, the orator of the tribe, and, in an harangue of the ordinary boastful style, lauded his own people for their prowess and nobility. When he had ended, Mahomet motioned to Thâbit ibn Cays that he should reply. Thâbit descanted on the glory of Mahomet as a messenger from Heaven, on the devotion of the Refugees, and on the faithful and generous friendship of the citizens of Medîna. He finished by threatening destruction against all who should refuse Islâm. Then Zibricân, the Bedouin bard, stood up, and recited poetry, in which he dilated on the greatness and unequalled hospitality of the Bani Tamîm. When he sat down, Hassân the son of Thâbit, by Mahomet's command, replied in glowing and well-measured verse. After dwelling upon the more ordinary topics, he ended thus:—

Their poet and orator worsted by Thâbit and Hassân.

Children of Dârim! contend not with us : Your boasting will turn to your shame.

Ye lie when ye contend with us for Glory. What are ye but our Servants, our Nurses, and our Attendants?

If ye be come to save your lives, and your property, that it may not be distributed as booty;—

Then make not unto God an equal, embrace Islâm, and abandon the wild manners of the Heathen.

The strangers were astonished at the beauty of Hassân's poetry, and abashed at the force and point of the concluding verses. 'By the Lord!' they said, 'how rich is this man's

[1] Al Acra said: 'Give us permission to speak; for, verily, from me praise is an ornament and reproach a disgrace.' 'Nay,' replied the Prophet, 'thou speakest falsely; that may be said of the Great and Almighty God alone.'

G G

fortune! His poet, as well as his orator, surpasseth ours in eloquence.

Mahomet liberated their prisoners, and, having entertained them hospitably, dismissed their Chief with rich presents and provisions for the way. All the branches of the tribe which had not yet given in their adhesion were now converted.[1]

But the Prophet did not forget the first rude and impatient address of the Bedouin deputation. To guard against such familiarity for the future, the following divine commandment was promulgated :—

O ye that believe! Go not in advance (in any matter) before God and his Prophet; and fear God, for God heareth and knoweth. O ye that believe! Raise not your voices above the voice of the Prophet; nor speak loudly in discourse with him as the loud speech of one of you with another, lest your works become vain, and ye perceive it not. Verily, they that lower their voices in the presence of the Apostle of God, are those whose hearts God hath disposed unto piety; these shall have pardon and an abundant reward. Verily as to those that call unto thee from outside of the private apartments, the most part of them understand not. If they had waited patiently, until thou wentest forth unto them, it had been better for them. But God is forgiving and merciful.

The tax-gatherer deputed to the Bani Mustalick, on approaching their encampment, was encountered by a large body of the tribe who went forth on camels to meet him. Apprehending violence, he fled back to Medîna; and Mahomet was preparing a party to avenge the affront, when a deputation appeared to explain the circumstance. They had in reality held steadily to the profession of Islâm, and what had been mistaken for hostile preparations were (they said) marks of joy and welcome. The deputation was received with courtesy. The tax-gatherer was reprehended, and his misconduct deemed not unworthy of a special revelation.

---

[1] Sprenger gives an anecdote which, though of very doubtful authority, illustrates the spirit of the times. One of the prisoners was a beautiful female, to whom Mahomet offered terms of marriage, which, however, she declined. When her husband came with the deputation, he turned out to be a black and ill-favoured person; whereupon the Moslems were so displeased at her refusal of the Prophet, that they began to abuse and curse her. But Mahomet interfered to excuse her, and bade them refrain.

Marginal notes:

Mahomet liberates their prisoners.

Notice of deputation in the Corân.

Sura xlix.

Deputation from Bani Mustalick. May, A.D. 630.

Another of his followers was then deputed by Mahomet to levy the tithes and to instruct the people in their religious duties.[1]

During the summer of this year several lesser expeditions were undertaken for the chastisement of rebellious or recusant tribes.   Marked only by the ordinary features of surprise and the capture of prisoners and plunder, it is unnecessary to burden the page with their details.   The largest was directed against a combination of the Abyssinians with the people of Jedda, the nature of which is not clearly explained.   It was, however, regarded by the Prophet of sufficient importance to require the services of an army of three hundred men.   This force reached an island on the shore of the Red Sea which the enemy had made their rendezvous, and forced them to retire.[2]

Expeditions during summer of A.H. IX. A.D. 630.

Abyssinians attacked at Jedda. July.

About the same time, Ali was sent, in command of two hundred horse, to destroy the temple of Fuls belonging to the Bani Tay, a tribe divided between the profession of Idolatry and the Christian faith.   He performed his mission effectually, and returned with many prisoners and laden with plunder.   Amongst the prisoners was the daughter of Hâtim Tay, the Christian Bedouin so famous for his generosity. This chieftain had died many years before ; and his son Adî, on the first alarm of Ali's approach, had fled with his family to Syria.   His sister prostrated herself at the feet of Mahomet, and told her plaintive story.   She was at once released, and presented with a change of raiment and a camel, on which, joining the first Syrian caravan, she went in quest of her brother.   At her solicitation, Adî presented himself before the Prophet, and, having embraced Islâm, was again appointed to the chiefship of his tribe.

Campaign against Bani Tay.

Conversion of son of Hâtim Tay. July.

The submission of the poet, Káb son of Zoheir, took

---

[1] The passage in the Corân relating to this incident is in immediate continuation of that just quoted, and runs as follows: 'O ye that believe! if an evil man come unto you with intelligence, make careful enquiry, lest ye injure a people through inadvertence, and afterwards repent of what ye have done. And know that, verily, the Apostle of God is amongst you. If he were to listen to you in many matters, ye would fall into sin,' &c.

[2] The circumstance is remarkable, and not the less so on account of the brevity of the Secretary and the silence of the other biographers. *Apparently,* a body of Abyssinians had crossed the Red Sea to join the Arabs of Jedda in opposing Mahomet. Were the eyes of the Negûs now opened to the futility of the expectation that Mahomet would support Christianity?

place about this time. His father was one of the most distinguished poets of Arabia; and the poetical mantle descended upon several members of his family. After the capture of Mecca his brother wrote from thence to warn Káb of the fate which had overtaken certain of the poets there, and urged him either to sue for terms at Medîna, or seek for himself elsewhere a secure asylum. Káb was imprudent enough to reply in verses significant of displeasure at his brother's conversion. Mahomet, highly incensed, gave utterance to threats ominous for the safety of Káb. Again the poet was warned, and urged by his brother to delay no longer. At last, in despair, he resolved to present himself before Mahomet and seek for pardon. So a stranger one day appeared unexpectedly in the Mosque: addressing the Prophet he said: 'Káb the son of Zoheir cometh unto thee repentant and believing. Wilt thou give him quarter if I bring him to thee?' The promise having been vouchsafed, the stranger made known that he himself was Káb. To signalise his gratitude, Káb presented to Mahomet the famous 'Poem of the Mantle,' in which he lauded the generosity and glory of his benefactor. When reciting it in the assembly, he came to this verse,—

Verily, the Prophet is a light to illuminate the world,
A naked sword from out of the armoury of God,—

Mahomet, unable to restrain his admiration and delight, took his own mantle from off his shoulders and threw it over the poet. The precious gift (from which the poem derived its name) was treasured up with care. It passed into the hands of the Caliphs, and was by them preserved, as one of the regalia of the empire, until Baghdad was sacked by the Tartars; and, under the name of the *Khirca Sharîfa,* a relic is even now exhibited at Constantinople as the self-same mantle. To gain over such a poet was no empty triumph, for Káb wielded a real power which was now thrown as a fresh weight into the scale of Islâm.

Deputa-
tions from
Arab
tribes.
A.H. IX., X.
A.D. 630,
631.
The Mosque of Mahomet began this year to be the scene of frequent embassies from all quarters of Arabia. His supremacy was everywhere recognised; and from the most distant parts of the Peninsula—from Yemen and Hadhramaut, from Mahra, Omân, and Bahrein, from the borders of Syria and the outskirts of Persia—the tribes hastened to

prostrate themselves before the rising potentate, and by an early submission to secure his favour. They were uniformly treated with consideration and courtesy; their representations were received in public in the court of the Mosque, which formed the hall of audience; and there whatever matters required the commands of Mahomet—the collection and transmission of tithes and tribute, the grant of lands, the recognition or conferment of authority and office, the adjustment of international disputes—were all discussed and settled. Simple though its exterior, and unpretending its forms and usages, more absolute power was exercised, and affairs of greater importance transacted, in the court-yard of the Mosque of Mahomet, than in many an imperial palace.

The messengers and embassies were quartered by Mahomet in the houses of the chief citizens of Medîna, by whom they were hospitably entertained. On departure they always received an ample sum for the expenses of the road, and generally some further present corresponding with their rank. A written treaty often guaranteed certain privileges to the tribe, and not unfrequently a teacher was sent back with the embassy to instruct the newly converted people in the duties of Islâm and the requirements of Mahomet, and to see that every remnant of idolatry was obliterated. For the rest a large amount of independence was left to the rulers of powerful tribes, and such distant provinces as Bahrein and Omân; but, though allowed themselves to collect the tithes, the amount must nevertheless, as a rule, be remitted to Medîna. In some cases this demand created discontent; but before the Prophet's death the irresistible combination of temporal with spiritual power had overcome all opposition. *Mode in which they were treated.*

These embassies having commenced in the ninth year of the Hegira, it is styled in tradition 'the Year of deputations;' but they were almost equally numerous in the tenth year. It would be tedious and unprofitable to enumerate them all. Those that have been already mentioned, or which are incidentally noticed hereafter, afford a sufficient specimen of the rest. *The ninth year of the Hegira, called Year of deputations.*

I have before, in the chapter on the relation of Islâm to Christianity, described the remarkable embassy from the Christians of Najrân which about this period visited Medîna. *Embassy from Najrân.*

CHAPTER XXVIII.

CAMPAIGN OF TABÛK; AND OTHER EVENTS IN THE SECOND HALF OF THE NINTH YEAR OF THE HEGIRA.

October, A.D. 630, *to April,* A.D. 631.

Gathering of Roman feudatories on Syrian border.

DURING the summer of the year A.D. 630, a force had been despatched from Medîna towards the Syrian frontier; it was directed, apparently, against certain disaffected clans of the Bani Odzra and Balî, who since the operations of Khâlid in that quarter were now, at least nominally, adherents of Mahomet. Whether to guard against the recurrence of similar marauding inroads, or in consequence of the rumour of Mahomet's growing power and pretensions, the Roman emperor, who is said to have been then at Hims, directed the feudatory tribes of the border to assemble for its protection. This precautionary measure was magnified by travellers and traders arriving from Syria into the assemblage of a great and threatening army. A year's pay, they said, had been advanced by the Kaiser, in order that the soldiers might be well furnished for a long campaign; the tribes of the Syrian desert, the Bani Lakhm, Judzâm, and Ghassân, were flocking around the Roman eagles, and the vanguard was already at Balcâa. Mahomet at once resolved to meet the danger with

Mahomet projects counter-expedition. Autumn, A.H. IX. A.D. 630.

the largest force he could collect. His custom at other times had been to conceal to the very last the object of an intended march, or by pretending to make preparations for a campaign in some other direction, to lull the suspicions of his enemy. But the journey now in contemplation was so distant, and the heat of the season so excessive, that timely warning was deemed necessary in order that the necessities of the way might be foreseen and provided for.

All his adherents and allies, the inhabitants of Mecca as well as the Bedouin tribes, received from Mahomet an urgent summons to join the army.   But the Arabs of the desert and the citizens of Medîna showed little alacrity in obeying the command.   The anticipated hardships of the journey, the long-continued drought and overpowering heat, and perhaps the memory of the execution done by the Roman phalanx at Mûta, made them loth to quit the ease and shelter of their homes.   Multitudes pleaded inability and other frivolous excuses.   These pleas were accepted when tendered by any from amongst the men of Medîna; for Mahomet, conscious of the debt of gratitude he owed their city, always treated them with tenderness.   But the Arab tribes were refused permission to remain behind.

On the other hand, extraordinary eagerness pervaded the ranks of all the earnest and faithful Moslems.   Tithes and free-will offerings poured in from every direction, and many of the chief men at Medîna vied with one another in the costliness of their gifts.   The contribution of Othmân surpassed all others, and amounted to one thousand golden dinars.   From these sources carriage and supplies were provided for the poorer soldiers; but they did not suffice for all who longed to share in the merit, or in the spoils, of the campaign.   A party for whom, after every effort, Mahomet could make no provision, retired in tears from his presence, and their names are embalmed in tradition under the title of *The Weepers*.[1]

At last the army was marshalled and encamped in the outskirts of the city.   Abu Bakr was appointed to conduct prayers in the encampment until the Prophet himself should assume command.   Muhammad son of Maslama was placed in charge of the city; Ali also was left behind to take care of the Prophet's family, as well as to check any rising of disaffection.   Abdallah ibn Obey pitched a separate camp for his numerous adherents near the main army; but eventually, as it would appear with the consent of Mahomet, he remained behind.

---

[1] *Bakkâ-ûn.*   The same word as in Judges ii. 1, 5, where a place is named *Bochim,* or 'Weepers,' because the children of Israel wept there.   See also Ps. lxxxiv. 6, 'the valley of *Baca,*' or weeping.   *The Weepers* are noticed in Sura ix. v. 94, in allusion to the present occasion.

Army marches for Tabûk. September, October, A.D. 630.

The army, after all these diminutions, was probably the largest effective force ever before put in motion in Arabia. Its numbers are given, though probably with some exaggeration, at thirty thousand, of whom no less than ten thousand are said to have been cavalry. The march was marked alone by the heat and discomfort of the way, and by the want of water. A curious scene occurred at the valley of Hejer,

Valley of Hejer.

whose rocky sides were hewn out (according to local tradition) into dwellings, by the rebellious and impious Thamudites. The army having alighted there and drawn water from its refreshing fountains, began to prepare their food, when suddenly a proclamation was made through the ranks that none should drink of the water or use it for their ablutions, that the dough which had been kneaded should be given to the camels, and that no one should go forth alone by night: 'Enter not the houses of the transgressors, except with lamentation, lest that overtake you which happened unto them.' On the morrow, a plentiful shower of rain, ascribed to the miraculous intervention of the Prophet, compensated for the loss of the wells of Hejer.[1]

Halt at Tabûk: Mahomet opens communications with surrounding tribes.

Having reached Tabûk, where there was plenty of shade and water, the army halted. The rumours of the Roman invasion had by this time melted away. There was nothing at the present moment to threaten the border, or engage in that direction the attention of Mahomet. So he contented himself with sending a strong detachment under Khâlid to Dûma, and with receiving the adhesion of the Jewish and Christian tribes on the shores of the Ælanitic Gulf, towards the east of which he was now encamped.

[1] The story, however, is not confirmed by Wâckidi. Hishâmi deals greatly in the marvellous regarding the journey. He tells a tale of two men who, neglecting Mahomet's caution, went out by night alone, and were maltreated by the evil spirits,—one having his neck wrenched, and the other being carried away by the wind to the hills of the Bani Tai. So also the following: By the way, they came to a trickling fountain, at which hardly two or three men could have slaked their thirst. Mahomet bade none to touch it before himself. But the prohibition was not attended to. Coming up, he found it empty, and cursed the men who had disobeyed him. Then he took up a little of the water in his hand, and, sprinkling the rock, wiped it with his hand and prayed over it. Floods of water immediately gushed forth, with a noise as it had been thunder, and all drank thereof. Mahomet said: 'Whosoever of you shall survive the longest, will hear of this valley being greener with trees and verdure than any other round about;'—meaning that the great stream now created would be permanent.

To the chief of these, John, the Christian Prince of Ayla (or Acaba), Mahomet addressed a letter, summoning him to submit on pain of being attacked by his great army.[1]   The Prince, with a cross of gold upon his forehead, hastened to the camp of Mahomet and, offering the present of a mule and a shawl, bowed himself reverentially in his presence. He was received with kindness, and Bilâl was commanded to entertain him hospitably.   The following treaty was concluded with him :—

'In the name of God the Gracious and Merciful: A compact of peace from God, and from Mahomet the Prophet and Apostle of God, granted unto Yuhanna (John) the son of Rûbah, and unto the people of Ayla.   For them who remain at home, and for those that travel abroad by sea or by land, there is the guarantee of God and the guarantee of Mahomet the Apostle of God, and for all that are with them, whether they belong to Syria or to Yemen or to the sea-coast.   Whoso contraveneth this treaty, his wealth shall not save him; it shall be the fair prize of him that taketh it. Now it shall not be lawful to hinder the men of Ayla from any springs which they have been in the habit of frequenting, nor from any passage they desire to make, whether by

(margin note: Treaty with John, Christian Prince of Ayla.)

---

[1] I have no reason to doubt the genuineness of this letter. It is as follows: *'To John ibn Rûbah and the Chiefs of Aylah.*   Peace be on you! I praise God for you, beside whom there is no Lord.   I will not fight against you until I have written thus unto you. Believe, or else pay tribute. And be obedient unto the Lord and his Prophet, and unto the messengers of his Prophet. Honour them and clothe them with excellent vestments, not with inferior raiment. Specially clothe Zeid with excellent garments. As long as my messengers are pleased, so likewise am I. Ye know the tribute. If ye desire to have security by sea and by land, obey the Lord and his Apostle, and he will defend you from every demand, whether by Arab or foreigner, saving the demand of the Lord and his Apostle. But if ye oppose and displease them, I will not accept from you a single thing, until I have fought against you and taken captive your little ones and slain the elder; for I am the Apostle of the Lord in truth. Believe in the Lord and in his Prophets. And believe in the Messiah son of Mary; verily he is the Word of God: I believe in him that he was a messenger of God. Come then, before trouble reach you.   I commend my messengers to you. Give to Harmala three measures of barley ; and indeed Harmala hath interceded for you. As for me, if it were not for the Lord and for this (intercession of Harmala), I would not have sent any message at all unto you, until ye had seen the army. But now, if ye obey my messengers, God will be your protector, and Mahomet, and whosoever belongeth unto him. Now my messengers are Sharahbîl, &c. Unto you is the guarantee of God and of Mahomet his Apostle, and peace be unto you if ye submit. And convey the people of Macna back to their land.'

sea or by land. This is the writing of Juheim and Sharahbîl, by command of the Apostle of God.'[1]

He is dismissed with honour.

In token of his approbation, Mahomet presented John with a mantle of striped Yemen stuff, and dismissed him honourably. The tribute was fixed at the yearly sum of a golden dinar for every family, or for the whole town of Ayla three hundred dinars.

Terms made with Jews of Macna, Adzrûh, and Jarbâ.

At the same time deputations from the Jewish settlements of Macna, Adzrûh, and Jarbâ presented themselves with a tender of submission to the Prophet. To each was given a rescript, specifying the amount of their tribute, and binding them to afford refuge and aid to any Moslem travellers or merchants who might stand in need of their good offices.[2]

Mahomet returns to Medina. A.H. IX. December, A.D. 630.

Having concluded these matters, Mahomet quitted Tabûk after having halted there for twenty days, and returned to Medîna. He reached home in the beginning of Ramadhân, or December, A.D. 630.

Khâlid conquers Dûma, and takes Chief prisoner to Medîna.

Meanwhile Khâlid had been travelling across the desert from Tabûk to Dûma, with four hundred and twenty horse, the flower of the army. So rapidly did he march, and so unexpectedly appear before Dûma, that Okeidar, the Christian chief, was surprised by him while hunting with his followers a wild cow. Khâlid pursued the party, and after a short struggle, in which the chief's brother was killed, took Okeidar captive. His life was spared on condition that the

---

[1] The treaty is evidently genuine. The original was no doubt retained as a precious charter of right by the chiefs of Ayla. We are told that Omar II. refrained from raising the tribute, which was below the proper amount, in deference to the guarantee given in this treaty.

[2] These treaties are genuine and interesting. The following was copied by Wâckidi, apparently from the original: 'In the name of God, &c. This writing is from Mahomet the Prophet to the people of Adzrûh. They are included in the truce of God and in the truce of Mahomet. They are to pay one hundred dinars every year, in Rajab, full weight and good money. And God is their guarantee that they shall behave towards the Moslems with probity and kindness. Whoever of the Moslems taketh refuge with them from danger and in quest of assistance, in case there should be ground of fear for such Moslems, and they are themselves in security, they are to protect them until they hear that Mahomet is preparing to set out for their aid.' A proof of the authenticity of this document is that 'Mahomet' is mentioned throughout by his simple name without either the affix *Prophet* or *Apostle*, or the reverential addition, 'Prayers and blessings be on him.' Such affixes are, in general, later additions by the pious transcriber.

gates of Dûma should be at once thrown open. The city was ransomed at two thousand camels, eight hundred sheep, four hundred suits of mail, and as many stand of arms. With this booty, and carrying with him Okeidar and another brother, Khâlid returned to Medîna.

The Christian chief, wearing a golden cross, and clothed in raiment of silk or velvet inwrought with gold, which attracted the admiration of the simple citizens of Medîna, was brought to the Prophet, who pressed him to embrace Islâm. The inducements presented by the new religion proved too strong for his faith in Christianity, and he was admitted to the favoured terms of a Moslem ally.[1]

The Chief embraces Islâm.

When Mahomet returned to Medîna, those of his followers who had remained behind without permission came forward to exculpate themselves. Mahomet reserved his reproaches for a special revelation. He thus avoided the odium that would have attached to a personal rebuke proceeding directly from himself, while the admonition came with all the force of a message from Heaven. The 9th Sura, the latest of all in chronological order, abounds with invectives against the disaffected 'hypocrites' generally, who still lingered in Medîna, and against those in particular who had neglected the order to join in the late expedition. The following passages will suffice as examples:—

Malingerers chided in Corân.

O ye that believe ! What ailed you that when it was said unto you, *Go forth to war in the ways of God*, ye inclined heavily towards the earth ? What ! do ye prefer the present life before

Sura ix.

---

[1] Wâckidi says he took the following copy *from the original at Dûma*: 'In the name of God, &c. ;—from Mahomet the Prophet of God to Keidar (when he accepted Islâm and put away from him the images and idols, by the hand of Khâlid, the Sword of God,) regarding Dûma of the waters of Jandal and its environs : to Mahomet belongeth the unoccupied land with its streams and fountains, its unenclosed and fallow ground, and the armour, weapons, camels, and forts ; and to you belongeth the occupied land with the fruit-bearing date-trees, and springs of water, after payment of the fifth. Your cattle shall not be molested in grazing on the waste lands ; that which is ordinarily exempt from tithe shall not be taxed ; the old date-trees shall not be taxed,—excepting the tenth thereof : so as that they observe prayer regularly, and pay the tithes faithfully. A true and faithful treaty. God is witness thereto, and all that are present of the Moslems.' This may be taken as a type of the treaties made with converted tribes. Okeidar revolted after Mahomet's death. The 'images and idols' may have been either those in use amongst the heathen part of the community, or such as belonged to the worship of Jesus and the Virgin.

that which is to come? If ye go not forth to war, he will punish you with a grievous punishment, and he will substitute another people for you : and ye shall not hurt him at all; for God is over all things powerful.   *   *   *

If it had been plunder close at hand, and an easy journey, they had surely followed thee. But the way seemed long unto them. They will swear unto thee by God, *If we had been able we had surely gone forth with you.* They destroy their own souls, for God knoweth they are liars. The Lord pardon thee ! Wherefore didst thou give them leave, until thou hadst distinguished those that speak the truth, and known the liars? [1]   *   *   *

If they had gone forth with thee, they had only added weakness to you, and had run to and fro amongst you, stirring up sedition. And amongst you, some had listened to them; for God knoweth the unjust. Verily they sought to stir up sedition aforetime; and they disturbed thy affairs until the Truth came, and the command of God was made manifest, although they were averse therefrom.[2] Among them there is that saith, *Give me leave to remain, and throw me not into temptation.* What ! have they not fallen into temptation already? Verily, Hell shall compass the Unbelievers round about.[3]

And the hypocrites.

The hypocrites, and the persons who privately scoffed and jested at the Faith and at those who spent their money in its propagation, are reprobated bitterly. Mahomet might pray for them seventy times; it would avail nothing with God for their pardon :—

They said, *Go not forth to war in the heat.* Say, the fire of Hell is a fiercer heat, if they understood. Wherefore they shall laugh little and weep much, for that which they have wrought.

Mahomet not to pray for them on their death.

These unfaithful followers are never more to be allowed the opportunity of going forth to fight with Mahomet :—

[1] From this it would appear that Mahomet repented (or affected to repent) afterwards that he had so easily and indiscriminately accepted the excuses of those to whom he gave permission to remain behind.

[2] Alluding to the conduct of the 'disaffected' at the battle of Ohod, or perhaps to the affair at the Mustalick expedition.

[3] Tradition assigns this last verse to the case of a man who begged Mahomet to excuse him from the campaign, as he feared the attractions of the Greek women. But a great number of the stories belonging to this campaign may be suspected (on the analogy of similar traditions regarding other texts) to have been fabricated for the purpose of illustrating such passages of the Corân.

'Neither do thou ever pray over any of them that shall die, nor stand over his grave, for they do reject God and his Prophet, and they shall die transgressors.'

The Arabs of the desert, who were the chief offenders, because they had stayed away notwithstanding the direct refusal of leave, are censured unsparingly for their disobedience ;—ignorant, stubborn, unbelieving, fickle,—' they watched but the changes of fortune.'

Bedouins specially reprobated.

Turn from them. They are an abomination. Their resting-place shall be Hell-fire, the reward of that which they have wrought.

Those believers who had not dissembled their fault, but honestly confessed it, were the most leniently dealt with :—

Such as confessed, more leniently treated.
Sura ix.

And others have acknowledged their offences ; they have mingled a good action with another that is evil. Haply God will be turned unto them, for God is forgiving and merciful. Take offerings of their substance, that thou mayst cleanse them and purify them thereby ; and pray for them, for thy prayers will restore tranquillity unto them. And there are others waiting the command of God, whether He will punish them, or whether He will be turned unto them, for God is knowing and wise.

The last verse refers to Káb ibn Málik, a poet, who had done good service to Mahomet, and to two other believers, who had incurred his special displeasure. They had no pretext to offer for their absence from the army, and their bad example had encouraged the hesitating and disaffected citizens in their neglect of the Prophet's summons; the latter could not with any show of justice be reprimanded or punished, if the far more serious offence of these his professed followers were passed over. A ban was therefore placed upon them. They were cut off from all intercourse with the people, and even with their own wives and families. Fifty days passed thus miserably, and the lives of the three men became a burden to them. At length Mahomet relented ; and, by the delivery of the following revelation, received them back into his favour :—

Káb and his two companions: ban put upon them.

Verily, God is reconciled unto the Prophet, and unto the Refugees and the men of Medîna, those who followed him in the hour of difficulty, after that the hearts of a part of them had nearly swerved. Thereafter He turned to them, for He is com-

Sura ix.

passionate unto them and merciful. And He is likewise reconciled unto the Three;—those that were left behind, so that the earth became straitened unto them with all its spaciousness, and their souls became straitened within them, and they felt that there was no refuge from God but by fleeing unto Him; —then He turned unto them, for God is easy to be reconciled, and merciful.

Káb received back into favour.

After the promulgation of this passage, Káb was again treated by Mahomet as before with kindness and consideration.

Mahomet destroys a Mosque at Coba.

The displeasure of the Prophet was also at this time kindled against a party at Coba, who had built a Mosque there, and desired Mahomet that he would come and consecrate it by praying in it himself. As he was at the moment preparing to start for Tabûk, he deferred to comply with their request until his return. Meanwhile he received information that the new Mosque was built with a sectarian and hostile bias, to draw off men from the original Mosque at Coba, and even to afford shelter to certain disaffected persons. On his return from Tabûk, therefore, he not only sent a party to destroy the new edifice, but gave utterance to the following command from the Almighty :—

Sura ix.

There are men who have builded a Mosque with evil purpose, out of unbelief, to make divisions among the Unbelievers, and as a lurking place for him that hath fought against God and his Apostle aforetime.[1] Yet they will swear, *Verily we intended nothing but good.* But God beareth witness that they are Liars. Stand not up (for prayer) therein for ever. There is a Mosque which from the first day hath been founded upon Piety. It is more just that thou shouldest stand up therein ;—Therein are men that love to be purified : for God loveth the Pure. What, therefore ? Whether is he better that hath builded his foundations upon the fear of God and His good pleasure, or he that hath built his foundations upon the brink of a crumbling bank, to be swept away with him into the fire of Hell : for God doth not guide the race of transgressors. The building which they have built shall not cease to be a cause of doubting in their hearts, until their hearts be cut in pieces. And God is knowing and wise.

---

[1] The biographers do not mention who is here alluded to. The *Commentators* specify Abu Aámir the hermit, who, after the battle of Honein, is said to have fled to Syria; but this is doubtful.

About two months after the return of Mahomet from Tabûk, Abdallah ibn Obey, the leader of the disaffected citizens at Medîna, died. Mahomet had almost uniformly followed the advice given to him on his first arrival in the city, to deal tenderly with this chief. Excepting the rupture which occurred on his return from the Bani Mustalick, and one or two other occasions when Abdallah openly took the part of his Jewish confederates, the Prophet was careful to avoid any harsh or humiliating treatment which might have driven him, with his numerous and influential adherents, into open and active opposition. This course was observed to the last. Mahomet prayed over his corpse, thereby professing to recognise Abdallah as having been a faithful Moslem; he walked behind the bier to the grave, and waited there till the ceremonies of the funeral were ended.

Death of Abdallah ibn Obey.

After Abdallah's death, there was no one left in the ranks of the disaffected party possessed of any power or influence. There was none whom Mahomet needed longer to treat with delicacy or caution. The faction had died out. Those who had hitherto been lukewarm or disloyal soon embraced, heart and soul, the cause of Islâm, and the power of Mahomet became fully and finally consolidated in Medîna.

Faction of disaffected dies with him.

The campaign to Tabûk was the last expedition undertaken during the Prophet's lifetime. Mahomet's authority was now unquestioned northwards to the Syrian confine, equally as in the south as far as the still recusant Tâyif. It seemed almost as if the need of fighting had gone by. The following tradition shows how little the real spirit of Islâm, as aggressive and tending necessarily to universal conquest, had yet dawned upon the understanding of the people; although indeed the principles from which such a conclusion was legitimately to be deduced, had long been inculcated by Mahomet. Looking around them, and seeing no enemy remain,—the Romans even having retired and left them alone in their deserts, the followers of the Prophet began to sell their arms, saying: 'The wars for religion now are ended.' But Mahomet saw better into the future. When it was told him, he forbade the sale, saying: 'There shall not cease from the midst of my people a party engaged in fighting for the truth, even until Antichrist appear.'

War to be carried on by Islâm till Antichrist appear.

Provision
made for
study of
theology.

Pointing to this normal state of warfare, is the following passage in the Corân, which makes provision, notwithstanding, for the maintenance of students and teachers of religion :—

Sura ix.

It is not necessary that the whole body of Believers should go forth to war. If a certain number from every party go not forth to war, it is that they may give themselves to study in religion, and may admonish their people when they return unto them (from the wars), so that they may take heed unto themselves.

CHAPTER XXIX.

EMBASSY FROM TÂYIF; AND PILGRIMAGE OF ABU BAKR.

A.H. IX.—*December*, A.D. 630, *to March*, A.D. 631.

It was now ten months since Mahomet had raised the siege of Tâyif. The citizens were wedded to idolatry, and still maintained a sullen isolation.

Tâyif resists Mahomet's authority.

Orwa, a chief of Tâyif, whom the reader will remember as one of the ambassadors of the Coreish to the Moslem camp at Hodeibia, was absent during the siege of his native city, having gone to Yemen to be instructed in the use of warlike engines for its defence. On his return, finding that all Mecca and the surrounding tribes, excepting the men of Tâyif, had submitted to Mahomet, and being himself favourably impressed with what he had seen of the new religion and its followers at Hodeibia, Orwa went in quest of the Prophet to Medîna, and there embraced Islâm. His first generous impulse was to return to Tâyif, and invite his fellow-citizens to share in the blessings imparted by the new faith. Mahomet, well knowing their bigotry and ignorance, warned him repeatedly of the danger he would incur; but Orwa, presuming on his popularity at Tâyif, persisted in the design. Arriving in the evening, he made public his conversion, and called upon the people to join him. They retired to consult upon the matter. In the morning, ascending the top of his house, he cried out aloud at the pitch of his voice the call to prayer. Hearing this, the rabble ran together; and some discharged arrows at him, by one of which he was mortally wounded in the arm. His family and friends rallied around him, but it was too late. He had offered up, he said, his blood unto its

Martyrdom of Orwa. A.H. IX. A.D. 630.

master for the sake of his people : he blessed God, with his dying breath, for the honour of martyrdom ; and he prayed his friends to bury him by the side of the Moslems who had fallen at Honein.   When the tidings reached Mahomet, he lauded the memory of the martyr : ' He may be compared,' was his exclamation, ' to the prophet Yâsîn, who summoned his people to believe in the Lord, and they slew him.'

Tâyif sends embassy to Mahomet.
A.H. IX.
December,
A.D. 630.

The martyrdom of Orwa compromised the inhabitants of Tâyif, and forced them to continue the hostile course they had previously been pursuing.   But they began to suffer severely from the marauding attacks of the Bani Hawâzin under Mâlik.   That chief, according to his engagement, had maintained an unceasing predatory warfare against them. The cattle were cut off in their pasture lands, and at their watering places ; and at last no man was safe beyond the walls of the city.   ' We have not strength,' they said among themselves, ' to fight against the Arab tribes all around, that have plighted their faith to Mahomet, and bound themselves to fight in his cause.'   So they sent a deputation to Medîna, consisting of six chiefs with fifteen or twenty followers, who reached their destination a fortnight after the return of the army from Tâbuk.   Mughîra (nephew of the martyr Orwa), meeting the embassy in the outskirts of the city, hastened to announce the approach of the strangers to the Prophet, who received them gladly, and pitched a tent for their accommodation close by the Mosque.   Every evening after supper he visited them there, and instructed them in the faith, till it was dark.   They freely communicated their apprehensions to him.   As for themselves, they were quite ready at once to destroy their great idol, Tâghia (or Lât) ; but the ignorant amongst the men, and especially the women, were devoted to the worship, and would be alarmed at its demolition.   If the idol were left for three years, and the people meanwhile familiarised with the requirements of Islâm, the wishes of the Prophet might then without difficulty be carried into effect.   But Mahomet would not consent.   Two years,— one year,—six months,—were asked successively, and successively refused.   ' The grace of one month might surely be conceded ;' but Mahomet was firm.   Islâm and the idol could not co-exist.   The idol must fall without a single day's delay.

They then begged to be excused performance of the daily prayers, and that some one else might be deputed to destroy the image. ' As for the demolition of the idol with your own hands,' replied Mahomet, ' I will dispense with that; but prayer is indispensable. Without prayer religion would be naught.' ' In that case,' said they, ' we shall perform it, though it be a degradation.' They also pleaded hard that the forest of Wajj, a famous preserve for the chase in the vicinity of Tâyif, should be declared inviolate. To this Mahomet acceded: and the embassy, having finally tendered their allegiance, were dismissed with a rescript to the effect ' that neither the trees nor the wild animals of Wajj should be meddled with. Whoever was found transgressing there should be scourged, and his garments seized. If he transgressed again, he should be sent to the Prophet. This was the command of Mahomet the Apostle of God.'

Abu Sofiân and Mughîra, both men of influence with the tribe, were deputed by Mahomet to accompany the strangers, and destroy their idol. Mughîra, wielding a pickaxe, and surrounded by a guard of armed men from amongst his immediate relatives, proceeded to the work, and, amid the cries and lamentations of the women, with his own hand hewed the image to the ground. The debts of the martyr Orwa were defrayed from the jewels and spoil of the temple. Tâyif is remarkable as the only place where a strong demonstration of popular feeling attended the fate of any of the idols of Arabia. Everywhere else they appear to have been destroyed without sympathy and without a pang. *Having been admitted to terms, their idol is destroyed by Mughîra.*

The sacred season of pilgrimage now again drew near. Mahomet had hitherto abstained from being present at its ceremonies because the great mass of the pilgrims were heathens, and idolatrous practices mingled with the holy rites. The same cause kept him away from the present festival. But he resolved that this should be the last in which the pilgrimage was dishonoured by unworthy customs and the holy places polluted by the presence of unbelievers. He was now strong enough to banish heathenism entirely and for ever from his native city. When thus purified, the ceremonies might, without compromising his holy office, be performed by himself in the succeeding year. *Mahomet stays away from yearly pilgrimage. A.H. IX. March. A.D. 631.*

The caravan of pilgrims from Medîna was therefore limited *Abu Bakr's pilgrim-*

age. The 'Release' committed to Ali for publication

on the present occasion to three hundred men, with Abu Bakr as their chief.   Shortly after its departure the opening verses of the 9th Sura were revealed, with the view of carrying out the object above explained.   The passage is styled *Barâat*, that is *liberty* or *release*, because Mahomet is therein discharged, after the expiry of four months, from any obligations otherwise devolving upon him towards the heathen Arabs.   This important revelation was committed to Ali, who was despatched after the caravan.   When Ali had come up with the pilgrims and communicated the nature of his errand, Abu Bakr enquired whether the Prophet had put him in command over the pilgrimage.   'No,' replied Ali; 'but he hath directed me to recite the divine behest in the hearing of all the people.'

The *Release*. 10th Dzul Hijj, A.H. IX. March 20, A.D. 631.

Towards the close of the pilgrimage, on the great day of sacrifice, at the place of casting stones near Minâ,[1] Ali read aloud to the multitudes who crowded round him in the narrow pass, the heavenly command, as follows:—

Sura ix.

A DISCHARGE by God and his Apostle, in reference to those of the Idolaters with whom ye have entered into treaty.

Go to and fro in the earth securely four months.   And know that ye cannot hinder God, and that verily God will bring disgrace upon the Unbelievers;—

And an ANNOUNCEMENT from God and his Apostle unto the People, on the day of the greater Pilgrimage, that God is discharged from (liability to) the Idolaters,—and his Prophet likewise.   Now, if ye repent, that will be better for you; but if ye turn your backs, know that ye cannot hinder God; and acquaint those who disbelieve with the tidings of a grievous punishment;—Excepting those of the Idolaters with whom ye have entered into treaty, and who thereafter have not failed you in any thing, and have not helped any one against you.   Fulfil unto these their treaty, until the expiration of their term; for God loveth the pious.

And when the forbidden months have elapsed, then fight against the Idolaters, wheresoever ye find them; take them captive, besiege them, and lay in wait for them in every ambush; but if they repent, and establish Prayer, and give the Tithes, leave them alone, for God is gracious and merciful.   And if any of the Idolaters ask a guarantee of thee, give it unto him, until he shall have heard the Word of God; then convey him back unto his place of security.   This because they are a people that do not understand.   *   *   *

_____
[1] See Burton, ii. 282, and his picture of the spot.

O ye that believe! Verily the Unbelievers are unclean. Wherefore, let them not approach the holy Temple after this year. And if ye fear poverty, God will enrich you of His abundance, if He pleaseth, for God is knowing and wise.

Having finished the recitation of this passage, Ali con- Ali an-
tinued : 'I have been commanded to declare unto you that Prophet's
no Unbeliever shall enter Paradise. No idolater shall after commands.
this year perform the pilgrimage; and no one shall make the circuit of the Holy house naked. Whosoever hath a treaty with the Prophet, it shall be respected till its termination. Four months are permitted to every tribe to return to their territories in security. After that the obligation of the Prophet ceaseth.'

The vast concourse of pilgrims listened peaceably till Ali Concourse
ended. Then they broke up and departed every man to his quietly.
home, publishing to all the tribes throughout the Peninsula the inexorable ordinance which they had heard from the lips of Ali.

The passage just quoted completed the system of Maho- Annihila-
met so far as concerned its relations with idolatrous tribes idolatry
and races. The few cases of truce excepted, uncompro- clared mis-
mising warfare was declared against them all. No trace of sion of
idolatry was to survive within the expanding circle of the influence of Islâm. And as Islâm was the universal faith intended for all mankind, so its mission was now plainly set forth to be the absolute annihilation of idolatry throughout the world.

In juxtaposition with this passage, though evidently And re-
revealed in an altogether different connection, we find Judaism
the following verses declaratory of the final principles on and Chri-
which the professors of Judaism and Christianity were to be dependent
treated. After long neglect and silence, the Corân now position.
notices Jews and Christians, only to condemn them to a perpetual vassalage :—

Fight against those who do not believe in God nor in the last Sura ix.
day, and who forbid not that which God hath forbidden, and profess not the true religion,—those, namely, who have received the Scriptures (that is both Jews and Christians) until they pay tribute with the hand, and are humbled. The Jews say that Ezra is the Son of God, and the Christians that the Messiah is the Son of God. This is their saying, with their mouths. They imitate the saying of the Unbelievers before them. God destroy them ! How have they devised lying vanities ! They have taken their priests and their monks as lords besides God,—and also the Messiah the son of Mary. Yet they were not bidden but to worship the one God ;—There is no God but He, far exalted above that with which they associate Him ! They seek to extinguish the light of God with their mouths. But God refuseth to do otherwise than make His light perfect, even though the Unbelievers be averse therefrom. He it is that hath sent His Apostle with the true guidance, and the religion of truth, that He may make it superior to all other religions, even though the Idolaters be averse therefrom. O ye that believe ! Verily many of the Priests and Monks devour the wealth of the people in vanity, and obstruct the way of God. And those that treasure up gold and silver, and spend it not in the way of God, announce unto them a grievous punishment ;—On the day on which it (*i.e.* the gold and silver) shall be heated in the fire of Hell, and their foreheads and their sides and their backs shall be seared therewith,—This is that which ye have treasured up for yourselves, wherefore taste that which ye have treasured up !

Contempt with which Judaism and Christianity are cast aside.

Thus, with threats of abasement and with bitter curses, Mahomet parted finally from the Jews and Christians, whom he had so long deceived with vain professions of attachment to their Scriptures, and from whose teaching he had borrowed that which was most valuable in his own. Having reached the pinnacle of prosperity and power, he cast contemptuously aside the supports to which he so greatly owed his elevation.

CHAPTER XXX.

EMBASSIES OF SUBMISSION RECEIVED AT MEDÎNA.

A.H. IX. AND X.—A.D. 630, 631.

Ætat. 62, 63.

THE life of Mahomet was drawing to a close; but his work was also near completion. The proof was amply shown in the stream of submissive embassies which from all quarters of Arabia now flowed uninterruptedly towards Medîna.

Numerous embassies during tenth year of Hegira.

The adhesion of Tâyif and the destruction of its famous idol produced a wide and powerful effect in the south and east of the Peninsula. Within a few months after those events, and before the close of the ninth year of the Hegira, many of the chiefs and princes of Yemen and Mahra, of Omân, Bahrein, and Yemâma, had signified by letter or by embassy their conversion to Islâm and submission to the Prophet.

Embassies from south and east. A.H. IX. and X. December, A.D. 630, to March. A.D. 631.

Some of them had been converted even earlier. On his return from the siege of Tâyif, towards the close of the eighth year of the Hegira, Mahomet sent Amru with a despatch to Jeyfar king of Omân, summoning him and his brother to make profession of the true faith. At first they gave answer 'that they would be the weakest among the Arabs, if they made another man possessor of their property.' But as Amru was about to depart, they repented, and, calling him back, embraced Islâm. The people followed their example, and without demur paid their tithes to Amru, who continued till the Prophet's death to be his representative in Omân. He was supported by a companion, who instructed the people in the Corân and superintended the assessment of the tithes. This province, which had hitherto been under the suzerainty of Persia, was so distant that Mahomet allowed

Conversion of Omân; A.H. VIII. February, A.D. 630.

the Prince to distribute the tithes among his own poor—a concession which no doubt facilitated the introduction of the new faith.

Conversion of Himyarite princes of Mahra and Yemen ;

At the same time, another legate was deputed to the Himyarite princes professing the Christian faith in Yemen. He carried with him a letter in which Mahomet expressed his belief in Moses and Jesus, but denied the Trinity, and the divinity of Christ. Their reply, accepting the new religion with all its conditions, reached the Prophet after his return from Tabûk ; and he acknowledged it in a despatch, praising the alacrity of their faith, setting forth the legal demands of Islâm, and commending his tithe collectors to their favour.[1]

And of Bahrein and Hejer.

Simultaneously with the mission of Amru, or a little later, Mahomet sent Alâ ' the Hadhramite' towards the Persian

---

[1] The instructions which Mahomet gave to his envoy are curious. He was to be particular in his purification and prayers on reaching the country. He was to take the Prophet's despatch in his right hand and place it in the right hand of the princes. He was to recite Sura xcviii, and then call upon them to submit, saying that he was able to refute every argument and book they could adduce against Islâm. Then he was to repeat the passage in Sura xlii., in which it is asserted that there is no real con roversy between Mahomet and Christians. A strange part of the instructions was, to call upon the people, after they believed, to produce three sticks,—two of which were gilded white and yellow, and one a black knotted cane,—which they used to worship. These he was to burn publicly in the market-place. The people, who spoke the Himyar tongue, were to translate their creed, &c., into Arabic. Mahomet's despatch is as follows : ' *From Mahomet, the Apostle of God to Hârith, &c.* I praise God on your behalf,—that God beside whom there is no other. Now, your messenger hath reached me at Medina, on my return from the land of Greece ; and he hath conveyed to me your letter, and given me intelligence regarding your conversion and your fighting against the Idolaters. Now, verily hath the Lord guided you with the right direction, that ye should amend your lives, obey God and his Apostles, set up prayer, pay the tithes, and from your booty set aside a fifth as the share of God and his Apostle.' Then follows a detail of the tithes. ' This is what is obligatory, and whoever exceedeth it will be for his merit. Every one that shall fulfil this, and believe in Islâm, and assist the Believers against the Idolaters. he verily is one of the Faithful : he shareth in what they share, and is responsible for that for which they are responsible. Thus it shall be with all Jews and Christians who embrace Islâm. But such as will not abandon Judaism and Christianity, shall pay tribute, every adult male and female, whether bond or free, a full golden dinar, or its equivalent in cloth. Whosoever payeth this, shall be embraced in the guarantee of God and his Apostle : whoever refuseth shall be their enemy.'

Then he commends his messengers, readers, and tithe collectors, to the Princes' good offices,—specifying Muâdz as their chief, and desiring that the tithe and tribute should be made over to him. He forbids oppression, ' for

Gulf with a letter to Mundzir, chief of Bahrein. Mundzir at once embraced Islâm, and forwarded a reply to Mahomet saying, 'that of the people of Hejer to whom he had read the Prophet's letter, some were delighted with the new religion, but others displeased with it; and that among his subjects there were Jews and Magians, regarding whom he solicited instructions.' A rescript was granted by Mahomet securing Mundzir in the government of his province so long as he administered it well, and directing that tribute should be levied from the Jews and Magians. To the Magians he dictated a separate despatch, inviting them to believe in the Corân : ' If they declined, toleration would be extended to them on the payment of tribute; but in such case, their women would not be taken in marriage by Believers, nor would that which they killed be lawful as food to any Moslem.' [1] Alâ remained at the court of Mundzir as the representative of Mahomet.

Among the tribes of Bahrein which sent embassies to Medîna before the close of the ninth year of the Hegira, were the Bani Bakr, who had so gloriously overthrown the forces of Persia about twenty years before; the Abd al Cays; and the Bani Hanîfa, a Christian branch of the Bani Bakr, who inhabited Yemâma. One of the deputation from the Bani Hanîfa was Museilama who, from what he then saw, conceived the idea that he too might successfully set up pretensions to be a Prophet. When the customary presents were distributed amongst them, the deputies solicited a share for him, saying that he had been left behind to guard the baggage. Mahomet commanded that he should have the same as the rest,—' for his position,' he said, ' is none the worse among you because of his present duty.' These words were afterwards converted by Museilama to his own ends.

Embassies from Bani Hanîfa and other Christian tribes. End of A.H. IX. Beginning of A.D. 631.

Mahomet is the protector of the poor as well as of the rich amongst you.' The tithe is not for Mahomet or his family : it is a means of purifying the rest of the giver's property, and is to be devoted to the poor and the wayfarer.

The deputation from Hamadân sang as they approached Mahomet : ' We have come to thee from the plains of Al Rîf; in the hot whirlwinds of summer and Kharîf' (*i.e.* 'autumnal harvest,' a word familiar to the Indian administrator). Mahomet's reply secured to them their hills and dales, &c.

[1] This passage refers to the distinction made by Mahomet in favour of the Jews and Christians, whose women may be taken in marriage, and what is killed and cooked by them eaten, by the Moslems. These privileges are refused to the Magians.

Christian tribe desired to demolish its church.

On the departure of the Bani Hanîfa, the Prophet gave them a vessel with some water in it remaining over from his ablutions, and said to them: 'When ye reach your country, break down your church, sprinkle its site with this water, and in place of it build up a Mosque.' These commands they carried into effect, and abandoned Christianity without compunction. To another Christian tribe, as we have already seen, he prohibited the practice of baptism, so that, although the adults continued to be nominally Christian, their children grew up with no profession but that of the Corân. It is no wonder that Christianity (which, as I have shown before, never had obtained in Arabia a firm and satisfactory footing) now warred against and, where her adherents remained faithful, reduced to tribute,—her distinctive rite prohibited wherever the professors were passive and careless, —her churches demolished and their sites purified before they could be used again for worship by the Moslem converts,—it is no wonder that Christianity, thus insulted and trampled under foot, languished, and soon disappeared from the Peninsula.[1]

Deputations from south. Beginning of A.H. X. April and May, A.D. 632.

The tenth year of the Hegira opened with fresh deputations from the south. The Bani Morâd and Zobeid, inhabiting the seacoast of Yemen, the Bani Khaulân who lived in the hilly country of that name, and the Bani Bajîla, were among the first whose embassies appeared at Medîna. The latter tribe at Mahomet's command, and, with the aid of an armed party deputed by Mahomet, destroyed the famous image of Dzul Kholasa, of which the Temple, from the popularity of its worship, was called the 'Káaba of Yemen.'

Submission of Bani Azd and people of Jorsh.

About this time, a party of fifteen or twenty men of the Bani Azd from Yemen presented themselves, with Surad, one of their chiefs. This person was recognised by Mahomet as the ruler of his clan, and a commission was given him to war against the heathen of his neighbourhood. The

[1] The following tradition is illustrative of Mahomet's relations with our faith at this period. Among the Bani Abd al Cays was a Christian named Jarûd. He said: 'O Prophet, I have hitherto followed the Christian faith, and I am now called on to change it. Wilt thou be *surety* for me in the matter of my religion!' 'Yea,' replied Mahomet, 'I am thy surety that God hath guided thee to a better faith than it.' On this Jarûd and his comrades embraced Islâm.

injunction was promptly fulfilled. After besieging Jorsh, the chief city of the idolaters, for more than a month without success, Surad made the feint of retiring to a hill. The enemy falling into the snare pursued him, and in a pitched battle sustained a signal defeat. The people of Jorsh immediately sent an embassy of submission to Medîna.

From Hadhramaut, two princes of the Bani Kinda, Wâil and Al Ashâth, the former chief of the coast, the latter of the interior, visited the Prophet at the head of a brilliant cavalcade, arrayed in garments of Yemen stuff lined with silk. 'Will ye embrace Islâm?' said Mahomet to them, after he had received their salutations in the Mosque. 'Yea; it is for that end that we have come.' 'Then why all this silk about your necks?' The silken lining was forthwith torn out and cast aside.[1] To mark his delight at the arrival of the embassy, Mahomet desired Bilâl to call aloud the summons for general prayer.[2] When the citizens were assembled, the Prophet introduced the strangers to the congregation: 'O People!' he said ; 'this is Wâil ibn Hejr, who hath come unto you from the region of Hadhramaut, out of desire to embrace Islâm.' He then presented Wâil with a patent securing him in his rights, in terms as follows: 'Since thou hast believed, I confirm thee in possession of all thy lands and fortresses. One part in every ten shall be taken from thee: a just collector shall see to it. I guarantee that thou shalt not be injured in this respect so long as the faith endureth. The Prophet, and all believers, shall be thine allies.' Muâvia, son of Abu Sofiân, was desired to escort Wâil to his house and entertain him there. On his way, the haughty Prince displayed what Mahomet styled 'a remnant of heathenism.' He would not allow Muâvia to mount behind him : the ground was scorching from the mid-day sun, yet he refused the use even of his sandals to his host, who was obliged to walk barefooted by the camel: 'What would my subjects in Yemen say,' he exclaimed in disdain, 'if they heard that a common man had worn the sandals of the king ! Nay, but I will drive the camel gently, and thou shalt walk in my shade.' Such insolent demeanour was altogether foreign

Chiefs of Bani Kinda from Hadhramaut visit Medina.

---

[1] Mahomet disapproved of silk and velvet for men's attire.

[2] *i.e.* the same as for the Friday service, at which all attended, joined in the 'common' prayer, and heard the s.rmon.

to the *brotherhood* of Islâm : but it was tolerated by Mahomet, for the accession was too valuable to be imperilled.

Al Ashâth marries Abu Bakr's daughter.

The other chief, Al Ashâth, sealed his adhesion to the cause of Mahomet by marrying Omm Farwa, Abu Bakr's daughter. The marriage was not then consummated, her parents declining that the bride should leave them for so distant a home as Hadhramaut.[1]

Muâdz sent forth with band of collectors and teachers to southern Arabia.

The supremacy of Islâm being thus widely recognised in the south of Arabia, Mahomet sent forth a band of officers charged with the instruction of the people, and the collection of the public dues. Over them he placed Muâdz, who had by this time fulfilled his mission at Mecca. 'Deal gently with the people,' said the Prophet to Muâdz, as he dismissed him to his new scene of labour, 'and be not harsh. Scare them not, but rather cheer. Thou wilt meet with Jews and Christians who will ask thee : What is the key of Paradise? Reply : *Verily the key of Paradise is to testify that there is no God but the Lord alone. With Him there is no partner.*'[2] These envoys of Mahomet were invested to some extent with a judicial authority. Acceptance of the new faith implied of necessity the simultaneous recognition of its civil institutions. Every dispute must be brought to the test of the Corân or of the instructions of Mahomet, and the

[1] Al Ashâth joined the rebellion which broke out upon the death of Mahomet, but subsequently returned to his allegiance, was pardoned, and then received Omm Farwa for his wife.

A member of the royal family in the deputation besought Mahomet to pray that his stammer might be removed. This the Prophet did, and appointed him a portion from the tithes of Hadhramaut. Another tradition relates that this man was seized with a paralytic affection on his way home. His followers came and told Mahomet, who desired them to heat a needle and pierce his eyelid with it ; and this remedy healed him. Mahomet attributed the illness to something wrong which the chief must have said after leaving Medîna.

[2] Muâdz was inextricably involved in debt, and his creditors had been clamorous before Mahomet for payment. Muâdz surrendered all his property, but it fell far short of the claims. When Mahomet therefore sent him away, he said : 'Go, and perchance the Lord will relieve thy wants.' Muâdz would appear to have made good use of his position, for Omar, when shortly after he met him at Mecca performing the pilgrimage, reprimanded him for the state in which he appeared, followed by a retinue of slaves, &c. He is said to have been very particular in following the practice of Mahomet, and never spat on his right side. He was lame, and was obliged to stretch out his legs at prayer. The people (as they always imitated the Imam in all his postures) did the same, till he forbade them.

exponents of these became, therefore, the judges of the land.[1]

Towards the close of the Prophet's life, the sound of war had almost died away at Medîna. Only two expeditions of a hostile character were undertaken during the tenth year of the Hegira. The first, under command of Khâlid, set out against the Bani Hârith of Najrân, during summer. About a year before, a deputation consisting of the bishop and clergy of Najrân had visited Mahomet, and (as I have before recounted) had obtained terms of security on the payment of tribute.[2] Khâlid was now instructed to call on the rest of the people to embrace Islâm; if they declined he was, after three days, to attack and force them to submit. Having reached his destination, he sent mounted parties in all directions, with this proclamation: 'Ye people! embrace Islâm, and ye shall be safe.' They all submitted, and professed their belief in the new faith.[3] Mahomet in a despatch to Khâlid acknowledged with delight his report of these proceedings, and summoned him to return and bring with him a deputation from the Bani Hârith. An embassy from the tribe accordingly visited Medîna, and were treated with courtesy.

Najrân submits to Khâlid.
A.H. X.
June, A.D. 631.

As the Bani Nakhâ and some other tribes in Yemen still held out, Ali was sent in the winter at the head of three hundred well equipped horse, to reduce them to submission. Yemen had repeatedly sent forth armies to subdue the Hejâz; this was the first army the Hejâz had ever sent forth to conquer Yemen. Ali met with but feeble opposition. His detachments ravaged the country all around, and returned with spoil of every kind,—women, children, camels, and flocks. Driven to despair, the people drew together, and

Campaign of Ali in Yemen against Bani Nakhâ, &c.
A.H. X.
December, A.D. 631.

---

[1] Mahomet asked Muâlz, before he left, how he would adjudicate causes: 'By the book,' he replied. *But if not in the Book?* 'Then by thy precedent.' *But if there be no precedent?* 'Then I will diligently frame my own judgment; and I shall not fail therein.' Thereupon Mahomet clapped him on the breast and said: 'Praise be to God, who hath fulfilled in the messenger sent forth by his Apostle, that which is well pleasing to the Apostle of the Lord!'

[2] See p. 159. I conclude that the operations of Khâlid were directed against the portion of the Bani Hârith still idolaters; at all events not against the Christian portion already under treaty.

[3] Hishâmi tells this naïvely: 'So they, being worsted, believed, and embraced the invitation to profess their adhesion to the new faith. Thereupon Khâlid began to teach them the nature of Islâm, and the word of God, and the regulations of the Prophet.'

attacked Ali with a general discharge of stones and arrows. The Moslem line charging put them to flight with the slaughter of twenty men. Ali held back his troop from pursuit, and again summoned the fugitives to accept his terms. This they now hastened to do. The chiefs did homage, and pledged that the people would follow their example. Ali accepted their promise; he then retraced his steps with the booty, and, reaching Mecca in the spring, joined Mahomet in his last pilgrimage. The Bani Nakhâ fulfilled their pledge, and submitted themselves to Muâdz, the Prophet's envoy in Yemen. Two hundred of them set out to tender a personal allegiance to Mahomet. It was the last deputation received by him. They reached Medîna at the beginning of the eleventh year of the Hegira.

Numerous embassies and despatches.

Numerous other embassies are described by the Secretary of Wâckidi, who has devoted a long chapter to the subject, and a chapter also to the despatches and rescripts of the Prophet. Those which I have already described will afford a sufficient idea of the whole; further detail would be tedious and unprofitable. But one or two incidents of interest connected with them may be mentioned.

Bani Aámir. Abu Berâ applies to Mahomet for a cure.

The part played by the Bani Aámir at the massacre of Bîr Maûna, will be in the memory of the reader.[1] This tribe had taken little share with the rest of the Bani Hawâzin (of which they formed a branch) in the battle of Honein. It maintained, under its haughty chieftain Aámir, an independent neutrality. The aged chief of the tribe, Abu Berâ, still exhibited friendly feelings towards Mahomet, but with advancing years his influence had passed away. Labouring under an internal ailment, he sent his nephew Labîd, the poet of the tribe, to the Prophet, with the present of a beautiful horse, and an urgent request that he would point out a cure for his disease. Mahomet declined the gift, saying courteously: 'If I could ever accept the offering of an idolater, it would be that of Abu Berâ.' Then taking up a clod of earth, he spat upon it, and directed that Abu Berâ should dissolve it in water, and drink the mixture. Tradition tells us that when he had done this, he recovered from his sickness.[2]

---

[1] *Ante*, p. 287.

[2] Labîd is famous for his Möallaca, or 'suspended' poem. According to

The following year Aámir, at the solicitation of his tribe, presented himself before Mahomet and sought to obtain from him advantageous terms. 'What shall I have,' he asked, 'if I believe?' 'That which other believers have,' replied Mahomet, 'with the same responsibilities.' 'Wilt thou not give me the rule after thee?' 'Nay, that is not for thee nor for thy tribe.' 'Then assign unto me the Bedouin tribes; and do thou retain the rest.' 'This,' said Mahomet, 'I cannot do; but I will give thee the command over the cavalry, for thou excellest as a horseman.' Aámir turned away in disdain: 'Doth this man not know,' he cried, 'that I can fill his land from one end to the other with troops, both footmen and horse?' Mahomet was alarmed at the threat, for the Bani Aámir were a formidable tribe; he prayed accordingly for deliverance from this foe: 'O Lord! defend me against Aámir son of Tofail. O Lord! guide his tribe unto the truth; and save Islâm from his stratagems!' The haughty chieftain never reached his home; he sickened by the way, and died miserably in a deserted hut. The Bani Aámir shortly after gave in their adhesion to the Prophet.

Interview of Aámir ibn Tofail with Mahomet. Conversion of the Bani Aámir.
A.H. X.
A.D. 631, 632.

The Bani Júfi, a tribe inhabiting Yemen, had a deeply-rooted prejudice against eating the heart of any animal. Cays, one of their chief men, came to Mahomet with his brother, and professed belief in the Corân. They were told that their faith was imperfect until they broke through their heathenish scruples, and a roasted heart was placed before them. Cays took it up and ate it, trembling violently. Mahomet, satisfied with the test of his sincerity, presented him with a patent, which secured him in the rule over his people. But before Cays and his brother left the presence of Mahomet, the conversation turned upon the guilt of infanti-cide: 'Our mother Muleika,' said they, 'was full of good deeds and charity; but she buried a little daughter alive. What is her condition now?' 'The burier and the buried both in hell,' replied the Prophet. The brothers turned away in wrath. 'Come back,' Mahomet cried; 'mine own mother, too, is there with yours.' They would not listen. 'This man,' they said, as they departed, 'hath not only made

Prejudices of Bani Júfi.

another tradition, Mahomet gave Labíd a leather bottle of honey, of which Abu Berâ ate, and so he recovered.

us to eat the heart of animals, but saith that our mother is in hell: who would follow him?'

Two of
their chiefs
cursed by
Mahomet
for robbing
tithe
camels.
On their way home, they met one of Mahomet's followers returning to Medîna with a herd of camels which had been collected as tithe. They seized the man, left him bound, and carried off the camels. Mahomet was greatly offended; and he entered the names of the robbers in the commination (the repetition of which seems still to have been kept up) against the perpetrators of the massacre at Bîr Maûna. A second deputation from the same tribe visited Mahomet, and was well received. We do not hear more of Cays.[1]

[1] Mahomet is said to have healed the hand of the leader of the second deputation from a protuberance which had prevented him holding his camel's rein, by striking an arrow on it and then stroking it, when it disappeared. He changed the name of this chief's son from *Aziz* (glorious) to Abd al Rahmân; —saying: 'There is none *glorious* but the Lord.'

CHAPTER XXXI.

THE FAREWELL PILGRIMAGE.

Dzul Hijj, A.H. X.—*March*, A.D. 630.

Ætat. 63.

THE period for the Annual pilgrimage again approached. Nothing now appeared to hinder Mahomet from the fulfilment of its ceremonies. There was no longer the possibility of offence from idolatrous objects or the rites of heathenism. Every vestige of an image in Mecca and its outskirts had been cleared away. And after the threatening announcement of the previous year, none but professed believers might venture near. Mahomet had not performed the Greater pilgrimage since his flight from Mecca. He now announced his intention of going up to the coming festival.

Mahomet resolves to go up to Mecca on pilgrimage. A.H. X. March, A.D. 630.

Five days before the opening of Dzul Hijj, the month of pilgrimage, the Prophet assumed the pilgrim's garb in the manner already described; and, followed by vast multitudes, set out on the journey to Mecca. All his wives accompanied him. One hundred camels, marked by his own hands as victims, were led in solemn procession. Along the road, mosques had already sprung up at the various halting places; at each the people prayed, Mahomet leading the devotions. On the evening of the tenth day, he reached Sarif, an easy stage from Mecca; there he rested for the night, and on the following morning, having bathed, and mounted Al Caswa, he proceeded towards Mecca. He entered the upper suburbs by the same route which he had taken two years before; and, passing down the main street of the city, approached the Káaba. As he passed through the Bani Sheyba gate, with the Holy temple full in view, he raised his hands to heaven,

Journey from Medina to Mecca.

and said: ' *O Lord! add unto this House in the dignity and glory, the honour and the reverence, which already thou hast bestowed on it. And they that for the Greater pilgrimage and the Lesser frequent the same, increase them much in honour and dignity, in piety, goodness, and glory!* ' Then, mounted as he was on his camel, he performed the prescribed circuits, and other rites, and afterwards retired to a tent pitched for him in the valley.

Most of his followers perform Lesser pilgrimage only.

The greater part of the pilgrims had brought no victims with them. These were directed by Mahomet, after completing the customary forms of the Omra, or Lesser pilgrimage, to divest themselves of the pilgrim garb. They accompanied the Prophet and the others who had brought victims in the farther procession to Minâ and Arafât, but only as spectators. Ali, meanwhile, having returned from Yemen, received the same directions as the rest of those who had no victims: ' Go,' said Mahomet, ' and encircle the Holy house; then divest thyself of the pilgrim's garb as thy fellows have done.' But Ali was anxious to fulfil the full rites of the yearly festival; ' for,' said he, ' I have taken upon me vows to perform the same pilgrimage as the Prophet shall perform, whatever that might be.' Mahomet yielded, and allowed him to fulfil the Greater pilgrimage, and to be a sharer in the victims he had brought for himself.[1]

Mahomet's pilgrimage to Arafât. 8th Dzul Hijj.

On the 7th of Dzul Hijj, the day preceding the opening rites of the Greater pilgrimage, Mahomet, after the mid-day prayer, preached to the concourse assembled at the Káaba.

[1] The sacrifice of victims is an essential part of the Greater pilgrimage, but not of the Lesser. According to the rules of Islâm, the pilgrim must *resolve*, before he assumes the pilgrim's garb, which pilgrimage he will perform. In connection with this custom, there is a great mass of contradictory tradition as to whether Mahomet set out from Medina with the vows upon him of the Lesser pilgrimage, or the Greater, or of both together; and the question is very warmly discussed.

When Mahomet desired those who had no victims to conclude their pilgrimage with the Omra, or lesser festival, they objected, saying: ' How then can we go on with thee to Minâ, after quitting the holy state of a pilgrim and returning to the impurities of the world?' Mahomet told them that there was no harm in doing so, for that, if similarly circumstanced, he would have done it himself; and that if he had foreseen these objections, he would not have brought any victims. Perhaps it was Mahomet's wish to show that visiting Mecca at the time of the Greater pilgrimage did not necessarily involve participation in the pilgrimage, the observance of which was reserved for special occasions.

Next day, followed by the whole multitude of pilgrims, and shaded from the sun's glare by Bilâl, who walked at his side with a screen (a staff with a piece of cloth attached), he proceeded to Minâ, where he performed the ordinary prayers, and passed the night in a tent.   The following morning at sunrise, he moved onwards and, passing Mozdalifa, reached Arafât, an abrupt conical hill, about two hundred feet high, in the middle of the valley, which, though elsewhere narrow, and on the farther side pent in by lofty granite peaks, here spreads out bare and stony to the breadth of nearly a mile.[1] On the summit of the sacred mount, the Prophet, standing erect upon his camel, said : ' The entire valley of Arafât is the holy station for pilgrimage, excepting only the vale of Urana.'   After he had bowed himself in prayer, he recited certain passages of the Corân, regarding the ceremonies of pilgrimage, and concluded with the verse : ' *This day have I perfected your Religion unto you, and fulfilled my mercy upon you, and appointed Islâm for you to be your religion.*'

As the sun was going down, Mahomet quitted Arafât.   Mahomet returns to

[1] See the pictures of this hill in Ali Bey and Burton. The following is the description of it by the latter : ' A mass of coarse granite split into large blocks, with a thin coat of withered thorns, about one mile in circumference, and rising abruptly from the low gravelly plain (a dwarf wall at the southern base forming the line of demarcation) to the height of one hundred and eighty or two hundred feet. It is separated by Batn Arna, a sandy vale, from the spurs of the Tâif hills. Nothing can be more picturesque than the view it affords of the blue peaks behind, and the vast encampment scattered over the barren yellow plain below.' So also Ali Bey : ' Arafât is a small mountain of granite rock, the same as those that surround it ; it is about one hundred and fifty feet high, and is situated at the foot of a higher mountain to the E.S.E., in a plain about three quarters of a mile in diameter, surrounded by barren mountains.' The ' Hadjee,' who has recently published an account of his pilgrimage in the *Bombay Times*, says : ' Round the foot of Arafât, which is completely detached from the adjoining mountains, are a number of trees, a thick growth of underwood, and a little grass, which are nourished by the water that escapes from the canal of Mecca which passes behind the hill.' But before the canal was made, the place must have been wild and bare of any growth but thorny bushes.

The popular tradition for the exclusion of the vale of Urana (or Arna) is given thus by Burton : ' This vale is not considered " standing ground " because Satan once appeared to the Prophet as he was traversing it.' The last pilgrimage is regarded as the type of all succeeding ones : there is accordingly a tendency to make Mahomet foresee this, and provide anticipatory instructions on all possible points. These must be received with caution : take, *e.g.*, the following tradition : Mahomet, as he went through the various rites, said : ' Observe, and learn of me the ceremonies which ye should practise, for I know not whether after this I shall ever perform another pilgrimage.'

Mozdalifa.
9th Dzul
Hijj.

Retracing his steps, with Osâma son of Zeid seated behind him on his camel, he travelled hastily back by the bright moonlight along the narrow valley to Mozdalifa, where he said the sunset and evening prayers both together: in this, and every other point, his example has been closely imitated by all pilgrims, to the present day. He passed the night at Mozdalifa, and very early in the morning sent forward the women and the children, lest the crowds of pilgrims that followed should impede their journey:[1] but, touching them on the shoulder as they went, he said: 'My children, have a care that ye throw not the stones at Acaba until the sun arise.'

Completes
the pil-
grimage at
Minâ. 10th
Dzul Hijj.

As the dawn of the tenth day of the month broke, Mahomet arose to perform the early morning prayer; after which, he mounted his camel, and took his stand on a certain spot, saying: 'This place, and the whole of Mozdalifa, is the station of pilgrimage, excepting only the vale of Muhassir.'[2] Then, with Fadhl son of Abbâs seated behind him, he proceeded onwards amid a heavy fall of rain to Minâ, shouting as he went the pilgrim's cry:—

Labbeik! O Lord! Labbeik! Labbeik!
There is none other God but Thee. Labbeik!
Praise, blessing, and dominion be to Thee. Labbeik!
Therein may no one share with Thee. Labbeik! Labbeik![3]

He ceased not to utter these ejaculations till he had reached Minâ, and cast stones (an ancient rite) at certain projecting corners of the valley.[4] Afterwards, he slew the victims brought for sacrifice, and then ended the pilgrimage by shaving the hair of his head and partly also of his face, and

---

[1] The 'Hadjee' gives a vivid description of the utter confusion which prevails on the hurried return of the multitude from Arafât to Mozdalifa; and it would seem that the same prevailed even in the time of Mahomet.

[2] I do not know the origin of the allusion here to this valley; it is according to Burton on the road to Minâ. A picture of Mozdalifa will be found in Ali Bey.

[3] For this expression, see *ante,* p. 368.

[4] See pp. xxiii. and 468. There are two or three spots at which stones are thus cast, called the greater and lesser Shaitân, or *devils.* The tradition is that Abraham here met the devil and repulsed him by similar means. There are minute traditions as to the kind of stone to be used on this occasion. Abdallah son of Abbâs picked up some gravel for Mahomet to throw; and the Prophet said: 'Yes: just such as this is the kind to throw. Take care that ye increase not the size. Verily they that have gone before you have come to naught, because of thus adding to the rites of their religion.'

paring his nails; the hair and parings he ordered to be burned.[1] The scanty dress of pilgrimage was now put away, perfumes were burned, the flesh of the victims and other cattle was distributed for food; and Ali, riding the Prophet's white mule, made proclamation that, the restrictions of the pilgrim state being ended, it was now a day for eating and enjoyment, and for the remembrance of God. Mahomet remained at Minâ from the 10th to the 12th of Dzul Hijj. Every evening as the sun declined he repaired to the prescribed spots at Acaba and repeated the rite of casting stones.

On the second of these three days, the Prophet mounted his camel, and, taking up a central and prominent position in the Minâ valley,[2] addressed the vast crowd of pilgrims in a memorable speech, which was looked upon by the people, and perhaps was felt by Mahomet himself, as his parting exhortation. Fragments of the discourse have been preserved; of these the following passages are the most important:— *Parting exhortations at Minâ. 11th Dzul Hijj.*

YE PEOPLE! Hearken to my words; for I know not whether, after this year, I shall ever be amongst you here again.[3]

Your Lives and Property are sacred and inviolable amongst one another until the end of time.

The Lord hath ordained to every man the share of his inheritance: a Testament is not lawful to the prejudice of heirs.

The child belongeth to the Parent: and the violator of Wedlock shall be stoned. Whoever claimeth falsely another for his father, or another for his master, the curse of God and the Angels, and of all Mankind, shall rest upon him.

Ye People! Ye have rights demandable of your Wives, and they have rights demandable of you. Upon them it is incumbent not to violate their conjugal faith, neither to commit any act of open impropriety;—which things if they do, ye have authority to shut

---

[1] Another tradition says that the hair was all caught by his followers. This idea must have grown up in after days, when a single hair of the Prophet was treasured as a relic and talisman.

[2] 'He stood between the two places for casting stones.' Burton mentions two such spots. Ali Bey's plan gives the chief one, or 'the Devil's house,' on the Mecca side of Minâ, and 'two small columns raised by the Devil,' in the middle of the narrow street of the village of Minâ. The position of Mahomet while delivering this famous discourse was thus within Minâ itself, but somewhat on the side of Mecca.

[3] So Hishâmi. The words, however, may be an afterthought of tradition. There is no other intimation that Mahomet felt his strength to be decaying at this time, or that either he or his followers anticipated his end to be near.

them up in separate apartments and to beat them with stripes, yet not severely. But if they refrain therefrom, clothe them and feed them suitably. And treat your Women well : for they are with you as captives and prisoners ; they have not power over anything as regards themselves. And ye have verily taken them on the security of God : and have made their persons lawful unto you by the words of God.

And your Slaves! See that ye feed them with such food as ye eat yourselves ; and clothe them with the stuff ye wear. And if they commit a fault which ye are not inclined to forgive, then sell them, for they are the servants of the Lord, and are not to be tormented.

Ye People! hearken to my speech and comprehend the same. Know that every Moslem is the brother of every other Moslem. All of you are on the same equality ; (and, as he pronounced these words, he raised his arms aloft and placed the forefinger of one hand on the forefinger of the other).[1] Ye are one Brotherhood.

Know ye what month this is ?—What territory this is ?—What day ? To these questions, the People gave appropriate answers,— 'The Sacred month,—the Sacred territory,—the Great day of pilgrimage.' After each reply, Mahomet added : '*Even thus sacred and inviolable hath God made the life and the property of each of you unto the other, until ye meet your Lord.*

'Let him that is present, tell it unto him that is absent. Haply, he that shall be told, may remember better than he who hath heard it.'

Abolition of the intercalary year.

Mahomet then proceeded to recite the verses which abolish the triennial intercalation of the year, and fix the month of pilgrimage according to the changing seasons of the lunar year :—

Sura ix.

Verily, the number of the months with God is twelve months, according to the Book of God, on the day in which He created the Heavens and the Earth. Of these, four are sacred :—this is the true Religion.

Verily, the changing of the months is an excess of infidelity, which causeth the Unbelievers to err. They make a month common in one year, and they make it sacred in another year, that they may equalise the number which God hath made sacred. Thus do they make common that which God hath hallowed.

'And now,' continued Mahomet, 'on this very day hath time performed its cycle, and returned to the disposition thereof

---

[1] Intending thereby to teach that all were absolutely upon the same level.

existing at the moment when God created the Heavens and the Earth.

'Ye People!　Truly Satan despaireth of being worshipped in your land for ever.　But if in some indifferent matter, which ye might be disposed to slight, he could secure obedience, verily he would be well pleased.　Wherefore beware of him!

'Verily, I have fulfilled my mission.　I have left that amongst you,—a plain command, the Book of God, and manifest Ordinances —which, if ye hold fast, ye shall never go astray.'

Then, looking up to heaven, Mahomet said: '*O Lord! I have delivered my message and fulfilled my mission.*' 'Yea,' cried all the people who crowded round him, 'yea, verily thou hast.'　'*O Lord! I beseech thee bear thou witness unto it.*'　And with these words, the Prophet, having concluded his address, dismissed the great assembly.

Mahomet takes God to witness that he has fulfilled his mission.

After staying three days at Minâ, the concourse broke up and proceeded to Mecca.　Mahomet desired the mass of the pilgrims to travel thither by day.　He himself accompanied his wives on the journey by night.　On reaching Mecca, he went straightway to the Káaba, and performed the seven circuits of it on his camel.　He next visited the well Zemzem close by, and calling for a pitcher of its water, drank part of its contents; then he rinsed his mouth in the pitcher, and desired that the water remaining in it should be thrown back into the well.　After this, taking off his shoes, he ascended the doorway of the Holy temple, and prayed within its walls.[1]　Having now ended all the ceremonies, and being fatigued with the journey, he stopped at the house of one who kept date-water for the pilgrims to drink, and desired the beverage to be furnished to him.　The son of Abbâs, who accompanied him, interposed: 'The hands of the passers-by,' he said, 'have been in this all day, and fouled it: come unto my father's house, where we have some that is

Returns to Mecca. Further ceremonies there.

---

[1] Mahomet regretted that he had entered the Káaba on this occasion, and when asked the reason said: 'I have this day done a thing which I wish I had left undone.　I have entered the Holy house.　And haply some of the people, when on pilgrimage, may not be able to enter therein, and may turn back grieved in heart (*i.e.* at not having completed the pilgrimage fully after their Prophet's example).　And, in truth, the command given unto me was only to encircle the Káaba: it is not incumbent on any one to enter it.'　This appears to be founded upon the notion before explained, that Mahomet *intended* this pilgrimage to be the final type and exemplar for all future pilgrims.

clean and pure for thee.' But the Prophet, refusing to drink of any other, quenched his thirst upon the spot.[1]

Returns to
Medina.

Three days more were spent at Mecca, and then Mahomet with his followers returned to Medîna.

[1] Water in which dates or raisins have been steeped or washed is called Nabîdz. So accurately do the pilgrims follow their Prophet, that some regard the rites of the pilgrimage as not properly completed unless Nabîdz be drunk as it was by Mahomet.

CHAPTER XXXII.

THE PRETENDERS WHO ROSE UP AGAINST MAHOMET.

Opening of A.H. XI.—*April and May,* A.D. 632.

THE eleventh year of the Hegira opened in peacefulness at Medîna. Mahomet was now chiefly occupied in the issue of despatches, the nomination of envoys and governors, and the consolidation of his authority in the more distant regions of Arabia. The native chiefs or princes were ordinarily maintained in the government of their respective territories when they were found suited to the Prophet's purpose. Instructors and collectors of the tithes were also deputed as his representatives, charged with political and judicial functions.

Opening of A.H. XI. March 29, A.D. 632.

Bâdzân, the Persian governor who, as we have seen, had early submitted himself to Mahomet, died about this time. His son Shahr was continued in the government of Sanâ and the surrounding district. But the other provinces hitherto combined under his authority, as Mâreb, Najrân, and Hamâdân, were divided by Mahomet among different governors, of whom some were natives of the several districts, and others persons specially deputed from Medîna.

Death of Bâdzân and division of his territories.

But a new cause of danger began suddenly to cloud the horizon. Three claimants of the prophetic office arose, in various quarters of Arabia, to dispute with Mahomet the supreme authority. Their assumptions were not, however, developed till near the close of his life, and the tidings which he received of their proceedings were hardly of so grave a nature as perhaps to raise serious apprehensions in his mind. I shall not, therefore, do more than very briefly notice these remarkable impostors.

Three impostors arise, claiming prophetic office.

Moment
propitious
for such
preten-
sions.

Besides the temptation to follow in the steps of Mahomet occasioned by his marvellous success, the present moment was especially propitious for the assertion of such claims. The Bedouin tribes, and distant people who had but lately succumbed to the new religion, began to find its rites irksome and its restraints unpalatable. How deep and general was the discontent, is evident from the almost universal rebellion which followed immediately on the Prophet's death, and which probably would never have been fully stifled had not the energies and passions of the Arabs been directed to foreign conquest. Mahomet was now well stricken in years, and strangers might perceive in him the marks of advancing infirmity. His death could not be far distant. No provision had been made for a successor nor for the permanent maintenance at Medîna of a supreme authority over the Peninsula. If any one were bold enough to assert that he had received a divine commission like that of Mahomet, why should his efforts not be crowned with similar success?

Tuleiha.
His re-
bellion
crushed by
Khâlid.

The least important of the three impostors who now started with these notions, was Tuleiha, chief of the Bani Asád, a warrior of note and influence in Nejd.[1] His tribe once journeying through the desert were overpowered by thirst, when Tuleiha announced to them that water would be found at a certain spot. The discovery confirmed the claims to inspiration (or at least to divination) which he had already made. Subsequent to the death of Mahomet he broke out into open rebellion, and was defeated, after a severe engagement, by Khâlid. On Omar's summoning the conquered rebels to join his standard, Tuleiha submitted, and afterwards with his tribe fought bravely on the side of Islâm.

Museilama.
His ad-
vances in-
dignantly
rejected by
Mahomet.

Museilama has already been noticed as having accompanied the deputation of the Bani Hanîfa to Medîna. He was a man of small stature and of insignificant appearance, but ready and powerful in speech. Following the example of Mahomet, he gave forth verses professed to have been received from heaven, and he pretended also to work miracles.[2] He claimed an authority and mission concurrent with

[1] Vide p. 284.

[2] He had learned the art of sleight of hand, &c. from conjurors. One of his *miracles* was to slip an egg into a narrow-mouthed phial. None of the

that of the Prophet of Medîna; and he deceived the people
of Yemâma by alleging that the claim had been admitted.[1]
Mahomet, hearing the rumour of his insolent pretensions,
sent him a summons to submit to Islâm. Museilama returned reply that he, too, was a prophet like Mahomet
himself: 'I demand therefore that thou divide the earth
with me; as for the Coreish, they are a people that have no
respect for justice.' When this letter was read before him,
Mahomet turned with indignation to the messengers: '*And
what do ye yourselves say to this?*' he asked. 'We say,'
they replied, 'even as Museilama doth.' '*By the Lord!*'
exclaimed Mahomet, '*if it were not that Ambassadors are
secure, and their lives inviolate, I would have beheaded both
of you!*' Then he indited the following answer: 'I have
received thine epistle, with its lies and its fabrications against
God. Verily the earth is the Lord's; He causeth such of his
servants as he pleaseth to inherit the same. Prosperity shall
attend the pious. Peace be to him that followeth the true
Direction!' The rebellion and the fate of Museilama belong
to the Caliphate of Abu Bakr.

Aswad, the third impostor, differed from the others *Rebellion
in not only advancing his pretensions, but in casting off the* of Aswad.
Mussulman yoke, while Mahomet was yet alive. A prince
of wealth and influence in the South, he assumed the garb of
a magician, and gave out that he was in communication with
the unseen world. He prosecuted his claims at the first
secretly, and gained over the chieftains in the neighbourhood
who were dissatisfied with the distribution of power made by
Mahomet on the death of Bâdzân. About the close of the
tenth year of the Hegira, he openly raised the standard of
rebellion, and drove out the officers of Mahomet, who fled for
refuge to the nearest friendly country. Advancing on Najrân,
which rose in his favour, he suddenly fell upon Sanâ, where,
having killed Shahr the son of Bâdzân, he put his army to
flight, married his widow, and established himself in undisputed authority. The insurrection, fanned by this sudden
success, spread like wild-fire, and the greater part of the

---

verses attributed to him are worth quoting. Sprenger says that the name,
signifying 'the little Moslem,' was given him in contempt.

[1] See the words of Mahomet which he is said to have drawn into this
construction—*ante*, p. 473.

Peninsula lying between the provinces of Bahrein, Tâif, and the coast, was soon subject to the Usurper.

Crushed about the time of Mahomet's death.

At what period intimation of this rebellion reached Mahomet, and what was the nature of the intelligence received, is not apparent. The accounts could not have been very alarming, for the Prophet contented himself with despatching letters to his officers on the spot, in which he desired them, according to their means, either to assassinate the Pretender, or to attack him in battle. Fortunately for the cause of Islâm, Aswad, in the pride of conquest, had already begun to slight the commanders to whose bravery he was indebted for his success. The agents of Mahomet opened up secret negotiations with them; and, favoured by the tyrant's wife, who detested him, and burned to avenge her late husband's death, plotted the assassination of Aswad. The Usurper was slain, according to tradition, on the very night preceding the death of Mahomet. The insurrection immediately ceased; and, excepting the disquiet occasioned by some bands of the rebel army which continued to infest the country, the authority of Mahomet's name was fully re-established.

CHAPTER XXXIII.

SICKNESS AND DEATH OF MAHOMET.

Mohurram, A.H. XI.—*June,* A.D. 632.

Ætat. 63.

MAHOMET, now sixty-three years of age, was to outward appearance in ordinary health, when on the last Monday of the month Safar (unaware of the storm lowering in the South) he commanded his followers to make themselves ready for an expedition against the Roman border. It was more than a year and a half since any important campaign had been undertaken. The inroad upon Tabûk was the last occasion on which Mahomet had called out a general levy of his followers. But he had by no means lost sight of the necessity for maintaining a warlike spirit in his people. It was essential to the permanence of Islâm that its aggressive course should be continuously pursued, and that its claim to universal supremacy, if not to universal acceptance, should be enforced at the point of the sword. Within the limits of Arabia this work appeared now to be accomplished. It remained to gain over the Christian and idolatrous tribes of the Syrian desert, and then in the name of the Lord to throw down the gauntlet of war before the empires of Rome and Persia, which, having treated with contempt the summons of the Prophet addressed to them in solemn warning four years ago, were now ripe for chastisement.

First principles of Islâm required continuing prosecution of war.

The present incursion was intended to strike terror into the tribes of the border, and to wipe out the memory of the reverse at Mûta, which still rankled in the heart of Mahomet. Accordingly, on the day following the general summons above mentioned, it was declared that Osâma, son of Zeid the

Osâma appointed to command army destined for Syrian border. A.H. XI.

May 25,
A.D. 632.
beloved friend of Mahomet slain at Mûta, was notwith-standing his extreme youth (hardly yet twenty years of age) to command the army. Having called him to the Mosque, the Prophet thus addressed him: 'Lead the army unto the place where thy father was killed, and let them destroy it utterly. Lo! I have made thee commander over this army. Fall suddenly at early dawn upon the people of Obna, and devour them with fire. Hasten thy march so that thine onset may precede the tidings of thee. If the Lord grant thee victory, then shorten thy stay amongst them. Take with thee guides, and send before thee scouts and spies.'

Banner
presented
to him,
and camp
formed at
Jorf.
May 27.
On the Wednesday following, Mahomet was seized with a violent headache and fever; but it passed off. The next morning he found himself sufficiently recovered to bind with his own hand upon the flagstaff a banner for the army. He presented it to Osâma with these words: 'Fight thou beneath this banner in the name of the Lord, and for His cause. Thus thou shalt discomfit and slay the people that disbelieveth in the Lord!' The camp was then formed at Jorf; and the whole body of the fighting men, not excepting even Abu Bakr and Omar, were summoned to join it. But the attention of the city was soon occupied by a more engrossing subject, which suspended for a time the preparations of Osâma's force.

Mahomet
attributes
illness to
poisoned
meat eaten
at Kheibar.
Mahomet had not hitherto suffered from any serious illness. About the close of the sixth year of the Hegira, (as has been already told) he ailed temporarily from loss of appetite and a pining depression of health and spirits, ascribed to the incantations of the Jews. Again, in the middle of the seventh year, his system sustained a shock from partaking of poisoned meat at Kheibar, for which he was cupped, and the effects of which he complained of periodically ever after. Indeed the present attack was attributed by Mahomet himself directly to this cause. When he had been now for several days sick, the mother of Bishr (who had died from the effects of the same poison) came to enquire after his health; she condoled with him on the violence of the fever, and remarked that the people said it was the pleurisy. 'Nay,' answered Mahomet, 'the Lord would never permit that sickness to seize his Apostle, for it cometh of Satan. This, verily, is the effect of that which

I ate at Kheibar, I and thy son. The artery of my back feeleth as though it would just now burst asunder.'

Whether his constitution was really impaired by the poison, or whether this was merely the Prophet's fancy, it is certain that the frailties of age were imperceptibly stealing upon him. His vigorous, well-knit frame began to stoop. Though frugal, if not abstemious in his habits, and in all things (the harem excepted) temperate, yet during the last twenty years of his life there had been much to tax his mind and body. At Mecca, hardship, rejection, persecution, confinement, exile; at Medîna, the anxieties of a cause for some years doubtful, and now the cares of a daily extending empire, all pressed heavily upon him. Nor must we forget the excitement and agitation (possibly of an epileptic character) which occasionally overpowered him in the moments of imagined inspiration and intercourse with unseen visitants. 'Ah! thou that art dearer to me than father or mother!' exclaimed Abu Bakr to Mahomet as he entered one day from his wives' apartments into the Mosque; 'alas! grey hairs are hastening upon thee;' and his eyes filled with tears as he saw the Prophet raise his beard with his hand, and gaze upon it. 'Yes,' said Mahomet, 'it is the travail of inspiration that hath done this. The Suras *Hûd,* and the *Inevitable,* and the *Striking,* with their fellows, have made white my hair.'

Circumstances affecting strength of his constitution.

But Mahomet did not yield to the infirmities of old age. To the very last he maintained the severe simplicity of robuster years. 'The people throng about thee in the Mosque,' said his uncle Abbâs to him;—'what if we make for thee an elevated seat, that they may not trouble thee?' But Mahomet forbade it: 'Surely,' he said, 'I will not cease from being in the midst of them, dragging my mantle behind me thus,[1] and covered with their dust, until that the Lord give me rest from amongst them.'

Increasing infirmity.

Mahomet himself was latterly not unconscious (if we may believe the traditions of Ayesha) of the premonitions of decay. He used frequently to repeat the 110th Sura, as follows :—

Conviction that his end was near.

When the help of God shall come, and the Victory,
And thou shalt see men entering the religion of God in troops;
Then celebrate the praises of thy Lord, and ask pardon of Him,
    for He is merciful.

---

[1] *i.e.* hurrying along and being jostled by the crowd.

These expressions he would refer to the multitudes now flocking to the faith from Yemen and the farther coasts of Arabia. He would furthermore declare that the sign received from the Lord of the completion of his work was thus fulfilled, and that it remained for him now only 'to busy himself in the praises of his Lord and to seek for pardon.'[1]

Attacked by illness, Mahomet visits the burial ground.

When attacked by his last illness, Mahomet, though probably feeling it to be serious, did not at the first succumb; for a day or two he still maintained the custom he had prescribed to himself of visiting his wives' apartments in rotation. One night lying restless on his bed, he arose softly, cast his clothes about him, and, followed only by a servant, walked to the burial ground, in the outskirts of the city. There he waited long absorbed in meditation. At last winding up his thoughts, he prayed aloud for those who were buried there, apostrophising thus: '*Verily, both ye and I have received the fulfilment of that which our Lord did promise us. Blessed are ye! for ye enjoy a lot far preferable to the lot of those that are left behind. Temptation and trial approach like portions of a dark night following one upon another, each portion darker than that preceding it. O Lord! grant pardon unto them that are buried here!*' Then he turned and departed to his house. By the way, he told his attendant that he too was himself hastening to the grave: 'The choice hath verily been offered me of continuance in this life, with Paradise thereafter, or to meet my Lord at once; and I have chosen to meet my Lord.'

Ayesha's raillery when he seeks commiseration.

In the morning, passing by the door of Ayesha, who was suffering from a severe headache, he heard her moaning: 'My head!—oh, my head!'[2] He entered and said: 'Nay,

[1] The traditions of this period abound in anticipations of Mahomet's decease. But few of these seem founded on fact. Take the following as a specimen. When the 110th Sura was revealed, Mahomet called Fâtima, and said: 'My daughter! I have received intimation of my approaching end.' Fâtima burst into tears. 'Why weepest thou, my child?' continued the Prophet; 'be comforted, for verily thou art the first of my people that shall rejoin me.' Whereupon Fâtima dried her tears and smiled pleasantly. As Fâtima died within six months after her father, it is easy to see how this tale grew up. Similar are the traditions in glorification of Fâtima: *e.g.* where Mahomet calls her 'the Queen of all the females of Paradise after Mary the Mother of Jesus;' and the prediction of divisions, sects, intestine war, &c. A shade of the same tendency will be observed in the prayer at the burial ground, which, notwithstanding, I have given entire.

[2] It may be necessary here to warn the reader that we have now reached a

Ayesha, it is rather I that have need to cry *My head, my head!*' Then in a tenderer strain : 'But wouldst thou not desire to be taken whilst I am yet alive; so that I might pray over thee, and wrapping thee, Ayesha, in thy winding sheet, thus commit thee to the grave?' 'That happen to another,' exclaimed Ayesha, 'and not to me!' archly adding: 'Ah, that is what thou art desirous of! Truly, I can fancy thee, after having done all this and buried me, return straightway hither to my house, and spend that very evening in sporting in my place with another wife!' The Prophet smiled at Ayesha's raillery, but his sickness pressed on him too heavily to admit of a rejoinder in the same strain; and so again with a sad complaint of the grievous ailment in his head, he returned to the apartment of Meimûna, whose day it was.

Mahomet had not been long there before the fever returned upon him with increasing violence. So calling his wives around him, he said: 'Ye see that I lie very sick : I am not able to visit your houses in turn; if it be pleasing to you, I will remain in the house of Ayesha.' All agreed to the proposal. His clothes having been wrapped loosely around him, and his head bound about with a napkin, the Prophet walked with the support of Ali and Abbâs to the apartment of Ayesha. Though hardly yet twenty years of age, and though she had never before tended any one in sickness, Ayesha waited with the utmost solicitude and tenderness on the death-bed of her aged husband. *Mahomet retires to Ayesha's house.*

For seven or eight days, the fever, although unchecked, did not confine Mahomet entirely to the house. He was able to move into the Mosque (the door of his apartment opening into its courts) and lead, though feebly, the public prayers. He had been ill about a week, when perceiving that the sick- *He chides the people for murmuring at Osâma's appointment.*

point in Mahomet's biography which has become specially the arena for contending traditions of party and faction. *First*, Ayesha, who had the closest opportunities by far of all others for watching the last moments of Mahomet, has made the most of her position; throughout her statements there is a patent endeavour to exclude even the mention of Ali and his partisans. There is, *secondly*, the party of Ali, who (with the view of strengthening their dogma that the divine right of succession was vested in their hero and his posterity) would attribute to him every important part in the scene. And, *lastly*, there are the Abbassides (holding the right of succession to reside in the near relatives of the Prophet and their heirs), whose tendency is to magnify Abbâs and his family. Every tradition is coloured by these factions; and it is necessary to steer very cautiously among them.

ness gained ground, and was aggravated by occasional fits of swooning, he resolved upon an effort to address the people, whose murmurs at the appointment of the youth Osâma, in supersession of the chiefest of the Refugees and Citizens, to the command of the Syrian army had reached his ears. ' Fetch me,' he said, ' seven skins of water from as many different wells, that I may bathe and then go forth unto them.' They procured the water, and, seating him in Haphsa's bathing vessel, poured it upon him from the skins till he held up his hand and cried ' Enough !' Meanwhile the people, both men and women, had assembled in the Mosque ; it was told the Prophet that they had come together, and that many wept. Being now refreshed by the bath, he went forth to them, his head bandaged, and a sheet drawn loosely round him, and seated himself in the pulpit. After prayer, and an exordium in the usual style, he proceeded : ' Ye people ! What is this which hath reached me, that some amongst you murmur against my appointment of Osâma to command the Syrian army ? Now, if ye blame my appointment of Osâma, verily heretofore ye blamed likewise my appointment of his father Zeid before him. And I swear by the Lord, that he verily was well fitted for the command, and that his son after him is well fitted also. Truly Osâma is one of the men most dearly beloved by me, even as his father was. Wherefore, do ye treat him well, for he is one of the best amongst you.'

He directs private doors leading into the Mosque to be closed.

After a pause he continued : ' Verily, the Lord hath offered unto one of his servants the choice betwixt this life and that which is nigh unto Himself ; and the servant hath chosen that which is nigh unto his Lord.' Mahomet by this saying intended to communicate by way of euphemism to the people, his anticipation that the illness would prove his last.[1] But they were slow of apprehension. Abu Bakr alone perceived his meaning, and burst into tears. Mahomet, in accents of affection, desired him not to weep. Then turning

---

[1] It is likely that the expression used by Mahomet regarding the *choice* of death or life was of a more general nature, such as ' that he preferred to depart and be near his Lord' (something, perhaps, in the manner of Paul's words, Philip. i. 21) ;—which tradition would easily and naturally convert into the mysterious phrase ' that he had *made election* of Paradise.' Against the text it might be urged that after such a declaration the people ought to have been more prepared for the Prophet's death when it did happen. But the

to the people, he said: 'Verily the chiefest among you all for love and devotion to me is Abu Bakr. If I were to choose a bosom friend it would be he: but Islâm hath made a closer brotherhood amongst us all. Now let every door that leadeth into the Mosque be closed, excepting only the door of Abu Bakr.' Accordingly the relatives of Mahomet and the chief men, whose houses skirted the quadrangle of the Mosque, closed their inward doors, that of Abu Bakr alone remaining open. Thus the busy hum and tread were hushed as became the precincts of death, and the courts of the Mosque were frequented only by worshippers at the hour of prayer, and by knots of whispering followers enquiring anxiously after the Prophet's health.

As he was about to re-enter Ayesha's room, Mahomet turned again, and, in testimony of his gratitude to the people of Medîna, thus addressed the assembly: 'Ye that are refugees from Mecca and other quarters, hearken to me! Ye increase, and throng into the city daily. But the men of Medîna do not increase. They will remain ever as they are this day. And verily they are dear unto me, for among them I found a refuge. Wherefore honour their honourable men, and treat well their excellent ones.' Then, having urged the early departure of the Syrian expedition, he retired into the room of Ayesha.

Mahomet commends citizens of Medina to his followers' care.

The exertion and excitement of delivering this address aggravated the Prophet's sickness. On the following day, when the hour of public prayer came round, he called for water to perform the preparatory ablutions; but, on attempting to rise, he found that his strength had failed, so he commanded that Abu Bakr should conduct the prayers in his stead; and having given this order he fell back and swooned away. Soon recovering, he enquired whether the commission had been conveyed to his friend. Ayesha replied: 'O Prophet! Truly Abu Bakr is a man of a tender heart, and weepeth readily. The people would with difficulty hear his voice.' 'Command that he lead the prayers,' repeated Mahomet in a loud and imperious tone. Ayesha, still clinging to the hope that Mahomet would be able himself to perform

Abu Bakr appointed to lead public prayers while Mahomet is laid aside.

scene after his death was justified by the immediate circumstances, and is to my apprehension quite consistent with even a more explicit statement by Mahomet than this, of his forebodings.

the duty, began again in a similar strain. Displeased and irritated, Mahomet exclaimed : 'Truly, ye resemble the foolish women in the story of Joseph :[1] give command forthwith as I desire.' The command was given, and Abu Bakr conducted the public prayers during the few remaining days of the Prophet's life.[2]

Mahomet thus sig-nified transfer to him as his deputy of ruling power.

Closely joined together as is spiritual authority in Islâm with temporal command, the right of presiding at public prayer was always recognised in early times as the mark of the chief secular power. There can be little doubt that Mahomet by nominating Abu Bakr to this duty, intended the delegation of the supreme authority to him while he himself was laid aside, if not to mark him as successor after death. It is related that on one occasion Abu Bakr happened not to be present when the summons to prayer was sounded by Bilâl, and that Omar having received, as he erroneously believed, the command of Mahomet to officiate in his room, stood up in the Mosque, and in his powerful voice commenced the *Takbîr*, ' Great is the Lord !' preparatory to the public service. Mahomet, overhearing this from his apartment, called aloud with energy : 'No! No! No! The Lord and the whole body of Believers forbid it ! None but Abu Bakr ! Let no one lead the prayers but only he !'

While thus unable to leave the room of Ayesha, Mahomet

---

[1] See Sura xii. The Commentators refer this expression to the scene in which the women of Egypt cut their hands in astonishment at the beauty of Joseph.

[2] Tradition is quite unanimous as to this scene. The only point on which I have ventured to deviate from it, is the *motive* of Ayesha. She herself says that she objected simply from the fear that people would ever after dislike her father for having stood up in the Prophet's place, and would attribute any evil that might happen to ill-luck arising out of such usurpation. This I believe to be an afterthought. Ayesha was ambitious enough, and no doubt rejoiced greatly at this indication of her father to the chief command. But she was also overcome at the moment by concern for her husband, and could not bear the admission that he was so dangerously ill as the nomination appeared to imply. It seemed to her to be a foreboding of his end : an inauspicious forestalling of the succession. Hence she deprecated the idea.

One set of traditions makes her to propose that Omar should conduct the prayers in her father's stead. This is unlikely ; but, supposing it to be true, her proposal may have arisen from the same cause;—she knew well that Mahomet would not pass over Abu Bakr, and may from false modesty, or it may be real delicacy, have suggested that Omar, and not her father, should be nominated to the invidious post.

was too weak to attend to any public business. Yet the He urges despatch of Osâma's army.
Syrian expedition weighed upon his mind; and he kept
saying to those around him: 'Send off quickly the army of
Osâma.' He also enjoined that all embassies which might
arrive, should be treated with the same consideration, and
receive the same largesses, as he had himself been wont to
bestow.

On the night of Saturday, the sickness assumed a very Increase of illness. Saturday night, 11th Rabi I. A.H. XI. June 6, A.D. 632.
serious aspect. The fever rose to such a pitch that the hand
could hardly be kept upon his skin from its burning heat.
His body was racked with pain; restless and moaning, he
tossed about upon his bed. Alarmed at a severe paroxysm
of the disease, Omm Salma, one of his wives, screamed aloud.
Mahomet rebuked her: 'Quiet!' he said. 'No one crieth
out thus but an unbeliever.' During the night, Ayesha
sought to comfort him, and suggested that he should seek
for consolation in the same lessons he had so often taught to
others when in sickness: 'O Prophet!' she said, 'if one of
us had moaned thus, thou wouldst surely have found fault
with it.' 'Yes,' he replied, 'but I burn with the fever-heat
of any two of you together.' 'Then,' exclaimed one, 'thou
shalt surely have a double reward.' 'Yes,' he answered,—
'I swear by him in whose hands is my life, that there is not
upon the earth a believer afflicted with any calamity or
disease, but the Lord thereby causeth his sins to fall from
him, even as leaves are shed from a tree in autumn.' At
another time he said: 'Suffering is an expiation for sin.
Verily, if the believer suffer but the scratch of a thorn, the
Lord raiseth his rank thereby, and wipeth away from him a
sin.' 'Believers,' he would affirm, 'are tried according to
their faith. If a man's faith be strong, so are his sufferings;
if he be weak, they are proportioned thereunto. Yet in any
case, the suffering shall not be remitted until he walk upon
earth without the guilt of a single transgression cleaving
unto him.'

Omar, approaching the bed, placed his hand on Mahomet's Sayings of Mahomet on his death-bed.
forehead, and suddenly withdrew it from the greatness of the
heat: 'O Prophet!' he said, 'how violent is the fever upon
thee!' 'Yea, verily,' replied Mahomet, 'but I have been
during the night season repeating in praise of the Lord
seventy Suras, and among them the seven long ones.' Omar

answered: 'But the Lord hath forgiven thee all thy sins, the former and the latter; now then, why not rest and take thine ease?' 'Nay,' replied Mahomet, 'for wherefore should I not be a faithful servant unto Him?'

An attendant, while Mahomet lay covered up, put his hand below the sheet and, feeling the excessive heat, made a remark similar to that of Omar. Mahomet replied: 'Even as this affliction prevaileth now against me, so shall my reward hereafter be enlarged.' 'And who are they,' asked another, 'that suffer the severest trials?' 'The prophets and the righteous,' said Mahomet; and then he made mention of one prophet having been destroyed by lice, and of another who was tried with poverty, so that he had but a rag to cover his nakedness withal; 'yet each of them rejoiced exceedingly in his affliction, even as one of you in great spoil would rejoice.'

Osâma visits him. Sunday, 12th Rabi I. June 7.

On the Sunday, Mahomet lay in a very weak and helpless state. Osâma, who had delayed his departure to see what the issue of the sickness might be, came in from Jorf to visit him. Removing the clothes from the Prophet's face, he stooped down and kissed him, but there was no audible response. Mahomet only raised his hands to heaven in the attitude of blessing, and then placed them upon Osâma. So he returned to the camp.

Mahomet physicked by his wives.

During some part of this day, Mahomet complained of pain in his side, and the suffering became so great, that he fell into a state of unconsciousness. Omm Salma advised that physic should be given him. Asma,[1] sister of Meimûna, prepared a draught after an Abyssinian recipe, and they forced it into his mouth. Reviving from its effects he felt the unpleasant taste in his mouth, and cried: 'What is this that ye have done to me? Ye have even given me physic!' They confessed that they had done so, and enumerated the ingredients of which Asma had compounded it.[2] 'Out upon you!' he exclaimed angrily; 'this is a remedy for the pleurisy, which she hath learned in the land of Abyssinia; but that is not a disease which the Lord will suffer to attack me. Now shall ye all partake of the same dose. Let not one remain in the house without being physicked, even as ye

---

[1] See *ante*, pp. 403, 410.

[2] Indian wood and a little *Wars* seed mixed with some drops of olive oil.

have physicked me, excepting only my uncle Abbâs.' So all the women arose, and they poured the physic, in presence of the dying Prophet, into each other's mouths.[1]

After this, the conversation turning upon Abyssinia, Omm Salma and Omm Habîba, who had both been exiles there, spoke of the beauty of a cathedral in that country, called the church of *Maria,* and of the wonderful pictures on its walls. Mahomet listened quietly to them, and then said ; ' These verily are the people who, when a good man hath lived amongst them, build over his tomb a place of worship, and then adorn it with their pictures. These, in the eyes of the Lord, are the worst part of all creation.' He stopped, and covered himself with the bedclothes; then casting them off in the restlessness and perhaps delirium of the fever,[2] he said: ' The Lord destroy the Jews and Christians![3] Let his anger be kindled against those that turn the tombs of their Prophets into places of worship! O Lord, let not my tomb be ever an object of worship! Let there not remain any faith but that of Islâm throughout Arabia!'[4]

Mahomet in fever curses Jews and Christians.

[1] This scene is well attested. How strangely it must have contrasted with the solemnity of the Prophet's death-bed! Meimûna pleaded that she was under a vow of fasting, and could not, therefore, allow anything, even medicine, to pass her lips; but the excuse was unavailing. Another tradition represents Mahomet as grounding his displeasure at being forced to take physic, on the fact that ' he was then fasting.' He had, perhaps, made some vow to this effect in reference to his sickness.

[2] ' He kept drawing the clothes over his face, and then pulling them off again.'

[3] Some authorities omit the *Christians* from this tradition,

[4] *Lit.,* ' Let there not remain two Religions,' &c.

See *ante,* pp. 160, 395. The facts there given prove that there was no *command* recognised by his people as such, given by the Prophet for the expulsion of the Jews from Arabia. Had there been, Abu Bakr and Omar would no doubt have made it one of their first objects to fulfil the order,—existing treaties and engagements notwithstanding. A command of Mahomet was never questioned during his life, much less after his death. I conclude that either the sentence is a fabrication, or that having been uttered in delirium, it was not felt to be binding. If uttered at all, even in delirium, it is a significant index of the current of Mahomet's thoughts.

According to some traditions Mahomet said that he had three injunctions to deliver ; one concerned the treatment of the embassies arriving at Medîna (see *ante,* p. 501); the second directed the ejection of Jews and Christians from Arabia ; before he could explain the third, he became unconscious. Other injunctions are mentioned, as kindness to slaves ; paying tithes ; observing prayer, &c.

Mahomet calls for writing materials.

About this time, recognising Omar, and some other chief men in the room, he called out: 'Fetch me hither ink and paper, that I may record for you a writing which shall hinder you from going astray for ever.' Omar said: 'He wandereth in his mind. Is not the Corân sufficient for us?' But the women wished that the writing materials should be brought; and a discussion ensued. Thereupon one said: 'What is his condition at this present moment? Come, let us see whether he speaketh deliriously or not.' So they went and asked him what his wishes were regarding the writing he had spoken of; but he no longer desired to indite it. 'Leave me thus alone,' he said, 'for my present state is better than that ye call me to.'[1]

He distributes alms.

In the course of the day, Mahomet called Ayesha to him, and said: 'Where is that gold which I gave unto thee to keep?' On her replying that it was by her, he desired that she should spend it at once in charity. Then he dozed off in a half conscious state, and some time after asked if she had done as he desired her. On her saying that she had not yet done so, he called for the money (which was apparently a portion of the tithe income); she placed it in his hand, and counted six golden dinars. He directed that it should be divided among certain indigent families; and then lying down he said: 'Now I am at peace. Verily it would not have become me to meet my Lord, and this gold in my possession.'[2]

---

[1] Either speaking incoherently, or meaning that he did not feel equal to the task. Abbâs is represented as lamenting the irreparable loss sustained by the absence of what Mahomet intended to dictate, and saying that his followers lost it through their quarrelling. But Mahomet was evidently wandering when he called for the writing materials. According to another tradition, when the women were about to bring the writing materials, Omar chided them: 'Quiet!' he said. 'Ye behave as women do always; when your master falleth sick ye burst into tears, and the moment he recovereth but a little, then ye begin embracing him.' Mahomet, jealous even on his death-bed of the good name of his wives, was aroused by these words, and said: 'Verily, they are better than ye are.' If this tradition be true, it shows that Mahomet was only partially delirious at the moment.

[2] The story is told in various ways, but the version in the text is probably correct. Some traditions unite the incident with one of those strange tales of Ayesha which contrast the Prophet's poverty with his benevolence; she was obliged (she says) to send to a neighbour to get oil for her lamp when Mahomet was on his death-bed. There are many traditions to show Mahomet's unwillingness to retain money in his possession. He used to give everything

All Sunday night the illness of Mahomet continued un- Improve-
abated. He was overheard praying. One of the ejacula- ment on
tions was to this effect: ' O my soul! Why seekest thou morning,
for refuge elsewhere than in God alone?'[1] The morning Rabi ;.
brought some measure of relief. The fever and the pain June 8.
abated; and there was an apparent return of strength.

The dangerous crisis of the Prophet's sickness on the Mahomet
preceding night having become known throughout the city, comes out
the Mosque was crowded in the morning at the hour of prayer;
prayer, by men and women who came seeking anxiously for
tidings. Abu Bakr, as usual, led the devotions; as Imâm he
stood in the place of Mahomet before the congregation, his
back turned towards them.[2] He had ended the first *Rakáat,*
or series of prostrations, and the people had just stood up
again for a second, when the curtain of Ayesha's door (to
the left of the audience, and a little way behind Abu Bakr)
slowly moved aside, and Mahomet himself appeared. As he
entered the assembly, he whispered in the ear of Fadhl son
of Abbâs, who with a servant supported him: ' The Lord
verily hath granted unto me refreshment[3] in prayer; ' and
he looked around him with a gladsome smile marked by all
who at the moment caught a glimpse of his countenance.[4]
That smile no doubt was the index of deep emotion in his
heart. What doubts or fears may have crossed the mind
of Mahomet as he lay on the bed of death, and felt that the
time was drawing nigh when he must render an account to
that God whose messenger he professed to be,—tradition
affords us no grounds even to conjecture. The rival claims
of Aswad and Museilama had perhaps suggested misgivings
such as those which had long ago distracted his soul. What

away in charity; and did not even like retaining money in his house over the
night. All this is probably exaggerated.

[1] In all his previous illnesses, Mahomet had prayed for his recovery. This
prayer, according to tradition, signified that now his expectation was to
depart.

[2] It will be remembered that in Mahometan prayers, the whole congregation, the Imâm (leader) included, look towards Mecca. The people are ranged
in rows behind the Imâm, and follow his motions.

[3] *Lit.,* ' Cooling of the eyes.'

[4] That is by the portion of the congregation in a line with the door, who
were standing sideways to it, and by all the ranks behind them. Those in
front had their backs partly towards him; but some of them also may probably
have turned round to see the cause of the general sensation.

if he too were an impostor, deceiving himself and deceiving others also! If any doubts and questionings of this nature had arisen in his mind, the sight of the great congregation, in attitude devout and earnest, may have caused him comfort and reassurance. That which brings forth good fruit must itself be good. The mission which had transformed gross and debased idolaters into spiritual worshippers such as these, resigning every faculty to the service of the one great God; and which, wherever accepted and believed in, was daily producing the same wonderful change,—that mission must be divine, and the voice from within which prompted him to undertake it must have been the voice of the Almighty revealed through His ministering spirit. Perhaps it was a thought like this which passed at the moment through the mind of the Prophet, and lighted up his countenance with that smile of joy diffusing gladness over the crowded courts of the Mosque.

And takes his seat beside Abu Bakr.

Having paused thus for a moment at the door, Mahomet, supported as before, walked softly to the front where Abu Bakr stood. The people made way for him, opening their ranks as he advanced. Abu Bakr heard the rustle (for he never when at prayer turned himself or looked to the right hand or the left) and, apprehending the cause which alone at that time could create so great sensation, stepped backwards to join the congregation, and vacate the place of leader for the Prophet. But Mahomet motioned him to resume the post, and taking his hand moved forward to the pulpit. There he sat on the ground by the side of Abu Bakr, who resumed the service, and finished it in the customary form.

Abu Bakr goes to visit his wife at Al Sunh.

When the prayers were ended, Abu Bakr entered into conversation with Mahomet. He rejoiced to find him to all appearance convalescent. 'O Prophet,' he said, 'I perceive that by the grace of God thou art better to-day, even as we desire to see thee. Now this day is the turn of my wife, the daughter of Khârija; shall I go and visit her?'[1] Mahomet gave him permission. So he departed to her house at Al Sunh, a suburb of the upper city.

Mahomet speaks with

Mahomet then sat himself down for a little while in the

[1] This was the wife whom he had married at Medîna, from amongst the Bani Hârith, see ante, p. 179. The Moslems all followed Mahomet's custom of spending a day in succession with each of their wives.

court-yard of the Mosque near the door of Ayesha's apart- *the people around him.* ment, and addressed the people who, overjoyed to find him again in their midst, crowded round. He spoke with emotion, and with a voice still so powerful as to reach beyond the outer doors of the Mosque. 'By the Lord!' he said, 'as for myself, verily, no man can lay hold of me in any matter; [1] I have not made lawful anything excepting what God hath made lawful; nor have I prohibited aught but that which God in his book hath prohibited.' Osâma was there: when he came to bid farewell, Mahomet said to him: 'Go forward with the army; and the blessing of the Lord be with thee!' Then turning to the women who sat close by: 'O Fâtima my daughter!' he exclaimed, 'and Safiâ, my aunt! Work ye both that which shall procure you acceptance with the Lord: for verily I have no power with Him to save you in anywise.' Having said this, he arose and re-entered the room of Ayesha.

Mahomet, exhausted by the exertion he had undergone, *Mahomet retires exhausted to Ayesha's room.* lay down upon his bed; and Ayesha, seeing him to be very weak, raised his head from the pillow and laid it tenderly upon her bosom. At that moment, one of her relatives entered with a green tooth-pick in his hand. [2] Ayesha observed that the eye of Mahomet rested on it, and, knowing it to be such as he liked, asked whether he wished to have it. He signified assent. Chewing it a little to make it soft and pliable, she placed it in his hand. This pleased him; for he took up the tooth-pick and used it, rubbing his teeth with his ordinary vigour; then he put it down.

His strength now rapidly sank. He seemed to be aware *The hour of death draws near.* that death was drawing near. He called for a pitcher of water, and, wetting his face, prayed thus: 'O Lord, I beseech thee assist me in the agonies of death!' Then three times he ejaculated earnestly: 'Gabriel, come close unto me!'

At this time, he began to blow upon himself, perhaps in *Mahomet dies reclining on Ayesha's bosom.* the half-consciousness of delirium, repeating the while an ejaculatory form which he had been in the habit of praying

---

[1] In this expression probably originated the highly improbable traditions that Mahomet on this occasion called upon all claimants to state what demands they had against him; some creditors having claims of very trifling amount came forward, it is said, and he discharged their debts. The appeal somewhat resembles that of Samuel (1 Sam. xii. 3).

[2] In the east, the fresh and tender wood of trees is used for this purpose, cut into thin and narrow pieces.

over persons who were very sick. When he ceased, from weakness, Ayesha took up the task and continued to blow upon him and recite the same prayer. Then, seeing that he was very low, she seized his right hand and rubbed it (another practice of the Prophet when visiting the sick) repeating all the while the earnest invocation.[1] But Mahomet was too far gone to bear even this. He now wished to be in perfect quiet: ' Take off thy hand from me,' he said; ' that cannot benefit me now.' After a little he prayed in a whisper: ' Lord, grant me pardon ; and join me to the companionship

---

[1] The prayer was : ' *Take away evil and misfortune, O thou Lord of mankind! Grant a cure, for thou art the best Physician. There is no cure besides thine ; it leaveth nought of the disease behind.*'

I have omitted all mention of the incantation which Gabriel is said to have recited over the dying Prophet; the story of the Angel of death coming to ask permission before he proceeded to exercise his vocation upon him; the voices of unseen visitants wailing, &c. But I may subjoin the following tradition from Jáfar ibn Muhammad, as illustrative of Mahometan ideas on the subject :—' Three days before the death of Mahomet, Gabriel came down to visit him: " O Ahmad!" he said, " the Lord hath deputed me thus as an honour and dignity and a peculiar favour unto thee, that he may enquire of thee concerning that, which indeed he knoweth better than thou thyself: He asketh, *How thou findest thyself this day?*" " Gabriel!" replied the Prophet, " I find myself in sore trouble and agony." The next day, Gabriel again visited Mahomet, and accosted him in the same words ; Mahomet replied as before. On the third day, there descended with Gabriel the Angel of death; and there also alighted with him another angel, called Ismaíl, who inhabiteth the air, never ascending up to heaven, and never before having descended to the earth since its creation ; and he came in command of 70,000 angels, each one of which was in command of 70,000 more. Gabriel, preceding these, addressed Mahomet in the same words as before, and received the same reply. Then said Gabriel: " This, O Mahomet! is the Angel of death. He asketh of thee permission to enter. He hath asked permission of no man before, neither shall he ask permission of any after thee." Mahomet gave permission ; so the Angel of death entered the room, and stood before Mahomet, and said: " O Ahmad, Prophet of the Lord! Verily God hath sent me unto thee, and hath commanded me to obey thee in all that thou mayest direct. Bid me to take thy soul, and I will take it; bid me to leave it, and I will do accordingly." To which, Mahomet replied: " Wilt thou, indeed, do so, O Angel of death!" The angel protested that his mission was even so, to do only that which Mahomet might command. On this, Gabriel interposed, and said: " O Ahmad! verily the Lord is desirous of thy company." " Proceed, then," said Mahomet, addressing the Angel of death, " and do thy work, even as thou art commanded." Gabriel now bade adieu to Mahomet: " Peace be on thee," he said, " O Prophet of the Lord! This is the last time that I shall tread the earth; with this world now I have concern no longer." So the Prophet died; and there arose a wailing of celestial voices (the sound was audible, but no form was seen) saying: " *Peace be on you, ye inhabitants of this house, and mercy from the Lord and his blessing ! Every soul shall taste death,*" '—and so on.

on high.' Then at intervals: 'Eternity in Paradise!'—
'Pardon!' 'Yes; the blessed companionship on high!'
He stretched himself gently. Then all was still. His head
grew heavy on the breast of Ayesha. The Prophet of Arabia
was dead.

Softly removing his head from her bosom, Ayesha placed
it on the pillow, and rising up joined the other women, who
were beating their faces in bitter lamentation.

Ayesha replaces his head on the pillow.

The sun had but shortly passed the meridian. It was
only an hour or two since Mahomet had entered the Mosque
cheerful, and seemingly convalescent. He now lay cold in
death.

It was still but a little after midday.

CHAPTER XXXIV.

THE EVENTS WHICH FOLLOWED ON THE DEATH OF MAHOMET.

13th and 14th of Rabî, A.H. XI.—*June 8 and 9,* A.D. 632.

News of
Mahomet's
death
reaches
Abu Bakr.

THE news of the Prophet's death, spreading rapidly over Medîna, soon reached Abu Bakr in the suburb of Al Sunh. Immediately he mounted his horse, and rode back to the Mosque in haste.

Omar
wildly de-
claims that
Mahomet
had only
swooned
away.

Meanwhile, a strange scene was being enacted there. Shortly after Mahomet had breathed his last, Omar entered the apartment of Ayesha; and, lifting up the sheet which covered the body, gazed wistfully at the features of his departed master. All was so placid, so natural, so unlike death, that Omar could not believe the mournful truth. Starting up, he exclaimed wildly: 'The Prophet is not dead; he hath only swooned away.' Mughîra, who was standing by, vainly endeavoured to convince him that he was mistaken. 'Thou liest!' cried Omar, as, quitting the chamber of death, they entered the courts of the Mosque;—'the Apostle of God is not dead: it is thy seditious spirit which hath suggested this thine imagination. The Prophet of the Lord shall not die until he have rooted out every hypocrite and unbeliever.' The crowd which, at the rumour of the Prophet's death, rapidly gathered in the Mosque, was attracted by the loud and passionate tones of Omar, and flocked around him; he went on to harangue them in a similar strain. 'The disaffected people would persuade you, O Believers! that Mahomet is dead. Nay! but he hath gone to his Lord, even as Moses son of Imrân, who remained absent forty days, and then returned after his followers had said that he was dead. So, verily, by the Lord! the Prophet shall return, and of a certainty shall cut off the hands and feet of those who dare to say that he is dead.' Omar found a willing audience. It was but a little while before that Mahomet had been in the midst of them, at their head had joined in the public prayers on that very spot, and had gladdened their hearts by the hope of speedy convalescence. The echo of his voice was hardly yet silent in the courts of the Mosque. Sudden alternations of hope and despair disturb the equilibrium of the mind, and unfit it for the exercise of a calm and dispassionate judgment. The events of the day had been pre-eminently of the kind calculated to produce this effect upon the people, who, now carried away by the fervour of Omar, gladly persuaded themselves that he might be in the right.

Just then appeared Abu Bakr. Passing through the Mosque, he listened for a moment to the frenzied words of Omar, and, without pausing further, walked onwards to the door of Ayesha's room. Drawing the curtain softly aside, he asked leave to enter. 'Come,' they replied from within, 'for this day, no permission needeth to be asked.' Then he entered, and, raising the striped sheet which covered the bed, stooped down and kissed the face of his departed friend, saying: 'Sweet thou wert in life, and sweet art thou in death.' After a moment, he took the head between his hands, and, slightly lifting it, gazed on the well-known features, now fixed in death, and exclaimed: 'Yes, thou *art* dead! Alas, my friend, my chosen one! Dearer than father or mother to me! Thou hast tasted the bitter pains of death; and thou art too precious in the sight of the Lord, that he should give thee this cup a second time to drink!' Gently putting down the head upon its pillow, he stooped again and kissed the face; then replaced the covering on the body, and withdrew.

Abu Bakr visits scene of death;

Having left the room of Ayesha, Abu Bakr went at once to the spot within the courts of the Mosque, where Omar, in the same excited state as before, was haranguing the people. 'Silence!' cried Abu Bakr, as he drew near. 'Omar! sit thee down; be quiet!' But Omar went on, not heeding the remonstrance. So Abu Bakr, turning from him, began himself to address the assembly; no sooner did they hear his voice open with the customary exordium, than they all

Convinces Omar and the people that Mahomet is really dead.

quitted Omar and gave attention to the words of Abu Bakr, who proceeded thus: 'Hath not the Almighty revealed this verse unto his Prophet saying,—" *Verily thou shalt die, and they shall die?* "   And again, after the battle of Ohod,— " *Mahomet is no more than an Apostle; verily the other Apostles have deceased before him.   What then!   If he were to die, or to be killed, would ye turn back on your heels?* " Let him then know, whosoever worshippeth Mahomet, that Mahomet indeed is dead: but whoso worshippeth God, let him know that the Lord liveth and doth not die.'   The words of the Corân fell like a knell on the ears of Omar and all those who with him had buoyed themselves up with the delusive hope of Mahomet's return to life.   The quiet and reflecting mind of Abu Bakr had no doubt frequently recalled these passages during the Prophet's illness.   To the people in general they had not occurred, at least in connection with the present scene.   When they heard them now repeated, 'it was as if they had not known till that moment that such a revelation existed in the Corân;' and, the truth now bursting upon them, they sobbed aloud.   Omar himself would relate: 'By the Lord! it was so that, when I heard Abu Bakr reciting those verses, I was horror-struck, my limbs trembled, I dropped down, and I knew of a certainty that Mahomet indeed was dead.'

Army at Jorf breaks up and returns to Medina.

The greater part of the army, when the Prophet died, was at Jorf, three miles distant from Medîna.   Encouraged by his seeming convalescence that morning in the Mosque, they had rejoined their camp.   Osâma, mindful of his master's strict injunction, had given the order for immediate march, and his foot was already in the stirrup, when a swift messenger from his mother Omm Ayman announced the Prophet's death.   The army, stunned by the intelligence, at once broke up, and returned to Medîna.   Osâma, preceded by the standard-bearer, went direct to the Mosque, and planted the great banner at the door of Ayesha's house.

Citizens of Medina assemble.

It was now towards the afternoon when one came running hastily to Abu Bakr and Omar with the tidings that the chief men of Medîna, with Sád ibn Obâda at their head, had assembled in one of the halls of the city, and were proceeding to choose Sád for their leader: 'If ye, therefore, desire to have the command, come quickly thither before the matter shall have been settled, and opposition become dangerous.' Immediately on hearing this report, Abu Bakr, after giving strict command that the family and near relatives of the Prophet should be left undisturbed while they washed the corpse and laid it out, hurried, in company with Omar and Abu Obeida, to the hall where the people had assembled. There was urgent necessity for their presence. The men of Medîna were brooding over their supersession by the once dependent strangers whom they had received as refugees from Mecca: 'Let them have their own chief,' was the general cry; 'but as for us, we shall have a chief for ourselves.' Sád, who lay sick and covered over in a corner of the hall, had already been proposed for the chiefship of the Medîna citizens, when suddenly Abu Bakr and his party entered. Omar, still in a state of excitement, was on the point of giving vent to his feelings in a speech which he had been preparing, when Abu Bakr, afraid of his rashness and impetuosity, held him back, and himself addressed the people. Omar used in after days to say that Abu Bakr anticipated all his arguments, and expressed them in language the most eloquent and persuasive. ' Ye men of Medîna!' he said, 'all that ye speak of your own excellence is true. There is no people upon earth deserving all this praise more than ye do. But the Arabs will not recognise the chief command elsewhere than in our tribe of the Coreish. We are the *Ameers*; ye are our *Wazeers*.'[1] 'Not so,' shouted the indignant citizens, ' but there shall be an Ameer from amongst us, and an Ameer from amongst you.' 'That can never be,' said Abu Bakr ; and he repeated in a firm, commanding voice : ' *We* are the Ameers; *you* are our Wazeers. We are the noblest of the Arabs by descent; and the foremost in the glory of our City. There! Choose ye whom ye will of these two (pointing to Omar and Abu Obeida) and do allegiance to him.'[2] 'Nay !' cried Omar, in words which rose high and clear above the growing tumult of the assembly; 'did not the Prophet himself command that *thou*, O Abu Bakr,

Abu Bakr sworn fealty to, as Caliph.

---

[1] *Ameer*, Chief, or Leader. *Wazeer*, or *Vizier*, Deputy, Councillor.

[2] There was nothing in the antecedents of Abu Obeida to sustain a claim to the Caliphate. He was simply named by Abu Bakr as being the only other Coreishite present. He subsequently bore a conspicuous part in the conquest of Syria.

shouldst lead the prayers? Thou art our master, and to thee we pledge our allegiance—thou whom the Prophet loved the best amongst us all!' and so saying he seized the hand of Abu Bakr, and, striking it, pledged faith to him. The words of Omar touched a chord which vibrated in every Believer's heart, and his example had the desired effect; the opposition vanished, and Abu Bakr was saluted as the *Caliph* (or successor) of the departed Prophet.[1]

Body of Mahomet washed and laid out.

Meanwhile Ali, Osâma, and Fadhl the son of Abbâs, with one or two of the Prophet's servants, had been busily employed in the room of Ayesha. There on the spot on which he breathed his last, they washed the body of Mahomet and laid it out.[2] The garment in which he died was left upon him: two sheets of fine white cloth were wound around it; and above all was cast a covering of striped Yemen stuff. Thus the body remained during the night, and until the time of burial.

Speech of Omar. Allegiance publicly sworn to Abu Bakr. Tuesday, 14th Rabî I. June 9.

On the morrow, when the people had assembled in the Mosque, Abu Bakr and Omar came forth to meet them. Omar first addressed the great assemblage: 'O ye people! that which I spoke unto you yesterday was not the truth. Verily, I find that it is not borne out by the Book which the Lord hath revealed, nor by the covenant which we made with His Apostle. As for me, verily I hoped that the Apostle of the Lord would continue yet a while amongst us, and speak in our ears a word such as might seem good unto him and be a perpetual guide unto us. But the Lord hath chosen for His Apostle the portion which is with Himself, in preference to

---

[1] Khalifa or Caliph signifies 'Successor.'

[2] As usual, when the name of Ali is introduced, tradition is overspread with fiction. A heavenly voice was heard ordering the attendants not to make bare the Prophet's body, for the eyes of any one that looked upon his nakedness would forthwith be destroyed. When Ali raised the limbs, they yielded to his touch, as if unseen hands were aiding him; another, essaying to do the same, found the weight insupportable. Thus Fadhl, who had ventured on the task, was well nigh dragged down, and called out for help: 'Haste thee, Ali! Hold, for my back is breaking with the weight of this limb.' Abbâs refused to enter the room at the time, 'because Mahomet had desired always to be hid from him while he bathed.'

Besides the three named in the text (who, as the nearest and most intimate friends, naturally superintended the washing of the body), one of the Medîna citizens, Aws ibn al Khawla, was admitted by Ali into the room. Another son of Abbâs is also named by some authorities as having been present. The servants employed on the occasion were Shakrân and Sâlih.

that which is with you. And truly the inspired Word which directed your Prophet is with us still. Take it, therefore, for your guide and ye shall never go astray. And now, verily, hath the Lord placed the administration of your affairs in the hands of him that is the best amongst us; the Companion of His Prophet, the sole companion, *the Second of the two when they were in the cave alone.* Arise! Swear fealty to him!' Forthwith the people crowded round, and one by one they swore allegiance upon the hand of Abu Bakr.

The ceremony being ended, Abu Bakr arose and said: 'Ye people! now, verily, I have become the Chief over you, although I am not the best amongst you. If I do well, support me; if I err, then set me right. In truth and sincerity is faithfulness, and in falsehood perfidy. The weak and oppressed among you in my sight shall be strong, until I restore his right unto him, if the Lord will; and the strong oppressor among you shall be weak, until I wrest from him that which he hath usurped. Now hearken to me; when a people leaveth off to fight in the ways of the Lord, verily He casteth them away in disgrace. Know also that wickedness never aboundeth in any nation, but the Lord visiteth that nation with calamity. Wherefore obey me, even as I shall obey the Lord and His Apostle. Whensoever I disobey them, obedience is no longer obligatory upon you. Arise to prayers! and the Lord have mercy on you!'

Speech of Abu Bakr on his inauguration.

The homage done to Abu Bakr was almost universal. Sád ibn Obâda, deeply chagrined at being superseded, is said by some to have remained altogether aloof.[1] It is probable that Ali, while the people were swearing allegiance, remained in his own house or in the chamber of death. It is alleged by his adherents, that he expected the Caliphate for himself; but there was nothing in his previous position, nor in the language and actions of the Prophet towards him, which should have led to this anticipation. It is possible, indeed, that, as the husband of Mahomet's only surviving daughter, he may have conceived that a claim existed by succession. Whatever his expectations were, it is certain that

Discontent of Ali and Fâtima.

---

[1] It is even said that he retired in disgust to Syria, where he died. Tabari, on the other hand, relates that he submitted to Abu Bakr, and acknowledged his authority.

he considered himself aggrieved when Abu Bakr denied the
title of his wife to inherit the Prophet's share in the lands of
Fadak and of Kheibar.   Fâtima failed in producing any
evidence of her father's intention to bestow this property on
her, and the Caliph justly held that it should be reserved for
those purposes of State to which Mahomet had in his life-
time devoted it.

Fâtima re-
nounces
society of
Abu Bakr.

Fâtima took the denial of this her supposed right so much
to heart that she held no intercourse with Abu Bakr during
the short remainder of her life.   It was probably she who
stirred up Ali and his friends to form a faction the influence
of which proved in after days disastrous to the interests
of Islâm.   Whether Ali swore allegiance at the first to his
new chief, or refused to do so, it was certainly not till
Fâtima's death, six months after that of her father, that Ali
recognised with any cordiality the title of Abu Bakr to the
Caliphate.[1]

[1] Some traditions say that he swore allegiance at the first, with the rest;
others, that he refused to do so till after Fâtima's death.

The traditions of Fâtima's deep grief at the loss of her father, and of her
joy at his prophecy that she would soon rejoin him in heaven, &c., ill accord
with the sordid manner in which she urged her claim to the property.   ' On
the day after her father's death,' we learn from Wâckidi, ' Fâtima repaired with
Ali to Abu Bakr, and said: "Give me the inheritance of my father the
Prophet."   Abu Bakr enquired whether she meant his household goods or his
landed estates.   "*Fadak* and *Kheibar*," she replied, "and the tithe lands at
Medîna,—my inheritance therein, even as thy daughters will inherit of thee
when thou diest."   Abu Bakr replied: "Verily, thy father was better than
my daughters are.   But the Prophet hath said, *No one shall be my heir; that
which I leave shall be for alms.*   Now, therefore, the family of Mahomet shall
not eat of that property; for, by the Lord, I will not alter a tittle of that
which the Prophet ordained; all shall remain as it was in his lifetime.
But," continued he, "if thou art certain that thy father gave thee this
property, I will accept thy word, and fulfil thy father's direction."   She
replied that she had no evidence excepting that of the maid-servant Omm
Ayman, who had told her that her father had given her Fadak.   Abu Bakr,
therefore, maintained his decision.'

CHAPTER XXXV.

THE BURIAL OF MAHOMET.

WHEN Abu Bakr had ended his speech, preparations were made for the burial of the Prophet. The people differed regarding the place most fitting for his grave. Some urged that the body should be buried in the Mosque close by the pulpit; and some, beneath the spot where as their Imâm he had so long led the daily prayers; while others wished to inter him beside his followers in the grave-yard without the city. Abu Bakr, with whom as Caliph the matter now rested, approved none of these proposals: for, said he, 'I have heard it from the lips of Mahomet himself, that in whatsoever spot a prophet dieth, there also should he be buried.' He therefore gave command that the grave should be dug where the body was still lying within the house of Ayesha. *Grave prepared in Ayesha's house. Tuesday, 14th Rabi I. June 9.*

Another question arose as to the form in which the tomb should be prepared. Two fashions prevailed in Arabia: in one kind, the bottom or pavement of the grave was flat; in the other, the bottom was partly excavated for the reception of the body, a ledge being left on one side of the vault or cavity. The former was the plan followed at Mecca, the latter at Medîna; and for each there was a separate grave-digger. Both were now summoned. The man of Medîna first appearing, dug the grave in the vaulted form; and so this fashion is followed by all Mahometans to the present day. *Grave dug in vaulted fashion.*

The body of Mahomet remained upon the bier for four-and-twenty hours, namely, from the afternoon or the evening of Monday to the same hour on the following day. On Tuesday, it was visited by all the inhabitants of the city. *Body visited by people. Orations of Abu Bakr and Omar.*

They entered in companies by the door of Ayesha's apartment which opened into the Mosque; and, after gazing once more on the countenance of their Prophet and praying over his remains, retired by the opposite entrance. The room was crowded to the utmost at the time when Abu Bakr and Omar entered together. They prayed as follows: 'Peace be upon thee, O Prophet of God; and the mercy of the Lord and His blessing! We bear testimony that the Prophet of God hath delivered the message revealed to him; hath fought in the ways of the Lord until that God brought forth His religion unto victory; hath fulfilled His words, commanding that He alone in his unity is to be worshipped; hath drawn us to himself, and been kind and tender-hearted to Believers; hath sought no recompense for delivering to us the Faith, neither hath he sold it for a price at any time!' And all the people said, *Amen! Amen!* The women followed in companies, when the men had departed; and then even the children crowded round the bier for a last look at their Prophet's face.

Burial.

In the evening the final rites were paid to the remains of Mahomet. A red mantle, worn by him, was first spread as a soft covering at the bottom of the grave; then the body was lowered into its last resting-place by the same loving hands that had washed and laid it out. The vault was built over with unbaken bricks, and the grave filled up.[1]

Ayesha continued to occupy apartment next the grave.

Ayesha continued as before to live in her house thus honoured as the Prophet's cemetery. She occupied a room adjoining that which contained the grave, but partitioned off

---

[1] There is wonderful rivalry, at least among the traditionists, as to which person was the last to quit the interior of the tomb. Mughîra asserts that, having dropped his ring into the grave, he was allowed to go down and pick it up, and thus was the last. Others hold that Ali sent down his son Hasan to fetch the ring. Others, that Ali denied the story of the ring altogether. Some allege that one or other of the sons of Abbâs was 'the first to enter, and the last to leave, the grave.' These variations form a good example of the Alyite and Abbasside influences.

I must not omit a tradition which seems to me to illustrate the naturalness of Omar's scepticism regarding the Prophet's death. Omm Salma says: 'I did not believe that Mahomet was really dead, till I heard the sound of the pickaxes at the digging of the grave, from the next room.' Ayesha also says that the sound of the pickaxes was the first intimation she had of the approaching interment. She had apparently retired, with the other wives, to an adjoining apartment.

from it. When her father died, he was buried close by the Prophet in the same apartment, and in due time Omar also. It is related of Ayesha that she used to visit this room unveiled till the burial of Omar, when (as if a stranger had been introduced) she never entered unless veiled and fully dressed.[1]

[1] Ayesha tells us, she once dreamt that three moons fell from the heavens into her bosom, which she hoped portended the birth of an heir. After her husband's death, Abu Bakr told her that the grave of Mahomet in her house was the first and best of the moons; the other two were the graves of Abu Bakr himself and of Omar. She survived the Prophet forty-seven years.

Wâckidi says there was no wall at first round Mahomet's house. Omar surrounded it with a low wall, which Abdallah ibn Zobeir increased.

CHAPTER XXXVI.

CAMPAIGN OF OSÂMA ON THE SYRIAN BORDER.   CONCLUDING OBSERVATIONS.

Campaign of Osâma.
A.H. XI.
May, June,
A.D. 632.

THE first concern of Abu Bakr, on assuming the Caliphate, was to despatch the Syrian army, and thus fulfil the dying wish of Mahomet. But the horizon was lowering all around; and many urged that the Moslem force should not be sent just yet upon this distant expedition. Even Omar joined in the cry: 'Scatter not the Believers; rather keep our soldiers here together: we may yet have need of them to defend the city.' 'Never!' replied Abu Bakr; 'the command of the Prophet shall be carried out, even if I be left here in the city all alone a prey to the wolves and beasts of the desert.' Then they besought that a more experienced soldier might be appointed to the chief command. Abu Bakr arose in wrath. 'Out upon thee!' he cried, as he seized Omar by the beard; 'hath the Prophet of the Lord named Osâma to the leadership, and dost thou counsel me to take it from him!' The Caliph would admit of no excuse and no delay; the force was soon marshalled again at Jorf. Abu Bakr repaired to the camp, and, treating Osâma with the profound respect due to a commander appointed by Mahomet himself, begged permission that Omar might be left behind at Medîna as his counsellor. The request was granted. Abu Bakr then, bidding Osâma farewell, exhorted him to go forward in the name of the Lord, and fulfil the commission he had received at the Prophet's hands. The army marched; and the Caliph, with Omar alone, returned to Medîna.

His triumphal return to Medina.

Within twenty days of his departure from Jorf, Osâma had overrun the province of Belcâa. In fire and blood, he avenged his father's death and the disastrous field of Mûta.

'They ravaged the land,' says the historian, 'with the well-known cry of *Yâ Mansur Amit* ("Strike, ye conquerors!"), they slew all who ventured to oppose them in the field, and carried off captive the remainder. They burned the villages, the fields of standing corn, and the groves of palm-trees; and there went up behind them, as it were, a whirlwind of fire and smoke.'[1] Having thus fulfilled the Prophet's last command, they retraced their steps. It was a triumphal procession as they approached Medîna; Osâma rode upon his father's horse, and the banner, bound so lately by Mahomet's own hand, floated before him. Abu Bakr and the citizens went forth to meet him, and received the army with acclamations of joy. Attended by the Caliph, and the chief companions of the Prophet, Osâma proceeded to the Mosque, and offered up prayer with thanksgiving for the success which had so richly crowned his arms.[2]

The rapid spread of Mussulman conquest.

With the return of Osâma's army to Medîna a new era opens upon us. The Prophet had hardly departed this life when Arabia was convulsed by the violent endeavour of its tribes to shake off the trammels of Islâm, and regain their previous freedom. The hordes of the desert rose up in rebellion, and during the first year of his Caliphate Abu Bakr had to struggle for the very existence of the faith. Step by step the wild Bedouins were subdued and forced to tender their submission. By a master-stroke of policy, they were induced again to take up their arms, and aroused, by the prospect of boundless spoil, to wield them on the side of Islâm. Like blood-hounds eager for the chase, they were let forth upon mankind—the whole world their prey. They gloried in the belief that they were the hosts of God, destined for the conversion of His elect and for the destruc-

---

[1] Wâckidi represents Osâma as killing in battle the very man that slew his father.

[2] The tidings of this bloody expedition alarmed Heraclius, and he sent a strong force into Belcâa. The attention of Abu Bakr had first to be directed nearer home. Reinforced by the army of Osâma, he had to quell the fierce spirit of insurrection rising all around. But a year had not elapsed, when he was again in a position to take the field in Syria, and to enter on the career of conquest which quickly wrested from the Empire that fair province.

tion of His enemies. The pretexts of religion thus disguised or gilded every baser motive. The vast plunder of Syria was accepted as but the earnest of a greater destiny yet in store. Once maddened by the taste of blood into a wild and irresistible fanaticism, the armies of Arabia swept their enemies everywhere before them. Checked towards the north by the strongholds of the Bosphorus, the surging wave spread to the east and to the west with incredible rapidity, till in a few short years it had engulfed in common ruin the earliest seats of Christianity and the faith of Zoroaster.

Earnest-
ness of
primitive
Moslems
after Ma-
homet's
death,
argument
for his
sincerity.

But this is a province of history upon which it is not my object to enter. In some respects, indeed, it might be connected indirectly with the subject of these volumes. The simplicity and earnestness of the early Caliphs, and the first burst of zeal and devotion exhibited by his followers after the Prophet's death, are strong evidence of their belief in his sincerity: and the belief of these men must carry undeniable weight in the formation of our own estimate of his character, since the opportunities they enjoyed for testing the grounds of their conviction were both close and long-continued. It is enough that I allude to the consideration, as strengthening generally the view of Mahomet's character which in this volume I have sought to support.

CHAPTER XXXVII.

THE PERSON AND CHARACTER OF MAHOMET.

It may be expected that, before bringing this work to a close, I should gather into one review the chief traits in the character of Mahomet, which at different stages of his life, and from various points of view, have in the course of the history been presented to the reader. This I will now briefly attempt.[1]

General review of Mahomet's character.

The person of Mahomet, as he appeared in the prime of life, has been pourtrayed in an early chapter; and though advancing age may have somewhat relaxed the outlines of his countenance and affected the vigour of his carriage, yet the general aspect remained unaltered to the end. His form, though little above the ordinary height, was stately and commanding. The depth of feeling in his dark black eye, and the winning expression of a face otherwise attractive, gained the confidence and love even of strangers. His features often unbended into a smile full of grace and condescension. 'He was,' says an admiring follower, 'the handsomest and bravest, the brightest-faced and most generous of men. It was as though the sun-light beamed in his countenance.' Yet when anger kindled in his piercing glance, the object of his displeasure might well quail before it: his stern frown was the augury of death to many a trembling captive.

Personal appearance.

---

[1] Most of the illustrations in this chapter are taken from the Section of Wâckidi on the 'appearance and habits of the Prophet.' In the Supplement to this Chapter will be found a selection of traditions on the subject taken from the same Section.

His gait.　In the later years of his life, the erect figure of Mahomet began to stoop. But his step was still firm and quick. His gait has been likened to that of one descending rapidly a hill. When he made haste, it was with difficulty that his followers kept pace with him. He never turned round even if his mantle caught in a thorny bush, so that his attendants might talk and laugh freely behind him secure of being un-observed.

His habits thorough.　Thorough and complete in all his actions, he never took in hand any work without bringing it to a close. The same habit pervaded his manner in social intercourse. If he turned in conversation towards a friend, he turned not partially, but with his full face and his whole body. ' In shaking hands, he was not the first to withdraw his own ; nor was he the first to break off in converse with a stranger, nor to turn away his ear.'

Simplicity of his life.　A patriarchal simplicity pervaded his life. His custom was to do everything for himself. If he gave an alms he would place it with his own hand in that of the petitioner. He aided his wives in their household duties; he mended his clothes; he tied up the goats; he even cobbled his sandals. His ordinary dress was of plain white cotton stuff, made like his neighbours'; but on high and festive occasions he wore gar-ments of fine linen, striped or dyed in red. He never re-clined at meals. He ate with his fingers; and, when he had finished, he would lick them before he wiped his hands. The indulgences to which he was most addicted were ' Women, scents, and food.' In the first two of these, Ayesha tells us, he had his heart's desire; and when she adds that he was straitened in the third, we can only attribute the saying to the vivid contrast between the frugal habits at the rise of Islâm, and the luxurious living which rapidly followed in the wake of conquest and prosperity. Mahomet, with his wives, lived (as we have seen) in a row of low and homely cottages built of unbaked bricks; the apartments were separated by walls of palm-branches rudely daubed with mud; curtains of leather, or of black hair-cloth, supplied the place of doors and windows. His abode was to all easy of access—' even as the river's bank to him that draweth water.' Yet we have shown that he maintained the state and dignity of real power.

No approach was suffered to familiarity of action or of speech. The Prophet must be addressed in subdued accents and in a reverential style. His word was absolute; his bidding law.

Urbanity and kindness of disposition.

A remarkable feature was the urbanity and consideration with which Mahomet treated even the most insignificant of his followers. Modesty and kindliness, patience, self-denial, and generosity, pervaded his conduct, and riveted the affections of all around him. He disliked to say *No*; if unable to answer a petitioner in the affirmative, he preferred silence. 'He was more bashful,' says Ayesha, 'than a veiled virgin; and if anything displeased him, it was rather from his face, than by his words, that we discovered it; he never smote any one but in the service of the Lord, not even a woman or a servant.' He was not known ever to refuse an invitation to the house even of the meanest, nor to decline a proffered present however small. When seated by a friend, 'he did not haughtily advance his knees towards him.' He possessed the rare faculty of making each individual in a company think that *he* was the favoured guest. When he met any one rejoicing he would seize him eagerly and cordially by the hand. With the bereaved and afflicted he sympathised tenderly. Gentle and unbending towards little children, he would not disdain to accost a group of them at play with the salutation of peace. He shared his food, even in times of scarcity, with others; and was sedulously solicitous for the personal comfort of every one about him. A kindly and benevolent disposition pervades all these illustrations of his character.

Friendship.

Mahomet was also a faithful friend. He loved Abu Bakr with the romantic affection of a brother; Ali, with the fond partiality of a father. Zeid, the Christian slave of Khadîja, was so strongly attached by the kindness of Mahomet who adopted him, that he preferred to remain at Mecca rather than return to his home with his own father: 'I will not leave thee,' he said, clinging to his patron, 'for thou hast been a father and a mother to me.' The friendship of Mahomet survived the death of Zeid, and Osâma was treated by him with distinguished favour for his father's sake. Othmân and Omar were also the objects of a special attachment; and the enthusiasm with which, at Hodeibia, the Prophet entered into 'the Pledge of the Tree' and swore that he would defend his beleaguered son-in-law with his last breath, was a signal proof of faithful friendship. Numerous other instances of Mahomet's ardent and unwavering regard might be adduced. And his affections were in no instance misplaced; they were ever reciprocated by a warm and self-sacrificing love.

Moderation and magnanimity.

In the exercise at home of a power absolutely dictatorial, Mahomet was just and temperate. Nor was he wanting in moderation towards his enemies, when once they had cheerfully submitted to his claims. The long and obstinate struggle against his pretensions maintained by the inhabitants of his native city, might have induced a haughty tyrant to mark his indignation in indelible traces of fire and blood. But Mahomet, excepting a few criminals, granted a universal pardon; and, nobly casting into oblivion the memory of the past, with all its mockery, affronts, and persecutions, he treated even the foremost of his opponents with a gracious and even friendly consideration. Not less marked was the forbearance shown to Abdallah and the disaffected party at Medîna, who for so many years persistently thwarted his schemes and resisted his authority, nor the clemency with which he received the submissive advances of the most hostile tribes, even in the hour of victory.

Cruelty towards enemies.

But the darker shades, as well as the brighter, must be depicted by the faithful historian. Magnanimity or moderation are nowhere discernible as features in the conduct of Mahomet towards such of his enemies as failed to tender a timely allegiance. Over the bodies of the Coreish who fell at Bedr, he exulted with a savage satisfaction; and several prisoners—accused of no crime but that of scepticism or political opposition—were deliberately executed at his command. The Prince of Kheibar, after being subjected to inhuman torture for the purpose of discovering the treasures of his tribe, was, with his cousin, put to death on the pretext of having treacherously concealed them, and his wife led away captive to the conqueror's tent. Sentence of exile was enforced by Mahomet with rigorous severity on two whole Jewish tribes residing at Medîna; and of a third, likewise his neighbours, the women and children were sold into captivity, while the men, amounting to six or eight hundred, were butchered in cold blood before his eyes.

In his youth Mahomet earned amongst his fellows the honourable title of 'the Faithful.' But in later years, however much sincerity and good faith may have guided his conduct in respect of his friends, craft and deception were certainly not wanting towards his foes. The perfidious attack at Nakhla, where the first blood in the internecine war with the Coreish was shed, although at the outset disavowed by Mahomet for its scandalous breach of the sacred usages of Arabia, was eventually justified by a revelation from heaven. Abu Basîr, the freebooter, was countenanced by the Prophet in a manner scarcely consistent with the letter, and certainly opposed to the spirit, of the truce of Hodeibia. The surprise which secured the easy conquest of Mecca, was designed with craftiness if not with duplicity. The pretext on which the Bani Nadhîr were besieged and expatriated (namely, that Gabriel had revealed their design against the Prophet's life) was feeble and unworthy of an honest cause. When Medîna was beleaguered by the Confederate army, Mahomet sought the services of Nueim, a traitor, and employed him to sow distrust amongst the enemy by false and treacherous reports; 'for,' said he, 'what else is War but a game of deception?' In his prophetical career, political and personal ends were frequently compassed by the flagrant pretence of *divine* revelations, which a candid examination would have shown him to be nothing more than the reflection of his own wishes. The Jewish and Christian systems, at first adopted honestly as the basis of his own religion, had no sooner served the purpose of establishing a firm authority, than they were ignored and virtually disowned. And what is perhaps worst of all, the dastardly assassination of political and religious opponents, countenanced and frequently directed in their cruel and perfidious details by Mahomet himself, leaves a dark and indelible stain upon his character.

In domestic life the conduct of Mahomet, with one grave exception, was exemplary. As a husband his fondness and devotion were entire, bordering at times upon jealousy. As a father he was loving and tender. In his youth he is said to have lived a virtuous life. At the age of twenty-five he married a widow forty years old, and during her lifetime

Craftiness and perfidy.

Domestic life; polygamy.

for five-and-twenty years he was a faithful husband to her alone. Yet it is remarkable that during this period were composed most of those passages of the Corân in which the black-eyed Houris reserved for believers in Paradise, are depicted in such glowing colours. Shortly after the death of Khadîja, the Prophet married again; but it was not till the mature age of fifty-four that he made the dangerous trial of polygamy, by taking Ayesha, yet a child, as the rival of Sauda. Once the natural limits of restraint were overpassed, Mahomet fell a prey to his strong passion for the sex. In his fifty-sixth year he married Haphsa; and the following year, in two succeeding months, Zeinab bint Khozeima and Omm Salma. But his desires were not to be satisfied by the range of a harem already in advance of Arab custom, and more numerous than was permitted to any of his followers; rather, as age advanced they were stimulated to seek for new and varied indulgence. A few months after his nuptials with Zeinab and Omm Salma, the charms of a second Zeinab were by accident discovered too fully before the Prophet's admiring gaze. She was the wife of Zeid, his adopted son and bosom friend; but he was unable to smother the flame she had kindled in his breast; and, by divine command, she was taken to his bed. In the same year he married a seventh wife, and also a concubine. And at last, when he was full threescore years of age, no fewer than three new wives, besides Mary the Coptic slave, were within the space of seven months added to his already well-filled harem. The bare recital of these facts may justify the saying of Ibn Abbâs: 'Verily the chiefest among the Moslems (meaning Mahomet) was the foremost of them in his passion for women;'—a fatal example imitated too readily by his followers, who adopt the Prince of Medîna, rather than the Prophet of Mecca, for their pattern.

Thus the social and domestic life of Mahomet, fairly and impartially viewed, is seen to be chequered by light and shade. While there is much to form the subject of nearly unqualified praise, there is likewise much which cannot be spoken of but in terms of severe reprobation.

Conviction of special providence. Proceeding now to consider the religious and prophetical character of Mahomet, the first point which strikes the biographer is his constant and vivid sense of a special and all-

pervading Providence. This conviction moulded his thoughts
and designs, from the minutest actions in private and social
life to the grand conception that he was destined to be the
Reformer of his people and of the world. He never entered
a company 'but he sat down and rose up with the mention
of the Lord.' When the first fruits of the season were
brought to him, he would kiss them, place them upon his
eyes, and say: 'Lord, as thou hast shown us the first, show
unto us likewise the last.' In trouble and affliction, as well
as in prosperity and joy, he ever saw and humbly acknowledged the hand of God. A fixed persuasion that every
incident, small and great, was ordered by the divine will, led
to the strong expressions of predestination which abound in
the Corân. It was the Lord who turned the hearts of mankind: and alike faith in the believer, and unbelief in the
infidel, were the result of the divine fiat. The hour and
place of every man's death, as all other events in his life,
were established by the same decree; and the timid believer
might in vain seek to avert the stroke by shunning the field
of battle. But this persuasion was far removed from the
belief in a blind and inexorable fate; for Mahomet held the
progress of events in the divine hand to be amenable to the
influence of prayer. He was not slow to attribute the conversion of a scoffer like Omar, or the removal of an impending misfortune (as when Medîna was delivered from the
Confederated hosts), to the effect of his own earnest petitions
to the Lord. On the other hand Mahomet was not altogether
devoid of superstition. He feared to sit down in a dark
place until a lamp had been lighted; and his apprehensions
were sometimes raised by the wind and clouds. He would
fetch prognostications from the manner in which a sword was
drawn from the scabbard. A special virtue was attributed
to being cupped an even number of times, and on a certain
day of the week and month. He was also guided by omens
drawn from dreams: but these may, perhaps, have been regarded by him as intimations of the divine will.

The growth in the mind of Mahomet of the conviction
that he was appointed to be a prophet and a reformer, was
intimately connected with his belief in a special Providence
embracing the spiritual as well as the material world; and
simultaneously with that conviction there arose an implicit

Mahomet's conflict at Mecca: his unwavering steadfastness.

confidence that the Almighty would crown his mission with success.   The questionings and aspirations of his inner soul were regarded by him as proceeding directly from God; the light which gradually illuminated his mind with a knowledge of the divine unity and perfections, and of the duties and destiny of man,—light amidst gross darkness,—must have emanated from the same source; and He who in his own good pleasure had thus begun the work would surely carry it through to a successful ending.   What was Mahomet himself but an instrument in the hand of the great Worker?   It was this belief which strengthened him, alone and unsupported, to brave for many weary years the taunts and persecutions of a whole people.   In estimating the signal moral courage thus displayed, it must not be overlooked that for what is ordinarily termed *physical* courage Mahomet was not remarkable.   It may be doubted whether he ever engaged personally in active conflict on the battle-field; though he accompanied his forces, he never himself led them into action, or exposed his person to avoidable danger.   And there were occasions on which (as when challenged by Abdallah to spare the Bani Cainucâa, alarmed by the altercation at the wells of Moraisî, or pressed by the mob at Jierrâna) he showed symptoms of a faint heart.   Yet even if this be admitted, it brings out in still higher relief the singular display of moral daring.   Let us for a moment look back to the period when a ban was proclaimed at Mecca against all citizens, whether professed converts or not, who espoused his cause; when with him these were shut up in the *Sheb* or quarter of Abu Tâlib; and there for three years, without prospect of relief, endured want and hardship.   Steadfast and mighty must have been the motives which enabled him, amidst all this opposition and apparent hopelessness of success, to maintain his principles unshaken.   No sooner was he released from confinement than, despairing of his native city, he went forth to Tâyif and summoned its rulers and inhabitants to repentance; he was solitary and unaided, but he had a message, he said, from his Lord.   On the third day he was driven out of the town with ignominy, blood trickling from wounds inflicted on him by the populace.   He retired to a little distance, and there poured forth his complaint to God: then he returned to Mecca, there to resume the same outwardly hopeless cause, with the same high confidence in its ultimate success. We search in vain through the pages of profane history for a parallel to the struggle in which for thirteen years the Prophet of Arabia, in the face of discouragement and threats, rejection and persecution, retained his faith unwavering, preached repentance, and denounced God's wrath against his godless fellow citizens. Surrounded by a little band of faithful men and women, he met insults, menace, and danger with a lofty and patient trust in the future. And when at last the promise of safety came from a distant quarter, he calmly waited until his followers had all departed, and then disappeared from amongst an ungrateful and rebellious people.

Not less marked was the firm front and unchanging faith in eventual victory, which at Medina bore him through seven years of mortal conflict with his native city; and enabled him, while his influence and authority were yet limited and precarious even in the city of his adoption, to speak and to act in the constant and undoubted expectation of victory.

And at Medina.

From the earliest period of his religious convictions, the idea of ONE great Being who guides with almighty power and wisdom the whole creation, while yet remaining infinitely above it, gained a thorough possession of his mind. Polytheism and idolatry, utterly at variance with this first principle of his faith, were indignantly condemned as levelling the Creator with the creature. On one occasion alone did Mahomet swerve from this position, when he admitted that the goddesses of Mecca might be adored as a medium of approach to God. But the inconsistency was soon perceived; and Mahomet at once retraced his steps. Never before nor afterwards did the Prophet deviate from the stern denunciation of idolatry.

Denunciation of polytheism and idolatry.

As he was himself the subject of convictions thus deep and powerful, it will readily be conceived that his exhortations were distinguished by a corresponding strength and cogency. Being a master too of eloquence, his language was cast in the purest and most persuasive style of Arabian oratory. His fine poetical genius exhausted the imagery of nature in the illustration of spiritual truths; and a vivid imagination enabled him to bring before his auditory the Resurrection and the Day of judgment, the joys of believers in Paradise, and the agonies of lost spirits in Hell, as close and impend-

Earnestness and honesty of Mahomet at Mecca.

ing realities. In ordinary address, his speech was slow, distinct, and emphatic ; but when he preached ' his eye would
redden, his voice rise high and loud, and his whole frame
become agitated with passion, even as if he were warning the
people of an enemy about to fall on them the next morning
or that very night.' In this thorough earnestness lay the
secret of his success. And if these stirring appeals had been
given forth as nothing more than what they really were, the
outgoings of a warm and active conviction, they would have
afforded no ground for cavil ; or, yet a step further, let him
have represented his appeals as the teaching of a soul guided
by natural inspiration, or even enlightened by divine influence,—such a course would not have differed materially
from that trodden by many a sincere, though it may be
erring, philanthropist in other ages and other lands. But, in
the development of his system, the claims of Mahomet to
inspiration far transcended any one of these assumptions.
His inspiration was essentially *oracular*. The Prophet himself was but the passive organ which received and transmitted a heavenly message. His revelations were not the fruit
of a subjective process in which a soul burning with divine
life and truth, seeks to impress the stamp of its own convictions on those around ; the process, on the contrary, was one
which Mahomet professed to be entirely external to himself,
and independent of his own reasoning, affections, and will.
The words of inspiration, whether purporting to be a portion
of the Corân or a simple message of direction, were produced as a real and objective intimation, conveyed immediately from the Almighty or through the angel Gabriel His
messenger. Such was the position assumed by Mahomet.
How far this conviction was fostered by epileptic or supernatural paroxysms (which do not, however, come prominently
to view at least in the later stages of his career) or by
cognate physiological phenomena, it is impossible to determine. We may readily admit that at the first Mahomet did
believe, or persuaded himself to believe, that his revelations
were dictated by a divine agency. In the Meccan period of
his life there certainly can be traced no personal ends or
unworthy motives belying this conclusion. Mahomet there
was nothing more than he professed to be, ' a simple
Preacher and a Warner ; ' he was the despised and rejected

prophet of a gainsaying people; and he had apparently no ulterior object but their reformation. He may have mistaken the right means for effecting this end, but there is no sufficient reason for doubting that he used those means in good faith and with an honest purpose.

But the scene changes altogether at Medîna. There the acquisition of temporal power, aggrandisement, and self-glorification mingled rapidly with the grand object of the Prophet's life; and they were sought after and attained by precisely the same instrumentality. Messages from heaven were freely brought down to justify political conduct, in precisely the same manner as to inculcate religious precept. Battles were fought, executions inflicted, and territories annexed, under pretext of the Almighty's sanction. Nay, even grosser actions were not only excused but encouraged by the divine approval or command. A special license was produced, allowing Mahomet a double number of wives; the discreditable affair with Mary the Coptic slave was justified in a separate Sura; and the passion for the wife of his own adopted son and bosom friend, was the subject of an inspired message in which the Prophet's scruples were rebuked by God, a divorce permitted, and marriage with the object of his unhallowed desires enjoined! If we say that such 'revelations' were believed by Mahomet sincerely to bear the divine sanction, it can be but in a modified and peculiar sense. He was not only responsible for that belief, but, in arriving at any such conviction, must have done violence to his judgment and the better principles of his nature.

At Medîna worldly motives mingle with spiritual objects.

As the necessary result of this moral obliquity, we trace from the period of Mahomet's arrival at Medîna a marked and rapid declension in the system he inculcated. Intolerance quickly took the place of freedom; force, of persuasion. The spiritual weapons designed at first for higher objects were no sooner prostituted to the purposes of temporal authority, than temporal authority was employed to impart a fictitious weight and power to those spiritual weapons. The name of the Almighty, impiously borrowed, imparted a terrible strength to the sword of the State; and the sword of the State yielded a willing return by destroying 'the enemies of God' and sacrificing them at the shrine of the new religion. 'Slay the unbelievers wheresoever ye find

Rapid moral declension the natural consequence.

them,' was now the watchword of Islâm. 'Fight in the ways of God until opposition be crushed and the Religion becometh the Lord's alone!' The warm and earnest devotion breathed by the Prophet and his followers at Mecca, soon became at Medîna dull and vapid; it degenerated into a fierce fanaticism, or evaporated in a lifeless round of cold and formal ceremonies. The Jewish faith, whose pure fountains were freely accessible to Mahomet, as well as the less familiar system of Christianity, were both, in spite of former protestations of faith and allegiance, cast aside without hesitation and without enquiry; for the course on which he had now entered was too profitable and too enticing to permit the exercise of any such nice research or close questioning as (perhaps he unconsciously felt) might have opened his eyes to the truth, and forced him either to retrace his steps, or to unveil himself before his own conscience in the dreadful form of an impostor. To what other conclusion can we come than that he was delivered over to the judicial blindness of a self-deceived heart; that, having voluntarily shut his eyes against the light, he was left miserably to grope in the darkness of his own choosing?

Benefits of Mahometanism;

And what have been the effects of the system which, established by such instrumentality, Mahomet has left behind him? We may freely concede that it banished for ever many of the darker elements of superstition for ages shrouding the Peninsula. Idolatry vanished before the battle-cry of Islâm; the doctrine of the unity and infinite perfections of God, and of a special all-pervading Providence, became a living principle in the hearts and lives of the followers of Mahomet, even as in his own. An absolute surrender and submission to the divine will (the idea conveyed by the very name of *Islâm*) was demanded as the first requirement of the religion. Nor are social virtues wanting. Brotherly love is inculcated towards all within the circle of the faith; infanticide is proscribed; orphans are to be protected, and slaves treated with consideration; intoxicating drinks are prohibited, and Mahometanism may boast of a degree of temperance unknown to any other creed.

Outweighed by its evils.

Yet these benefits have been purchased at a costly price. Setting aside considerations of minor import, three radical evils flow from the faith in all ages and in every country, and must continue to flow *so long as the Corân is the standard of belief.* FIRST : Polygamy, Divorce, and Slavery are maintained and perpetuated; striking at the root of public morals, poisoning domestic life, and disorganising society. SECOND : freedom of thought and private judgment in religion are crushed and annihilated. The sword still is and must remain the inevitable penalty for the renunciation of Islâm. Toleration is unknown. THIRD : a barrier has been interposed against the reception of Christianity. They labour under a miserable delusion who suppose that Mahometanism paves the way for a purer faith. No system could have been devised with more consummate skill for shutting out the nations over which it has sway from the light of truth. *Idolatrous* Arabia (judging from the analogy of other nations) might have been aroused to spiritual life, and to the adoption of the faith of Jesus; *Mahometan* Arabia is, to the human eye, sealed against the benign influences of the Gospel. Many a flourishing land in Africa and in Asia which once rejoiced in the light and liberty of Christianity, is now overspread by gross darkness and barbarism. It is as if their day of grace had come and gone, and there remained to them ' no more sacrifice for sins.' That a brighter day will yet dawn on these countries we may not doubt; but the history of the past and the condition of the present is not the less true and sad. The sword of Mahomet, and the Corân, are the most stubborn enemies of Civilisation, Liberty, and Truth, which the world has yet known.

In conclusion, I would warn the reader against seeking to portray to himself a character in all its parts consistent, as that of Mahomet. On the contrary, the strangest inconsistencies were blended (according to the wont of human nature) throughout his life. The student of history will trace for himself how the pure and lofty aspirations of Mahomet were first tinged, and then gradually debased, by a half unconscious self-deception; and how in this process truth merged into falsehood, sincerity into guile. The reader will observe that simultaneously with the anxious desire to extinguish idolatry and to promote religion and virtue in the world, there was fostered by the Prophet, in his own heart, a licentious self-indulgence; till in the end, assuming to be the favourite of Heaven, he justified himself by ' revelations'

Inconsistencies run through character of Mahomet.

from God in flagrant breaches of morality. He will remark that while Mahomet cherished a kind and tender disposition, 'weeping with them that weep' and binding to
his person the hearts of his followers by the ready and self-
sacrificing offices of love and friendship, he could yet take
pleasure in cruel and perfidious assassination, could gloat
over the massacre of an entire tribe, and savagely consign
the innocent babe to the fires of hell. Inconsistencies such
as these continually present themselves from the period of
Mahomet's arrival at Medîna; and it is by the study of them
that his character must be rightly apprehended. The key to
many such difficulties may be found, I believe, in the chapter
'on the belief of Mahomet in his own inspiration.' When
once he had dared to forge the name of the Most High God
as the seal and authority of his own words and actions, the
germ was laid from which the errors of his after life were
freely and fatally developed.

Conclusion.   MAHOMET and the CORÂN, the author of Islâm and the
instrument by which he achieved success, are themes worthy
the earnest attention of mankind. If I have at all succeeded in contributing some fresh materials towards the
formation of a correct judgment of either, many hours of
study, snatched not without difficulty from engrossing avoca-
tions, will have secured an ample recompense.

SUPPLEMENT TO CHAPTER XXXVII.

DESCRIPTION OF MAHOMET FROM THE BIOGRAPHY OF WÀCKIDY'S SECRETARY.

IN this appendix I place before the reader a selection from the traditions embodied by the Secretary of Wâckidy in the Section of his work on the person and character of Mahomet. They will, I trust, prove interesting in themselves, as well as illustrate the style of the Prophet's biographers.

Description of Mahomet in the Old Testament and the Gospel.— Mahomet was thus foretold: ' O Prophet! We have sent thee to be a Witness and a Preacher of good tidings, and a Warner, and a Defender of the Gentiles. Thou art my servant and my messenger. I have called thee *Al Mutawakkil* (he that trusteth in the Lord). He shall not be one that doeth iniquity, nor one that crieth aloud in the streets; he shall not recompense evil for evil, but he shall be one that passeth over and forgiveth. His kingdom shall be Syria. Mahomet is my elected servant; he shall not be severe nor cruel. I shall not take him away by death, till he make straight the crooked religion; and till the people say, *There is no God but the Lord alone.* He shall open the eyes of the blind, and the ears of the deaf, and the covered hearts.'

These are evident perversions of passages in Isaiah xlii. and lxi. In one set of traditions Ayesha represents them as prophecies from *the Gospel*, in ignorance apparently that they are quoted there (Matt. xii. 18) as applying to Jesus.

His disposition.—When Ayesha was questioned about Mahomet she used to say: ' He was a man just such as yourselves; he laughed often and smiled much.' *But how would he occupy himself at home?* ' Even as any of you occupy yourselves. He would mend his clothes, and cobble his shoes. He used to help me in my household duties; but what he did oftenest was to sew. If he had the choice between two matters, he would choose the easiest, so as that no sin accrued therefrom. He never took revenge excepting where the honour of God was concerned. When angry with any person he would say, " *What hath taken such a one that he should soil his forehead in the mud!* " '

Side notes:
Extracts from the Secretary of Wàckidy.

Prophecies regarding Mahomet.

His disposition.

His humility was shown by his riding upon asses, by his accepting the invitation even of slaves, and when mounted by his taking another behind him. He would say: 'I sit at meals as a servant doeth, and I eat like a servant: for I really am a servant;' and he would sit as one that was always ready to rise. He discouraged (supererogatory) fasting, and works of mortification. When seated with his followers, he would remain long silent at a time. In the Mosque at Medîna, they used to repeat pieces of poetry, and tell stories regarding the incidents that occurred in the 'days of ignorance,' and laugh; and Mahomet, listening to them, would smile at what they said.

Mahomet hated nothing more than lying; and whenever he knew that any of his followers had erred in this respect, he would hold himself aloof from them until he was assured of their repentance.

His speech.

His manner of speech.—He did not speak rapidly, running his words into one another, but enunciated each syllable distinctly, so that what he said was imprinted in the memory of every one who heard him. When at public prayers, it might be known from a distance that he was reading by the motion of his beard. He never read in a singing or chanting style; but he would draw out his voice, resting at certain places. Thus, in the prefatory words of a Sura, he would pause after *bismillâhi*, after *al Rahmân*, and again after *al Rahîm*.

Gait.

His walking.—One says that at a funeral he saw Mahomet walking, and remarked to a friend how rapidly he moved along; it seemed as if he 'were doubling up the ground.' He used to walk so rapidly that the people half ran behind him, and could hardly keep up with him.

Habits in eating.

His eating.—He never ate reclining, for Gabriel had told him that such was the manner of kings; nor had he ever two men to walk behind him. He used to eat with his thumb and his two forefingers; and when he had done he would lick them, beginning with the middle one. When offered by Gabriel the valley of Mecca full of gold, he preferred to forego it; saying, that when he was hungry he would come before the Lord lowly, and when full, with praise.

Moderation.

Excellence of his Morals.—A servant maid being once long in returning from an errand, Mahomet was annoyed and said: 'If it were not for the law of retaliation, I should have punished you with this toothpick' (*i.e.* with an inappreciably light punishment).

Customs at prayer.

Mahomet at Prayers.—He used to stand for such a length of time at prayer that his legs would swell. When remonstrated with, he said : 'What ! Shall I not behave as a thankful servant should?' He never yawned at prayer. When he sneezed he did so with a subdued voice, covering his face. At funerals he never rode: he would remain silent on such occasions, as if conversing with himself, so that the people used to think he was holding communication with the dead.

While he accepted presents, he refused to use anything that had been offered as alms; neither would he allow any one in his family to use what had been brought as alms; 'for,' said he, 'alms are the impurity of mankind' (*i.e.* that which cleanses their impurity). His scruples on this point were so strong, that he would not eat even a date picked up on the road, lest perchance it might have dropped from a tithe load. One day, little Hasan was playing by his grandfather when a basketful of dates was brought in; on enquiry, Mahomet found that they were tithes, and ordered them to be taken away and given to the poor Refugees. But Hasan, having taken up one to play with, had put it in his mouth; the Prophet, seeing this, opened the boy's mouth, and pulled it out, saying, 'the family of Mahomet may not eat of the tithes.' Refusal to make personal use of the tithes.

Food which he relished.—Mahomet had a special liking for sweetmeats and honey. A tailor once invited him to his house and placed before him barley bread, with stale suet; there was also a pumpkin in the dish; now Mahomet greatly relished the pumpkin. His servant Anas used to say as he looked at the pumpkin: 'Dear little plant, how the Prophet loved thee!' He was also fond of cucumbers and of undried dates. Food relished.

When a lamb or a kid was being cooked, Mahomet would go to the pot, take out the shoulder and eat it. Abu Râfi tells us: 'I once slew a kid and dressed it. The Prophet asked me for the forequarter and I gave it to him. "*Give me another,*" he said; and I gave him the second. Then he asked for a third. "O Prophet!" I replied, "there are but two forequarters to a kid." "*Nay,*" said Mahomet, "*hadst thou remained silent, thou wouldst have handed to me as many forequarters as I asked for.*"'

He used to eat moist dates and cooked food together. What he most relished was a mess of bread cooked with meat, and a dish of dates dressed with butter and milk. When he ate fresh dates he would keep the bad dates in his hand. One asked on a certain occasion that he would give him the dates so rejected. '*Not so,*' he answered; '*what I do not like for myself, I do not like to give to thee.*' Once a tray of fresh dates was brought to him; he sat down on his knees, and taking them up by handfuls, sent a handful to each of his wives; then taking another handful, he ate it himself. He kept throwing the stones on his left side, and the domestic fowls came and ate them up.

Mahomet used to have sweet (rain) water kept for his use.

Food dis- liked.

Food which he disliked.—On Mahomet's first arrival at Medîna, Abu Ayûb used to send him portions of baked food. On one occasion the dinner was returned uneaten, without even the marks of the Prophet's fingers. On being asked the reason, he explained that he had refrained from the dish because of the onions that were in it, for the angel which visited him disliked onions; but others he said might freely eat of them. So also as to garlic; he would never allow it to pass his lips; '*for*,' said he, '*I have in- tercourse with one* (meaning Gabriel) *with whom ye have not.*' He disliked flour made of almonds, saying that it was 'spendthrift's food.' He would never partake of the large lizard, for he thought it might have been the beast into which a party of the children of Israel were changed; but he said there was no harm in others eating it.

When drinking milk Mahomet once said, 'When a man eateth let him pray thus: *O Lord! grant Thy blessing upon this, and feed me with better than this!* But to whomsoever the Lord giveth milk to drink, let him say: *O Lord! grant Thy blessing upon this, and vouchsafe unto me an increase thereof;* for there is no other thing which combineth both food and drink save milk alone.'

Women and scents.

Mahomet's fondness for women and scents.—A great array of traditions are produced to prove that the Prophet liked these of all things in the world the best.

Ayesha used to say: 'The Prophet loved three things— women, scents, and food; he had his heart's desire of the two first, but not of the last.' In respect to scents, traditions have been already quoted in the Supplement to Chapter XVII.

Straitened means at Medîna.

Narrowness of his means at Medîna.—A long chapter is de- voted to this subject, containing many such traditions as the fol- lowing. Fâtima once brought Mahomet a piece of bread; it was the first that had passed his lips for three days. Ayesha tells us that for months together Mahomet did not get a full meal. 'Months used to pass,' she says again, 'and no fire would be lighted in Mahomet's house either for baking bread or cooking meat. *How then did ye live?* By the "two black things" (dates and water), and by what the citizens used to send unto us; the Lord requite them! Such of them as had milch cattle would send us a little milk. The Prophet never enjoyed the luxury of two kinds of food the same day; if he had flesh there was nothing else; and so if he had dates; so likewise if he had bread. We possessed no sieves, but used to bruise the grain and blow off the husks. One night Abu Bakr sent Mahomet the leg of a kid. Ayesha held it while the Prophet cut off a piece for himself in the dark ; and in his turn the Prophet held it while Ayesha cut off a piece for herself. " *What*," exclaimed the listeners, " *and ye ate without a lamp !* " " Yea," replied Ayesha ; "had we possessed oil for a lamp, think ye not that we should have lighted it for our food ? " '

Abu Hureira explains the scarcity thus : ' It arose,' he says, ' from the great number of Mahomet's visitors and guests ; for he never sat down to food but there were some followers with him. Even the conquest of Kheibar did not put an end to the scarcity ; because Medîna has an intractable soil, which is ordinarily cultivated for dates only, the staple food of its inhabitants. There did not exist in the country means of support sufficient for the greatly increased population. Its fruits were the commonest products of the soil, which want little water ; and such water as was needed the people used to carry on their backs, for in these days they had few camels. One year, moreover, a disease (premature shedding) smote the palms, and the harvest failed. It is true that a dish used to be sent for the Prophet's table from the house of Sád ibn Obâda, every day until his death, and also in the same manner by other Citizens ; and the Refugees used to aid likewise ; but the claims upon the Prophet increased greatly, from the number of his wives and dependents.'

l have repeatedly noticed these opinions, and have attributed them to the frugal habits of Mahomet compared with the sudden growth of wealth and splendour in the Caliphate. The products of the surrounding country were no doubt at first inadequate to the wants of the great numbers who flocked with Mahomet to Medîna. But it is evident that although Mahomet, in the early years of the Hegira, may have been reduced to common fare, he could hardly have ever suffered *want*, especially with so many devoted followers about him. It was the vivid contrast between the luxury prevalent in the days when tradition was growing up, and the simple life of Mahomet, which mainly gave rise to these ideas. Thus Abd al Rahmân, when in after years he used to fare sumptuously on fine bread and every variety of meats, would weep while looking at his richly furnished table and thinking of the Prophet's straitened fare. Another upbraids his comrade who could not live without bread made of the finest flour : ' What !' said he ; ' the Prophet of the Lord, to the last hour of his life, never had two full meals on the same day, of bread and of oil ; and behold thou and thy fellows vainly luxuriate on the delicacies of this life, as if ye were children ! '

Appear-
ance,
habits, &c. *On Mahomet's personal appearance and habits.*—The chief traditions on this head have been embodied in the text. The following are of a more special character.

He used to wear two garments. His *izâr* (under-garment) hung down three or four inches below his knees. His mantle was not wrapped round him so as to cover his body, but he would draw the end of it under his shoulder.

He used to divide his time into three parts: one was given to God, the second allotted to his family, the third to himself. When public business began to press upon him he gave up one half of the latter portion to the service of others.

When he pointed he did so with his whole hand; and when he was astonished he turned his hand over (with the palm upwards). In speaking with another, he brought his hand near to the person addressed; and he would strike the palm of the left, on the thumb of the right, hand. Angry, he would avert his face; joyful, he would look downwards. He often smiled, and, when he laughed, his teeth used to appear white as hailstones.

In the interval allotted to others, he received all that came to him, listened to their representations, and occupied himself in disposing of their business and in hearing what they had to tell him. He would say on such occasions: 'Let those that are here give information regarding that which passeth to them that are absent; and they that cannot themselves appear to make known their necessities, let others report them to me in their stead; the Lord will establish the feet of such in the day of judgment.'

Seal of
prophecy. *The seal of prophecy on the back of Mahomet.*—This, says one, was a protuberance on the Prophet's back of the size and appearance of a pigeon's egg. Abdallah ibn Sarjas describes it as having been as large as his closed fist, with moles round about it. Abu Ramtha, whose family were skilled in surgery, offered to remove it, but Mahomet refused, saying: '*The Physician thereof is He who placed it where it is.*' According to another tradition, Mahomet said to Abu Ramtha: '*Come hither and touch my back;*' which Abu Ramtha did, drawing his fingers over the prophetical seal, and behold (says he) there was a collection of hairs upon the spot.

I have not noticed this 'Seal' in the body of the work, because it is so surrounded with supernatural tales that it is extremely difficult even to conjecture what it really was. It is said to have been the *divine* seal which, according to the predictions of the Scriptures, marked Mahomet as the last of the Prophets. How far Mahomet himself encouraged this idea it is

impossible to say.   From the traditions quoted above, it would
seem to have been nothing more than a mole of unusual size;
and the saying of Mahomet that ' God had placed it there ' was
probably the germ of the supernatural associations which grew
up concerning it.   Had the Prophet really attributed any divine
virtue to this mole, he would have spoken very differently to one
who offered to lance or remove it.

On his hair.—It reached, a follower tell us, to his shoulders;   Hair.
according to another to the tip of his ears.   His hair used to
be combed; it was neither curling nor smooth.   He had, says
one, four curled locks.   His hair was ordinarily parted, but
he did not care if it was not so.   According to another tradition, ' The Jews and Christians used to let their hair fall down,
while the heathen parted it.   Now Mahomet loved to follow the
people of the Book in matters concerning which he had no
express command.   So he used to let down his hair without
parting it.   Subsequently, however, he fell into the habit of
parting it.'

On his being cupped.—Some of the many traditions on this   Cupping.
head have been quoted elsewhere.   It was a cure which Gabriel
directed him to make use of.   He had the blood buried lest the
dogs should get at it.   On one occasion Mahomet having fainted
after being cupped, an Arab is said to have gone back from the
profession of Islâm; (because the bodily weakness so exhibited
was inconsistent with the prophetic office?)

On his moustache.—Mahomet used to clip his moustache.   A   Moustache.
Magian once came to him and said: ' You ought to clip your beard
and allow your moustaches to grow.'   ' Nay,' said the Prophet,
' for my Lord hath commanded me to clip the moustaches and
allow the beard to grow.'

On his dress.—Various traditions are quoted on the different   Dress.
colours he used to wear,—white chiefly, but also red, yellow, and
green.   He sometimes put on woollen clothes.   Ayesha, it is
said, exhibited a piece of woollen stuff in which she swore that
Mahomet died.   She adds that he once had a black woollen
dress; and she still remembered, as she spoke, the contrast between the Prophet's fair skin, and the black cloth.   ' The odour
of it, however, becoming unpleasant, he cast it off,—for he loved
sweet odours.'

He entered Mecca on the taking of the city (some say) with
a black turban.   He had also a black standard.   The end of his
turban used to hang down between his shoulders.   He once
received the present of a scarf for a turban, which had a figured
or spotted fringe; and this he cut off before wearing it.   He was

very fond of striped Yemen stuffs. He used to wrap his turban many times round his head, and 'the lower edge of it used to appear like the soiled clothes of an oil-dealer.'

He once prayed in a silken dress, and then cast it aside with abhorrence, saying: '*Such stuff it doth not become the pious to wear.*' On another occasion, as he prayed in a figured or spotted mantle, the spots attracted his notice; when he had ended he said: '*Take away that mantle, for verily it hath distracted me in my prayers, and bring me a common one.*' His sleeve ended at the wrist. The robes in which he was in the habit of receiving embassies, and his fine Hadhramaut mantle, remained with the Caliphs; when worn or rent these garments were mended with fresh cloth; and in after times the Caliphs used to wear them at the festivals. When he put on new clothes (either an under-garment, a girdle, or a turban) the Prophet would offer up a prayer such as this: 'Praise be to the Lord who hath clothed me with that which shall hide my nakedness and adorn me while I live. I pray Thee for the good that is in this, and the good that hath been made for it; and I seek refuge from the evil that is in the same, and from the evil that hath been made for it.'

Mahomet had a piece of tanned leather which was ordinarily spread for him in the Mosque to pray upon. He had also a mat of palm-fibre for the same purpose: this was always taken, after the public prayers, into his wives' apartments for him to use there.

Golden ring.

On his golden ring.—Mahomet had a ring made of gold; he used to wear it, with the stone inwards, on his right hand. The people began to follow his example and make rings of gold for themselves. Thereupon the Prophet, ascending the pulpit, sat down and, taking off the ring, said: '*By the Lord, I will not wear this ring ever again;*' so saying, he threw it from him. And all the people did likewise. According to another tradition, he cast it away because it had distracted his attention when preaching; or, again, because the people were attracted by it. He then pro-hibited the use altogether of golden signet rings.

Silver ring.

On his silver ring.—The purport of these traditions will be noticed in the appendix.

Shoes.

On his shoes.—His servant, Anas, had charge of his shoes and of his water-pot. After his master's death Anas used to show his shoes. They were after the Hadhramaut pattern, with two thongs. In the year 100 or 110 A.H., one went to buy shoes at Mecca, and tells us that the shoemaker offered to make them exactly after the model of Mahomet's, which he said he had seen in the possession of Fâtima, granddaughter of Abbâs. His shoes used to be cobbled. He was in the habit of praying with his shoes on. On one occasion, having taken them off at prayers, all the people did likewise; but Mahomet told them there was no necessity, for he had merely taken off his own because Gabriel had apprised him that there was some dirty substance attaching to them (cleanliness being required in all the surroundings at prayer). The thongs of his shoes once broke and they mended them for him by adding a new piece; after the service Mahomet desired his shoes to be taken away and the thongs restored as they were; for,' said he, 'I was distracted at prayer thereby.'

On his tooth-picks.—Ayesha tells us that Mahomet never lay down, by night or by day, but on waking he applied the tooth-pick to his teeth before he performed ablution. He used it so much as to wear away his gums. The tooth-pick was always placed conveniently for him at night, so that, when he got up in the night to pray, he might use it before his lustrations. One says that he saw him with the tooth-pick in his mouth, and that he kept saying *áâ, áâ*, as if about to vomit. His tooth-picks were made of the green wood of the palm-tree. He never travelled without one.

His articles of toilet.—I have noticed these in the Supplement to Chapter XVII. He very frequently oiled his hair, poured water on his beard, and applied antimony to his eyes.

His armour.—Four Sections are devoted to the description of Mahomet's armour,—his swords, coats of mail, shields, lances, and bows.

The Prophet used to snuff *simsim* (sesamum), and wash his hands in a decoction of the wild plum-tree. When he was afraid of forgetting anything, he would tie a thread on his finger or his ring.

On his horses, &c.—The first horse which Mahomet ever possessed was one he purchased of the Bani Fazâra, for ten owckeas (ounces of silver); and he called its name *Sakb* (running water), from the easiness of its paces. Mahomet was mounted on it at the battle of Ohod, when there was but one other horse from Medîna on the field. He had also a horse called *Sabáha*: he raced it and it won, and he was greatly rejoiced thereat. He had a third horse named *Murtajis* (neigher).

When the white mule arrived from Muckoukas, Mahomet sent it to his wife Omm Salma; and she gave some wool and palm-fibre, of which they made a rope and halter. Then the Prophet brought forth a garment, doubled it fourfold, and throwing it over the back of the beast, straightway mounted it, with one of his followers behind him. This mule survived till the reign of Muâvia. Farwah (the Syrian governor said to have died a martyr) sent the Prophet a mule called *Fizza*, and he gave it to Abu

Marginal notes: Tooth-picks. Articles of toilet. Armour. Miscellaneous. Horses.

N N

Bakr; also an ass, which died on the march back from the Farewell pilgrimage. He had another ass called *Yáfûr*. Ali was anxious to breed a mule similar to that of Mahomet; but Mahomet told him that 'no one would propose so unnatural a cross save he who lacked knowledge.'

Riding camels.

His riding camels.—Besides Al Caswa, Mahomet had a camel called Adhba, which in speed outstripped all others. Yet one day an Arab passed it when at its fleetest pace. The Moslems were chagrined at this; but Mahomet reproved them, saying: 'It is the property of the Lord, that whensoever men exalt anything, or seek to exalt it, then the Lord putteth down the same.'

Milch camels.

His milch camels.—Mahomet had twenty milch camels, the same that were plundered at Al Ghâba. Their milk was for the support of his family: every evening they gave two large skinsful. Omm Salma relates: 'Our chief food when we lived with Mahomet was milk. The camels used to be brought from Al Ghâba every evening. I had one called Arîs, and Ayesha one called Al Samra. The herdman fed them at Al Jûania, and brought them to our homes in the evening. There was also one for Mahomet.

Hind and Asma, two herdmen, used to feed them, one day at Ohod, the other at Himna. They beat down leaves from the wild trees for them, and on these the camels fed during the night. They were milked for the guests of the Prophet, and his family got what was over. If the evening drew in and the camels' milk was late in being brought, Mahomet would say: 'The Lord make thirsty him who maketh thirsty the family of Mahomet at night.'

Milch flocks.

His milch flocks.—Mahomet had seven goats which Omm Ayman used to tend (this probably refers to an early period of his residence at Medîna). His flocks grazed at Ohod and Himna alternately, and were brought back to the house of that wife whose turn it was for Mahomet to be in her abode. A favourite goat having died, the Prophet desired its skin to be tanned.

Mahomet attached a peculiar blessing to the possession of goats. 'There is no house,' he would say, 'possessing a goat, but a blessing abideth thereon; and there is no house possessing three goats, but the angels pass the night there praying for its inmates until the morning.'

Servants.

Mahomet's servants.—Fourteen or fifteen persons are mentioned who served the Prophet at various times. His slaves he always freed.

Houses.

The houses of his wives.—Abdallah ibn Yazîd relates that he saw the houses in which the wives of the Prophet dwelt, at the time when Omar ibn al Azîz governor of Medîna (about A.H. 100) demolished them. They were built of unburnt bricks, and had separate apartments made of palm-branches, daubed (or built up) with mud: he counted nine houses, each having separate apartments, in the space extending from the house of Ayesha and the gate of Mahomet to the house of Asma daughter of Hosein. Observing the dwelling-place of Omm Salma, he questioned her grandson concerning it; and he told him that when the Prophet was absent on the expedition to Dûma, Omm Salma built up an addition to her house with a wall of unburnt bricks. When Mahomet returned, he went in to her and asked what new building this was. She replied: 'I purposed, O Prophet, to shut out the glances of men thereby!' Mahomet answered: 'O Omm Salma! verily, the most unprofitable thing that eateth up the wealth of a Believer is building.' A citizen of Medîna, present at the time, confirmed this account, and added that the curtains (anglo-indice, *purdas*) of the doors were of black hair-cloth. He was present, he said, when the despatch of the Caliph Abd Al Malîk (A.H. 86–88) was read aloud, commanding that these houses should be brought within the area of the Mosque, and he never witnessed sorer weeping than there was amongst the people that day. One exclaimed: 'I wish, by the Lord! that they would leave these houses alone thus as they are; then would those that spring up hereafter in Medîna, and strangers from the ends of the earth, come and see what kind of building sufficed for the Prophet's own abode, and the sight thereof would deter men from extravagance and pride.'

There were four houses of unburnt bricks, the apartments being of palm-branches; and five houses made of palm-branches built up with mud and without any separate apartments. Each was three Arabian yards in length. Some say that they had leather curtains for the doors. One could reach the roof with the hand.

The house of Hâritha was next to that of Mahomet. Now whenever Mahomet took to himself a new wife, he added another house to the row, and Hâritha was obliged successively to remove his house, and to build on the space beyond. At last this was repeated so often that the Prophet said to those about him: 'Verily, it shameth me to turn Hâritha over and over again out of his house.'

Mahomet's private property.—There were seven gardens which Properties. Mukheiríck the Jew left to Mahomet. Omar ibn al Azîz, the Caliph, said that, when governor of Medîna, he ate of the fruit of these, and never tasted sweeter dates. Others say that these gardens formed a portion of the confiscated estates of the Bani Nadhîr. They were afterwards dedicated perpetually to pious purposes.

Mukheirîck is said to have been a learned Jewish priest and a leader of the Cainucâa, who 'recognised Mahomet by his marks, and identified him as the promised Prophet.' But the love of his own religion prevailed, so that he did not openly join Islâm. Nevertheless, on the day of Ohod he put on his armour, notwithstanding it was the Sabbath day, and went forth with the Moslems and was killed. His corpse was found and was buried near the Moslems; but he was not prayed over, nor did Mahomet beg mercy for his soul then or afterwards; the utmost he would say of him was, '*Mukheirîck, the best of the Jews!*' He had large possessions in groves and gardens, and left them all to Mahomet.

Mahomet had three other properties:—

I. The confiscated lands of the Bani Nadhîr. The produce of these was appropriated to his own wants. One of the plots was called *Mashruba Omm Ibrahîm*, the 'summer garden of (Mary) the mother of Ibrahîm,' where the Prophet used to visit her.

II. Fadak; the fruits of this were reserved as a fund for indigent travellers.

III. The fifth share, and the lands received by capitulation, in Kheibar. This was divided into three parts. Two were devoted for the benefit of the Moslems generally (*i.e.* for State purposes); the proceeds of the third, Mahomet assigned for the support of his own family; and what remained over he added to the fund for the use of the Moslems.

Wells.   *The wells from which Mahomet drank.*—A variety of wells are enumerated out of which Mahomet drank, and on which he invoked a blessing, spitting into them. One night as he sat by the brink of the well called Gharsh, he said: 'Verily, I am sitting beside one of the fountains of Paradise.' He praised its water above that of all other wells, and not only drank of it but bathed in it. He also drank from the fountain of Budháa, taking up the water in both his hands and sipping it. He would send the sick to bathe in this fountain, 'and when they had bathed, it used to be as if they were loosed from their bonds.'

The well called Ruma belonged to a man of the Bani Mozeina. Mahomet said that it would be a meritorious deed if any one were to buy this well and make it free to the public. Othmân, hearing this, purchased the well for 400 dinars, and attached a pulley to it. Mahomet, again happening to pass the well, was apprised of what Othmân had done. He prayed the Lord to grant him a reward in Paradise, and calling for a bucket of water he drank therefrom, and praised the water, saying that it was both cold and sweet.

APPENDIX.

———•◇•———

SOURCES FOR THE BIOGRAPHY OF MAHOMET.
THE CORAN AND TRADITION.

CONFIDENCE in a narrative must vary with the medium through which it has been transmitted. The exploits of Hercules carry less conviction than the feats of the heroes of Troy ; while, again, the wanderings of Ulysses and the adventures of the early founders of Rome, are regarded with incomparably less trust than the history of the Peloponnesian war or the fortunes of Julius Cæsar. Thus there are three great divisions of ancient narrative. Legendary tales are based upon ideal materials, and it is doubtful whether they shadow forth facts or only myths and notions. Tradition and the rhapsodies of bards, have for their object actual or supposed events ; but the impression of these events is liable to become distorted from the imperfection of the vehicle which conveys them to posterity. It is to contemporary history alone, or to history deriving its facts from contemporary records, that we accord a reliance which, proportioned to the means and the fidelity of the observer who recorded the events, may rise to absolute certainty. *(Ancient story either legendary, traditional, or contemporary.)*

The narrative which we now possess of the origin of Islâm does not belong exclusively to any one of these classes. It is *legendary*, for it contains multitudes of wild myths, such as the ' Light of Mahomet,' and the Cleansing of his Heart. It is *traditional*, since the main material of the story was handed down by oral recitation not recorded until Islâm had attained to a full growth. But it possesses also some of the elements of *History*, because there are certain contemporary records of undoubted authenticity, to which we can still refer. Moreover, Moslem tradition is of a peculiar and systematic character, and in some respects carries an authority superior to that of common tradition. *(Evidence of rise of Islâm belongs to all three classes.)*

From such imperfect and incoherent materials it might be supposed difficult, if not impossible, to frame a uniform and consistent account of the Arabian Prophet, the various points of which shall be supported by sufficient evidence or probability. It will be my attempt to elucidate this topic; to enquire into the available sources for such a narrative; and the degree of credit to which they are severally entitled.

Sources specified.

We have two main treasuries from which may be drawn materials for tracing the life of Mahomet and the rise of Islâm. These are the CORÂN, and TRADITION. Two minor classes may be added, namely, contemporary documents, and Arab poetry; but these have been, for the most part, transmitted also by Tradition, and may with propriety be treated as coming under the same head.

Value, absolute and comparative.

What dependence, then, can be placed on these sources? What is their individual merit as furnishing historical evidence, and what their comparative value in relation to each other? The solution of these questions will form the subject of this essay.

CORÂN. In what manner preserved during Mahomet's life-time.

The CORÂN consists exclusively of the revelations or commands which Mahomet professed, from time to time, to receive through Gabriel, as a message direct from God; and which, under an alleged divine direction, he delivered to those about him.[1] At the moment of inspiration or shortly after, each passage was recited by Mahomet before the friends or followers who happened to be present, and was generally committed to writing by some one amongst them, at the time or afterwards, upon palm-leaves, leather, stones, or such other rude material as conveniently came to hand.[2] These divine messages continued throughout the three-

---

[1] According to the strict Mahometan doctrine every syllable of the Corân is of divine origin. Some of the wild rhapsodical Suras first composed by Mahomet (as the 91st, 100th, 102nd, and 103rd) do not bear marks of having been so intended. But when Mahomet's die was cast of assuming the Most High as the speaker of his revelations, then these earlier Suras also came to be regarded as emanating directly from the Deity. Hence Mahometans rigidly include *every word* of the Corân, at whatever stage delivered, in the category of 'Thus saith the Lord.' And it is one of their arguments against our Scriptures, that they are not exclusively oracles from the mouth, and spoken in the person, of God.

[2] In the latter part of his career, the Prophet had many Arabic amanuenses; some of them occasional as Ali and Othmân; others official as Zeid ibn Thâbit, who learned Hebrew expressly to conduct as Secretary such business as Mahomet had in that language. In Wâckidi's collection of despatches, the several amanuenses are named, and they amount to fourteen. Some say there were four-and-twenty followers whom Mahomet used more or less as scribes; others as many as forty-two. In his early Meccan life, he could not have had these facilities; but even then Khadîja, Waraca, Ali, or Abu Bakr, who could all read, might have recorded his revelations. At Medîna, Obey ibn Kâb is mentioned as one who used to record the inspired recitations of Mahomet.

and-twenty years of his prophetical life, so that the last portion did not appear till near the time of his death. The canon was then closed; but the contents during the Prophet's life-time were never as a whole systematically arranged or even collected together. We have no certain knowledge how the originals were preserved. That there did not exist any special depository for them, is evident from the mode in which, after Mahomet's death, the various fragments had to be sought for. Much of the Corân possessed only a temporary interest, arising out of circumstances which soon ceased to be important; and it is doubtful whether the Prophet intended passages of this nature to be used for public or private worship, or to be maintained at all in currency. Such portions it is little likely he would take pains to preserve. Whether he retained under his own eye and custody the more important parts, we have no indication; perhaps he regarded them as sufficiently safe in the current copies, guarded by the almost miraculous tenacity of the Arab memory. The later, and the more important, revelations were probably left with the scribes who recorded them, or laid up in the habitation of some one of the Prophet's wives.[1] However this may have been, it is very certain that, when Mahomet died, there was nowhere any deposit of the complete series of original transcripts, and it may be questioned whether the *original* or first transcripts themselves were then generally in existence.

But the preservation of the Corân during the life-time of Mahomet was not dependent on any such uncertain archives. The divine revelation was the corner-stone of Islâm. The recital of a passage from it formed an essential part of daily prayer public and private; and its perusal and repetition were enforced as a duty and a privilege fraught with religious merit. This is the universal voice of early tradition, and may be gathered also from the revelation itself. The Corân was accordingly committed to memory more or less by *every* adherent of Islâm, and the extent

Committed to memory by early Moslems;

Another, Abdallah ibn Sád, was excepted from the Meccan amnesty, because he is said to have falsified revelations dictated to him by the Prophet.

It is also evident that the revelations were recorded, because they are called throughout the Corân *Kitâb*, *i.e.* 'the Writing,' 'Scriptures.' The name *Corân* signifies simply 'recitation,' and does not necessarily imply a written original.

[1] If the originals were retained by Mahomet, they must needs have been in the custody of one of his wives; since at Medina the Prophet had no special house of his own, but dwelt by turns in the abode of each of his wives. As Omar committed his exemplar to the keeping of his daughter Haphsa, one of the widows of Mahomet, this may have been done in imitation of the Prophet's own practice. The statement made by Sale that the fragmentary revelations were cast promiscuously into a chest, is not borne out by any good authority that I have met with.

to which it could be recited was one of the chief distinctions of nobility in the early Moslem empire.[1] The custom of Arabia favoured the task. Passionately fond of poetry, yet possessed of but limited means and skill in committing to writing the effusions of their bards, the Arabs had long been habituated to imprint these, as well as the tradition of genealogical and other tribal events, on the living tablets of their hearts. The recollective faculty was thus cultivated to the highest pitch; and it was applied, with all the ardour of an awakened spirit, to the Corân. Such was the tenacity of their memory, and so great their power of application, that several of Mahomet's followers, according to early tradition, could, during his life-time, repeat with scrupulous accuracy the entire revelation.[2]

But not in any fixed order of parts.

We are not, however, to assume that the entire Corân was at this period repeated in any fixed order. The present compilation, indeed, is held by the Moslems to follow the arrangement pre-scribed by Mahomet; and early tradition might appear to imply some known sequence.[3] But this cannot be admitted; for had any fixed order been observed or sanctioned by the Prophet, it would unquestionably have been preserved in the subsequent collection. Now the Corân, as handed down to our time, follows

[1] Thus among a heap of warrior martyrs, he who had been the most versed in the Corân was honoured with the first burial. The person who in any company could most faithfully repeat the Corân, was of right entitled to be the *Imâm*. or conductor of the public prayers (a post ordinarily implying also temporal command) and to pecuniary rewards. Thus after the usual distribu-tion of the spoils taken on the field of Cadesia, A.H. 14, the residue was divided among those who knew most of the Corân.

[2] Four or five such persons are named; and several others also who could very nearly repeat the whole before Mahomet's death.

[3] Thus we read of certain Companions. who could repeat the whole Corân in a *given time*, which might be held to imply some usual connection of the parts; but the original tradition may have intended such portions only as were commonly used by Mahomet in public worship, and these may have followed, both in copying and repetition from memory, some understood order; or the tradition may refer to a later period when the order had been fixed by means of Omar's compilation. There was no fixed order observed (as in the regular course of 'Lessons' in Christian worship) in the portions of the Corân recited at the public prayers. The selection of a passage was dependent on the will and choice of the Imâm. Thus Abu Hureira one day took credit to himself for remembering which Sura the Prophet had read the day before; and on urgent occasions we hear of a short Sura being used. It is only in *private* recitals that the whole, or large portions, of the Corân are said to have been recited consecutively.

The common idea of the Mahometans that the Corân was fixed by Mahomet as we have it now, originates in the tradition that Gabriel had an annual recitation of the whole Corân with the Prophet, as well as in the desire to augment the authority of the book as it now stands.

in the disposition of its several parts no intelligible arrangement whatever, either of subject or time; and it is inconceivable that Mahomet should have enjoined its recital invariably in this order. We must even doubt whether the number of the Suras, or chapters, was determined by Mahomet as we now have them.[1] The internal sequence at any rate of the contents of the several Suras cannot, in most cases, have been that which was enforced by the Prophet. The constant chaotic mingling of subjects, disjoined as well by chronology as by the sense; a portion produced at Medîna sometimes immediately preceding a passage revealed long before at Mecca; a command placed directly after a later one which cancels or modifies it; or an argument suddenly disturbed by the interjection of a sentence foreign to its purport; all this forbids us to believe that the present, or indeed any complete, arrangement was in use during Mahomet's life-time.

On the other hand, there is no reason to doubt that several at least of the Suras are precisely the same, both in matter and order, as Mahomet left them;[2] and that the remainder, though often resembling a mosaic of various material rudely dovetailed

Fragments from which Corân was compiled, are exactly as Maho-

---

[1] But there is reason to believe that the chief of the Suras, including all the passages in most common use, were fixed and known by a name or distinctive mark. Some of them are spoken of, in early and well authenticated traditions, as having been referred to by Mahomet himself. Thus he recalled his followers from Medîna, at the discomfiture of Honein, by shouting to them as 'the men of the *Sura Bacr* ' (*i.e.* Sura ii.).

Several persons are stated by tradition to have learnt by heart a *certain number of Suras* in Mahomet's life-time. Thus Abdallah ibn Masûd learned seventy Suras from the Prophet's own mouth, and Mahomet on his death-bed repeated seventy Suras, 'among which were the Seven long ones.' These traditions signify a recognised division of at least some part of the revelation into Suras, if not a usual order in repeating the Suras themselves.

The liturgical use of the Suras by Mahomet, must no doubt have in some measure fixed their form, and probably also their sequence. But I fail to follow Sprenger in his conclusions as to 'double' Suras, and Suras 'in groups' (*mathâni* and *natzâir*).

[2] Where whole Suras were revealed at once, this would naturally be the case; but short passages were often given out in driblets, and even single verses, as occasion required. With regard to these, it is asserted in some traditions that Mahomet used to direct his amanuensis to enter them ' in the Sura which treated of such and such a subject.' This, if an authentic tradition (and it is probably founded on fact), would indicate that Mahomet intended the Corân to be arranged according to its matter, and not chronologically.

There are also several Suras which from the unity of subject, or from the form of composition, are evidently complete and integral. Such are the history of Joseph, Sura xii.; and the psalm descriptive of Paradise, Sura lv., quoted at p. 81.

The traditions just cited as to the number of Suras which some of the Companions could repeat, and which Mahomet himself repeated on his death-bed, imply the existence of such Suras in a complete and finished form.

met com-
posed th€m.

together, is yet composed of genuine fragments, generally of considerable length, and each for the most part following the connection in which it was recited at the public prayers, and committed to memory or to paper from the mouth of the Prophet by his followers.[1] The irregular interposition and orderless disposal of the smaller fragments have indeed frequently destroyed the sequence, and produced a perplexing confusion. Still, the fact remains, that the fragments themselves were strictly and exclusively Mahomet's own composition, and were learned or recorded under his instructions ; and this fact stamps the Corân, not merely as formed out of the Prophet's *words* and *sentences*, but to a large extent as his in relation to the *context* likewise.

Ability to write common among early Moslems both of Mecca and Medina.

However retentive the Arab memory, we should still have regarded with distrust a transcript made entirely from that source. But there is good reason for believing that many fragmentary copies, embracing amongst them the whole Corân, or nearly the whole, were made by Mahomet's followers during his life. Writing was without doubt generally known at Mecca long before Mahomet assumed the prophetical office. Many of his followers are expressly mentioned as employed by the Prophet at Medîna in writing his letters or despatches. And, though himself delighting in the title of the ' illiterate Prophet,' and abstaining by necessity or design from the use of penmanship, he by no means looked with a jealous eye upon the art. Some of the poorer Meccan captives taken at Bedr were offered their release on condition that they would teach a certain number of the ignorant citizens of Medîna to write. And although the people of Medîna were not so generally educated as those of Mecca, yet many are distinctly noticed as having been able to write before Islâm.[2] The ability thus existing, it may be safely inferred that the verses which were so indefatigably committed to memory, would be likewise committed carefully to writing.

Transcripts of portions of Corân

We also know that when a tribe first joined Islâm, Mahomet was in the habit of deputing one or more of his followers to teach

---

[1] Anecdotes are told of some who in reciting the Corân were in the habit of omitting, especially when tired, passages from the similar termination of the verses ; and of others who, having been guilty of such omission, could spontaneously correct themselves. (*Homoioteleuta* are of very frequent recurrence in the Corân, from the rhythm of the verses being often formed by the repetition of common-place phrases at their close, such as the attributes of ·God, &c.) These anecdotes certainly suppose a settled order of the parts repeated ; and though the period referred to is subsequent to Mahomet's death, yet the habit of such connected repetition was most probably formed during his life-time, and before the collection into one volume.

[2] Thus, to cite one of a score of instances, Wâckidi says that ' Abu Abbâs used to write Arabic before the rise of Islâm, while as yet writing was rare among the Arabs.'

them the Corân and the requirements of the faith. We are frequently informed that they carried *written* instructions with them on the latter point, and they would naturally provide themselves also with transcripts of the more important parts of the Revelation, especially those upon which the ceremonies of Islâm were founded, and such as were usually recited at the public prayers. Besides the reference in the Corân to its own existence in a written form, we have express mention made in the authentic traditions of Omar's conversion, of a copy of the 20th Sura being used by his sister's family for social and private devotional reading.[1] This refers to a period preceding, by three or four years, the emigration to Medîna. If transcripts of the revelations were made, and in common use, at that early time when the followers of Islâm were few and oppressed, it is certain that they must have multiplied exceedingly when the Prophet came to power, and his Book formed the law of the greater part of Arabia.

common among early Moslems;

But such transcripts were (like the portions committed to memory) mere fragments compiled, if compiled at all, with little or no connection of subject and date. The Suras chiefly used in public worship, or the most favourite for private perusal and recitation, would be those of which the greatest number of copies existed. Transcripts of the earliest Suras, and of those of evanescent interest, if extant at all, would be few in number.

But incomplete and fragmentary.

Such was the condition of the text of the Corân during Mahomet's life-time, and such it remained for about a year after his death, imprinted upon the hearts of his people, and fragmentary transcripts increasing daily. The two sources would correspond closely with each other; for the Corân, even while the Prophet was yet alive, was regarded with a superstitious awe as containing the very words of God; so that any variations would be reconciled by a direct reference to Mahomet himself,[2] and after his death to the originals where they existed, or copies from the same, and to the memory of the Prophet's confidential friends and amanuenses.

State of Corân up to the year after Mahomet's death.

It was not till the overthrow of Moseilama, when a great carnage took place amongst the Moslems at Yemâma, and large numbers of the best reciters of the Corân were slain, that a misgiving arose in Omar's mind as to the uncertainty which would be experienced regarding the text, when all those who had received it from the original source, and thence stored it in their

Corân collected, A.H. XI. by Zeid; his text authoritative during Caliphates

---

[1] 'The Corân, . . . none shall touch the same, excepting such as are clean.' This is from an early Meccan Sura, and the passage was referred to by the sister of Omar when at his conversion he desired to take her copy of Sura xx. into his hands.

[2] We meet with instances of such references in case of doubt to Mahomet made by Omar, Abdallah ibn Masûd, and Obey ibn Káb.

memories, should have passed away. 'I fear,' said he, addressing the Caliph Abu Bakr, 'that slaughter may again wax hot
amongst the reciters of the Corân, in other fields of battle; and
that much may be lost therefrom. Now, therefore, my advice is,
that thou shouldest give speedy orders for the collection of the
Corân.' Abu Bakr agreed, and thus made known his wishes to
Zeid ibn Thâbit, a citizen of Medîna, and the Prophet's chief
amanuensis: 'Thou art a young man, and wise; against whom
no one amongst us can cast an imputation; and thou wert wont
to write down the inspired revelations of the Prophet of the
Lord. Wherefore now search out the Corân, and bring it together.' So new and unexpected was the enterprise that Zeid at
first shrank from it, and doubted the propriety, or even lawful-
ness, of attempting that which Mahomet had neither himself done
nor commanded to be done. At last he yielded to the joint
entreaties of Abu Bakr and Omar, and seeking out the fragments
of the Corân from every quarter, 'gathered it together, from date-
leaves, and tablets of white stone, and from the breasts of men.'[1]
By the labours of Zeid, these scattered and confused materials
were reduced to the order and sequence in which we now find
them, and in which it is said that Zeid used to repeat the Corân
in the presence of Mahomet. The original copy prepared by
Zeid was probably kept by Abu Bakr during the short remainder
of his reign. It then came into the possession of Omar who (probably following Mahomet's example) committed it to the custody
of his daughter Haphsa, the Prophet's widow. The compilation
of Zeid, as embodied in this exemplar, continued during Omar's
ten years' Caliphate to be the standard and authoritative text.

Recension
in Oth-
mân's Cali-
phate
(some time
after A.H.
33;)

But variety of expression either prevailed in the previous
transcripts and modes of recitation, or soon crept into the copies
which were made from Zeid's edition. Mussulmans were scandalised. The Corân sent down from heaven was ONE, but
where was now its unity? Hodzeifa, who had warred both
in Armenia and Adzerbâijan and had observed the different
readings of the Syrians and of the men of Irâc, alarmed at the
number and extent of the variations, warned Othmân to interpose, and 'stop the people, before they should differ regarding
their Scripture, as did the Jews and Christians.' The Caliph
was persuaded, and to remedy the evil had recourse again to

---

[1] Other traditions add, fragments of parchment or paper, pieces of leather,
and the shoulder and rib bones of camels and goats. Leather was frequently
used for writing, and many of Mahomet's treaties and letters were recorded on
it. There is a curious tradition regarding a man who used a leather letter,
received from Mahomet, for the purpose of mending his bucket, and whose
family were thence called the 'children of the *cobbler*.'

Zeid, with whom he associated a syndicate of three Coreish. The original copy of the first edition was obtained from Haphsa's depository, the various readings were sought out from the different provinces, and a careful recension of the whole set on foot. In case of difference between Zeid and his coadjutors, the voice of the latter, as conclusive of the Coreishite idiom, was to preponderate; and the new collation was thus assimilated exclusively to the Meccan dialect, in which the Prophet had given utterance to his inspiration.[1] Transcripts were multiplied and forwarded to the chief cities in the empire, and the previously existing copies were all, by the Caliph's command, committed to the flames. The old original was returned to Haphsa's custody.

The recension of Othmân has been handed down to us unaltered. So carefully, indeed, has it been preserved, that there are no variations of importance—we might almost say no variations at all—among the innumerable copies of the Corân scattered throughout the vast bounds of the empire of Islâm. Contending and embittered factions, taking their rise in the murder of Othmân himself within a quarter of a century from the death of Mahomet, have ever since rent the Mahometan world. Yet but ONE CORÂN has been current amongst them; and the consentaneous use by them all in every age up to the present day of the same Scripture, is an irrefragable proof that we have now before us the very text prepared by command of the unfortunate Caliph.[2]

Remains unaltered to the present day.

[1] It is one of the maxims of the Moslem world, supported perhaps by the revelation itself (Sura xi. 2), that the Corân is incorruptible, and that it is preserved from error and variety of reading by the miraculous interposition of God himself. In order, therefore, to escape the scandal and inconsistency of the transaction here detailed, it is held that the Corân, as to its external form, was revealed in seven dialects of the Arabic tongue.

[2] The Moslems would have us believe that some of the *self-same copies,* penned by Othmân or by his order, are still in existence. The copy which the Caliph held in his hand when he was murdered, is said to have been preserved in the village of Antartus. Others hold that leaves of it were treasured up in the grand Mosque of Cordova, and Edrisi describes the ceremonies with which they were treated; they were finally transferred to Fez or Telemsan. Ibn Batûta, when in the fourteenth century he visited Basra, declares that this MS. was then in its Mosque, and that the marks of the Caliph's blood were still visible at the words, ' God shall avenge thee against them' (Sura ii. v. 138). [Tradition states that the unfortunate Caliph's blood did run down to these words.] Other of Othmân's originals are said to be preserved in Egypt, Morocco, and Damascus; as well as at Mecca and Medîna. The Medina copy, it is said, has a note at the end, relating that it was compiled by the injunctions of Othmân; and the compilers' names are also given. But it appears very unlikely that any of Othmân's copies can have escaped the innumerable changes of dynasty and party to which every part of the Moslem world has been subjected. Any very ancient copy would come to be called that of Othmân.

There is probably in the world no other work which has remained twelve centuries with so pure a text. The various readings are wonderfully few in number, and are chiefly confined to differences in the vowel points and diacritical signs. But these marks were invented at a later date. They did not exist at all in the early copies, and can hardly be said to affect the text of Othmân.[1]

I. Was Othmân's text a faithful reproduction of Abu Bakr's edition ?

Since, then, we possess the undoubted text of Othmân's recension, it remains to be enquired whether that text was an honest reproduction of Abu Bakr's edition, with the simple reconcilement of unimportant variations. There is the fullest ground for believing that it was so. No early or trustworthy traditions throw suspicion upon Othmân of tampering with the Corân in order to support his own claims. The Sheeahs of later times, indeed, pretend that Othmân left out certain Suras or passages which favoured Ali. But this is incredible. He could not possibly have done so without being observed at the time ; and it cannot be imagined that Ali and his followers (not to mention the whole body of the Mussulmans who fondly regarded the Corân as the word of God) would have permitted such a proceeding.

Reasons for believing that it was so.

In support of this position, the following arguments may be adduced. *First* : When Othmân's edition was prepared, no open breach had taken place between the Omeyads and the Alyites. The unity of Islâm was still complete and unthreatened. Ali's pretensions were as yet undeveloped. No sufficient object can, therefore, be assigned for the perpetration by Othmân of an offence which Moslems regard as one of the blackest dye. *Second* : On the other hand, Ali, from the very commencement of Othmân's reign, had an influential party of adherents, strong enough in the end to depose the Caliph, to storm his palace in the heart of Medîna, and to put an end to his life. Can we conceive that these men would have remained quiet, when the very evidence of their leader's superior claims was being openly expunged from the book of God ? *Third* : At the time of the recension, there were still multitudes alive who had the Corân, as originally

---

[1] There are, however, instances of variation in the letters themselves, and these not confined to difference in the dots, but extending sometimes to the *form* of the letters also ; but these too are immaterial. This almost incredible· purity of text, in a book so widely scattered over the world, and continually copied by people of different tongues and lands, is without doubt owing mainly to Othmân's recension and the official promulgation and maintenance of his edition. To countenance a various reading was an offence against the State, and punished. We need not wonder that, when such means were resorted to, perfect uniformity of text has been maintained. To compare (as the Moslems are. fond of doing) their pure text with the various readings of our Scriptures, is to compare things between which there is no analogy.

delivered, by heart; and cf the supposed passages favouring Ali
—had any ever existed—there would have been numerous transcripts in the hands of his family and followers.   Both of these
sources must have proved an effectual check upon any attempt at
suppression. *Fourth*: The party of Ali shortly after assumed
an independent attitude, and he himself succeeded to the Caliphate.   Is it conceivable that either Ali, or his party, when thus
arrived at power, would have tolerated a mutilated Corân—mutilated expressly to destroy his claims?   Yet we find that they
used the same Corân as their opponents, and raised no shadow of
an objection against it.[1]   The insurgents are indeed said to have
made it one of their complaints against Othmân that he had
caused a new edition to be made, and had committed the old
copies of the sacred volume to the flames; but these proceedings
were objected to simply as unauthorised and sacrilegious.   No
hint was dropped of alteration or omission.   Such a supposition,
palpably absurd at the time, is altogether an after-thought of the
modern Sheeas.

We may then safely conclude that Othman's recension was,
what it professed to be, namely, the reproduction of Abu Bakr's
edition, with a more perfect conformity to the dialect of Mecca,
and possibly a more uniform arrangement of the component parts
—but still a faithful reproduction.   The most important question
yet remains, viz., *Whether Abu Bakr's edition was itself an authentic and complete collection of Mahomet's Revelations.*   The following considerations warrant the belief that it was authentic and
in the main as complete as at the time was possible.

First.—We have no reason to doubt that Abu Bakr was a
sincere follower of Mahomet, and an earnest believer in the divine
origin of the Corân.   His faithful attachment to the Prophet's
person, conspicuous for the last twenty years of his life, and his
simple, consistent, and unambitious deportment as Caliph, admit

[Margin: II. Was Abu Bakr's edition a faithful copy of Mahomet's revelations?]

[Margin: Reasons for believing that it was so. First.—Sincerity and faith of]

[1] So far from objecting to Othmân's revision, Ali multiplied copies of the
edition.   Among other MSS. supposed to have been written by Ali, one is said
to have been preserved at Meshed Ali as late as the fourteenth century, which
bore his signature.   Some leaves of the Corân, said to have been copied by
him, are now in the Lahore *Tosho-Khâna*; others in the same repository are
ascribed to the pen of his son, Husein.   Without leaning upon such uncertain
evidence, it is sufficient for our argument that copies of Othmân's Corân were
notoriously *used and multiplied by Ali's partisans*, and have been so used and
multiplied to the present day.   Ali was moreover deeply versed in the Corân,
and his memory (if tradition be true) would amply have sufficed of itself to
detect, if not to restore, any passage that had been tampered with.   Ali said of
himself: 'There is not a verse in the Corân, of which I do not know the
matter, the parties to whom it refers, and the place and time of its revelation,
whether by night or by day, whether in the plains or upon the mountains.'

Abu Bakr
and early
Moslems. no other supposition. Firmly believing the revelations of his friend to be the revelations of God himself, his first object would be to secure a pure and complete transcript of them. A similar argument applies with almost equal force to Omar and the other agents in the revision. The great mass of Mussulmans were undoubtedly sincere in their belief. From the scribes themselves, employed in the compilation, down to the humblest Believer who brought his little store of writing on stones or palm-leaves, all would be influenced by the same earnest desire to reproduce the very words which their Prophet had declared as his message from the Lord. And a similar guarantee existed in the feelings of the people at large, in whose soul no principle was more deeply rooted than an awful reverence for the supposed word of God. The Corân itself contains frequent denunciations against those who should presume to 'fabricate anything in the name of the Lord,' or conceal any part of that which He had revealed. Such an action, represented as the very worst description of crime, we cannot believe that the first Moslems, in the early ardour of their faith and love, would have dared to contemplate.

Second.—Corân, as delivered by Mahomet, yet fresh in memory of his followers.

Second.—The compilation was made within two years of Mahomet's death. We have seen that several of his followers had the entire revelation (excepting perhaps some obsolete fragments) by heart; that *every* Moslem treasured up more or less some portions in his memory; and that there were official Reciters of it, for public worship and tuition, in all countries to which Islâm extended. These formed a living link between the Revelation fresh from Mahomet's lips. and the edition of it by Zeid. Thus the people were not only sincere and fervent in wishing for a faithful copy of the Corân: they were also in possession of ample means for realising their desire, and for testing the accuracy and completeness of the volume placed in their hands by Abu Bakr.

Third.—It must have corresponded with numerous transcripts in daily use.

Third.—A still greater security would be obtained from the fragmentary transcripts which existed in Mahomet's life-time, and which must have greatly multiplied before the Corân was compiled. These were in the possession, probably, of all who could read. And as we know that the compilation of Abu Bakr came into immediate and unquestioned use, it is reasonable to conclude that it embraced and corresponded with every extant fragment; and *therefore*, by common consent, superseded them. We hear of no fragments, sentences, or words intentionally omitted by the compilers, nor of any that differed from the received edition. Had any such been discoverable, they would undoubtedly have been preserved and noticed in those traditional repositories which treasured up the minutest and most trivial acts and sayings of the Prophet.

Fourth.—The contents and the arrangement of the Corân speak forcibly for its authenticity. All the fragments that could be obtained have, with artless simplicity, been joined together. The patchwork bears no marks of a designing genius or moulding hand. It testifies to the faith and reverence of the compilers, and proves that they dared no more than simply collect the sacred fragments and place them in juxtaposition. Hence the interminable repetitions; the palling reiteration of the same ideas, truths, and doctrines; hence scriptural stories and Arab legends, told over and over again with little verbal variation; hence the pervading want of connection, and the startling chasms between adjacent passages. Again, the frailties of Mahomet, supposed to have been noticed by the Deity, are all with evident faithfulness entered in the Corân. Not less undisguised are the frequent verses contradicted or abrogated by later revelations.[1] The editor plainly contented himself with compiling and copying out in a continuous form, but with scrupulous accuracy, the fragmentary materials within his reach. He neither ventured to select from repeated versions of the same incident, nor to reconcile differences, nor by the alteration of a single letter to connect abrupt transitions of context, nor by tampering with the text to soften discreditable appearances. Thus we possess every internal guarantee of confidence.

But it may be objected,—If the text of Abu Bakr's Corân was pure and universally received, how came it to be so soon corrupted, and to require, in consequence of its variations, an extensive recension? Tradition does not afford sufficient light to determine the cause of these discrepancies. They may have been owing to various readings in the older fragmentary transcripts, which remained in the possession of the people; they may have originated in the diverse dialects of Arabia, and the different modes of pronunciation and orthography; or they may have sprung up naturally in the already vast domains of Islâm, before strict uniformity was officially enforced. It is sufficient for us to know that in Othmân's revision recourse was had to the *original* exemplar of the first compilation, and that there is otherwise every security, internal and external, that we possess a text the same as that which Mahomet himself gave forth and used.

While, however, it is maintained that we now have the Corân

---

[1] Though the convenient doctrine of abrogation is acknowledged in the Corân, yet the Mussulman doctors endeavour as far as possible to explain away such contradictions. Still they are obliged to allow that the Corân contains no fewer than 225 verses cancelled by later ones.

some passages once revealed but subsequently cancelled.

as it was left by Mahomet, there is no ground for asserting that passages, once put forth as inspired, may not at some subsequent period have been changed or withdrawn *by the Prophet himself.* On the contrary, repeated examples of such withdrawal are noticed in tradition; and alterations (although no express instances are given) seem to be clearly implied. The Corân itself recognises the withdrawal of certain passages, after they had been promulgated as a part of the Revelation: ' Whatever verses We cancel, or *cause thee to forget,* We give thee better in their stead, or the like thereof.'

Any passages which Mahomet, thus finding to be inconvenient, or otherwise inexpedient for publication, withdrew from the original transcripts before coming into circulation, will, of course, not be found in our present Corân; nor would an altered passage remain but in its altered form. But this does not in any measure affect the value of the Corân as an exponent of Mahomet's opinions, or at least of the opinions he finally professed to hold; since what we now have, though possibly corrected and modified by himself, is still *his own.*

Nor some obsolete, suppressed, or ephemeral passages.

It is, moreover, not impossible that verses which had been allowed to fall into abeyance and become obsolete, or the suppression of which Mahomet himself desired, may have been sought out by the blind zeal of his followers, and, with pious veneration for everything believed to be the word of God, entered in Zeid's collection. On the other hand, many early passages of ephemeral interest may, without any design on the part of Mahomet, have entirely disappeared in the lapse of time; and, no trace being left, they must necessarily have been omitted from the compilation. But these are mere hypotheses, of which we have no instances.

CONCLUSION. Corân is authentic record of Mahomet's revelations.

The conclusion, which we may now with confidence draw, is that the editions of Abu Bakr and of Othmân were not only faithful, but, so far as the materials went, complete; and that whatever omissions there may have been, were not on the part of the compilers intentional. The real drawback to the inestimable value of the Corân as a contemporary and authentic record of Mahomet's character and actions, is the want of arrangement and connection which pervades it; so that, in enquiring into the meaning and force of a passage, no certain dependence can be placed upon the adjacent sentences as the true context. But, bating this serious defect, we may upon the strongest presumption affirm that every verse in the Corân is the genuine and unaltered composition of Mahomet himself, and conclude with at least a close approximation to the verdict of Von Hammer: *That we hold the*

Corân to be as surely Mahomet's word, as the Mahometans hold it to be the word of God.

The importance of this deduction can hardly be over-estimated. The Corân becomes the ground-work and the test of all enquiries into the origin of Islâm and the character of its founder. Here we have a storehouse of *Mahomet's own words recorded during his life*, extending over the whole course of his public career, and illustrating his religious views, his public acts, and his domestic character. By this standard of his own making we may safely judge his life and actions, for it must represent either what he actually thought, or that which he affected to think. And so true a mirror is the Corân of Mahomet's character, that the saying became proverbial among the early Moslems, *His character is the Corân.* 'Tell me,' was the curious enquiry often put to Ayesha, as well as to Mahomet's other widows, 'tell me something about the Prophet's disposition.' 'Thou hast the Corân,' replied Ayesha; 'art thou not an Arab, and readest the Arabic tongue?' 'Yea, verily.' 'Then why takest thou the trouble to enquire of me? For the Prophet's disposition is no other than the Corân itself.' Of Mahomet's biography the Corân is the key-stone.

Importance of Corân as furnishing contemporary evidence of Mahomet's words and character.

Having gained this firm position, we proceed to enquire into the credibility and authority of the other source of early Mahometan history, viz., TRADITION. This must necessarily form the chief material for the biography of the Prophet. It may be possible to establish from the Corân the outlines and some of the details of his life, but tradition alone enables us to determine their relative position, and to weave them into the tissue of intermediate affairs.

TRADITION, the chief material of early Moslem history,

Mahometan tradition consists of the sayings of the friends and followers of the Prophet, handed down by an alleged chain of narrators to the period when they were collected, recorded, and classified. The process of transmission was for the most part oral. It may be sketched as follows.

Described.

After the death of Mahomet, the main employment of his followers was arms. The pursuit of pleasure, and the formal round of religious observances, filled up the intervals of active life, but afforded scanty exercise for the higher faculties of the mind. The tedium of long and irksome marches, and the lazy period from one campaign to another, fell listlessly upon a simple and semi-barbarous race. These intervals were occupied, and that tedium beguiled, chiefly by calling up the past in familiar conversation or more formal discourse. On what

Habits of the early Moslems favoured growth of tradition.

topic, then, would the early Moslems more enthusiastically descant than on the acts and sayings of that wonderful man who had called them into existence as a conquering nation, and had placed in their hands 'the keys both of this World and of Paradise?'

Lapse of time invested Mahomet with supernatural attributes.

Thus the converse of Mahomet's followers would be much about him. The majesty of his character gained greatness by contemplation; and as time gradually removed him farther from them, the lineaments of the mysterious mortal who was wont to hold familiar intercourse with the messengers of heaven, rose into dimmer but more gigantic proportions. The mind was unconsciously led on to think of him as endowed with supernatural power and surrounded by supernatural agency. Here was the material out of which Tradition grew luxuriantly. When there was at hand no standard of fact whereby these recitals might be tested, the Memory was aided by the unchecked efforts of the Imagination; and as days rolled on imagination gained the ascendency.

Superstitious reverence with which traditions of Companions were regarded by succeeding generation.

Such is the result which the lapse of time would naturally have upon the minds and the narratives of the 'COMPANIONS' of Mahomet—more especially of those who, being young when he died, lived long into the next generation. And then another race sprang up who had never seen the Prophet, who looked up to his contemporaries with a superstitious reverence, and listened to their stories of him as to the tidings of a messenger from the other world. 'Is it possible, father of Abdallah! that thou hast been with Mahomet?' was the question addressed by a pious Moslem to Hodzeifa, in the Mosque of Kufâ; 'didst thou really see the Prophet, and wert thou on terms of familiar intercourse with him?' 'Son of my uncle! it is indeed as thou sayest.' 'And how wert thou wont to behave towards the Prophet?' 'Verily, we used to labour hard to please him.' 'Well, by the Lord!' exclaimed the ardent listener, 'had I been but alive in his time, I would not have allowed him to put his blessed foot upon the earth, but would have borne him on my shoulders wherever he listed.' On another occasion, the youthful Obeida listened to a Companion who was reciting before an assemby how the Prophet's head was shaved at the Pilgrimage, and the hair distributed amongst his followers; the young man's eyes glistened as the speaker proceeded, and he interrupted him with the impatient exclamation: 'Would that I had even a single one of those blessed hairs! I would cherish it for ever, and prize it beyond all the gold and silver in the world.' Such were the natural feelings of fond devotion with which the Prophet came to be regarded by the generation which followed the 'Companions.'

As the tale of the Companions was thus taken up by their followers, distance began to invest it with an increasing charm, while a living faith and warm imagination were fast degenerating into superstitious credulity. This second generation are termed in the language of the patristic lore of Arabia, SUCCESSORS. Here and there a *Companion* survived till near the end of the first century; but, for all practical purposes, they had passed from the stage before the commencement of its last quarter. Their first *Successors*, who were in some measure also their contemporaries, flourished in the latter half of the same century, and some of the older may have survived for a time even in the second.[1]

Successors belong to latter half of first century.

Meanwhile a new cause was at work, which gave to the tales of Mahomet's Companions a fresh and an adventitious importance.

The Arabs, a simple and unsophisticated race, found in the Corân ample provisions for the regulation of their affairs, religious, social, and political. But the aspect of Islâm soon underwent a mighty change. Scarcely was the Prophet buried when his followers issued forth from their barren Peninsula armed with the warrant of the Corân, to impose the faith of Islâm upon all the nations of the earth. Within a century they had, as a first step to universal subjugation, conquered every land that intervenes from the banks of the Oxus to the farthest shores of Northern Africa, and had enrolled the great majority of their peoples under the standard of the Corân. This vast empire differed widely from the Arabia of Mahomet's time; and that which sufficed for the patriarchal simplicity of the early Arabs, was found altogether inadequate for the multiplying wants of their descendants. Crowded cities, like Fostât, Kûfa, and Damascus, required elaborate laws for the guidance of their courts of justice: widening political relations demanded a system of international equity: the speculations of a people before whom Literature was throwing open her arena, and the controversies of eager factions on nice points of doctrine, were impatient of the narrow limits which confined them :—all called loudly for the enlargement of the scanty and naked dogmas of the Corân, and for the development of its rudimental code of ethics.

Wants of expanding empire required enlargement of administrative code of Corân.

---

[1] For practical purposes, the age of the Companions may be limited to the first half or three-quarters of the Seventh century. Thus, supposing a Companion to have reached his sixty-third year in A.D. 674, he would have been only twenty years of age at the Prophet's death, and but ten years of age at the time of the Flight. A margin of ten or twelve additional years may be left for cases of great age and unusual memory.

Corân at first sole authoritative rule of conduct.

And yet by the first principles of Islâm, the standard of Law, Theology, and Politics, was the Corân alone. By it Mahomet himself ruled. To the Corân in his teaching he always referred. From the Corân he professed to derive his opinions, and upon it to ground his decisions. If he, the Messenger of the Lord, and the Founder of the faith, was thus bound by the heavenly Revelation, how much more the Caliphs, his uninspired successors! But new and unforeseen circumstances were continually arising, for which the Corân had made no provision. It no longer sufficed for its original object. How, then, were its deficiencies to be supplied?

Deficiency supplied by SUNNAT, or sayings and practice of Mahomet.

The difficulty was resolved by adopting the CUSTOM or ' SUNNAT ' of Mahomet—that is, his *sayings* and his *practice*—as supplementary of the Corân. The recitals regarding the life of the Prophet now acquired an unlooked-for value. *He* had never held himself infallible, except when directly inspired of God; but this new doctrine assumed that a heavenly and unerring guidance pervaded every word and action of his prophetic life. Tradition was thus invested with the force of law, and with something of the authority of inspiration. It was in great measure owing to the rise of this theory, that, during the first century of Islâm, the cumbrous recitals of tradition so far outstripped the dimensions of reality. The prerogative now claimed for Tradition stimulated the growth of fabricated evidence, and led to the preservation of every kind of story, spurious or real, touching the Prophet. Before the close of the century it had imparted an incredible impulse to the search for traditions, and had in fact given birth to the new profession of *Collectors*. Men devoted their lives to the business. They travelled from city to city, and from tribe to tribe, over the whole Mahometan world; sought out by personal enquiry every vestige of Mahomet's biography yet lingering among the *Companions*, the *Successors*, and their descendants; and committed to writing the tales and reminiscences with which they were wont to edify their wondering and admiring auditors. They also established schools of tradition in all the leading cities, and there held lectures, and recited their Collections of tradition together with the authorities on which they rested. Each circle of pupils took notes from their master's oral delivery; and thus the compilations of the most popular Collectors were preserved and spread abroad.

Legendary tales of strolling storytellers.

I need here only allude to another body of so-called tradition, namely, the legendary tales of the strolling minstrel or storyteller. This personage has always been popular in the East; and in the early days of Islâm he had special opportunities for the exercise of his vocation. As he travelled from city to city and village to village, crowds gathered around, and hung upon his lips while he recited in glowing terms some episode of the Prophet's life, his birth and childhood, the heavenly journey, or the battle of Bedr. Great latitude both in detail and colouring was allowed to these story-tellers, whose object was at once to entertain and edify. Such tales, no doubt, formed the ground-work of the biographical legends so popular all over the Mahometan world. They are still recited on special occasions (as the birth and childhood of Mahomet in the first ten days of Râbi i.); and they form the staple of the modern biographies of the Prophet. It is needless to add that, being utterly uncritical, they are possessed as historical sources of no authority whatever.[1]

It was soon found that the work of collecting and propagating authoritative traditions too closely affected the public interests, and the political aspect of the empire, to be left entirely to private responsibility and individual zeal. About a hundred years after Mahomet, the Caliph Omar II. issued circular orders for the formal collection of all extant tradition. The task thus begun, continued to be vigorously prosecuted; but we possess no authentic remains of any compilation of an earlier date than the middle or end of the second century of the Hegira. Then, indeed, ample materials had been amassed, and they have been handed down to us both in the shape of *Biographies* and of *General collections* which bear upon every imaginable point of Mahomet's character, and detail the minutest incidents of his life.

General collections of biographical tradition.

It thus appears that the traditions we now possess remained generally in an unrecorded form for at least the greater part of a century. It is not indeed asserted that some of Mahomet's sayings may not have been noted down in writing during his life-time, and from that source copied and propagated afterwards. But the evidence in favour of any such record is meagre, suspicious, and contradictory. And few and uncertain as are the statements of any such practice, there was a motive to invent them in the additional credit with which the traditions of a Companion supposed to have committed them to writing, would be invested.

Tradition not recorded till latter part of first century.

It is hardly possible that, if the writing down of Mahomet's sayings had prevailed as a custom during his life, we should not have had frequent intimation of the fact, with notices of the writers, and special references to the nature, contents, and peculiar authority of their records. But no such references or quotations

[1] See Sprenger, i. 341; and for samples of these legends as current at the present time, an article in the *Calcutta Review* on Biographies of Muhammad for India, No. xxxiv., Art. 6.

are anywhere to be found. It cannot be objected that the Arabs trusted so implicitly to their memory that they regarded oral to be as authoritative as recorded narratives, and therefore would not notice the latter; for we see that Omar was afraid lest even the Corân, believed by him to be divine and itself the subject of heavenly care, should become defective if left to the memory of man. Just as little weight, on the other hand, should be allowed to the tradition that Mahomet *prohibited* his followers from noting down his words; though it is not easy to see how these could have gained currency at all, had it been the regular and constant practice of any persons to record his sayings. The truth appears to be that there was at the first no such practice; and that the story of the prohibition, though spurious, embodies the after-thought of serious Mahometans as to what Mahomet *would have said*, had he foreseen the loose and fabricated stories that sprang up, and the danger his people would fall into of allowing *Tradition* to supersede the *Corân*. The evils of Tradition, in truth, were as little thought of as its value was perceived, till many years after Mahomet's death.

Even if recorded memoranda kept in Mahomet's life-time, none can be connected with extant traditions.

But even admitting all that has been advanced, it would prove no more than that *some of the Companions used to keep memoranda* of the Prophet's sayings. Now, unless it were possible to connect any given traditions with such memoranda, the concession would be useless. But it is not, so far as I know, demonstrable of any single tradition or class of traditions now in existence, that they were copied from such memoranda, or have been derived in any way from them. To prove, therefore, that *some* traditions were at first recorded, will not help us to a knowledge of whether any of these still exist, or to discriminate them from such as rest on a purely oral basis. The very most that could be urged from the premises is, that our present collections *may* contain *some* traditions founded upon a recorded original, and handed down in writing; but we are unable to single out any individual tradition as so accredited. The entire mass of extant tradition rests in this respect on the same uncertain ground, and the uncertainty of any one portion (apart from internal evidence of probability) attaches equally to the whole. We cannot, with the least show of likelihood, affirm confidently of any tradition that it was recorded till nearly the end of the first century of the Hegira.

Mahometan tradition not only uncertain, but affected by

We see, then, how entirely Tradition, as now possessed by us, rests its authority on the *memory* of those who handed it down; and how dependent it must have been upon their convictions and their prejudices. For, in addition to the common frailty of

APPENDIX. EFFECT ON TRADITION OF POLITICAL FACTIONS. 569

human recollection rendering unrecorded evidence notoriously bias and prejudice. infirm, and to the errors or exaggerations which always distort a narrative transmitted orally through many witnesses, there exist in Mahometan tradition abundant indications of actual fabrication; and there may everywhere be traced the indirect but not less powerful and dangerous influence of a latent bias, which insensibly gave its colour and its shape to all the stories of their Prophet treasured up in the memories of Believers.

To form an adequate conception of the value and defects of Historical review necessary. Tradition, the nature and extent of these influences must be thoroughly understood; and for this purpose it is necessary that the reader should possess an outline of the political aspect of the empire of Islâm from the death of Mahomet to the period at which our *written* authorities commence. Such an outline I will now endeavour to supply.

Mahomet survived for ten years the era of his *Hegira* or During first two Caliphates, faction unknown. flight to Medîna. The Caliphates of Abu Bakr and Omar occupied the thirteen succeeding years, during which the new-born empire, animated by the one ruling passion of enforcing an universal submission to Islâm, was unbroken by schism. The distorting medium of Faction had not yet interposed betwixt us and Mahomet. The chief tendency to be dreaded in tradition as transmitted through this period, or originating in it, is one which was then perhaps even stronger and more busy than in the approaching days of civil broil, namely, the disposition to exalt the character of Mahomet, and to endow it with super-human attributes.

The weak and vacillating reign of Othmân gave birth to the A.H. 23–35. Effect on tradition of divisions following murder of Othmân;— not unfavourable. conspiracy of Ali and his party, who, by the murder of the aged Prince, caused a fatal rent in the unity of the empire, and left it a prey to contending factions of new competitors for the Caliphate. The immediate effect of this disunion was not unfavourable to the historical value of Tradition. For although each party would be tempted to colour their recollections by their own factious bias, they must still do so in the face of a hostile criticism. And, while as yet there were alive on either side eye-witnesses of the Prophet's actions, both parties would be cautious in advancing what might be liable to dispute, and eager to denounce and expose every false statement of their opponents.[1]

[1] Othmân (when Caliph) commanded, saying: 'It is not permitted to any one to relate a tradition as from the Prophet, which he hath not already heard in the time of Abu Bakr or Omar. And verily nothing hinders me from repeating traditions of the Prophet's sayings (although I be one of those endowed with the most retentive memory amongst all his Companions) but that I have heard him say, *Whoever shall repeat of me that which I have not said, his resting-place*

A.H. 35–40.
Omeyad
Caliphates
favourable
to truthful
tradition.

The Caliphate of Ali, after a troubled and doubtful existence of four-and-a-half years, was terminated by assassination, and the opposing faction of the Omeyads then gained undisputed supremacy. During the protracted sovereignty of this Dynasty, that is for nearly one hundred years, the influence of the ruling power directly opposed the superstitious dogmas of the adherents of Mahomet's more immediate family. The authority of a line which derived its descent from Abu Sofiân, long the grand opponent of the Prophet, may have softened the asperity of Tradition regarding the conduct of their progenitor, while it aided in the chorus of glory to Mahomet. But it would be tempted to none of those distorting fabrications the object of which was to make out a divine right of succession in favour of the uncle or the descendants of the Founder of Islâm; and which, for that end, invested their heroes with virtues, and attributed to them actions, which never had existence. Such in the process of time were the motives, and such was the practice, of the partisans of the houses of Ali and Abbâs, the son-in-law and the uncle of Mahomet. In the early part, however, of the Omeyad succession, these insidious tendencies had but little room for play. The fiction of divine right, even had it been thought of, contradicted too directly the knowledge and convictions of the early Moslems to have met with support. The unqualified opposition of a large section of Mahomet's most intimate friends to Ali himself shows how little ground there was for regarding him as the peculiar favourite of Heaven. The Khârijites, or sectarians of the theocratic principle and the extreme opponents of the Omeyads, went the length of condemning and rejecting Ali for the scandalous crime of parleying with the denounced Muâvia. It is hence evident that the extravagant pretensions of the Alyites and Abbassides were not entertained, or even dreamt of, in the early part of the Omeyad Caliphate.

Type then
cast never
after mate-
rially al-
tered.

During this century the main fabric of Tradition grew up, and assumed permanent shape. Towards its close, all surviving traditions began to be systematically sought out, and publicly put upon record. The type then moulded could not but be maintained, in its chief features at least, ever after. Subsequent sectaries might strive to re-cast it; their efforts could secure but a very partial success, because the only standard they possessed was formed under the influence of the Omeyad princes. In

shall be in Hell.' This tradition, if well founded, gives pretty clear intimation that, even before Othmân's murder, fabricated traditions were propagated by opponents to shake his authority, and that the unfortunate Caliph endeavoured to check the practice by forbidding the currency of traditions not already known in the Caliphates of his two predecessors.

the traditional impress of this period, although the features of the Prophet were magnified into majestic and supernatural dimensions, yet the character of his friends and followers, and the general events of early Islâm, were undoubtedly preserved with very tolerable accuracy, and thus a broad basis of historical truth has been maintained.

But in the latter part of the period now before us, an undercurrent of great volume and intensity commenced to flow. The adherents of the house of Ali, beaten in the field and in all their rebellious attempts to dethrone the Omeyads, were driven to other expedients; and the key-stone of their new machinations was the divine right of the family of the Prophet to both temporal and spiritual rule. They established secret associations, and sent forth emissaries in every direction, to decry the Omeyads as godless usurpers, and to canvass for the Alyite pretender of the day. These claims were ever and anon strengthened by the mysterious report that the divine Imâm of Ali's race was about to step forth from his hidden recess, and stand confessed the Conqueror of the world. Such attempts, however, issued in no more permanent results than a succession of rebellions, massacres, and fruitless civil wars, until another party leagued themselves in the struggle. These were the Abbassides, who desired to raise to the throne some descendant of the Prophet's uncle, Abbâs. They combined with the Alyites in denouncing as usurpers the present dynasty, which, though sprung from the Coreish, was but distantly related to Mahomet. By their united endeavours they at length succeeded in supplanting the Omeyads; when the Alyites found themselves over-reached, and an Abbasside Caliph was raised to the throne.

Alyites and Abbassides conspire to supplant Omeyad line;

It is not difficult to perceive how much Tradition must have been affected by these unwearied conspirators. *Perverted tradition* was, in fact, the chief instrument employed to accomplish their ends. By it they blackened the memory of the forefathers of the Omeyads, and exalted the progenitors of the Abbassides. By it they were enabled almost to deify Ali, and to assert their principle that the right of empire vested solely in the near relatives of the Prophet, and in their descendants. For these ends no device was spared. The Corân was misinterpreted, and tradition falsely coloured, distorted, and fabricated. Their operations were concealed. Studiously avoiding the eye of any one likely to oppose them, they canvassed in the dark. Thus they were safe from criticism; and the stories and glosses of their traditional schools gradually acquired the character of prescriptive evidence.

And for that object fabricate and pervert tradition.

In the 136th year of the Hegira, the Abbassides were installed

Accession of the Abbassides, A.H. 136;

in the Caliphate ; and the factious teaching, which had hitherto flourished only in the distant satrapies of Persia or, when it ventured near the throne, lurked in the purlieus of crowded cities, now stalked forth with the prestige of sovereignty. The Omeyads were persecuted even to extirpation, and their names and descent overwhelmed with obloquy.

Under whom the first biography of Mahomet was compiled.

It was under the auspices of the first two Abbasside Caliphs that the earliest biography of which we have any remains was composed; that, namely, of IBN ISHÂC. It is cause for little wonder that this author followed in the steps of his patrons ; and that, while lauding their ancestors, he sought to stigmatise the Omeyads, and to denounce as miscreants those of their forefathers who acted a prominent part in the first scenes of Islâm.

Intolerant Caliphate of Al Mâmûn. A.H. 198-218

The fifth Caliph from this period was the famous Al Mâmûn, who, during a reign of twenty years, countenanced with princely support the pursuits of literature. He affected a combination with the followers of Ali, who had been bitterly persecuted by his predecessors ; [1] and he adopted with enthusiasm the peculiar teaching of the Motazelites—a sect whom the learned Weil applauds as the *Rationalists* of Islâm. But however freely this Caliph may have derided the doctrine of the eternity of the Corân, and in opposition to orthodox believers asserted the freedom of the human will, he was not a whit less bigoted or intolerant than his predecessors. He not only declared Ali to be the noblest of mortals, and Muâvia the basest, but he denounced and severely punished any one who should venture to speak evil of the one, or attribute good to the other. He made strenuous efforts to impose his theological views upon all. He went so far as to establish even a species of inquisition, and visited with penalties those who dared to differ from him. Unhappily for us, this very reign was the busiest age of the traditional writers, and the period at which (excepting only that of Ibn Ishâc) the earliest extant biographies of Mahomet were composed. It was under Al Mâmûn that WÂCKIDI,

Its baneful influence on tradition.

IBN HISHÂM, and MADAINI, lived and wrote. Justly, indeed, may we grieve over this as a coincidence fraught with evil to the interests of historical truth. 'We look upon it, ' says Weil, ' as a great misfortune, that the very three oldest Arabic histories, which are nearly the only sources of authority for the

---

[1] When the Abbassides reached the throne, they cast aside the Alyite platform from which they had made the fortunate ascent. They were then obliged in self-defence to crush with an iron hand every rising of the Alyites, who found to their cost that they had become the unconscious tools for raising to power a party with whom they had in reality as little fellow-feeling as with the Omeyads. They deserved their fate.

first period of Islâm, were written under the Government of
Mâmûn. At a period when every word in favour of Muâvia
rendered the speaker liable to death, and when all were declared
outlaws who would not acknowledge Ali to be the most distinguished of mankind, it was not possible to compose, with even
the smallest degree of impartiality, a history of the Companions
of Mahomet and of his successors.'

But besides the biographers of Mahomet, the *Collectors of
general tradition*, who likewise flourished at this period, came
within the circle of Abbasside influence, and some of them under
the direct patronage of Al Mâmûn. This class, as shown above,
travelled over the whole empire, and searched after every kind of
tradition which bore the slightest relation to their Prophet. The
mass of narrations gathered by this laborious process was sifted
by a pseudo-critical canon, founded on the general repute of the
narrators who formed the chain from Mahomet downwards ; and
the approved residuum was published under the authority of the
Collector's name. Such collections were far more popular than
the biographical or historical treatises. They formed, in fact,
and still form, the ground-work of the different theological schools
of Islâm ; and, having been used universally and studied continuously from the period of their appearance, exist to the
present day in an authentic and genuine shape. Copies of them
abound in all Moslem countries ; whereas the early biographies
are either not extant at all, or can only be procured with
difficulty.

General collections of tradition made under similar influences.

The six standard *Sunni* collections were compiled exclusively
under the Abbasside Caliphs, and the earliest of them partly
during the reign of Al Mâmûn. The four canonical collections of
the *Sheeahs* were prepared somewhat later, and are incomparably
less trustworthy than the former, because their paramount object
is to build up the divine *Imâmat* or headship of Ali and his
descendants.

Two schools; Sunni, and Sheeah.

That the Collectors of tradition rendered an important
service to Islâm, and even to history, cannot be doubted. The
vast flood of tradition, poured forth from every quarter of the
Moslem empire, and daily gathering volume from innumerable
tributaries, was composed of the most heterogeneous elements ;
without the labours of the traditionists it must soon have formed
a chaotic mass in which truth and error, fact and fable, would
have mingled together in undistinguishable confusion. It is a
legitimate inference from the foregoing sketch, that Tradition in
the second century embraced a large element of truth. That
even respectably derived traditions often contained much that

Service rendered by Collectors.

was exaggerated and fabulous, is an equally fair conclusion. It is proved by the testimony of the Collectors themselves, that thousands and tens of thousands of traditions were current in their times which possessed not even the shadow of authority.

Immense proportion of fictitious matter in current tradition;

The prodigious amount of base and fictitious material may be gathered from the estimate even of Mahometan criticism. To quote again from Dr. Weil : ' Reliance upon oral traditions, at a time when they were transmitted by memory alone, and every day produced new divisions among the professors of Islâm, opened up a wide field for fabrication and distortion. There was nothing easier, when required to defend any religious or political system, than to appeal to an oral tradition of the Prophet. The nature of these so-called traditions, and the manner in which the name of Mahomet was abused to support all possible lies and absurdities, may be gathered most clearly from the fact that Bokhâri, who travelled from land to land to gather from the learned the traditions they had received, came to the conclusion, after many years' sifting, that out of 600,000 traditions, ascertained by him to be then current, only 4,000 were authentic ! And of this selected number, the European critic is compelled, without hesitation, to reject at least one-half.' Similar appears to have been the experience of the other intelligent compilers of the day. Thus Abu Dâûd, out of 500,000 traditions which he is said to have amassed, threw aside 495,200, and retained as trustworthy only 4,800.[1]

Rejected even by Mahometan Collectors.

Anecdote of Bokhâri.

The heavenly vision which induced Bokhâri to commence his pious and herculean task, is sufficiently significant of the urgent necessity which then existed for searching out and preserving the grains of truth scattered here and there amid the chaff. These are his words : ' In a dream I beheld the Messenger of the Lord (Mahomet), from whom I seemed to be driving off the flies. When I awoke I enquired of an interpreter of dreams the meaning of my vision. *It is*, he replied, *that thou shalt drive away lies far from him.* This it was which induced me to compile the *Sahîh.*' And well, indeed, in the eyes of Mahometans, did he fulfil the heavenly behest; for, to this day, the SAHÎH BOKHÂRI is regarded by them as one of the most authentic treasuries of tradition.

Collectors, though unsparing in rejection of

It is evident, then, that some species of criticism was practised by the Compilers ; and that, too, so unsparingly that out of every hundred traditions on an average ninety-nine were

_____

[1] Even of this number a portion is spoken of as doubtful. ' I wrote down,' says Abu Dâûd, ' five hundred thousand traditions respecting the Prophet, from which I selected those, to the number of four thousand eight hundred, contained in this book. I have entered herein the authentic, *those which seem to be authentic, and those which are nearly so.*'

rejected. But the European reader will be grievously deceived if he at all regards such criticism, rigorous as it was, in the light of a sound and discriminating investigation into the credibility of the traditional elements. It was not the *subject-matter* of a tradition, but simply the *names* attached thereto, which decided the question of credit. Its authority must rest on some Companion of the Prophet, and on the character of each individual in the long chain of witnesses through whom it was handed down.[1] If these were unimpeachable, the tradition *must be received*. No inherent improbability, however glaring, could exclude a narration thus attested from its place in the authentic collections. The compilers would not venture upon the open sea of criticism, but steered slavishly by this single miserable canon. They dared not enquire into internal evidence. To have arraigned the motives of the first author or subsequent rehearsers of a story, discussed its probability, and brought it to the test of historical evidence, would have been a strange and uncongenial task. The spirit of Islâm would not brook free enquiry and real criticism. The blind faith of Mahomet and his followers spurned the aids of investigation and of evidence. *Thus saith the Prophet of the Lord*, and every rising doubt must be smothered, every question vanish. If doubts did arise, and questions were entertained, by any rash philosopher, the sword was unsheathed to dispel and silence them. The temporal power was so closely welded with the dogmas of Islâm, that it had no option but to enforce with a stern front and iron hand an implicit acquiescence in those dogmas. Upon the apostate Moslem the sentence of death—an award resting on the Prophet's authority—was rigorously executed by the civil power; and between the heterodoxy of the free-thinker, and the lapse of the renegade, there existed but a vague and narrow boundary. To the combination, or rather the *unity*, of the spiritual and political elements in the unvarying type of Mahometan government, must be attributed that utter absence of candid and free investigation into the origin and truth of Islâm, which so painfully characterises the Moslem mind even to the present day. The faculty of criticism has been annihilated by the sword.

untrustworthy traditions, did not discriminate by any intelligent canon;

Political element of Islâm extinguished free enquiry and real criticism.

Upon the other hand, there is no reason to doubt that the Collectors were sincere and honest in doing that which they professed to do. It may well be admitted that they sought out in good faith all traditions actually current, enquired carefully

But they were honest in accomplishing what they professed.

---

[1] Out of 40,000 men, who are said to have been instrumental in handing down Tradition, Bokhâri and Muslim acknowledged the authority of only 2,000 by receiving their traditions. Later collectors were far less scrupulous.

into the authorities on which they rested, and recorded them with scrupulous accuracy. The sanctions of religion were at hand to enforce diligence and caution. Thus Bokhâri, who, as we have just seen, commenced his work at a supposed divine monition, was heard to say ' that he never inserted a tradition in his *Sahîh*, until he had made an ablution, and offered up a prayer of two *rakâats*.' The prepossessions of the several Collectors would undoubtedly influence them in accepting or rejecting the chain of witnesses to any traditions; but there is no reason to suppose that they at all tampered with the traditions themselves. Thus a Sheeah collector would cast aside a tradition received from Ayesha through an Omeyad channel; whilst one of Omeyad predilections would discard every traditional chain in the links of which he discovered an emissary of the house of Ali. But neither the one nor the other was likely to *fabricate* a tradition; or to tamper with a narration, whatever its purport or bearing might be, if only it were attested by an unexceptionable chain of names.

Guarantees and evidence of their honesty. The honesty of the compilers is warranted by the style and contents of their works. The complete series of witnesses, by which every tradition is traced up through each stage of transmission to one of the Prophet's Companions, is invariably prefixed to it; and we cannot but admit the authority which even the names of at least the later witnesses in such a chain would impart.[1] These could not be feigned names, but were the names of real characters, many of them personages of note. The traditional collections were openly published, and the credit of the compilers would have been endangered by the fabrication of such evidence. The Collector was likewise, in general, the centre of a school of traditional learning which, as it were, challenged the public to test its authorities. So far, then, as this kind of attestation can give weight to hearsay, that weight may be readily conceded. Again, the simple manner in which the most contradictory traditions are accepted, and placed side by side, is a guarantee of sincerity. All that could be collected seem to have been thrown together with scrupulous fidelity. Each tradition, though it be a bare repetition, or possibly the direct opposite, of a dozen preceding it, is noted down unquestioned, with its special chain of witnesses; whilst no account whatever is made of the most violent improbabilities, of incidents plainly fabulous,

---

[1] A tradition is always given in the direct form of speech in which it is supposed to have been originally uttered. Thus: ' A informed me, saying that B had spoken to the effect that C had told him, saying D mentioned that he heard E relate that he had listened to F, who said, *I heard G enquiring of Ayesha*, "*What food did the Prophet of the Lord like?*" *and she replied*, "*Verily, he loved sweetmeats and honey, and greatly relished the pumpkin.*" '

or even of patent contradictions.[1] Now this is evidence at least of an honest design. Pains would otherwise have been taken to exclude or to soften down opposing statements; and we should not have found so much allowed to be credible tradition, which either on the one hand or on the other must have crossed the views and prejudices of the compiler. If we suppose *design*, we must suppose at the same time a less even-handed admission of contrary traditions.

Conceding, then, the general honesty of the collectors in making their selection, upon an untenable principle indeed, yet *bonâ fide* from existing materials, let us now turn to their selected compilations, and enquire whether they contain any authentic elements of the life of Mahomet; and if so, how and to what extent these have become commingled with adventitious or erroneous matter.

How far do the collections of tradition contain elements of truth?

In the first place, how far does the present text afford ground for confidence that its contents are identical with the supposed evidence originally given by contemporary witnesses? To place the case in the strongest point of view, we shall suppose a class of traditions purporting to have been *written* by the Companions, and to have been recorded afresh at every successive stage of transmission. There is a peculiarity in traditional composition which, even upon this supposition, would render it always of doubtful authority; namely, that each tradition is short and abrupt, and completely isolated from every other. The isolation extends not simply to the traditions themselves as finally compiled by the collector, but to their whole history and descent throughout the long period preceding their collection. At every point each tradition was completely detached and independent; and this, coupled with the generally brief and fragmentary character of the statements made in them, deprives us of the checks and critical appliances which are brought to bear on a continuous composition. There is little or no context whereby to judge the soundness of a tradition. Each witness in the chain, though professing simply to repeat the words of the first narrator, is in effect an independent authority; and we cannot tell how far, and at what stages, variations may or may not have been allowed, or fresh matter interpolated by any of them. Even were we satisfied of the integrity of all the witnesses, we are unacquainted with their views of the liberty with which tradition might be treated. The style of the narrations marks them for the most

Fragmentary and isolated character of each tradition prevents application of ordinary checks.

---

[1] The biographers of Mahomet, when they relate contradictory or varying narratives, sometimes add an expression of their own opinion as to which is preferable. They also sometimes mark doubtful stories by the addition: ' The Lord knows whether this be false or true.'

part as communicated, at the first, with the freedom of social conversation, and with much of the looseness of hearsay; and a similar informality and looseness may have attached to any of the steps of their subsequent transmission.

Each tradition regarded as a unit, to be, without investigation of its parts, accepted or rejected as a whole.

Again, each tradition was not only isolated, but was held by the collectors to be an *indivisible unit*, and as such received or rejected. If the traditional links were unexceptionable, the tradition must be accepted *as it stood*, whole and entire. There could be no sifting of component parts. Whatever in each tradition might be true, and whatever might be fictitious,—the probable and the fabulous,—composed an indissoluble whole; so that the acceptance or rejection of one portion involved the acceptance or rejection of every portion, as equally credible or undeserving of credit. The power of eradicating interpolated words, or of excluding such parts of a tradition as were evidently unfounded or erroneous, was thus renounced. The good seed and the tares were reaped together, and the latter vastly predominated.

Exclusively oral character of early tradition deprives it of all check against error and fabrication.

Such is the uncertainty that would attach to tradition, even if we should concede that it had been recorded from the first. But (as we have seen) there is no ground for believing that the practice of writing down traditions was observed in the first days of Islâm, or became general until the greater part of a century had elapsed. The existence of an early record would have afforded *some* check; but, as the facts stand, there is no check at all. A record would have at least fixed the terms in which the evidence is given; whereas tradition purely oral is affected by the character and habits, the associations and the prejudices, of each witness in the chain of repetition. No precaution could hinder the commingling in oral tradition of mistaken or fabricated matter with what at the first may have been trustworthy evidence. The flood-gates of error, exaggeration, and fiction were thrown wide open; and we need only look to the experience of every country and every age, to be satisfied that but little dependence can be placed on the recital of historical incident, and none whatever upon supernatural tales, conveyed for any length of time through such a channel. That Islâm forms no exception to the general principle is amply proved by the puerile extravagances and splendid fabrications which adorn or darken the pages of its early history. The critical test applied by the collectors had no reference whatever to these pregnant sources of error; and, though it may have rejected multitudes of modern fabrications, it failed to place the earlier traditions upon any certain basis, or to supply the means of discerning between the actual and the fictitious, between the offspring of the imagination and the sober evidence of fact.

It remains to examine the traditional collections with reference to their contents and internal probability. And here we fortunately have in the Corân a standard of comparison which has been already proved a genuine and contemporary document.

Tradition tested by correspondence with Corân.

We find accordingly that in its main historical outlines the Corân is at one with the received traditional collections. It notices, either directly or incidentally, those topics which, from time to time, most interested Mahomet; and with these salient points, tradition is found upon the whole to tally. The statements and allusions of this description in the Corân, though themselves comparatively few, are linked more or less with a vast variety of important incidents which refer as well to the Prophet individually and his domestic relations as to public events and the progress of Islâm. A just confidence is thus imparted that a large amount of historical truth has been conveyed by tradition.

Main historical and biographical outlines agree.

Upon the other hand, there are subjects in which the Corân is directly at variance with Tradition. For example, there is no position more satisfactorily established by the Corân than that Mahomet did not in any part of his career perform miracles, or lay claim to the power of performing them. Yet tradition abounds with miraculous acts belying the plain declarations of the Corân; and, moreover, such miracles, if at all based on fact, would undoubtedly have been mentioned in the Corân itself, which omits nothing, however trivial, calculated to strengthen the prophetical claim. Here, then, in matters of simple narration and historical incident, we find tradition discredited by the Corân.

Disagreement in certain important points, as power to work miracles.

The result of the comparison, then, is precisely that which we have already arrived at *à priori*, from the foregoing historical review. But, though it strengthens our conclusion, the comparison does not afford us much help in the practical treatment of Tradition itself. Excepting in a limited number of events, it furnishes us with no rule for eliminating falsehood. Facts which we know from the Corân to be well founded, and tales which we know to be fabricated, are indiscriminately woven together; and of both the fabric and colour are so uniform, that we are at a loss for any means of distinguishing the one from the other. The biographer of Mahomet continually runs the risk of substituting for the realities of history some puerile fancy or extravagant invention. In striving to avoid this danger he is exposed to the opposite peril of rejecting as pious fabrications, what may in reality be important historical fact.

Perplexing alternative.

Opinion of Dr. Sprenger too favourable to tradition.

It is, indeed, the opinion of Dr. Sprenger that 'although the nearest view of the Prophet which we can obtain is at a distance of one hundred years,' and although this long vista is formed of a medium *exclusively* Mahometan, yet our knowledge of the bias of the narrators ' enables us to correct the media, and to make them almost achromatic.' The remark is true to some extent; but its full application would carry us much beyond the truth. The difficulties of the task cannot without danger be underrated. To bring to a right focus the various lights of Tradition, to reject those that are fictitious, to restore to a proper direction the rays reflected by a false and deceptive surface, to calculate the extent of aberration, and make due allowance for a thousand disturbing influences;—this is indeed a work of entanglement and complication, which would require for its perfect accomplishment a finer discernment, and a machinery of nicer complexion, than human nature can boast. Nevertheless, it is right that an attempt should be made, however imperfect the success that may attend it.

An attempt to lay down tests for discriminating what is reliable in tradition.

It is possible that, by a comprehensive consideration of the subject, and a careful discrimination of the several sources of error, we may reach at the least a fair approximation to the truth. With this view I will endeavour to lay down some principles which may prove useful to the enquirer in separating the true from the false in Mahometan tradition.

Traditional evidence *ex-parte.* Tests must depend on internal examination.

The grand defect in the traditional evidence regarding Mahomet consists in its being wholly *ex-parte.* It is the statement of a witness regarding himself, in which the license of partiality and self-interest is unchecked by any opposing party, and the sanction even of a neutral audience is wanting. But what is thus defective in the process, may in some measure be corrected or repaired by a close scrutiny of the record. By analysing the evidence, and by considering the position and qualifications of the witnesses, we may find internal grounds for credit or for doubt; while, in reference to some classes of statements, it may even appear that a Mahometan public would itself supply the place of an impartial censor. In this view, the points on which the probability of a tradition will mainly depend, appear to be *first*, whether there existed a bias among the Mahometans generally on the subject narrated; *second*, whether there are traces of any special interest, prejudice, or design, on the part of the narrator; and *third*, whether the narrator had opportunity for personally knowing the facts. These topics will perhaps best be discussed by considering the *Period* to which a narration relates, and then the *Subject* of which it treats.

Two divisions; *period* and *subject* of events narrated.

I. PERIOD.

I. A.—The PERIOD to which a tradition purports to refer, is a point of vital importance. The original authors of all reliable tradition were the *Companions* of Mahomet himself. But Mahomet was above threescore years old when he died; and few of his Companions, from whom traditions have come down, were of equal age,—hardly any of them older. In proportion to their years, the number of aged men was small and the period short during which they survived Mahomet; and these are precisely the considerations by which their influence, in the formation of tradition, must be limited also. The great majority were young; and in proportion to their youth was the number that survived longest, and gave the deepest impress to tradition.[1] We may, then, fix the term of Mahomet's own life as the extreme backward limit within which our witnesses range themselves. In other words, we have virtually no original witnesses who lived at a period anterior to Mahomet; few, if any, were born before him; the great majority, many years after him. They are not, therefore, trustworthy witnesses for events preceding Mahomet's birth, or for details of his childhood; few of them, even, for the incidents of his youth. They could not by any possibility possess a personal knowledge of these things; and to admit that they gained their information at second-hand, is to impair the value of their testimony as that of contemporary witnesses.

First.— Up to entrance of Mahomet on public life. All witnesses younger, and most of them much younger, than Mahomet;

Their personal knowledge cannot therefore go farther back than his youth at earliest.

B.—But, again, the value of evidence depends upon the degree in which the facts are noticed by the witness at the time of their occurrence. If the attention were not specially attracted, it would be in vain to expect a full and careful report; and, after the lapse of many years, the utmost that could be looked for from such a witness, would be a bare general outline. This principle applies forcibly to the biography of Mahomet up to the time when he became the prominent leader of a party. Before, there was nothing remarkable about him. A poor orphan, a quiet, inoffensive citizen, he was perhaps of all the inhabitants of Mecca the least likely to have the eyes of his neighbours turned upon him, and their memory and imagination busy in noting the events of his life, and conjuring up anticipations of coming greatness. The remark may be extended, not merely to the era when he first

Attention not attracted till Mahomet had publicly assumed prophetic office.

---

[1] Abu Bakr, for instance, was within two years of Mahomet's age; but then he survived him only two-and-a-half years. Most of the elderly Companions either died a natural death, or were killed in action before the practice of tradition came into vogue. Thus Wâckidi: 'The reason why many of the chief men of the Companions have left few traditions, is that they died before there was any necessity for referring to them. The chiefest among the Companions, Abu Bakr, Othmân, Talha, &c., gave forth fewer traditions than others. *There did not issue from them, anything like the number of traditions that did from the younger Companions.*'

made pretensions to inspiration (for that excited the regard of a few only among his earliest adherents); but to the entire interval preceding the period when he stood forth *publicly* to assume the prophetic rank, opposed polytheism, and came into open collision with the chiefs of Mecca. Then, indeed, he began to be narrowly watched; and thenceforward the Companions of the Prophet are not to be distrusted on the score at least of insufficient attention.

For events prior to Mahomet's public life circumstantiality ground of suspicion.

c.—It follows that, in all cases affected by either of the foregoing rules, circumstantiality will be a strong token of fabrication. And we shall do well to adopt the analogous canon of Christian criticism, that any tradition whose origin is not strictly contemporary with the facts related, *is worthless exactly in proportion to the particularity of detail.*[1] This will relieve us of a vast number of extravagant stories, in which the minutiæ of close narrative and sustained colloquy in early passages of the Prophet's life are preserved with the pseudo-freshness of yesterday.

Exception in favour of leading outlines of Mahomet's life.

D.—It will, however, be just to admit an exception for the main outlines of Mahomet's life, which under ordinary circumstances his friends and acquaintance would naturally remember or might learn from himself, and would thus be able in after days to call up with tolerable accuracy. Such, for instance, are the death of his father, his nurture as an infant by the Bani Sád, his mother's journey with him to Medîna, and the expedition with his uncle to Syria while yet a boy. A still wider exception must be allowed in favour of public personages and national events, even preceding Mahomet's birth; because the attention of the people at large would be actively directed to these topics, while the patriarchal habits of the Arabs and their spirit of clanship would be propitious to their tenacious recollection. Thus the conversation of Mahomet's grandfather with Abraha the Abyssinian invader, is far more likely to be founded in fact than any of the much later conversations which Mahomet himself is said to have had with the monks on either of his journeys to Syria; and yet the leading facts regarding these journeys there is no reason to doubt.

Public events;

And national history.

Under the same exception will fall those genealogical and historical facts, the preservation of which for several centuries by

[1] The remarks of Alford are strikingly illustrative of Mahometan tradition: 'As usual in traditional matter, on our advance to later writers, we find more and more particular accounts given; the year of John's life, the reigning Emperor, &c., under which the Gospel was written.' But Christian traditionists were mere tyros in the art of discovering such particulars in comparison with the Mahometans, at the talisman of whose pen distance vanishes, and even centuries deliver up the minutest details which they had engulfed.

the memory alone, is so wonderful a phenomenon in the story of Arabia. Here poetry, no doubt, aided the retentive faculty. The rhapsodies of the bard were at once caught up by his admiring clan, and soon passed into the mouths even of the children. In such poetry were preserved the names of the chieftains, their feats of bravery, their glorious liberality, the unparalleled nobility of their breeds of camel and horse. Many of these odes became national, and carried with them the testimony, not of the tribe alone, but of the whole Arab family. Thus poetry, the passion for genealogical and tribal reminiscences, and the singular capacity of imprinting them indelibly on the memory for generations, have secured to us the interwoven details of many centuries with a minuteness and particularity that would excite suspicion were not their reality in many instances established by other evidence and by internal coincidence.[1]

E.—A second marked section of time is that which intervenes between Mahomet's entrance on public life, and the taking of Mecca. Here indeed we have two opposing parties, marshalled against each other in mortal strife, whose statements might have been a check one upon the other. But during this interval, or very shortly after, one of the parties was wholly extirpated. Its chief leaders were nearly all killed in battle, and the remainder went over to the victors. We have therefore no surviving evidence whatever on the side of Mahomet's enemies. Not a single advocate was left to explain their actions, often misrepresented by hatred, or to rebut the accusations and charges imputed to them by Mahomet and his followers. On the other hand, we have no witnesses of any kind against Mahomet and his party, whose one-sided assertions of innocence and justice might perhaps otherwise have been often liable to question. The intemperate and unguarded language of the fathers of tradition is

Second period.— From entrance on public life to taking of Mecca, *i.e.* B.H. 10 to A.H. 8.

No surviving evidence on side of Meccans; or against Mahomet and his party.

---

[1] M. Caussin de Perceval who, with incredible labour, has sought out and arranged these facts into a uniform history, thus expresses his estimate of the Arab genealogical traditions : 'J'ai dit que toutes les généalogies Arabes n'étaient point certaines ; on en trouve en effet un grand nombre d'évidemment incomplètes. Mais il en est aussi beaucoup d'authentiques, et qui remontent, sans lacune probable, jusqu'à environ six siècles avant Mahomet. C'est un phénomène vraiment singulier chez un peuple inculte et en général étranger à l'art de l'écriture, comme l'étaient les Arabes, que cette fidélité à garder le souvenir des ancêtres. Elle prenait sa source dans un sentiment de fierté, dans l'estime qu'ils faisaient de leur noblesse. Les noms de aïeux, gravés dans la mémoire des enfants, étaient les archives des familles. À ces noms se rattachaient nécessairement quelques notions sur la vie des individus, sur les événements dans lesquels ils avaient figuré; et c'est ainsi que les traditions se perpétuaient d'âge en âge.'

sufficient proof that, in speaking of adversaries, their opinion was seldom impartial, and their judgment not always unerring.

To what degree Meccan party, as finally incorporated with Moslems, proved a check upon misrepresentation.

F.—It may be urged in reply, that the great body of the hostile Meccans who eventually went over to Islâm, would still form a check upon any material misrepresentation of their party. It may be readily admitted that they did form some check on the perversion of public opinion in matters not vitally connected with the credit of Islâm and its Founder. Their influence would also tend to preserve the reports of their own individual actions, and perhaps those of their friends and relatives, in as favourable a light as possible. But this influence at best was partial. It must be borne in mind that the enemies of the Prophet who now joined his ranks acquired at the same time, or very shortly after, all the *esprit de corps* of Islâm.[1] And, long before the stream of tradition commenced, these very men had learned to look back upon the heathenism of their own Meccan career with horror and contempt. The stains of the Moslem's previous life were, on his conversion, washed away, and imparted no tarnish to his subsequent character. He had sinned ' ignorantly in unbelief ;' but now, both in his own view and in the eyes of his comrades, he was *another man*. He might now, therefore, well speak of his mad opposition to ' the Prophet of the Lord' and the divine message, with as hearty a reprobation as other men ; nay, the violence of reaction might make his language even stronger. Such are the witnesses who constitute our only check upon the *ex-parte* story told by Mahometans of their long struggle with the idolaters of Mecca.

Evidence against opponents of Mahomet to be received with caution.

G.—It is therefore incumbent upon us, in estimating the folly, injustice, and cruelty attributed to the opponents of the Prophet, to make much allowance for the exclusively hostile character of the evidence. We may, also, suspect exaggeration in the statements of hardship and persecution suffered by the Moslems at their hands. Above all, the history of those who died in unbelief, before the conquest of Mecca, and under the ban of Mahomet, must be subject to a rigid criticism. For such men as Abu Jahl and Abu Lahab, hated and cursed by their Prophet, what Mahometan dare be the advocate? To the present day, the hearty ejaculation, *May the Lord curse him !* is linked by every Moslem with the mention of such ' enemies of the Lord, and of his Prophet.' What voice would be raised to correct the pious exaggerations of the faithful in the stories of their

---

[1] Thus Abu Sofiân, himself the leader in the last stage of opposition to Mahomet, became a zealous Moslem, and fought under the banners of his own son in the first Syrian campaign.

execrable deeds, or to point out the just causes of provocation which they may have received? Impious attempt, and mad perversity! Again and again was the sword of Omar brandished over the neck of the luckless offender, for conduct far more excusable, and far less dangerous to Islâm.

H.—Precisely similar limitations must be brought to bear on the evidence against the Jewish inhabitants in the vicinity of Medîna, whom Mahomet either expatriated, brought over to his faith, or utterly extirpated. The various Arab tribes also, whether Christian or Pagan, whom Mahomet at different times of his life attacked, come more or less under the same category.

So also with Jewish, Christian, and Pagan tribes of Arabia.

I.—The same considerations apply also, though in a modified form, to the 'Hypocrites,' or disaffected population of Medîna, who covertly opposed the claim of Mahomet to temporal authority over that city. The Prophet did not wage the same war of defiance with these as he did with his Meccan opponents, but sought to counteract their influence by skilful tactics. Neither was this class so suddenly rooted out as the idolaters of Mecca; they rather vanished gradually before the increasing authority of Islâm. Still its leaders are held in abhorrence by the traditionists, and the historian must keep a jealous eye on the testimony against them.

Similar considerations apply to Hypocrites, or disaffected inhabitants of Medina.

II.—The SUBJECT-MATTER of tradition itself, considered both as regards the motives of its authors and the views of early Mahometan society generally, will help us to an estimate of their credibility. The chief aspects in which this argument may be treated refer to *personal*, *party*, and *national* bias.

II. SUBJECT-MATTER as affected by personal, party, or national, bias.

A.—*Individual* prepossession and self-interested motives would cause exaggeration, false colouring, and even invention. Besides the more obvious cases falling under this head, there is a fertile class which originates in the ambition of the narrator to be associated with Mahomet. The name of the Prophet threw veneration and nobility around every object connected with it. The friendship of Mahomet imparted a rank and dignity acknowledged by the universal voice of Islâm. It is difficult to conceive the reverence and court enjoyed by his widows, friends, and servants. Interminable enquiries were put to them; and their responses were received with implicit deference. All who possessed personal knowledge of the Prophet, and especially those who had been honoured with his familiar acquaintance, were admitted by common consent into the envied circle of Moslem aristocracy; and many a picturesque scene is sketched by the traditionists of the crowds which listened to these men as they delivered their testimony in the Mosques of Kufâ or

1. Personal ambition of being associated with Mahomet.

Damascus.   The sterling value of such qualifications would
induce imitation.   Some who may have had but a distant and
superficial knowledge of Mahomet would be tempted, by the consideration it imparted, to counterfeit a more perfect intimacy;
and the endeavour to support their equivocal position by particularity of detail, would lead the way to loose and unfounded
narratives of the life and character of the Prophet.   Equally
misleading was the ambition, traceable throughout the traditions
of the Companions, of being closely connected with any of the
supposed mysterious visitations or supernatural actions of
Mahomet.   To be *noticed* in the Revelation was the highest
honour that mortal man could aspire to; and in any way to be
linked with the heavenly phases of the Prophet's life, reflected a
portion of the divine lustre on the fortunate aspirant.[1]   Thus
a premium was put upon the invention or exaggeration of super-
human incidents.

Exaggera-
tion of per-
sonal merit
in cause of
Islâm.

    B.—Under the same head are to be classed the attempts of
narrators to exaggerate their labours and exploits, and to multiply their losses and perils in the service of the Prophet.   The
tendency thus to appropriate a superior, and often an altogether
unwarrantable, merit is obvious on the part of many of the
Companions of Mahomet.[2]   A reference to this tendency may be
even occasionally employed by the critic in exculpation of the
Prophet from questionable actions.   For example, Amr ibn
Omeya, in narrating his mission by Mahomet to assassinate Abu

    [1] Thus Ayesha's party having been long delayed when with the Prophet
on a certain expedition, the verse permitting the substitution of sand for
lustration was in consequence revealed.   The honour conferred by this indirect connection with a divine revelation is thus eulogised: ' This is not the
least of the divine favours poured out upon you, ye house of Abu Bakr!'
    [2] We have many examples of the glory and honour lavished upon those
who had suffered persecution at Mecca.   Thus when Omar was Caliph, Khobâb
showed him the scars of the stripes he had received from the unbelieving
Meccans twenty or thirty years before.   Omar seated him upon his throne,
saying that there was but one man who was more worthy of this favour than
Khobâb, namely, Bilâl.   But Khobâb replied: ' And why is he more worthy than
I am ?   He had his friends among the idolaters whom the Lord raised up to
elp him.   But I had none to help me.   I well remember one day they took
me and kindled a fire, and threw me therein upon my back; and a man stamped
with his foot upon my chest, my back being all the while upon the ground.
And when they uncovered my back, lo! it was blistered and white.'
    The same principle led the Moslems to magnify the hardships which
Mahomet himself endured.   It appears to lie at the bottom of Ayesha's strange
exaggerations of the Prophet's poverty and frequent starvation, which she
carries so far as to say that she had not even oil to burn in her chamber while
Mahomet lay dying there!   The subsequent affluence and luxuries of the
conquering nation, also, led them by reaction to contrast with fond regret their
present state with their former simplicity and want, and even to weep at the

Sofiân, so magnifies the dangers and exploits of his adventure as might have involved that dark mission itself in suspicion, were there not collateral proof to support it.

It may be here objected,—Would not untrue or exaggerated tales like these receive a check from other parties, free from the interested motives of the narrator? They would to some extent. But to prove a negative position is generally difficult, and it would not often be attempted without some strong impelling cause, especially in the early spread of Islâm when the public mind was in the highest degree impressible and credulous. Such traditions, then, were likely to be opposed only when they interfered with the private claims of others, or ran counter to public opinion in which case they would fall into discredit and oblivion. Otherwise they would be carried down upon the traditional stream of mingled legend and truth, and with it find a place in the unquestioning record of the second century.

Small chance of exaggerations and fictions being checked.

c.—We have undoubted evidence that the bias of PARTY effected a deep and abiding impress upon tradition. Where this spirit tended to produce or embellish a tale adverse to the interests of another party, and the denial of the facts involved nothing prejudicial to the honour of Islâm, endeavour might be made to rebut the fictitious statement, and the discussion so produced would subserve the purity of tradition. But this could seldom occur. The tradition would often affect that section alone in whose favour it originated, and therefore would not be controverted at all. The story would probably at the first be confined within the limits of the party which it concerned, and no opportunity would be afforded for its contradiction until it had taken root and acquired a prescriptive claim. Under any circumstances, the considerations advanced in the preceding paragraph are equally applicable here; so that without doubt a vast collection of exaggerated tales have come down to us, which owe their existence to party spirit.

2. Party.—Likelihood of party traditions coming into general currency.

By the bias of party is not to be understood simply the influence of faction, but likewise the partiality and prejudice of the lesser circles which formed the ramifications of Mussulman society. The former we are less in danger of overlooking.

Prejudicial influence of lesser associations of Tribe, Family, Patron, &c.

remembrance. Thus of the same Khobâb, it is recorded: He had a winding-sheet made ready for himself of fine Coptic cloth; and he compared it with the wretched pall of Hamza (killed at Ohod); and he contrasted his own poverty when he possessed not a dinar, with his present condition: 'and now I have in my chest by me in the house 40,000 ounces of gold. Verily, I fear that the sweets of the present world have hastened upon us. Our companions have received their reward in Paradise; but truly I dread lest my reward consist in these benefits I have obtained after their departure.'

Where the full development of faction, as in the case of the Abbassides and Omeyads, has laid bare the passions and excesses to which it gave rise, the reader is on his guard against misrepresentation; he receives with caution the unnaturally dark or resplendent phases of such characters as Ali and Abbâs, Muâvia and Abu Sofiân. But, though on a less extensive scale, the influences of tribe, of family, and of the smaller associations of party clustering around the several heroes of Islâm, were equally real and effective. The spirit of clanship, which ran so high among the Arabs that Mahomet endeavoured in vain to supplant it by the brotherhood of the faith, perpetuated the confederacies and antipathies of ante-Mahometan Arabia far down into the annals of Islâm, and often exerted a potent influence upon the destinies even of the Caliphate. It cannot be doubted that these combinations and prejudices imparted a strong and often deceptive hue to the sources of tradition. As an example, may be specified the rivalry which led the several families or parties to compete with each other for the earliest converts to Islâm until they arrived at the conclusion, and consequently propagated the tradition, that some of their patrons or ancestors were Mahometans before Mahomet himself.

3. National bias; common to whole of Islâm, and therefore most fatal. D.—We now come to the class of motives incomparably the most dangerous to the purity of Tradition, namely, those which were *common to the whole Moslem body.* In the previous cases the bias was confined to a fragment, and the remainder of the nation might form a check upon the fractional aberration. But here the bias was universal, pervading the *entire medium* through which we have received tradition, and leaving us, for the correction of its divergencies, no check whatever.

Tendency to exalt Mahomet, and ascribe to him supernatural attributes. To this class must be assigned all traditions the object of which is to glorify Mahomet, and to invest him with supernatural attributes. Although in the Corân the Prophet disclaims the power of working miracles, yet he implies that there existed a continuous intercourse between himself and the agents of the other world. The whole Corân, indeed, assumes to be a message from the Almighty, communicated through Gabriel. Besides being the medium of revelation, that favoured angel is often referred to as bringing directions from the Lord for the guidance of his Prophet in the common concerns of life. The supposed communication with heavenly messengers, thus countenanced by Mahomet himself, was implicitly believed by his followers, and led them even during his life-time to regard him with superstitious awe. On a subject so impalpable to sense and so congenial with the imagination, it may be fairly assumed that reason had little share in controlling the fertile productions of fancy; that the conclusions of his susceptible and credulous followers far exceeded the premises granted by Mahomet; that even simple facts were construed by excited faith as pregnant with supernatural power and unearthly companionship; and that, after the object of their veneration had passed from their sight, fond devotion perpetuated and enhanced the fascinating legends. If the Prophet gazed into the heavens, or looked wistfully to the right hand or to the left, it was Gabriel with whom he was holding mysterious converse. Passing gusts raised a cloud from the sandy track; the pious Believer exulted in the conviction that it was the dust of Gabriel and his mounted squadrons scouring the plain, and going before them to shake the foundations of some doomed fortress. On the field of Bedr, three stormy blasts swept over the marshalled army; again, it was Gabriel with a thousand horse flying to the succour of Mahomet, while Michael and Serâfîl each with a like angelic troop wheeled to the right and to the left of the Moslem front. Nay, the very dress and martial uniform of these helmed angels are detailed by the earliest and most trustworthy biographers with as much *naïveté* as if they had been veritable warriors of flesh and blood; and the heads of the enemy were seen to drop off before the Moslem swords had even touched them, because the unseen scymitars did the work more swiftly than the grosser steel of Medîna! Such is a specimen of the vein of legend and extravagance which runs throughout even the purest sources of tradition.

It will frequently be a question, extremely difficult to decide, what portions of these supernatural stories either originated in Mahomet himself, or received his countenance; and what portion owed its birth, after he was gone, to the excited imagination of his followers. No doubt facts have not seldom been thus adorned or distorted by a superstitious fancy. The subjective conceptions of the fond believer have been reflected back upon the biography of the Prophet, and have encircled even the realities of his life, as in the pictures of our saints, with a lustrous halo. The false colouring and fictitious light so intermingle with the picture, as often to place its details altogether beyond the reach of analytical criticism.[1]

Difficulty of discriminating what originated with Mahomet himself, in supernatural tales.

[1] The corpse of Sâd lay in an empty room. Mahomet entered alone, picking his steps carefully, as if he walked in the midst of men seated closely on the ground. On being asked the cause of so strange a proceeding, he replied: 'True, there were no men in the room, but it was so filled with angels, all seated on the ground, that I found nowhere to sit down, until one of the angels spread out his wing for me on the ground, and I sat thereon.' It is almost impossible to say what in this is Mahomet's own, and what has been concocted for him. For other supernatural tales connected with the same occasion, vide *ante*, p. 335.

Miracles.

E.—To the same universal desire of Mahomet's glorification must be ascribed the unquestioned miracles with which even the earliest biographies abound. They are such as the following: A tree from a distance moves towards the Prophet, ploughing up the earth as it advances, and then similarly retires; oft-repeated attempts to murder him are miraculously averted; distant occurrences are instantaneously revealed, and future events foretold; a large company is fed from victuals hardly adequate for the supply of a single person; prayer draws down immediate showers from heaven, or causes their equally sudden cessation. A frequent class of miracles is for the Prophet to touch the udders of dry goats which immediately distend with milk; and by his command to make floods of water well up from parched fountains, gush forth from empty vessels, or issue from betwixt his fingers. With respect to all such stories, it is sufficient to say that they are opposed to the clear declarations and pervading sense of the Corân.

That it contains the recital of a miracle does not necessarily discredit an entire tradition.

It by no means, however, follows that, because a tradition relates a miracle, the collateral incidents are thereby discredited. It may be that the facts were fabricated to illustrate or embellish a popular miracle; but it is also possible that the miracle was invented to adorn, or to account for, well-founded facts. In the former case, the supposed facts are worthless; in the latter, they may be true and valuable. In the absence of other evidence, the main drift and apparent design of the narrative is all that can guide the critic between these alternatives.

Tales and legends how far ascribable to Mahomet.

F.—The same propensity to fabricate the marvellous must be borne in mind when we peruse the childish tales and extravagant legends put by tradition into the mouth of Mahomet. The Corân, it is true, imparts a far wider basis of likelihood to the narration by Mahomet of such tales, than to his assumption of miraculous powers. When the Prophet ventured to place such fanciful and unworthy fictions as those of 'Solomon and the Genii,' of 'the Seven sleepers,' or 'the Adventures of Dzûl Carnein,' in the pages of a *divine* Revelation, to what puerilities might he not stoop in the familiarity of social conversation! It must, on the other hand, be remembered that Mahomet was taciturn, laconic, and reserved, and is therefore not likely to have given forth more than an infinitesimal part of the masses of legend and fable which tradition represents as gathered from his lips. These are probably the growth of successive ages, each of which added its contribution to the nucleus of the Prophet's pregnant words, if indeed there ever was such a nucleus at all. For example, the germ of the elaborate pictures and gorgeous scenery of the Prophet's heavenly journey lies in a very short and simple recital in the Corân. That he subsequently expanded this germ, and amused or edified his Companions with the minutiæ which have been brought down to us by tradition, is *possible*. But it is also possible, and (by the analogy of Mahomet's miracles) far more probable, that the vast majority of these fancies have no other origin than the heated imagination of the early Mussulmans.[1]

G.—Connected indirectly with Mahomet's life, but immediately with the credit and the evidence of Islâm, is another class of narrations which would conjure up on all sides prophecies regarding the Founder of the faith and anticipations of his approach. These probably, for the most part, depended upon some general declaration or incidental remark of the Prophet himself, which his enthusiastic followers deemed themselves bound to prove and illustrate. For example, the Jews are often accused in the Corân of wilfully rejecting Mahomet, 'although they recognised him as they did one of their own sons.' Tradition provides us, accordingly, with an array of Jewish rabbins and Christian monks, who found it written in their books that the last of the Prophets was at this time about to rise at Mecca, and who asserted that not only his name, but his personal appearance, manners, and character were therein depicted to the life, so that recognition could not but be instantaneous; and among other absurd particulars, the very city of *Medina* is pointed out by name as the place where he would take refuge from the persecution of his people! Again, the Jews are in the Corân accused of grudging that a Prophet should arise among the Arabs, and that their nation should thus be robbed of its prophetic dignity. Wherefore, in fit illustration we have numerous stories of Mahomet having been recognised by the rabbins, and of attempts made by them to kill him; and this, too, long before he had any suspicion himself that he was to be a Prophet, nay *during his very infancy!* It is enough to have alluded to this class of fabrications.

Supposed anticipations of Mahomet by Jews and Christians.

H.—Such unblushing inventions will lead us to receive with suspicion the whole series of tales in which it is pretended that Mahomet and his religion were *foreshadowed*, so that pious men anticipated, long before the Prophet arose, many of the peculiar rites and doctrines of Islâm. It was a fond conceit of Mahomet that Islâm is as old as Adam, and has from the beginning been

Anticipations of Islâm.

[1] Sprenger holds that the narrative, in its main features, emanated from Mahomet himself, because (says he) *There is no event in his life, on which we have more numerous and genuine traditions than on his nightly journey.* The fact is significant, but the conclusion doubtful.

the faith of all good men, who looked forward to himself as the Prophet charged with winding up all previous dispensations. It was therefore natural for his credulous followers to carry out this idea, and to invest the memory of any serious-minded man or earnest enquirer who preceded Mahomet with some of the dawning rays of the divine effulgence about to burst upon the world.

I.—To the same spirit we may attribute the palpable endeavour to make Mahometan tradition and the legends of Arabia *tally with the Scriptures of the Old Testament, and with Jewish tradition.* This canon has little application to the biography of Mahomet himself, but it has a wide and most effective range in reference to the legendary history of his ancestors and of early Arabia. The desire to regard, and possibly the endeavour to prove, the Prophet of Islâm a descendant of Ishmael, began even in his life-time. Many Jews, versed in the Scriptures, and won over by the inducements of Islâm, pandered their knowledge to the service of Mahomet and his followers. Jewish tradition had long been well known in Medîna and in the countries over which Islâm early spread, and the Mahometan system was now made to fit upon it; for Islâm did not ignore, but merely superseded, Judaism and Christianity, as the whole does a part, or rather as that which is complete swallows up what is inchoate. Hence arose such absurd anachronisms as the attempts to identify Cahtân with Joktan (between whom, at the most moderate estimate, fifteen centuries intervene); and thus were forged the earlier links of the Abrahamic genealogy of Mahomet, and numberless tales of Ishmael and the Israelites, cast in a semi-Jewish semi-Arab mould. These, though pretending to be original traditions, can generally be recognised as plagiarisms from rabbinical lore, or as Arabian legends forced into accommodation with them.

J.—Of analogous nature may be classed the traditions which affirm that the Jews and Christians mutilated or interpolated their Scriptures. After repeated examination of the Corân, I have been unable to discover any grounds for believing that Mahomet himself ever expressed a doubt in regard either to the authority or the genuineness of the Old and New Testaments, as extant in his time. He was profuse in assurances that his system entirely corresponded with both, and that he had been foretold by former prophets; and, as perverted Jews and Christians were at hand to confirm his words, and as the Bible was little known among the generality of his followers, such assurances were implicitly believed. But as Islâm spread abroad and began to include countries where the Holy Scriptures were

Side notes:

History of Prophet's ancestors, and of early Arabia, borrowed from Jewish Scripture and tradition.

Traditions as to Jewish and Christian Scriptures being mutilated and interpolated.

familiarly read, the discrepancies between them and the Corân became patent. The sturdy believer, with an easy conscience, laid the blame at the door of the dishonest Jews and Christians, the former of whom their Prophet had accused in the Corân of 'hiding' and 'dislocating' the prophecies regarding himself; and, according to the Moslem wont, a host of stories with details of Jewish fabrication soon grew up, exactly suited to the charge.[1]

If it appear strange that extravagant and unreasonable stories of the kind alluded to in the last few paragraphs should not have been contradicted by the more upright and reasonable Mahometans of the first age, and thus nipped in the bud, it must be remembered that criticism and freedom of opinion were completely stifled under the crushing dogmas of Islâm. Any simpleton might fancy, and every designing man could with ease invent, such tales; when once current, the attempt to disprove them would be difficult and dangerous. Supposing that they contradicted no well-known fact or received dogma, by what arguments were they to be rebutted? If any one, for instance, had contended that human experience was opposed to the marvellous foreknowledge of the Jews regarding Mahomet, he would have been scouted as an infidel. Honest enquiry, as it would have sapped the foundations of Islâm, was not tolerated. Who would have dared to argue that a miraculous tale which did honour to Mahomet was in itself improbable, that the narrator might have laboured under a false impression, or that in the Corân itself miraculous powers were disclaimed by the Prophet? The argument would have placed the neck of the heretic in jeopardy; for it has been already shown that the faith and the polity of Islâm were one, and that free opinions and

Why such extravagant and unfounded traditions were not contradicted.

[1] As examples of these traditions take the following. A Copt, reading his uncle's Bible, was struck by finding two leaves closely glued together. On opening them, he discovered copious details regarding Mahomet, as a Prophet immediately about to appear. His uncle was displeased at his curiosity and beat him, saying that the Prophet had not yet arisen. Again, a narrator relates that there was, in the kingdom of Syria, a Jew who, while busied on the Sabbath perusing the Old Testament, perceived on one of the leaves the name of the blessed Prophet in four places; and out of spite he cast that leaf into the fire. On the following day, he found the same name written in eight places: again he burnt the pages. On the third, he found it written in twelve places. The man marvelled exceedingly. He said within himself: 'The more I remove this name from the Scripture, the more do I find it written therein. I shall soon have the whole Bible filled with the same.' At last he resolved to proceed to Medîna and see the Prophet. He arrived soon after Mahomet's death, embraced his garments, 'and expired in the arms of his love.'

heresy were synonymous with conspiracy, treason, and rebellion.[1] And thus, under the shelter of the civil arm and of the fanatical credulity of the people, these marvellous legends grew up in perfect security from the attacks of doubt and of rational enquiry.

Traditions unfavourable to Mahomet became obsolete.

к.—The converse is likewise true ; that is to say, traditions, founded upon good evidence, and undisputed because notorious in the first days of Islâm, gradually fell into disrepute, or were entirely rejected, because they appeared to dishonour Mahomet, or to countenance some heretical opinion. The nature of the case renders it impossible to prove this position so fully as the preceding, since there can have survived but little trace of such traditions as were early and entirely dropped. But we discover vestiges of a spirit that would necessarily produce such results, working even in the second and third centuries. We have seen that the momentary lapse and compromise of Mahomet with the idolatry of Mecca is well supported by the earliest and the best authorities. But theologians began to deem the opinion dangerous or heretical that Mahomet should have thus degraded himself 'after he had received the truth ;' and the occurrence is therefore denied, or entirely omitted, by some of the earliest and most of the later biographers, though the facts are so patent that the more candid fully admit them.[2] The principle thus found in existence in the second and third centuries, may be presumed to have been at work also in the first.

Pious frauds

L.—The system of *pious frauds* is not abhorrent from the axioms of Islâm. Deception, in the current theology of Maho-

[1] This is well illustrated by the treatment which the 'hypocrites' or 'disaffected' are represented as receiving even during Mahomet's life-time. On the expedition to Tabûk, Mahomet prayed for rain, which accordingly descended. A perverse doubter, however, said: 'It was but a chance cloud that happened to pass.' Shortly after, the Prophet's camel strayed; again the doubter said: 'Doth not Mahomet deem himself a Prophet? He professeth to bring intelligence to you from the Heavens; yet is he unable to tell where his own camel is!' 'Ye servants of the Lord!' exclaimed his comrade, 'there is a plague in this place. and I knew it not. Get out from my tent, enemy of the Lord! Wretch, remain not in my presence!' Mahomet had of course, in due time, *supernatural* intimation conveyed to him not only of the doubter's speech, but of the spot where the camel was; and the doubter afterwards repented, and was confirmed in the faith. Omar's sword was readily unsheathed to punish such sceptical temerity, and Mahomet himself once and again visited it in the early part of his Medîna career with condign punishment.

[2] The author of the *Mawâhib Alladoniya* traces the omission of the passage to fear of heresy and injury to Islâm. ' It is said that this story is of an heretical character and has no foundation. But it is not so ; it is really well founded.' 'Again (another author) rejects it on the ground that if it had really happened, many of those who had believed would have become apostates, which was not the case.'

metans, is under certain circumstances allowable.   The Prophet allowable in Islám. himself, by precept as well as by example, encouraged the notion that to tell an untruth is on some occasions allowable ; and what occasion would approve itself as more justifiable, nay meritorious, than that of furthering the interests of Islâm?   The early Moslems would suppose it to be fitting and right that a divine religion should be supported by the evidence of miracles, and they no doubt believed that they were doing God service by building up such testimony in its favour.   The case of our own religion, whose purer morality renders such attempt the less excusable, shows that pious fabrications of this description easily commend themselves to the conscience, wherever there is the inclination and the opportunity for their perpetration.

There were indeed conscientious persons among the early Difficulty of distin- Moslems, who would probably have scrupled at such open fraud ; guishing but these are the very individuals from whom we have the fewest conscien- traditions.   We read of some cautious and scrupulous Com- tious wit- panions who, perceiving the difficulty of reciting accounts of nesses. their Prophet with perfect accuracy, and perhaps in disgust at the barefaced effrontery of the ordinary propagators of garbled and unfounded traditions, abstained entirely from repeating the sayings of Mahomet.[1]   But regarding those Companions from whom the great mass of tradition is drawn, and their immediate successors, it does not appear that we are now in possession of any satisfactory means for dividing them into separate classes,

---

[1] Thus Omar declined to give certain information, saying : ' If it were not that I feared lest I should add to the facts in relating them, or take therefrom, verily I would tell you.'   Similar traditions are given regarding Othmân. Abdallah ibn Masûd was so afraid of repeating Mahomet's words wrongly, that he always guarded his relation by the conditional clause—' He spake something like this, or near unto it ;' but one day, as he repeated a tradition, the uncon- ditional formula of repetition—' *thus spake the Prophet of the Lord* '—escaped his lips, and he became oppressed with anguish, so that the sweat dropped from his forehead.   Then he said : ' If the Lord so will, the Prophet may have said more than that, or less, or near unto it.'   Again Sád was asked a question, and he kept silence, saying : ' *I fear that if I tell you one thing, ye will go and add thereto, as from me, a hundred.*'   Thus also one enquired of Abdallah ibn Zobeir : ' Why do we not hear thee telling anecdotes regarding the Prophet, as such and such persons tell?'   He replied : ' It is very true that I kept close by the Prophet from the time I first believed (and therefore am intimately acquainted with his words) ; but I heard him say, " Whosoever shall repeat a lie concerning me, his resting-place shall be in hell-fire."'   So in explaining why several of the principal Companions had left no traditions, Wâckidi writes : ' From some there are no remains of tradition regarding the Prophet, although they were more in his company, sitting and hearing him, than others who have left us many traditions, *and this we attribute to their fear* (of giving forth erroneous traditions).

of which the trustworthiness would vary to any great extent. With respect, indeed, to some it is known that they were more constantly than others with Mahomet, and had therefore better opportunities for acquiring information; some, like the garrulous Ayesha, were specially given to gossiping tales and trifling frivolities; but none of them, so far as we can judge, was free from the tendency to glorify Mahomet at the expense of truth, or could be withheld from the marvellous by the most glaring violations of probability or of reason. Such at least is the impression derived from their evidence in the shape *in which it has reached us.*

Examples of capricious fabrication.

M.—The aberrations from truth hitherto noticed are presumed to have proceeded from some species of bias, the nature of which I have been endeavouring to trace. But the testimony of the Companions, as delivered to us, is so unaccountably fickle and capricious that, even where no motive whatever can be guessed at, and where there were the fullest opportunities of observation, traditions often flatly contradict one another. For instance, a score of persons affirm that Mahomet dyed his hair: they mention the substances used; some not only maintain that they were eye-witnesses of the fact during the Prophet's life, but after his death produced relics of hair on which the dye was visible. A score of others, possessing equally good means of information, assert that he never dyed his hair, and that moreover he had no need to do so, as his grey hairs were so few that they might be counted.[1] Again, with respect to his *Signet ring*—a matter involving no faction, family interest, or dogma—tradition is most discordant. One party relate that, feeling the want of a seal for his despatches, the Prophet had a signet ring prepared for that purpose of pure silver. Another party assert that Khâlid ibn Sáîd made for himself an iron ring plated with silver; and that Mahomet, taking a fancy to it, appropriated it to his own use. A third tradition states that the ring was brought by Amr ibn Sáîd from Abyssinia; and a fourth that Muâdz ibn Jabal had it engraved for himself in Yemen. One set of traditions hold that Mahomet wore this ring on his

---

[1] Even the exact number of his white hairs is given by different authorities variously, as 17, 18, 20, or 30. Some say that when he oiled his head they appeared; others that the process of oiling concealed them. As to the colour used, the accounts also differ. One says he employed Henna and Katam which gave a reddish tinge, but that he liked yellow best; another mentions a jet-black dye, while others say the Prophet forbade this; *e.g.* Mahomet said: 'Those who dye their hair black like the crops of pigeons, shall never smell the smell of Paradise.' 'In the day of judgment, the Lord will not look upon him who dyes his hair black.'

right hand, another on his left; one that he wore the seal inside, others that he wore it outside; one that the inscription upon it was, *The truth of God*, while the rest declare that it was *Muhammad, Prophet of God*. These traditions all refer to one and the same ring; because it is repeatedly added that, after Mahomet's death, it was worn by Abu Bakr, by Omar, and by Othmân, and was lost by the latter in the well Arìs. There is yet another tradition that neither the Prophet nor any of his immediate successors ever wore a ring at all. Now these varying narratives are not given doubtfully, as conjectures which might either be right or wrong; but they are told with the full assurance of certainty, and with such minute particulars and circumstantiality as to leave the impression on the simple reader's mind that each of the narrators had the most intimate acquaintance with the subject.

To what tendency then or habit of mind, but the sheer love of story-telling, are we to attribute such gratuitous and wholesale fabrications? We may, therefore, from all this fairly conclude that tradition cannot be received with too much caution, or exposed to too rigorous a criticism; and that no important statement should be accepted as securely proved by tradition only, unless there be some farther ground of probability, analogy, or collateral evidence in its favour. *Unsupported tradition is insufficient evidence.*

III. I will now proceed to mention the considerations which should be regarded as *confirming* the credit of a tradition. *III. Considerations confirming tradition.*

A.—General agreement between traditions independent one of another, or which, though traceable to a common origin, have descended by different chains of witnesses, may be regarded as a presumption of credibility. The sources of tradition were numerous; and the stream reaches us through many separate channels. Evidence of this description may therefore afford a cumulative presumption that matter common to many separate traditions was currently reported or believed at the period immediately succeeding Mahomet's death. But, on the other hand, close agreement may be a ground of distrust; it may argue that, though attributed to different sources, the traditions really belong to one and the same family, perhaps of spurious origin, long subsequent to the time of Mahomet. If the uniformity be so great as to exclude circumstantial variety, it will be strong ground for believing that either the common source of such traditions is not of old date, or that the channels of their conveyance have not been kept distinct. Some degree of incidental discrepancy must be looked for, and will improve rather than injure the character of the evidence. Thus the frequent variations as *Agreement between independent traditions.*

to the day of the week on which remarkable events occurred, are just what we should expect in independent traditions having their origin in hearsay; and the simplicity with which these are placed in juxtaposition speaks strongly for the honesty of the Collectors as having gathered them *bonâ fide* from various and independent sources, as well as having refrained from any attempt to blend or harmonise them.

Agreement between portions of independent traditions.

A like argument may be applied to the several parts of a tradition. Certain portions of distinct versions of the same subject-matter may agree almost verbally together, while other portions may contain circumstantial variations; and it is possible that the latter may have a *bonâ fide* independent origin, which the former could not pretend to. Thus the story of Mahomet's infantile days, which professes to have been derived from his nurse Halîma, has been handed down to us in three distinct traditions. 'These three accounts,' says Sprenger, 'agree almost literally in the marvellous, but they differ in the facts.' The *marvellous* was derived from a common source of fabrication, but the *facts* from original authorities. Hence the uniformity of the one, and the variation in the other.

Verbal coincidence may point to a common written original.

Entire verbal coincidence may sometimes involve a species of evidence peculiar to itself; it may point to a common *recorded* original of date older probably than that at which most of the other traditions were reduced to writing. There being no reason to believe that any such documents were framed till long after Mahomet's death, they can assume none of the merit of contemporaneous remains. But they may claim the advantage of a greater antiquity of record than the mass of ordinary tradition, as in the case of the history by Zohri of the Prophet's military conquests, which was probably recorded about the close of the first century.

Correspondence with the Corân a valuable confirmation.

B.—Correspondence at any point with facts mentioned in the Corân will generally impart credit to the traditional narrative. Some of the most important incidents connected with Mahomet's battles and campaigns, as well as a variety of domestic and political matters, are thus attested. Such apparent confirmation may however be deceptive, for the allusion in the Corân may have *given rise* to the tradition. The story may have originated in some illustrative supposition or paraphrastic comment on the text; and, gradually changing its character, have been transmitted to posterity as a recital of fact. Take for example the following verse in the Corân: *Remember the favour of thy Lord unto thee, when certain men designed to stretch forth their hands upon thee, and the Lord held back from thee their hands.* By some this passage is supposed to refer to Mahomet's escape from Mecca; but, the craving after the circumstantial and marvellous not being satisfied with this reasonable interpretation, several different occasions have been invented on which the *hand* of the enemy, in the very act of brandishing a sword over Mahomet's head, was miraculously stayed by Gabriel.[1] Again, the discomfiture of the army of Abraha shortly before the birth of Mahomet, is thus poetically celebrated in Sura cv. : *And did not the Lord send against them flocks of little birds, which cast upon them small clay stones, and made them like unto the stubble of which the cattle have eaten ?* This appears to be only a highly coloured metaphor setting forth the general destruction of the army by the ravages of small-pox or some similar pestilence. But it has afforded a starting point for the extravagances of tradition, which gives a detailed statement of the species of bird, the size and material of the little stones, the precise mode in which they struck the enemy, the exact kind of wound inflicted, &c., as if the portent had but just occurred within sight of the narrators ; and yet the whole has evidently no other foundation than the verse above quoted which the credulous Moslems, interpreting literally, deemed it necessary to clothe with ample illustration. Such are examples of the numberless puerile legends which, though purely imaginary, have been reared upon a Corânic basis.[2]

c.—When a tradition contains statements in disparagement of Mahomet, such as an indignity shown to him by his followers ; or an insult from his enemies after his emigration (for then the period of his humiliation had passed, and that of his exaltation

Disparagement of Mahomet a ground of credibility.

---

[1] In the attack upon the Bani Ghatafân, we learn from Wâckidi that whilst Mahomet was resting under a tree, the enemy's leader came stealthily up, and, snatching his sword, exclaimed : ' Who is there to defend thee against me this day ? ' ' The Lord,' replied the Prophet. Immediately Gabriel struck the foe a blow upon his chest, which caused the sword to fall from his hand ; thereupon Mahomet in his turn seized the sword and retorted the question on his adversary, who forthwith became a convert ; 'and *with reference to this,*' it is added, ' was *Sura* v. 12 *revealed* ' (*i.e.* the verse quoted in the text).

The tale is a second time clumsily repeated by the biographers almost in the same terms, on the occasion of his expedition to Dzât al Ricâ ; and here Hishâmi adds : ' With special reference to this event, Sura v. 12 was revealed ; but others attribute the passage to the attempt of Amr ibn Jahsh, one of the Bani Nadhîr,' who (as is pretended) tried to roll down a stone upon the Prophet from the roof of a house.

Thus we have three or four different incidents to which the text is applied, *some of which are evidently fabricated to suit the passage itself.*

[2] As illustrative of similarly fabricated stories in the early history of the Church, the legend of St. Paul's battle with the wild beasts may be referred to as growing out of 1 Cor. xv. 32. See Stanley *in loco.*

arrived) ; his failure in any enterprise or laudable endeavour ; or, in fine, anything at variance either in fact or doctrine with the principles and tendencies of Islâm, then there will be strong reason for admitting it as authentic ; because, otherwise, it seems hardly possible that such a tradition could be fabricated, or, having been fabricated, that it could obtain currency among the followers of Mahomet. At the same time we must be careful not to apply the rule to all that is considered *by ourselves* discreditable or opposed to morality. Cruelty however inhuman, and revenge the most implacable, *when practised against infidels*, were regarded by the first followers of Islâm as highly meritorious ; and the rude civilisation of Arabia admitted with complacency a coarseness of language and behaviour, which we should look upon as reprehensible indecency. These and similar exceptions must be made from this canon of otherwise universal application.

Treaties contemporaneously recorded.

D.—There is embodied in tradition a source of information far more authentic than any yet alluded to, though unfortunately of very limited extent,—I mean the transcripts of treaties purporting to have been dictated by Mahomet, and engrossed in his presence.

Their authority far superior to that of ordinary tradition ;

It has been already shown that ordinary traditions were not recorded in the time of Mahomet ; and that, even were we to admit an occasional resort to early notes or memoranda, there is no evidence regarding their subsequent fate, nor any criteria for distinguishing traditions so derived from those that originated and were long sustained by purely oral means. To a very different category belong the treaties of Mahomet. They consist of compacts entered into with surrounding tribes, which were at the time reduced to writing, and attested by one or more of his followers. They are of course confined to the period succeeding the Prophet's acquisition of political influence, and from their nature are limited to the recital of a few simple facts. But these facts again form valuable points of support to the traditional outline ; and, especially where they detail the relations of Islâm with the neighbouring Jewish and Christian tribes, are possessed of the highest interest.

Especially in regard to Jewish and Christian tribes.

In Wâckidi's biography there is a section expressly devoted to the transcription of such treaties, and it contains two or three scores of them. Over and again, the author (at the end of the second or beginning of the third century) states that he had copied these from the *original* documents, or recorded their purport from the testimony of those who had seen them. ' They were still in force,' writes Sprenger, ' in the time of Hârûn al Rashîd (A.H. 170–193), and were then collected.' This is quite conceivable, for they were often recorded upon leather, and would invariably be preserved with care as charters of privilege by those in whose favour they were concluded. Some of the most interesting, as the terms allowed to the Jews of Kheibar and to the Christians of Najrân, formed the bases of political events in the Caliphates of Abu Bakr and Omar; the concessions made in others to Jewish and Christian tribes, are satisfactory proof that they were not fabricated by Mahometans; while it is equally clear that they would never have been acknowledged if counterfeited by a Jewish or a Christian hand. Whenever, then, there is fair evidence in favour of such treaties, they may be placed, as to historical authority, almost on a par with the Corân itself.

The narrative of official deputations to Mahomet is sometimes stated to have been derived from the family or tribe which sent the embassy, and which had preserved a written memorial of the circumstances. Accounts so obtained may undoubtedly be viewed as founded on fact, for the family or clan would naturally treasure up in the most careful way any memorials of the manner in which the Prophet had received and honoured them, although there would no doubt be a tendency in such statements to self-aggrandisement.[1]

Written details of embassies preserved in several tribes which sent them.

E.—Another traditionary source, supported by authority peculiar to itself, consists of the verses and poetical fragments attributed to the time of Mahomet. Some of these profess to be the composition of persons who died before the Prophet, as Abu Tâlib, his uncle; others, of those who survived him, as Hassân the poet of Medîna. There can be no question as to the great antiquity of these remains, though we may not always be able to fix with exactness the period of their composition. With respect to those which purport to be of date preceding the rise to power of Mahomet, when we consider the poetical habits of the nation, their faculty of preserving poetry by memory,[2] the ancient style and language of the pieces themselves, and the likelihood that carefully composed verses were from the first

Poetical remains have special authority. 1. Those ascribed to a period before the rise of Mahomet.

---

[1] Thus Wâckidi: 'My informant, Muhammad ibn Yahya, relates, *that he found it in the writings* of his father, that,' &c.; and again 'Amr the Odzrite says, he *found it written in the papers* of. his father, that,' &c.; proceeding with the narrative of a deputation from the tribe to Mahomet.

[2] Burckhardt's testimony shows that the faculty still remains. 'Throughout every part of the Arabian desert, poetry is equally esteemed. Many persons are found who make verses of true measure, although they cannot either read or write; yet as they employ on such occasions chosen terms only, and as the purity of their vernacular language is such as to preclude any grammatical errors, these verses, after passing from mouth to mouth, may at last be committed to paper, and will most commonly be found regular and correct. I presume that the greater part of the regular poetry of the Arabs, which has descended to us, is derived from similar compositions.'

committed for greater security to writing, it cannot certainly be deemed improbable that such poems or fragments should in reality have been composed by the parties to whom they are ascribed. It is, on the other hand, quite possible that poetry of date long after the death of Mahomet, but descriptive of some passage in his life, may gradually have come to be regarded as composed upon the occasion by a contemporary poet, or as the actual effusion of the actors in the scene to whom, by poetical fiction, the modern author attributed it. As a general rule, it may be laid down that wherever there is betrayed an anticipation of Mahomet's prophetical dignity or victories, the poetry may at once be concluded as an after-thought, triumphant Islâm having reflected some rays of its refulgence upon the bare points of its early career. Tried by this rule, there are fragments which may be ascribed, as more or less genuine, to the men whose names they bear; but there is also much which, from patent anachronism either in fact or spirit, is evidently the composition of a later age.[1]

Poets who survived Mahomet.

Pieces said to have been recited by poets who survived Mahomet, there is every reason for believing to be the composition of the persons to whom they are ascribed. But whether they were composed before the Prophet's death, even when so represented, is a more difficult question; and their authority as historical documents will in some measure be regulated accordingly. Under any circumstances they must be of great value, as

[1] The following glaring anachronism shows with what caution poetry of this class must be received. When Mahomet with his followers performed the pilgrimage to Mecca under the treaty of Hodeibia, the leader of his camel, as he encircled the Káaba, shouted verses of hostile defiance against the Coreish, who had retired by compact to the overhanging rocks and thence viewed the Prophet and his people. Among these verses was the couplet: ' We shall slay you on the score of the interpretation of it (the Corán), as we slew you on the score of its revelation ' (*i.e.* for rejecting it). Now this evidently belongs to a period long subsequent, when, Islâm having been broken up into parties, men fought against each other for their several ' interpretations ' of the Corán, and looked back to the struggle with the idolaters of Mecca as to a bygone era. Yet the verses are ascribed both by Wâckidi and Hishâmi to the Hodeibia armistice, *i.e.* a period anterior even to the conquest of Mecca.— Vide *ante*, p. 401.

As a further example, I may refer to the rhetorical contest before Mahomet held between his own followers and the embassy of the Bani Tamîm. Anticipations of universal conquest are developed in the orations of the Mahometan party. Thus the threat is used by Thâbit ibn Keis that the Moslems ' *would fight against all the world till they were converted.*' This was language appropriate only to the time when the Arabs had begun to fight and conquer beyond Arabia. The speeches and poems were no doubt composed afterwards as suitable to the occasion, and, like the orations of classical history, attributed to the speakers of the original scene.—Vide *ante*, p. 449.

the work of Mahomet's contemporaries. Wherever they bear upon historical events, they are of much use as adding confirmation to the corresponding traditions; for, whether handed down by writing, or by memory alone, their poetical form is a material safeguard against change or interpolation. As examples, may be specified the odes of Hassân ibn Thâbit on the 'Battle of the Ditch,' and on 'the taking of Mecca;' and the poem of Káb ibn Mâlik, descriptive of the oath of fealty by the Medîna converts at the 'second pledge of Acaba,' in which are mentioned the names of the twelve leaders chosen by the Prophet. Besides illustrating specific facts, this early poetry is often instructive, from its exhibition of the *spirit* of the first Moslems towards their unconverted brethren, and the biting satire and virulent abuse employed against the enemies of Islâm.

But while these poetical pieces attest many facts we are already acquainted with, they reveal none which, without them, we should not have known. They are valuable because *confirmatory of tradition*, and as the earliest literary remains of a period which contained the germ of such mighty events, they deserve our best attention; but they give us little fresh insight into the history or character of the Prophet. *Their poetry useful as confirmatory of tradition.*

Such, then, are the criteria which should be applied to Mahometan tradition. It is obvious that the technical rule of 'respectable names,' used by the Collectors as the connecting chain of evidence, can carry no authority with us; that every tradition, separately subjected to close examination, must stand or fall upon its own merits; and that, even after its reception as *generally* credible, the component parts are still severally liable, upon a close scrutiny of internal evidence, to suspicion and rejection. The sure light of the Corân will be the pole-star of the historian; and by it he will judge tradition. Where in its absence tradition stands alone, he will maintain a jealous guard against the misleading tendencies which I have endeavoured to explain, and will reject whatever bears their traces. In the remainder he will find ample and trustworthy materials for the biography of the Prophet. *Conclusion.*

I will now notice briefly the EARLY HISTORIANS OF MAHOMET. We have seen that towards the end of the first century of the Hegira, the general practice first commenced of recording Mahometan tradition. One of the persons known to have been employed in this task was *Zohri*, who died A.H. 124, aged 72. It has been even stated that both he and his master Orwa (who died as early as A.H. 94), composed regular biographies of *EARLY BIOGRAPHIES. Zohri, and other compilers of biographical collections.*

Mahomet; but the grounds are uncertain. Be this as it may, there is no doubt that Zohri at least made separate collections of the traditions bearing on certain episodes of the Prophet's life, certainly on that relating to his military career. It is conjectured by Sprenger, that such compilations gave rise to the uniformity of narrative and coincidence of expression observable in many parts of the various biographies of Mahomet, and especially in the history of his expeditions and battles. The supposition is probable; at all events the work of Zohri was of such source. He lived at the court of the Omeyad Caliphs, and there is hence every reason to believe that his accounts are as unbiassed as could be expected from any Mussulman author. There is nothing of Zohri extant in independent form, but he is largely quoted by subsequent biographers; and their account of Mahomet's military operations is probably in great part the reproduction of materials collated by him.

Biographies compiled in second century A.H.

Two other authors are mentioned as having written biographies of Mahomet early in the second century, namely MÙSA IBN OCKBA and ABU MÁSHAR. Neither of their works is extant; but the latter is extensively referred to by Tabari. To these may be added, as no longer available, the histories of ABU ISHÂC, who died A.H. 188, and MADAINI, who survived to the beginning of the third century. Though the latter published many works on Mahomet, not one of them is now known to exist.

Extant biographies.

Difference between biographies and ordinary traditional collections.

The earliest biographical writers, whose treatises are extant more or less in their original state, are:—I. Ibn Ishâc; II. Ibn Hishâm; III. Wâckidi, and his Secretary; IV. Tabari. These works, though professing, like the traditional collections, to be composed exclusively of trustworthy traditions, differ from them in the following particulars.[1]

First.— The former confined to biographical matter chronologically arranged.

Firstly.—The traditional matter is confined to biographical subjects, and is arranged in chronological order. Commencing with anticipatory and genealogical notices, the work advances to the birth of Mahomet, and traces with some degree of method the various periods of his life. To each stage a separate chapter is devoted; and all traditions, which have any bearing whatever on the subject, are thrown together in that chapter, and arranged with more or less of intelligible sequence. The practice of the Collectors as to the quotation of their authorities is generally observed; namely, that each separate tradition must be supported by its original witness, and the chain of witnesses specified by name which connects the biographer with that authority. This induces the same motley and fragmentary appearance which

---

[1] Biographical works are called *Siyar* (or *Sîrat*), while the general *Collections* of tradition are termed *Hadîth* (or *Hadees*).

marks the traditional *collections*. The biography of Mahomet, in fact, resembles a collection of 'table talk.' It is a compilation rather than an original composition.

Secondly.—Traditions are sometimes fused together, or reduced into a uniform story. Such is more particularly the case in descriptions of Mahomet's military life, where the expeditions are often detailed in an unbroken narrative, the authorities for which are generally thrown together at the beginning.

Second.—Traditions sometimes formed into connected narrative.

Thirdly.—This process at times induces some degree of critical examination of the several traditions so collected. Where the authorities differ, we find the biographer occasionally stating his opinion as to which is the correct exposition of fact. Verbal differences are sometimes mentioned, and various readings noted. Satisfactory evidence is thus afforded of the labour bestowed by the biographers in bringing together all authentic tradition which could illustrate their subject, and of the accuracy with which they recorded it.

Third.—A measure of critical collation.

The following account of the four authors whose works are more or less extant, will enable the reader to form an estimate of their value as biographical authorities.

I. Muhammad ibn Ishâc is the earliest biographer of whom any extensive remains, the authorship of which can certainly be distinguished, have reached us. He died A.H. 151, fifteen years after the overthrow of the Omeyad dynasty. His work was published under the auspices and influence of the Abbasside Princes, and was in fact composed 'for the use' of the Caliph Al Mansûr, the second of that line. Its accuracy has been impugned. But from the portions which have come down to us there seems no ground for believing that he was less careful than other traditionists: while the high character generally ascribed to him, and the fact of his being uniformly quoted with confidence by later authors, leave little doubt that the aspersions cast upon him have no good foundation.

Muham-mad ibn Ishâc;

In the biographical dictionary of Ibn Khallicân we find the following testimonies in his favour: 'Muhammad ibn Ishâc is held by the majority of the learned as a sure authority in the traditions, and none can be ignorant of the high character borne by his work, *the Maghâzi* (military expeditions). '*Whoever wishes to know the early Moslem conquests,*' says Zohri, '*let him refer to Ibn Ishâc;*' and Al Bokhâri himself cites him in his history. Al Shâfi said: '*Whoever wishes to obtain a complete acquaintance with the early Moslem conquests, must borrow his information from Ibn Ishâc.*' Safyân ibn Oyaina declared that he never met any one who cast suspicions on Ibn Ishâc's recitals; and Shôba ibn al Hajjâj

Testimonies to his authority.

was heard to say : ' *Muhammad ibn Ishâc is the Commander of the Faithful,*' meaning that he held that rank as a traditionist. * * * Al Sâjî mentions that Zohri's pupils had recourse to Muhammad ibn Ishâc, whenever they had doubts respecting the exactness of any of the traditions delivered by their master ; such was the confidence they placed in his excellent memory. It is stated that Yahya ibn Mâîn, Ahmad ibn Hanbal, and Yahya Sáîd al Kattân, considered Muhammad ibn Ishâc as a trustworthy authority, and quoted his traditions in proof of their legal doctrines. * * * It was from Ibn Ishâc's works that Ibn Hishâm extracted the materials of his biography of the Prophet, and every person who has treated on this subject has been obliged to take Ibn Ishâc for his authority and guide.

Ibn Ishâc one of the two chief sources of subsequent biographies.

These testimonies are conclusive of the popularity of Ibn Ishâc in the Moslem world, and of his general respectability as a writer. But the surest proof of his character and authority is that his statements have been embodied in all subsequent biographies of Mahomet, excepting that of Wâckidi who in comparison with others quotes sparingly from him ; and that in fact the two works of Ibn Ishâc and Wâckidi contain between them the chief materials on which later writers have drawn for authentic details of the Prophet's life.

Though not extant, its materials largely available in Ibn Hishâm's biography.
Ibn His-hâm :

No copy of Ibn Ishâc's biography, in the form of its original composition, is now available. But the materials have been so extensively adopted by Ibn Hishâm, and wrought into his history in so complete and unaltered a form, that we have probably not lost much by the absence of the work itself.

II. Ibn Hishâm, who died A.H. 213 (or 218), made the labours of Ibn Ishâc the basis of his biography of Mahomet. Copies of this work are extant, and are known to the European historians of the Prophet.[1]

His character.

The following extract from Ibn Khallicân will place before the reader all that it is necessary to know regarding the life of this author : ' Ibn Hishâm, the author of the *Sîrat al Râsul,* or *Biography of the Prophet,* is spoken of in these terms by Abu'l-Câsim-al-Suhaili, in his work entitled *Al Raud al Unuf,* which is a commentary on the *Sîrat.* He was celebrated for his learning, and possessed superior information in genealogy and grammar. His native place was Old Cairo, but his family were of Basra. He composed a genealogical work on the tribe of

[1] ' Even of this work copies are rare.'—*Sprenger.* The fact is that the literary public among Mahometans do not affect the early and original sources of their Prophet's life, and hardly ever use them. They prefer the modern biographies with their marvellous tales.

Himyar and its princes; and I have been told that he wrote another work, in which he explained the obscure passages of poetry cited in (Ibn Ishâc's) biography of the Prophet. His death occurred at Old Cairo A.H. 213. This Ibn Hishâm is the person who extracted and drew up the "History of the Prophet" from Ibn Ishâc's work, entitled "The Wars and Life of Mahomet." Al Suhaili explained its difficulties in a commentary, and it is now found in the hands of the public under the title of *Sîrat ibn Hishâm*, *i.e.* "The Biography of Mahomet, by Ibn Hishâm."'

There is reason to suspect that Ibn Hishâm was not quite so honest as his great authority Ibn Ishâc. Certainly one instance throws suspicion upon him as a witness, disinclined at least to tell the *whole* truth. We find in a subsequent biographer, Tabari, *a quotation from Ibn Ishâc*, in which is described the temporary lapse of Mahomet into idolatry; and the same incidents are also given by Wâckidi from other original sources. But no notice whatever of the fact appears in the biography of Ibn Hishâm, though it is professedly based upon the work of Ibn Ishâc. His having thus studiously omitted all reference to so important an incident, for no other reason apparently than because he fancied it to be discreditable to the Prophet, cannot but lessen our confidence generally in his book. Still, it is evident from a comparison of his text with the quotations made by Tabari from the same passages of Ibn Ishâc (the two ordinarily tallying word for word with each other) that whatever he did excerpt from his author was faithfully and accurately quoted. *Suspicions of his candour and fidelity.*

The arrangement and composition of Ibn Hishâm are careful, if not elaborate. The traditions are well classified, and the narrative proceeds with much of the regularity of an ordinary biography. The frequent fusion of traditions, however, renders it sometimes difficult to single out the separate authorities, and to judge of them on their individual merits. *Arrangement and composition.*

An abridged edition of Ibn Hishâm's work was made at Damascus A.H. 707 (A.D. 1307), by one Ahmad ibn Ibrahîm. The abridgment consists chiefly in the omission of the authorities, *i.e.* of the series of witnesses leading up to the Companion who first gave forth the tradition. A beautiful manuscript, *in the handwriting of the abbreviator himself*, was met with by Dr. Sprenger in Delhi, and has been used as an authoritative copy both by Dr. Sprenger and myself. *Abridgment used by the author.*

III. WÂCKIDI—or as his full name runs *Muhammad ibn Omar, al Wâckidi*—was born at Medina about A.H. 130, and died A.H. *WÂCKIDI:*

207. He studied and wrote exclusively under the Abbassides. He enjoyed their patronage, and passed a part of his life at their court, having in his later days been appointed a Câzi of Baghdad. In judging therefore of his learning and prejudices, we must always bear in mind that the influence of the Abbasside dynasty bore strongly and continuously upon him. His traditional re-searches were vast, and his works voluminous. The following is from Ibn Khallicân: 'Al Wâckidi was a man eminent for learning, and the author of some well-known works on the conquests of the Moslems, and other subjects. His *Kitab al Redda*, a work of no inferior merit, contains an account of the apostacy of the Arabs on the death of the Prophet, and of the wars between his followers and Tuleiha al Aswad and Museilama, the false prophets. * * * His Secretary, Muhammad ibn Sád, and a number of other distinguished men, delivered traditional information on his authority. He held the post of *Kâdi* in the eastern quarter of Baghdad, and was appointed by the Caliph Al Mâmûn to fill the same office at Askar al Mahdi. The traditions received from him are considered of feeble authority, and doubts have been expressed on the subject of his veracity. Al Mâmûn testified a high respect for him, and treated him with marked honour.'

Notwithstanding the extraordinary fertility of his pen, none of the works of Wâckidi have reached us in their original form, with the exception of the *Maghâzi*, or 'History of the Wars of the Prophet,' a copy of which was recently discovered in Syria, and has now been published in the *Bibliotheca Indica*.

Happily, his Secretary, MUHAMMAD IBN SÁD, profited by the labours of his master, and through him we enjoy largely the results. The Secretary is thus described by Ibn Khallicân: 'Muhammad ibn Sád was a man of the highest talents, merit, and eminence. He lived for some time with Al Wâckidi in the character of a Secretary, and for this reason became known by the appellation The Secretary of Wâckidi. * * * He composed an excellent work in fifteen volumes on the different classes of Mahomet's Companions and the Successors; it contains also a history of the Caliphs, brought down to his own time. He left also a smaller edition. His character as a veracious and trust-worthy historian is universally admitted. It is said that the complete collection of Wâckidi's works remained in the possession of four persons, the first of whom was his Secretary, Muhammad ibn Sád. This distinguished writer displayed great acquirements in the sciences, the traditions, and traditional literature; most of his books treat of the traditions and law. The Khatîb Abu Bakr, author of the 'History of Baghdad,' speaks of him in these terms:

His character and writings.

The 'Maghâzi' his only work extant in original form.

But the most important results of his labours preserved in writings of his Secretary Muhammad ibn Sád.

'We consider Muhammad ibn Sád as a man of unimpeached integrity, and the traditions which he delivered are a proof of his veracity, for in the greater part of the information handed down by him, we find him discussing it passage by passage.' At the age of sixty-two he died at Baghdad, A.H. 230, and was interred in the cemetery outside the Damascus gate. *The Secretary of Wâckidi.*

In the fifteen volumes here noticed, the Secretary is supposed to have embodied the researches of his master, together with the fruits of his own independent labour. The first volume has, fortunately for the interests of literature and of truth, been preserved to us in an undoubtedly genuine form. It contains the *Sirat* or 'Biography of Mahomet,' with detailed accounts of the learned men of Medîna, and of all the Companions of the Prophet who were present at Bedr. For a copy of this invaluable volume we are indebted to the indefatigable research of Dr. Sprenger, who discovered it in a library at Cawnpore. This manuscript is written in an ancient but very distinct character, and is in excellent preservation. It was transcribed at Damascus, A.H. 718 (A.D. 1318), by a scholar named Hakkâri, who traces up, link by link, from the pupil to the master (by whom it was successively taught, or by whom copied) the guarantee of the authenticity of the volume, till the chain reaches to the Secretary, Muhammad ibn Sád himself.[1] *His works.* *Discovery of MS. of the Secretary's volume containing biography of Mahomet and his Companions.*

This treatise (if we except some special narratives, as portions of the military expeditions) is composed entirely of detached traditions, which are arranged in chapters according to subject, and in fair chronological order. The chain of authority is generally traced in detail to the fountain-head for each tradition, separately; and so carefully is every fragment of a tradition bearing on each subject treasured up and gathered together, that we often find a dozen or more traditions reiterated in detail one after another, though they are all couched perhaps in precisely the same words, or in expressions closely resembling one another. We likewise meet continually with the most contradictory authorities placed side by side without any remark; and sometimes (but the occasion is comparatively rare) the author gives his opinion as to their relative credibility. *Composed mainly of detached traditions.*

Wâckidi is said to have been a follower of the Alyite sect. Like others, he probably yielded to the prevailing influences of the day, which tended to exalt the Prophet's son-in-law as well as all the progenitors of the Abbasside race. But there is not the slightest ground for doubting that his character is equal, if not *Authority of Wâckidi and his Secretary.*

[1] This rare MS. is now in my possession, and I purpose depositing it in the library of the India Office. There is but one other copy believed to be extant, which is in the library of Gotha.

R R

superior, to that of any other historian of his time. Of the biography compiled by his Secretary, at all events, Sprenger has well vindicated the authority and faithfulness. ' There is no trace,' says he, ' of a sacrifice of truth to design, or of pious fraud, in his work. It contains few miracles ; and even those which are recorded in it admit of an easy explanation.' Concurring to a certain extent in this praise, I do not hesitate to designate the compilation as the fruit of an honest endeavour to bring together the most credible authorities current at the end of the second century, and to depict the life of Mahomet with as much truth as from such sources was possible ; it is marked by at least as great sincerity as we may expect to find in any extant Mahometan author. But Sprenger's admiration carries him too far, when he affirms that the miracles it contains are either few in number or of easy explanation. They are, on the contrary, nearly as numerous as those we find in Ibn Hishâm. It is very evident that the criticism of Wâckidi and his Secretary extended little, if at all, beyond that of their contemporaries. They were mere compilers of current traditions ; and these, if attested by reputable names, were received, however fabulous or extravagant, with a blind and implicit credulity.

TABARI.

IV. TABARI, or *Abû Jáfar ibn Jarîr al Tabari*, flourished in the latter part of the third century of the Moslem era. The following is from Ibn Khallicân : ' Al Tabari was an Imâm (or leader) in many various branches of knowledge, such as Corânic interpretation, traditions, jurisprudence, history, &c. He composed some fine works on various subjects, and these productions are a testimony of his extensive information and great abilities. He was one of the *Mujtahid Imâms*, as he (judged for himself and) adopted the opinions of no particular doctor. * * * He is held to merit the highest confidence as a transmitter of traditional information, and his history is the most authentic and the most exact of any. * * * He was born A.H. 224 at Amul in Tabarestân, and he died at Baghdad A.H. 410.'

Volume containing biography of Mahomet discovered by Sprenger.

Tabari, happily styled by Gibbon 'the Livy of the Arabians,' composed annals not only of Mahomet's life, but of the progress of Islâm. The Arabic original of the latter has long been known, but it commences only with the Prophet's death. Of the previous chapters, hitherto available only through an untrustworthy Persian translation, no trace, until a very few years ago, could anywhere be found.

Here again the literary world is indebted to Dr. Sprenger who, having been before the Mutiny deputed by the Indian Government to examine the libraries of Lucknow, succeeded in tracing from amongst a heap of neglected manuscripts, a portion of the long-lost volume. It begins with the birth of Mahomet : but it terminates with the siege of Medîna, that is, five years before the Prophet's death. The remainder of the work is in all probability extant in India, and may yet reward the search of some future collector of manuscripts. The fortunate discovery is thus described by Sprenger :—

'One of the most important books, which it was my good luck to find during my late mission to Lucknow, is the fourth volume of the history of Tabari (who died in A.H. 310), of which I believe no other copy is known to exist. It is a volume in a small quarto of 451 pages, fifteen lines in a page. Ten pages are wanting. The writing is ancient and bold, and, though not without errors, generally very correct. I should say, from the appearance, the copy is 500 years old. The intrinsic merits of the work are not so great as might be expected. Two-thirds of the book consists of extracts from Ibn Ishâc and Wâckidi, and only one third or thereabouts contains original traditions. Some of these are very valuable, inasmuch as they contain information not to be found anywhere else.'[1]

The discovery of this portion of Tabari in its original language is, after that of Wâckidi and his Secretary, the most important event affecting the biography of Mahomet which has occurred for many years. It has a marked bearing on the sufficiency and completeness of our other early authorities,—Ibn Ishâc (as known to us through Ibn Hishâm) and Wâckidi.

Importance of discovery.

The estimate given by Dr. Sprenger (not an exaggerated one), that two-thirds of the work of Tabari are composed of extracts quoted formally from Ibn Ishâc and Wâckidi, proves not only that these two biographers were in his day held as trustworthy, but likewise that they were *the standard writers* and the *chief authorities* on the subject, up to at least the close of the third century. The remaining materials of Tabari, derived from a variety of sources, possess, as observed by Sprenger, a peculiar interest, because accessible in no other quarter. Yet these sources in no case bear the character of a complete and authoritative biography, but only of occasional or miscellaneous fragments, nor do they bring to light any new or important features in Mahomet's life. Quoted by Tabari, they are sometimes valuable as supplementary to the accounts given by Ibn Ishâc and Wâckidi, or confirmatory of them; but they are oftener symptomatic of the growth of a less honest and scrupulous selection than that of the earlier Collectors. Now as Tabari was an

Especially as proving completeness of our other authorities, Ibn Ishâc and Wâckidi.

---

[1] I have been fortunate enough to secure this MS. also, and purpose to place it with that of Wâckidi in the library of the India Office.

intelligent and diligent historian, and evidently neglected no useful and trustworthy sources within his reach, we are entitled to conclude that, beside Ibn Ishâc and Wâckidi, there were available in Tabari's time no other material works, or sources of essential importance, relating to the biography of Mahomet. Had any existed, they must have been within his reach, and if within his reach he would unquestionably have made use of them in his Annals.

Historical
sources
recounted.

To the three biographies, then, of IBN HISHÂM, of WÂCKIDI as rendered by his Secretary, and of TABARI, the judicious historian of Mahomet will, as his original authorities, confine himself. He will also receive with a similar respect, such traditions in the general Collections of the earliest traditionists—Bokhâri, Muslim, Tirmidzi, and others—as may bear upon his subject. But he will reject as evidence all later authors, to whose so-called traditions he will not allow any historical weight whatever.

No subse-
quent
works
carry his-
torical
weight.

In the absence of any History or Collection of traditions, compiled *before* the accession of the Abbassides, the works above specified present us with all the credible information regarding the Arabian Prophet which mankind are ever likely to obtain. It is clear that our authorities compiled with zeal and assiduity all traditions which could illustrate their subject. They were contemporary with those tradition-gatherers who compassed sea and land in the enthusiastic search after any trace of Mahomet yet lingering in the memories, or in the family archives, of his followers. Whatever authentic information really existed must already have become public and available. It cannot be imagined that, in the unwearied search of the second century, any trustworthy tradition could have escaped the Collectors; or, supposing this possible, that it could have survived that age in an unrecorded shape. Every day diminished the chance that any stray traditions should still be floating downward on the swift and troubled current of time. Later historians could not by any possibility add a single source of information to what these authors have given us. What they did add, and that abundantly, consisted of worthless and fictitious matter, gathered from the spurious traditions and tales of later times. After the era of our three biographers, the springs of fresh authority absolutely fail.

Opinion of
Sprenger.

The verdict of Sprenger is therefore just, and of the deepest importance: 'To consider late historians like Abulfeda as *authorities*, and to suppose that an account gains in certainty, because it is mentioned by several of them, is highly uncritical; and if such a mistake is committed by an Orientalist, we must accuse him of culpable ignorance in the history of Arabic literature.'

Our early authors were, besides, in an incomparably better position than men in later days, for judging of the character and authenticity of each tradition. However blind their reception of the supposed authorities that lay far back close to the fountainhead, they must have possessed the ability, as we are bound to concede to them the intention and desire, to test the credit and honesty of the tradition-mongers of their own age, and of that immediately preceding. An intimate acquaintance with the character and circumstances of these would often afford grounds for distinguishing recently fabricated or mistaken narratives from ancient and *bonâ fide* tradition; and for rejecting many infirm and worthless stories, which later historians, with the indiscriminate appetite so pitifully generated by Moslem credulity, have greedily devoured.

Early writers alone authoritative.

I have thus, as proposed, endeavoured to sketch the original sources for the biography of Mahomet. I have examined the Corân, and have admitted its authority as an authentic and contemporary record. I have enquired into the origin and history of Mahometan tradition, and shown that it contains the elements of truth; and I have endeavoured to indicate some canons, by which fact may be distinguished from the legend and fiction so closely commingled with it. I have enumerated those early biographical compilations which can alone be regarded as worthy of attention, and have shown that no later authors are possessed of an original and independent authority. The principles thus laid down, if followed with sagacity, perseverance, and impartiality, will enable the enquirer to arrive at a fair approximation to historical fact. Many Gordian knots regarding the Prophet of Arabia will remain unsolved, many paradoxes still vainly excite curiosity and baffle explanation; but the groundwork of his life will be laid down with confidence; the details will be substantially filled in with all reasonable amplitude; and the student will be able to determine with certainty the leading features of his character.

Review.

INDEX.

---◆---

LONDON: PRINTED BY
SPOTTISWOODE AND CO., NEW-STREET SQUARE
AND PARLIAMENT STREET

Printed in the United States
63212LVS00001B/39

9 780766 177413